Instructor's Solutions Manual

Elementary Geometry for College Students

FIFTH EDITION

Dan Alexander
Parkland College

Geralyn Koeberlein
Mahomet-Seymour High School

Prepared by

Geralyn Koeberlein
Mahomet-Seymour High School

Dan Alexander
Parkland College

BROOKS/COLE
CENGAGE Learning

Australia • Brazil • Japan • Korea • Mexico • Singapore • Spain • United Kingdom • United States

ISBN-13: 978-0-538-73769-2
ISBN-10: 0-538-73769-7

Brooks/Cole
20 Davis Drive
Belmont, CA 94002-3098
USA

Cengage Learning is a leading provider of customized learning solutions with office locations around the globe, including Singapore, the United Kingdom, Australia, Mexico, Brazil, and Japan. Locate your local office at: **www.cengage.com/global**

Cengage Learning products are represented in Canada by Nelson Education, Ltd.

To learn more about Brooks/Cole, visit **www.cengage.com/brookscole**

Purchase any of our products at your local college store or at our preferred online store **www.ichapters.com**

Printed in the United States of America
1 2 3 4 5   15 14 13 12 11

FD060

Contents

Suggestions for Course Design

The authors believe that this textbook would be appropriate for a 3-hour, 4-hour, or 5-hour course. Some instructors may choose to include all or part of Appendix A (Algebra Review) due to their students' background in algebra. There may also be a desire to include The Introduction to Logic, found at our website, as a portion of the course requirement. Inclusion of some laboratory work with a geometry package such as *Geometry Sketchpad* is an option for coursework.

3-hour course

Include most of Chapters 1-7. Optional sections could include:

Section 2.2   *Indirect Proof*
Section 2.3   *Basic Constructions Justified*
Section 2.6   *Symmetry and Transformation*
Section 3.5   *Inequalities in a Triangle*
Section 6.4   *Some Constructions and Inequalities for the Circle*
Section 7.5   *More Area Relationships in the Circle*

4-hour course

Include most of Chapters 1-7 and include all/part of at least one of these chapters:

Chapter 8   *Surfaces and Solids (Solid Geometry)*
Chapter 9   *Analytic Geometry (Coordinate Geometry)*
Chapter 10   *Introduction to Trigonometry*

5-hour course

Include most of Chapters 1-10 as well as topics desired from Appendix A and/or The Introduction to Logic (see website).

Daniel C. Alexander
Geralyn M. Koeberlein

Chapter-by-Chapter Commentary for Instructors

Chapter One: Preliminary Concepts

Section 1.1: Sets, Statements, and Reasoning

The student should be aware of the role of a statement in mathematics, its truth or falsity, and whether conclusions are obtained in a logical manner. Of the compound statements (conjunction, disjunction, and implication), your students need to be convinced that the conditional statement (or implication) plays the greatest role in their study of geometry. For the implication, the student must determine the hypothesis and conclusion as a prelude to the study of proof. The student should be able to distinguish and provide examples of the 3 types of reasoning (intuition, induction, and deduction). The Law of Detachment will play a central role in the study of geometry; however, emphasize for the student the difference between the valid and invalid form of this argument. Students will come to know a geometric figure as a set of points and define other geometric terms using the set concepts of union and intersection.

Section 1.2: Informal Geometry and Measurement

In this section, many terms of geometry are introduced. Although these will be repeated, it is still important to warn students that they must become familiar with this terminology. This is much like learning the "rules of the game" in order to play that game. Measuring the line segment with the ruler prepares the student intuitively for the Ruler Postulate and the Segment Addition Postulate. The measurement of angles with a protractor is also preparation for the principles of Section 1.4. Due to the fact that some students will have difficulty with measurement of angles (due to the dual scales), it may be worthwhile to prepare an activity sheet for practice.

Section 1.3: Early Definitions and Postulates

So that the student can understand the concept "branch of mathematics," he/she should be introduced to the four parts of a mathematical system. The basic terminology and symbolism for lines (and their subsets) must be given due attention in that these will be utilized throughout the textbook. The instructor should alert students to undefined terms as "building blocks." Also, characterize definitions and postulates as significant in that they lead to conclusions known as theorems, statements that can be proven. For the instructor, pens and pencils can be used to visualize relationships among lines, line segments, and rays. Table tops and pieces of cardboard can be used to represent planes.

Section 1.4: Angles and Their Relationships

It is most important, once again, that students be able not only to recognize the terminology for angles but to able to state definitions and principles in their own terms. Measuring angles with the protractor should enable the student to understand principles such as the Protractor Postulate and the Angle Addition Postulate. Constructions may also provide understanding of certain concepts (like congruence and angle bisector). Many examples will remind the student of the role played by algebra in the solution of problems of geometry. Students can be referred to the Algebra Appendix as needed.

Section 1.5: Introduction to Geometric Proof

The purpose of this section is to introduce the student to geometric proof. Many of the little things (hypothesis = Given information, order, statements and reasons, etc) are of tremendous importance as you prepare the student for proof. In the Fifth Edition, many of the techniques are emphasized in a new feature *Strategy for Proof*; be sure that your students are aware of these and utilize this feature. The two-column proof is used at this time in that it emphasizes all the written elements of proof.

Section 1.6: Relationships: Perpendicular Lines

The "perpendicular relationship" is most important to many later discoveries. For now, be sure that students know that this relation extends itself to combinations such as line-line, line-plane, and plane-plane. For the general concept of *relation*, we explore the reflexive, symmetric, and transitive properties . . . particularly those that relate geometric figures. Some discussion of *uniqueness* is productive in that it will provide background for the notion of auxiliary lines (introduced in a later section).

Section 1.7: The Formal Proof of a Theorem

Be sure that your students know *in order* the five written parts of the *written proof*: Statement of proof (the theorem), Drawing (from hypothesis), Given (from hypothesis), Prove (from conclusion), and Proof. The instructor must convince that the unwritten Plan for Proof is far and away the most important step; for this part, suggest scratch paper, reviewing the textbook, and use of the *Strategy for Proof* feature. Several theorems that have already been stated or proven in part are left as exercises; many of these have a similar counterpart (an example) in the textbook.

Chapter Two: Parallel Lines

Section 2.1: The Parallel Postulate and Special Angles

From the outset of Chapter 2, the instructor should emphasize that parallel lines must be coplanar. It is suggested that the instructor illustrate parallel and perpendicular (even skew lines) relationships by using pens and pencils for lines and pieces of construction paper or cardboard for planes. Even though it is nearly impossible for students to grasp the significance of this fact, tell students that the Parallel Postulate characterizes the branch of mathematics known as Euclidean Geometry (plane geometry). While this characterization suggest that "the earth is flat," it is adequate for our study even though spherical geometry is requires at the global level. Beginning with Postulate 11, students should be able to complete several statements of the form, "If two parallel lines are cut by a transversal, then . . . ."

Section 2.2: Indirect Proof

Note: If there is insufficient time allowed for the complete development of geometry from a theoretical perspective, this section can be treated as optional.

This section provides the opportunity to review the negation of a statement as well as the implication and its related statements (converse, inverse, and contrapositive). Based upon the deductive form Law of Negative Inference, the primary goal of this section is the introduction of the indirect proof. It is important that students be aware that the indirect proof is often used in proving negations and uniqueness theorems. In the construction of an indirect proof, the student often makes the mistake of assuming that the negation of the hypothesis (rather than negation of conclusion) is true.

Section 2.3: Proving Lines Parallel
Due to the similarity between statements of this section and those in Section 2.1, caution students that parallel lines were a *given* in Section 2.1. However, theorems in Section 2.3 *prove* that lines meeting specified conditions are parallel; that is, statements in this section take the form, "If . . . , then these lines are parallel." For this section, have students draw up a list of conditions that *lead to* parallel lines.

Section 2.4: The Angles of a Triangle
Students will need to become familiar with much of the terminology of triangles (sides, angles, vertices, etc). Also, students should classify triangles by using both side relationships (scalene, isosceles, etc) and angle relationships (obtuse, right, etc). Some persuasion may be needed to have students accept the use of an auxiliary line. For an auxiliary line, you must explain (1) its uniqueness, (2) verify its existence in a proof, and (3) explain "why" that particular line was chosen. The instructor cannot emphasize enough the role of the theorem, "The sum of the measures of the interior angles of a triangle is 180^0." Because of the relation of remaining theorems to Theorem 2.4.1, note that each statement is called a *corollary* of that theorem.

Section 2.5: Convex Polygons
Again terminology for the polygon must be given due attention. The student should be able to classify several polygons due to the number of sides (triangle, quadrilateral, pentagon, etc). Terms such as equilateral, equiangular, and regular should be known.
Rather than count the number of diagonals D for a polygon of n sides, the student should be able to use the formula $D = \dfrac{n(n-3)}{2}$. The student should be able to state and use formulas for the sum of the interior angles (or exterior angles) of a polygon; in trurn, the student should know and be able to apply formulas that lead to the measures of an interior angle or exterior angle of a regular polygon. Polygrams could be treated as optional.

Section 2.6: Symmetry and Transformations
Appealing to the student's intuitive sense of symmetry , the student can be taught that line symmetry exists when one-half of the figure is the mirror image (*reflection*) of the other half . . . with the line of symmetry as the mirror. For point symmetry, ask the student "is there a point (not necessarily on the figure) that is the midpoint of a line segment determined by 2 corresponding points on the figure in question." While a figure may have more than one line of symmetry, emphasize that the figure can have only one point of symmetry.
Transformations (slides, reflections, and rotations) always produce an image (figure) that is congruent to the original figure. In Chapter 3, many examples of pairs of congruent triangles can be interpreted as the result of a slide, reflection, or rotation of one triangle to produce another triangle (its image).

Chapter Three: Triangles

Section 3.1: Congruent Triangles

As you begin the study of congruent triangles, stress the need to pair corresponding vertices, corresponding sides, and corresponding angles. Also, students should realize that the methods for proving triangles congruent (SSS, SAS, ASA, and AAS) are useful through the remainder of their study of geometry. Due to the simplicity and brevity of some proof problems found in this section, encourage students to attempt proof without fear. Also, have students utilize suggestions found in the *Strategy for Proof* feature.

Section 3.2: Corresponding Parts of Congruent Triangles

Students should know the acronym CPCTC and know that it represents, "Corresponding Parts of Congruent Triangles are Congruent." Emphasize that CPCTC allows them to prove that a pair of line segments (or a pair of angles) are congruent; however, warn them that CPCTC cannot be cited as a reason unless a pair of congruent triangles have already been established. Let students know that CPCTC empowers them to take an additional step; for instance, proving that 2 line segments are congruent may enable the student to establish a midpoint relationship. Once terminology for the right triangle has been introduced, caution students that the HL method for proving triangles congruent is valid only for right triangles. In order to give it due attention, the Pythagorean Theorem is introduced here without proof. The connection of the Pythagorean Theorem to this section lies in the fact that it will later be used to prove the HL theorem.

Section 3.3: Isosceles Triangles

Students should become familiar with terms (base, legs, etc) that characterize the isosceles triangle. Students should know meanings of (and be able to differentiate between) these figures related to a triangle: an angle-bisector, the perpendicular-bisector of a side, an altitude, and a median. Of course, every triangle will three angle-bisectors, three altitudes, etc. With unsuspecting students, it may be best to show them that the three-perpendicular bisectors of sides (or three altitudes) can intersect at a point *outside* the triangle . . . perhaps a drawing session would help! The most important theorems of this section are converses: (1) If two sides of a triangle are congruent, then the angles opposite these sides are congruent. (2) If two angles of a triangle are congruent, then the sides opposite these angles are congruent.

Section 3.4: Basic Constructions Justified

Note: If there is insufficient time or constructions are not to be emphasized, this section can be treated as optional.

The first goal of this section is to validate (prove) the construction methods introduced in earlier sections. For instance, we validate the method for bisecting an angle through the use of congruent triangles and CPCTC. The second goal of this section is that of constructing line segments of a particular length or of constructing angles of a particular measure (such as 45^0 or 60^0).

Section 3.5: Inequalities in a Triangle

Note: If there is insufficient time or inequality relationships are not to be emphasized, this section can be treated as optional.

To enable the proofs of theorems in this section, we must begin with a concrete definition of the term *greater than*. Note that some theorems involving inequalities are referred to as *lemmas* because these theorems help us to prove other theorems. The inequality theorems involving the lengths of sides and measures of angles of a triangle are most important in that they will be applied in Chapters 4 and 6. For some students, the Triangle Inequality will later be applied in the coursework of trigonometry and calculus.

Chapter Four: Quadrilaterals

Section 4.1: Congruent Triangles

Alert students to the fact that principles of parallel lines, perpendicular lines, and congruent triangles are extremely helpful in developments of this chapter. Be sure to define the parallelogram, but caution students not to confuse this definition with any of several properties of parallelograms found in theorems of this section. These theorems have the form, "If a quadrilateral is a parallelogram, then . . . ." In Section 4.3, these properties will also characterize the rectangle, square, and rhombus . . . because each is actually a special type of parallelogram. The final topic (bearing of airplane or ship) can be treated as optional.

Section 4.2: The Parallelogram and Kite

In this section, parallelograms are *not* a given in the theorems of the form, "If a quadrilateral . . . , then the quadrilateral is a parallelogram." That is, we will be proving that certain quadrilaterals are parallelograms. Like the parallelogram, a kite has two pairs of congruent sides; by definition, the congruent pairs of sides in the kite are adjacent sides. A kite has its own properties (like perpendicular diagonals) as well.

Section 4.3: The Rectangle, Square, and Rhombus

Consider carefully the definition of each figure (rectangle, square, and rhombus); with each being a type of parallelogram, the properties of parallelograms are also those of the rectangle, square, and rhombus. Of course, each type of parallelogram found in this section has its own properties. For example, the rectangle and square have four right angles while the diagonals of a rhombus are perpendicular; as a consequence of these properties, the Pythagorean Theorem can be applied toward solving many problems involving these special types of parallelograms.

Section 4.4: The Trapezoid

Because the trapezoid has only two sides that are parallel, it does not assume the properties of parallelograms. If the trapezoid is isosceles, then it will have special properties such as congruent diagonals and congruent base angles. Remaining theorems describe the length of a median of a trapezoid and characterize certain quadrilaterals as trapezoids or isosceles trapezoids.

Quadrilateral types can be compared by use of a Venn Diagram or the following outline:
1. Quadrilaterals
    A. Parallelograms
        1. Rectangle
            a. Square
        2. Rhombus
    B. Kites
    C. Trapezoids
        1. Isosceles Trapezoids

Chapter Five: Similar Triangles

Section 5.1: Ratios, Rates, and Proportions
Note: For Chapter 5 work, the instructor may want to refer those students who need a review of the methods of solving quadratic equations to Appendix Section A.4.
In this section, emphasize the difference between a ratio (quotient comparing *like* units) and a rate (quotient comparing *unlike units)*. Students should understand that a proportion is an equation in which two ratios (or rates) are equal. Terminology for proportions (means, extremes, etc) are important in that the student better understands a property like the Means-Extremes Property.

Section 5.2: Similar Polygons
In this section, similar polygons are defined and their related terminology (corresponding sides, corresponding angles, etc) are introduced. The definition of similar polygons allows students to (1) equate measures of corresponding angles and (2) form proportions that compare lengths of corresponding sides. Thus, this section focuses upon problem-solving, including an ancient technique known as *shadow reckoning.*

Section 5.3: Proving Triangles Similar
Whereas Section 5.2 focuses upon problem solving, this section emphasizes methods for proving that triangles are similar. Due to its simplicity, the instructor should emphasize that the AA method for proving triangles similar should be used whenever possible. The definition of similar triangles forces two relationships among parts of similar triangles:
  (1.) CASTC means "Corresponding Angles of Similar Triangles are Congruent" while
  (2.) CSSTP means "Corresponding Sides of Similar Triangles are Proportional."
Other methods for proving triangles similar are SAS ~ and SSS ~ ; in application, these methods are difficult due to the necessity of showing lengths of sides to be proportional. Warn students not to use SAS and SSS (methods of proving triangles congruent) as reasons for claiming that triangles are similar.

Section 5.4: The Pythagorean Theorem
Theorem 5.3.1 leads to a proof of the Pythagorean Theorem and its converse. Students should be aware that many (more than 100) proofs exist for the Pythagorean Theorem. For emphasis, note that the Pythagorean Theorem allows one to find the length of a side of a right triangle; however, its converse enables one to conclude that a given triangle may be a right triangle. Because these are commonly applied, Pythagorean Triples such as (3,4,5) and (5,12,13) are best memorized by the student.

With c being the length of the longest side of a given triangle, this triangle is:

an *acute* triangle if $c^2 < a^2 + b^2$, a *right* triangle if $c^2 = a^2 + b^2$,

or an *obtuse* triangle if $c^2 > a^2 + b^2$.

Section 5.5: Special Right Triangles

In Section 5.4, some right triangles were special because of their integral lengths of sides (a,b,c). In this section, a right triangle with angle measures of 45^0, 45^0, and 90^0 always has congruent legs while the hypotenuse is $\sqrt{2}$ times as long as either leg. Also, a right triangle with angle measures of 30^0, 60^0, and 90^0 has a longer leg that is $\sqrt{3}$ times as long as the shorter leg while the hypotenuse is 2 as long as the shorter leg. These relationships, and their converses, also have applications in trigonometry and calculus.

Section 5.6: Segments Divided Proportionally

Note: In this section, Ceva's Theorem is optional in that it is not applied in later sections. The phrase *divided proportionally* can be compared to profit sharing among unequal partners in a business venture. This concept is, of course, the essence of numerous applications found in this section. The Angle-Bisector Theorem that states that an angle-bisector of an angle in a triangle leads to equal ratios among the parts of the lengths of the two sides forming the bisected angle and the lengths of parts of the third side.

Chapter Six: Circles

Section 6.1: Circles and Related Segments and Angles

Terminology for the circle is reviewed and extended in this section. Students will have difficulty with the definition of *congruent arcs* in that they must have both equal measures and lie within the *same* circle or *congruent* circles. Many of the principles of this section are intuitive and therefore easily accepted. Contrast the sides and vertex locations of the central angle and the inscribed angle. Stress these angle-measurement relationships in that further angle-measurement relationships will be added in Section 6.2.

Section 6.2: More Angle Measures in the Circle

The terms tangent and secant are introduced and will be given further attention in later sections as well as in the coursework of trigonometry and calculus. Again emphasize the new angle-measurement techniques with the circle. A summary of methods (Table 6.1) is provided for students.

Section 6.3: Line and Segment Relationships in the Circle

The early theorems in this section sound similar, yet make different assertions; for this reason, it may be best that students draw the hypothesis of each theorem to "see" that the conclusion must follow. Students will also need to distinguish the concepts of *common tangent for two circles* and *tangent circles*. Each of the relationships found in Theorems 6.3.5-6.3.7 is difficult to believe without proof; however, with the help of an auxiliary line, each proof of theorem is easily and quickly proved.

Section 6.4: Constructions and Inequalities for the Circle

Note: If there is insufficient time or constructions and inequality relationships are not to be emphasized, this section can be treated as optional.

Because the construction methods of this section are fairly involved, be sure to assign homework exercises that have students perform them. The inequality relationships involving circles are intuitive (easily believed); due to the difficulty found in constructing proofs of these theorems, the instructor may wish to treat proofs as optional.

Chapter Seven: Locus and Concurrence

Section 7.1: The Locus of Points

So that the term locus is less confusing for students, the instructor should tie this word to its Latin meaning "location." For the locus concept, quantity makes a difference; that is, students will need to see several examples. While construction of a locus is optional, a drawing of the locus is imperative. Theorems 7.1.1 and 7.1.2 are most important in that they lay the groundwork for later sections. The instructor should be sure to distinguish between the locus of points in a plane and the locus of points in space.

Section 7.2: The Concurrence of Lines

The discussion of locus leads indirectly to the notion of concurrence. In particular, the concurrence of the three angle-bisectors of a triangle follows directly from the first locus theorem in Section 7.1; in turn, a triangle has an inscribed circle whose center is the incenter of the triangle. Likewise, the three perpendicular-bisectors of the sides of a triangle are concurrent at the circumcenter of the triangle, the point that is the center of the circumscribed circle of every triangle. In this section, do not just have students memorize the terms incenter, circumcenter, orthocenter, and centroid, but also have them know which concurrency (angle-bisectors, etc) leads to each result.

Section 7.3: More About Regular Polygons

Based upon our findings in Section 7.2, the student should know that a circle can be inscribed in *every* triangle and also be circumscribed about *every* triangle. Futher, the center for both circles (inscribed and circumscribed) is the same point for the equilateral triangle and regular polygons in general. The new terminology for the regular polygon (center, radius, apothem, central angle, etc) should be memorized in that it will also be applied in Section 8.3.

Chapter Eight: Areas of Polygons and Circles

Section 8.1: Area and Initial Postulates

Even though most students say *area of a triangle,* they should realize that accurate description would be *area of triangular region.* Stress the difference between linear units (used to measure length) and square units (used to measure area). With each area formula serving as a "stepping stone" to the next formula, the given order for the area formulas is natural. Perhaps the most significant formula in the list is that of the parallelogram ($A = bh$) in that this is derived from the area of rectangle formula while it leads to the remaining formulas.

Section 8.2: Perimeter and Area of Polygons

Given its practical applications, the notion of perimeter should be reviewed and extended. Heron's Formula is difficult to state and apply; however, it is common to find the area of a triangle whose lengths of sides are known. The proof of Heron's Formula is found at the website that accompanies this textbook. Emphasize Theorem 8.2.3 and that the area formulas for the rhombus and kite are just special cases of this theorem.

Section 8.3: Regular Polygons and Area

In this section, we first consider formulas for the area of the equilateral triangle and square. For regular polygons in general, be sure to introduce or review the terminology (center, radius, apothem, central angle, etc) that was found in Section 7.3; if studied, the work of both Chapters 9 and 11 use this terminology as well. The ultimate goal of this section is to establish the formula for the area of a regular polygon, namely $A = \frac{1}{2} aP$.

Section 8.4: Circumference and Area of a Circle

Begin with the definition of π as a ratio and then provide some approximations of its value (such as $\frac{22}{7}$ and 3.1416). Using $\pi = \frac{C}{d}$, we can show that $C = \pi d$ and $C = 2\pi r$.

Using a proportion, we find the length of an arc of circle (as part of the circumference). Developed as the limit of areas of inscribed regular polygons, we show that the area of a circle is given by $A = \pi r^2$. Note that the concept of *limit* needs a few examples. For students to distinguish between $2\pi r$ and πr^2 (for circumference and area), have them compare units ... where r = 3 cm, $2\pi r = 2\pi \cdot 3$ cm = 6π cm (a linear measure) while $\pi r^2 = \pi \cdot 3$ cm $\cdot 3$ cm or 9π cm^2 (a measure of area).

Section 8.5: More Area Relationships in the Circle

Note: If there is insufficient time for the study of this section, it can be treated as optional in that none of the content is used in later sections.

Formulas for the area of a sector and segment depend upon the formula for the area of a circle; however, an understanding of these area concepts is far more important than the memorization of formulas. The area of segment applications require that the related central angle have a convenient measure such as 60^0, 90^0, or 120^0; otherwise, trigonometry would be necessary to solve the problem. When a triangle has perimeter P and inscribed circle of radius r, the area of the triangle is given by $A = \frac{1}{2} rP$.

Chapter Nine: Surfaces and Solids

Section 9.1: Prisms, Area, and Volume

The student needs to consider three-dimensional objects in this section and chapter; for that purpose, the instructor should use a set of models displaying various prisms and other solids or space figures. Students need to become familiar with prisms and related terminology. To calculate the lateral area and the total area of a prism, a student must apply formulas from Chapter 8. For the volume formula for a prism (V = Bh), emphasize that B is the area of the base and that V is always measured in *cubic units*.

Section 9.2: Pyramids, Area, and Volume

Again, the instructor should use a set of models to display various pyramids. Students need to become familiar with pyramids and related terminology, including the *slant height* of a regular pyramid. Calculating the lateral area and the total area of a pyramid requires the application of formulas from Chapter 8; to find the length of the slant height of a regular pyramid requires the use of the Pythagorean Theorem. Compare the formula for the volume of a pyramid ($V = \frac{1}{3}Bh$) to that of the prism ($V = Bh$).

Section 9.3: Cylinders and Cones

Comparing the prism to cylinder and the pyramid to cone will help to motivate students in learning the area and volume formulas of this section. Three-dimensional models will motivate the formula for the lateral area of cylinder and to explain the slant height of the right circular cone. The length of the slant height of the right circular cone can be found by using the Pythagorean Theorem. Compare volume formulas for the prism ($V = Bh$) and right circular cylinder ($V = Bh$ or $V = \pi r^2 h$); likewise compare the volume formulas for the pyramid ($V = \frac{1}{3}Bh$) and right circular cylinder ($V = \frac{1}{3}Bh$ or $V = \frac{1}{3}\pi r^2 h$). While the material involving solids of revolution is a preparatory topic for calculus, it can be treated as optional.

Section 9.4: Polyhedrons and Spheres

Students should recognize (or be told) that prisms and pyramids are merely examples of polyhedrons (or polyhedra). Students should verify Euler's Formula ($V + F = E + 2$) for polyhedra with a small number of vertices by using solid models from a kit. For the sphere, compare its terminology with that of the circle; however, note that a sphere also has tangent planes. To develop the volume of sphere formula, it is necessary to interpret the volume as the limit of the volumes of inscribed regular polyhedra with an increasing number of faces. Due to limitations, we only apply the surface area of sphere formula.

Chapter Ten: Analytic Geometry

Section 10.1: The Rectangular Coordinate System

The student should become familiar with the rectangular coordinate system and its related terminology. Warn students that the definitions for lengths of horizontal and vertical line segments are fairly important in the development of the chapter. For the formulas developed, P_1 is read *first* point and x_1 as the *value of x for the first point*. The Distance Formula and Midpoint Formulas must be memorized in that they will be used throughout Chapter 10; of course, these formulas also useful in later coursework as well.

Section 10.2: Graphs of Linear Equations and Slope

At first, a point-plot approach for graphing equations is used. However, graphing linear equations leads to graphs that are lines and, in turn, the notion of *slope* of a line. The student must memorize the Slope Formula. By sight, a student should be able to recognize that a given line has a positive, negative, zero, or undefined slope.

Many students have difficulty drawing a line based upon its provided slope; for this reason, it is important to treat slope as m = $\frac{rise}{run}$. To draw a line with slope m, move from one point to the second point by simultaneously using a vertical change (rise) that corresponds to the horizontal change (run). Using the slopes of two given lines, the student should be able to classify lines as parallel, perpendicular, or neither.

Section 10.3: Preparing to do Analytic Proofs
This section is a "warm up" for completing analytic proofs that follow in Section 10.4. Not to downplay the section, specific goals that need to be achieved are:
1. The student should know the formulas found in the summary on the first page.
2. The student should follow the suggestions for placement of a drawing so that the proof of the theorem can be completed. See the *Strategy for Proof.*
3. The student should study the relationship between desired theorem conclusion and formulas needed to obtain such conclusions. See the *Strategy for Proof.*

Section 10.4: Analytic Proofs
This section utilizes all formulas and suggestions from previous sections of Chapter 10. In each classroom, the instructor must warn students of the amount of rigor required. For instance, suppose that we are trying to prove a theorem such as, "If a quadrilateral is a parallelogram, then its diagonals bisect each other." Does the student provide a figure with certain vertices that is known to be a parallelogram *or* does that figure have to be proven a parallelogram before the proof can be continued? You may wish to prove each claim once and then accept it at a later time as given (not needing proof); if it was shown in an earlier section that the triangle with vertices at A(-a,0), B(a,0), and C(0,b) is isosceles, then it will be Given as such in a later proof.

Section 10.5: Equations of Lines
In this section, we use given information about a line (like slope and y-intercept) to find its equation. Students will need to memorize and apply both the Slope-Intercept and the Point-Slope forms of a line. Emphasize that solving systems of linear equations is the algebraic equivalent of finding the point of intersection of two lines using geometry. Emphasize that the method (algebra or geometry) used to find this point of intersection always leads to the same result. Point out that the Slope-Intercept and Point-Slope forms of a line can be used to prove further theorems by the analytic approach.

Chapter Eleven: Introduction to Trigonometry

Section 11.1: The Sine Ratio and Applications
Related to the right triangle, ask students to memorize the sine ratio of an angle in the form $\frac{opposite}{hypotenuse}$; while this seems rather informal, the remaining definitions of trigonometric ratios will be given in a similar form. While students are encouraged to use the calculator to

find sine ratios for angles, they should also know these results from memory: $\sin 0^0 = 0$, $\sin 30^0 = \frac{1}{2}$, $\sin 45^0 = \frac{\sqrt{2}}{2}$, $\sin 60^0 = \frac{\sqrt{3}}{2}$, and $\sin 90^0 = 1$.

Students should realize that the sine ratios increase as the angle measure increases. Emphasize the terms angle of elevation and angle of depression and be able to perform applications that require the use of the sine ratio.

Section 11.2: The Cosine Ratio and Applications

Ask students to memorize the cosine ratio of an angle in the form $\frac{adjacent}{hypotenuse}$.

In addition to using the calculator to find cosine ratios, students should memorize results such as $\cos 0^0 = 1$, $\cos 30^0 = \frac{\sqrt{3}}{2}$, etc. Students should recognize that an increase in angle measures produces a decrease in cosine measures. Students need to be able to complete applications that require the cosine ratio. The instructor should include and perhaps require that the student be able to prove the theorem $\sin^2 \theta + \cos^2 \theta = 1$. Emphasize that many geometry problems (such as Example 7 of this section) cannot be solved without the use of trigonometry.

Section 11.3: The Tangent Ratio and Other Ratios

Students should memorize the tangent ratio as $\frac{opposite}{adjacent}$ and memorize exact values for tan 0^0, tan 30^0, tan 45^0, etc. Some attention and discussion should be devoted to the claim that "tan 90^0 is undefined." Now that three ratios are available, some practice and discussion should be given to determination of the ratio needed to solve a particular problem. While the remaining ratios (cotangent, secant, and cosecant) are included for completeness, the students can solve all problems by using only the sine, cosine, and tangent ratios. The final ratios can be recalled as reciprocals of the first three; for instance, if $\sin \theta = \frac{a}{b}$, then $\csc \theta = \frac{b}{a}$.

Section 11.4: More Trigonometric Relationships

Only the most basic trigonometric identities are included in this section. Due to the Reciprocal Identities, remind students that only the sine, cosine, and tangent ratios are needed in application. The instructor should demonstrate the use of the calculator in finding a ratio such as sec 34^0 (as reciprocal of $\cos 34^0$). Because the Quotient Identities and Pythagorean Identities are easily proved, some time should be devoted to proving at least one identity of each type. The area formula, $A = \frac{1}{2} bc \sin \alpha$, is easily proved; however, students should probably focus on its application. Students should also know the general form of the the Law of Sines and the Law of Cosines; also, the student should be able to determine which form of each is used to solve a problem. In this textbook, we do not deal with ratios, identities, or formulas involving an obtuse angle.

Chapter 1 Line and Angle Relationships

SECTION 1.1: Sets, Statements, and Reasoning

1. **a.** Not a statement.
    b. Statement; true
    c. Statement; true
    d. Statement; false

2. **a.** Statement; true
    b. Not a statement.
    c. Statement; false
    d. Statement; false

3. **a.** Christopher Columbus did not cross the Atlantic Ocean.
    b. Some jokes are not funny.

4. **a.** Someone likes me.
    b. Angle 1 is not a right angle.

5. Conditional

6. Conjunction

7. Simple

8. Disjunction

9. Simple

10. Conditional

11. H: You go to the game.
    C: You will have a great time.

12. H: Two chords of a circle have equal lengths.
    C: The arcs of the chords are congruent.

13. H: The diagonals of a parallelogram are perpendicular.
    C: The parallelogram is a rhombus.

14. H: $\frac{a}{b} = \frac{c}{d}$ $(b \neq 0, d \neq 0)$
    C: $a \cdot d = b \cdot c$

15. H: Two parallel lines are cut by a transversal.
    C: Corresponding angles are congruent.

16. H: Two lines intersect.
    C: Vertical angles are congruent.

17. First, write the statement in "If, then" form. If a figure is a square, then it is a rectangle.
    H: A figure is a square.
    C: It is a rectangle.

18. First, write the statement in "If, then" form. If angles are base angles, then they are congruent.
    H: Angles are base angles of an isosceles triangle.
    C: They are congruent.

19. True

20. True

21. True

22. False

23. False

24. True

25. Induction

26. Intuition

27. Deduction

28. Deduction

29. Intuition

30. Induction

31. None

32. Intuition

33. Angle 1 looks equal in measure to angle 2.

34. $\overline{AM}$ has the same length as $\overline{MB}$.

35. Three angles in one triangle are equal in measure to the three angles in the other triangle.

36. The angles are not equal in measure.

37. *A Prisoner of Society* might be nominated for an Academy Award.

38. Andy is a rotten child.

39. The instructor is a math teacher.

40. Your friend likes fruit.

41. Angles 1 and 2 are complementary.

42. Kathy Jones will be a success in life.

43. Alex has a strange sense of humor.

44. None

45. None

46. None

47. June Jesse will be in the public eye.

48. None

49. Marilyn is a happy person.

50. None

51. Valid

52. Not valid

53. Not valid

54. Valid

55. **a.** True

   b. True

   c. False

SECTION 1.2: Informal Geometry and Measurement

1. $AB < CD$

2. $m\angle ABC < m\angle DEF$

3. Two; one

4. No

5. One; none

6. Three

7. $\angle ABC$, $\angle ABD$, $\angle DBC$

8. 23°, 90°, 110.5°

9. Yes; no; yes

10. $A\text{-}X\text{-}B$

11. $\angle ABC$, $\angle CBA$

12. Yes; yes

13. Yes; no

14. a, d

15. a, d

16. R; they are equal.

17. **a.** 3

   b. $2\frac{1}{2}$

18. **a.** 1.5

   b. 5

19. **a.** 40°

   b. 50°

20. **a.** 90°

   b. 25°

21. Congruent; congruent

22. Equal; yes

23. Equal

24. 2 inches

25. No

26. Yes

27. Yes

28. No

29. Congruent

30. Congruent

31. $\overline{MN}$ and $\overline{QP}$

32. Equal

33. $\overline{AB}$

34. $\angle ABD$

35. 22

36. 14

37. $x + x + 3 = 21$
$2x = 18$
$x = 9$

38. $x + y$

39. 124°

40. $2x + x = 180$
$3x = 180$
$x = 60$
$m\angle 1 = 120°$

41. 71°

42. 34°

43. $x + 2x + 3 = 72$
$3x = 69$
$x = 23$

44. $x + y$

45. $32.7 \div 3 = 10.9$

46.

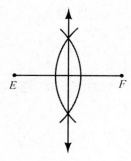

47. $x + y = 180$
$\underline{x - y = 24}$
$2x = 204$
$\quad x = 102$
$\quad y = 78$

48. $x + y = 67$
$\underline{x - y = 17}$
$2x = 84$
$\quad x = 42$
$\quad y = 25$

49. N 22° E

50. S 66° E

SECTION 1.3: Early Definitions and Postulates

1. AC

2. Midpoint

3. 6.25 ft · 12 in./ft = 75 in.

4. 52 in. ÷ 12 in./ft = $4\frac{1}{3}$ ft or 4 ft 4 in.

5. $\frac{1}{2}$ m · 3.28 ft/m = 1.64 feet

6. 16.4 ft ÷ 3.28 ft/m = 5 m

7. $18 - 15 = 3$ mi

8. $300 + 450 + 600 = 1350$ m
   1350 m ÷ 15 m/s = 90 s or 1 min 30 s

9. **a.** A-C-D
   b. A, B, C or B, C, D or A, B, D

10. **a.** Infinite
    b. One
    c. None
    d. None

11. $\overleftrightarrow{CD}$ means line CD;
    $\overline{CD}$ means segment CD;
    CD means the measure or length of $\overline{CD}$;
    $\overrightarrow{CD}$ means ray CD with endpoint C.

12. **a.** No difference
    b. No difference
    c. No difference
    d. $\overrightarrow{CD}$ is the ray starting at C and going to the right.
    $\overrightarrow{DC}$ is starting at D and going to the left.

13. **a.** m and t
    b. m and $\overrightarrow{AD}$ or $\overrightarrow{AD}$ and t

14. **a.** False
    b. False
    c. True
    d. True
    e. False

15. $2x + 1 = 3x - 2$
    $\quad -x = -3$
    $\quad\quad x = 3$
    $\quad AM = 7$

16. $2(x + 1) = 3(x - 2)$
    $2x + 2 = 3x - 6$
    $\quad -1x = -8$
    $\quad\quad x = 8$
    $\quad AB = AM + MB$
    $\quad AB = 18 + 18 = 36$

17. $2x + 1 + 3x = 6x - 4$
    $\quad 5x + 3 = 6x - 4$
    $\quad\quad -1x = -7$
    $\quad\quad\quad x = 7$
    $\quad\quad AB = 38$

18. No; Yes; Yes; No

19. **a.** $\overrightarrow{OA}$ and $\overrightarrow{OD}$
    b. $\overrightarrow{OA}$ and $\overrightarrow{OB}$ (There are other possible answers.)

20. $\overleftrightarrow{CD}$ lies on plane X.

21. a.

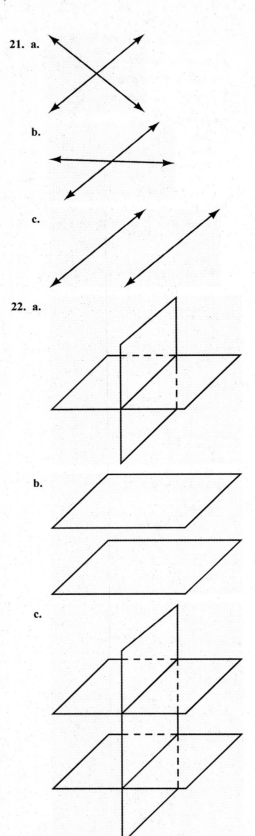

   b.

   c.

22. a.

   b.

   c.

23. Planes *M* and *N* intersect at $\overleftrightarrow{AB}$.

24. *B*

25. *A*

26. a. One

   b. Infinite

   c. One

   d. None

27. a. *C*

   b. *C*

   c. *H*

28. a. Equal

   b. Equal

   c. *AC* is twice *DC*.

29. Given: $\overline{AB}$ and $\overline{CD}$ as shown $(AB > CD)$
   Construct $\overline{MN}$ on line *l* so that
   $MN = AB + CD$

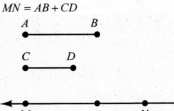

30. Given: $\overline{AB}$ and $\overline{CD}$ as shown $(AB > CD)$
   Construct: $\overline{EF}$ so that $EF = AB - CD$.

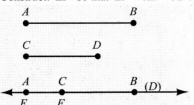

31. Given: $\overline{AB}$ as shown
   Construct: $\overline{PQ}$ on line *n* so that $PQ = 3(AB)$

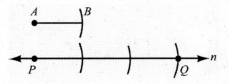

32. Given: $\overline{AB}$ as shown

Construct: $\overline{TV}$ on line n so that $TV = \frac{1}{2}(AB)$

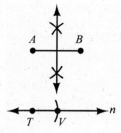

33. **a.** No

b. Yes

c. No

d. Yes

34. A segment can be divided into 2^n congruent parts where $n \geq 1$.

35. Six

36. Four

37. Nothing

38. **a.** One

b. One

c. None

d. One

e. One

f. One

g. None

39. $\frac{1}{3}a + \frac{1}{2}b$ or $\frac{2a+3b}{6}$

SECTION 1.4: Angles and Their Relationships

1. **a.** Acute

b. Right

c. Obtuse

2. **a.** Obtuse

b. Straight

c. Acute

3. **a.** Complementary

b. Supplementary

4. **a.** Congruent

b. None

5. Adjacent

6. Vertical

7. Complementary (also adjacent)

8. Supplementary

9. Yes; No

10. **a.** True

b. False

c. False

d. False

e. True

11. **a.** Obtuse

b. Straight

c. Acute

d. Obtuse

12. B is not in the interior of $\angle FAE$; the Angle-Addition Postulate does not apply.

13. $m\angle FAC + m\angle CAD = 180$
$\angle FAC$ and $\angle CAD$ are supplementary.

14. **a.** $x + y = 180$

b. $x = y$

15. **a.** $x + y = 90$

b. $x = y$

16. $62°$

17. $42°$

18. $2x + 9 + 3x - 2 = 67$
$5x + 7 = 67$
$5x = 60$
$x = 12$

19. $2x - 10 + x + 6 = 4(x - 6)$
$3x - 4 = 4x - 24$
$20 = x$
$x = 20$
$m\angle RSV = 4(20 - 6) = 56°$

20. $5(x + 1) - 3 + 4(x - 2) + 3 = 4(2x + 3) - 7$
$5x + 5 - 3 + 4x - 8 + 3 = 8x + 12 - 7$
$9x - 3 = 8x + 5$
$x = 8$
$m\angle RSV = 4(2 \cdot 8 + 3) - 7 = 69°$

21. $\dfrac{x}{2} + \dfrac{x}{4} = 45$

    Multiply by LCD, 4

    $2x + x = 180$

    $3x = 180$

    $x = 60;\ m\angle RST = 30°$

22. $\dfrac{2x}{3} + \dfrac{x}{2} = 49$

    Multiply by LCD, 6

    $4x + 3x = 294$

    $7x = 294$

    $x = 42;\ m\angle TSV = \dfrac{x}{2} = 21°$

23. $x + y = 2x - 2y$

  $x + y + 2x - 2y = 64$

    $-1x + 3y = 0$

    $3x - 1y = 64$

    $\begin{aligned} -3x + 9y &= 0 \\ 3x - y &= 64 \\ \hline 8y &= 64 \end{aligned}$

    $y = 8;\ x = 24$

24. $2x + 3y = 3x - y + 2$

  $2x + 3y + 3x - y + 2 = 80$

    $-1x + 4y = 2$

    $5x + 2y = 78$

    $\begin{aligned} -5x + 20y &= 10 \\ 5x + 2y &= 78 \\ \hline 22y &= 88 \end{aligned}$

    $y = 4;\ x = 14$

25. $\angle CAB \cong \angle DAB$

26. $x + y = 90$

    $x = 12 + y$

    $\begin{aligned} x + y &= 90 \\ x - y &= 12 \\ \hline 2x &= 102 \end{aligned}$

    $x = 51$

    $51 + y = 90$

    $y = 39$

27. $x + y = 180$

    $x = 24 + 2y$

    $x + y = 180$

    $x - 2y = 24$

    $\begin{aligned} -2x + 2y &= 360 \\ x - 2y &= 24 \\ \hline 3x &= 384 \end{aligned}$

    $x = 128;\ y = 52$

  $\angle\text{s are } 128° \text{ and } 52°.$

28. a. $(90 - x)°$

  b. $\left(90 - (3x - 12)\right)°$

  c. $90 - (2x + 5y) = (90 - 2x - 5y)°$

29. a. $(180 - x)°$

  b. $180 - (3x - 12) = (192 - 3x)°$

  c. $180 - (2x + 5y)$

    $(180 - 2x - 5y)°$

30. $x - 92 = 92 - 53$

    $x - 92 = 39$

      $x = 131$

31. $x - 92 + (92 - 53) = 90$

    $x - 92 + 39 = 90$

      $x - 53 = 90$

        $x = 143$

32. a. True

  b. False

  c. False

33. Given: Obtuse $\angle MRP$

  Construct: With $\overrightarrow{OA}$ as one side,

      an angle $\cong \angle MRP$.

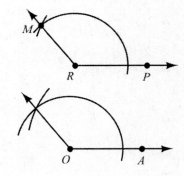

34. Given: Obtuse $\angle MRP$

Construct: $\overrightarrow{RS}$, the angle-bisector of $\angle MRP$.

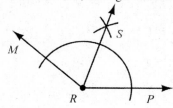

35. Given: Obtuse $\angle MRP$

Construct: Rays RS, RT, and RU so that $\angle MRP$ is divided into 4 $\cong$ angles.

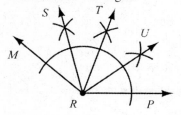

36. Given: Straight angle DEF

Construct: a right angle with vertex at E.

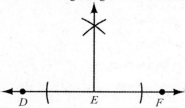

37. For the triangle shown, the angle bisectors are been constructed.

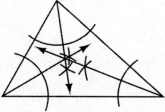

It appears that the angle bisectors meet at one point.

38. Given: Acute $\angle 1$

Construct: Triangle ABC which has

$\angle A \cong \angle 1$, $\angle B \cong \angle 1$ and base $\overline{AB}$.

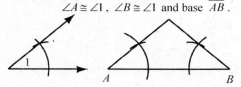

39. It appears that the two sides opposite $\angle$ s A and B are congruent.

40. Given: Straight angle ABC

Construct: Bisectors of $\angle ABD$ and $\angle DBC$.

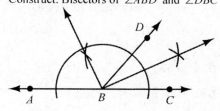

It appears that a right angle is formed.

41. a. 90°

b. 90°

c. Equal

42. Let $m \angle USV = x$, then $m \angle TSU = 38 - x$

$38 - x + 40 = 61$

$78 - x = 61$

$78 - 61 = x$

$x = 17$; $m \angle USV = 17°$

43.

$x + 2z + x - z + 2x - z = 60$

$4x = 60$

$x = 15$

If $x = 15$, then $m\angle USV = 15 - z$,

$m\angle VSW = 30 - z$, and

$m\angle USW = 3x - 6 = 3(15) - 6 = 39$

So $15 - z + 2(15) - z = 39$

$45 - 2z = 39$

$6 = 2z$

$z = 3$

44. a. 52°

b. 52°

c. Equal

45. $90 + x + x = 360$

$\qquad 2x = 270$

$\qquad x = 135°$

SECTION 1.5: Introduction to Geometric Proof

1. Division Property of Equality or Multiplication Property of Equality

2. Distributive Property $[x + x = (1+1)x = 2x]$

3. Subtraction Property of Equality

4. Addition Property of Equality

5. Multiplication Property of Equality

6. Addition Property of Equality

7. If 2 angles are supplementary, then the sum of their measures is 180°.

8. If the sum of the measures of 2 angles is 180°, then the angles are supplementary.

9. Angle-Addition Property

10. Definition of angle-bisector

11. $AM + MB = AB$

12. $AM = MB$

13. $\overrightarrow{EG}$ bisects $\angle DEF$

14. $m\angle 1 = m\angle 2$ or $\angle 1 \cong \angle 2$

15. $m\angle 1 + m\angle 2 = 90°$

16. $\angle 1$ and $\angle 2$ are complementary

17. $2x = 10$

18. $x = 7$

19. $7x + 2 = 30$

20. $\frac{1}{2} = 50\%$

21. $6x - 3 = 27$

22. $x = -20$

23. 1. Given

    2. Distributive Property

    3. Addition Property of Equality

    4. Division Property of Equality

24. 1. Given

    2. Subtraction Property of Equality

    3. Division Property of Equality

25. 1. $2(x + 3) - 7 = 11$

    2. $2x + 6 - 7 = 11$

    3. $2x - 1 = 11$

    4. $2x = 12$

    5. $x = 6$

26. 1. $\frac{x}{5} + 3 = 9$

    2. $\frac{x}{5} = 6$

    3. $x = 30$

27. 1. Given

    2. Segment-Addition Postulate

    3. Subtraction Property of Equality

28. 1. Given

    2. The midpoint forms 2 segments of equal measure.

    3. Segment-Addition Postulate

    4. Substitution

    5. Distributive Property

    6. Multiplication Property of Equality

29. 1. Given

    2. If an angle is bisected, then the two angles formed are equal in measure.

    3. Angle-Addition Postulate

    4. Substitution

    5. Distribution Property

    6. Multiplication Property of Equality

30. 1. Given

    2. Angle-Addition Postulate

    3. Subtraction Property of Equality

31. S1. M-N-P-Q on $\overline{MQ}$

    R1. Given

    2. Segment-Addition Postulate

    3. Segment-Addition Postulate

    4. $MN + NP + PQ = MQ$

32. **1.** $\angle TSW$ with $\overrightarrow{SU}$ and $\overrightarrow{SV}$; Given

    2. Angle-Addition Postulate

    3. Angle-Addition Postulate

    4. $m\angle TSW = m\angle TSU + m\angle USV + m\angle VSW$

33. $5 \cdot x + 5 \cdot y = 5(x + y)$

34. $5 \cdot x + 7 \cdot x = (5 + 7)x = 12x$

35. $(-7)(-2) > 5(-2)$ or $14 > -10$

36. $\dfrac{12}{-4} < \dfrac{-4}{-4}$ or $-3 < 1$

37. **1.** Given

    2. Addition Property of Equality

    3. Given

    4. Substitution

38. **1.** a = b   **1.** Given

    2. a − c = b − c   **2.** Subtraction Property of Equality

    3. c = d   **3.** Given

    4. a − c = b − d   **4.** Substitution

SECTION 1.6: Relationships: Perpendicular Lines

1. **1.** Given

    2. If 2 $\angle$ s are $\cong$, then they are equal in measure.

    3. Angle-Addition Postulate

    4. Addition Property of Equality

    5. Substitution

    6. If 2 $\angle$ s are = in measure, then they are $\cong$.

2. **1.** Given

    2. The measure of a straight angle is 180°.

    3. Angle-Addition Postulate

    4. Substitution

    5. Given

    6. The measure of a right $\angle = 90°$.

    7. Substitution

    8. Subtraction Property of Equality

    9. Angle-Addition Postulate

10. Substitution

11. If the sum of measures of 2 angles is 90°, then the angles are complementary.

3. **1.** $\angle 1 \cong \angle 2$ and $\angle 2 \cong \angle 3$

    2. $\angle 1 \cong \angle 3$

4. **1.** $m\angle AOB = m\angle 1$ and $m\angle BOC = m\angle 1$

    2. $m\angle AOB = m\angle BOC$

    3. $\angle AOB \cong \angle BOC$

    4. $\overrightarrow{OB}$ bisects $\angle AOC$

5. Given: Point N on line s.
Construct: Line m through N so that $m \perp s$.

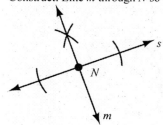

6. Given: $\overrightarrow{OA}$
Construct: Right angle BOA
    (Hint: Use the straightedge to extend $\overrightarrow{OA}$ to the left.)

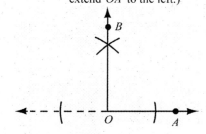

7. Given: Line ℓ containing point A
Construct: A 45° angle with vertex at A

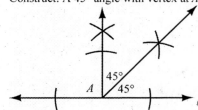

8. Given: $\overline{AB}$
   Construct: The perpendicular bisector of $\overline{AB}$

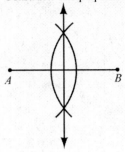

9. Given: Triangle *ABC*
   Construct: The perpendicular bisectors of each
   side, $\overline{AB}$, $\overline{AC}$, and $\overline{BC}$.

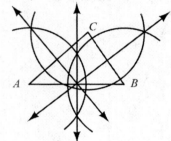

10. It appears that the perpendicular bisectors meet at one point.

11. 1. Given
    3. Substitution
    4. m∠1 = m∠2
    5. ∠1 ≅ ∠2

12. 1. Given
    2. m∠1 = m∠2 and m∠3 = m∠4
    3. Given
    4. m∠2 + m∠3 = 90
    5. Substitution
    6. ∠s 1 and 4 are comp.

13. No; Yes; No

14. No; No; Yes

15. No; Yes; No

16. No; No; Yes

17. No; Yes; Yes

18. No; No; No

19. a. perpendicular
    b. angles

c. supplementary

d. right

e. measure of angle

20. a. postulate
    b. union
    c. empty set
    d. less than
    e. point

21. a. adjacent
    b. complementary
    c. ray AB
    d. is congruent to
    e. vertical

22. In space, there are an infinite number of lines perpendicular to a given line at a point on the line.

23.

STATEMENTS	REASONS
1. $M - N - P - Q$ on $\overleftrightarrow{MQ}$	1. Given
2. $MN + NQ = MQ$	2. Segment-Addition Postulate
3. $NP + PQ = NQ$	3. Segment-Addition Postulate
4. $MN + NP + PQ = MQ$	4. Substitution

24. $AE = AB + BC + CD + DE$

25.

STATEMENTS	REASONS
1. ∠*TSW* with $\overrightarrow{SU}$ and $\overrightarrow{SV}$	1. Given
2. m∠*TSW* = m∠*TSU* + m∠*USW*	2. Angle-Addition Postulate
3. m∠*USW* = m∠*USV* + m∠*VSW*	3. Angle-Addition Postulate
4. m∠*TSW* = m∠*TSU* +m∠*USV* + m∠*VSW*	4. Substitution

26. $m\angle GHK = m\angle 1 + m\angle 2 + m\angle 3 + m\angle 4$

27. In space, there are an infinite number of lines that perpendicularly bisect a given line segment at its midpoint.

28. **1.** Given

    2. If 2 $\angle$s are comp., then the sum of their measures is 90°.

    3. Given

    4. The measure of an acute angle is between 0 and 90°.

    5. Substitution

    6. Subtraction Prop. of Eq.

    7. Subtraction Prop. of Inequality

    8. Addition Prop. of Inequality

    9. Transitive Prop. of Inequality

    10. Substitution

    11. If the measure of an angle is between 0 and 90°, then the angle is an acute $\angle$.

SECTION 1.7: The Formal Proof of a Theorem

1. H: A line segment is bisected.

    C: Each of the equal segments has half the length of the original segment.

2. H: Two sides of a triangle are congruent.

    C: The triangle is isosceles.

3. First write the statement in the "If, then" form. If a figure is a square, then it is a quadrilateral.

    H: A figure is a square.

    C: It is a quadrilateral.

4. First write the statement in the "If, then" form. If a polygon is a regular polygon, then it has congruent interior angles.

    H: A polygon is a regular polygon.

    C: It has congruent interior angles.

5. H: Each is a right angle.

    C: Two angles are congruent.

6. First write the statement in the "If, then" form. If polygons are similar, then the lengths of corresponding sides are proportional.

    H: Polygons are similar.

    C: The lengths of corresponding sides are proportional.

7. Statement, Drawing, Given, Prove, Proof

8. **a.** Hypothesis

    b. Hypothesis

    c. Conclusion

9. **a.** Given   **b.** Prove

10. a, c, d

11. Given: $\overleftrightarrow{AB} \perp \overleftrightarrow{CD}$
Prove: $\angle AEC$ is a right angle.

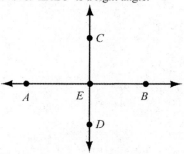

Figurer for exercises 11 and 12.

12. Given: $\angle AEC$ is a right angle
Prove: $\overleftrightarrow{AB} \perp \overleftrightarrow{CD}$

13. Given: $\angle 1$ is comp to $\angle 3$
       $\angle 2$ is comp to $\angle 3$
Prove: $\angle 1 \cong \angle 2$

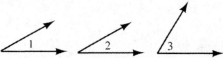

14. Given: $\angle 1$ is supp to $\angle 3$
       $\angle 2$ is supp to $\angle 3$
Prove: $\angle 1 \cong \angle 2$

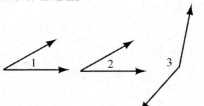

15. Given: Lines l and m
Prove: $\angle 1 \cong \angle 2$ and $\angle 3 \cong \angle 4$

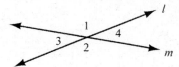

16. Given: ∠1 and ∠2 are right angles
    Prove: ∠1 ≅ ∠2

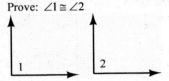

17. m∠2 = 55°, m∠3 = 125°, m∠4 = 55°

18. m∠1 = 133°, m∠3 = 133°, m∠4 = 47°

19.   m∠1 = m∠3
    $3x + 10 = 4x - 30$
         $x = 40$; m∠1 = 130°

20.   m∠2 = m∠4
     $6x + 8 = 7x$
         $x = 8$; m∠2 = 56°

21. m∠1 + m∠2 = 180°
      $2x + x = 180$
         $3x = 180$
           $x = 60$; m∠1 = 120°

22. m∠2 + m∠3 = 180°
     $x + 15 + 2x = 180$
            $3x = 165$
             $x = 55$; m∠2 = 110°

23. $\dfrac{x}{2} - 10 + \dfrac{x}{3} + 40 = 180$

    $\dfrac{x}{2} + \dfrac{x}{3} + 30 = 180$

    $\dfrac{x}{2} + \dfrac{x}{3} = 150$

    Multiply by 6

    $3x + 2x = 900$

    $5x = 900$

    $x = 180$; m∠2 = 80°

24. $x + 20 + \dfrac{x}{3} = 180$

    $x + \dfrac{x}{3} = 160$

    Multiply by 3

    $3x + x = 480$

$4x = 480$

$x = 120$; m∠4 = 40°

25. **1.** Given

   2. If 2 ∠s are comp., then the sum of their measures is 90.

   3. Substitution

   4. Subtraction Property of Equality

   5. If 2 ∠s are = in measure, then they are ≅.

26. Given: ∠1 is supp to ∠2
          ∠3 is supp to ∠2
    Prove: ∠1 ≅ ∠3

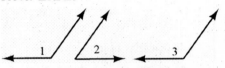

STATEMENTS	REASONS
1. ∠1 is supp to ∠2 ∠3 is supp to ∠2	1. Given
2. m∠1 + m∠2 = 180 m∠3 + m∠2 = 180	2. If 2 ∠s are supp., then the sum of their measures is 180.
3. m∠1 + m∠2 = m∠3 + m∠2	3. Substitution
4. m∠1 = m∠3	4. Subtraction Property of Equality
5. ∠1 ≅ ∠3	5. If 2 ∠s are = in measure, then they are ≅.

27. If 2 lines intersect, the vertical angles formed are congruent.
    Given: $\overleftrightarrow{AB}$ and $\overleftrightarrow{CD}$ intersect at E
    Prove: ∠1 ≅ ∠2

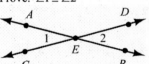

STATEMENTS	REASONS
1. $\overleftrightarrow{AB}$ and $\overleftrightarrow{CD}$ intersect at E	1. Given
2. ∠1 is supp to ∠AED ∠2 is supp to ∠AED	2. If the exterior sides of two adj. ∠s form a straight line, then these ∠s are supp.
3. ∠1 ≅ ∠2	3. If 2 ∠s are supp. to the same ∠, then these ∠s are ≅.

28. Any two right angles are congruent.
  Given: ∠1 is a rt. ∠ ;
      ∠2 is a rt. ∠
  Prove: ∠1 ≅ ∠2

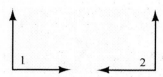

STATEMENTS	REASONS
1. ∠1 is a rt. ∠ ∠2 is a rt. ∠	1. Given
2. m∠1 = 90 m∠2 = 90	2. Measure of a right ∠ = 90.
3. m∠1 = m∠2	3. Substitution
4. ∠1 ≅ ∠2	4. If 2 ∠s are = in measure, then they are ≅.

29. 1. Given

  2. ∠ABC is a right ∠ .

  3. The measure of a rt. ∠ = 90 .

  4. Angle-Addition Postulate

  6. ∠1 is comp. to ∠2 .

30. If 2 segments are congruent, then their midpoints separate these segments into four congruent segments.
  Given: $\overline{AB} \cong \overline{DC}$
      M is the midpoint of $\overline{AB}$
      N is the midpoint of $\overline{DC}$
  Prove: $\overline{AM} \cong \overline{MB} \cong \overline{DN} \cong \overline{NC}$

A ●————— M ●————— B

D ●————— N ●————— C

STATEMENTS	REASONS
1. $\overline{AB} \cong \overline{DC}$	1. Given
2. $AB = DC$	2. If 2 segments are ≅, then their lengths are =.
3. $AB = AM + MB$ $DC = DN + NC$	3. Segment-Addition Post.
4. $AM + MB = DN + NC$	4. Substitution
5. M is the midpt of $\overline{AB}$ N is the midpt of $\overline{DC}$	5. Given
6. $AM = MB$ and $DN = NC$	6. If a pt. is the midpt of a segment, it forms 2 segments equal in measure.
7. $AM + AM = DN + DN$ or $2 \cdot AM = 2 \cdot DN$	7. Substitution
8. $AM = DN$	8. Division Prop. of Eq.
9. $AM = MB = DN = NC$	9. Substitution
10. $\overline{AM} \cong \overline{MB} \cong \overline{DN} \cong \overline{NC}$	10. If segments are = in length, then they are ≅.

31. If 2 angles are congruent, then their bisectors separate these angles into four congruent angles.

Given: $\angle ABC \cong \angle EFG$

$\overrightarrow{BD}$ bisects $\angle ABC$

$\overrightarrow{FH}$ bisects $\angle EFG$

Prove: $\angle 1 \cong \angle 2 \cong \angle 3 \cong \angle 4$

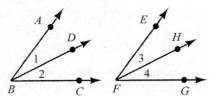

STATEMENTS	REASONS
1. $\angle ABC \cong \angle EFG$	1. Given
2. $m\angle ABC = m\angle EFG$	2. If 2 angles are $\cong$, then their measures are $=$.
3. $m\angle ABC = m\angle 1 + m\angle 2$ $m\angle EFG = m\angle 3 + m\angle 4$	3. Angle-Addition Post.
4. $m\angle 1 + m\angle 2$ $= m\angle 3 + m\angle 4$	4. Substitution
5. $\overrightarrow{BD}$ bisects $\angle ABC$ $\overrightarrow{FH}$ bisects $\angle EFG$	5. Given
6. $m\angle 1 = m\angle 2$ and $m\angle 3 = m\angle 4$	6. If a ray bisects an $\angle$, then 2 $\angle$s of equal measure are formed.
7. $m\angle 1 + m\angle 1$ $= m\angle 3 + m\angle 3$ or $2 \cdot m\angle 1 = 2 \cdot m\angle 3$	7. Substitution
8. $m\angle 1 = m\angle 3$	8. Division Prop. of Eq.
9. $m\angle 1 = m\angle 2$ $= m\angle 3 = m\angle 4$	9. Substitution
10. $\angle 1 \cong \angle 2 \cong \angle 3 \cong \angle 4$	10. If $\angle$s are $=$ in measure, then they are $\cong$.

32. The bisectors of two adjacent supplementary angles form a right angle.

Given: $\angle ABC$ is supp. to $\angle CBD$

$\overrightarrow{BE}$ bisects $\angle ABC$

$\overrightarrow{BF}$ bisects $\angle CBD$

Prove: $\angle EBF$ is a rt. $\angle$

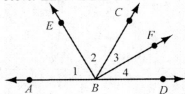

STATEMENTS	REASONS
1. $\angle ABC$ is supp to $\angle CBD$	1. Given
2. $m\angle ABC + m\angle CBD = 180$	2. The sum of the measures of supp angles is 180.
3. $m\angle ABC = m\angle 1 + m\angle 2$ $m\angle CBD = m\angle 3 + m\angle 4$	3. Angle-Addition Post.
4. $m\angle 1 + m\angle 2 + m\angle 3$ $+ m\angle 4 = 180$	4. Substitution
5. $\overrightarrow{BE}$ bisects $\angle ABC$ $\overrightarrow{BF}$ bisects $\angle CBD$	5. Given
6. $m\angle 1 = m\angle 2$ and $m\angle 3 = m\angle 4$	6. If a ray bisects an $\angle$, then 2 $\angle$s of equal measure are formed.
7. $m\angle 2 + m\angle 2 + m\angle 3$ $+ m\angle 3 = 180$ or $2 \cdot m\angle 2 + 2 \cdot m\angle 3 = 180$	7. Substitution
8. $m\angle 2 + m\angle 3 = 90$	8. Division Prop. of Eq.
9. $m\angle EBF = m\angle 2 + m\angle 3$	9. Angle-Addition Post.
10. $m\angle EBF = 90$	10. Substitution
11. $\angle EBF$ is a rt. $\angle$	11. If the measure of an $\angle$ is 90, then the $\angle$ is a rt. $\angle$.

33. The supplement of an acute angle is obtuse.

Given: $\angle 1$ is supp to $\angle 2$

$\angle 2$ is an acute $\angle$

Prove: $\angle 1$ is an obtuse $\angle$

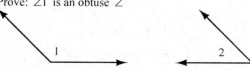

	STATEMENTS		REASONS
1.	$\angle 1$ is supp to $\angle 2$	1.	Given
2.	$m\angle 1 + m\angle 2 = 180$	2.	If 2 $\angle$s are supp., the sum of their measures is 180.
3.	$\angle 2$ is an acute $\angle$	3.	Given
4.	$m\angle 2 = x$ where $0 < x < 90$	4.	The measure of an acute $\angle$ is between 0 and 90.
5.	$m\angle 1 + x = 180$	5.	Substitution (#4 into #3)
6.	x is positive $\therefore m\angle 1 < \angle 180$	6.	If $a + p_1 = b$ and p_1 is positive, then $a < b$.
7.	$m\angle 1 = 180 - x$	7.	Substitution Prop of Eq. (#5)
8.	$-x < 0 < 90 - x$	8.	Subtraction Prop of Ineq. (#4)
9.	$90 - x < 90 < 180 - x$	9.	Addition Prop. or Ineq. (#8)
10.	$90 - x < 90 < m\angle 1$	10.	Substitution (#7 into #9)
11.	$90 < m\angle 1 < 180$	11.	Transitive Prop. of Ineq (#6 & #10)
12.	$\angle 1$ is an obtuse $\angle$	12.	If the measure of an angle is between 90 and 180, then the $\angle$ is obtuse.

REVIEW EXERCISES

1. Undefined terms, defined terms, axioms or postulates, theorems

2. Induction, deduction, intuition

3. 1. Names the term being defined.

    2. Places the term into a set or category.

    3. Distinguishes the term from other terms in the same category.

    4. Reversible

4. Intuition

5. Induction

6. Deduction

7. H: The diagonals of a trapezoid are equal in length.

    C: The trapezoid is isosceles.

8. H: The parallelogram is a rectangle.

    C: The diagonals of a parallelogram are congruent.

9. No conclusion

10. Jody Smithers has a college degree.

11. Angle A is a right angle.

12. C

13. $\angle RST$, $\angle S$, more than $90°$.

14. Diagonals are $\perp$ and they bisect each other.

15.

16.

17.
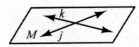

18. **a.** Obtuse   **b.** Right

19. **a.** Acute   **b.** Reflex

20. $2x + 15 = 3x - 2$
$17 = x$
$x = 17; \ m\angle ABC = 98°$

21. $2x + 5 + 3x - 4 = 86$
$5x + 1 = 86$
$5x = 85$
$x = 17; \ m\angle DBC = 47°$

22. $3x - 1 = 4x - 5$
$4 = x$
$x = 4; \ AB = 22$

23. $4x - 4 + 5x + 2 = 25$
$9x - 2 = 25$
$9x = 27$
$x = 3; \ MB = 17$

24. $2 \cdot CD = BC$
$2(2x + 5) = x + 28$
$4x + 10 = x + 28$
$3x = 18$
$x = 6; \ AC = BC = 6 + 28 = 34$

25. $7x - 21 = 3x + 7$
$4x = 28$
$x = 7$
$m\angle 3 = 49 - 21 = 28°$
$\therefore m\angle FMH = 180 - 28 = 152°$

26. $4x + 1 + x + 4 = 180$
$5x + 5 = 180$
$5x = 175$
$x = 35$
$m\angle 4 = 35 + 4 = 39°$

27. **a.** Point M

    b. $\angle JMH$

    c. $\overline{MJ}$

    d. $\overline{KH}$

28. $2x - 6 + 3(2x - 6) = 90$
$2x - 6 + 6x - 18 = 90$
$8x - 24 = 90$
$8x = 114$
$x = 14\frac{1}{4}$

$m\angle EFH = 3(2x - 6) = 3\left(28\frac{1}{2} - 6\right)$
$= 3 \cdot 22\frac{1}{2}$
$= 67\frac{1}{2}°$

29. $x + (40 + 4x) = 180$
$5x + 40 = 180$
$5x = 140$
$x = 28°$
$40 + 4x = 152°$

30. **a.** $2x + 3 + 3x - 2 + x + 7 = 6x + 8$

    b. $6x + 8 = 32$
$6x = 24$
$x = 4$

    c. $2x + 3 = 2(4) + 3 = 11$
$3x - 2 = 3(4) - 2 = 10$
$x + 7 = 4 + 7 = 11$

31. The measure of angle 3 is less than 50.

32. The four foot board is 48 inches. Subtract 6 inches on each end leaving 36 inches.
$4(n - 1) = 36$
$4n - 4 = 36$
$4n = 40$
$n = 10$
$\therefore$ 10 pegs will fit on the board.

33. S

34. S

35. A

36. S

37. N

38. **2.** $\angle 4 \cong \angle P$

    3. $\angle 1 \cong \angle 4$

    4. If 2 $\angle$ s are $\cong$, then their measures are $=$.

    5. Given

    6. $m\angle 2 = m\angle 3$

    7. $m\angle 1 + m\angle 2 = m\angle 4 + m\angle 3$

    8. Angle-Addition Postulate

    9. Substitution

    10. $\angle TVP \cong \angle MVP$

39. Given: $\overline{KF} \perp \overline{FH}$

∠JHK is a right ∠

Prove: ∠KFH ≅ ∠JHF

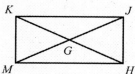

STATEMENTS	REASONS
1. $\overline{KF} \perp \overline{FH}$	1. Given
2. ∠KFH is a right ∠	2. If 2 segments are ⊥, then they form a right ∠.
3. ∠JHF is a right ∠	3. Given
4. ∠KFH ≅ ∠JHF	4. Any two right ∠s are ≅.

40. Given: $\overline{KH} \cong \overline{FJ}$

G is the midpoint of both $\overline{KH}$ and $\overline{FJ}$

Prove: $\overline{KG} \cong \overline{GJ}$

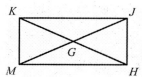

STATEMENTS	REASONS
1. $\overline{KH} \cong \overline{FJ}$ G is the midpoint of both $\overline{KH}$ and $\overline{FJ}$	1. Given
2. $\overline{KG} \cong \overline{GJ}$	2. If 2 segments are ≅, then their midpoints separate these segments into 4 ≅ segments.

41. Given: $\overline{KF} \perp \overline{FH}$

Prove: ∠KFH is comp to ∠JHF

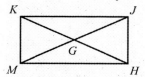

STATEMENTS	REASONS
1. $\overline{KF} \perp \overline{FH}$	1. Given
2. ∠KFH is comp. to ∠JFH	2. If the exterior sides of 2 adjacent ∠s form ⊥ rays, then these ∠s are comp.

42. Given: ∠1 is comp. to ∠M
∠2 is comp. to ∠M
Prove: ∠1 ≅ ∠2

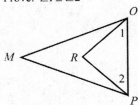

STATEMENTS	REASONS
1. ∠1 is comp. to ∠M	**1.** Given
2. ∠2 is comp. to ∠M	**2.** Given
3. ∠1 ≅ ∠2	**3.** If 2 ∠s are comp. to the same ∠, then these angles are ≅.

43. Given: ∠MOP ≅ ∠MPO
$\overrightarrow{OR}$ bisects ∠MOP
$\overrightarrow{PR}$ bisects ∠MPO
Prove: ∠1 ≅ ∠2

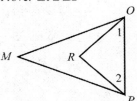

STATEMENTS	REASONS
1. ∠MOP ≅ ∠MPO	**1.** Given
2. $\overrightarrow{OR}$ bisects ∠MOP	**2.** Given
$\overrightarrow{PR}$ bisects ∠MPO	
3. ∠1 ≅ ∠2	**3.** If 2 ∠s are ≅, then their bisectors separate these ∠s into four ≅ ∠s.

44. Given: ∠4 ≅ ∠6
Prove: ∠5 ≅ ∠6

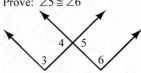

STATEMENTS	REASONS
1. ∠4 ≅ ∠6	**1.** Given
2. ∠4 ≅ ∠5	**2.** If 2 angles are vertical ∠s then they are ≅.
3. ∠5 ≅ ∠6	**3.** Transitive Prop.

45. Given: Figure as shown
Prove: ∠4 is supp. to ∠2

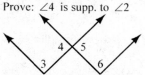

STATEMENTS	REASONS
1. Figure as shown	**1.** Given
2. ∠4 is supp. to ∠2	**2.** If the exterior sides of 2 adjacent ∠s form a line, then the ∠s are supp.

46. Given: ∠3 is supp. to ∠5
∠4 is supp. to ∠6
Prove: ∠3 ≅ ∠6

STATEMENTS	REASONS
1. ∠3 is supp to ∠5 ∠4 is supp to ∠6	**1.** Given
2. ∠4 ≅ ∠5	**2.** If 2 lines intersect, the vertical angles formed are ≅.
3. ∠3 ≅ ∠6	**3.** If 2 ∠s are supp to congruent angles, then these angles are ≅.

47. Given: $\overline{VP}$

Construct: $\overline{VW}$ such that $VW = 4 \cdot VP$

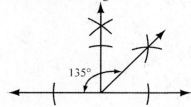

48. Construct a 135° angle.

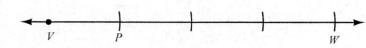

49. Given: Triangle PQR
Construct: The three angle bisectors.

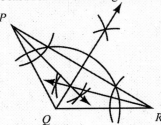

It appears that the three angle bisectors meet at one point inside the triangle.

50. Given: $\overline{AB}$, $\overline{BC}$, and $\angle B$ as shown
Construct: Triangle ABC

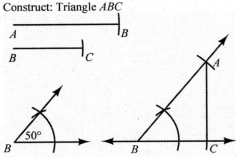

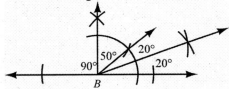

51. Given: $m\angle B = 50°$
Construct: An angle whose measure is 20°.

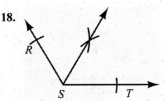

52. $m\angle 2 = 270°$

CHAPTER TEST

1. Induction

2. $\angle CBA$ or $\angle B$

3. $\overline{AP} + \overline{PB} = \overline{AB}$

4. a. Point

   b. Line

5. a. Right

   b. Obtuse

6. a. Supplementary

   b. Congruent

7. $m\angle MNP = m\angle PNQ$

8. a. Right

   b. Supplementary

9. Kianna will develop reasoning skills.

10. $3.2 + 7.2 = 10.4$ in.

11. a. $x + x + 5 = 27$
$$2x + 5 = 27$$
$$2x = 22$$
$$x = 11$$

   b. $x + 5 = 11 + 5 = 16$

12. $m\angle 4 = 35°$

13. a. $x + 2x - 3 = 69$
$$3x - 3 = 69$$
$$3x = 72$$
$$x = 24°$$

   b. $m\angle 4 = 2(24) - 3 = 45°$

14. a. $m\angle 2 = 137°$

   b. $m\angle 2 = 43°$

15. a. $2x - 3 = 3x - 28$
$$x = 25°$$

   b. $m\angle 1 = 3(25) - 28 = 47°$

16. a. $2x - 3 + 6x - 1 = 180$
$$8x - 4 = 180$$
$$8x = 184$$
$$x = 23°$$

   b. $m\angle 2 = 6(23) - 1 = 137°$

17. $x + y = 90$

18.

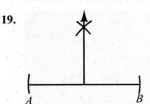

19.

20. **1.** Given

    2. Segment-Addition Postulate

    3. Segment-Addition Postulate

    4. Substitution

21. **1.** $2x - 3 = 17$

    2. $2x = 20$

    3. $x = 10$

22. **1.** Given

    2. 90°

    3. Angle-Addition Postulate

    4. 90°

    5. Given

    6. Definition of Angle-Bisector

    7. Substitution

    8. $m\angle 1 = 45°$

23. 108°

Chapter 2: Parallel Lines

SECTION 2.1: The Parallel Postulate and Special Angles

1. a. 108°

   b. 72°

2. a. 109°

   b. 71°

3. a. 68.3°

   b. 68.3°

4. a. 110.8°

   b. 110.8°

5. a. No

   b. Yes

   c. Yes

6. $\ell \parallel t$

7. Angle 9 appears to be a right angle.

8. a.

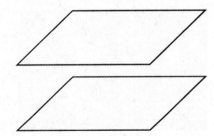

   b.

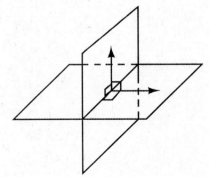

9. a. $m\angle 3 = 87°$; $\angle 3$ is vertical to $\angle 2$.

   b. $m\angle 6 = 87°$; $\angle 6$ corresponds to $\angle 2$.

   c. $m\angle 1 = 93°$; $\angle 1$ is supplementary to $\angle 2$.

   d. $m\angle 7 = 87°$; $\angle 7$ corresponds to $\angle 3$.

10. a. One

    b. One

11. a. $\angle 5$

    b. $\angle 5$

    c. $\angle 8$

    d. $\angle 5$

12. a. $m\angle B = 88°$; if 2 $\parallel$ lines are cut by a trans., then the interior $\angle$s on the same side of the transversal are supplementary.

    b. $m\angle C = 92°$; same reason as (a) using $\overline{AB} \parallel \overline{DC}$.

    c. $m\angle D = 88°$; same reason as (a).

13. a. $m\angle 2 = 68°$; $\angle 2$ is supp. to $\angle 1$.

    b. $m\angle 4 = 112°$; $\angle 4$ is vertical to $\angle 1$.

    c. $m\angle 5 = 112°$; $\angle 5$ is an alternate interior $\angle$ to $\angle 4$.

    d. $m\angle MOQ = 34°$

       $m\angle MON = m\angle 2 = 68°$

       $m\angle MOQ = \frac{1}{2}$ of $m\angle MON = 34°$.

14. If 2 $\parallel$ lines are cut by a trans., then the exterior angles on the same side of the transversal are supplementary.
$$(4x + 2) + (4x - 2) = 180$$
$$8x = 180$$
$$x = 22.5$$
$$m\angle 6 = 4(22.5) - 2 = 88°$$
$$m\angle 5 = 92°$$
$$\angle 5 \text{ is supp. to } \angle 6.$$

15. If 2 $\parallel$ lines are cut by a trans., then the alternate interior angles are congruent.
$$m\angle 3 = m\angle 6$$
$$x^2 - 3x = (x + 4)(x - 5)$$
$$x^2 - 3x = x^2 = 1x - 20$$
$$-3x = -1x - 20$$
$$-2x = -20$$
$$x = 10$$
$$m\angle 3 = (10)^2 - 3(10) = 70°$$
$$m\angle 4 = 110°$$
$$\angle 4 \text{ is supp. to } \angle 3.$$

16. Angles 2 and 8 are supp. because they are exterior angles on the same side of the trans.

Angles 1 and 2 are also supp. This leads to a system of 2 equations with 2 variables.

$$(5x + y) + (3x + y) = 180$$
$$(3x + y) + (3x + 5y) = 180$$

Simplifying yields

$$8x + 2y = 180$$
$$6x + 6y = 180$$

Dividing the second equation by –3 gives

$$8x + 2y = 180$$
$$-2x - 2y = -60$$

Addition leads to

$$6x = 120$$
$$x = 20$$

Using $8x + 2y = 180$ and $x = 20$, we have

$$8(20) + 2y = 180$$
$$160 + 2y = 180$$
$$2y = 20$$
$$y = 10$$

$$m\angle 8 = 3(20) + 5(10) = 110°$$

17. Angles 3 and 5 are supp. because they are interior angles on the same side of the transversal. Angles 5 and 6 are also supp. This leads to a system of 2 equations with 2 variables.

$$(6x + y) + (8x + 2y) = 180$$
$$(8x + 2y) + (4x + 7y) = 180$$

Simplifying yields,

$$14x + 3y = 180$$
$$12x + 9y = 180$$

Dividing the 2nd equation by –3 gives

$$14x + 3y = 180$$
$$-4x - 3y = -60$$

Addition gives

$$10x = 120$$
$$x = 12$$

Using $14x + 3y = 180$ and $x = 12$ we get

$$14(12) + 3y = 180$$
$$168 + 3y = 180$$
$$3y = 12$$
$$y = 4$$

$$m\angle 6 = 4(12) + 7(4) = 76°$$
$$\therefore m\angle 7 \text{ also} = 76°.$$

18. No

19.
1. Given
2. If 2 parallel lines are cut by a transversal, then the corresponding angles are $\cong$.
3. If 2 lines intersect, the vertical angles are $\cong$.
4. $\angle 3 \cong \angle 4$
5. $\angle 1 \cong \angle 4$

20.
1. Given
2. If 2 parallel lines are cut by a transversal, then the corresponding angles are $\cong$.
3. If 2 lines intersect, the vertical angles are $\cong$.
4. $m \parallel n$
5. If 2 parallel lines are cut by a transversal, then the corresponding angles are $\cong$.
6. $\angle 1 \cong \angle 4$; Transitive for $\cong$.

21. Given: $\overrightarrow{CE} \parallel \overrightarrow{DF}$; trans. $\overrightarrow{AB}$

$\overrightarrow{CX}$ bisects $\angle ACE$ and

$\overrightarrow{DE}$ bisects $\angle CDF$

Prove: $\angle KFH \cong \angle JHF$

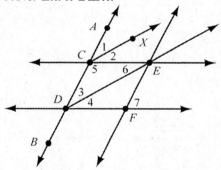

STATEMENTS	REASONS
1. $\overrightarrow{CE} \parallel \overrightarrow{DF}$; trans. $\overrightarrow{AB}$	1. Given
2. $\angle ACE \cong \angle ADF$	2. If 2 $\parallel$ lines are cut by a trans., then the corresponding $\angle$s are $\cong$.
3. $\overrightarrow{CX}$ bisects $\angle ACE$ $\overrightarrow{DE}$ bisects $\angle CDF$	3. Given
4. $\angle 1 \cong \angle 3$	4. If two $\angle$s are $\cong$, then their bisectors separate these $\angle$s into four $\cong$ $\angle$s.

22. Given: $\overleftrightarrow{CE} \parallel \overleftrightarrow{DF}$; trans. $\overleftrightarrow{AB}$

        $\overrightarrow{DE}$ bisects $\angle CDF$

Prove: $\angle 3 \cong \angle 6$

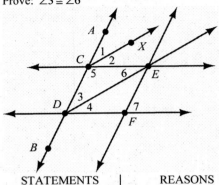

STATEMENTS	REASONS
1. $\overleftrightarrow{CE} \parallel \overleftrightarrow{DF}$; trans. $\overleftrightarrow{AB}$	1. Given
2. $\angle 6 \cong \angle 4$	2. If 2 ‖ lines are cut by a trans., then the alternate interior ∠s are ≅.
3. $\overrightarrow{DE}$ bisects $\angle CDF$	3. Given
4. $\angle 3 \cong \angle 4$	4. If a ray bisects an ∠, then 2 ≅ angles are formed.
5. $\angle 3 \cong \angle 6$	5. Transitive for ≅.

23. Given: $r \parallel s$; trans. T

        $\angle 1$ is a right ∠

Prove: $\angle 2$ is a right ∠

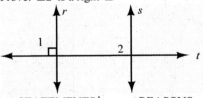

STATEMENTS	REASONS
1. $r \parallel s$; trans. t	1. Given
2. $\angle 1 \cong \angle 2$	2. If 2 ‖ lines are cut by a trans., then the corresponding ∠s are ≅.
3. $m\angle 1 = m\angle 2$	3. If 2 ∠s are ≅, then their measures are ≅.
4. $\angle 1$ is a right ∠	4. Given
5. $m\angle 1 = 90°$	5. The measure of a right angle = 90°.
6. $m\angle 2 = 90°$	6. Substitution
7. $\angle 2$ is a right ∠	7. If the measure of an ∠ = 90°, then the ∠ is a right ∠.

24. 96°   25. 93°

26. Given: $r \parallel s$ and $r \perp t$

    Prove: $s \perp t$

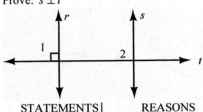

STATEMENTS	REASONS
1. $r \parallel s$; trans. t	1. Given
2. $\angle 1 \cong \angle 2$	2. If 2 ‖ lines are cut by a trans., then the corresponding ∠s are ≅.
3. $r \perp t$	3. Given
4. $\angle 1$ is a right ∠	4. If 2 lines are ⊥, they form a rt. ∠.
5. $m\angle 1 = 90°$	5. The measure of a right angle = 90°.
6. $m\angle 1 = m\angle 2$	6. If 2 ∠s are ≅, then their measures are =.
7. $m\angle 2 = 90°$	7. Transitive Property
8. $\angle 2$ is a right ∠	8. If the measure of an ∠ = 90°, then the ∠ is a right ∠.
9. $s \perp t$	9. If 2 lines form a rt. ∠, then they are ⊥.

27. **a.** $\angle 4 \cong \angle 2$ and $\angle 5 \cong \angle 3$

    b. 180°

    c. 180°

28. If two parallel lines are cut by a transversal, then the alternate exterior angles are congruent.
    Given: ℓ ∥ m ; trans t
    Prove: ∠1 ≅ ∠2

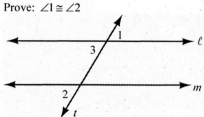

STATEMENTS	REASONS
1. ℓ ∥ m; trans. t	**1.** Given
2. ∠3 ≅ ∠2	**2.** If 2 ∥ lines are cut by a trans., then the corresponding ∠s are ≅.
3. ∠1 ≅ ∠3	**3.** If 2 lines intersect, then the vertical ∠s formed are ≅.
4. ∠1 ≅ ∠2	**4.** Transitive for ≅.

29. If two parallel lines are cut by a transversal, then the exterior angles on the same side of the transversal are supplementary.
    Given: ℓ ∥ m ; trans t
    Prove: ∠1 is supp. to ∠2

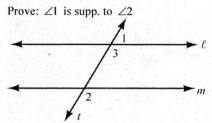

STATEMENTS	REASONS
1. ℓ ∥ m; trans. t	**1.** Given
2. ∠1 ≅ ∠3	**2.** If 2 ∥ lines are cut by a trans., then the corresponding ∠s are ≅.
3. m∠1 = m∠3	**3.** If 2 ∠s are ≅, then their measures are =.
4. ∠2 is supp. to ∠3	**4.** If the exterior sides of two adjacent ∠s form a straight line, then these angles are supp.
5. m∠1 + m∠2 = 180°	**5.** If 2 ∠s are supp., then the sum of their measures is 180°.
6. m∠2 + m∠1 = 180°	**6.** Substitution
7. m∠1 is supp. to ∠2	**7.** If the sum of the measures of 2 ∠s is 180°, then the ∠s are supp.

30. See the solution for #24.

31. No

32. Given: ℓ and point P not on ℓ
Construct: $\overleftrightarrow{PQ} \perp \ell$

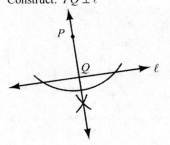

33. Given: Triangle ABC with 3 acute angles
Construct: $\overline{BD} \perp \overline{AC}$

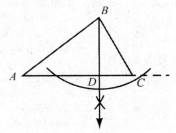

34. Given: Triangle MNQ with obtuse $\angle MNQ$
Construct: $\overrightarrow{NE} \perp \overline{MQ}$

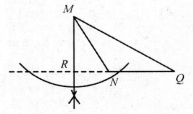

35. Given: Triangle MNQ with obtuse $\angle MNQ$
Construct: $\overline{MR} \perp \overline{NQ}$
(Hint: Extend $\overline{NQ}$)

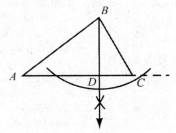

36. Lines s and m are parallel.

SECTION 2.2: Indirect Proof

1. If Juan wins the state lottery, then he will be rich.
   Converse: If Juan is rich, then he won the state lottery. FALSE.
   Inverse: If Juan does not win the state lottery, then he will not be rich. FALSE.
   Contrapositive: If Juan is not rich, then he did not win the state lottery. TRUE.

2. If $x > 2$, then $x \neq 0$.
   Converse: If $x \neq 0$, then $x > 2$. FALSE.
   Inverse: If $x \not> 2$, then $x = 0$. FALSE.
   Contrapositive: If $x = 0$, then $x \not> 2$. TRUE.

3. If the sum of the measures of two angles is 90°, then the two angles are complementary.
   Converse: If two angles are complementary, then the sum of their measures is 90°. TRUE.
   Inverse: If the sum of the measures of two angles is not 90°, then the two angles are not complementary. TRUE.
   Contrapositive: If two angles are not complementary, then the sum of their measures is not 90°. TRUE.

4. In a plane, if two lines are not perpendicular to the same line, then these lines are not parallel.
   Converse: In a plane, if two lines are not parallel, then these two lines are not perpendicular to the same line. TRUE.
   Inverse: In a plane, if two lines are perpendicular to the same line, then these lines are parallel. TRUE.
   Contrapositive: In a plane, if two lines are parallel, then these two lines are perpendicular to the same line. TRUE.

5. No conclusion.

6. Triangles ABC and DEF are not congruent.

7. $x = 5$

8. $x \leq 3$

9. (a) (b) (e)

10. a. Assume $AC = BC$

    b. Assume ℓ is parallel to m.

    c. Assume there are two perpendicular bisectors of a segment.

11. If $\angle$ A and $\angle$ B are vertical angles, then $\angle$ A and $\angle$ B are congruent.

12. If lines ℓ and m form right angles, then lines ℓ and m are perpendicular.

13. If a triangle is an equilateral triangle, then all sides of the triangle are congruent.

14. If a quadrilateral (figure with 4 sides) is a trapezoid, then 2 sides of the quadrilateral are parallel.

15. The areas of triangles ABC and DEF are equal.

16. Triangles RST and XYZ have the same shape.
    ℓ

17. Parallel

18. 45°

19. Given: $\angle 1 \not\cong \angle 5$
    Prove: $r \not\parallel s$

    Proof:
    Assume that $r \parallel s$. If they are $\parallel$, then $\angle 1 \cong \angle 5$ because they are corresponding angles. But this contradicts the Given information. Therefore, our assumption is false and $r \not\parallel s$.

20. Given: $\angle ABD \not\cong \angle DBC$
    Prove: $\overrightarrow{BD}$ does not bisect $\angle ABC$

    Proof:
    Assume that $\overrightarrow{BD}$ bisects $\angle ABC$. Then $\angle ABD \cong \angle DBC$ since an angle-bisector divides the angles into 2 congruent angles. But this contradicts the Given information. Therefore, our assumption is false and $\overrightarrow{BD}$ does not bisect $\angle ABC$.

21. Given: $m\angle 3 > m\angle 4$
    Prove: $\overline{FH}$ is not $\perp$ to $\overline{EG}$

    Proof:
    Assume that $\overline{FH} \perp \overline{EG}$. Then $\angle 3 \cong \angle 4$ and $m\angle 3 = m\angle 4$. But it is given that $m\angle 3 > m\angle 4$, which leads to a contradiction. Then the assumption that $\overline{FH} \perp \overline{EG}$ must be false and it follows that $\overline{FH}$ is not perpendicular to $\overline{EG}$.

22. Given: $MB > BC$; $AM = CD$
    Prove: B is not the midpoint of $\overline{AD}$
    Proof:
    Assume that B is the midpoint of $\overline{AD}$, then $AB = BD$. By the Segment-Addition Postulate, $AB = AM + MB$ and $BD = BC + CD$. By substitution we have $AM + MB = BC + CD$. Since $AM = CD$ and using subtraction we have $MB = BC$. But this contradicts the given information that $MB > BC$. Therefore our assumption is wrong and B is not the midpoint of $\overline{AD}$.

23. Assume that the angles are vertical angles. If they are vertical angles, then they are congruent. But this contradicts the hypothesis that the two angles are not congruent. Hence, our assumption must be false and the angles are not vertical angles.

24. Assume $x = 5$; then $x^2 = 25$. But this contradicts the hypothesis, $x^2 \neq 25$. Therefore, our assumption is false and $x \neq 5$.

25. Assume that the lines are parallel. If 2 lines are parallel and are cut by a transversal, then the alternate interior angles are congruent. But this contradicts the hypothesis and our assumption must be false. Hence, the lines are not parallel.

26. Assume $\sqrt{a^2 + b^2} = a + b$. Squaring both sides of the equation gives $a^2 + b^2 = a^2 + 2ab + b^2$. Simplifying gives $0 = 2ab$. This means that either $a = 0$ or $b = 0$. But this contradicts the hypothesis that a and b are both positive. Hence, our assumption must be false and

$$\sqrt{a^2 + b^2} \neq a + b.$$

27. Given: M is a midpoint of $\overline{AB}$.

A ●————————●————————● B
       A   M   B

Prove: M is the only midpoint of $\overline{AB}$.

Proof: If M is a midpoint of $\overline{AB}$, then

$AM = \dfrac{1}{2} \cdot AB$. Assume that N is also a midpoint

of $\overline{AB}$ so that $AN = \dfrac{1}{2} \cdot AB$. By substitution

$AM = AN$.

●————————●——●————————●
A   N   M   B

By the Segment-Addition Postulate,
$AM = AN + NM$. Using substitution again,
$AN + NM = AN$. Subtracting gives $NM = 0$.
But this contradicts the Ruler Postulate which states that the measure of a line segment is a positive number. Therefore, our assumption is wrong and M is the only midpoint for $\overline{AB}$.

28. Given: $\overleftrightarrow{CD} \perp \overleftrightarrow{AB}$ at D.

Prove: $\overleftrightarrow{CD}$ is the only line perpendicular to $\overleftrightarrow{AB}$ at D.

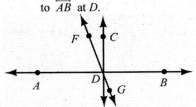

Proof: If $\overleftrightarrow{CD} \perp \overleftrightarrow{AB}$ at D, then $m\angle CDB = 90°$.
Assume there is another line, $\overleftrightarrow{FG}$, perpendicular to $\overleftrightarrow{AB}$ at D. Then $m\angle FDB = 90°$ also. By the Angle-Addition Postulate,
$m\angle FDB = m\angle FDC + m\angle CDB$. By substitution,
$90° = m\angle FDC + 90°$. By subtraction,
$m\angle FDC = 0°$. But this contradicts the Protractor Postulate which states that the measure of an angle must be a positive number. Hence, our assumption must be wrong and $\overleftrightarrow{CD}$ is the only perpendicular to $\overleftrightarrow{AB}$ at D.

29. Given: $a \parallel b$ and $c \parallel b$

Prove: $a \parallel c$

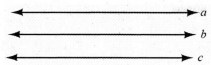

Proof: Assume that $a \not\parallel c$. Draw trans. t to intersect lines a, b, and c.

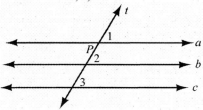

If $a \parallel b$, then $\angle 1 \cong \angle 2$ since they are corresponding angles. Likewise, since $c \parallel b$, $\angle 2 \cong \angle 3$. By the Transitive Prop. for $\cong$, $\angle 1 \cong \angle 3$ and hence $m\angle 1 = m\angle 3$. Because $a \not\parallel c$, a line can be drawn through point P parallel to c.

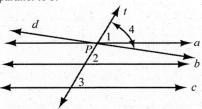

Then $\angle 4 \cong \angle 3$ by corresponding angles and $m\angle 4 = m\angle 3$. By substitution $m\angle 1 = m\angle 4$. But by the Angle-Addition Postulate, $m\angle 4 = m\angle 1 + m\angle 5$. By substitution again, $m\angle 1 = m\angle 1 + m\angle 5$. Subtracting gives us $m\angle 5 = 0$ which contradicts the Protractor Postulate that says the measure of an angle must be a positive number. Hence, our assumption is wrong and $a \parallel c$.

30. Given: ℓ and m are cut by a transversal t;

$\angle 1 \cong \angle 2$

Prove: $\ell \parallel m$

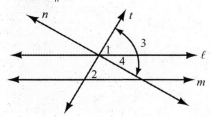

Proof: Assume $\ell \not\parallel m$. Then by the Parallel Postulate of a line, n, can be drawn through point P so that it is parallel to line m. If $n \parallel m$, then $\angle 2 \cong \angle 3$ since they are corresponding angles. But if $\angle 1 \cong \angle 2$ by Given, then $\angle 1 \cong \angle 3$ by Transitive for $\cong$. It follows then that $m\angle 1 = m\angle 3$. But $m\angle 3 = m\angle 1 + m\angle 4$ and by subtraction $m\angle 4 = 0$. This contradicts the Protractor Postulate which says the measure of an angle must be a positive number. Hence our assumption is wrong and $\ell \parallel m$.

SECTION 2.3: Proving Lines Parallel

1. $\ell \parallel m$

2. $\ell \parallel m$

3. $\ell \not\parallel m$

4. Cannot be determined

5. $\ell \not\parallel m$ (Sum = 181°)

6. Cannot be determined

7. $p \parallel q$

8. None

9. None

10. $\ell \parallel n$

11. $\ell \parallel n$

12. $\ell \parallel n$

13. None

14. $\ell \parallel m$

15. $\ell \parallel n$

16. $p \parallel q$

17. 1. Given

2. If 2 ∠s are comp. to the same ∠, then they are ≅.

3. $\overline{BC} \parallel \overline{DE}$

18. 1. Given

2. If 2 ∥ lines are cut by a trans., then the corresponding ∠s are ≅.

4. ∠3 ≅ ∠4

3. ℓ ∥ n ; If 2 lines are cut by a trans., so that corresponding ∠s are ≅, then the lines are ∥.

19. Given: $\overline{AD} \perp \overline{DC}$
        $\overline{BC} \perp \overline{DC}$
Prove: $\overline{AD} \parallel \overline{BC}$

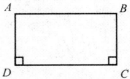

STATEMENTS	REASONS
1. $\overline{AD} \perp \overline{DC}$ and $\overline{BC} \perp \overline{DC}$	**1.** Given
2. $\overline{AD} \parallel \overline{BC}$	**2.** If 2 lines are each ⊥ to a third line, then these lines are ∥ to each other.

20. Given: m∠2 + m∠3 = 90 ;
        $\overrightarrow{BE}$ bisects ∠ABC and
        $\overrightarrow{CE}$ bisects ∠BCD
Prove: ℓ ∥ n

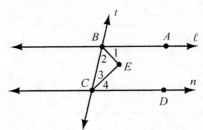

STATEMENTS	REASONS
1. m∠2 + m∠3 = 90	**1.** Given
2. $\overrightarrow{BE}$ bisects ∠ABC $\overrightarrow{CE}$ bisects ∠BCD	**2.** Given
3. m∠1 = m∠2 and m∠3 = m∠4	**3.** If a ray bisects an ∠, it forms 2 ∠s of equal measure.
4. m∠1 + m∠4 = 90	**4.** Substitution
5. m∠1 + m∠2 + m∠3 + m∠4 = 180	**5.** Addition Prop. of Equality
6. m∠ABC = m∠1 + m∠2 m∠BCD = m∠3 + m∠4	**6.** Angle-Addition Postulate
7. m∠ABC + m∠BCD = 180	**7.** Substitution
8. ∠ABC is supp. to ∠BCD	**8.** If the sum of measures of 2 ∠s is 180, then the ∠s are supp.
9. ℓ ∥ n	**9.** If 2 lines are cut by a transversal so that interior angles on the same side of the trans. are supplementary, then the lines are ∥.

21. Given: $\overline{DE}$ bisects $\angle CDA$

$\angle 3 \cong \angle 1$

Prove: $\overline{ED} \parallel \overline{AB}$

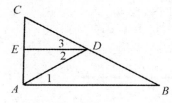

STATEMENTS	REASONS
1. $\overline{DE}$ bisects CDA	1. Given
2. $\angle 2 \cong \angle 3$	2. Bisecting an $\angle$ forms 2 $\cong$ angles.
3. $\angle 3 \cong \angle 1$	3. Given
4. $\angle 1 \cong \angle 2$	4. Transitive Propery of Equality
5. $\overline{ED} \parallel \overline{AB}$	5. If 2 lines are cut by a transversal so that alternate interior angles are congruent, then the lines are parallel.

22. Given: $\overline{XY} \parallel \overline{WZ}$; $\angle 1 \cong \angle 2$

Prove: $\overline{MN} \parallel \overline{XY}$

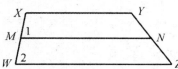

STATEMENTS	REASONS
1. $\overline{XY} \parallel \overline{WZ}$	1. Given
2. $\angle 1 \cong \angle 2$	2. Given
3. $\overline{MN} \parallel \overline{WZ}$	3. If 2 lines are cut by a trans. so that the corresponding $\angle$s are $\cong$, then these lines are $\parallel$.
4. $\overline{MN} \parallel \overline{XY}$	4. If two lines are each $\parallel$ to a third line, then these lines are $\parallel$.

23. $5x = 4(x+5)$

$5x = 4x + 20$

$x = 20$

24. $4x + 3 = 5(x-3)$

$4x + 3 = 5x - 15$

$-x = -18$

$x = 18$

25. $m\angle 3 + m\angle 5 = 180$

$$\frac{x}{2} + x = 180$$

Multiply by 2, the LCD

$x + 2x = 360$

$3x = 360$

$x = 120$

26. $m\angle 3 = m\angle 5$

$$\frac{x}{2} + 35 = \frac{3x}{4}$$

Multiply by 4, the LCD

$2x + 140 = 3x$

$x = 140$

27. $x^2 - 9 = x(x-1)$

$x^2 - 9 = x^2 - x$

$x = 9$

28. $2x^2 - 3x + 6 = 2x(x-1) - 2$

$2x^2 - 3x + 6 = 2x^2 - 2x - 2$

$-3x + 6 = -2x - 2$

$-x = -8$

$x = 8$

29. $(x+1)(x+4) + 16(x+3) - (x^2 - 2) = 180$

$x^2 + 5x + 4 + 16x + 48 - x^2 + 2 = 180$

$21x + 54 = 180$

$21x = 126$

$x = 6$

30. $(x^2 - 1)(x+1) + 185 - x^2(x+1) = 180$

$x^3 + x^2 - x - 1 + 185 - x^3 - x^2 = 180$

$-x + 184 = 180$

$-x = -4$

$x = 4$

31. If two lines are cut by a transversal so that the alternate exterior angles are congruent, then these lines are parallel.

Given: Lines ℓ and m and trans t;
$\angle 1 \cong \angle 2$
Prove: $\ell \parallel m$

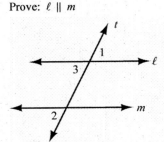

STATEMENTS	REASONS
1. Lines ℓ and m and trans. t $\angle 1 \cong \angle 2$	**1.** Given
2. $\angle 1 \cong \angle 3$	**2.** If 2 lines intersect, the vertical $\angle$s formed are $\cong$.
3. $\angle 2 \cong \angle 3$	**3.** Transitive for $\cong$.
4. $\ell \parallel m$	**4.** If lines are cut by a trans. so that the corresponding angles are $\cong$, then these lines are $\parallel$.

32. If two lines are cut by a transversal so that the exterior angles on the same side of the transversal are supplementary, then these lines are parallel.

Given: Lines ℓ and m and trans t;
$\angle 1$ is supp. to $\angle 2$
Prove: $\ell \parallel m$

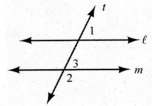

STATEMENTS	REASONS
1. Lines ℓ and m and trans. t $\angle 1$ is supp. to $\angle 2$	**1.** Given
2. $\angle 2$ is supp. to $\angle 3$	**2.** If the exterior sides of two adjacent $\angle$s form a straight line then these angles are supp.
3. $\angle 1 \cong \angle 3$	**3.** If 2 $\angle$s are supp. to the same $\angle$, then these $\angle$s are $\cong$.
4. $l \parallel m$	**4.** If lines are cut by a trans. so that the corresponding angles are $\cong$, then these lines are $\parallel$.

33. If two lines are parallel to the same line, then these lines are parallel to each other.

    Given: $a \parallel b$ and $c \parallel b$ with trans. t

    Prove: $a \parallel c$

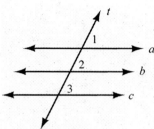

STATEMENTS	REASONS
1. $a \parallel b$ with trans. t	1. Given
2. $\angle 1 \cong \angle 2$	2. If 2 $\parallel$ lines are cut by a trans., then the corresponding $\angle$s are $\cong$.
3. $a \parallel b$ with trans. t	3. Given
4. $\angle 2 \cong \angle 3$	4. Same as (2).
5. $\angle 1 \cong \angle 3$	5. Transitive for $\cong$.
6. $a \parallel c$	6. If lines are cut by a trans. so that the corresponding angles are $\cong$, then these lines are $\parallel$.

34. In the figure, $n \parallel \ell$ and $n \parallel m$. ℓ must be $\parallel m$ because they move in the same direction.

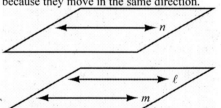

35. Given: Line l and P not on l

    Construct: The line through $P \parallel l$

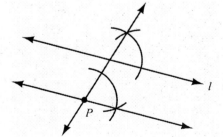

36. Given: $\overline{AB}$ and Q not on $\overline{AB}$

    Construct: The line through $Q \parallel \overline{AB}$

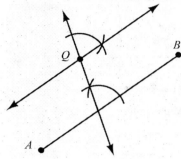

37. Given: $\overline{BC}$ and A not on $\overline{BC}$

    Construct: The line through $A \perp \overline{BC}$

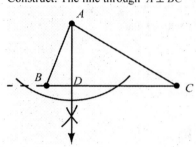

SECTION 2.4: The Angles of a Triangle

1. $m\angle C = 75°$

2. $m\angle A = 59°$

3. $m\angle B = 46°$

4. $m\angle A = m\angle C = 69°$

5.   a. Underdetermined

     b. Determined

     c. Overdetermined

6.   a. Overdetermined

     b. Overdetermined

     c. Underdetermined

7.   a. Equilateral Δ

     b. Isosceles Δ

8.   a. Isosceles Δ

     b. Scalene Δ

9.   a. Equiangular Δ

     b. Right Δ

10.   a. Obtuse Δ

     b. Acute Δ

11. If 2 $\angle$s of one $\vartriangle$ are $\cong$ to 2 $\angle$s of another $\vartriangle$, then the third $\angle$s are $\cong$.

12. If 2 $\angle$s of one $\vartriangle$ are $\cong$ to 2 $\angle$s of another $\vartriangle$, then the third $\angle$s are $\cong$.

13. $m\angle 1 = 122°$; $m\angle 2 = 58°$; $m\angle 5 = 72°$

14. $m\angle 1 = 106°$; $m\angle 4 = 51°$; $m\angle 5 = 51°$

15. $m\angle 2 = 57.7°$; $m\angle 3 = 80.8°$; $m\angle 4 = 41.5°$

16. $x = 108°$; $y = 44°$; $z = 47°$

17. $35°$

18. $108°$

19. $40°$

20. x

21. $x + x + \dfrac{x}{2} = 180$

     $2x + \dfrac{x}{2} = 180$

     Multiply by 2, the LCD

$4x + x = 360$

$5x = 360$

$x = 72$; $m\angle 1 = 72°$; $m\angle DAE = 36°$

22. $\dfrac{x}{2} + \dfrac{x}{2} + x = 180$

     Multiply by 2, the LCD

     $x + x + 2x = 360$

     $4x = 360$

     $x = 90$; $m\angle BAC = 90°$: $m\angle B = 45°$

23. $360°$

24. $7x + 4 + 5x + 2 = 90$

           $12x = 84$

             $x = 7°$

25. $3x = x + 90$ $(m\angle 3 = m\angle 1 + m\angle C)$

        $2x = 90$

         $x = 45°$

    $x + y = 90$; $y = 45°$

26. $x + \dfrac{x}{2} = 90$

     Multiply by 2, the LCD

     $2x + x = 180$

     $3x = 180$

     $x = 60$

27. $\dfrac{x}{2} + \dfrac{x}{3} = 90$

     Multiply by 6, the LCD

     $3x + 2x = 540$

     $5x = 540$

     $x = 108$

28. $8(x + 2) = 5x - 3 + 5(x + 1) - 2$

     $8x + 16 = 5x - 3 + 5x + 5 - 2$

     $8x + 16 = 10x$

         $16 = 2x$

         $x = 8°$

29. $x + 4y = 180$
$2y + 2x - y - 40 = 180$

$x + 4y = 180$ (Multiply by -2)
$2x + y = 220$

$-2x - 8y = -360$
$\underline{2x + y = 220}$
$-7y = -140$
$y = 20°$
$x + 4(20) = 180$
$x + 100 = 180$
$x = 100°$
$m\angle 2 = 80°$; $m\angle 3 = 40°$ $\therefore m\angle 5 = 60°$

30. Given: Equiangular $\triangle RST$ and
$\overrightarrow{RV}$ bisects $\angle SRT$
Prove: $\triangle RVS$ is a rt. $\triangle$

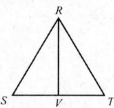

STATEMENTS	REASONS
1. $\triangle RST$ is equiangular	1. Given
2. $m\angle S = 60°$ and $m\angle SRT = 60°$	2. Each angle of an equiangular triangle is $60°$.
3. $\overrightarrow{RV}$ bisects $\angle SRT$	3. Given
4. $m\angle SRV = 30°$	4. If a ray bisects an angle, it divides the angle into 2 $\angle$s of equal measure.
5. $m\angle S + m\angle SRV$ $+ m\angle RVS = 180°$	5. The sum of measures of the $\angle$s in a triangle is $180°$.
6. $60 + 30 + m\angle RVS$ $= 180°$	6. Substitution
7. $m\angle RVS = 90°$	7. Subtraction Prop. of Equality
8. $\angle RVS$ is a right $\angle$	8. If the measure of an $\angle$ is $90°$, it is a rt. angle.
9. $\triangle RVS$ is a right $\triangle$	9. If a $\triangle$ has a right $\angle$, it is a right $\triangle$.

31. Given: $\overline{MN}$ and $\overline{PQ}$ intersect at K as shown;
$\angle M \cong \angle Q$
Prove: $\angle P \cong \angle N$

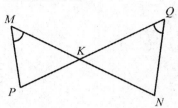

STATEMENTS	REASONS
1. $\overline{MN}$ and $\overline{PQ}$ intersect at K; $\angle M \cong \angle Q$	1. Given
2. $\angle MKP \cong \angle QKN$	2. If 2 lines intersect, the vertical $\angle$s formed are $\cong$.
3. $\angle P \cong \angle N$	3. If 2 $\angle$s one $\triangle$ are $\cong$ to 2 $\angle$s, of another $\triangle$, then the third $\angle$s are also $\cong$.

32. Right $\triangle$

33. a.

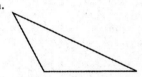

b. It is not possible to draw an equilateral right triangle.

34. a.

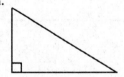

b. Not possible

35. $44°$

36. $115°$

37. $x + 2x + 33 = 180$
$3x = 147$
$x = 49$
$m\angle N = 49°$; $m\angle P = 98°$

38. Let $m\angle CBA = x$; $m\angle CAB = x + 24$
$x + x + 24 = 90$
$2x = 66$
$x = 33$
$m\angle B = 33°$; $m\angle A = 33 + 24 = 57°$

39. $2x + 110 = 180$

$2x = 70$

$x = 35$

$m\angle A = m\angle B = 35°$

40. $2x + 3x = 180$

$5x = 180$

$x = 36$

$3x = 108$

$m\angle A = m\angle B = 36°$

$m\angle C = 108°$

41. 75°

42. 360°

43. The three $\angle$s of an equiangular $\triangle$ must be equal in measure and their sum must be 180°. 180° divided three ways gives each angle a measure of 60°.

44. In a right triangle, the sum of the angle measures must be 180°. The right angle measures 90°. Therefore, the sum of the other 2 angles must equal 90°. Hence, they are complementary.

45. The measure of an exterior angle of a triangle equals the sum of measures of the two nonadjacent interior angles.

Given: $\triangle ABC$ with ext. $\angle BCD$

Prove: $m\angle BCD = m\angle A + m\angle B$

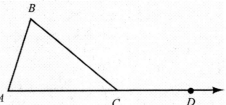

STATEMENTS	REASONS
1. $\triangle ABC$ with ext. $\angle BCD$	1. Given
2. $m\angle A + m\angle B$ $+ m\angle BCA = 180$	2. The sum of the measures of the $\angle$s in a $\triangle$ is 180.
3. $\angle BCA$ is supp. to $\angle BCD$	3. If the exterior sides of two adjacent $\angle$s form a straight line, then the angles are supp.
4. $m\angle BCA$ $+ m\angle BCD = 180$	4. If two $\angle$s are supp., then the sum of their measures is 180.
5. $m\angle BCA + m\angle BCD$ $= m\angle A + m\angle B$ $+ m\angle BCA$	5. Substitution
6. $m\angle BCD$ $= m\angle A + m\angle B$	6. Subtraction Prop. of Equality

46. If two angles of one triangle are congruent to two angles of another triangle, then the third angles are also congruent.

Given: $\angle A \cong \angle D$

$\angle B \cong \angle E$

Prove: $\angle C \cong \angle F$

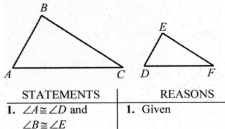

STATEMENTS	REASONS
1. $\angle A \cong \angle D$ and $\angle B \cong \angle E$	1. Given
2. $m\angle A = m\angle D$ and $m\angle B = m\angle E$	2. If 2 $\angle$s are $\cong$, then their measures are =. in a $\triangle$ is 180.
3. $m\angle A + m\angle B$ $+ m\angle C = 180$ and $m\angle D + m\angle E$ $+ m\angle F = 180$	3. The sum of the measures of the $\angle$s of a $\triangle$ is 180.
4. $m\angle A + m\angle B$ $+ m\angle C = m\angle D$ $+ m\angle E + m\angle F$	4. Substitution
5. $m\angle C = m\angle F$	5. Subtraction Prop. of Equality
6. $\angle C \cong \angle F$	6. If 2 $\angle$s are = in measure, then they are $\cong$.

47. Prove by indirect method: A triangle cannot have more than 1 right angle.

Proof: Assume that a triangle does have more than one right angle. Then the sum of the measures of the interior angles would be greater than 180°. But this contradicts the fact that the sum of the measures of the angles of a triangle is 180°. Therefore, our assumption is wrong and a triangle cannot have more than 1 right angle.

48. Given: $\overleftrightarrow{AB}$, $\overleftrightarrow{DE}$, and $\overrightarrow{CF}$ as shown;

$\overleftrightarrow{AB} \parallel \overleftrightarrow{DE}$; $\overrightarrow{CG}$ bisects $\angle BCF$ while

$\overrightarrow{FG}$ bisects $\angle CFE$

Prove: $\angle G$ is a right angle

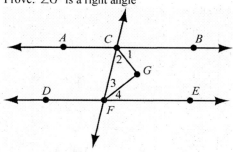

STATEMENTS	REASONS
1. $\overleftrightarrow{AB}$, $\overleftrightarrow{DE}$ and $\overrightarrow{CF}$ $\overleftrightarrow{AB} \parallel \overleftrightarrow{DE}$	1. Given
2. $\angle BCF$ is supp. to $\angle CFE$	2. If 2 $\parallel$ lines are cut by a trans., then the interior $\angle$s on the same side of the trans. are supp.
3. $m\angle BCF + m\angle CFE = 180$	3. If 2 $\angle$s are supp., then the sum of their measures is 180.
4. $m\angle BCF = m\angle 1 + m\angle 2$ and $m\angle CFE = m\angle 3 + m\angle 4$	4. Angle-Addition Postulate
5. $m\angle 1 + m\angle 2 + m\angle 3 + m\angle 4 = 180$	5. Substitution
6. $\overrightarrow{CG}$ bisects $\angle BCF$ and $\overrightarrow{FG}$ bisects $\angle CFE$	6. Given
7. $m\angle 1 = m\angle 2$ and $m\angle 3 = m\angle 4$	7. If a ray bisects an $\angle$, it divides the $\angle$ into 2 $\angle$s of = measure.
8. $m\angle 2 + m\angle 2 + m\angle 3 + m\angle 3 = 180$ or $2 \cdot m\angle 2 + 2 \cdot m\angle 3 = 180$	8. Substitution
9. $m\angle 2 + m\angle 3 = 90$	9. Division Prop. of Equality
10. $m\angle 2 + m\angle 3 + m\angle G = 180$	10. The sum of the measures of the $\angle$s of a $\triangle$ is 180.
11. $90 + m\angle G = 180$	11. Substitution
12. $m\angle G = 90$	12. Subtraction Prop. of Equality
13. $\angle G$ is a right angle.	13. If the measure of an $\angle$ is 90, then it is a right $\angle$.

49. $2b = m\angle M + 2a$

$\qquad (m\angle RPM = m\angle M + m\angle MNP)$

$\therefore m\angle M = 2b - 2a$

$b = 42 + a$

$\qquad (m\angle QPR = m\angle Q + m\angle QNP)$

$m\angle M = 2(42 + a) - 2a \qquad$ (Substitution)

$m\angle M = 84 - 2a + 2a$

$m\angle M = 84°$

50. $135°$

SECTION 2.5: Convex Polygons

1. Increase

2. Decrease

3. $x = 113°$; $y = 67°$; $z = 36°$

4. In a pentagon the sum of the $\angle$ measures is
   $180(5-2) = 540$. $540 - 93 - 93 = 354$.
   354 divided by 3 equals 118.
   $m\angle EDC = 118°$

For #5 and #6 use $D = \dfrac{n(n-3)}{2}$

5. a. 5

   b. 35

6. a. 9

   b. 20

For #7 and #8 use $S = 180(n-2)$

7. a. 540°

   b. 1440°

8. a. 720°

   b. 1080°

For #9 and #10 use $I = \dfrac{180(n-2)}{n}$

9. a. 90°

   b. 150°

10. a. 120°

    b. 144°

For #11 and #12 use $E = \dfrac{360}{n}$

11. a. 90°

    b. 30°

12. a. 60°

    b. 36°

For #13 and #14 use $S = 180(n-2)$

13. a. 7

    b. 9

14. a. 13

    b. 15

For #15 and #16 use $I = \dfrac{180(n-2)}{n}$

15. a. $108 = \dfrac{180(n-2)}{n}$
    $108n = 180n - 360$
    $-72n = -360$
    $n = 5$

    b. $144 = \dfrac{180(n-2)}{n}$
    $144n = 180n - 360$
    $-36n = -360$
    $n = 10$

16. a. $150 = \dfrac{180(n-2)}{n}$
    $150n = 180n - 360$
    $-30n = -360$
    $n = 12$

    b. $168 = \dfrac{180(n-2)}{n}$
    $168n = 180n - 360$
    $-12n = -360$
    $n = 30$

For #17 and #18 use $n = \dfrac{360}{E}$

17. a. 15

    b. 20

18. a. 8

    b. 40

19. $\dfrac{360}{8} = 45°$ which is the measure of an exterior
    angle; the measure of each interior angle is 135°.

20. $\dfrac{360}{5} = 72°$

21.

22.

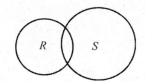

23.

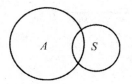

24.

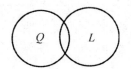

25.

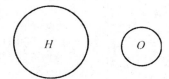

26.

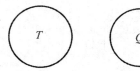

27. Given: Quad *RSTQ* with ext. ∠s at *R* and *T*
Prove: m∠1 + m∠2 = m∠3 + m∠4

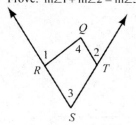

STATEMENTS	REASONS
1. Quad *RSTV* with ext. ∠s at *R* and *T*	1. Given
2. m∠QRS + m∠3 + m∠STQ + m∠4 = 360	2. The sum of the measures of the angles in a quad. is 360.
3. ∠1 is supp. to ∠QRS ∠2 is supp. to ∠QTS	3. If the exterior sides of two adjacent angles form a straight line, then these angles are supp.
4. m∠1 + m∠QRS = 180 m∠2 + m∠QTS = 180	4. If 2 ∠s are supp., then the sum of their measures is 180.
5. m∠1 + m∠QRS + m∠2 + m∠QTS = 360	5. Addition Prop. of Equality
6. m∠QRS + m∠3 + m∠STQ + m∠4 = m∠1 + m∠QRS + m∠2 + m∠QTS	6. Substitution
7. m∠1 + m∠2 = m∠3 + m∠4	7. Subtraction Prop. of Equality

28. Given: Regular hexagon *ABCDEF*
with diagonal $\overline{AC}$ and ext. $\angle 1$
Prove: $m\angle 2 + m\angle 3 = m\angle 1$

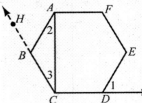

STATEMENTS	REASONS
1. Regular hexagon *ABCDEF* with diagonals $\overline{AC}$ and ext $\angle 1$	1. Given
2. Extend $\overline{BC}$ through *B* to a point *H*	2. A line can be extended infinitely.
3. $m\angle ABH = m\angle 1$	3. The exterior angles of a regular polygon are equal in measure.
4. $m\angle ABH = m\angle 2 + m\angle 3$	4. The measure of an exterior $\angle$ of a $\triangle$ equals the sum of the measures of the nonadjacent interior angles.
5. $m\angle 2 + m\angle 3 = m\angle 1$	5. Substitution

29. Given: Quad. *RSTV* with diagonals
$\overline{RT}$ and $\overline{SV}$ intersecting at *W*
Prove: $m\angle 1 + m\angle 2 = m\angle 3 + m\angle 4$

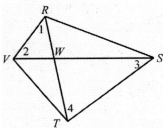

STATEMENTS	REASONS
1. Quad *RSTV* with diagonals $\overline{RT}$ and $\overline{SV}$ intersecting at *W*.	1. Given
2. $m\angle RWS = m\angle 1 + m\angle 2$	2. The measure of an ext. $\angle$ of a $\triangle$ equals the sum of the measures of the non-adjacent interior $\angle$s of the $\triangle$.
3. $m\angle RWS = m\angle 3 + m\angle 4$	3. Same as (2)
4. $m\angle 1 + m\angle 2 = m\angle 3 + m\angle 4$	4. Substitution

30. Given: Quad. *ABCD* with $\overline{BA} \perp \overline{AD}$
and $\overline{BC} \perp \overline{DC}$
Prove: $\angle$s *B* and *D* are supp.

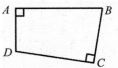

STATEMENTS	REASONS
1. Quad *ABCD* with $\overline{BA} \perp \overline{AD}$ and $\overline{BC} \perp \overline{DC}$	1. Given
2. $m\angle A$ and $\angle C$ are right $\angle$s	2. If 2 lines are $\perp$, they form a rt. $\angle$.
3. $m\angle A = 90$ and $m\angle C = 90$	3. Measure of a rt. $\angle = 90$.
4. $m\angle A + m\angle B + m\angle C + m\angle D = 360$	4. The sum of the angle measures in a quad. $= 360$.
5. $90 + m\angle B + 90 + m\angle D = 360$	5. Substitution
6. $m\angle B + m\angle D = 180$	6. Subtraction Prop. of Eq.
7. $\angle$s *B* and *D* are supp.	7. If the sum of the measures of 2 angles is 180, then the $\angle$s are supp.

31. a. 90°, 90°, 120°, 120°, 120°

    b. 90°, 90°, 90°, 135°, 135°

32. a. $180 - \dfrac{(n-2)180}{n}$

    b. $\dfrac{180n}{n} - \dfrac{180n - 360}{n} = \dfrac{180n - 180n + 360}{n}$
$$= \dfrac{360}{n}$$

33. 36°

34. 90°

35. The resulting polygon is also a REGULAR polygon.

36. Equilateral

For #37 and #38 use $I = \dfrac{180(n-2)}{n}$

37. 150°

38. 120°

39. a. $n - 3$

    b. $\dfrac{n(n-3)}{2}$

40. Draw $\overline{BC}$ in the concave quadrilateral *ABCD*. Since the sum of the angle measures in each of the two triangles formed is 180°, the sum of the interior angle measures of the quadrilateral must equal 180° times 2 or 360°.

41. 221°   **42. a.** No   **b.** Yes

43. a. No   **b.** Yes

SECTION 2.6: Symmetry and Transformations

  1. M, T, X

  2. I, K, V

  3. N, X

  4. S, Z

  5. (a), (c)

  6. (b), (c)

  7. (a), (b)

  8. (b), (c)

  9. MOM

10. WOW, MAM

11. a.

    b.

12. a.

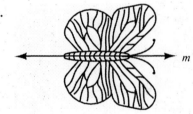

    b.

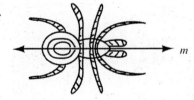

13. a.

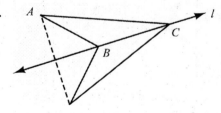

    b.

14. **a.**

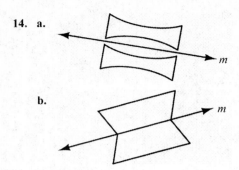

    b.

15. **a.** $m\angle D = 63°$

    b. Yes

    c. Yes

16. **a.** Yes

    b. Yes

    c. $WX = 1.8$ cm

17. WHIM

18. DECODE

19. SIX

20. HOW

21. WOW

22. FRED

23. **a.** clockwise

    b. counterclockwise

24. **a.** counterclockwise

    b. clockwise

25. 62,365 kilowatt hours

26. 62270

27. **a.** line

    b. none

    c. line

28. **a.** line

    b. point or line

    c. point or line

29. (b), (c)

30. (a), (b), (d)

31. **a.** 12

    b. 6

    c. 4

    d. 3

32. **a.** 36

    b. 8

    c. 4

    d. 3

33. $\dfrac{x}{5} + 20 = \dfrac{x}{2} + 5$

    Multiply by 10, the LCD

    $2x + 200 = 5x + 50$

    $150 = 3x$

    $x = 50$

34. $\dfrac{5x}{6} = 130$

    $5x = 780$

    $x = 156$

CHAPTER REVIEW

1. **a.** $\overline{BC} \parallel \overline{AD}$

    b. $\overline{AB} \parallel \overline{CD}$

2. $m\angle 3 = 110°$

3. $2x + 17 = 5x - 94$
$$111 = 3x$$
$$37 = x$$

4. $m\angle A = 50°$ (corresponds to $\angle DCE$)

    $\therefore$ $m\angle BCA = 55°$

        $m\angle BCD = 75°$ and $m\angle D = 75°$

        $m\angle DEF = 50 + 75 = 125°$

5. $130 + 2x + y = 180$
$150 + 2x - y = 180$

    $\begin{aligned} 2x + y &= 50 \\ 2x - y &= 30 \\ \hline 4x &= 80 \\ x &= 20 \end{aligned}$

    $130 + 2(20) + y = 180$
    $130 + 40 + y = 180$
    $y = 10$

6. $2x + 15 = x + 45$
$\quad\quad x = 30$

$3y + 30 + 45 = 180$
$\quad\quad 3y + 75 = 180$
$\quad\quad\quad 3y = 105$
$\quad\quad\quad\quad y = 35$

7. $\overline{AE} \parallel \overline{BF}$

8. None

9. $\overline{BE} \parallel \overline{CF}$

10. $\overline{BE} \parallel \overline{CF}$

11. $\overline{AC} \parallel \overline{DF}$ and $\overline{AE} \parallel \overline{BF}$

12. $\quad x = 120°$ (corr. $\angle$);
$\quad\quad x = y + 50$
$\quad 120 = y + 50$
$\quad\quad\quad y = 70°$

13. $x = 32°$; $y = 30°$

14. $\quad\quad 2x - y = 3x + 2y$
$\quad -1x - 3y = 2 \quad\quad$ (Multiply by 3)
$\quad\quad\quad 3x - y = 80$

$\quad\quad -3x - 9 = 0$
$\quad\quad\underline{\quad 3x - y = 80}$
$\quad\quad\quad -10y = 80$
$\quad\quad\quad\quad\quad y = -8$

$\quad\quad 3x + 8 = 80$
$\quad\quad\quad 3x = 72$
$\quad\quad\quad\quad x = 24$

15. $2a + 2b + 100 = 180$
$\quad\quad 2a + 2b = 80$
$\quad\quad\quad a + b = 40 \quad (\div \text{ by } 2)$
$\quad (a + b) + x = 180$
$\quad\quad\quad 40 + x = 180$
$\quad\quad\quad\quad\quad\quad x = 140°$

16. $x^2 - 12 = x(x - 2)$
$\quad x^2 - 12 = x^2 - 2x$
$\quad\quad -12 = -2x$
$\quad\quad\quad x = 6$

17. $x^2 - 3x + 4 + 17x - x^2 - 5 = 111$
$\quad\quad\quad\quad\quad 14x - 1 = 222$
$\quad\quad\quad\quad\quad\quad 14x = 112$
$\quad\quad\quad\quad\quad\quad\quad x = 8$

$m\angle 3 = 69°$; $m\angle 4 = 67°$; $m\angle 5 = 44°$

18. $3x + y + 5x + 10 = 180$
$\quad\quad 3x + y = 5y + 20$
$\quad\quad 3x + y = 170 \quad$ (Multiply by 4)
$\quad\quad 3x - 4y = 20$

$\quad\quad 32x + 4y = 680$
$\quad\quad\underline{\quad 3x - y = 80}$
$\quad\quad\quad 35x = 700$
$\quad\quad\quad\quad x = 20$

$\quad 8(20) + y = 170$
$\quad\quad 160 + y = 170$
$\quad\quad\quad\quad y = 10$

$m\angle C = 5(10) + 20 = 70° \therefore m\angle B = 110°$

19. S

20. N

21. N

22. S

23. S

24. A

25.

Number of sides	8	12	20	15	10	16	180
Measure of each ext. $\angle$	45	30	18	24	36	22.5	2
Measure of each int. $\angle$	135	150	162	156	144	157.5	178
Number of diagonals	20	54	170	90	35	104	15,930

26.

27.

28. Not possible

29.

30. Statement: If 2 angles are right angles, then the angles are congruent.
Converse: If 2 angles are congruent, then the angles are right angles.
Inverse: If 2 angles are not right angles, then the angles are not congruent.
Contrapositive: If 2 angles are not congruent, then the angles are not right angles.

31. Statement: If it is not raining, then I am happy.
Converse: If I am happy, then it is not raining.
Inverse: If it is raining, then I am not happy.
Contrapositive: If I am not happy, then it is
raining.

32. Contrapositive

33. Given: $\overline{AB} \parallel \overline{CF}$
        $\angle 2 \cong \angle 3$
Prove: $\angle 1 \cong \angle 3$

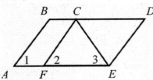

STATEMENTS	REASONS
1. $\overline{AB} \parallel \overline{CF}$	**1.** Given
2. $\angle 1 \cong \angle 2$	**2.** If 2 ∥ lines are cut by a trans., then the corresponding ∠s are ≅.
3. $\angle 2 \cong \angle 3$	**3.** Given
4. $\angle 1 \cong \angle 3$	**4.** Transitive Prop. of Congruence

34. Given: $\angle 1$ is comp. to $\angle 2$
        $\angle 2$ is comp. to $\angle 3$
Prove: $\overline{BD} \parallel \overline{AE}$

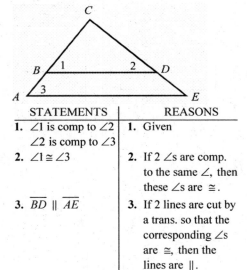

STATEMENTS	REASONS
1. $\angle 1$ is comp to $\angle 2$ $\angle 2$ is comp to $\angle 3$	**1.** Given
2. $\angle 1 \cong \angle 3$	**2.** If 2 ∠s are comp. to the same ∠, then these ∠s are ≅.
3. $\overline{BD} \parallel \overline{AE}$	**3.** If 2 lines are cut by a trans. so that the corresponding ∠s are ≅, then the lines are ∥.

35. Given: $\overline{BE} \perp \overline{DA}$
        $\overline{CD} \perp \overline{DA}$
Prove: $\angle 1 \cong \angle 2$

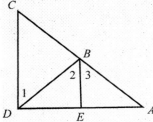

STATEMENTS	REASONS
1. $\overline{BE} \perp \overline{DA}$ $\overline{CD} \perp \overline{DA}$	**1.** Given
2. $\overline{BE} \parallel \overline{CD}$	**2.** If 2 lines are each ⊥ to a 3rd line, then these lines are parallel to each other.
3. $\angle 1 \cong \angle 2$	**3.** If 2 ∥ lines are cut by a trans., then the alternate interior ∠s are ≅.

36. Given: $\angle A \cong \angle C$
        $\overline{DC} \parallel \overline{AB}$
Prove: $\overline{DA} \parallel \overline{CB}$

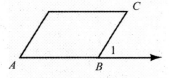

STATEMENTS	REASONS
1. $\angle A \cong \angle C$	**1.** Given
2. $\overline{DC} \parallel \overline{AB}$	**2.** Given
3. $\angle C \cong \angle 1$	**3.** If 2 ∥ lines are cut by a trans., then the alt. int. ∠s are congruent.
4. $\angle A \cong \angle 1$	**4.** Transitive Prop. of Congruence
5. $\overline{DA} \parallel \overline{CB}$	**5.** If 2 lines are cut by a trans. so that corr. ∠s are ≅, then these lines are ∥.

37. Assume $x = -3$.

38. Assume the sides opposite these angles are ≅.

39. Given: $m \not\parallel n$

Prove: $\angle 1 \not\cong \angle 2$

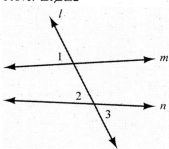

Indirect Proof:
Assume that $\angle 1 \cong \angle 2$. Then $m \parallel n$ since congruent corr. angles are formed. But this contradicts our hypothesis. Therefore, our assumption must be false and it follows that $\angle 1 \not\cong \angle 2$.

40. Given: $\angle 1 \not\cong \angle 3$

Prove: $m \not\parallel n$

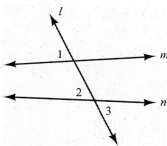

Indirect Proof:
Assume that $m \parallel n$. Then $\angle 1 \cong \angle 3$ since alt. ext. angles are congruent when parallel lines are cut by a transversal. But this contradicts the given fact that $\angle 1 \not\cong \angle 3$. Therefore, our assumption must be false and it follows that $m \not\parallel n$.

41. Given: $\triangle ABC$

Construct: The line through C parallel to $\overline{AB}$.

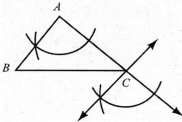

42. Given: $\overline{AB}$

Construct: An equilateral triangle ABC with side $\overline{AB}$.

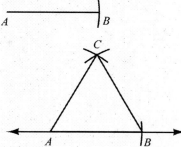

43. **a.** B, H, W

    b. H, S

44. **a.** Isosceles triangle, Circle, Regular pentagon

    b. Circle

45. Congruent

46. **a.**

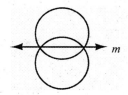

    b.

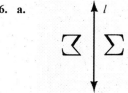

47. 90°

CHAPTER TEST

1. **a.** $\angle 5$

    b. $\angle 3$

2. **a.** $m\angle 2 + m\angle 8 = 68 + 112 = 180°$
$m\angle 6 + m\angle 9 = 68 + 110 = 178°$
$r \parallel s$

    b. $m\angle 2 + m\angle 8 = 68 + 112 = 180°$
$m\angle 6 + m\angle 9 = 68 + 110 = 178°$
$l \not\parallel m$

3. not Q

4. $\angle R$ and $\angle S$ are not both right angles.

5. a. If $r \parallel s$ and $s \parallel t$,

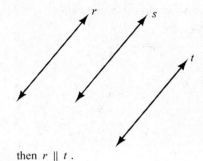

then $r \parallel t$.

b. If $a \perp b$ and $b \perp c$,

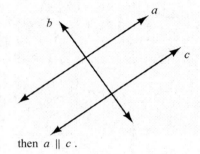

then $a \parallel c$.

6.

7. a. $65 + 79 + x = 180$
$144 + x = 180$
$x = 36$

$m\angle B = 36°$

b. $2x + x + 2x + 15 = 180$
$5x + 15 = 180$
$5x = 165$
$x = 33$

$m\angle B = 33°$

8. a. Pentagon

b. Use $D = \dfrac{n(n-3)}{2}$; 5

9. a. Equiangular hexagon

b. Use $I = \dfrac{180(n-2)}{n}$; 120°

10. A: line; D: line; N: point; O: both; X: both

11. a. Reflection

b. Slide

c. Rotation

12. $\angle 1 \cong \angle 2$ and $\angle 4 \cong \angle 3$
$m\angle C = 61°$

13. $x + 28 = 2x - 26$
$x = 54$

14. $m\angle 3 = 80°$ so $m\angle 4 = 50°$

15. $m\angle 3 = 63°$
$m\angle 2 = x$
$x + 2x + 63 = 180$
$3x = 117$
$x = 39$
$m\angle 2 = 39°$; $m\angle 1 = 78°$

16. **1.** Given

2. $\angle 2 \cong \angle 3$

3. Transitive Prop. of Congruence

4. $\ell \parallel n$

17. Given: $\triangle MNQ$ with $m\angle N = 120°$
Prove: $\angle M$ and $\angle Q$ are not complementary

M

N   *Q*

Indirect Proof:
Assume that $\angle M$ and $\angle Q$ are complementary.
By definition $m\angle M + m\angle Q = 90°$. Also,
$m\angle M + m\angle Q + m\angle N = 180°$ because these are
the three angles of $\triangle MNQ$. By substitution,
$90° + m\angle N = 180°$, so it follows that
$m\angle N = 90°$. But this leads to a contradiction
because it is given that $m\angle N = 120°$. The
assumption must be false, and it follows that
$\angle M$ and $\angle Q$ are not complementary.

18. **1.** Given

2. 180°

3. $m\angle 1 + m\angle 2 + 90° = 180°$

4. 90°

S5. $\angle 1$ and $\angle 2$ are complementary.

R5. Definition of complementary angles.

19. $m\angle = 21°$

Chapter 3: Triangles

SECTION 3.1: Congruent Triangles

1. $\angle A$; $\overline{AB}$; No; No

2. $a = 10$; $b = 8$; $c = 11$

3. $m\angle A = 72°$

4. $m\angle E = 38°$

5. SAS

6. $\triangle BCA \cong \triangle EDF$

7. $\triangle AED \cong \triangle FDE$

8. $\overline{RS} \cong \overline{RS}$

9. SSS

10. ASA

11. AAS

12. SAS

13. ASA

14. SAS

15. ASA

16. SAS

17. SSS

18. ASA

19. a. $\angle A \cong \angle A$

    b. ASA

20. a. $\overline{MP} \cong \overline{MP}$

    b. SSS

21. $\overline{AD} \cong \overline{EC}$

22. $\angle WVY \cong \angle ZVX$

23. $\overline{MO} \cong \overline{MO}$

24. $\angle E \cong \angle J$

25. 1. Given

    2. $\overline{AC} \cong \overline{AC}$

    3. SSS

26. 1. Given

    2. If 2 parallel lines are cut by a transversal, then the alternate interior angles are $\cong$.

    3. $\overline{AD} \parallel \overline{BC}$

    4. $\angle DAC \cong \angle BCA$

    5. Identity

    6. $\triangle ABC \cong \triangle CDA$

27. Given: $\overrightarrow{PQ}$ bisects $\angle MPN$;
    $\overline{MP} \cong \overline{NP}$
    Prove: $\triangle MQP \cong \triangle NQP$

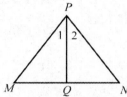

STATEMENTS	REASONS
1. $\overrightarrow{PQ}$ bisects $\angle MPN$	1. Given
2. $\angle MPQ \cong \angle NPQ$	2. If a ray bisects an $\angle$, it forms 2 $\cong$ $\angle$s.
3. $\overline{MP} \cong \overline{NP}$	3. Given
4. $\overline{PQ} \cong \overline{PQ}$	4. Identity
5. $\triangle MQP \cong \triangle NQP$	5. SAS

28. Given: $\overline{PQ} \perp \overline{MN}$ and $\angle 1 \cong \angle 2$
    Prove: $\triangle MQP \cong \triangle NQP$

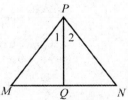

STATEMENTS	REASONS
1. $\overline{PQ} \perp \overline{MN}$ and $\angle 1 \cong \angle 2$	1. Given
2. $\angle PQM \cong \angle PQN$	2. If 2 lines are $\perp$, they form $\cong$ adjacent $\angle$s.
3. $\overline{PQ} \cong \overline{PQ}$	3. Identity
4. $\triangle MQP \cong \triangle NQP$	4. ASA

29. Given: $\overline{AB} \perp \overline{BC}$ and
    $\overline{AB} \perp \overline{BD}$;
    also $\overline{BC} \cong \overline{BD}$
    Prove: $\triangle ABC \cong \triangle ABD$

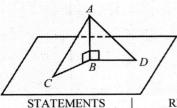

STATEMENTS	REASONS
1. $\overline{AB} \perp \overline{BC}$ and $\overline{AB} \perp \overline{BD}$	1. Given
2. $\angle ABC$ is a right $\angle$ and $\angle ABD$ is a right $\angle$	2. If 2 lines are $\perp$, then they meet to form a right $\angle$.
3. $\angle ABC \cong \angle ABD$	3. Any two right $\angle$s are $\cong$.
4. $\overline{BC} \cong \overline{BD}$	4. Given
5. $\overline{AB} \cong \overline{AB}$	5. Identity
6. $\triangle ABC \cong \triangle ABD$	6. SAS

30. Given: $\overline{PN}$ bisects $\overline{MQ}$;
    $\angle$s M and Q are right angles
    Prove: $\triangle PQR \cong \triangle NMR$

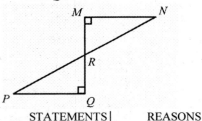

STATEMENTS	REASONS
1. $\overline{PN}$ bisects $\overline{MQ}$	1. Given
2. $\overline{MR} \cong \overline{QR}$	2. If a segment bisects a segment, then two $\cong$ segments are formed.
3. $\angle$s M and Q are right angles	3. Given
4. $\angle M \cong \angle Q$	4. Any 2 right $\angle$s are $\cong$.
5. $\angle MRN \cong \angle QRP$	5. If 2 lines intersect, the vertical $\angle$s formed are $\cong$.
6. $\triangle PQR \cong \triangle NMR$	6. ASA

31. Given: $\angle VRS \cong \angle TSR$
    $\overline{RV} \cong \overline{TS}$
    Prove: $\triangle RST \cong \triangle SRV$

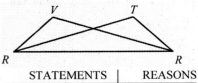

STATEMENTS	REASONS
1. $\angle VRS \cong \angle TSR$ and $\overline{RV} \cong \overline{TS}$	1. Given
2. $\overline{RS} \cong \overline{RS}$	2. Identity
3. $\triangle RST \cong \triangle SRV$	3. SAS

32. Given: $\overline{VS} \cong \overline{TR}$
    $\angle TRS \cong \angle VSR$
    Prove: $\triangle RST \cong \triangle SRV$

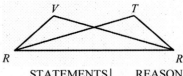

STATEMENTS	REASONS
1. $\overline{VS} \cong \overline{TR}$	1. Given
2. $\angle TRS \cong \angle VSR$	2. Given
3. $\overline{RS} \cong \overline{RS}$	3. Identity
4. $\triangle RST \cong \triangle SRV$	4. SAS

33. Yes; SAS or SSS

34. No

35. No

36. Yes; AAS

37. **a.** $\triangle CBE$, $\triangle ADE$, $\triangle CDE$

    b. $\triangle ADC$

    c. $\triangle CBD$

38. If 2 angles of one triangle are congruent to 2 angles of another triangle, then the third angles are also congruent.

39. Given: Plane M; C is the midpoint of $\overline{EB}$;
$\overline{AD} \perp \overline{BE}$ and
$\overline{AB} \parallel \overline{ED}$

Prove: $\triangle ABC \cong \triangle DEC$

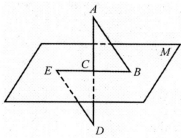

STATEMENTS	REASONS
1. Plane M; C is the midpoint of $\overline{EB}$	1. Given
2. $\overline{EC} \cong \overline{CB}$	2. The midpoint of a a segment divides the segment into 2 $\cong$ segments.
3. $\overline{AD} \perp \overline{BE}$	3. Given
4. $\angle ACB$ is a right $\angle$ $\angle DCE$ is a right $\angle$	4. If 2 lines are $\perp$, they meet to form a right $\angle$.
5. $\angle ACB \cong \angle DCE$	5. Any two right angles are $\cong$.
6. $\overline{AB} \parallel \overline{ED}$	6. Given
7. $\angle ABC \cong \angle DEC$	7. If 2 $\parallel$ lines are cut by a trans., then the alternate interior $\angle$s are $\cong$.
8. $\triangle ABC \cong \triangle DEC$	8. ASA

40. Given: $\overline{SP} \cong \overline{SQ}$; $\overline{ST} \cong \overline{SV}$
Prove: $\triangle SPV \cong \triangle SQT$ and
$\triangle TPQ \cong \triangle VQP$

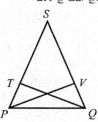

STATEMENTS	REASONS
1. $\overline{SP} \cong \overline{SQ}$; $\overline{ST} \cong \overline{SV}$	1. Given
2. $\angle S \cong \angle S$	2. Identity
3. $\triangle SPV \cong \triangle SQT$	3. SAS
4. $\overline{PV} \cong \overline{QT}$	4. If 2 $\triangle$s are $\cong$, then the corresponding parts are $\cong$.
5. $\overline{PQ} \cong \overline{PQ}$	5. Identity
6. $SP = SQ$; $ST = SV$	6. If 2 segments are $\cong$, they are $\cong$ in measure.
7. $SP = ST + PT$ and $SQ = SV + QV$	7. Segment-Addition Postulate
8. $ST + PT = SV + QV$	8. Substitution
9. $PT = QV$	9. Subtraction Prop. of Equality
10. $\overline{PT} \cong \overline{QV}$	10. If 2 segments are = in measure, they are $\cong$.
11. $\triangle TPQ \cong \triangle VQP$	11. SSS

41.

STATEMENTS	REASONS
1. $\angle ABC; \overline{RS}$ is the $\perp$ bisector of $\overline{AB}; \overline{RT}$ is the $\perp$ bisector of $\overline{BC}$	1. Given
2. $\angle RSA \cong \angle RSB$ and $\angle RTB \cong \angle RTC$	2. $\perp$ lines form $\cong$ adj. $\angle$s
3. $\overline{AS} \cong \overline{BS}; \overline{BT} \cong \overline{TC}$	3. Bisecting a seg. forms 2 $\cong$ segments.
4. $\overline{RS} \cong \overline{RS}$ and $\overline{RT} \cong \overline{RT}$	4. Identity
5. $\triangle RSA \cong \triangle RSB$ and $\triangle RTB \cong \triangle RTC$	5. SAS
6. $\overline{AR} \cong \overline{BR}$ and $\overline{BR} \cong \overline{RC}$	6. If 2 triangles are $\cong$, the corresponding sides are $\cong$.
7. $\overline{AR} \cong \overline{RC}$	7. Transitive Property for Congruence

SECTION 3.2: Corresponding Parts of Congruent Triangles

1. Given: $\angle 1$ and $\angle 2$ are right $\angle$s .
$\overline{CA} \cong \overline{DA}$
Prove: $\triangle ABC \cong \triangle ABD$

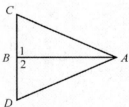

STATEMENTS	REASONS
1. $\angle 1$ and $\angle 2$ are right $\angle$s and $\overline{CA} \cong \overline{DA}$	1. Given
2. $\overline{AB} \cong \overline{AB}$	2. Identity
3. $\triangle ABC \cong \triangle ABD$	3. HL

2. Given: $\angle 1$ and $\angle 2$ are right $\angle$s
$\overline{AB}$ bisects $\angle CAD$
Prove: $\triangle ABC \cong \triangle ABD$

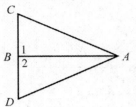

STATEMENTS	REASONS
1. $\angle 1$ and $\angle 2$ are right $\angle$s and $\overline{AB}$ bisects $\angle CAD$	1. Given
2. $\angle CAB \cong \angle DAB$	2. If a ray bisects an $\angle$, it forms 2 $\cong$ $\angle$s.
3. $\overline{AB} \cong \overline{AB}$	3. Identity
4. $\triangle ABC \cong \triangle ABD$	4. ASA

3. Given: P is the midpoint of both $\overline{MR}$ and $\overline{NQ}$
Prove: $\triangle MNP \cong \triangle RQP$

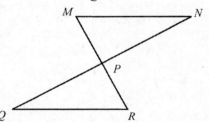

STATEMENTS	REASONS
1. P is the midpoint of $\overline{MR}$ and $\overline{NQ}$	1. Given
2. $\overline{MP} \cong \overline{PR}$ and $\overline{QP} \cong \overline{PN}$	2. Midpoint of a segment forms 2 $\cong$ segments.
3. $\angle MPN \cong \angle RPQ$	3. If 2 lines intersect, the vertical $\angle$s are $\cong$.
4. $\triangle MNP \cong \triangle RQP$	4. SAS

4. Given: $\overline{MN} \parallel \overline{QR}$ and $\overline{MN} \cong \overline{QR}$
Prove: $\triangle MNP \cong \triangle RQP$

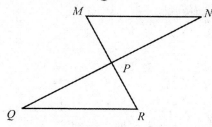

STATEMENTS	REASONS
1. $\overline{MN} \parallel \overline{QR}$	1. Given
2. $\angle M \cong \angle Q$ and $\angle N \cong \angle Q$	2. If 2 $\parallel$ lines are cut by a trans., then the alternate interior $\angle$s are $\cong$.
3. $\overline{MN} \cong \overline{QR}$	3. Given
4. $\triangle MNP \cong \triangle RQP$	4. ASA

5. Given: $\angle R$ and $\angle V$ are right $\angle$s.
$\angle 1 \cong \angle 2$
Prove: $\triangle RST \cong \triangle VST$

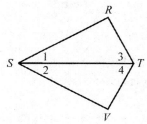

STATEMENTS	REASONS
1. $\angle R$ and $\angle V$ are right $\angle$s and $\angle 1 \cong \angle 2$	1. Given
2. $\angle R \cong \angle V$	2. All right $\angle$s are $\cong$.
3. $\overline{ST} \cong \overline{ST}$	3. Identity
4. $\triangle RST \cong \triangle VST$	4. AAS

6. Given: $\angle 1 \cong \angle 2$ and $\angle 1 \cong \angle 2$
Prove: $\triangle RST \cong \triangle VST$

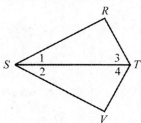

STATEMENTS	REASONS
1. $\angle 1 \cong \angle 2$ and $\angle 3 \cong \angle 4$	1. Given
2. $\overline{ST} \cong \overline{ST}$	2. Identity
3. $\triangle RST \cong \triangle VST$	3. ASA

7. Given: $\overline{SR} \cong \overline{SV}$ and $\overline{RT} \cong \overline{VT}$
Prove: $\triangle RST \cong \triangle VST$

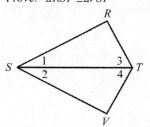

STATEMENTS	REASONS
1. $\overline{SR} \cong \overline{SV}$ and $\overline{RT} \cong \overline{VT}$	1. Given
2. $\overline{ST} \cong \overline{ST}$	2. Identity
3. $\triangle RST \cong \triangle VST$	3. SSS

8. Given: $\angle R$ and $\angle V$ are right $\angle$s.
$\overline{RT} \cong \overline{VT}$
Prove: $\triangle RST \cong \triangle VST$

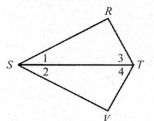

STATEMENTS	REASONS
1. $\angle R$ and $\angle V$ are right $\angle$s and $\overline{RT} \cong \overline{VT}$	1. Given
2. $\overline{ST} \cong \overline{ST}$	2. Identity
3. $\triangle RST \cong \triangle VST$	3. HL

9. $m\angle 2 = 48°$; $m\angle 3 = 48°$
$m\angle 5 = 42°$; $m\angle 6 = 42°$

10. $4x + 3 + 6x - 3 = 90$
$ 10x = 90$
$ x = 9$

$m\angle 1 = 39°$; $m\angle 2 = 51°$
$m\angle 3 = 51°$; $m\angle 4 = 39°$
$m\angle 5 = 39°$; $m\angle 6 = 39°$

11. **1.** Given

2. If 2 lines are $\perp$, then they form right $\angle$s.

3. Identity

4. $\triangle HJK \cong \triangle HJL$

5. $\overline{KJ} \cong \overline{JL}$

12. **1.** $\overrightarrow{HJ}$ bisects ∠KHL

2. If a ray bisects an ∠ , if forms 2 ≅ ∠s .

3. Given

4. If 2 lines are ⊥ , then they form ≅ adjacent ∠s .

5. $\overline{HJ} \cong \overline{HJ}$

6. △HJK ≅△HJL

7. CPCTC

13. Given: ∠s *P* and *R* are rt. ∠ s

   M is the midpoint of $\overline{PR}$

Prove: ∠*N* ≅ ∠*Q*

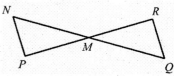

STATEMENTS	REASONS
1. ∠s *P* and *R* are rt. ∠s	1. Given
2. ∠*P* ≅ ∠*R*	2. All rt. ∠s are ≅ .
3. *M* is the midpoint of $\overline{PR}$	3. Given
4. $\overline{PM} \cong \overline{MR}$	4. Midpoint of a segment forms 2 ≅ segments.
5. ∠*NMP* ≅ ∠*QMR*	5. If 2 lines intersect, the vertical angles formed are ≅ .
6. △*NPM* ≅△*QRM*	6. ASA
7. ∠*N* ≅ ∠*Q*	7. CPCTC

14. Given: *M* is the midpoint of $\overline{NQ}$;

   $\overline{NP} \parallel \overline{RQ}$ with trans. $\overline{PR}$

Prove: $\overline{NP} \cong \overline{QR}$

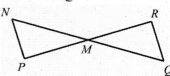

STATEMENTS	REASONS
1. *M* is the midpoint of $\overline{PR}$	1. Given
2. $\overline{NM} \cong \overline{MQ}$	2. The midpoint of a divides the segment into 2 ≅ segments.
3. $\overline{NP} \parallel \overline{RQ}$ with trans. $\overline{PR}$	3. Given
4. ∠*P* ≅ ∠*R*	4. If 2 lines are cut by a trans, then the alt int. ∠s are ≅ .
5. ∠*NMP* ≅ ∠*QMR*	5. If 2 lines intersect, the vertical angles formed are ≅ .
6. △*NPM* ≅△*QRM*	6. AAS
7. $\overline{NP} \cong \overline{QR}$	7. CPCTC

15. Given: ∠s 1 and 2 are rt. ∠ s

   H is the midpoint of $\overline{FK}$

   and $\overline{FG} \parallel \overline{HJ}$

Prove: $\overline{FG} \cong \overline{HJ}$

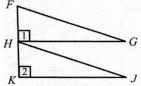

STATEMENTS	REASONS
1. ∠s 1 and 2 are rt. ∠s	1. Given
2. ∠1 ≅ ∠2	2. All rt. ∠s are ≅ .
3. *H* is the midpoint of $\overline{FK}$	3. Given
4. $\overline{FH} \cong \overline{HK}$	4. The midpoint of a segment forms 2 ≅ segments.
5. $\overline{FG} \parallel \overline{HJ}$	5. Given
6. ∠*GFH* ≅ ∠*JHK*	6. If 2 ∥ lines are cut by a trans., then the corresponding angles are ≅ .
7. △*FHG* ≅△*HKJ*	7. ASA
8. $\overline{FG} \cong \overline{HJ}$	8. CPCTC

16. Given: $\overline{DE} \perp \overline{EF}$; $\overline{CB} \perp \overline{AB}$
      $\overline{AB} \parallel \overline{FE}$ and
      $\overline{AC} \cong \overline{FD}$
   Prove: $\overline{EF} \cong \overline{BA}$

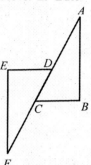

STATEMENTS	REASONS
1. $\overline{DE} \perp \overline{EF}$ $\overline{CB} \perp \overline{AB}$	**1.** Given
2. $\angle E$ is a rt. $\angle$ $\angle B$ is a rt. $\angle$	**2.** If 2 lines are $\perp$, then they meet to form a rt. $\angle$.
3. $\angle E \cong \angle B$	**3.** Any 2 rt. $\angle$s are $\cong$.
4. $\overline{AB} \parallel \overline{FE}$	**4.** Given
5. $\angle F \cong \angle A$	**5.** If 2 $\parallel$ lines are cut by a trans., then the alt. int. $\angle$s are $\cong$.
6. $\overline{AC} \cong \overline{FD}$	**6.** Given
7. $\triangle FED \cong \triangle ABC$	**7.** AAS
8. $\overline{EF} \cong \overline{BA}$	**8.** CPCTC

17. $c = 5$

18. $c = 13$

19. $b = 8$

20. $a = 8$

21. $c = \sqrt{41}$

22. $b = \sqrt{15}$

23. Given: $\overline{DF} \cong \overline{DG}$
      $\overline{FE} \cong \overline{EG}$
   Prove: $\overline{DE}$ bisects $\angle FDG$

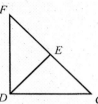

STATEMENTS	REASONS
1. $\overline{DF} \cong \overline{DG}$ and $\overline{FE} \cong \overline{EG}$	**1.** Given
2. $\overline{DE} \cong \overline{DE}$	**2.** Identity
3. $\triangle FDE \cong \triangle GDE$	**3.** SSS
4. $\angle FDE \cong \angle GDE$	**4.** CPCTC
5. $\overline{DE}$ bisects $\angle FDG$	**5.** If a ray divides an $\angle$ into 2 $\cong$ $\angle$s, then the ray bisects the angle.

24. Given: $\overrightarrow{DE}$ bisects $\angle FDG$
      $\angle F \cong \angle G$
   Prove: E is the midpoint of $\overline{FG}$

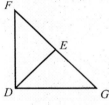

STATEMENTS	REASONS
1. $\overrightarrow{DE}$ bisects $\angle FDG$	**1.** Given
2. $\angle FDE \cong \angle GDE$	**2.** If a ray bisects an $\angle$, then it forms 2 $\cong$ $\angle$s.
3. $\angle F \cong \angle G$	**3.** Given
4. $\overline{DE} \cong \overline{DE}$	**4.** Reflexive
5. $\triangle FDE \cong \triangle GDE$	**5.** AAS
6. $\overline{DE} \cong \overline{DE}$	**6.** CPCTC
7. E is the midpoint of $\overline{FG}$	**7.** If a point divides a segment into 2 $\cong$ segments, then the point is a midpoint.

25. Given: *E* is the midpoint of $\overline{FG}$;

$\overline{DF} \cong \overline{DG}$

Prove: $\overline{DE} \perp \overline{FG}$

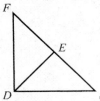

STATEMENTS	REASONS
1. *E* is the midpoint of $\overline{FG}$	1. Given
2. $\overline{FE} \cong \overline{EG}$	2. The midpoint of a segment forms 2 $\cong$ segments.
3. $\overline{DF} \cong \overline{DG}$	3. Given
4. $\overline{DE} \cong \overline{DE}$	4. Reflexive
5. $\triangle FDE \cong \triangle GDE$	5. SSS
6. $\angle DEF \cong \angle DEG$	6. CPCTC
7. $\overline{DE} \perp \overline{FG}$	7. If 2 lines meet to form $\cong$ adj. $\angle$s, then the lines are $\perp$.

26. Given: $\angle$s *MQP* and *NPQ* are rt. $\angle$s ;

$\overline{MQ} \cong \overline{NP}$

Prove: $\overline{MP} \cong \overline{NQ}$

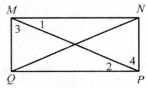

STATEMENTS	REASONS
1. $\angle$s *MQP* and *NPQ* are rt. $\angle$s	1. Given
2. $\angle MQP \cong \angle NPQ$	2. Any 2 rt. $\angle$s are $\cong$.
3. $\overline{MQ} \cong \overline{NP}$	3. Given
4. $\overline{QP} \cong \overline{QP}$	4. Identity
5. $\triangle MQP \cong \triangle NPQ$	5. SAS
6. $\overline{MP} \cong \overline{NQ}$	6. CPCTC

27. Given: $\angle 1 \cong \angle 2$

$\overline{MN} \cong \overline{QP}$

Prove: $\overline{MQ} \parallel \overline{NP}$

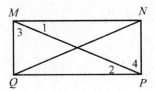

STATEMENTS	REASONS
1. $\angle 1 \cong \angle 2$ and $\overline{MN} \cong \overline{QP}$	1. Given
2. $\overline{MP} \cong \overline{MP}$	2. Identity
3. $\triangle NMP \cong \triangle QPM$	3. SAS
4. $\angle 3 \cong \angle 4$	4. CPCTC
5. $\overline{MQ} \parallel \overline{NP}$	5. If 2 lines are cut by a trans. so that the alt. int. $\angle$s are $\cong$, then the lines are $\parallel$.

28. Given: $\overline{MN} \parallel \overline{QP}$

$\overline{MQ} \parallel \overline{NP}$

Prove: $\overline{MQ} \cong \overline{NP}$

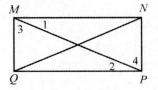

STATEMENTS	REASONS
1. $\overline{MN} \parallel \overline{QP}$	1. Given
2. $\angle 1 \cong \angle 2$	2. If 2 $\parallel$ lines are cut by a trans., then the alt. int. $\angle$s are $\cong$.
3. $\overline{MQ} \parallel \overline{NP}$	3. Given
4. $\angle 3 \cong \angle 4$	4. Same as (2).
5. $\overline{MP} \parallel \overline{MP}$	5. Identity
6. $\triangle MQP \cong \triangle PNM$	6. ASA
7. $\overline{MQ} \cong \overline{NP}$	7. CPCTC

29. Given: $\overrightarrow{RW}$ bisects $\angle SRU$;
also $\overline{RS} \cong \overline{RU}$
Prove: $\triangle TRU \cong \triangle VRS$

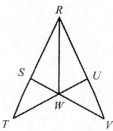

STATEMENTS	REASONS
1. $\overrightarrow{RW}$ bisects $\angle RSU$	1. Given
2. $\angle SRW \cong \angle URW$	2. If a ray bisects an $\angle$ then 2 $\cong$ $\angle$s are formed.
3. $\overline{RS} \cong \overline{RU}$	3. Given
4. $\overline{RW} \cong \overline{RW}$	4. Identity
5. $\triangle RSW \cong \triangle RUW$	5. SAS
6. $\angle RSW \cong \angle RUW$	6. CPCTC
7. $\angle TRV \cong \angle VRS$	7. Identity
8. $\triangle TRU \cong \triangle VRS$	8. ASA

30. Given: $\overline{DB} \perp \overline{BC}$ and $\overline{CE} \perp \overline{DE}$;
$\overline{AB} \cong \overline{AE}$
Prove: $\triangle BDC \cong \triangle ECD$

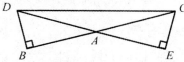

STATEMENTS	REASONS
1. $\overline{DB} \perp \overline{BC}$ and $\overline{CE} \perp \overline{DE}$	1. Given
2. $\angle DBA$ is a rt. $\angle$ $\angle CEA$ is a rt. $\angle$	2. If 2 lines are $\perp$, then they meet to form a rt. $\angle$.
3. $\angle DBA \cong \angle CEA$	3. Any 2 rt. $\angle$s are $\cong$.
4. $\overline{AB} \parallel \overline{AE}$	4. Given
5. $\angle DAB \cong \angle CAE$	5. If 2 lines intersect, the vertical $\angle$s formed are $\cong$.
6. $\triangle ACE \cong \triangle ADB$	6. ASA
7. $\overline{DB} \cong \overline{CE}$	7. CPCTC
8. $\overline{DC} \cong \overline{DC}$	8. Identity
9. $\triangle BDC \cong \triangle ECD$	9. HL

31. a. 8

b. 37°

c. 53°

32. a. 28°

b. 56°

c. 24

33. $x^2 = 45^2 + 750^2$
$x^2 = 2025 + 562,500$
$x^2 = 564,525$
$x \approx 751$ ft

34. $(AB)^2 = (AC)^2 + (CB)^2$
$(AB)^2 = 5^2 + 12^2$
$(AB)^2 = 25 + 144$
$(AB)^2 = 169$
$AB \approx 13$ mi
$(AC + CB) - AB = 5 + 12 - 13 = 4$ mi

35. Given: Regular pentagon $ABCDE$
with diagonals $\overline{BE}$ and $\overline{BD}$
Prove: $\overline{BE} \cong \overline{BD}$
(Hint: First prove $\triangle ABE \cong \triangle CBD$)

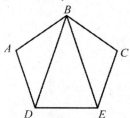

STATEMENTS	REASONS
1. Regular pentagon $ABCDE$ with diagonals $\overline{BE}$ and $\overline{BD}$	1. Given
2. $\overline{AB} \cong \overline{BC} \cong \overline{CD} \cong \overline{AE}$	2. All sides of a reg. pentagon are $\cong$.
3. $\angle A \cong \angle C$	3. The interior $\angle$s of reg. polygons are $\cong$.
4. $\triangle ABE \cong \triangle CBD$	4. SAS
5. $\overline{BE} \cong \overline{BD}$	5. CPCTC

36. $\overline{AB} \cong \overline{AE}$ in $\triangle ABE$. If $m\angle ABE = m\angle AEB$ and $m\angle A = 108°$, then $m\angle ABE = 36°$. Likewise $m\angle CBD = 36°$. Since $m\angle ABC = 108°$, then $m\angle EBD = 36°$. Yes, $\overrightarrow{BE}$ and $\overrightarrow{BD}$ trisect $\angle ABC$.

SECTION 3.3: Isosceles Triangles

1. Isosceles

2. $\angle T \cong \angle U$

3. $\overline{VT} \cong \overline{VU}$

4. Perimeter $= 10 + 10 + 8 = 28$

5. $m\angle U = 69°$

6. $m\angle V = 180 - 2(69) = 42°$

7. $m\angle V = 180 - 2(72) = 36°$

8. $m\angle T = \frac{1}{2}(180 - 40) = 70°$

9. $L = E$ (equivalent)

10. A is a subset of S.

11. R and S are disjoint; so $R \cap S = \varnothing$

12. I and R intersect.

13. Underdetermined

14. Determined

15. Overdetermined

16. Overdetermined

17. Determined

18. Overdetermined

19. The measure of the vertex angle plus the measure of the 2 base angles equals 180°. Therefore, the measure of the 2 base angles must equal 100°. Since the base angles are equal in measure, each base angle measures 55°.

20. $m\angle A + m\angle ABD + m\angle ADB = 180$
    $40 + m\angle ABD + m\angle ADB = 180$
    $m\angle ABD + m\angle ADB = 140°$
    But since the base angles of an isosceles △ are
    $\cong$, $m\angle ABD = m\angle ADB = 70°$. Since $\angle ABD$ and
    $\angle ADB$ are bisected, $m\angle ABC = 35°$ and
    $m\angle ADC = 35°$. But $m\angle s$ CBD and CDB are
    also $= 35°$. But
    $m\angle CBD + m\angle 1 + m\angle CDB = 180°$. Therefore,
    $m\angle 1 = 110°$.

21. $m\angle 2 = 68°$ (Base $\angle$s in an isosceles △ are $\cong$)
    Also, $m\angle 1 + m\angle 2 + m\angle 3 = 180$
    $m\angle 1 + 68 + 68 = 180$
    $m\angle 1 + 136 = 180$
    $m\angle 1 = 44°$

22. $\frac{1}{2} \cdot m\angle 3 = \frac{1}{2} \cdot m\angle 2 = \frac{1}{2} \cdot 68 = 34°$

    $m\angle 4 = 180 - 34 - 34 = 112°$

23. $\frac{1}{2} \cdot m\angle 3 = 34°$

    $m\angle 1 = 180 - 68 - 68 = 44°$

    $\frac{1}{2} \cdot m\angle 1 = 22°$

    $m\angle 5 = 180 - 34 - 22 = 124°$

24. $m\angle 3 = m\angle 2 = 2x$
    $m\angle 1 = 180 - 2x - 2x = 180 - 4x$
    $\frac{1}{2} \cdot m\angle 3 = x$ and $\frac{1}{2} \cdot m\angle 1 = 90 - 2x$
    $m\angle 5 = 180 - x - (90 - 2x)$
    $m\angle 5 = 180 - x - 90 + 2x$
    $m\angle 5 = 90 + x$

25. Let the measure of the vertex angle be x. Then the measure of the base angles are each $x + 12$.
    $x + (x + 12) + (x + 12) = 180$
    $3x + 24 = 180$
    $3x = 156$
    $x = 52$

    $m\angle A = 52°$; $m\angle B = 64°$; $m\angle C = 64°$

26. Let the measure of each base angle be x. Then the measure of the vertex angle is $5 + \frac{1}{2} \cdot x$

    $x + x + \left(5 + \frac{1}{2} \cdot x\right) = 180$

    $\frac{5}{2} \cdot x + 5 = 180$

    $\frac{5}{2} \cdot x = 175$

    $\frac{2}{5} \cdot \frac{5}{2} \cdot x = 175 \cdot \frac{2}{5}$

    $x = 70$

    $m\angle A = 40°$; $m\angle B = 70°$; $m\angle C = 70°$

27. 26

28. 10.9

29. 12

30. 20

31. Yes

32. Yes

33. 1. Given

    2. $\angle 3 \cong \angle 2$

    3. $\angle 1 \cong \angle 2$

    4. If 2 $\angle$s of one △ are $\cong$, then the opposite sides are $\cong$.

34. **1.** $\overline{AB} \cong \overline{AC}$

2. If 2 sides of one △ are ≅, then opposite ∠s are ≅.

3. If the exterior sides of two adjacent ∠s form a line, then the ∠s are supplementary.

4. ∠6 ≅ ∠7

35. Given: ∠1 ≅ ∠3
$\overline{RU} \cong \overline{VU}$
Prove: △STU is isosceles

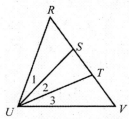

STATEMENTS	REASONS
1. ∠1 ≅ ∠3	**1.** Given
2. $\overline{RU} \cong \overline{VU}$	**2.** Given
3. ∠R ≅ ∠V	**3.** If 2 sides of a △ are ≅, then the ∠s opposite these sides are also ≅.
4. △RUS ≅ △VUT	**4.** ASA
5. $\overline{SU} \cong \overline{TU}$	**5.** CPCTC
6. △STU is isosceles	**6.** If a △ has 2 sides ≅, it is an isosceles △.

36. Given: $\overline{WY} \cong \overline{WZ}$;
M is the midpoint of $\overline{YZ}$;
$\overline{MX} \perp \overline{WY}$ and $\overline{MT} \perp \overline{WZ}$
Prove: $\overline{MX} \cong \overline{MT}$

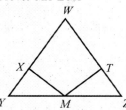

STATEMENTS	REASONS
1. $\overline{WY} \cong \overline{WZ}$	**1.** Given
2. ∠Y ≅ ∠Z	**2.** If 2 sides of a △ are ≅, then the ∠s opposite these sides are also ≅.
3. *M* is the midpoint of $\overline{YZ}$	**3.** Given
4. $\overline{YM} \cong \overline{MZ}$	**4.** The midpoint of a segment forms 2 ≅ segments.
5. $\overline{MX} \perp \overline{WY}$ and $\overline{MT} \perp \overline{WZ}$	**5.** Given
6. ∠YXM is a rt. ∠ ∠ZTM is a rt. ∠	**6.** If 2 lines are ⊥, then they meet to form a right ∠.
7. ∠YXM ≅ ∠ZTM	**7.** Any 2 right ∠s are ≅.
8. △XYM ≅ △TZM	**8.** AAS
9. $\overline{MX} \cong \overline{MT}$	**9.** CPCTC

37. Given: Isosceles △MNP with vertex *P*;
Isosceles △MNQ with vertex *Q*
Prove: △MQP ≅ △NQP

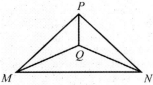

STATEMENTS	REASONS
1. Isosceles △MNP with vertex *P*	**1.** Given
2. $\overline{MP} \cong \overline{NP}$	**2.** An isosceles △ has 2 ≅ sides.
3. Isosceles △MNQ with vertex *Q*	**3.** Given
4. $\overline{MQ} \cong \overline{NQ}$	**4.** Same as (2)
5. $\overline{PQ} \cong \overline{PQ}$	**5.** Identity
6. △MQP ≅ △NQP	**6.** SSS

38. a. For $\triangle BAT$,
$$P = 12.3 + 12.3 + 7.6 = 32.2$$

b. For $\triangle ARB$,
$$P = 12.3 + 7.6 + 7.6 = 27.5$$

c. For $\triangle RBT$,
$$P = 7.6 + 7.6 + 4.7 = 19.9$$

39. a.
$$20 + 2x = 180$$
$$2x = 160$$
$$x = 80°$$
$$m\angle T = 80°$$

b. $m\angle ARB = 180 - 80 = 100°$

c. Since $\overline{BR} \cong \overline{AR}$, then $m\angle RBA = m\angle A$.
$$m\angle RBA + m\angle A + m\angle BRA = 180°$$
$$2 \cdot m\angle A + 100 = 180°$$
$$2 \cdot m\angle A = 80°$$
$$m\angle A = 40°$$

40. $\triangle PMN$ is an isosceles $\triangle$ with
$m\angle PMN = m\angle PNM = 72°$. Since both of these
$\angle$s are bisected,

$m\angle PMB = m\angle BMN = m\angle PNA = m\angle ANM = 36°$.
Therefore, the isosceles triangles in the drawing
are: $\triangle PMN$, $\triangle PBM$, $\triangle PAN$, $\triangle MQN$, $\triangle AQM$,
$\triangle BQN$, $\triangle MBN$, and $\triangle NAM$.

41. 75° each

42. The altitude of an isosceles triangle divides the
triangle into 2 triangles which are congruent by
HL. The base of an isosceles triangle is divided
into 2 segments which are congruent by CPCTC.
Therefore, the altitude meets the base at the
midpoint of the base which means the altitude is
also the median to the base of the triangle.

43. The bisector of the vertex angle of an isosceles
triangle divides the triangle into two congruent
triangles by SAS. The base of the isosceles
triangle is divided into two segments which are
congruent by CPCTC. Therefore, the bisector of
the vertex angle bisects the base.

44. The angle bisectors of the base angles of an
isosceles triangle divide the base angles into four
congruent angles. Since two angles in the triangle
formed by the angle bisectors are congruent, the
opposite sides are also congruent. Therefore, the
triangle is an isosceles triangle.

45. Proof: The Given implies $\overline{XZ} \cong \overline{YZ} \cong \overline{ZW}$.
Then a = e and f = d.

$a + b + e = 180$ But if a = e, then

$a + b + a = 180$ or

$\qquad b = 180 - 2a$ Also

$\qquad b + c = 180$ so

$180 - 2a + c = 180$ or

$\qquad c = 2a$ Also

$\qquad c + f + d = 180$ so

$2a + d + d = 180$ or

$2a + 2d = 180$ or

$\qquad a + d = 90$

If a + d = 90, then $m\angle XYW$ must = 90.

$\therefore \triangle XYW$ is a right $\triangle$

46. The Given implies that
$\overline{XZ} \cong \overline{YZ} \cong \overline{ZW}$.

If a = e = 66, then b = 48; c = 132;

f = d = 24. Since e + f = 90, $\triangle XYW$ is a

right $\triangle$. Also, XW = 2(7.8) = 15.6.

Using the Pythagorean Theorem,

$$XY = \sqrt{(15.6)^2 - (14.3)^2}$$
$$XY = 6.2$$

Perimeter = 15.6 + 14.3 + 6.2

Perimeter = 36.1 inches

SECTION 3.4: Basic Constructions Justified

1.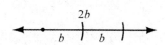
b

$2b$
b b

2. $b+c$

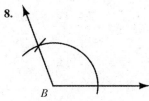
b c

3.

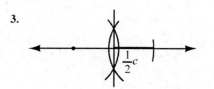
$\frac{1}{2}c$

4.

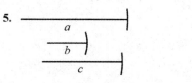
b $a-b$

5.

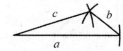
a

b

c

c b

a

6.

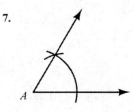
a a

b

7.

A

8.

B

9.

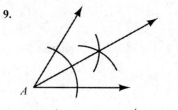
A

10.

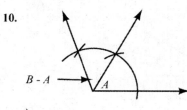
$B-A$ A

11.

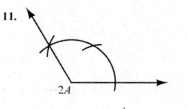
$2A$

12.

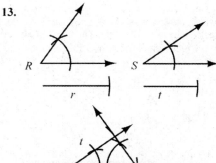

13.

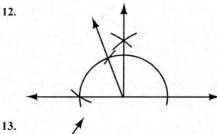
R S

r t

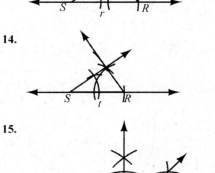
t

S r R

14.

S t R

15.

$45°$

16.

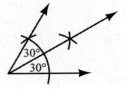

17.

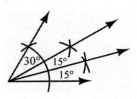

18.

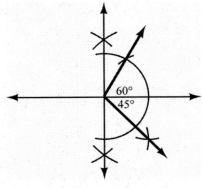

19. Construct a 90° angle; bisect it to form two 45° ∠s . Bisect one of the 45° angles to get a 22.5° ∠ .

20. Construct a 90° angle. Using one side of the 90° angle, construct a 60° angle. The 90° and 60° will form a 150° angle. Bisect the 150° angle to get a 75° angle.

21.

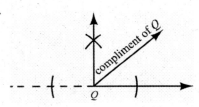

22.

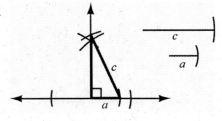

23.

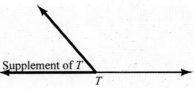

24.

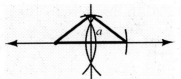

25.

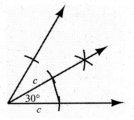

26.

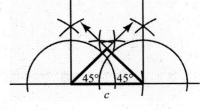

27.

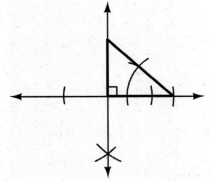

28.

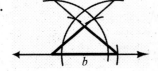

29. Given: Line *m*, with point *P* on *m*

$\overline{PQ} \cong \overline{PR}$ (by construction)

$\overline{QS} \cong \overline{RS}$ (by construction)

Prove: $\overleftrightarrow{SP} \perp m$

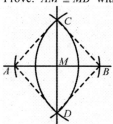

STATEMENTS	REASONS
1. Line *m* with point *P* on line *m* $\overline{PQ} \cong \overline{PR}$ and $\overline{QS} \cong \overline{RS}$	1. Given
2. $\overline{SP} \cong \overline{SP}$	2. Identity
3. $\triangle SPQ \cong \triangle SPR$	3. SSS
4. $\angle SPQ \cong \angle SPR$	4. CPCTC
5. $\overleftrightarrow{SP} \perp m$	5. If 2 lines intersect to form $\cong$ adjacent $\angle$s, then the lines are $\perp$.

30. Given: $\overline{AB}$ with $\overline{AC} \cong \overline{BC} \cong \overline{AD} \cong \overline{BD}$ (by construction)

Prove: $\overline{AM} \cong \overline{MB}$ with $\overline{CD} \perp \overline{AB}$

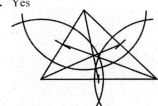

STATEMENTS	REASONS
1. $\overline{AB}$ with $\overline{AC} \cong \overline{BC} \cong \overline{AD} \cong \overline{BD}$	1. Given
2. $\overline{CD} \cong \overline{CD}$	2. Identity
3. $\triangle ACD \cong \triangle BCD$	3. SSS
4. $\angle ACM \cong \angle BCM$	4. CPCTC
5. $\overline{CM} \cong \overline{CM}$	5. Identity
6. $\triangle ACM \cong \triangle BCM$	6. SAS
7. $\overline{AM} \cong \overline{MB}$ and $\angle CMA \cong \angle CMB$	7. CPCTC
8. $\overline{CD} \perp \overline{AB}$	8. If 2 lines intersect to form $\cong$ adj. $\angle$s, then the lines are $\perp$.

31. 120°

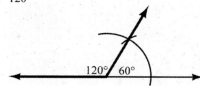

32. 135°

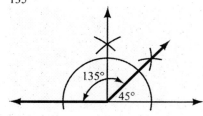

33. 150°

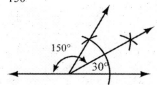

34. Yes

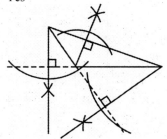

35. Yes

36. Yes

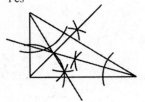

37. Yes

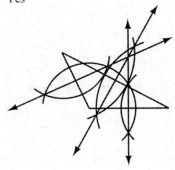

38. The three medians, the three angle-bisectors, and the three perpendicular bisectors are the same segments.

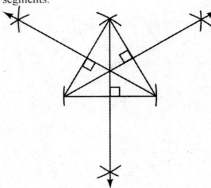

39. Point D is on the angle-bisector.

40. By AAS, $\triangle BCD \cong \triangle BED$.

Then $\overline{BC} \cong \overline{BE}$, so BE = a

Also, BE + EA = AB

So a + EA = c and EA = c − a

SECTION 3.5: Inequalities in a Triangle

1. False

2. True

3. True

4. False

5. True

6. True

7. False

8. False

9. True

10. False

11. **a.** Not possible

   b. Possible

12. **a.** Not possible

   b. Possible

13. **a.** Possible

   b. Not possible (8 + 9 = 17)

   c. Not possible (8 + 9 < 18)

14. **a.** Not possible

   b. Not possible

   c. Possible

15. Scalene right triangle $(m\angle Z = 90°)$

16. Equilateral acute triangle $(m\angle X = m\angle Y = m\angle Z = 60°)$

17. Isosceles obtuse triangle $(m\angle Z = 100°)$

18. Isosceles acute triangle $(m\angle Z = 70°)$

19. 4 cm

20. 10 cm

21. Largest $\angle$ is 72° (two of these); smallest is 36°

22. Largest $\angle$ is 96°; smallest is 42° (two of these).

23. Nashville

24. Salina

25. **1.** $m\angle ABC > m\angle DBE$ and $m\angle CBD > m\angle EBF$

   3. Angle-Addition Postulate

   4. $m\angle ABD > m\angle DBF$

26. **1.** Equilateral $\triangle ABC$ and D-B-C

   2. An equilateral $\triangle$ is also an equiangular $\triangle$ that has 3 $\angle$s of equal measure.

   4. $m\angle C > m\angle D$

5. $DA > AC$; If the measure of one $\angle$ of a $\triangle$ is greater than the measure of a second $\angle$, then the side which is opposite the first $\angle$ is longer than the side which is opposite the second $\angle$.

27. Given: Quadrilateral $RSTU$ with diagonal $\overline{US}$
$\angle R$ and $\angle TUS$ are right angles
Prove: $TS > UR$

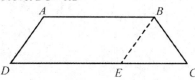

STATEMENTS	REASONS
1. Quad. $RSTU$ with diagonal $\overline{US}$; $\angle R$ and $\angle TUS$ are right angles.	1. Given
2. $TS > US$	2. Shortest distance from a point to a line is the $\perp$ distance.
3. $US > UR$	3. Same as (2)
4. $TS > UR$	4. Transitive Prop. of Inequality

28. Given: Quadrilateral $ABCD$
$\overline{AB} \cong \overline{DE}$
Prove: $DC > AB$

STATEMENTS	REASONS
1. Quad. $ABCD$ with $\overline{AB} \cong \overline{DE}$	1. Given
2. $AB = DE$	2. If 2 segments are $\cong$, then their measures are $=$.
3. $DC = DE + EC$	3. Segment-Addition Postulate
4. $DC = AB + EC$	4. Substitution
5. EC is a positive number	5. The measure of a segment must be positive.
6. $DC > AB$	6. If $a = b+c$ and c is positive, then $a > b$.

29. $BC < EF$

30. $NQ < QP$

31. $2 < x < 10$

32. $6 < x < 20$

33. $x + 2 < y < 5x + 12$

34. The diagonal of a square is not equal in length to the length of any of the sides of the square.
Given: $ABCD$ is a square
Prove: $AC \neq AB$

Proof: In square $ABCD$, $\angle B$ is a rt. $\angle$. Assume that $AC = AB$. But this contradicts the fact that the shortest distance from a point to a line is the $\perp$ distance. (That is, $AB < AC$.) Hence, our assumption must be wrong and $AC \neq AB$. Likewise, AC cannot equal the length of any of the sides of the square.

35. Given: $\triangle MPN$ is **not** isosceles
Prove: $PM \neq PN$

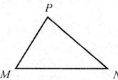

Proof: Assume $PM = PN$. Then $\triangle MPN$ is isosceles. But that contradicts the hypothesis. Thus, our assumption must be wrong and $PM \neq PN$.

36. Proof: Assume $\overline{ZW}$ is $\perp$ to $\overline{XY}$. If $\overline{ZW}$ bisects $\angle$ XZY, then $\triangle$ XZW $\cong$ $\triangle$ YZW by ASA. Then $\overline{XZ} \cong \overline{YZ}$ by CPCTC. But that contradicts the Given information that $\triangle$ XYZ scalene. $\therefore$ our assumption is wrong and $\overline{ZW}$ is not perpendicular to $\overline{XY}$.

37. The length of the median from the vertex of an isosceles triangle is less than the length of either of the legs.

Given: $\triangle ABC$ is isosceles with $\overline{AB} \cong \overline{BC}$

$\overline{BD}$ is the median to $\overline{AC}$

Prove: $BD < AB$ and $BD < BC$

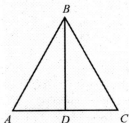

STATEMENTS	REASONS
1. $\triangle ABC$ is isosceles with $\overline{AB} \cong \overline{BC}$	1. Given
2. D is the midpoint of $\overline{AC}$	2. Median is drawn from a vertex to the midpoint of the opposite side.
3. $\overline{AD} \cong \overline{DC}$	3. Midpoint of a segment forms 2 $\cong$ segments.
4. $\overline{BD} \cong \overline{BD}$	4. Identity
5. $\triangle ABD \cong \triangle CBD$	5. SSS
6. $\angle BDA \cong \angle BDC$	6. CPCTC
7. $\overline{BD} \perp \overline{AC}$	7. If 2 lines intersect to form $\cong$ adjacent $\angle$s, the lines are $\perp$.
8. $BD < AB$ and $BD < BC$	8. Shortest distance from a point to a line is the $\perp$ distance.

38. The length of an altitude of a triangle that does not contain a right angle is less than the length of either side containing the same vertex as the altitude.

Given: $\triangle ABC$ with altitude $\overline{BD}$ to $\overline{AC}$

Prove: $BD < AB$ and $BD < BC$

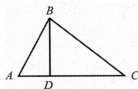

STATEMENTS	REASONS
1. $\triangle ABC$ with altitude $\overline{BD}$ to $\overline{AC}$	1. Given
2. $\overline{BD} \perp \overline{AC}$	2. Altitude of a $\triangle$ is the line segment drawn from a vertex $\perp$ to the opp. side.
3. $BD < AB$ and $BD < BC$	3. Shortest distance from a point to the line is the $\perp$ distance.

CHAPTER REVIEW

1. Given: $\angle AEB \cong \angle DEC$
    $\overline{AE} \cong \overline{ED}$
Prove: $\triangle AEB \cong \triangle DEC$

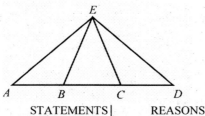

STATEMENTS	REASONS
1. $\angle AEB \cong \angle DEC$	**1.** Given
2. $\overline{AE} \cong \overline{ED}$	**2.** Given
3. $\angle A \cong \angle D$	**3.** If 2 sides of a $\triangle$ are $\cong$, then the $\angle$s opposite these sides are also $\cong$.
4. $\triangle AEB \cong \triangle DEC$	**4.** ASA

2. Given: $\overline{AB} \cong \overline{EF}$
    $\overline{AC} \cong \overline{DF}$
    $\angle 1 \cong \angle 2$
Prove: $\angle B \cong \angle E$

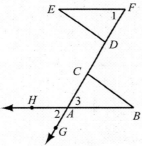

STATEMENTS	REASONS
1. $\overline{AB} \cong \overline{EF}$	**1.** Given
2. $\overline{AC} \cong \overline{DF}$; $\angle 1 \cong \angle 2$	**2.** Given
3. $\angle 2 \cong \angle 3$	**3.** If 2 lines intersect, then the vertical $\angle$s formed are $\cong$.
4. $\angle 1 \cong \angle 3$	**4.** Transitive Prop. for $\cong$.
5. $\triangle ABC \cong \triangle FED$	**5.** SAS
6. $\angle B \cong \angle E$	**6.** CPCTC

3. Given: $\overline{AD}$ bisects $\overline{BC}$
    $\overline{AB} \perp \overline{BC}$
    $\overline{DC} \perp \overline{BC}$
Prove: $\overline{AE} \cong \overline{ED}$

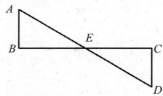

STATEMENTS	REASONS
1. $\overline{AB} \cong \overline{EF}$	**1.** Given
2. $\overline{AC} \cong \overline{DF}$; $\angle 1 \cong \angle 2$	**2.** Given
3. $\angle 2 \cong \angle 3$	**3.** If 2 lines intersect, then the vertical $\angle$s formed are $\cong$.
4. $\angle 1 \cong \angle 3$	**4.** Transitive Prop. for $\cong$.
5. $\triangle ABC \cong \triangle FED$	**5.** SAS
6. $\angle B \cong \angle E$	**6.** CPCTC

4. Given: $\overline{OA} \cong \overline{OB}$
    $\overline{OC}$ is the median to $\overline{AB}$
Prove: $\overline{OC} \perp \overline{AB}$

STATEMENTS	REASONS
1. $\overline{OA} \cong \overline{OB}$	**1.** Given
2. $\overline{OC}$ is the median to $\overline{AB}$	**2.** Given
3. C is the midpoint of $\overline{AB}$	**3.** The median of a $\triangle$ is a segment drawn from a vertex to the midpoint of the opp. side.
4. $\overline{AC} \cong \overline{CB}$	**4.** Midpoint of seg. form 2 $\cong$ segments.
5. $\overline{OC} \cong \overline{OC}$	**5.** Identity
6. $\triangle AOC \cong \triangle BOC$	**6.** SSS
7. $\angle OCA \cong \angle OCB$	**7.** CPCTC
8. $\overline{OC} \perp \overline{AB}$	**8.** If 2 lines meet to form $\cong$ adj. $\angle$s, then the lines are $\perp$.

5. Given: $\overline{AB} \cong \overline{DE}$

        $\overline{AB} \parallel \overline{DE}$

        $\overline{AC} \cong \overline{DF}$

Prove: $\overline{BC} \parallel \overline{FE}$

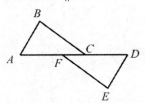

STATEMENTS	REASONS
1. $\overline{AB} \cong \overline{DE}$ and $\overline{AB} \parallel \overline{DE}$	1. Given
2. $\angle A \cong \angle D$	2. If 2 ∥ lines are cut by a trans., then the alt. int. ∠s are ≅.
3. $\overline{AC} \cong \overline{DF}$	3. Given
4. $\triangle BAC \cong \triangle EDF$	4. SAS
5. $\angle BCA \cong \angle EFD$	5. CPCTC
6. $\overline{BC} \parallel \overline{FE}$	6. If 2 lines are cut by a trans. so that alt. int. ∠s are ≅, then the lines are ∥.

6. Given: *B* is the midpoint of $\overline{AC}$

        $\overline{BD} \perp \overline{AC}$

Prove: $\triangle ADC$ is isosceles

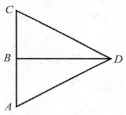

STATEMENTS	REASONS
1. *B* is the midpoint of $\overline{AC}$	1. Given
2. $\overline{CB} \cong \overline{BA}$	2. Midpoint of a segment forms 2 ≅ segments.
3. $\overline{BD} \perp \overline{AC}$	3. Given
4. $\angle DBC \cong \angle DBA$	4. If 2 lines are ⊥, they meet to form ≅ adj. ∠s.
5. $\overline{BD} \cong \overline{BD}$	5. Identity
6. $\triangle CBD \cong \triangle ABD$	6. SAS
7. $\overline{DC} \cong \overline{DA}$	7. CPCTC
8. $\triangle ADC$ is isosceles	8. If a △ has 2 ≅ sides, it is an isos. △.

7. Given: $\overline{JM} \perp \overline{GM}$

        $\overline{GK} \perp \overline{KJ}$

        $\overline{GH} \cong \overline{HJ}$

Prove: $\overline{GM} \cong \overline{JK}$

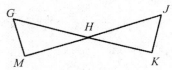

STATEMENTS	REASONS
1. $\overline{JM} \perp \overline{GM}$ and $\overline{GK} \perp \overline{KJ}$	1. Given
2. $\angle M$ is a rt. ∠ and $\angle K$ is a rt. ∠	2. If 2 lines are ⊥, they meet to form a rt. ∠.
3. $\angle M \cong \angle K$	3. Any 2 rt. ∠s are ≅.
4. $\overline{GH} \cong \overline{HJ}$	4. Given
5. $\angle GHM \cong \angle JHK$	5. If 2 lines intersect, the vertical ∠s formed are ≅.
6. $\triangle GHM \cong \triangle JHK$	6. AAS
7. $\overline{GM} \cong \overline{JK}$	7. CPCTC

8. Given: $\overline{TN} \cong \overline{TR}$

        $\overline{TO} \perp \overline{NP}$

        $\overline{TS} \perp \overline{PR}$

        $\overline{TO} \cong \overline{TS}$

Prove: $\angle N \cong \angle R$

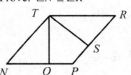

STATEMENTS	REASONS
1. $\overline{TN} \cong \overline{TR}$	1. Given
2. $\overline{TO} \perp \overline{NP}; \overline{TS} \perp \overline{PR}$	2. Given
3. $\angle TON$ is a rt. ∠ and $\angle TSR$ is a rt. ∠.	3. If 2 lines are ⊥, they meet to form a rt. ∠.
4. $\overline{TO} \cong \overline{TS}$	4. Given
5. $\triangle TON \cong \triangle TSR$	5. HL
6. $\angle N \cong \angle R$	6. CPCTC

9. Given: $\overline{YZ}$ is the base of an isosceles triangle
$\overline{XA} \parallel \overline{YZ}$

Prove: $\angle 1 \cong \angle 2$

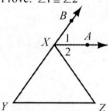

STATEMENTS	REASONS
1. $\overline{YZ}$ is the base of an isosceles △	1. Given
2. $\angle Y \cong \angle Z$	2. Base ∠s of an isos. △ are ≅.
3. $\overline{XA} \parallel \overline{YZ}$	3. Given
4. $\angle 1 \cong \angle Y$	4. If 2 ∥ lines are cut by a trans., then the corresp. ∠s are ≅.
5. $\angle 2 \cong \angle Z$	5. If 2 ∥ lines are cut by a trans., then the corresp. ∠s are ≅.
6. $\angle 1 \cong \angle 2$	6. Transitive Prop. for ≅.

10. Given: $\overline{AB} \parallel \overline{DC}$
$\overline{AB} \cong \overline{DC}$
C is the midpoint of $\overline{BE}$

Prove: $\overline{AC} \parallel \overline{DE}$

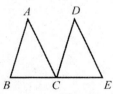

STATEMENTS	REASONS
1. $\overline{AB} \cong \overline{DE}$ and $\overline{AB} \parallel \overline{DC}$	1. Given
2. $\angle B \cong \angle DCE$	2. If 2 ∥ lines are cut by a trans., then the corresp. ∠s are ≅.
3. $\overline{AB} \cong \overline{DC}$	3. Given
4. C is the midpoint of $\overline{BE}$	4. Given
5. $\overline{BC} \cong \overline{CE}$	5. Midpoint of a seg. forms 2 ≅ segments.
6. $\triangle ABC \cong \triangle DCE$	6. SAS
7. $\angle ACB \cong \angle E$	7. CPCTC
8. $\overline{AC} \parallel \overline{DE}$	8. If 2 lines are cut by a trans. so that the corresp. ∠s are ≅, then the lines are ∥.

11. Given: $\angle BAD \cong \angle CDA$
$\overline{AB} \cong \overline{CD}$

Prove: $\overline{AE} \cong \overline{ED}$

STATEMENTS	REASONS
1. $\angle BAD \cong \angle CDA$	1. Given
2. $\overline{AB} \cong \overline{CD}$	2. Given
3. $\overline{AD} \cong \overline{AD}$	3. Identity
4. $\triangle BAD \cong \triangle CDA$	4. SAS
5. $\angle 1 \cong \angle 2$	5. CPCTC
6. $\overline{AE} \cong \overline{ED}$	6. If 2 ∠s of a triangle are ≅, then the sides opp. these ∠s are also ≅.

12. Given: $\overline{BE}$ is altitude to $\overline{AC}$
$\overline{AD}$ is altitude to $\overline{CE}$
$\overline{BC} \cong \overline{CD}$

Prove: $\overline{BE} \cong \overline{AD}$

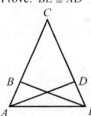

STATEMENTS	REASONS
1. $\overline{BE}$ is altitude to $\overline{AC}$ $\overline{AD}$ is altitude to $\overline{CE}$	1. Given
2. $\overline{BE} \perp \overline{AC}$ and $\overline{AD} \perp \overline{CE}$	2. An altitude is a line segment drawn from a vertex ⊥ to opp. side.
3. $\angle CBE$ is a rt. ∠ and $\angle CDA$ is a rt. ∠	3. If 2 lines are ⊥, they meet to form a rt. ∠.
4. $\angle CBE \cong \angle CDA$	4. Any 2 rt. ∠s are ≅.
5. $\overline{BC} \cong \overline{CD}$	5. Given
6. $\angle C \cong \angle C$	6. Identity
7. $\triangle CBE \cong \triangle CDA$	7. ASA
8. $\overline{BE} \cong \overline{AD}$	8. CPCTC

13. Given: $\overline{AB} \cong \overline{CD}$

     $\angle BAD \cong \angle CDA$

     Prove: $\triangle AED$ is isosceles

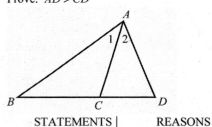

STATEMENTS	REASONS
1. $\overline{AB} \cong \overline{CD}$	1. Given
2. $\angle BAD \cong \angle CDA$	2. Given
3. $\overline{AD} \cong \overline{AD}$	3. Identity
4. $\triangle BAD \cong \triangle CDA$	4. SAS
5. $\angle CAD \cong \angle BDA$	5. CPCTC
6. $\overline{AE} \cong \overline{ED}$	6. If 2 $\angle$s of a $\triangle$ are $\cong$, then the sides opp. these $\angle$s are also $\cong$.
7. $\triangle AED$ is isosceles	7. If a $\triangle$ has 2 $\cong$ sides, it is an isosceles $\triangle$.

14. Given: $\overrightarrow{AC}$ bisects $\angle BAD$

     Prove: $AD > CD$

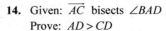

STATEMENTS	REASONS
1. $\overrightarrow{AC}$ bisects $\angle BAD$	1. Given
2. $m\angle 1 \cong m\angle 2$	2. If a ray bisects an $\angle$, it forms 2 $\angle$s of = measure.
3. $m\angle ACD > m\angle 1$	3. The measure of an ext. $\angle$ of a $\triangle$ is greater than the measure of either of the nonadjacent interior angles.
4. $m\angle ACD > m\angle 2$	4. Substitution
5. $AD > CD$	5. If the measure of one angle of a $\triangle$ is greater than the measure of a second angle, then the side which is opposite the 1st angle is longer than the side which is opp. the second angle.

15. a. $\overline{PR}$

     b. $\overline{PQ}$

16. $\overline{BC}$, $\overline{AC}$, $\overline{AB}$

17. $\angle R$, $\angle Q$, $\angle P$

18. $\overline{AD}$

19. (b)

20. 5 and 35

21. 20°

22. 115°

23. $3x + 10 = \dfrac{5}{2}x + 18$

     $\dfrac{1}{2}x = 8$

     $x = 16$

     $m\angle 4 = \dfrac{5}{2}(16) + 18 = 58°$

     $m\angle C = 64°$

24. $10 + x + 6 + 2x - 3 = 40$
$$3x + 13 = 40$$
$$3x = 27$$
$$x = 9$$
$AB = 10$; $BC = 15$; $AC = 15$: the triangle is isosceles.

25. Either $AB = BC$ or $AB = AC$ or $BC = AC$.
If $AB = BC$, $y + 7 = 3y + 5$
$$-2y = -2$$
$$y = 1$$
If $AB = AC$, $y + 7 = 9 - y$
$$2y = 2$$
$$y = 1$$
If $BC = AC$, $3y + 5 = 9 - y$
$$4y = 4$$
$$y = 1$$
If $y = 1$, $AB = 8$; $BC = 8$; $AC = 8$; the triangle is also equilateral.

26. If $m\angle 1 = 5x$, then the $m\angle 2 = 180 - 5x$
$m\angle 4 = m\angle 2 = 180 - 5x$.
But $m\angle 3 = m\angle 4$, therefore
$$2x + 12 = 180 - 5x$$
$$7x = 168$$
$$x = 24$$
$m\angle 2 = 180 - 5(24) = 60°$

27. Construct an angle that measures 75°.

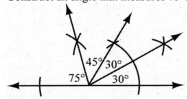
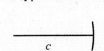

28. Construct a right triangle that has acute angle A and hypotenuse of length c.

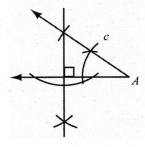

29. Construct another isosceles triangle in which the base angles are half as large as the given base angles.

CHAPTER TEST

1. a. Since $\triangle ABC \cong \triangle DEF$, then $m\angle A \cong m\angle D$, $m\angle B \cong m\angle E$ and $m\angle C \cong m\angle F$.
$m\angle A \cong 37°$ and $m\angle E \cong 68°$
$m\angle F = 180 - 37 - 68 = 75°$

b. Since $\triangle ABC \cong \triangle DEF$, then $\overline{AB} \cong \overline{DE}$, $\overline{BC} \cong \overline{EF}$, and $\overline{AC} \cong \overline{DF}$.
$AB = 7.3$, $BC = 4.7$, and $AC = 6.3$
$EF = 4.7$ cm

2. a. $\overline{XY}$

b. $\angle Y$

3. a. SAS

b. ASA

4. Corresponding parts of congruent triangles are congruent.

5. a. No

b. Yes

6. Yes

7. a. $c = 10$

b. $b = \sqrt{c^2 - a^2}$
$b = \sqrt{8^2 - 6^2}$
$b = \sqrt{64 - 36}$
$b = \sqrt{28} = 2\sqrt{7}$

8. a. $\overline{AM} \cong \overline{BM}$

b. No

9. a. $m\angle V = 180 - 71 - 71 = 38°$

    b. $7x + 2 = 9(x - 2)$
        $7x + 2 = 9x - 18$
        $20 = 2x$
        $x = 10$
        $m\angle T = 7(10) + 2 = 72°$
        $m\angle U = 9(10 - 2) = 72°$
        $m\angle V = 180 - 72 - 72 = 36°$

10. a. $VU = 7.6$ in.

    b. $4x + 1 = 6x - 10$
        $11 = 2x$
        $x = \dfrac{11}{2}$
        $VT = 4\left(\dfrac{11}{2}\right) + 1 = 23$
        $TU = 2\left(\dfrac{11}{2}\right) = 11$
        $VU = 6\left(\dfrac{11}{2}\right) - 10 = 23$
        $P = 23 + 11 + 23 = 57$

11. a. Construct an angle that measures 60°.

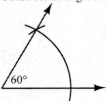

    b. Construct an angle that measures 60°.

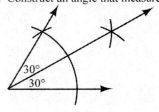

12.

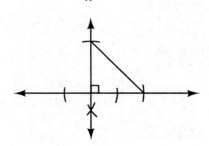

13. a. $\overline{BC}$

    b. $\overline{CA}$

14. $m\angle V > m\angle U > m\angle T$

15. $EB = \sqrt{(AE)^2 + (AB)^2}$
    $EB = \sqrt{(4+3)^2 + 5^2}$
    $EB = \sqrt{49 + 25} = \sqrt{74}$
    $DC = \sqrt{(AD)^2 + (AC)^2}$
    $DC = \sqrt{4^2 + (5+2)^2}$
    $DC = \sqrt{16 + 49} = \sqrt{65}$
    $EB > DC$ since $EB = \sqrt{74}$ and $DC = \sqrt{65}$.

16.

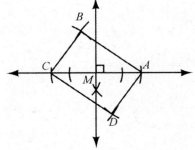

$\overline{DA}$

17.

STATEMENTS	REASONS
1. $\angle R$ and $\angle V$ are rt. $\angle$s	1. Given
2. $\angle R \cong \angle V$	2. All rt. $\angle$s are $\cong$
3. $\angle 1 \cong \angle 2$	3. Given
4. $\overline{ST} \cong \overline{ST}$	4. Identity
5. $\triangle RST \cong \triangle VST$	5. AAS

18. **R1.** Given

    R2. If 2 $\angle$s of a $\triangle$ are $\cong$, the opposite sides are $\cong$.

    S3. $\angle 1 \cong \angle 3$

    R4. ASA

    S5. $\overline{US} \cong \overline{UT}$

    S6. $\triangle STU$ is an isosceles triangle

19. Let each leg = a, and half the base = b.

    Then 2a + 2b = 32 or a + b = 16 or a = 16 − b.

    But $\sqrt{8^2 + b^2}$ = a   so

    $\sqrt{8^2 + b^2}$ = 16 − b   Squaring both sides
    gives $8^2 + b^2 = 256 - 32b + b^2$ or

    64 − 256 = −32b

    −192 = −32b

    b = 6 ∴ a = 10

Chapter 4: Quadrilaterals

SECTION 4.1: Properties of a Parallelogram

1. a. $AB = DC$

    b. $m\angle A = m\angle C$

2. a. $AD = BC$

    b. $m\angle B = m\angle D$

3. a. 8

    b. 5

    c. 70°

    d. 110°

4. a. 17.9

    b. 12.7

    c. 58°

    d. 122°

5. In parallelogram $ABCD$, $AB = DC$.
    Therefore,
    $$3x + 2 = 5x - 2$$
    $$4 = 2x$$
    $$x = 2$$
    $$AB = DC = 8$$
    $$BC = AD = 9$$

6. In parallelogram $ABCD$, $\angle A \cong \angle C$. Therefore,
    $$2x + 3 = 3x - 27$$
    $$30 = x$$
    $$m\angle A = m\angle C = 63°$$
    $$m\angle B = m\angle D = 117°$$
    (Consecutive $\angle$s in a parallelogram are
    supplementary.)

7. $m\angle A + m\angle B = 180°$; Consecutive angles in a
    parallelogram are supp.
    $$2x + 3 + 3x - 23 = 180$$
    $$5x - 20 = 180$$
    $$5x = 200$$
    $$x = 40°$$
    $$m\angle A = m\angle C = 83°$$
    $$m\angle B = m\angle D = 97°$$

8. $\dfrac{2x}{5} + \dfrac{x}{2} = 180$

    Multiply by 10, the LCD

    $4x + 5x = 1800$

    $9x = 1800$

$x = 200$; $m\angle A = m\angle C = 80°$;

$m\angle B = m\angle D = 100°$

9. $\dfrac{2x}{3} = \dfrac{x}{2} + 20$

    Multiply by 6, the LCD

    $4x = 3x + 120$

    $x = 120$; $m\angle A = m\angle C = 80°$;

    $m\angle B = m\angle D = 100°$

10. $m\angle A + m\angle B = 180°$; consecutive angles in a
    parallelogram are supp.
    $\angle A \cong \angle C$; opposite $\angle$s in a parallelogram
    are $\cong$.
    $$2x + y + 2x + 3y - 20 = 180$$
    $$2x + y = 3x - y + 16$$
    Simplifying yields
    $$4x + 4y = 200$$
    $$-1x + 2y = 16$$
    Dividing top equation by 4
    $$1x + 1y = 50$$
    $$-1x + 2y = 16$$
    Adding both equations
    $$3y = 66$$
    $$y = 22$$
    Substituting $y = 22$ into $x + y = 50$ gives
    $x = 28$.
    $$m\angle A = m\angle C = 78°$$
    $$m\angle B = m\angle D = 102°$$

11. $\overline{AC}$

12. $\angle B$

13. a. $\overline{VY}$

    b. 16

14. a. $\overline{VX}$

    b. 12

15. True

16. False

17. True

18. False

19. The resulting quadrilateral appears to be a
    parallelogram.

20. It appears that these segments bisect each other.

71

21. Parallelogram

22. Parallelogram

23. **1.** Given

    2. $\overline{RV} \perp \overline{VT}$ and $\overline{ST} \perp \overline{VT}$

    3. $\overline{RV} \parallel \overline{ST}$

    4. *RSTV* is a parallelogram

24. **1.** Given

    2. ∠s *Z* and *y* are supp.

    3. $\overline{WZ} \parallel \overline{XY}$

    4. *WXYZ* is a parallelogram

25. Given: Parallelogram *RSTV*
     with $\overline{XY} \parallel \overline{VT}$

    Prove: $\angle 1 \cong \angle S$

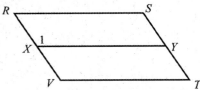

STATEMENTS	REASONS
1. Parallelogram *RSTV*	**1.** Given
2. $\overline{RS} \parallel \overline{VT}$	**2.** Oppposite sides of a parallelogram are ∥.
3. $\overline{XY} \parallel \overline{VT}$	**3.** Given
4. $\overline{RS} \parallel \overline{XY}$	**4.** If 2 lines are each ∥ to a third line, then the lines are all ∥.
5. *RSYX* is a parallelogram	**5.** If a quadrilateral has opposite sides ∥, then the quad. is a parallelogram.
6. $\angle 1 \cong \angle S$	**6.** Opposite angles of a parallelogram are ≅.

26. Given: Parallelogram *ABCD*
     with $\overline{DE} \perp \overline{AB}$ and $\overline{FB} \perp \overline{AB}$

Prove: $\overline{DE} \cong \overline{FB}$

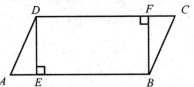

STATEMENTS	REASONS
1. Parallelogram *RSTV*	**1.** Given
2. $\overline{AB} \parallel \overline{DC}$	**2.** Oppposite sides of a parallelogram are ∥.
3. $\overline{DE} \perp \overline{AB}$ and $\overline{FB} \perp \overline{AB}$	**3.** Given
4. $\overline{DE} \parallel \overline{FB}$	**4.** If 2 lines are each ⊥ to the same line, then the 2 lines all ∥.
5. *DEBF* is a parallelogram	**5.** If a quadrilateral has opposite sides ∥, then the quad. is a parallelogram.
6. $\overline{DE} \cong \overline{FB}$	**6.** Opposite sides of a parallelogram are ≅.

27. The opposite angles of a parallelogram are congruent.
Given: Parallelogram *ABCD*
Prove: $\angle BAD \cong \angle BCD$ and
     $\angle ABC \cong \angle ADC$

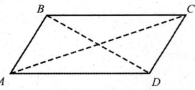

STATEMENTS	REASONS
1. Parallelogram *ABCD*	**1.** Given
2. Draw diagonal $\overline{BD}$	**2.** Through 2 points there is exactly one line.
3. △*ABD* ≅ △*CDB*	**3.** A diagonal of a parallelogram separates it into 2 ≅ △s.
4. $\angle BAD \cong \angle BCD$	**4.** CPCTC
5. Draw in diagonal $\overline{AC}$	**5.** Same as (2)
6. △*ABC* ≅ △*CDA*	**6.** Same as (3)
7. = m∠*A* + m∠*B*	**7.** CPCTC

28. The opposite sides of a parallelogram are congruent.
Given: Parallelogram $ABCD$
Prove: $\overline{AB} \cong \overline{CD}$ and $\overline{BC} \cong \overline{AD}$

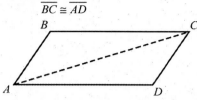

STATEMENTS	REASONS
1. Parallelogram $ABCD$	1. Given
2. Draw in diagonal $\overline{CD}$	2. Through 2 points there is exactly one line.
3. $\triangle ABC \cong \triangle CDA$	3. A diagonal of a parallelogram separates it into 2 $\cong$ $\triangle$s.
4. $\overline{AB} \cong \overline{CD}$ and $\overline{BC} \cong \overline{AD}$	4. CPCTC

29. The diagonals of a parallelogram bisect each other.
Given: Parallelogram $ABCD$
Prove: $\overline{AC}$ bisects $\overline{BD}$ and $\overline{BD}$ bisects $\overline{AC}$

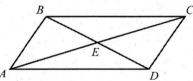

STATEMENTS	REASONS
1. Parallelogram $ABCD$	1. Given
2. $\overline{AB} \cong \overline{CD}$	2. Opposite sides of a parallelogram are $\cong$.
3. $\overline{AB} \parallel \overline{CD}$	3. Opposite sides of a parallelogram are parallel.
4. $\angle ABD \cong \angle CBD$ and $\angle BAC \cong \angle DCA$	4. If 2 $\parallel$ lines are cut by a trans., then alternate interior $\angle$s are $\cong$.
5. $\triangle ABE \cong \triangle CDE$	5. ASA
6. $\overline{BE} \cong \overline{ED}$ and $\overline{AE} \cong \overline{EC}$	6. CPCTC
7. $\overline{AC}$ bisects $\overline{BD}$ and $\overline{BD}$ bisects $\overline{AC}$	7. If a segment divides another segment into 2 $\cong$ segments, then the segment is bisected.

30. The consecutive angles of a parallelogram are supplementary.
Given: Parallelogram $ABCD$
Prove: $\angle A$ and $\angle B$ are supplementary

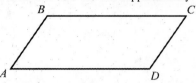

STATEMENTS	REASONS
1. Parallelogram $ABCD$	1. Given
2. $\overline{BC} \parallel \overline{AD}$	2. Oppposite sides of a parallelogram are parallel.
3. $\angle A$ and $\angle B$ are supplementary	3. If 2 $\parallel$ lines are cut by a trans., then the interior $\angle$s on the same side of the trans. is supp.

31. $\angle P$ is a right angle.

32. $\triangle DEC$ is a right triangle; $\triangle ADE$ and $\triangle BCE$ are isosceles triangles.

33. $\overline{RT}$

34. $\angle RST$ and $\angle RVT$

35. 255 mph

36. 80°

37. $\overline{AC}$

38. $\overline{AC}$ and $\overline{BD}$ should bisect each other.

39. $x + 16 + 2(x + 1) + \dfrac{3x}{2} \cdot 11 + \dfrac{7x}{3} \cdot 16 = 360$

$x + 2x + 2 + \dfrac{3x}{2} \cdot 11 + \dfrac{7x}{3} = 360$

$3x + \dfrac{3x}{2} + \dfrac{7x}{3} = 369$

Multiply by 6, the LCD

$18x + 9x + 14x = 2214$

$41x = 2214$

$x = 54$; $m\angle A = 70°$; $m\angle B = 110°$; $m\angle C = 70°$; $m\angle D = 110°$; $ABCD$ is a parallelogram.

40. In $\square ABCD$ let AB = CD = a; BC = AD = b;

diagonal BD = d; diagonal AC = D. Draw
$\overline{BE} \perp \overline{AD}$ and $\overline{CF} \perp$ to the extension

of $\overline{AD}$. Call the heights, h. Let AE = DF = x.

In rt. $\triangle$ ABE, $a^2 = h^2 + x^2$

In rt. $\triangle$ BED, $d^2 = h^2 + (b \bullet x)^2 = h^2 + b^2 \bullet 2bx + x^2$;
In rt. $\triangle$ ACF, $D^2 = h^2 + (b + x)^2 = h^2 + b^2 + 2bx + x^2$

$d^2 + D^2 =\ h^2 + b^2 \bullet 2bx + x^2 + h^2 + b^2 + 2bx + x^2$

$d^2 + D^2 = 2h^2 + 2b^2 + 2x^2$

$d^2 + D^2 = 2(h^2 + x^2) + 2b^2$

$d^2 + D^2 = 2a^2 + 2b^2$

SECTION 4.2: The Parallelogram and Kite

1. **a.** Yes

    b. No

2. **a.** No

    b. No

3. Parallelogram

4. Kite

5. **a.** Kite

    b. Parallelogram

6. **a.** Kite

    b. Congruent

7. $\overline{AC}$

8. $\overline{YW}$

9. 6.18

10. 15.3

11. **a.** 8

    b. 7

    c. 6

12. **a.** 16

    b. 20

    c. 12

13. 10

14. 25.4

15. **a.** Yes; diagonal separating kite into 2 $\cong$ $\triangle$.

    b. No

16. **a.** No

    b. Yes

17. Parallel and congruent

18. Bisect each other

19. **1.** Given

    2. Identity

    3. $\triangle NMQ \cong \triangle NPQ$

    4. CPCTC

    5. $MNPQ$ is a kite

20. **1.** Quad. *ABCD* with midpoints *E*, *F*, *G* and *H* of the sides.

    3. The segment that joins the midpoints of two sides of a $\triangle$ is $\parallel$ to the third side of the $\triangle$.

    4. $\overline{EF} \parallel \overline{HG}$

21. Given: *M-Q-T* and *P-Q-R* so that
       MNPQ and *QRST* are parallelograms
    Prove: $\angle N \cong \angle S$

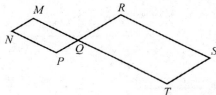

STATEMENTS	REASONS
1. *M-Q-T* and *P-Q-R* so that *MNPQ* and *QRST* are parallelograms.	1. Given
2. $\angle N \cong \angle MQP$	2. Opposite $\angle$s in a parallelogram are $\cong$.
3. $\angle MPQ \cong \angle RQT$	3. If 2 lines intersect, the vertical $\angle$s formed are $\cong$.
4. $\angle RQT \cong \angle S$	4. Same as (2)
5. $\angle N \cong \angle S$	5. Transitive Prop. for $\cong$.

22. Given: Parallelogram *WXYZ* with
      diagonals $\overline{WY}$ and $\overline{XZ}$
    Prove: △*WMX* ≅ △*YMZ*

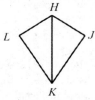

STATEMENTS	REASONS
1. Parallelogram *WXYZ* with $\overline{WY}$ and $\overline{XZ}$	**1.** Given
2. $\overline{WY}$ and $\overline{XZ}$ bisect each other	**2.** Diagonals of a parallelogram bisect each other.
3. $\overline{WM} \cong \overline{MY}$ and $\overline{ZM} \cong \overline{MX}$	**3.** If a segment is bisected, 2 ≅ segments are formed.
4. ∠*WMX* ≅ ∠*ZMY*	**4.** If 2 lines intersect the vertical ∠s formed are ≅.
5. △*WMX* ≅ △*YMZ*	**5.** SAS

23. Given: Kite *HJKL* with diagonal $\overline{HK}$
    Prove: $\overrightarrow{HK}$ bisects ∠*LHJ*

STATEMENTS	REASONS
1. Kite *HJKL* with diagonal $\overline{HK}$	**1.** Given
2. $\overline{LH} \cong \overline{HJ}$ and $\overline{LK} \cong \overline{JK}$	**2.** A kite is a quad. with 2 distinct pairs of ≅ adjacent sides.
3. $\overline{HK} \cong \overline{HK}$	**3.** Identity
4. △*LHK* ≅ △*JHK*	**4.** SSS
5. ∠*LHK* ≅ ∠*JHK*	**5.** CPCTC
6. $\overrightarrow{HK}$ bisects ∠*LHJ*	**6.** If a ray divides an ∠ into 2 ≅ ∠s, then the ray bisects the ∠.

24. Given: Parallelogram *MNPQ* with *T* the midpoint
      of $\overline{MN}$ and *S* the midpoint of $\overline{QP}$
    Prove: △*QMS* ≅ △*NPT* and
       MSPT is a parallelogram

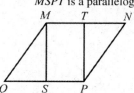

STATEMENTS	REASONS
1. Parallelogram *MNPQ*	**1.** Given
2. $\overline{MN} \cong \overline{QP}$ and $\overline{MQ} \cong \overline{NP}$	**2.** Opposite sides of a parallelogram are ≅.
3. *T* is the midpoint of $\overline{MN}$ and *S* is the midpoint of $\overline{QP}$	**3.** Given
4. $\overline{QS} \cong \overline{TN}$ and $\overline{MT} \cong \overline{SP}$	**4.** If 2 segments are ≅, then their midpoints separate into 4 ≅ segments.
5. ∠*Q* ≅ ∠*N*	**5.** Opposite ∠s of a parallelogram are ≅.
6. △*QMS* ≅ △*NPT*	**6.** SAS
7. $\overline{MS} \cong \overline{TP}$	**7.** CPCTC
8. *MSPT* is a parallelogram	**8.** If a quad. has both pairs of opposite sides ≅, then the quad. is a parallelogram.

25. If both pairs of opposite sides of a quadrilateral are congruent, then the quadrilateral is a parallelogram.
Given: Quad. *ABCD* with
$\overline{AB} \cong \overline{CD}$ and $\overline{BC} \cong \overline{AD}$
Prove: *ABCD* is a parallelogram

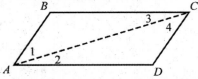

STATEMENTS	REASONS
1. Quad *ABCD* with $\overline{AB} \cong \overline{CD}$ and $\overline{BC} \cong \overline{AD}$	1. Given
2. Draw in $\overline{AC}$	2. Through 2 points there is exactly one line.
3. $\overline{AC} \cong \overline{AC}$	3. Identity
4. $\triangle ABC \cong \triangle CDA$	4. SSS
5. $\angle 1 \cong \angle 4$ and $\angle 2 \cong \angle 3$	5. CPCTC
6. $\overline{AB} \| \overline{CD}$ and $\overline{BC} \| \overline{AD}$	6. If 2 lines are cut by a trans. so that alt. int. $\angle$s are $\cong$, then the lines are $\|$.
7. *ABCD* is a parallelogram	7. If a quad. has both pairs of opposite sides $\|$, the quad. is a parallelogram.

26. If the diagonals of a quadrilateral bisect each other, then the quadrilateral is a parallelogram.
Given: Quad. *ABCD* with
$\overline{AC}$ and $\overline{BD}$ bisecting each other
Prove: *ABCD* is a parallelogram

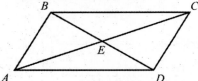

STATEMENTS	REASONS
1. Quad. *ABCD* with $\overline{AC}$ and $\overline{BD}$ bisecting each other	1. Given
2. $\overline{AE} \cong \overline{EC}$ and $\overline{BE} \cong \overline{ED}$	2. If a segment is bisected, 2 $\cong$ segments are formed.
3. $\angle AEB \cong \angle CED$	3. If 2 lines intersect then the vertical $\angle$s formed are congruent.
4. $\triangle AEB \cong \triangle CED$	4. SAS
5. $\overline{AB} \cong \overline{CD}$	5. CPCTC
6. $\angle BAE \cong \angle DCE$	6. CPCTC
7. $\overline{AB} \| \overline{CD}$	7. If 2 lines are cut by a trans. so that the alt. int. $\angle$s are $\cong$, then the lines are $\|$.
8. *ABCD* is a parallelogram	8. If two sides of a quad. are both $\cong$ and $\|$, then the quad. is a parallelogram.

27. In a kite, one diagonal is the perpendicular bisector of the other diagonal.

    Given: Kite *ABCD* with diagonals $\overline{AC}$ and $\overline{BD}$

    Prove: $\overline{BD} \perp \overline{AC}$ and
    $\overline{BD}$ bisects $\overline{AC}$

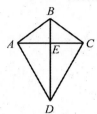

STATEMENTS	REASONS
1. Kite *HJKL* with diagonals $\overline{AC}$ and $\overline{BD}$	1. Given
2. $\overline{AB} \cong \overline{BC}$ and $\overline{AD} \cong \overline{CD}$	2. A kite is a quad. with 2 distinct pairs of $\cong$ adjacent sides.
3. $\overline{BD} \cong \overline{BD}$	3. Identity
4. $\triangle ABD \cong \triangle CBD$	4. SSS
5. $\angle ABD \cong \angle CBD$	5. CPCTC
6. $\overline{BE} \cong \overline{BE}$	6. Identity
7. $\triangle ABE \cong \triangle CBE$	7. SAS
8. $\angle BEA \cong \angle BEC$	8. CPCTC
9. $\overline{BD} \perp \overline{AC}$	9. If 2 lines intersect to form $\cong$ adjacent $\angle$s, then the lines are $\perp$.
10. $\overline{AE} \cong \overline{EC}$	10. CPCTC
11. $\overline{BD}$ bisects $\overline{AC}$	11. If a segment divides into 2 $\cong$ segments, then the segment is bisected.

28. One diagonal of a kite bisects 2 of the angles of the kite.

    Given: Kite *ABCD* with diagonal $\overline{BD}$

    Prove: $\overrightarrow{BD}$ bisects $\angle ABC$
    $\overrightarrow{DB}$ bisects $\angle ADC$

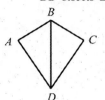

STATEMENTS	REASONS
1. Kite *ABCD* with diagonal $\overline{BD}$	1. Given
2. $\overline{AB} \cong \overline{BC}$ and $\overline{AD} \cong \overline{CD}$	2. A kite is a quad. with 2 distinct pairs of $\cong$ adjacent sides.
3. $\overline{BD} \cong \overline{BD}$	3. Identity
4. $\triangle ABD \cong \triangle CBD$	4. SSS
5. $\angle ABD \cong \angle CBD$ $\angle ADB \cong \angle CDB$	5. CPCTC
6. $\overrightarrow{BD}$ bisects $\angle ABC$ $\overrightarrow{DB}$ bisects $\angle ADC$	6. If a ray divides an $\angle$ into 2 $\cong$ $\angle$s, then the ray bisects the $\angle$.

29.
$$MN = \frac{1}{2} \cdot ST$$
$$2y - 3 = \frac{1}{2} \cdot 3y$$
$$2y - 3 = \frac{3}{2}y$$
$$\frac{1}{2}y = 3$$
$$y = 6$$
$$MN = 9$$
$$ST = 18$$

30.
$$MN = \frac{1}{2} \cdot ST$$
$$x^2 + 5 = \frac{1}{2} \cdot x(2x + 5)$$
$$2x^2 + 10 = x(2x + 5)$$
$$2x^2 + 10 = 2x^2 + 5x$$
$$10 = 5x$$
$$x = 2$$
$$MN = 9$$
$$ST = 18$$

31. If M and N are the midpoints of $\overline{RS}$ and $\overline{RT}$ and if $RM = RN$, then $RS = RT = 4x + 2$. But if $m\angle R = 60°$ and $RS = RT$, then $m\angle S = m\angle T = 60°$. Triangle RST is equiangular and therefore equilateral. Therefore
$$4x + 2 = 5x - 3$$
$$x = 5$$
If $x = 5$, $RM = 11$ and $ST = 22$.

32. $\dfrac{3x}{2} + 2 = \dfrac{9x}{4} \cdot 3$

$5 = \dfrac{9x}{4} \cdot \dfrac{3x}{2}$

Multiply by 4, the LCD

$20 = 9x \cdot 6x$

$20 = 3x$

$x = \dfrac{20}{3}$ or $6\dfrac{2}{3}$

33. $\dfrac{x}{3} + 3 = \dfrac{x}{6} + 5$

$\dfrac{x}{3} = \dfrac{x}{6} + 2$

Multiply by 6, the LCD

$2x = x + 12$

$x = 12$; $AD = 7$; $AB = 7$; $BC = DC = 10$

Perimeter $= 2(7) + 2(10) = 34$

34. a. The measure of the angle formed by the bisectors of $\angle RST$ and $\angle STV$ is 115

b. The measure of the angle formed by the bisectors of $\angle SRV$ and $\angle RST$ is 65°.

35. $m\angle B = 360 - m\angle A - m\angle C - m\angle D$
$\qquad = 360 - 30 - 30 - 30$
$\qquad = 270°$

36. From Exercise 33, $m\angle B = 270°$ so $m\angle ABC = 90°$.

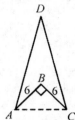

$\triangle ABC$ forms a 45°-45°-90° relationship. Since $AB = BC = 6$, then $AC = 6\sqrt{2}$ in.

37. The segment which joins the midpoints of 2 sides of a triangle has a length which equals one-half the length of the third side.

Given: $\triangle ABC$ with M the midpoint of $\overline{AB}$ and
    N the midpoint of $\overline{AC}$

Prove: $MN = \frac{1}{2} \cdot BC$

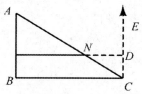

STATEMENTS	REASONS
1. Through C construct $\overline{CE} \parallel \overline{AB}$ midpoints of $\overline{AB}$	1. Parallel Postulate
2. Extend $\overline{MN}$ to meet $\overline{CE}$ at D	2. Through 2 points there is exactly one line.
3. $\triangle ABC$ with M the midpoint $\overline{AB}$ and N the midpoint of $\overline{AC}$	3. Given
4. $\overline{AN} \cong \overline{NC}$	4. The midpoint of a segments forms 2 $\cong$ segments.
5. $\angle A \cong \angle NCD$	5. If 2 $\parallel$ lines are cut by a trans., then the alt. int. $\angle$s are $\cong$.
6. $\angle ANM \cong \angle CND$	6. If 2 lines intersect then the vertical $\angle$s formed are $\cong$.
7. $\triangle ANM \cong \triangle CND$	7. ASA
8. $\overline{MN} \cong \overline{ND}$	8. CPCTC
9. $MN = DN$	9. If 2 segments are $\cong$, then their measures are $\cong$.
10. $MN + ND = MD$	10. Segment-Addition Postulate
11. $MN + MN = MD$ or $2 \cdot MN = MD$	11. Substitution
12. $MN = \frac{1}{2} \cdot MD$	12. Division Prop. of Equality
13. $\overline{MN} \parallel \overline{ND}$	13. The segment which joins the midpoint of two sides of a $\triangle$ is $\parallel$ to the third side.
14. $BMDC$ is a parallelogram.	14. If 2 sides of a quad. are both $\cong$ and $\parallel$, then the quad. is a parallelogram.
15. $\overline{MD} \cong \overline{BC}$	15. Opposite sides of a parallelogram are $\cong$.
16. $MD = BC$	16. Same as (9)
17. $MN = \frac{1}{2} \cdot BC$	17. Substitution

38. When the midpoints of the consecutive sides of a quadrilateral are joined in order, the resulting quadrilateral is a parallelogram.

Given: Quad. *ABCD* with *M*, *N*, *O*, *P* the

midpoints of $\overline{AB}$, $\overline{BC}$, $\overline{CD}$,

and $\overline{AD}$, respectively.

Prove: *MNOP* is a parallelogram

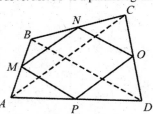

STATEMENTS	REASONS
1. Quad. *ABCD* with *M*,*N*,*O*,*P* the midpoints of $\overline{AB}$ $\overline{BC}$, $\overline{CD}$, $\overline{AD}$	1. Given
2. Draw in $\overline{AC}$	2. Through 2 points there is exactly one line.
3. In △*ABC*, $\overline{MN} \parallel \overline{AC}$	3. The segment which joins the midpoints of two sides of a △ is ∥ to the third side.
4. In △*ACD*, $\overline{OP} \parallel \overline{AC}$	4. Same as (3)
5. $\overline{MN} \parallel \overline{OP}$	5. If 2 lines are each ∥ to a 3rd line, then these lines are ∥ to each other.
6. Draw in $\overline{BD}$	6. Same as (2)
7. In △*ABD*, $\overline{MP} \parallel \overline{BD}$	7. Same as (3)
8. In △*CBD*, $\overline{NO} \parallel \overline{BD}$	8. Same as (3)
9. $\overline{MP} \parallel \overline{NO}$	9. Same as (5)
10. *MNOP* is a parallelogram	10. If a quad. has both paris of opposite sides ∥, it is a parallelogram.

SECTION 4.3: The Rectangle, Square and Rhombus

1. $m\angle A = 60°$; $m\angle ABC = 120°$

2. The parallelogram is a rhombus.

3. The parallelogram is a rectangle.

4. The parallelogram is a square.

5. The quadrilateral is a rhombus.

6. The rhombus is a square.

7. $\overline{MN} \parallel$ to both $\overline{AB}$ and $\overline{DC}$; $MN = AB = DC$

8. $CD = 5$; $AD = 12$; $AC = 13$

9. $2x + 7 = 3x + 2$
    $x = 5$
    $AD = BC = 3(5) + 4 = 19$

10. $x + y = 2x - y - 1$
    $3x - 3y + 1 = x + 2y$

    $-1x + 2y = -1$ Multiply by 2
    $2x - 5y = -1$

    $\begin{array}{r} -2x + 4y = -2 \\ 2x - 5y = -1 \\ \hline -1y = -3 \\ y = 3 \end{array}$

    $-1x + 2(3) = -1$
    $-1x + 6 = -1$
    $-1x = -7$
    $x = 7$

11. $NQ = 10$; $MP = 10$

12. $NQ = \sqrt{117}$; $MP = \sqrt{117}$

13. $QP = \sqrt{72} = 6\sqrt{2}$
    $MN = \sqrt{72} = 6\sqrt{2}$

14. $MQ = 8$; $NP = 8$

15. $AD = \sqrt{41}$

16. $AB = \sqrt{61}$

17. $AD = \sqrt{34}$

18. $BC = \sqrt{74}$

19. 5

20. 5

21. True

22. True

23. 1. Given

    4. The line joining the midpoints of two sides of a △ is ∥ to the third side.

    5. If 2 lines are each ∥ to a third line, then the 2 lines are ∥.

    6. Same as (2)

    7. Same as (3)

    8. Same as (4)

    9. Same as (5)

    10. *ABCD* is a parallelogram

24. 1. Rect. *WXYZ* with diagonals $\overline{WY}$ and $\overline{XZ}$

    2. $\overline{WY} \cong \overline{XZ}$

    4. Identity

    5. SSS

    6. $\angle 1 \cong \angle 2$; CPCTC

25. (a)

26. (b)

27. $AC^2 = 52^2 + 39^2$
$AC^2 = 2704 + 1521$
$AC^2 = 4225$
$AC = 65$
$DC^2 = 65^2 - 25^2$
$DC^2 = 4225 - 625$
$DC^2 = 3600$
$DC = 60$
$P = 52 + 39 + 25 + 60 = 176$

28. Let the length of one side of the square = *x*.
$x^2 = \left(3\sqrt{2}\right)^2 + \left(3\sqrt{2}\right)^2$
$x^2 = 18 + 18$
$x^2 = 36$
$x = 6$
$P = 4(6) = 24$

29. A rectangle is a parallelogram. Therefore, the opposite angles are congruent and the consecutive angles are supplementary. If a rectangle has one right angle which measures 90°, the other three angles must also be 90°. Therefore, all the angles in a rectangle are right angles.

30. A rhombus is a parallelogram with adjacent sides congruent. Since a parallelogram has opposite sides congruent, then all the sides of a rhombus must be congruent.

31. A square can be defined as a rhombus with a right angle. If all the sides of a rhombus are congruent (#16), then all sides of a square must be congruent since the square is a rhombus.

32. The diagonals of a square are perpendicular.
Given: *ABCD* is a square.
Prove: $\overline{BD} \perp \overline{AC}$

STATEMENTS	REASONS
1. *ABCD* is a square	1. Given
2. *ABCD* is a rectangle	2. A square is a rectangle with 2 adjacent sides ≅.
3. $\overline{AB} \cong \overline{BC}$	3. Same as (2)
4. *ABCD* is a parallelogram	4. A rectangle is a parallelogram with a rt. ∠.
5. $\overline{BD}$ bisects $\overline{AC}$	5. Diagonals of a parallelogram bisect each other.
6. $\overline{AE} \cong \overline{EC}$	6. If a seg. is bisected, 2 ≅ segments are formed.
7. $\overline{BE} \cong \overline{BE}$	7. Identity
8. $\triangle ABE \cong \triangle CBE$	8. SSS
9. $\angle BEA \cong \angle BEC$	9. CPCTC
10. $\overline{BD} \perp \overline{AC}$	10. If 2 lines meet to form ≅ adj. ∠s, lines are ⊥.

33. A diagonal of a rhombus bisects two angles of the rhombus.

Given: *ABCD* is a rhombus

Prove: $\overrightarrow{AC}$ bisects $\angle BAD$

and $\overrightarrow{CA}$ bisects $\angle BCD$

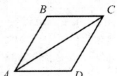

STATEMENTS	REASONS
1. *ABCD* is a rhombus	1. Given
2. $\overline{AB} \cong \overline{BC} \cong \overline{CD} \cong \overline{AD}$	2. All sides of a rhombus are ≅.
3. *ABCD* is a parallelogram	3. A rhombus is a parallelogram with 2 ≅ adj. sides.
4. $\angle B \cong \angle D$	4. Opposite angles of a parallelogram are ≅.
5. $\triangle ABC \cong \triangle ADC$	5. SAS
6. $\angle BAC \cong \angle DAC$ and $\angle BCA \cong \angle DCA$	6. CPCTC
7. $\overrightarrow{AC}$ bisects $\angle BAD$ and $\overrightarrow{CA}$ bisects $\angle BCD$	7. If a ray divides an $\angle$ into 2 ≅ $\angle$s, then the ray bisects the $\angle$.

34. If the diagonals of a parallelogram are congruent, then the parallelogram is a rectangle.

Given: Parallelogram *ABCD* with

$\overline{AC} \cong \overline{BD}$

Prove: *ABCD* is a rect.

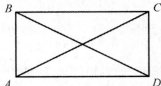

STATEMENTS	REASONS
1. Parallelogram *ABCD* with $\overline{AC} \cong \overline{BD}$	1. Given
2. $\overline{AB} \cong \overline{CD}$	2. Opposite sides of parallelogram are ≅.
3. $\overline{AD} \cong \overline{AD}$	3. Identity
4. $\triangle BAD \cong \triangle CDA$	4. SSS
5. $\angle BAD \cong \angle CDA$	5. CPCTC
6. $m\angle BAD \cong m\angle CDA$	6. If 2 $\angle$s are ≅, then their measures are =.
7. $\angle BAD$ is supp. to $\angle CDA$	7. Consecutive $\angle$s in a parallelogram are supp.
8. $m\angle BAD + m\angle CDA = 180$	8. If 2 $\angle$s are supp., then the sum of their measures is 180.
9. $m\angle BAD + m\angle BAD = 180$ or $2 \cdot m\angle BAD = 180$	9. Substitution
10. $m\angle BAD = 90$	10. Division Prop. of Eq.
11. $\angle BAD$ is a rt. $\angle$.	11. If the measure of an $\angle$ is 90, then the $\angle$ is a rt. $\angle$.
12. *ABCD* is a rect.	12. If a parallelogram has a rt. $\angle$, then the parallelogram is a rect.

35. If the diagonals of a parallelogram are perpendicular, then the parallelogram is a rhombus.
    Given: *ABCD* is a parallelogram
    with $\overline{BD} \perp \overline{AC}$
    Prove: *ABCD* is a rhombus

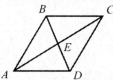

STATEMENTS	REASONS
1. *ABCD* is a parallelogram with $\overline{BD} \perp \overline{AC}$	1. Given
2. $\angle BEA \cong \angle BEC$	2. If 2 lines are $\perp$, then they meet to form $\cong$ adj. $\angle$s.
3. $\overline{BD}$ bisects $\overline{AC}$	3. Diagonals of a parallelogram bisect each other.
4. $\triangle BAD \cong \triangle CDA$	4. If a segment is bisected, then 2 $\cong$ segments are formed.
5. $\overline{BE} \cong \overline{BE}$	5. Identity
6. $\triangle BEA \cong \triangle BEC$	6. SAS
7. $\overline{AB} \cong \overline{BC}$	7. CPCTC
8. *ABCD* is a rhombus.	8. If a parallelogram has 2 adj. sides $\cong$, then the parallelogram is a rhombus.

36. If the diagonals of a parallelogram are congruent and also perpendicular, then the parallelogram is a square.
    Given: *ABCD* is a parallelogram with $\overline{BD} \cong \overline{AC}$; also $\overline{BD} \perp \overline{AC}$
    Prove: *ABCD* is a square

STATEMENTS	REASONS
1. *ABCD* is a parallelogram with $\overline{BD} \cong \overline{AC}$	1. Given
2. *ABCD* is a rectangle	2. From Exercise 34, if the diagonals of a parallelogram are $\cong$ then the parallelogram is a rect.
3. $\overline{BD} \perp \overline{AC}$	3. Given
4. $\angle BEA \cong \angle BEC$	4. If 2 lines are $\perp$, then they meet to form $\cong$ adj. $\angle$s.
5. $\overline{BD}$ bisects $\overline{AC}$	5. Diagonals of a parallelogram bisect each other.
6. $\overline{AE} \cong \overline{EC}$	6. If a segment is bisected, then 2 $\cong$ segment are formed.
7. $\overline{BE} \cong \overline{BE}$	7. Identity
8. $\triangle BEA \cong \triangle BEC$	8. SAS
9. $\overline{AB} \cong \overline{BC}$	9. CPCTC
10. *ABCD* is a square	10. If a rectangle has 2 adj. sides $\cong$, then the rectangle is a square.

37. If the midpoints of the sides of a rectangle are joined in order, then the quadrilateral formed is a rhombus.
Given: Rect. *ABCD* with *M, N, O,* and *P*
　　　 the midpoints of the sides.
Prove: *MNOP* is a rhombus

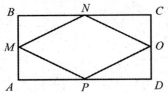

STATEMENTS	REASONS
1. Rect. *ABCD* with *M, N, O* and *P* the midpoints of the sides.	1. Given
2. *MNOP* is a parallelogram	2. From Exercise 36 of Section 4.2, when the midpoints of the consecutive sides of a quadrilateral are joined in order, the resulting quadrilateral is a parallelogram.
3. ∠s *A* and *B* are rt. ∠s	3. All angles of a rect. are rt. ∠s.
4. $\angle A \cong \angle B$	4. Any 2 right ∠s are ≅.
5. $\overline{MB} \cong \overline{MA}$	5. The midpoint of a segment forms 2 ≅ segments.
6. $\overline{BC} \cong \overline{AD}$	6. Opposite sides of a parallelogram are ≅.
7. $\overline{BN} \cong \overline{AP}$	7. If two segments are ≅, then their midpoints separate these segments into four ≅ segments.
8. △*MBN* ≅ △*MAP*	8. SAS
9. $\overline{MN} \cong \overline{MP}$	9. CPCTC
10. *MNOP* is rhombus	10. If a parallelogram has 2 adj. sides ≅, then the parallelogram is a rhombus.

38. Let the length of the brace = *x*.
$$x^2 = 8^2 + 12^2$$
$$x^2 = 64 + 144$$
$$x^2 = 208$$
$$x = 14.4 \text{ ft}$$

39. Let the length of the ramp = *x*.
$$x^2 = 4^2 + 20^2$$
$$x^2 = 16 + 400$$
$$x^2 = 416$$
$$x = 20.4 \text{ ft}$$

40. a. In rect. *ABCD*, diagonals $\overline{AC}$ and $\overline{BD}$ are ≅.
Because *ABCD* is also a parallelogram, the diagonals bisect each other at *M*. With *M* the midpoint of $\overline{AC}$ and $\overline{BD}$,
$\overline{DM} \cong \overline{CM} \cong \overline{BM} \cong \overline{AM}$. (If 2 segments are congruent, their midpoints separate these segments into four congruent segments.) In the drawing, ∠*ABC* is a rt. ∠. Then *M* is the midpoint of hypotenuse $\overline{AC}$ of rt. △*ABC* and *CM* = *BM* = *AM*.

b. If *AC* = 6 and *BC* = 8, then *AB* = 10 and *AM* = *MB* = 5. Because the midpoint *M* of the hypotenuse is equidistant from all vertices of rt. △*ABC*, *CM* = 5.

41. Rhombus

42. Draw the described square. AB = BC = CD = AD = 8. AE = 10. Let CE = x; then ED = 8 • x.
Using the Pythagorean Theorem on △ AED we get $10^2 = 8^2 + (8 • x)^2$ or 100 = 64 + 64 • 16x + x^2. This simplifies to
$$x^2 • 16x + 28 = 0$$
$$(x • 2)(x • 14) = 0$$
x = 2 or x = 14; reject x = 14
Now use the Pythagorean Theorem on △ BCE.
$$(BE)^2 = 8^2 + 2^2 = 68$$
$$BE = \sqrt{68} = 2\sqrt{17}$$

43. Draw the described square including $\overline{EC}$ and
$\overline{ED}$. AB = BC = CD = AD = BE = AE = 8.
$m\angle ABD = m\angle BEA = m\angle EAB = 60$.
$m\angle EBC = m\angle EAD = 30$. Because
$\triangle BEC$ and $\triangle AED$ are isosceles,
$m\angle BEC = m\angle BCE = 75$ and
$m\angle AED = m\angle ADE = 75$. Thus,
$m\angle ECD = m\angle EDC = 15$.
$\therefore m\angle DEC = 150°$.

SECTION 4.4: The Trapezoid

1. $m\angle D = 180 - 58 = 122°$
$m\angle B = 180 - 125 = 55°$

2. $m\angle A = 180 - 118 = 62°$
$m\angle C = 180 - 63 = 117°$

3. The trapezoid is an isosceles trapezoid.

4. The trapezoid is an isosceles trapezoid.

5. The quadrilateral is a rhombus.

6. $\triangle WMA \cong \triangle ZMD$. Therefore, $WA = DZ$ and
$\triangle XNB \cong \triangle YNC$. By CPCTC, $BX = YC$. In rect.
$WZYX$, $WX = MN = ZY$ or $MN = \frac{1}{2}(WX + ZY)$.
But if WA and BX are subtracted from WX and
added to ZY, then $MN = \frac{1}{2}(AB + DC)$.

7. Trapezoid

8. Yes

9. **a.** Yes

   b. No

10. **a.** Yes

   b. No

11. $MN = \frac{1}{2}(AB + DC)$
$= \frac{1}{2}(7.3 + 12.1)$
$= 9.7$

12. $MN = \frac{1}{2}(AB + DC)$
$6.3 = \frac{1}{2}(AB + 7.5)$
$12.6 = AB + 7.5$
$AB = 5.1$

13. $MN = \frac{1}{2}(AB + DC)$
$9.5 = \frac{1}{2}(8.2 + DC)$
$19 = 8.2 + DC$
$DC = 10.8$

14. $MN = \frac{1}{2}(AB + DC)$
$5x + 3 = \frac{1}{2}(7x + 5 + 4x - 2)$
$10x + 6 = 7x + 5 + 4x - 2$
$10x + 6 = 11x + 3$
$-1x = -3$
$x = 3$

15. $MN = \frac{1}{2}(AB + DC)$
$= \frac{1}{2}(6x + 5 + 8x - 1)$
$= \frac{1}{2}(14x + 4)$
$= 7x + 2$

16. $MN = \frac{1}{2}(AB + DC)$
$= \frac{1}{2}(x + 3y + 4 + 3x + 5y - 2)$
$= \frac{1}{2}(4x + 8y + 2)$
$= 2x + 4y + 1$

17. Given: $ABCD$ is an isosceles trapezoid.
Prove: $\triangle ABE$ is isosceles

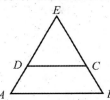

STATEMENTS	REASONS
1. $ABCD$ is an isosceles trap.	1. Given
2. $\angle A \cong \angle B$	2. Lower base angles of an isosceles trap. are $\cong$.
3. $\overline{EB} \cong \overline{EA}$	3. If 2 $\angle$s of a $\triangle$ are $\cong$, then the sides opposite these $\angle$s are also $\cong$.
4. $\triangle ABE$ is isosceles	4. If a $\triangle$ has 2 $\cong$ sides, it is an isosceles $\triangle$.

18. Given: Isosceles $\triangle ABE$ with $\overline{AE} \cong \overline{BE}$;
D and C are midpoints of
$\overline{AE}$ and $\overline{BE}$, respectively
Prove: $ABCD$ is an isosceles trapezoid

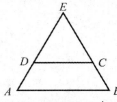

STATEMENTS	REASONS
1. Isosceles $\triangle ABE$ with $\overline{AE} \cong \overline{BE}$; D and C are midpoints of $\overline{AE}$ and $\overline{BE}$, respectively	**1.** Given
2. $\overline{DC} \parallel \overline{AB}$	**2.** The segment joining the midpoints of 2 sides of a $\triangle$ is $\parallel$ to the third side of the $\triangle$.
3. $\overline{AD} \cong \overline{CB}$	**3.** The midpoint of 2 $\cong$ segments form 4 $\cong$ segments.
4. $ABCD$ is a trapezoid	**4.** If a quad. has one pair of $\parallel$ sides, the quad. is a trapezoid.
5. $ABCD$ is an isosceles trapezoid	**5.** If a trapezoid has the nonparallel sides $\cong$, then the trapezoid is an isosceles trapezoid.

19. $h = 8$

20. $WX = 33$

21. $(QP)^2 = (MQ)^2 + (MP)^2$
$13^2 = 5^2 + (MP)^2$
$169 = 25 + (MP)^2$
$144 = (MP)^2$
$12 = MP$

22. $MN = \frac{1}{2}(RV + ST)$
$MN = \frac{1}{2}(17 + 13)$
$MN = 15$
$(RN)^2 = (RM)^2 + (MN)^2$
$(RN)^2 = 8^2 + 15^2$
$(RN)^2 = 289$
$RN = 17$

23. $h = \frac{1}{2}(20 + 24)$
$h = 22$ ft

24. $AB = \frac{1}{2}(225 + 515)$
$AB = 370$ mi

25. $AB = BC$
$2x + 3 = x + 7$
$x = 4$
$EF = DE = 3x + 2$
$EF = 3(4) + 2 = 14$

26. $AB = BC$
$2x + 3y = x + y + 7$
$x + 2y = 7$
$DE = EF$
$2x + 3y + 3 = 5x - y + 2$
$-3x + 4y = -1$

$x + 2y = 7$ Multiply by 3
$-3x + 4y = -1$

$3x + 6y = 121$
$\underline{-3x + 4y = -1}$
$10y = 20$
$y = 2$
$x + 2(2) = 7$
$x + 4 = 7$
$x = 3$

27. The diagonals of an isosceles trapezoid are congruent.
Given: Trap. $ABCD$ is an isos. trap.
with $\overline{AB} \cong \overline{CD}$
Prove: $\overline{AC} \cong \overline{BD}$

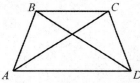

STATEMENTS	REASONS
1. Trap. $ABCD$ is an isos. trap. with $\overline{AB} \cong \overline{CD}$	**1.** Given
2. $\angle BAD \cong \angle CDA$	**2.** Base $\angle$s of a isos. trap. are $\cong$.
3. $\overline{AD} \cong \overline{AD}$	**3.** Identity
4. $\triangle BAD \cong \triangle CDA$	**4.** SAS
5. $\overline{BD} \cong \overline{AC}$	**5.** CPCTC

28. The median of a trapezoid is parallel to each base.
Given: Trap. *ABCD* with median $\overline{MN}$.
Prove: $\overline{MN} \parallel \overline{BC}$ and $\overline{MN} \parallel \overline{AD}$

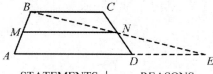

STATEMENTS	REASONS
1. Trap. *ABCD* with median $\overline{MN}$	**1.** Given
2. Draw $\overrightarrow{BN}$ and extend $\overline{AD}$ $\overrightarrow{BN}$ intersects $\overrightarrow{AD}$ at *E*.	**2.** Through any 2 points there is exactly one line.
3. *M* is midpoint of $\overline{AB}$ and *N* is midpoint of $\overline{CD}$ and	**3.** The median of a trap. joins the midpoints of the non-parallel sides.
4. In △*ABE*, $\overline{MN} \parallel \overline{AD}$	**4.** The segment joining the midpoints of 2 sides of a △ is ∥ to the 3rd sides.
5. $\overline{BC} \parallel \overline{AD}$	**5.** A trap. has one pair of ∥ sides.
6. $\overline{MN} \parallel \overline{BC}$	**6.** If two lines are each ∥ to a 3rd line, then these lines are each ∥ to each other.

29. If 2 consecutive angles of a quadrilateral are supplementary, the quadrilateral is a trapezoid.
Given: Quadrilateral *ABCD* with ∠*A* is supp. to ∠*B*
Prove: *ABCD* is a trapezoid

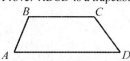

STATEMENTS	REASONS
1. Quad. *ABCD* with ∠*A* is supp. to ∠*B*	**1.** Given
2. $\overline{BC} \parallel \overline{AD}$	**2.** If 2 lines are cut by a trans. so that the interior ∠s on the same side of the trans. are supp., then these lines are ∥.
3. *ABCD* is a trapezoid	**3.** If a quad had 2 ∥ sides, then the quad. is a trapezoid.

30. If two base angles of a trapezoid are congruent, the trapezoid is an isosceles trapezoid.
Given: Trapezoid *RSTV* with $\overline{RS} \parallel \overline{VT}$ and ∠*V* ≅ ∠*T*
Prove: *RSTV* is an isosceles trapezoid

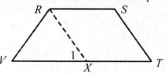

STATEMENTS	REASONS
1. Trap. *RSTV* with $\overline{RS} \parallel \overline{VT}$ and ∠*V* ≅ ∠*T*	**1.** Given
2. Draw $\overline{RX} \parallel \overline{ST}$	**2.** Through a point not on a line there is only one line ∥ to the given line.
3. ∠1 ≅ ∠*T*	**3.** If 2 ∥ lines are cut by a trans., then the corresponding ∠s are ≅.
4. ∠1 ≅ ∠*V*	**4.** Transitive Property
5. $\overline{RV} \parallel \overline{RX}$	**5.** If 2 ∠s of 1 △ are ≅, then the opposite sides are ≅.
6. *RSTX* is a parallelogram	**6.** If both pairs of opposite sides are ∥, then the quadrilateral is a parallelogram.
7. $\overline{RX} \parallel \overline{ST}$	**7.** Opposite sides of a parallelogram are ≅.
8. $\overline{RV} \parallel \overline{ST}$	**8.** Transitive Property
9. *RSTV* is an isosceles trap.	**9.** If a trapezoid has the nonparallel sides, then the trapezoid is an isosceles trapezoid.

31. If three parallel lines intercept congruent segments on one transversal then they intercept congruent segments on any transversal.

Given: Parallel lines *a*, *b*, and *c* cut by transversal *t* so that $\overline{AB} \cong \overline{BC}$; also transversal *m* is drawn

Prove: $\overline{DE} \cong \overline{EF}$

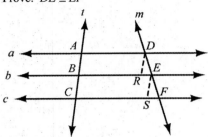

STATEMENTS	REASONS
1. Parallel lines *a*, *b*, and *c* cut by transversal *t* so that $\overline{AB} \cong \overline{BC}$; also transversal *m* is drawn	1. Given
2. Through *D* and *E* draw $\overline{AB} \cong \overline{BC}$ and $\overline{DE} \cong \overline{EF}$.	2. Through a point not on a line there is only one line ∥ to the given line.
3. *ABRD* is a parallelogram *BCSE* is a parallelogram	3. A quad. with opposite sides ∥ to the given line.
4. $\overline{AB} \cong \overline{DR}$ and $\overline{BC} \cong \overline{ES}$	4. Opposite sides of a parallelogram are ≅.
5. $\overline{DR} \cong \overline{ES}$	5. Transitive Property for ≅.
6. $\angle RDE \cong \angle SEF$ $\angle DER \cong \angle EFS$	6. If 2 ∥ lines are cut by a transversal, then the corresponding ∠s are ≅.
7. $\triangle DER \cong \triangle EFS$	7. AAS
8. $\overline{DE} \parallel \overline{EF}$	8. CPCTC

32. If the midpoints of the sides of an isosceles trapezoid are joined in order, then the quadrilateral formed is a rhombus.

Given: Isosceles trap. *ABCD* with *M*, *N*, *O* and *P* the midpoints of the sides

Prove: *MNOP* is a rhombus

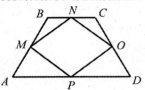

STATEMENTS	REASONS
1. Isosceles trap. *ABCD* with *M*, *N*, *O*, and *P* the midpoints of the sides.	1. Given
2. *MNOP* is a parallelogram	2. From Exercise 36 of 4.2, when the midpoints of the consecutive sides of a quad. are joined in order, the resulting quad. is parallelogram.
3. $\overline{BN} \cong \overline{NC}$	3. Midpoint of a segment forms 2 ≅ segments.
4. $\overline{AB} \cong \overline{CD}$	4. The non-parallel sides of an isos. trap. are ≅.
5. $\overline{MB} \cong \overline{CO}$	5. If segments are ≅, then their midpoints separate these segments into 4 ≅ segments.
6. $\angle B \cong \angle C$	6. Base angles of an isos. trap. are ≅.
7. $\triangle MBN \cong \triangle OCN$	7. SAS
8. $\overline{MN} \cong \overline{NO}$	8. CPCTC
9. *MNOP* is a rhombus	9. If a parallelogram has 2 ≅ adj. sides, then the parallogram is a rhombus.

33. Given: $\overline{EF}$ is the median of trapezoid $ABCD$

Prove: $EF = \frac{1}{2}(AB + DC)$

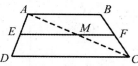

STATEMENTS	REASONS
1. $\overline{EF}$ is the median of trapezoid $ABCD$	1. Given
2. $\overline{AB} \parallel \overline{DC}$	2. Trapezoid has one pair of $\parallel$ sides.
3. $\overline{EF}$ is $\parallel$ to both $\overline{AB}$ and $\overline{DC}$	3. The median of a trap. is $\parallel$ to each base.
4. E is the midpoint of $\overline{AD}$ and F is the midpoint of $\overline{BC}$	4. The median of a trap. joins the midpoints of the nonparallel sides.
5. $\overline{AE} \cong \overline{ED}$	5. The midpoint of a segment forms 2 $\cong$ segments.
6. $\overline{AM} \cong \overline{MC}$	6. If 3 (or more) parallel lines intercept $\cong$ segments on one transversal, then they intercept $\cong$ segments on any transversal.
7. M is the midpoint of $\overline{AC}$	7. If a point divides a segment into 2 $\cong$ segments, then the point is the midpoint.
8. In $\triangle ADC$, $EM = \frac{1}{2}(DC)$ and in $\triangle ABC$, $MF = \frac{1}{2}(AB)$	8. The segment that joins the midpoints of two sides of a $\triangle$ is $\parallel$ to the third side and has a length equal to one-half the length of the third side.
9. $EM + MF = \frac{1}{2}(AB) + \frac{1}{2}(DC)$	9. Addition Property of Equality
10. $EM + MF = \frac{1}{2}(AB + DC)$	10. Distrubutive Property
11. $EF = EM + MF$	11. Segment Addition Postulate
12. $EF = \frac{1}{2}(AB + DC)$	12. Substitution

34. a. $MF = \frac{1}{2}(12.8) = 6.4$

b. $EM = \frac{1}{2}(18.4) = 9.2$

c. $EF = 6.4 + 9.2 = 15.6$

d. $EF = \frac{1}{2}(12.8 + 18.4) = \frac{1}{2}(31.2) = 15.6$; Yes.

35. a. $AB = 2(3.5) = 7$

b. $DC = 2(7.1) = 14.2$

c. $EF = 7.1 + 3.5 = 10.6$

d. $EF = \frac{1}{2}(7 + 14.2) = \frac{1}{2}(21.2) = 10.6$; Yes

36. Since $\overline{AB} \parallel \overline{DC}$ and $\overline{CE} \parallel \overline{DA}$, $ADCE$ is a parallelogram. Therefore, $m\angle A = 56°$, $m\angle DCE = 56°$, $m\angle D = 124°$, and $m\angle AEC = 124°$. Since $m\angle B = 56°$, $m\angle DCB = 124°$. $m\angle DCF = m\angle FCB = 62°$ since $\angle DCB$ was bisected. Therefore, $m\angle FCE = 6°$.

37. **a.** $AS = 3$ ft

b. $VD = 12$ ft

c. $CD = 13$ ft

d. $DE = \sqrt{73}$ ft

38. **a.** $GN = 2.75$ ft

b. DK

39. depth $= \dfrac{1}{2}(3 + 13) = 8$ ft

40. Using the Pythagorean Theorem,
$$(DC)^2 = 24^2 + (13 - 3)^2$$
$$(DC)^2 = 576 + 100$$
$$(DC)^2 = 676$$
$$DC = 26$$

41. If $\angle A$ is supp to $\angle B$, then

$$\dfrac{x}{3} + 50 + \dfrac{x}{2} + 10 = 180$$

$$\dfrac{x}{3} + \dfrac{x}{2} = 120$$

Multiply by 6, the LCD

$$2x + 3x = 720$$

$$5x = 720$$

$$x = 144$$

If $\angle B$ is supp to $\angle C$, then

$$\dfrac{x}{3} + 50 + \dfrac{x}{5} + 50 = 180$$

$$\dfrac{x}{3} + \dfrac{x}{5} = 80$$

Multiply by 15, the LCD

$$5x + 3x = 1200$$

$$8x = 1200$$

$$x = 150$$

Possible values of x are 144 or 150.

CHAPTER REVIEW

1. A

2. S

3. N

4. S

5. S

6. A

7. A

8. A

9. A

10. N

11. S

12. N

13. $2(2x + 3) + 2(5x - 4) = 96$
$$4x + 6 + 10x - 8 = 96$$
$$14x - 2 = 06$$
$$14x = 98$$
$$x = 7$$
$$AB = DC = 2(7) + 3 = 17$$
$$AD = BC = 5(7) - 4 = 31$$

14. $2x + 6 + x + 24 = 180$
$$3x + 30 = 180$$
$$3x = 150$$
$$x = 50$$
$$m\angle C = m\angle A = 2(50) + 6 = 106°$$

15. The sides of a parallelogram measure 13 since $5^2 + 12^2 = (\text{side})^2$. Perimeter is 52.

16. $4x = 2x + 50$
$$2x = 50$$
$$x = 25$$
$$m\angle M = 4(25) = 100°$$
$$m\angle P = 180 - 100 = 80°$$

17. $\overline{PN}$

18. Kite

19. $m\angle G = m\angle F = 180 - 108 = 72°$
$$m\angle E = 108°$$

20. Median $= \dfrac{1}{2}(12.3 + 17.5)$
$$= \dfrac{1}{2}(29.8)$$
$$= 14.9 \text{ cm}$$

21. $15 = \dfrac{1}{2}(3x + 2 + 2x - 7)$
$$30 = 5x - 5$$
$$35 = 5x$$
$$x = 7$$
$$MN = 3(7) + 2 = 23$$
$$PO = 2(7) - 7 = 7$$

22. If $\overline{FJ} \cong \overline{FH}$ and M and N are their midpoints,
then $FM = NH$ or

$$2y + 3 = 5y - 9$$
$$-3y = -12$$
$$y = 4$$

$$FM = 2(4) + 3 = 11$$
$$FN = NH = 5(4) - 9 = 11$$
$$JH = 2(4) = 8$$

The perimeter of $\triangle FMN = 26$.

23. Since M and N are midpoints, $\overline{MN} \parallel \overline{JH}$ and

$MN = \dfrac{1}{2} \cdot JH$. There fore, $MN = 6$,

$m\angle FMN = 80°$ and $m\angle FNM = 40°$.

24. Since M and N are midpoints, $MN = \dfrac{1}{2} \cdot JH$.

Therefore $x^2 + 6 = \dfrac{1}{2} \cdot 2x(x + 2)$

$$x^2 + 6 = x(x + 2)$$
$$x^2 + 6 = x^2 + 2x$$
$$6 = 2x$$
$$x = 3$$

$$MN = 15$$
$$JH = 30$$

25. Given: $ABCD$ is a parallelogram
$\overline{AF} \cong \overline{CE}$
Prove: $\overline{DF} \parallel \overline{EB}$

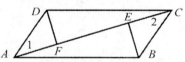

STATEMENTS	REASONS
1. $ABCD$ is a parallelogram	1. Given
2. $\overline{AD} \cong \overline{CB}$	2. Opp. sides of a parallelogram are $\cong$.
3. $\overline{AD} \parallel \overline{CB}$	3. Opp. sides of a parallelogram are $\parallel$.
4. $\angle 1 \cong \angle 2$	4. If 2 $\parallel$ lines are cut by a trans., then the alt. int. $\angle$s are $\cong$.
5. $\overline{AF} \cong \overline{CE}$	5. Given
6. $\triangle DAF \cong \triangle BCE$	6. SAS
7. $\angle DFA \cong \angle BEC$	7. CPCTC
8. $\overline{DF} \parallel \overline{EB}$	8. If 2 lines are cut by a trans. so that alt. ex. $\angle$s are $\cong$, then the lines are $\parallel$.

26. Given: $ABEF$ is a rect., $BCDE$ is a rect.
$\overline{FE} \cong \overline{ED}$
Prove: $\overline{AE} \cong \overline{BD}$ and $\overline{AE} \parallel \overline{BD}$

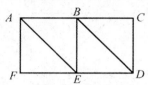

STATEMENTS	REASONS
1. $ABEF$ is a rect.	1. Given
2. $ABEF$ is a parallelogram	2. A rect. is a parallelogram with a rt. $\angle$.
3. $\overline{AF} \cong \overline{BE}$	3. Opp. sides of a parallelogram are $\cong$.
4. $BCDE$ is a rect.	4. Given
5. $\angle F$ and $\angle BED$ are rt. $\angle$s	5. Same as (2)
6. $\angle F \cong \angle BED$	6. Any 2 rt. $\angle$s are $\cong$.
7. $\overline{FE} \cong \overline{ED}$	7. Given
8. $\triangle AFE \cong \triangle BED$	8. SAS
9. $\overline{AE} \cong \overline{BD}$	9. CPCTC
10. $\angle AEF \cong \angle BDE$	10. CPCTC
11. $\overline{AE} \parallel \overline{BD}$	11. If lines are cut by a trans. so that the corresp. $\angle$s are $\cong$, then the lines are $\parallel$.

27. Given: $\overline{DE}$ is a median in $\triangle ADC$
$\overline{BE} \cong \overline{FD}$ and $\overline{EF} \cong \overline{FD}$
Prove: $ABCF$ is a parallelogram

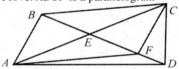

STATEMENTS	REASONS
1. $\overline{DE}$ is a median of $\triangle ADC$	1. Given
2. E is the midpoint of $\overline{AC}$	2. Median of a $\triangle$ is a line segment drawn from a vertex to the midpoint of the opp. side.
3. $\overline{AE} \cong \overline{EC}$	3. Midpoint of a segment forms 2 $\cong$ segments.
4. $\overline{BE} \cong \overline{FD}$ and $\overline{EF} \cong \overline{FD}$	4. Given
5. $\overline{BE} \cong \overline{EF}$	5. Transitive Prop. for $\cong$
6. $ABCF$ is a parallelogram	6. If the diagonals of a quad. bisect each other then the quad is a parallelogram.

28. Given: △*FAB* ≅ △*HCD*

          △*EAD* ≅ △*GCB*

Prove: *ABCD* is a parallelogram

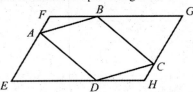

STATEMENTS	REASONS
1. △*FAB* ≅ △*HCD*	1. Given
2. $\overline{AB} \cong \overline{DC}$	2. CPCTC
3. △*EAD* ≅ △*GCB*	3. Given
4. $\overline{AD} \cong \overline{BC}$	4. CPCTC
5. *ABCD* is a parallelogram	5. If a quad. has both pairs of opp. sides ≅, then the quad is a parallelogram.

29. Given: *ABCD* is a parallelogram

          $\overline{DC} \cong \overline{BN}$

          ∠3 ≅ ∠4

Prove: *ABCD* is a rhombus

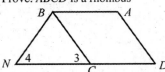

STATEMENTS	REASONS
1. *ABCD* is a parallelogram	1. Given
2. $\overline{DC} \cong \overline{BN}$	2. Given
3. ∠3 ≅ ∠4	3. Given
4. $\overline{BN} \cong \overline{BC}$	4. If 2 ∠s of a △ are ≅, then the sides opp. these ∠s are also ≅.
5. $\overline{DC} \cong \overline{BC}$	5. Transitive Prop. for ≅.
6. *ABCD* is a rhombus	6. If a parallelogram has 2 ≅ adj. sides, then the parallelogram is a rhombus

30. Given: △*TWX* is an isosceles with base $\overline{WX}$

          $\overline{RY} \parallel \overline{WX}$

Prove: *RWXY* is an isosceles trapezoid

STATEMENTS	REASONS
1. △*TWX* is isosceles with base $\overline{WX}$	1. Given
2. ∠*W* ≅ ∠*X*	2. Base ∠s of an isos. △ are ≅.
3. $\overline{RY} \parallel \overline{WX}$	3. Given
4. ∠*TRY* ≅ ∠*W* and ∠*TYR* ≅ ∠*X*	4. If 2 ∥ lines are cut by a trans., then the corresp. ∠s are ≅.
5. ∠*TRY* ≅ ∠*TYR*	5. Transitive Prop. for ≅.
6. $\overline{TR} \cong \overline{TY}$	6. If 2 ∠s of a △ are ≅, then the side opp. these ∠s are also ≅.
7. $\overline{TW} \cong \overline{TX}$	7. Isosceles △ has 2 ≅ sides.
8. *TR* = *TY* and *TW* = *TX*	8. If 2 segments are ≅, then they are equal in length.
9. *TW* = *TR* + *RW* and *TX* = *TY* + *YX*	9. Segment-Addition Post.
10. *TR* + *RW* = *TY* + *YX*	10. Substitution
11. *RW* = *YX*	11. Subtraction Prop. of Eq.
12. $\overline{RW} \cong \overline{YX}$	12. If segments are ≅ in length, then they are ≅.
13. *RWXY* is an isosceles trapezoid.	13. If a quad. has one pair of ∥ sides and the non-parallel sides are ≅, then the quad. is an isos. trap.

31.

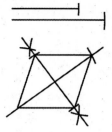

32. a. $\overline{AB} \perp \overline{BC}$

    b. $AC = 13$

33. a. $\overline{WY} \perp \overline{XZ}$

    b. $WY = 30$

34. a. Kites, rectangles, squares, rhombi, isosceles trapezoids

    b. Parallelograms, rectangles, squares, rhombi

35. a. Rhombus

    b. Kite

CHAPTER TEST

1. a. Congruent

    b. Supplementary

2. 18.8 cm

3. $CD = AB$. Let $x = AE$.
$$(AE)^2 + (DE)^2 = (AD)^2$$
$$x^2 + 4^2 = 5^2$$
$$x^2 = 9$$
$$x = 3$$
$$EB = AB - AE = 9 - 3 = 6$$

4. $m\angle S = 57°$
$m\angle R = 180 - 57 = 123°$
$\overline{VS}$ is longer.

5. $VT = 3x - 1$, $TS = 2x + 1$, $RS = 4(x - 2)$
$$3x - 1 = 4(x - 2)$$
$$x = 7$$

6. a. Kite

    b. Parallelogram

7. a. Altitude

    b. Rhombus

8. a. The line segments are parallel.

    b. $MN = \dfrac{1}{2}(BC)$

9. $MN = \dfrac{1}{2}(BC)$
$$7.6 = \dfrac{1}{2}(BC)$$
$$BC = 15.2 \text{ cm}$$

10. $MN = 3x - 11$
$BC = 4x + 24$
$$MN = \dfrac{1}{2}(BC)$$
$$3x - 11 = \dfrac{1}{2}(4x + 24)$$
$$x = 23$$

11. Let $x = AC$. $AD = 12$ and $DC = 5$
$$5^2 + 12^2 = x^2$$
$$x^2 = 169$$
$$x = 13$$
$$AC = 13$$
Or use the Pythagorean Triple (5, 12, 13).

12. a. $\overline{RV}$, $\overline{ST}$

    b. $\angle R$ and $\angle V$ (or $\angle S$ and $\angle T$)

13. $MN = \dfrac{1}{2}(RS + VT)$
$$= \dfrac{1}{2}(12.4 + 16.2)$$
$$= 14.3 \text{ in.}$$

14. $VT = 2x + 9$, $MN = 6x - 13$, $RS = 15$
$$MN = \dfrac{1}{2}(RS + VT)$$
$$6x - 13 = \dfrac{1}{2}(15 + 2x + 9)$$
$$6x - 13 = x + 12$$
$$5x = 25$$
$$x = 5$$

15. S1. Kite $ABCD$; $\overline{AB} \cong \overline{AD}$ and $\overline{BC} \cong \overline{DC}$

    R1. Given

    S3. $\overline{AC} \cong \overline{AC}$

    R4. SSS

    S5. $\angle B \cong \angle D$

    R5. CPCTC

16. S1. Trap. $ABCD$ with $\overline{AB} \parallel \overline{DC}$ and $\overline{AD} \cong \overline{BC}$

    R1. Given

    R2. Congruent

    R3. Identity

    R4. SAS

    S5. $\overline{AC} \cong \overline{DB}$

17. $x - 1 = y - 3$

Using $y = 2x - 4$, we get

$x - 1 = 2x - 4 - 3$

$x - 1 = 2x - 7$

$x = 6;$ $y = 2(6) - 4 = 8;$

$RS = 8;$ $ST = 5;$ $TV = 5;$ $RV = 8$

Perimeter of $RSTV = 2(8) + 2(5) = 26$

Chapter 5: Similar Triangles

SECTION 5.1: Ratios, Rates and Proportions

1. a. $\dfrac{12}{15} = \dfrac{4}{5}$

   b. $\dfrac{12 \text{ inches}}{15 \text{ inches}} = \dfrac{4}{5}$

   c. $\dfrac{1 \text{ foot}}{18 \text{ inches}} = \dfrac{12 \text{ inches}}{18 \text{ inches}} = \dfrac{2}{3}$

   d. $\dfrac{1 \text{ foot}}{18 \text{ ounces}}$ is incommensurable

2. a. $\dfrac{20}{36} = \dfrac{5}{9}$

   b. $\dfrac{24 \text{ ounces}}{52 \text{ ounces}} = \dfrac{6}{13}$

   c. $\dfrac{20 \text{ ounces}}{2 \text{ pounds}} = \dfrac{20 \text{ ounces}}{32 \text{ ounces}} = \dfrac{8}{5}$

   d. $\dfrac{2 \text{ pounds}}{20 \text{ ounces}} = \dfrac{32 \text{ ounces}}{20 \text{ ounces}} = \dfrac{5}{8}$

3. a. $\dfrac{15}{24} = \dfrac{5}{8}$

   b. $\dfrac{2 \text{ feet}}{3 \text{ yards}} = \dfrac{2 \text{ feet}}{6 \text{ feet}} = \dfrac{1}{3}$

   c. $\dfrac{2 \text{ meters}}{150 \text{ cm}} = \dfrac{200 \text{ cm}}{150 \text{ cm}} = \dfrac{4}{3}$

   d. $\dfrac{2 \text{ meters}}{1 \text{ pound}}$ is incommensurable

4. a. $\dfrac{24}{32} = \dfrac{3}{4}$

   b. $\dfrac{12 \text{ in.}}{2 \text{ yards}} = \dfrac{12 \text{ in.}}{72 \text{ in.}} = \dfrac{1}{6}$

   c. $\dfrac{150 \text{ cm}}{2 \text{ meters}} = \dfrac{150 \text{ cm}}{200 \text{ cm}} = \dfrac{3}{4}$

   d. $\dfrac{1 \text{ gallon}}{24 \text{ miles}}$ is incommensurable

5. a. $12x = 36$
      $x = 3$

   b. $21x = 168$
      $x = 8$

6. a. $5(x-1) = 30$
      $5x - 5 = 30$
      $5x = 35$
      $x = 7$

   b. $12(x+1) = 60$
      $12x + 12 = 60$
      $12x = 48$
      $x = 4$

7. a. $24(x-3) = 8(x+3)$
      $24x - 72 = 8x + 24$
      $16x = 96$
      $x = 6$

   b. $18(x+1) = 6(4x-1)$
      $18x + 18 = 24x - 6$
      $24 = 6x$
      $x = 4$

8. a. $x^2 = 144$
      $x = \pm 12$

   b. $x^2 = 64$
      $x = \pm 8$

9. a. $x^2 = 28$
      $x = \pm\sqrt{28} = \pm 2\sqrt{7} \approx \pm 5.29$

   b. $x^2 = 18$
      $x = \pm\sqrt{18} = \pm 3\sqrt{2} \approx \pm 4.24$

10. a. $(x+1)(x+2) = 30$
       $x^2 + x3 + 2 = 30$
       $x^2 + 3x - 28 = 0$
       $(x+7)(x-4) = 0$
       $x + 7 = 0 \quad \text{or} \quad x - 4 = 0$
       $x = -7 \quad \text{or} \quad x = 4$

    b. $(x-2)(x+2) = 60$
       $x^2 - 4 = 60$
       $x^2 = 64$
       $x = \pm 8$

11. a. $(x+1)(2x)=10x$

$$2x^2+2x=10x$$
$$2x^2-8x=0$$
$$2x(x-4)=0$$

$2x=0$ or $x-4=0$

$x=0$ or $\quad\quad x=4$

Reject $x=0$ because that would give 0 in the denominator.

b. $(2x+1)(3x-1)=14(x+1)$

$$6x^2+1x-1=14x+14$$
$$6x^2-13x-15=0$$
$$(6x+5)(1x-3)=0$$

$6x+5=0\quad$ or $\quad x-3=0$

$\quad x=-\dfrac{5}{6}\quad$ or $\quad\quad x=3$

12. a. $(x+1)(x-1)=14$

$$x^2-1=14$$
$$x^2=15$$
$$x=\pm\sqrt{15}$$

b. $(x+1)(x-2)=15$

$$x^2-1x-2=15$$
$$x^2-1x-17=0$$

$a=1;\ \ b=-1;\ \ c=-17$

$$x=\frac{-b\pm\sqrt{b^2-4ac}}{2a}$$
$$x=\frac{-(-1)\pm\sqrt{(-1)^2-4(1)(-17)}}{2(1)}$$
$$x=\frac{1\pm\sqrt{1+68}}{2}$$
$$x=\frac{1\pm\sqrt{69}}{2}$$

13. a. $\quad\ \ 3(x+1)=2x^2$

$$3x+3=2x^2$$
$$2x^2-3x-3=0$$

$a=2;\ \ b=-3;\ \ c=-3$

$$x=\frac{-b\pm\sqrt{b^2-4ac}}{2a}$$
$$x=\frac{-(-3)\pm\sqrt{(-3)^2-4(2)(-3)}}{2(2)}$$
$$x=\frac{3\pm\sqrt{9+24}}{4}$$
$$x=\frac{3\pm\sqrt{33}}{4}\approx 2.19\text{ or }-0.69$$

b. $5(x+1)=2x(x-1)$

$$5x+1=2x^2-2x$$
$$0=2x^2-7x-5$$

$a=2;\ \ b=-7;\ \ c=-5$

$$x=\frac{-b\pm\sqrt{b^2-4ac}}{2a}$$
$$x=\frac{-(-7)\pm\sqrt{(-7)^2-4(2)(-5)}}{2(2)}$$
$$x=\frac{7\pm\sqrt{49+40}}{4}$$
$$x=\frac{7\pm\sqrt{89}}{4}\approx 4.11\text{ or }-0.61$$

14. a. $(x+1)(x-1)=x^2$

$$x^2-1=x^2$$
$$0\neq-1$$

There is no solution.

b. $(x+2)(x-2)=2x^2$

$$x^2-4=2x^2$$
$$-4=x^2$$

x^2 cannot equal a negative number. Therefore, there is no solution.

15. $\dfrac{300\text{ m}}{47.7\text{ sec}}=6.3$ m/sec

16. $13\dfrac{1}{3}\div 4=3\dfrac{1}{3}$ yards for each dress

17. $\dfrac{4\text{ eggs}}{3\text{ cups of milk}}=\dfrac{14\text{ eggs}}{x\text{ cups of milk}}$

$$4x=42$$
$$x=\frac{42}{4}\text{ or }10\frac{1}{2}\text{ cups of milk}$$

18. $\dfrac{168\text{ worksheets}}{28\text{ students}}=\dfrac{x\text{ worksheets}}{32\text{ students}}$

$$28x=5376$$
$$x=192\text{ worksheets}$$

19. $\dfrac{20\text{ outlets}}{6\text{ rooms}}=\dfrac{x\text{ outlets}}{7\text{ rooms}}$

$$6x=140$$
$$x\approx24\text{ oulets}$$

20. $\dfrac{15\text{ secretaries}}{4\text{ copy machines}}=\dfrac{23\text{ secretaries}}{x\text{ copy machines}}$

$$15x=92$$
$$x\approx6\text{ copy machines}$$

21. a.
$$\frac{BD}{AD} = \frac{AD}{DC}$$
$$\frac{6}{AD} = \frac{AD}{8}$$
$$(AD)^2 = 48$$
$$AD = \sqrt{48} = 4\sqrt{3} \approx 6.93$$

b.
$$\frac{BD}{AD} = \frac{AD}{DC}$$
$$\frac{BD}{6} = \frac{6}{8}$$
$$8(BD) = 36$$
$$BD = \frac{36}{8} = 4\frac{1}{2}$$

22. a.
$$\frac{BD}{AB} = \frac{AB}{BC}$$
$$\frac{6}{AB} = \frac{AB}{16}$$
$$(AB)^2 = 96$$
$$AD = \sqrt{96} = 4\sqrt{6} \approx 9.80$$

b.
$$\frac{BD}{AB} = \frac{AB}{BC}$$
$$\frac{15 - DC}{10} = \frac{10}{15}$$
$$15(15 - DC) = 100$$
$$225 - 15 \cdot DC = 100$$
$$-15 \cdot DC = -125$$
$$DC = 8\frac{1}{3}$$

23. Let $2x$, $3x$, and $5x$ represent the salaries of a secretary, salesperson, and vice president.
$$2x + 3x + 5x = 124,500$$
$$10x = 124,500$$
$$x = 12,450$$
Secretary's salary is \$24,900; salesperson's salary is \$37,350; vice-president's salary is \$62,250.

24. Let $2x$, $3x$, $4x$, and $6x$ represent the measure of each angle in the quadrilateral.
$$2x + 3x + 4x + 6x = 360$$
$$15x = 360$$
$$x = 24$$
The angles measure $48°$, $72°$, $96°$, and $144°$.

25. Let the first angle have measure x so that the complementary angle has measure $90 - x$. Then
$$\frac{x}{90 - x} = \frac{4}{5}$$
$$5x = 4(90 - x)$$
$$5x = 360 - 4x$$
$$9x = 360$$
$$x = 40; \ 90 - x = 50$$
The angles measure $40°$ and $50°$.
Alternate method: Let the measures of the two angles be $4x$ and $5x$. Then
$$4x + 5x = 90$$
$$9x = 90$$
$$x = 10; \ 4x = 40; \ 5x = 50$$
The angles measure $40°$ and $50°$.

26. Let the first angle have measure x so that the supplementary angle has measure $180 - x$. Then
$$\frac{x}{180 - x} = \frac{2}{7}$$
$$7x = 2(180 - x)$$
$$7x = 360 - 2x$$
$$9x = 360$$
$$x = 40$$
$$180 - x = 140$$
Alternate method: Let the measure of the two angles be $2x$ and $7x$. Then
$$2x + 7x = 180$$
$$9x = 180$$
$$x = 20$$
$$2x = 40$$
$$7x = 140$$
The angles measure $40°$ and $140°$.

27.
$$\frac{2.54 \text{ cm}}{1 \text{ in.}} = \frac{x \text{ cm}}{12 \text{ in.}}$$
$$x = 2.54(12)$$
$$x = 30.48 \text{ cm}$$

28.
$$\frac{2.2 \text{ pounds}}{1 \text{ kg}} = \frac{12 \text{ pounds}}{x \text{ kg}}$$
$$2.2x = 12$$
$$x = 5\frac{5}{11} = 5.\overline{45} \text{ kg}$$

29.
$$\frac{7}{3} = \frac{6}{YZ}$$
$$7 \cdot YZ = 18$$
$$YZ = 2\frac{4}{7} \approx 2.57$$

30.
$$\frac{2 \cdot XY}{XY} = \frac{MQ}{3\frac{1}{2}}$$
$$2 = \frac{MQ}{3\frac{1}{2}}$$
$$MQ = 7$$

31.
$$\frac{a}{b} = \frac{3}{4}$$
$$4a = 3b$$
$$4a - 3b = 0$$

$$\frac{a-2}{b-1} = \frac{2}{3}$$
$$3(a-2) = 2(b-1)$$
$$3a - 6 = 2b - 2$$
$$3a - 2b = 4$$
Solve the system
$4a - 3b = 0$ Multiply by -2
$3a - 2b = 4$ Multiply by 3

$$-8a + 6b = 0$$
$$9a - 6b = 12$$
Add these equations to get
$1a = 12$;
Substitute 12 in for a to get $4(12) - 3b = 0$
$$48 - 3b = 0$$
$$48 = 3b$$
$$b = 16$$

32.

$$\frac{a}{b} = \frac{2}{3}$$

$$2b = 3a$$

$$b = \frac{3}{2}a$$

$$\frac{a-2}{b-2} = \frac{3}{5}$$

$$5a - 10 = 3b - 6$$

$$5a - 10 = 3\left(\frac{3}{2}a\right) - 6$$

$$5a = \frac{9}{2}a + 4$$

$$10a = 9a + 8$$

$$a = 8; b = \frac{3}{2}(8) = 12$$

33. Let the measure of angle be x.

Complement $= 90 - x$

Supplement $= 180 - x$

$$\frac{90 - x}{180 - x} = \frac{1}{3}$$

$$270 - 3x = 180 - x$$

$$-2x = -90$$

$x = 45$; the measure of the $\angle$ is 45°

34. Let the measure of the angle be x;
the measure of the complement is $90 - x$;
the measure of the supplement is $180 - x$.
If the ratio of the measure of the complement to
the measure of its supplement is 1:4, then

$$\frac{90 - x}{180 - x} = \frac{1}{4}$$
$$4(90 - x) = 1(180 - x)$$
$$360 - 4x = 180 - 1x$$
$$180 = 3x$$
$$x = 60$$
The measure of the angle is 60°.

35.
$$\frac{1 \text{ in.}}{3 \text{ ft}} = \frac{x \text{ in.}}{12 \text{ ft}}$$
$$3x = 12$$
$$x = 4 \text{ in.}$$

$$\frac{1 \text{ in.}}{3 \text{ ft}} = \frac{y \text{ in.}}{14 \text{ ft}}$$
$$3y = 14$$
$$y = 4\frac{2}{3} \text{ in.}$$

The blue print should be 4 in. by $4\frac{2}{3}$ in.

36.
$$\frac{1}{L} = \frac{L-1}{1}$$
$$1 = L^2 - L$$
$$L^2 - L - 1 = 0$$
Using the Quadratic Formula gives
$$L = \frac{1 \pm \sqrt{(-1)^2 - 4(1)(-2)}}{2(1)}$$
$$L = \frac{1 \pm \sqrt{1 + 4}}{2}$$
$$L = \frac{1 \pm \sqrt{5}}{2}$$

Reject $\frac{1 - \sqrt{5}}{2}$ because it is a negative number.

Therefore, $L = \frac{1 + \sqrt{5}}{2}$.

37. a.
$$\frac{5}{L} = \frac{L-5}{5}$$
$$L^2 - 5L = 25$$
$$L^2 - 5L - 25 = 0$$
$$L = \frac{5 \pm \sqrt{25 - 4(1)(-25)}}{2(1)}$$
$$L = \frac{5 \pm \sqrt{125}}{2}$$
$$L = \frac{5 \pm 5\sqrt{5}}{2}$$

Reject $\frac{5 - 5\sqrt{5}}{2}$ because it is a negative number.

Therefore, $L = \frac{5 + 5\sqrt{5}}{2}$.

b. $L \approx 1.62W$
$L \approx 1.62(5) \approx 8.1$

38. If $\dfrac{a}{b} = \dfrac{c}{d}$ and a, b, c, d are nonzero,

then ad = bc by the Means-Extreme Property.

Divide each side by cd to get $\dfrac{ad}{cd} = \dfrac{bc}{cd}$.

Simplifying gives $\dfrac{a}{c} = \dfrac{b}{d}$.

39. If $\dfrac{a}{b} = \dfrac{c}{d}$ where $b \neq 0$ and $d \neq 0$, add 1 to both

sides to get $\dfrac{a}{b} + 1 = \dfrac{c}{d} + 1$ or

$$\frac{a}{b} + \frac{b}{b} = \frac{c}{d} + \frac{d}{d} \text{ or}$$

$$\frac{a+b}{b} = \frac{c+d}{d}$$

SECTION 5.2: Similar Polygons

1. a. Congruent

b. Proportional

2. a. No

b. Yes

3. a. Yes

b. No

4. a. No

b. Yes

5. a. $\triangle ABC \sim \triangle XTN$

b. $\triangle ACB \sim \triangle NXT$

6. a. $\angle C$

b. $\overline{XN}$

7. Yes; Yes. Spheres have the same shape; one is generally an enlargement of the other.

8. $ABCDE \sim MNPQR$

9. a. $m\angle N = 82°$

b. $m\angle N = 42°$

c. $\dfrac{NP}{RS} = \dfrac{NM}{RQ}$
$\dfrac{NP}{7} = \dfrac{9}{6} \text{ or } \dfrac{3}{2}$
$2 \cdot NP = 21$
$NP = 10\dfrac{1}{2}$

d. $\dfrac{MP}{QS} = \dfrac{MN}{RQ}$
$\dfrac{12}{QS} = \dfrac{9}{6} \text{ or } \dfrac{3}{2}$
$3 \cdot QS = 24$
$QS = 8$

10. a. $m\angle B = 23°$

b. $m\angle RPC = 67°$

c. $\dfrac{AC}{PC} = \dfrac{AB}{PR}$
$\dfrac{AC}{5} = \dfrac{26}{13} \text{ or } \dfrac{2}{1}$
$AC = 10$

d. $\dfrac{CB}{CR} = \dfrac{AB}{PR}$
$\dfrac{CB}{12} = \dfrac{26}{13} \text{ or } \dfrac{2}{1}$
$CB = 24$

11. **a.** Yes

  b. Yes

  c. Yes

12. **a.** Symmetric

  b. Transitive

  c. Reflexive

13. $\dfrac{HK}{KF} = \dfrac{HJ}{FG}$

  $\dfrac{4}{FG} = \dfrac{6}{8}$ or $\dfrac{3}{4}$

  $3 \cdot FG = 16$

  $FG = 5\dfrac{1}{3}$

14. $\dfrac{HJ}{FG} = \dfrac{HK}{KF}$

  $\dfrac{HJ}{5} = \dfrac{6}{8}$ or $\dfrac{3}{4}$

  $4 \cdot HJ = 15$

  $HJ = 3\dfrac{3}{4}$

15. $m\angle K = 360 - (55 + 128 + 98)$

  $m\angle K = 79°$

16. $m\angle A = m\angle H$, $m\angle B = m\angle J$, $m\angle C = m\angle K$,

  $m\angle D = m\angle L$

  $x + x + 50 + 2x - 45 + x + 35 = 360$

  $5x + 40 = 360$

  $5x = 320$

  $x = 64°$

17. $\dfrac{AB}{HJ} = \dfrac{BC}{JK}$

  $\dfrac{n}{n+3} = \dfrac{5}{10}$ or $\dfrac{1}{2}$

  $n + 3 = 2n$

  $n = 3$

18. $\dfrac{AD}{DC} = \dfrac{HL}{LK}$

  $\dfrac{8}{6} = \dfrac{12}{LK}$

  $LK = 9$

  Using the Pythagorean Theorem,

  $(HK)^2 = 9^2 + 12^2$

  $(HK)^2 = 81 + 144$

  $(HK)^2 = 225$

  $HK = 15$

19. $2x + 4 = 68$

  $2x = 64$

  $x = 32$

  $m\angle L = 3x - 6$

  $m\angle L = 3(32) - 6$

  $m\angle L = 90°$

20. Parallelograms

21. Let $BC = x$; then $CE = x$ and $CA = x + 6$.

  $\dfrac{4}{x} = \dfrac{6}{x+6}$

  $6x = 4(x + 6)$

  $6x = 4x + 24$

  $2x = 24$

  $x = 12;\ BC = 12$

22. Let $DB = BC = x$; then $AB = x + 8$.

  $\dfrac{5}{8} = \dfrac{x}{x+8}$

  $8x = 5(x + 8)$

  $8x = 5x + 40$

  $3x = 40$

  $x = \dfrac{40}{3} = 13\dfrac{1}{3}$

  $AB = x + 8 = 13\dfrac{1}{3} + 8 = 21\dfrac{1}{3}$

23. Let $BC = x = CE$; then $AE = 20 - x$

  $\dfrac{x}{4} = \dfrac{20}{20-x}$

  $x(20 - x) = 80$

  $20x - x^2 = 80$

  $x^2 - 20x + 80 = 0$

  $a = 1,\ b = -20,\ c = 80$

  $x = \dfrac{-b \pm \sqrt{b^2 - 4ac}}{2a}$

  $x = \dfrac{20 \pm \sqrt{400 - 4(1)(80)}}{2(1)}$

  $x = \dfrac{20 \pm \sqrt{400 - 320}}{2}$

  $x = \dfrac{20 \pm \sqrt{80}}{2}$

  $x = \dfrac{20 \pm 4\sqrt{5}}{2}$

  $x = 10 \pm 2\sqrt{5}$

  $BC = 10 + 2\sqrt{5}$ or $10 - 2\sqrt{5}\ \approx 14.47$ or 5.53.

24. Let $AE = x = BD$; then $AB = x + 4$

$$\frac{x}{x+4} = \frac{x}{18}$$
$$x(x+4) = 72$$
$$x^2 + 4x - 72 = 0$$
$$a = 1, b = 4, c = -72$$
$$x = \frac{-b \pm \sqrt{b^2 - 4ac}}{2a}$$
$$x = \frac{-4 \pm \sqrt{16 - 4(1)(-72)}}{2(1)}$$
$$x = \frac{-4 \pm \sqrt{16 + 288}}{2}$$
$$x = \frac{-4 \pm \sqrt{304}}{2}$$
$$x = \frac{-4 \pm 4\sqrt{19}}{2}$$
$$x = -2 \pm 2\sqrt{19}$$
$$AE = -2 + 2\sqrt{19} \approx 6.72$$

$(-2 - 2\sqrt{19}$ is rejected because it is negative.)

25. Quadrilateral $MNPQ \sim$ quadrilateral $WXYZ$

$$\frac{6}{9} = \frac{50}{n}$$
$$6n = 9 \cdot 50$$
$$6n = 450$$
$$n = 75$$

26. Let $x =$ the length of the longest side of $WXYZ$.
$$\frac{5}{7} = \frac{8}{x}$$
$$5x = 56$$
$$x = \frac{56}{5}$$

27. Let $x =$ the height.
$$\frac{72}{6} = \frac{30}{x}$$
$$72x = 180$$
$$x = \frac{5}{2} = 2.5 \text{ in.}$$

28. Let $x =$ the distance.
$$\frac{3\frac{1}{2}}{3} = \frac{2\frac{1}{2}}{x}$$
$$x\left(3\frac{1}{2}\right) = 3\left(2\frac{1}{2}\right)$$
$$x\left(\frac{7}{2}\right) = \frac{15}{2}$$
$$x = \frac{15}{2} \cdot \frac{2}{7}$$
$$x = \frac{15}{7} = 2\frac{1}{7} \text{ in.}$$

29. Let $x =$ the boy's height.

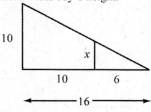

$$\frac{6}{x} = \frac{16}{10} \text{ or } \frac{8}{5}$$
$$8x = 30$$
$$x = \frac{30}{8} \text{ or } 3\frac{3}{4}, \text{ the boy is 3 ft 9 in.}$$

30. Let $x =$ the height above the ground.

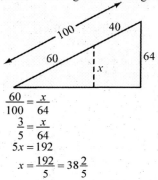

$$\frac{60}{100} = \frac{x}{64}$$
$$\frac{3}{5} = \frac{x}{64}$$
$$5x = 192$$
$$x = \frac{192}{5} = 38\frac{2}{5}$$

The kite is $38\frac{2}{5}$ feet above the ground.

31. Let the height of the tree be x.

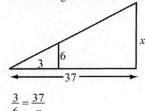

$$\frac{3}{6} = \frac{37}{x}$$
$$\frac{1}{2} = \frac{37}{x}$$
$$x = 74$$

The height of the tree is 74 feet.

32. Let x = the number of feet from the floor to the garage door; then $10 - x$ represents the number of feet from the door to the ceiling.

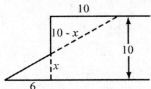

$$\frac{10-x}{x} = \frac{10}{6} \text{ or } \frac{5}{3}$$
$$3(10-x) = 5x$$
$$30 - 3x = 5x$$
$$30 = 8x$$
$$x = \frac{30}{8} \text{ or } 3\frac{3}{4}$$

The door is $3\frac{3}{4}$ feet above the floor.

33. No. The sides of quadrilateral *ABCD* are not proportional to quadrilateral *.DCFE.*

34. Yes

35. a. Yes

b. Yes

36. a. 2

b. Yes

37. In rhombus ARST, if AR = RS = TS = AT = x, then TC = 6 − x and RB = 10 − x. The

proportion to use is $\dfrac{TC}{TS} = \dfrac{RS}{BR}$ or

$$\frac{6-x}{x} = \frac{x}{10-x}$$
$$x^2 = (6-x)(10-x)$$
$$x^2 = 60 - 16x + x^2$$
$$16x = 60$$
$$x = 3.75$$

38. Let AB = x and use the proportion

$$\frac{EA}{AB} = \frac{ED}{DC}$$

$$\frac{2}{x} = \frac{8}{6}$$

$$8x = 12$$

$$x = 1.5; \text{ AB} = 1.5; \text{ BG} = .5; \text{ GH} = 4; \text{ BH} = 4.5$$

Use the Pythagorean Theorem on $\triangle$ BHC.

$(BC)^2 = 6^2 + (4.5)^2$

$(BC)^2 = 36 + 20.25$

$(BC)^2 = 56.25$

BC = 7.5

Perimeter of ABCD = 6 + 6 + 7.5 + 1.5 = 21

SECTION 5.3: Proving Triangles Similar

1. CASTC

2. CSSTP

3. a. True

b. True

4. a. True

b. False

5. SSS ~

6. AA

7. SAS ~

8. SSS ~

9. SAS ~

10. SAS ~

11. 1. Given

2. If 2 lines are $\perp$, they form right angles.

3. All right angles are $\cong$.

4. Opposite $\angle$s of a $\square$ are $\cong$.

5. AA

12. 1. Given

3. If 2 $\parallel$ lines are cut by a transversal, the corresponding $\angle$s are $\cong$.

4. Opposite sides of a parallelogram are $\parallel$.

5. Same as (3).

6. AA

13. 1. Given

    2. Definition of midpoint

    3. If a line segment joins the midpoints of two sides of a $\triangle$, its length is $\frac{1}{2}$ the length of the third side.

    4. Division Prop. of Eq.

    5. Substitution

    6. SSS ~

14. 1. Given

    3. Substitution

    4. Identity

    5. SAS

15. 1. $\overline{MN} \perp \overline{NP}$ and $\overline{QR} \perp \overline{RP}$

    2. If two lines are $\perp$, then they form a rt. $\angle$.

    3. $\angle N \cong \angle QRP$

    4. Identity

    S5. $\triangle MNP \sim \triangle QRP$

    R5. AA

16. 1. $\overline{MN} \parallel \overline{QR}$

    2. If 2 $\parallel$ lines are cut by a transversal, the corresponding $\angle$s are $\cong$.

    3. $\angle N \cong \angle QRP$

    S4. $\triangle MNP \sim \triangle QRP$

    R4. AA

17. 1. $\angle H \cong \angle F$

    2. If two $\angle$s are vertical $\angle$s, then they are $\cong$.

    S3. $\triangle HJK \sim \triangle FGK$

    R3. AA

18. 1. $\overline{HJ} \perp \overline{JF}$ and $\overline{HG} \perp \overline{FG}$

    2. If 2 lines are $\perp$, then they form a rt. $\angle$.

    3. If 2 $\angle$s are rt. $\angle$s, then they are $\cong$.

    4. If 2 $\angle$s are vertical $\angle$s, then they are $\cong$.

    S5. $\triangle HJK \sim \triangle FGK$

    R5. AA

19. 1. $\dfrac{RQ}{NM} = \dfrac{RS}{NP} = \dfrac{QS}{MP}$

    2. $\triangle RQS \sim \triangle NMP$

    3. $\angle N \cong \angle R$

20. S1. $\dfrac{DG}{DE} = \dfrac{DH}{DF}$

    R1. Given

    2. Identity

    3. SAS ~

    S4. $\angle DGH \cong \angle E$

    R4. CASTC

21. S1. $\overline{RS} \parallel \overline{UV}$

    R1. Given

    2. 2 $\parallel$ lines are cut by a transversal, alternate interior $\angle$s are $\cong$.

    3. $\triangle RST \sim \triangle VUT$

    S4. $\dfrac{RT}{VT} = \dfrac{RS}{VU}$

    R4. CSSTP

22. 1. Given

    2. $\angle B \cong \angle DCE$

    3. $\overline{AC} \parallel \overline{DE}$

    4. If 2 $\parallel$ lines are cut by a transversal, the corresponding $\angle$s are $\cong$.

    5. AA

    S6. $\dfrac{AB}{DC} = \dfrac{BC}{CE}$

    R5. SSS ~

23. Let $EB = x$.

$$\frac{x}{6} = \frac{6}{8}$$
$$8x = 36$$
$$x = \frac{36}{8} = 4\frac{1}{2}$$
$$EB = 4\frac{1}{2}$$

24. Let $DE = x$.

$$\frac{6}{x} = \frac{12}{10} \text{ or } \frac{6}{5}$$
$$x = 5$$
$$DE = 5$$

25. Let $DB = x$; then $AB = DB + AD = x + 4$.

$$\frac{AC}{DE} = \frac{AB}{DB}$$
$$\frac{10}{8} = \frac{x+4}{x}$$
$$8(x+4) = 10x$$
$$8x + 32 = 10x$$
$$2x = 32$$
$$x = 16$$
$$DB = 16$$

26. If $BC = 12$ and $EC = 4$, then $BE = 8$.
Let $DB = x$, then $AB = x + 5$

$$\frac{x}{x+5} = \frac{8}{12}$$
$$12x = 8(x+5)$$
$$12x = 8x + 40$$
$$4x = 40$$
$$x = 10$$
$$DB = 10$$

27. Let $EB = x$. Since $\triangle CDE \sim \triangle CBA$, then
$CB = CE + EB = 6 + x$ and
$AC = AD + DC = 8 + 10 = 18$.

$$\frac{CD}{CB} = \frac{CE}{AC}$$
$$\frac{10}{6+x} = \frac{6}{18}$$
$$\frac{10}{6+x} = \frac{1}{3}$$
$$30 = 6 + x$$
$$x = 24$$
$$EB = 24$$

28. Let $CE = x$. Since $\triangle CDE \sim \triangle CBA$, then
$CB = CE + EB = x + 12$.

$$\frac{CE}{CA} = \frac{CD}{CB}$$
$$\frac{x}{16} = \frac{10}{x+12}$$
$$x^2 + 12x - 160 = 0$$
$$(x-8)(x-20) = 0$$
$$x - 8 = 0 \quad \text{or} \quad x + 20 = 0$$
$$x = 8 \quad \text{or} \quad x = -20; \text{ reject } x = -20$$
$$CE = 8$$

29. Since $\triangle ABF \sim \triangle CBD$, then.

$$m\angle C + m\angle B + m\angle AFB = 180°$$
$$45° + x + 4x = 180°$$
$$5x = 135°$$
$$x = 27°$$

30.
$$\frac{m\angle A}{m\angle CDB} = \frac{1}{3}$$
$$3m\angle A = m\angle CDB$$
Let $m\angle A = x$ and $m\angle CDB = 3x$.
$$x + 3x + 44 = 180$$
$$4x + 44 = 180$$
$$4x = 136$$
$$x = 34°$$
$$m\angle A = 34°$$

31. Given: $\overline{AB} \parallel \overline{DF}$ and $\overline{BD} \parallel \overline{FG}$
Prove: $\triangle ABC \sim \triangle EFG$

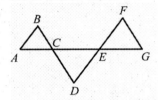

STATEMENTS	REASONS
1. $\overline{AB} \parallel \overline{DF}$ and $\overline{BD} \parallel \overline{FG}$	1. Given
2. $\angle A \cong \angle FEG$ and $\angle BCA \cong \angle G$	2. If 2 ∥ lines are cut by a trans., then the corresponding ∠s are ≅ .
3. $\triangle ABC \sim \triangle EFG$	3. AA

32. Given: $\overline{RS} \perp \overline{AB}$ and $\overline{CB} \perp \overline{AC}$
Prove: $\triangle BSR \sim \triangle BCA$

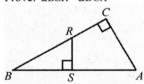

Proof: If $\overline{RS} \perp \overline{AB}$ and $\overline{CB} \perp \overline{AC}$, then $\angle BSR$
and $\angle C$ are right angles and therefore congruent.
Both $\triangle$s have $\angle B$ as a common angle.
Therefore, $\triangle BSR \sim \triangle BCA$ by AA.

33. "The lengths of the corresponding altitudes of similar triangles have the same ratio as the lengths of any pair of corresponding sides."

Given: $\triangle DEF \sim \triangle MNP$

$\overline{DG}$ and $\overline{MQ}$ are altitudes

Prove: $\dfrac{DG}{MQ} = \dfrac{DE}{MN}$

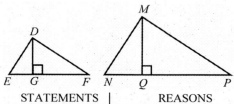

STATEMENTS	REASONS
1. $\triangle DEF \sim \triangle MNP$ $\overline{DG}$ and $\overline{MQ}$ are altitudes.	1. Given
2. $\overline{DG} \perp \overline{EF}$ and $\overline{MQ} \perp \overline{NP}$	2. An altitude is a segment drawn from a vertex $\perp$ to the opposite side.
3. $\angle DGE$ and $\angle MQN$ are rt. $\angle$s	3. $\perp$ lines form a rt. $\angle$.
4. $\angle DGE \cong \angle MQN$	4. Right $\angle$s are $\cong$.
5. $\angle E \cong \angle N$	5. If two $\triangle$s are $\sim$ then the corresponding $\angle$s are $\cong$.
6. $\triangle DGE \sim \triangle MQN$	6. AA
7. $\dfrac{DG}{MQ} = \dfrac{DE}{MN}$	7. Corresp. sides of $\sim$ $\triangle$s are proportional.

34. Given: $\overline{RS} \parallel \overline{YZ}$ and $\overline{RU} \parallel \overline{XZ}$

Prove: $RS \cdot ZX = ZY \cdot RT$

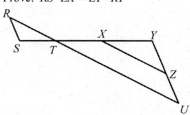

Proof: If $\overline{RS} \parallel \overline{YZ}$, $\angle S \cong \angle Y$ since they are alternate interior $\angle$s. If $\overline{Rt} \parallel \overline{XZ}$,

$\angle RTS \cong \angle YXZ$ since they are alt. ext. $\angle$s.

$\triangle RTS \sim \triangle ZXY$ by AA. With corresponding sides

of $\sim$ $\triangle$s proportional, $\dfrac{RS}{ZY} = \dfrac{RT}{ZX}$. Hence,

$RS \cdot ZX = ZY \cdot RT$.

35. $\dfrac{QP}{QS} = \dfrac{QM}{QR}$

$\dfrac{12}{QS} = \dfrac{9}{6}$

$9QS = 72$

$QS = 8$

36. $\dfrac{AD}{AE} = \dfrac{AB}{AF}$

$\dfrac{12}{AE} = \dfrac{7}{5}$

$7AE = 60$

$AE = \dfrac{60}{7}$ or $8\dfrac{4}{7}$

37. $\dfrac{XY}{YZ} = \dfrac{TY}{YW} = \dfrac{XT}{WZ}$

$\dfrac{120}{40} = \dfrac{XT}{50}$

$3 = \dfrac{XT}{50}$

$XT = 150$ feet

38. $\triangle ABC \sim \triangle ADB$

$\dfrac{AB}{AC} = \dfrac{AD}{AB}$

$\dfrac{AB}{8} = \dfrac{2}{AB}$

$(AB)^2 = 16$

$AB = 4$

39. The altitude drawn to the hypotenuse of a right triangle separates the right triangle into two right triangles which are similar to each other and to the original triangle.

    Given: Right △*ABC* with right ∠ at *ACB*; $\overline{CD}$ is the altitude to $\overline{AB}$.

    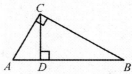

    Prove: △*ADC* ~△*CDB* ~△*ACD*

    Proof: Draw the three △s separately.

    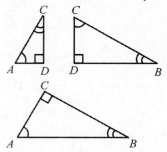

    By hypothesis, $\overline{CD}$ is the altitude to $\overline{AB}$. $\overline{CD}$ is then ⊥ to $\overline{AB}$ which means ∠*CDA* is a rt. ∠. By hypothesis, ∠*ACB* is a rt. ∠ in △*ABC*. Therefore, ∠*CDA* ≅ ∠*ACB*. ∠*A* is common to both △*ADC* and △*ACB*. By AA, △*ADC* ~△*ACB*. Since ∠*CDB* is also a right ∠, ∠*CDB* ≅ ∠*ACD*. In △*CDB* and △*ACB*, ∠*B* is the common angle. By AA, △*CDB* ~△*ACB*. For △*CDA* and △*CDB*, both have a right ∠. ∠*ACD* ≅ ∠*CBD* because "If 2 angles of one △ (△*ADC*) are congruent to 2 angles of another △ (△*ACB*), then the 3rd angles are also ≅. Thus by AA, △*ADC* ~△*CBD*. Hence the two right △s formed by the altitude to the hypotenuse are similar to each other and each is similar to the original right △.

40. The line segment which joins the midpoints of two sides of a triangle forms a triangle which is similar to the original triangle.

    Given: △*ACD* with *B* and *E* the midpoints of $\overline{AC}$ and $\overline{AD}$, respectively.

    Prove: △*ABE* ~△*ACD*

    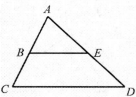

    Proof: By hypothesis, △*ACD* has *B* and *E* to be the midpoints of $\overline{AC}$ and $\overline{AD}$, respectively. $\overline{BE}$ is parallel to $\overline{CD}$ since the segment joining the midpoints of 2 sides of a triangle is parallel to the 3rd side. ∠*ABE* ≅ ∠*C* and ∠*AEB* ≅ ∠*D* since they are corresponding angles. By AA, then △*ABE* ~△*ACD*.

SECTION 5.4: The Pythagorean Theorem

1. $\triangle RST \sim \triangle RVS \sim \triangle SVT$

2. $\dfrac{TV}{SV} = \dfrac{SV}{VR}$

3. $\dfrac{RT}{RS} = \dfrac{RS}{RV}$ or $\dfrac{RV}{RS} = \dfrac{RS}{RT}$

4. $\dfrac{TR}{TS} = \dfrac{TS}{TV}$

5. $\dfrac{RV}{6} = \dfrac{6}{8}$
   $8 \cdot RV = 36$
   $RV = 4.5$

6. $\dfrac{RT}{6} = \dfrac{6}{4}$
   $4 \cdot RT = 36$
   $RT = 9$

7. **a.** $(DF)^2 = (DE)^2 + (EF)^2$
   $(DF)^2 = 8^2 + 6^2$
   $(DF)^2 = 64 + 36$
   $(DF)^2 = 100$
   $DF = 10$
   Or, $(6, 8, 10)$ is a multiple of a Pythagorean Triple, $(3, 4, 5)$; therefore $DF = 10$.

   b. $(DF)^2 = (DE)^2 + (EF)^2$
   $(DF)^2 = 5^2 + 3^2$
   $(DF)^2 = 25 + 9$
   $(DF)^2 = 34$
   $DF = \sqrt{34} \approx 5.83$

8. **a.** $(DF)^2 = (DE)^2 + (EF)^2$
   $13^2 = (DE)^2 + 5^2$
   $169 = (DE)^2 + 25$
   $(DE)^2 = 144$
   $DE = 12$
   Or, $(5, 12, 13)$ is a Pythagorean Triple; therefore $DE = 12$.

   b. $(DF)^2 = (DE)^2 + (EF)^2$
   $12^2 = (DE)^2 + (6\sqrt{3})^2$
   $144 = (DE)^2 + 108$
   $(DE)^2 = 36$
   $DE = 6$

9. **a.** $(DF)^2 = (DE)^2 + (EF)^2$
   $17^2 = 15^2 + (EF)^2$
   $289 = 225 + (EF)^2$
   $(EF)^2 = 64$
   $EF = 8$
   Or, $(8, 15, 17)$ is a Pythagorean Triple; therefore $EF = 8$.

   b. $(DF)^2 = (DE)^2 + (EF)^2$
   $12^2 = (8\sqrt{2})^2 + (EF)^2$
   $144 = 128 + (EF)^2$
   $(EF)^2 = 16$
   $EF = 4$

10. **a.** $(DF)^2 = (DE)^2 + (EF)^2$
    $(DF)^2 = 12^2 + 5^2$
    $(DF)^2 = 144 + 25$
    $(DF)^2 = 169$
    $DF = 13$
    Or, $(5, 12, 13)$ is a Pythagorean Triple; therefore $DF = 13$.

    b. $(DF)^2 = (DE)^2 + (EF)^2$
    $(DF)^2 = 12^2 + 6^2$
    $(DF)^2 = 144 + 36$
    $(DF)^2 = 180$
    $DF = \sqrt{180} = 6\sqrt{5} \approx 13.42$

11. **a.** $5^2 = 3^2 + 4^2$
    Yes

    b. $6^2 \neq 4^2 + 5^2$
    No

    c. $13^2 = 5^2 + 12^2$
    Yes

    d. $15^2 \neq 6^2 + 13^2$
    No

12. **a.** $17^2 = 8^2 + 15^2$
    Yes

    b. $19^2 \neq 10^2 + 13^2$
    No

    c. $10^2 = 6^2 + 8^2$
    Yes

    d. $20^2 \neq 11^2 + 17^2$
    No

13. Let c be the longest side.

 a. $5^2 = 3^2 + 4^2$
  Right △

 b. $6^2 < 4^2 + 5^2$
  Acute △

 c. $\left(\sqrt{7}\right)^2 = 2^2 + \left(\sqrt{3}\right)^2$
  Right △

 d. No △

14. Let c be the longest side.

 a. $(2.5)^2 = (1.5)^2 + 2^2$
  Right △

 b. $29^2 = 20^2 + 21^2$
  Right △

 c. $16^2 > 10^2 + 12^2$
  Obtuse △

 d. $9^2 > 5^2 + 7^2$
  Obtuse △

15. Let x = the distance from the base of the antenna.

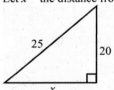

$25^2 = x^2 + 20^2$
$625 = x^2 + 400$
$\quad x^2 = 225$
$\quad\ x = 15$ ft
Or (15, 20, 25) is a multiple of the Pythagorean Triple, (3, 4, 5).

16. Let x = the length of the string.

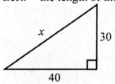

$x^2 = 30^2 + 40^2$
$x^2 = 900 + 1600$
$x^2 = 2500$
$\ x = 50$ ft
Or (30, 40, 50) is a multiple of the Pythagorean Triple (3, 4, 5).

17. Let x = the length of rope needed.

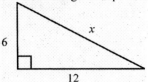

$x^2 = 6^2 + 12^2$
$x^2 = 36 + 144$
$x^2 = 180$
$\ x = \sqrt{180} = 6\sqrt{5} \approx 13.4$ meters

18. Let x = the distance form the balloon to the ground.

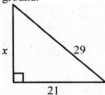

$29^2 = x^2 + 21^2$
$841 = x^2 + 441$
$\quad x^2 = 400$
$\quad\ x = 20$ ft
Or (20, 21, 29) is a Pythagorean Triple.

19. Let x = the height of the raised mid-sections.

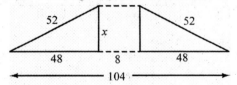

$52^2 = x^2 + 48^2$
$2704 = x^2 + 2304$
$\quad x^2 = 400$
$\quad\ x = 20$ ft
Or (20, 48, 52) is a multiple of the Pythagorean Triple (5, 12, 13).

20. Let x = the height of the raised mid-sections.

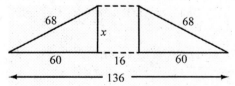

$68^2 = x^2 + 60^2$
$4624 = x^2 + 3600$
$\quad x^2 = 1024$
$\quad\ x = 32$ ft
Or (32, 60, 68) is a multiple of the Pythagorean Triple (8, 15, 17).

21. Let x = the length of the rectangle.

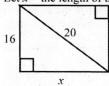

$$20^2 = 16^2 + x^2$$
$$400 = 256 + x^2$$
$$x^2 = 144$$
$$x = 12 \text{ cm}$$

Or (12, 16, 20) is a multiple of the Pythagorean Triple (3, 4, 5).

22.
$$(2x+3)^2 = x^2 + (2x+2)^2$$
$$4x^2 + 12 + 9 = x^2 + 4x^2 + 8x + 4$$
$$0 = x^2 - 4x - 5$$
$$0 = (x-5)(x+1)$$
$$x = 5 \text{ or } x = -1; \text{ reject } x = -1.$$

The lengths are 5, 12, and 13.

23.
$$(2x)^2 = (x+3)^2 + (x+1)^2$$
$$4x^2 = x^2 + 6x + 9 + x^2 + 2x + 1$$
$$4x^2 = 2x^2 + 8x + 10$$
$$2x^2 - 8x - 10 = 0$$
$$x^2 - 4x - 5 = 0$$
$$(x-5)(x+1) = 0$$
$$x = 5 \text{ or } x = -1; \text{ reject } x = -1.$$

The base is 8; the altitude is 6; the diagonals are 10.

24. Since the diagonals of a rhombus are perpendicular and since they bisect each other, 2 sides of a right $\triangle$ have lengths 3 and 4. The length of the hypotenuse is 5 by the Triple (3, 4, 5). Therefore, each side of the rhombus has length 5.

25. Since the diagonals of a rhombus are perpendicular and since they bisect each other, one side of the right triangle has length 9 and the hypotenuse has length 12.

Let x represent the length of the other side of the right triangle.
$$12^2 = x^2 + 9^2$$
$$144 = x^2 + 81$$
$$x^2 = 63$$
$$x = \sqrt{63} = 3\sqrt{7}$$

The length of the other diagonal is $6\sqrt{7} \approx 15.87$ in.

26. Let the length of each leg be x.
$$10^2 = x^2 + x^2$$
$$100 = 2x^2$$
$$x^2 = 50$$
$$x = \sqrt{50} = 5\sqrt{2}$$

27. Let the length of the hypotenuse be x.
$$x^2 = (6\sqrt{2})^2 + (6\sqrt{2})^2$$
$$x^2 = 72 + 72$$
$$x^2 = 144$$
$$x = 12 \text{ in.}$$

28. In right $\triangle ABC$, $AC = 6$ using the multiple of (3, 4, 5) which is (6, 8, 10). $AM = 3$ and $MC = 3$.

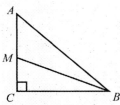

In rt. $\triangle MCB$, let $MB = x$, then
$$x^2 = 3^2 + 8^2$$
$$x^2 = 9 + 64$$
$$x^2 = 73$$
$$x = \sqrt{73}$$
$$MB = \sqrt{73}$$

29. In rt. $\triangle ACB$, $AC = 8$ using the triple (8, 15, 17).

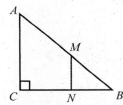

Since M and N are midpoints, $\overline{MN} \parallel \overline{AC}$. Since $\overline{MN} \parallel \overline{AC}$, $MN = \frac{1}{2} \cdot AC$. Therefore, $MN = 4$.

30. A triangle whose lengths are 6, 8, and 10 is a right triangle. The altitude to the 10 inch side is the altitude to the hypotenuse. Let the lengths of the 2 segments of the hypotenuse be x and $10 - x$. Let the length of the altitude to the hypotenuse be H. Using the fact that the length of each leg of a right triangle is the geometric mean for the length of the hypotenuse and the length of the segment on the hypotenuse adjacent to that leg, we have

$$\frac{x}{6} = \frac{6}{10}$$
$$10x = 36$$
$$x = \frac{36}{10} = \frac{18}{5} = 3\frac{3}{5}$$

If $x = 3\frac{3}{5}$, then $10 - x = 6\frac{2}{5}$.

Now, if the length of the altitude to the hypotenuse of a right triangle is the geometric mean of the lengths of the segments of the hypotenuse, we have

$$\frac{\frac{18}{5}}{H} = \frac{H}{\frac{32}{5}}$$
$$H^2 = \frac{18}{5} \cdot \frac{32}{5} = \frac{576}{25}$$
$$H = \frac{24}{5} \text{ or } 4\frac{4}{5}$$

30. Alternate Solution:
The altitude to the 10 inch side separates it into two parts whose lengths are x and $10 - x$. The length of the altitude is H. Using the Pythagorean Theorem twice, we have $x^2 + H^2 = 6^2$ and $(10 - x)^2 + H^2 = 8^2$. Subtracting the first equation from the second gives

$$100 - 20x + x^2 + H^2 = 64$$
$$\underline{\quad\quad\quad x^2 + H^2 = 36\quad}$$
$$100 - 20x \quad\quad\quad = 28$$
$$-20x = -72$$
$$x = \frac{72}{20} = \frac{18}{5} \text{ or } 3\frac{3}{5}$$

To find H, substitute $\frac{18}{5}$ in for x in

$$x^2 + H^2 = 6^2$$
$$\left(\frac{18}{5}\right)^2 + H^2 = 36$$
$$\frac{324}{25} + H^2 = 36$$
$$H^2 = 36 - \frac{324}{25} \text{ or } \left(\frac{900}{25} - \frac{624}{25}\right) = \frac{576}{25}$$
$$H = \frac{24}{5} \text{ or } 4\frac{4}{5}$$

31. A triangle whose lengths are 10, 24, and 26 is a right triangle. The altitude to the 26 inch side is the altitude to the hypotenuse. Let the lengths of the 2 segments of the hypotenuse be x and $26 - x$. Let the length of the altitude to the hypotenuse be H. Using the fact that the length of each leg of a right triangle is the geometric mean for the length of the hypotenuse and the length of the segment on the hypotenuse adjacent to that leg, we have

$$\frac{x}{10} = \frac{10}{26}$$
$$26x = 100$$
$$x = \frac{100}{26} = \frac{50}{13} = 3\frac{11}{13}$$

If $x = 3\frac{11}{13}$, then $26 - x = 22\frac{2}{13}$.

Now, if the length of the altitude to the hypotenuse of a right triangle is the geometric mean of the lengths of the segments of the hypotenuse, we have

$$\frac{\frac{50}{13}}{H} = \frac{H}{\frac{288}{13}}$$
$$H^2 = \frac{50}{13} \cdot \frac{288}{13} = \frac{14,400}{169}$$
$$H = \frac{120}{13} \text{ or } 9\frac{3}{13}$$

31. Alternate Solution:
The altitude to the 26 inch side separates it into two parts whose lengths are x and $26 - x$. The length of the altitude is H. Using the Pythagorean Theorem twice, we have $x^2 + H^2 = 10^2$ and $(26 - x)^2 + H^2 = 24^2$. Subtracting the first equation from the second gives

$$676 - 52x + x^2 + H^2 = 576$$
$$\underline{\quad\quad\quad x^2 + H^2 = 100\quad}$$
$$676 - 52x \quad\quad\quad = 476$$
$$-52x = -200$$
$$x = \frac{200}{52} = \frac{50}{13} \text{ or } 3\frac{11}{13}$$

To find H, substitute $\frac{50}{13}$ in for x in

$$x^2 + H^2 = 10^2$$
$$\left(\frac{50}{13}\right)^2 + H^2 = 100$$
$$\frac{2500}{169} + H^2 = 100$$
$$H^2 = 100 - \frac{2500}{169} \text{ or } \left(\frac{16,900}{169} - \frac{2500}{169}\right)$$
$$H^2 = \frac{14,400}{169}$$
$$H = \frac{120}{13} \text{ or } 9\frac{3}{13}$$

32. In rt. $\triangle ABC$, if $BC = 3$ and $AB = 4$, then
$AC = 5$, using the Triple (3, 4, 5).
In rt. $\triangle ACD$, if $AC = 5$ and $DC = 12$, then
$DA = 13$ using the Triple (5, 12, 13).

33. In rt. $\triangle RST$, if $RS = 6$ and $ST = 8$, then
$RT = 10$ using the Pythagorean Triple (6, 8, 10).
In rt. $\triangle RTU$, $RT = 10$ and $RU = 15$; let
$UT = x$ and use the Pythagorean Theorem.
$$15^2 = 10^2 + x^2$$
$$225 = 100 + x^2$$
$$x^2 = 125$$
$$x = \sqrt{125} = 5\sqrt{5} \approx 11.18$$

34. Given: $\triangle ABC$ is not a right $\triangle$
Prove: $a^2 + b^2 \neq c^2$

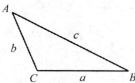

Proof: Assume $a^2 + b^2 = c^2$. Then $\triangle ABC$ must
be a right $\triangle$. But this contradicts our hypothesis.
Therefore, our assumption is wrong and
$a^2 + b^2 \neq c^2$.

35. $a = p^2 - q^2$
$\therefore a^2 = (p^2 - q^2)^2 = p^4 - 2p^2q^2 + q^4$
$b = 2pq$
$\therefore b^2 = (2pq)^2 = 4p^2q^2$
$c = p^2 + q^2$
$c^2 = (p^2 + q^2)^2 = p^4 + 2p^2q^2 + q^4$
Now, $a^2 + b^2 = (p^4 - 2p^2q^2 + q^4) + 4p^2q^2$
$\qquad\qquad = p^4 + 2p^2q^2 + q^4$
$\qquad\qquad = c^2$
$\qquad \therefore c^2 = a^2 + b^2$

36.

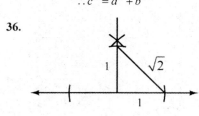

37.

38. The length of each side of the square would be
12. Therefore the perimeter would be 48.

39. $m\angle ACF = 60°$

40. The altitude to the 8 inch side separates it into
two parts whose lengths are x and $8 - x$. Let the
length of the altitude be H.

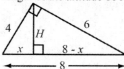

Using the Pythagorean Theorem twice, we have
$x^2 + H^2 = 4^2$ and $(8 - x)^2 + H^2 = 6^2$
Subtracting the first equation from the second, we
have
$$64 - 16x + x^2 + H^2 = 36$$
$$\underline{\qquad\quad x^2 + H^2 = 16}$$
$$64 - 16x \qquad\quad = 20$$
$$-16x = -44$$
$$x = \frac{44}{16} = \frac{11}{4}$$

To find H, substitute $\frac{11}{4}$ in for x.
$$x^2 + H^2 = 4^2$$
$$\left(\frac{11}{4}\right)^2 + H^2 = 16$$
$$H^2 = 16 - \frac{121}{16}$$
$$H^2 = \frac{256}{16} - \frac{121}{16}$$
$$H^2 = \frac{135}{16}$$
$$H = \frac{\sqrt{135}}{4} = \frac{3\sqrt{15}}{4} \approx 2.90$$

41. $TS = 13$ using the Pythagorean Triple (5, 12, 13).
$$(RT)^2 = (RS)^2 + (TS)^2$$
$$(RT)^2 = 13^2 + 13^2$$
$$(RT)^2 = 169 + 169$$
$$(RT)^2 = 338$$
$$RT = \sqrt{338} = 13\sqrt{2} \approx 18.38$$

42. If (a, b, c) is a Pythagorean Triple, then
$a^2 + b^2 = c^2$. If n is a natural number, then
$$(na)^2 + (nb)^2 = n^2a^2 + n^2b^2$$
$$= n^2(a^2 + b^2)$$
$$= n^2c^2$$
$$= (nc)^2$$

43. Theorem 5.4.2: The length of the altitude to the hypotenuse of a right triangle is the geometric mean of the lengths of the segments of the hypotenuse.

Given: Right $\triangle ABC$ with right $\angle$ at ACB; $\overline{CD} \perp \overline{AB}$.

Prove: $\dfrac{AD}{CD} = \dfrac{CD}{DB}$

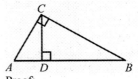

Proof:

By hypothesis, $\overline{CD} \perp \overline{AB}$ which means $\angle CDA$ is a rt. $\angle$. By hypothesis, $\angle ACB$ is a rt. $\angle$ in $\triangle ABC$. Therefore, $\angle CDA \cong \angle ACB$. $\angle A$ is common to both $\triangle ADC$ and $\triangle ACB$. By AA, $\triangle ADC \sim \triangle ACB$. Since $\angle CDB$ is also a right $\angle$, $\angle CDB \cong \angle ACD$. In $\triangle CDB$ and $\triangle ACB$, $\angle B$ is the common angle. By AA, $\triangle CDB \sim \triangle ACB$. For $\triangle CDA$ and $\triangle CDB$, both have a right $\angle$. $\angle ACD \cong \angle CBD$ because "If 2 angles of one $\triangle$ ($\triangle ADC$) are congruent to 2 angles of another $\triangle$ ($\triangle ACB$), then the 3rd angles are also $\cong$. Thus by AA, $\triangle ADC \sim \triangle CBD$. Therefore $\dfrac{AD}{CD} = \dfrac{CD}{DB}$ by CSSTP.

44. Lemma 5.4.3: The length of each leg of a right triangle is the geometric mean of the length of the hypotenuse and the length of the segment of the hypotenuse adjacent to the leg.

Given: $\triangle ABC$ with right $\angle ACB$; 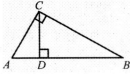 $\overline{CD} \perp \overline{AB}$.

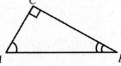

Prove: $\dfrac{AB}{AC} = \dfrac{AC}{AD}$

By hypothesis, $\overline{CD} \perp \overline{AB}$ which means $\angle CDA$ is a rt. $\angle$. By hypothesis, $\angle ACB$ is a rt. $\angle$ in $\triangle ABC$. Therefore, $\angle CDA \cong \angle ACB$. $\angle A$ is common to both $\triangle ADC$ and $\triangle ACB$. By AA, $\triangle ADC \sim \triangle ACB$. By CSSTP, $\dfrac{AB}{AC} = \dfrac{AC}{AD}$.

SECTION 5.5: Special Right Triangles

1. **a.** $BC = a$

   b. $AB = \sqrt{a^2 + a^2} = a\sqrt{2}$

2. **a.** $AC = 1$

   b. $BC = 1$

3. **a.** $YZ = a\sqrt{3}$

   b. $XY = 2a$

4. **a.** $XZ = a$

   b. $YZ = a\sqrt{3}$

5. $YZ = 8$ and $XY = 8\sqrt{2} \approx 11.31$

6. Since $\overline{XZ} \cong \overline{YZ}$, $m\angle X = 45°$ and $m\angle Y = 45°$. Using the 45°-45°-90° $\triangle$ with lengths a, a, $a\sqrt{2}$, we can set $10 = a\sqrt{2}$. Solve for a to get $a = 5\sqrt{2}$. So $XZ = YZ = 5\sqrt{2} \approx 7.07$.

7. $XZ = 10$; $YZ = 10$

8. $XZ = 12$; $YZ = 12$

9. $DF = 5\sqrt{3} \approx 8.66$ and $FE = 10$

10. $ED = 6$; $FD = 6\sqrt{3} \approx 10.39$

11. $ED = 12$; $FE = 24$

12. If $m\angle E = 2 \cdot m\angle F$ and $m\angle E + m\angle F = 90°$, then $2 \cdot m\angle F + m\angle F = 90°$ or $3 \cdot m\angle F = 90°$ or $m\angle F = 30°$. Therefore $m\angle E = 60°$. Using the 30°-60°-90° $\triangle$, with lengths a, $a\sqrt{3}$, and $2a$, we can set $2a = 12\sqrt{3}$. Solve for a: $a = 6\sqrt{3}$. $DE = 6\sqrt{3} \approx 10.39$ and $DF = 6\sqrt{3} \cdot \sqrt{3} = 18$.

13. In right $\triangle HLK$, if $m\angle HKL = 30°$ and $LK = 6\sqrt{3}$, then $HL = 6$ and $HK = 12$. $MK = 6$ since the diagonals of a rectangle bisect each other.

14. If $m\angle STV = 150°$, then $m\angle STR = 30°$ and $m\angle SRT = 60°$. Using the 30°-60°-90° reference $\triangle$ with lengths a, $a\sqrt{3}$, and $2a$, we can set $2a = 6\sqrt{2}$. Solving for a gives $a = 3\sqrt{2}$. $RS = 3\sqrt{2} \approx 4.24$ and $ST = 3\sqrt{2} \cdot \sqrt{3} = 3\sqrt{6} \approx 7.35$.

15. $AC = 6$ and $AB = 6\sqrt{2} \approx 8.49$.

16. If $MP = PN$, then $m\angle M = m\angle N = 45°$. In the 45°-45°-90° $\triangle$ with lengths a, a, $a\sqrt{2}$, we can set $a\sqrt{2} = 10\sqrt{2}$. Therefore $a = 10$. $PM = PN = 10$.

17. $RS = 6$ and $RT = 6\sqrt{3} \approx 10.39$.

18. Since $\overline{XY} \cong \overline{XZ} \cong \overline{YZ}$, $\triangle XYZ$ is an equilateral $\triangle$ and therefore equiangular. If $\overline{ZW} \perp \overline{XY}$, $\triangle ZWY$ is a 30°-60°-90° $\triangle$. $WY = 3$ and $ZW = 3\sqrt{3} \approx 5.20$.

19. Since the diagonals of a square are perpendicular, bisect each other, and are congruent, $\triangle DEC$ is a 45°-45°-90° $\triangle$. Using the 45°-45°-90° $\triangle$ with the lengths a, a, $a\sqrt{2}$, we can set $a\sqrt{2} = 5\sqrt{3}$. Solving for a gives $a = \frac{5\sqrt{3}}{\sqrt{2}} = \frac{5\sqrt{3}}{\sqrt{2}} \cdot \frac{\sqrt{2}}{\sqrt{2}} = \frac{5\sqrt{6}}{2}$. $DB = 2 \cdot a = 5\sqrt{6} \approx 12.25$.

20. In the 30°-60°-90° $\triangle$, $MN = 6$ and $MP = 3\sqrt{3} \approx 5.20$. In the 45°-45°-90° $\triangle$, $PQ = 3\sqrt{3} \approx 5.20$ $MQ = 3\sqrt{3} \cdot \sqrt{2} = 3\sqrt{6} \approx 7.35$ $NQ = NP + PQ$ $NQ = 3 + 3\sqrt{3} \approx 8.20$

21. From vertex Z, draw an altitude to $\overline{XY}$; call the altitude $\overline{ZW}$. In the 30°-60°-90° $\triangle$, $WX = 6$ and $ZW = 6\sqrt{3}$. In the 45°-45°-90° $\triangle$, $\overline{YW} = 6\sqrt{3}$. $XY = YW + WX = 6\sqrt{3} + 6 \approx 16.39$.

22. If $DB = AB$ in rhombus $ABCD$, then $AB = BC = DC = AD = DB = 8$. Since the diagonals of a rhombus are perpendicular and bisect each other, $\triangle DEC$ is a rt. $\triangle$ with $DE = 4$ and $DC = 8$. Let $EC = x$. Using the Pythagorean Theorem we have $8^2 = 4^2 + x^2$ $64 = 16 + x^2$ $x^2 = 48$ $x = \sqrt{48} = 4\sqrt{3}$ $AC = 2 \cdot EC = 8\sqrt{3} \approx 6.93$.

23. 45°

24. 30°

25. 60°; $200^2 + x^2 = 400^2$
$$x^2 = 400^2 - 200^2$$
$$x^2 = 120,000$$
$$x \approx 346$$
The jogger travels $(200 + 346) - 400 = 146$ feet further.

26. In a half of an hour, Thelma has traveled 6 miles and Gina has traveled 12 miles. A 30°-60°-90° △ is formed. Therefore, $GT = 6\sqrt{3} \approx 10.4$ miles.

27. In rt. $\triangle BCA$, $CA = 6$. In rt. $\triangle DCA$, let $DC = x$ and $DA = 2x$. Using the Pythagorean Theorem we have
$$(2x)^2 = x^2 + 6^2$$
$$4x^2 = x^2 + 36$$
$$3x^2 = 36$$
$$x^2 = 12$$
$$x = \sqrt{12} = 2\sqrt{3}$$
$$DC = 2\sqrt{3} \approx 3.46$$
In isosceles $\triangle BDA$,
$$DB = DA = 2 \cdot x = 4\sqrt{3} \approx 6.93.$$

28. In right $\triangle BCA$, $m\angle B = 30°$ and $m\angle DAC = 30°$. In right $\triangle DCA$, let $DC = x$.
$$AC = 10 = x\sqrt{3}$$
$$\frac{10}{\sqrt{3}} = x$$
$$DC = \frac{10\sqrt{3}}{3} \approx 5.77$$
In rt. $\triangle BCA$, $BC = 10\sqrt{3} \approx 17.32$
Therefore,
$$DB = BC - DC = 10\sqrt{3} - \frac{10\sqrt{3}}{3} \approx 11.55.$$

29. Since $\triangle MNQ$ is equiangular and $\overrightarrow{NR}$ bisects $\angle MNQ$ and $\overrightarrow{QR}$ bisects $\angle MQN$, $m\angle RQN = 30° = m\angle RNQ$. From R, draw an altitude to $\overline{NQ}$. Name the altitude $\overline{RP}$. $NR = RQ = 6$. In 30-60-90 $\triangle RPQ$, $RP = 3$ and $PQ = 3\sqrt{3}$. NQ therefore equals $6\sqrt{3} \approx 10.39$.

30. Since $\triangle STV$ is an isosceles right triangle, $ST = TV = x$. Using the Pythagorean Theorem, we have
$$20^2 = x^2 + x^2$$
$$400 = 2x^2$$
$$x^2 = 200$$
$$x = \sqrt{200} = 10\sqrt{2}$$
$$TV = 10\sqrt{2}$$
Since $M + N$ are midpoints of $\overline{ST}$ and $\overline{SV}$ respectively, $MN = \frac{1}{2} \cdot TV$. Therefore,
$$MN = 5\sqrt{2} \approx 7.07.$$

31. In right $\triangle ACB$, $AC = 6$ and $BC = 6\sqrt{3}$. In right $\triangle ACD$, let $DC = x$. Then $AC = 6 = x\sqrt{3}$. If $6 = x\sqrt{3}$, then $x = \frac{6}{\sqrt{3}} = \frac{6\sqrt{3}}{3} = 2\sqrt{3}$.
$$BD = BC - DC = 6\sqrt{3} - 2\sqrt{3}$$
$$BD = 4\sqrt{3} \approx 6.93.$$

32. In right $\triangle ACD$, if $AC = 2\sqrt{3}$, then $DC = 2$ and $AD = 4$. If $AD = 4$, then $BD = 4$ because they are sides of the isosceles $\triangle ABD$.

33. Draw in altitude $\overline{CD}$. In right $\triangle CDB$, if $BC = 12$, then $CD = 6$ and $DB = 6\sqrt{3}$. In right $\triangle ACD$, if $CD = 6$, then $AD = 6$ and $AC = 6\sqrt{2}$. $AB = 6 + 6\sqrt{3} \approx 16.39$.

34. In the trapezoid $MNPQ$, if $m\angle M = 120°$, then $m\angle MQP = m\angle NPQ = 60°$. Also
$$m\angle MQT = m\angle TQP = m\angle TPQ = m\angle TNP$$
$$= m\angle NTP = m\angle MTQ = 30°$$
Draw in altitude $\overline{TR}$ to $\overline{QP}$. In right $\triangle TRP$, if $RP = 6$, then $TR = 2\sqrt{3}$ and $TP = 4\sqrt{3}$. In isosceles $\triangle TNP$, draw altitude $\overline{NS}$. In right $\triangle NSP$, if $SP = 2\sqrt{3}$, then $NS = 2$ and $NP = 4$. Therefore, the perimeter of $MNPQ = 4 + 8 + 4 + 12 = 28$.

35. **a.** $\triangle BCF$ forms a 30°-60°-90° △. Since $AB = 6$ in., $BF = 6\sqrt{3}$ in.

    b. $CF = 12$ in.

36. **a.** $\triangle BCF$ forms a 30°-60°-90° △. Since $AB = x$ cm, $BF = x\sqrt{3}$ cm.

    b. $CF = 12$ cm

37. Draw $\overline{XV}$. YV = VZ = 2; XZ = 5.

    Using the Pythagorean Theorem on $\triangle$ XYV,

    $$XV = \sqrt{3^2 + 2^2} = \sqrt{13}$$

    Let VW = x; WZ = y and XW = 5 − y

    In $\triangle$ XVW, $x^2 + (5-y)^2 = (\sqrt{13})^2$

    In $\triangle$ VWZ, $x^2 + y^2 = 2^2$ or $x^2 = 4 - y^2$.

    By substitution and squaring $(5-y)$,

    $4 - y^2 + 25 - 10y + y^2 = 13$

    $29 - 10y = 13$

    $-10y = -16$

    $y = 1.6$

    Using $x^2 = 4 - y^2$

    $x^2 = 4 - (1.6)^2$

    $x^2 = 4 - 2.56 = 1.44$

    $x = 1.2$; VW = 1.2

38. Draw $\overline{DF} \perp \overline{AB}$. Because $\triangle$ DEC is an

    isosceles $\triangle$ and AECB is a square, DF = 11

    and FB = 4. In rt. $\triangle$ DFB,

    $(DB)^2 = 11^2 + 4^2$

    $(DB)^2 = 121 + 16$

    $(DB)^2 = 137$

    $DB = \sqrt{137}$

SECTION 5.6: Segments Divided Proportionately

1. Let $5x$ = the amount of ingredient A;
   $4x$ = amount of ingredient B;
   $6x$ = amount of ingredient C.
   $5x + 4x + 6x = 90$
   $\quad\quad 15x = 90$
   $\quad\quad\quad x = 6$
   30 ounces of ingredient A;
   24 ounces of ingredient B;
   36 ounces of ingredient C.

2. Let $2x$ = the amount of chemical A;
   $1x$ = amount of chemical B;
   $3x$ = amount of chemical C.
   $2x + 1x + 3x = 72$
   $\quad\quad\quad 6x = 72$
   $\quad\quad\quad\quad x = 12$
   24 grams of chemical A;
   12 grams of chemical B;
   36 grams of chemical C.

3. **a.** Yes

   b. Yes

4. **a.** No

   b. Yes

5. Let $EF = x$, $FG = y$, and $GH = z$
   $AD = 5 + 4 + 3 = 12$ so that

   $\dfrac{AB}{AD} = \dfrac{EF}{EH} \quad\quad \dfrac{BC}{AD} = \dfrac{FG}{EH} \quad\quad \dfrac{CD}{AD} = \dfrac{GH}{EH}$

   $\dfrac{5}{12} = \dfrac{x}{10} \quad\quad \dfrac{4}{12} = \dfrac{y}{10} \quad\quad \dfrac{3}{12} = \dfrac{z}{10}$

   $12x = 50 \quad\quad 12y = 40 \quad\quad 12z = 30$

   $x = \dfrac{50}{12} = 4\dfrac{1}{6} \quad y = \dfrac{40}{12} = 3\dfrac{1}{3} \quad z = \dfrac{30}{12} = 2\dfrac{1}{2}$

   $EF = 4\dfrac{1}{6} \quad\quad FG = 3\dfrac{1}{3} \quad\quad GH = 2\dfrac{1}{2}$

6. Let $FG = x$ and $GH = y$

   $\dfrac{AB}{EF} = \dfrac{BC}{FG} \quad\quad\quad \dfrac{BC}{EF} = \dfrac{CD}{GH}$

   $\dfrac{7}{6} = \dfrac{5}{x} \quad\quad\quad \dfrac{7}{6} = \dfrac{4}{y}$

   $7x = 30 \quad\quad\quad 7y = 24$

   $x = \dfrac{30}{7} = 4\dfrac{2}{7} \quad\quad y = \dfrac{24}{7} = 3\dfrac{3}{7}$

   $FG = 4\dfrac{2}{7} \quad\quad\quad GH = 3\dfrac{3}{7}$

   $EH = EF + FG + GH$;

   $EH = 6 + 4\dfrac{2}{7} + 3\dfrac{3}{7} = 13\dfrac{5}{7}$.

7. $\dfrac{4}{x} = \dfrac{5}{12-x}$

   $5x = 4(12 - x)$

   $5x = 48 - 4x$

   $9x = 48$

   $x = \dfrac{48}{9} = 5\dfrac{1}{3}$

   $DE = 5\dfrac{1}{3}$

   $EF = 12 - 5\dfrac{1}{3} = 6\dfrac{2}{3}$

8.
$$\frac{5}{x-2} = \frac{x}{7}$$
$$x(x-2) = 35$$
$$x^2 - 2x - 35 = 0$$
$$(x-7)(x+5) = 0$$
$$x-7 = 0 \quad \text{or} \quad x+5 = 0$$
$$x = 7 \quad \text{or} \quad x = -5; \text{ reject } x = -5.$$
$$BC = 7 \; ; \; DE = 5 \; .$$

9. Let $EC = x$.
$$\frac{5}{12} = \frac{7}{x}$$
$$5x = 84$$
$$x = \frac{84}{5} \text{ or } 16\frac{4}{5}; \; EC = 16\frac{4}{5}$$

10. Let $EC = x$; then $AE = 20 - x$
$$\frac{6}{10} = \frac{20-x}{x}$$
$$6x = 10(20-x)$$
$$6x = 200 - 10x$$
$$16x = 200$$
$$x = \frac{200}{16} = 12\frac{1}{2}$$
$$EC = 12\frac{1}{2}$$

11.
$$\frac{a-1}{2a+2} = \frac{a}{4a-5}$$
$$(a-1)(4a-5) = a(2a+2)$$
$$4a^2 - 9a + 5 = 2a^2 + 2a$$
$$2a^2 - 11a + 5 = 0$$
$$(2a-1)(a-5) = 0$$
$$a = \frac{1}{2} \text{ or } a = 5$$

If $a = \frac{1}{2}$, then $AD = \frac{1}{2} - 1$ which is a negative

number. $\therefore a \neq \frac{1}{2}$. If $a = 5$, then $AD = 5 - 1 = 4$.

12.
$$\frac{5}{a+3} = \frac{a+1}{3(a-1)}$$
$$(a+3)(a+1) = 5 \cdot 3(a-1)$$
$$a^2 + 4a + 3 = 15a - 15$$
$$a^2 - 11a + 18 = 0$$
$$(a-9)(a-2) = 0$$
$$a-9 = 0 \quad \text{or} \quad a-2 = 0$$
$$a = 9 \quad \text{or} \quad a = 2$$
$$EC = 24 \text{ or } EC = 3 \; .$$

13. **a.** No

  b. Yes

14. **a.** Yes

  b. No

15. Let $TV = x$.
$$\frac{8}{12} = \frac{6}{x}$$
$$8x = 72$$
$$x = 9$$
$$TV = 9$$

16. Let $WT = x$; then $TV = 9 - x$.
$$\frac{9}{12} = \frac{x}{9-x}$$
$$12x = 9(9-x)$$
$$12x = 81 - 9x$$
$$21x = 81$$
$$x = \frac{81}{21} = 3\frac{6}{7}$$
$$WT = 3\frac{6}{7}$$

17. Let $NP = x = MQ$.
$$\frac{x}{12} = \frac{8}{x}$$
$$x^2 = 96$$
$$x = \sqrt{96} = 4\sqrt{6}$$
$$NP = 4\sqrt{6} \approx 9.80$$

18. If NP = 4, MN = 8, PQ = 3, and MQ = 6, then

$$\frac{NP}{MN} = \frac{PQ}{MQ}$$. This implies that

$\overrightarrow{NQ}$ bisects $\angle$ PNM. If $m\angle P = 63$ and

$m\angle M = 27$, then $m\angle PNM = 90$.

$\therefore m\angle PNQ = 45°$

19. If NP = 6, MN = 9, PQ = 4, and MQ = 6, then

$$\frac{NP}{MN} = \frac{PQ}{MQ}$$. This implies that

$\overrightarrow{NQ}$ bisects $\angle$ PNM. If $m\angle P = 62$ and

$m\angle M = 36$, then $m\angle PNM = 82$.

$\therefore m\angle QNM = 41°$

20. In right $\triangle ABC$, $BC = 12$ since (12, 16, 20) is a multiple of the Triple (3, 4, 5).
Let $DB = x$; then $DC = 12 - x$.
Since $\angle BAC$ is bisected, we can write this proportion: $\dfrac{x}{12-x} = \dfrac{20}{16}$ or $\dfrac{5}{4}$

$$4x = 60 - 5x$$
$$9x = 60$$
$$x = \frac{60}{9} = 6\frac{2}{3}$$
$$DB = 6\frac{2}{3}$$

$$DC = 12 - x = 5\frac{1}{3}.$$

21. $\dfrac{AC}{CE} = \dfrac{AD}{DE}$; $\dfrac{DC}{CB} = \dfrac{DE}{EB}$

22. **a.** $\overline{EC}$

   b. $\overline{DB}$

   c. $\overline{FB}$

23. If $RS = 6$ and $RT = 12$, then $\triangle RST$ is a 30-60-90 $\triangle$ and $ST = 6\sqrt{3}$. Let $SV = x$. Then $VT = 6\sqrt{3} - x$.

$$\frac{6}{12} = \frac{x}{6\sqrt{3} - x}$$
$$36\sqrt{3} - 6x = 12x$$
$$36\sqrt{3} = 18x$$
$$x = 2\sqrt{3}$$
$$SV = 2\sqrt{3} \approx 3.46$$
$$VT = 6\sqrt{3} - 2\sqrt{3} = 4\sqrt{3} \approx 6.93$$

24. Let $AC = x$. If $AD = 4$ and $DB = 6$, then $AB = 10$.

$$\frac{AD}{AC} = \frac{AC}{AB}$$
$$\frac{4}{x} = \frac{x}{10}$$
$$x^2 = 40$$
$$x = \sqrt{40} = 2\sqrt{10}$$
$$AC = 2\sqrt{10} \approx 6.32$$

25.
$$\frac{x-6}{2-x} = \frac{3}{x+2}$$
$$(x-6)(x+2) = 3(2-x)$$
$$x^2 - 4x - 12 = 6 - 3x$$
$$x^2 - 1x - 18 = 0$$
$$a = 1, b = -1, c = -18$$
$$x = \frac{-b \pm \sqrt{b^2 - 4ac}}{2a}$$
$$x = \frac{1 \pm \sqrt{1^2 - 4(1)(-18)}}{2(1)}$$
$$x = \frac{1 \pm \sqrt{1 + 72}}{2}$$
$$x = \frac{1 + \sqrt{73}}{2} \text{ or } x = \frac{1 - \sqrt{73}}{2}$$

Reject both because each will give a negative number for the length of a side.

26.
$$\frac{2x}{3x-1} = \frac{x}{x+1}$$
$$2x^2 + 2x = 3x^2 - x$$
$$0 = x^2 - 3x$$
$$0 = x(x-3)$$
$$x = 0 \text{ or } x = 3 \text{; reject } x = 0.$$
Therefore, $x = 3$.

27. **a.** True

   b. True

28. **a.** 1

   b. 1

29.
$$\frac{3}{4} \cdot \frac{4}{5} \cdot \frac{3}{RK} = 1$$
$$\frac{9}{5RK} = 1$$
$$RK = \frac{9}{5} = 1.8$$

30.
$$\frac{RG}{GS} \cdot \frac{SH}{HT} \cdot \frac{KT}{KR} = 1$$
$$\frac{2}{3} \cdot \frac{3}{4} \cdot \frac{KT}{KR} = 1$$
$$\frac{KT}{KR} = 2$$

31. **1.** Given

   2. Means-Extremes Property

   3. Addition Property of Equality

   4. Distributive Property

   5. Means-Extremes Property

   6. Substitution

32. Given: $\triangle RST$ with $\overrightarrow{XY} \parallel \overline{RT}$ and
$\overrightarrow{YZ} \parallel \overline{RS}$

Prove: $\dfrac{RX}{XS} = \dfrac{ZT}{RZ}$

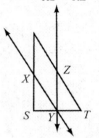

STATEMENTS	REASONS
1. $\triangle RST$ with $\overrightarrow{XY} \parallel \overline{RT}$	**1.** Given
2. $\dfrac{RX}{XS} = \dfrac{YT}{XY}$	**2.** If a line is $\parallel$ to one one side of a $\triangle$, and intersects the other two sides, then it divides these sides proportionally.
3. $\overrightarrow{YZ} \parallel \overline{RS}$	**3.** Given
4. $\dfrac{YT}{SY} = \dfrac{ZT}{RZ}$	**4.** Same as (2).
5. $\dfrac{RX}{XS} = \dfrac{ZT}{RZ}$	**5.** Substitution

33. Given: $\triangle RST$ with M the midpoint of $\overline{RS}$;
$\overline{MN} \parallel \overline{ST}$

Prove: N is the midpoint of $\overline{RT}$

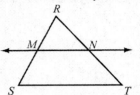

STATEMENTS	REASONS
1. $\triangle RST$ with M the midpoint of $\overline{RS}$ $\overline{MN} \parallel \overline{ST}$	**1.** Given
2. $RM = MS$	**2.** The midpoint of a segment divides the segment into 2 segments of equal measure.
3. $\dfrac{RM}{MS} = \dfrac{RN}{NT}$	**3.** If a line is $\parallel$ to one one side of a $\triangle$, and intersects the other two sides, then it divides these sides proportionally.
4. $\dfrac{MS}{MS} = 1 = \dfrac{RN}{NT}$	**4.** Substitution
5. $RN = NT$	**5.** Mean-Extremes Property
6. N is the midpoint of $\overline{RT}$	**6.** If a point divides a segment into 2 segments of equal measure, then the point is a midpoint.

34. Given: Trapezoid $ABCD$ with
median $\overline{MN}$

Prove: $MN = \dfrac{1}{2}(AB + CD)$

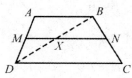

STATEMENTS	REASONS
1. Trapezoid $ABCD$ with median $\overline{MN}$	1. Given
2. M is the midpoint of $\overline{AD}$ N is the midpoint of $\overline{BC}$	2. The median of a trap. is a segment that joins the midpoints of the two nonparallel sides.
3. $\overline{MN} \parallel \overline{AB}$ and $\overline{MN} \parallel \overline{DC}$	3. The median of a trap is $\parallel$ to each base.
4. X is the midpoint of $\overline{MN}$	4. If a line is $\parallel$ to one one side of a $\triangle$, and passes through the midpoint of a second side, then it will pass through the midpoint of the third side.
5. $MX = \dfrac{1}{2} AB$ $XN = \dfrac{1}{2} CD$	5. The segment that joins the midpoints of 2 sides of a $\triangle$ is $\parallel$ to the 3rd side and has a length equal to one half the length of the 3rd side.
6. $MX + XN = \dfrac{1}{2} AB + \dfrac{1}{2} CD$	6. Addition Property of Equality
7. $MX + XN = MN$	7. Segment Addition Postulate
8. $MN = \dfrac{1}{2} AB + \dfrac{1}{2} CD$	8. Substitution
9. $MN = \dfrac{1}{2}(AB + CD)$	9. Distributive Property

35. Given: $\triangle XYZ$; $\overline{YW}$ bisects $\angle XYZ$
$\overline{WX} \cong \overline{WZ}$

Prove: $\triangle XYZ$ is isosceles

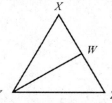

STATEMENTS	REASONS
1. $\triangle XYZ$; $\overline{YW}$ bisects $\angle XYZ$	1. Given
2. $\dfrac{YX}{YZ} = \dfrac{WX}{WZ}$	2. If a ray bisects one $\angle$ of a $\triangle$, then it divides the opposite side into segments that are proportional to the two sides which form that angle.
3. $\overline{WX} \cong \overline{WZ}$	3. Given
4. $WX = WZ$	4. If two segments are $\cong$, then their measures are equal. into four $\cong$ $\angle$s.
5. $\dfrac{YX}{YZ} = \dfrac{WX}{WX} = 1$	5. Substitution
6. $YX = YZ$	6. Means-Extremes Property
7. $\overline{YX} \cong \overline{YZ}$	7. If 2 segments are equal in measure, they are $\cong$.
8. $\triangle XYZ$ is isosceles	8. If 2 sides of a $\triangle$ are $\cong$, then the $\triangle$ is isosceles.

36. Since $\dfrac{AC}{CD} = \dfrac{6}{3} = \dfrac{AB}{DB} = \dfrac{2}{1}$, let $DB = x$ and

$AB = 2x$.

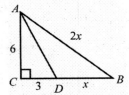

Using the Pythagorean Theorem with $\triangle ACB$, we have

$$6^2 + (3+x)^2 = (2x)^2$$
$$36 + 9 + 6x + x^2 = 4x^2$$
$$0 = 3x^2 - 6x - 45$$
$$0 = x^2 - 2x - 15$$
$$0 = (x-5)(x+3)$$

$x - 5 = 0$ or $x + 3 = 0$

  $x = 5$ or $x = -3$; reject $x = -3$

$BD = 5$ and $AB = 10$

37. If $\triangle ABC$ is isosceles and

$m\angle ABC = m\angle C = 72°$, then $m\angle A = 36°$. Since

$\overrightarrow{BD}$ bisects $\angle ABC$, $m\angle ABD = m\angle DBC = 36°$.

$m\angle BDC = 72°$ so that $\triangle BDC$ is also isosceles with $BD = BC$. $\triangle ADB$ is also isosceles with $BD = AD$.

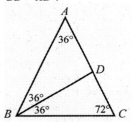

Since $\triangle ABC$ is isosceles, $AB = AC = 1$. Let $BC = x$ which makes $AD = x$, too. Then $DC = 1 - x$. Since $\angle ABC$ has been bisected, we can write the proportion

$$\frac{x}{1-x} = \frac{1}{x}$$
$$x^2 = 1 - x$$
$$x^2 + x - 1 = 0$$
$$a = 1, b = 1, c = -1$$
$$x = \frac{-1 \pm \sqrt{1^2 - 4(1)(-1)}}{2(1)}$$
$$x = \frac{-1 \pm \sqrt{1+4}}{2}$$
$$x = \frac{-1 \pm \sqrt{5}}{2}; \text{ reject } \frac{-1-\sqrt{5}}{2} \text{ because it is}$$

negative.

$$BC = \frac{-1+\sqrt{5}}{2} \approx 0.62$$

38. In rt. $\triangle TSR$, if $m\angle R = 30°$ and $TS = 6$, then $RT = 12$. $\triangle NST$ is a 30°-60°-90° $\triangle$ and $\triangle NSM$ is a 30°-60°-90° $\triangle$.

$\overline{NT}$ is the side opposite the 30° $\angle$ in $\triangle NST$

$\therefore NT = 3$.

$\overline{MN}$ is the side opposite the 30° $\angle$ in $\triangle NSM$

$\therefore MN = 3$.

RM must then $= 6$ since $RM + MN + NT = 12$.

39. a. Let $CD = x$. Then $DB = 5 - x$.

$$\frac{CD}{CA} = \frac{DB}{BA}$$
$$\frac{x}{4} = \frac{5-x}{6}$$
$$4(5-x) = 6x$$
$$20 - 4x = 6x$$
$$10x = 20$$
$$x = 2$$
$$CD = 2$$
$$DB = 5 - 2 = 3$$

b. Let $CE = x$. Then $EA = 4 - x$.

$$\frac{CE}{BC} = \frac{EA}{BA}$$
$$\frac{x}{5} = \frac{4-x}{6}$$
$$5(4-x) = 6x$$
$$20 - 5x = 6x$$
$$11x = 20$$
$$x = \frac{20}{11}$$
$$CE = \frac{20}{11}$$
$$EA = 4 - \frac{20}{11} = \frac{24}{11}$$

c. Let $BF = x$. Then $FA = 6 - x$.

$$\frac{BF}{BC} = \frac{FA}{CA}$$
$$\frac{x}{5} = \frac{6-x}{4}$$
$$5(6-x) = 4x$$
$$30 - 5x = 4x$$
$$9x = 30$$
$$x = \frac{10}{3}$$
$$BF = \frac{10}{3}$$
$$FA = 6 - \frac{10}{3} = \frac{8}{3}$$

d. $\dfrac{BD}{DC} \cdot \dfrac{CE}{EA} \cdot \dfrac{AF}{FB} = \dfrac{3}{2} \cdot \dfrac{\frac{20}{11}}{\frac{24}{11}} \cdot \dfrac{\frac{8}{3}}{\frac{10}{3}} = \dfrac{3}{2} \cdot \dfrac{20}{24} \cdot \dfrac{8}{10} = 1$

40. **a.** Using the Pythagorean Theorem,

$$(TR)^2 = (TX)^2 + (RX)^2$$
$$13^2 = 12^2 + (RX)^2$$
$$(RX)^2 = 169 - 144$$
$$(RX)^2 = 25$$
$$RX = 5$$
$$(ST)^2 = (TX)^2 + (XS)^2$$
$$15^2 = 12^2 + (XS)^2$$
$$(XS)^2 = 225 - 144$$
$$(XS)^2 = 81$$
$$XS = 9$$

b. Using the Pythagorean Theorem,

$$(TR)^2 = (RY)^2 + (TY)^2$$
$$13^2 = \left(\frac{168}{15}\right)^2 + (TY)^2$$
$$(TY)^2 = 169 - \frac{3136}{25}$$
$$(TY)^2 = \frac{1089}{25}$$
$$TY = \frac{33}{5}$$
$$(RS)^2 = (RY)^2 + (YS)^2$$
$$14^2 = \left(\frac{168}{15}\right)^2 + (YS)^2$$
$$(YS)^2 = 196 - \frac{3136}{25}$$
$$(YS)^2 = \frac{1764}{25}$$
$$YS = \frac{42}{5}$$

c. Using the Pythagorean Theorem,

$$(RS)^2 = (SZ)^2 + (ZR)^2$$
$$14^2 = \left(\frac{168}{13}\right)^2 + (ZR)^2$$
$$(ZR)^2 = 196 - \frac{28,224}{169}$$
$$(ZR)^2 = \frac{4900}{169}$$
$$ZR = \frac{70}{13}$$
$$(ST)^2 = (SZ)^2 + (TZ)^2$$
$$15^2 = \left(\frac{168}{13}\right)^2 + (TZ)^2$$
$$(TZ)^2 = 225 - \frac{28,224}{169}$$
$$(TZ)^2 = \frac{9801}{169}$$
$$TZ = \frac{99}{13}$$

d. $\dfrac{RX}{XS} \cdot \dfrac{SY}{YT} \cdot \dfrac{TZ}{ZR} = \dfrac{5}{9} \cdot \dfrac{\frac{42}{5}}{\frac{33}{5}} \cdot \dfrac{\frac{99}{13}}{\frac{70}{13}}$

$$= \frac{5}{9} \cdot \frac{42}{33} \cdot \frac{99}{70}$$
$$= \frac{5 \cdot (2 \cdot 3 \cdot 7) \cdot 9 \cdot 11}{9 \cdot (3 \cdot 11) \cdot 7 \cdot 2 \cdot 5}$$
$$= 1$$

CHAPTER REVIEW

1. False

2. True

3. False

4. True

5. True

6. False

7. True

8. **a.** $x^2 = 18$

$$x = \pm\sqrt{18} = \pm 3\sqrt{2} \approx \pm 4.24$$

b. $7(x-5) = 3(2x-3)$
$$7x - 35 = 6x - 9$$
$$x = 26$$

c. $6(x+2) = 2(x+4)$
$$6x + 12 = 2x + 8$$
$$4x = -4$$
$$x = -1$$

d. $7(x+3) = 5(x+5)$
$$7x + 21 = 5x + 25$$
$$2x = 4$$
$$x = 2$$

e. $(x-2)(x-1) = (x-5)(2x+1)$
$$x^2 - 3x + 2 = 2x^2 - 9x - 5$$
$$x^2 - 6x - 7 = 0$$
$$(x-7)(x+1) = 0$$
$$x = 7 \text{ or } x = -1$$

f. $\qquad 5x(x+5) = 9(4x+4)$
$$5x^2 + 25x = 36x + 36$$
$$5x^2 - 11x - 36 = 0$$
$$(5x+9)(x-4) = 0$$
$$x = -\frac{9}{5} \text{ or } x = 4$$

g. $(x-1)(3x-2) = 10(x+2)$

$$3x^2 - 5x + 2 = 10x + 20$$
$$3x^2 - 15x - 18 = 0$$
$$x^2 - 5x - 6 = 0$$
$$(x-6)(x+1) = 0$$

$x = 6$ or $x = -1$

h. $(x+7)(x-2) = 2(x+2)$

$$x^2 + 5x - 14 = 2x + 4$$
$$x^2 + 3x - 18 = 0$$
$$(x+6)(x-3) = 0$$

$x = -6$ or $x = 3$

9. Let x = cost of the six containers.

$$\frac{4}{2.52} = \frac{6}{x}$$
$$4x = 15.12$$
$$x = 3.78$$

The six containers cost $3.78.

10. Let x = the number of packages you can buy for $2.25.

$$\frac{2}{0.69} = \frac{x}{2.25}$$
$$0.69x = 4.50$$
$$x = \frac{450}{69} = 6\frac{12}{23}$$

With $2.25, you can buy 6 packages of M&M's.

11. Let x = cost of the rug that is 12 square meters.

$$\frac{20}{132} = \frac{12}{x}$$
$$20x = 1584$$
$$x = 79.20$$

The 12 square meters rug will cost $79.20.

12. Let the measure of the sides of the quadrilateral be $2x, 3x, 5x$ and $7x$.

$$2x + 3x + 5x + 7x = 68$$
$$17x = 68$$
$$x = 4$$

The length of the sides are 8, 12, 20 and 28.

13. Let the width of the similar rectangle be x.

$$\frac{18}{12} = \frac{27}{x}$$
$$\frac{3}{2} = \frac{27}{x}$$
$$3x = 54$$
$$x = 18$$

The width of the similar rectangle is 18.

14. Let x and y be the lengths of the other two sides.

$$\frac{6}{15} = \frac{8}{x} = \frac{9}{y}$$

$$\frac{2}{5} = \frac{8}{x} \quad \text{and} \quad \frac{2}{5} = \frac{9}{y}$$
$$2x = 40 \qquad\qquad 2y = 45$$
$$x = 20 \qquad\qquad y = \frac{45}{2} = 22\frac{1}{2}$$

The other two sides have lengths 20 and $22\frac{1}{2}$.

15. Let the measure of the angle be x; the measure of the supplement would be $180 - x$; the measure of the complement would be $90 - x$.

$$\frac{180 - x}{90 - x} = \frac{5}{2}$$
$$2(180 - x) = 5(90 - x)$$
$$360 - 2x = 450 - 5x$$
$$3x = 90$$
$$x = 30$$

The measure of the supplement is 150°.

16. a. SSS ~

b. AA

c. SAS ~

d. SSS ~

17. Given: $ABCD$ is a parallelogram;
$\overline{DB}$ intersects $\overline{AE}$ at pt. F

Prove: $\dfrac{AF}{EF} = \dfrac{AB}{DE}$

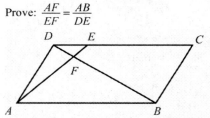

STATEMENTS	REASONS
1. $ABCD$ is a parallelogram $\overline{DB}$ intersects $\overline{AE}$ at pt. F	**1.** Given
2. $\overline{DC} \parallel \overline{AB}$	**2.** Opp. sides of a parallelogram are $\parallel$.
3. $\angle CDB \cong \angle ABD$	**3.** If 2 $\parallel$ lines are cut by a trans., then the alt. int. $\angle$s $\cong$.
4. $\angle DEF \cong \angle BAF$	**4.** Same as (3).
5. $\triangle DFE \sim \triangle BFA$	**5.** AA
6. $\dfrac{AF}{EF} = \dfrac{AB}{DE}$	**6.** Corresp. sides of $\sim$ $\triangle$s are proportional.

18. Given: $\angle 1 \cong \angle 2$

Prove: $\dfrac{AB}{AC} = \dfrac{BE}{CD}$

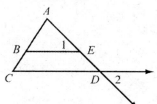

STATEMENTS	REASONS
1. $\angle 1 \cong \angle 2$	1. Given
2. $\angle ADC = \angle 2$	2. If 2 lines intersect, then the vertical $\angle$s formed are $\cong$.
3. $\angle ADC \cong \angle 1$	3. Transitive Prop. for Congruence.
4. $\angle A \cong \angle A$	4. Identity.
5. $\triangle BAE \sim \triangle CAD$	5. AA
6. $\dfrac{AB}{AC} = \dfrac{BE}{CD}$	6. Corresp. sides of $\sim$ $\triangle$s are proportional.

19. Since the $\triangle$ s are $\sim$, $m\angle A = m\angle D$.

$50 = 2x + 40$

$10 = 2x$

$x = 5$

$m\angle D = 2(5) + 40 = 50°$

$m\angle E = 33°$

$m\angle F = 180 - 33 - 50 = 97°$

20. With $\angle B \cong \angle F$, and $\angle C \cong \angle E$,

$\triangle ABC \sim \triangle DFE$. It follows that

$\dfrac{AB}{DF} = \dfrac{AC}{DE} = \dfrac{BC}{FE}$

Substituting in gives

$\dfrac{AB}{2} = \dfrac{9}{3}$ or $\dfrac{3}{1}$ and $\dfrac{9}{3}$ or $\dfrac{3}{1} = \dfrac{BC}{4}$

$AB = 6$ and $BC = 12$.

21. $\dfrac{BD}{AD} = \dfrac{BE}{EC}$; let $AB = x$

$\dfrac{6}{x} = \dfrac{8}{4}$ or $\dfrac{2}{1}$

$2x = 6$

$x = 3$

22. $\dfrac{BD}{BA} = \dfrac{DE}{AC}$; let $AC = x$; $BA = 12$

$\dfrac{8}{12} = \dfrac{2}{3} = \dfrac{3}{x}$

$2x = 9$

$x = 4\dfrac{1}{2}$

$AC = 4\dfrac{1}{2}$

23. $\dfrac{BD}{BA} = \dfrac{BE}{BC}$; let $BC = x$; $BD = 8$

$\dfrac{8}{10}$ or $\dfrac{4}{5} = \dfrac{5}{x}$

$4x = 25$

$x = 6\dfrac{1}{4}$

$BC = 6\dfrac{1}{4}$

24. Since $\overrightarrow{GJ}$ bisects $\angle FGH$, we can write the proportion $\dfrac{FJ}{FG} = \dfrac{JH}{GH}$; let $JH = x$.

$\dfrac{7}{10} = \dfrac{x}{8}$

$10x = 56$

$x = \dfrac{56}{10} = 5\dfrac{3}{5}$

$JH = 5\dfrac{3}{5}$

25. Since $\overrightarrow{GJ}$ bisects $\angle FGH$, and $GF : GH = 1 : 2$,

we can write the proportion $\dfrac{GF}{GH} = \dfrac{FJ}{JH}$; let

$JH = x$.

$\dfrac{1}{2} = \dfrac{5}{x}$

$x = 10$

$JH = 10$

26. Since $\overrightarrow{GJ}$ bisects $\angle FGH$, we can write the proportion $\dfrac{FG}{GH} = \dfrac{FJ}{JH}$; let $FJ = x$ and

$JH = 15 - x$.

$\dfrac{8}{12} = \dfrac{x}{15 - x}$

$\dfrac{2}{3} = \dfrac{x}{15 - x}$

$2(15 - x) = 3x$

$30 - 2x = 3x$

$30 = 5x$

$x = 6$

$FJ = 6$

27. Let $MK = x$, then $\dfrac{MK}{HJ} = \dfrac{EM}{FH}$.

$\dfrac{x}{5} = \dfrac{6}{10}$ or $\dfrac{3}{5}$

$x = 3$

$MK = 3$

Let $EO = y$ and $OM = 6 - y$.

Then $\dfrac{y}{2} = \dfrac{6-y}{8}$

$8y = 2(6 - y)$

$8y = 12 - 2y$

$10y = 12$

$y = \dfrac{12}{10} = 1\dfrac{1}{5}$

$EO = 1\dfrac{1}{5}$

$EK = 9$

28. If a line bisects one side of a triangle and is parallel to a second side, then it bisects the third side.

Given: $\overrightarrow{DE}$ bisects $\overline{AC}$

$\overrightarrow{DE} \parallel \overline{BC}$

Prove: $\overrightarrow{DE}$ bisects $\overline{AB}$

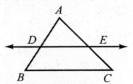

STATEMENTS	REASONS
1. $\overrightarrow{DE}$ bisects $\overline{AC}$	1. Given
2. $AE = EC$	2. Bisecting a segment forms 2 segments of equal measure.
3. $\overrightarrow{DE} \parallel \overline{BC}$	3. Given
4. $\dfrac{AD}{DB} = \dfrac{AE}{EC}$	4. If a line is parallel to one side of a triangle and intersects the other sides, then it divides these sides proportionally.
5. $AD \cdot EC = DB \cdot AE$	5. Means-Extremes Prop.
6. $AD = DB$	6. Division Prop. of Eq.
7. $\overrightarrow{DE}$ bisects $\overline{AB}$	7. If a segment has been divided into 2 segments of equal measure, the segment has been bisected.

29. The diagonals of a trapezoid divide themselves proportionally.

Given: $ABCD$ is a trapezoid with $\overline{BC} \parallel \overline{AD}$ and diagonals $\overline{BD}$ and $\overline{AC}$

Prove: $\dfrac{BE}{ED} = \dfrac{EC}{AE}$

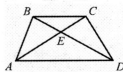

STATEMENTS	REASONS
1. $ABCD$ is a trapezoid with $\overline{BC} \parallel \overline{AD}$ and diagonals $\overline{BD}$ and $\overline{AC}$.	1. Given
2. $\angle CBE \cong \angle ADE$ and $\angle BCE \cong \angle DAE$	2. If 2 $\parallel$ lines are cut by a trans., then the alt. int. $\angle$s are $\cong$.
3. $\triangle BCE \cong \triangle DAE$	3. AA
4. $\dfrac{BE}{ED} = \dfrac{EC}{AE}$	4. Corresponding sides of $\sim$ $\triangle$s are proportional.

30. a. $\dfrac{BD}{AD} = \dfrac{AD}{DC}$

Let $DC = x$.

$\dfrac{3}{5} = \dfrac{5}{x}$

$3x = 25$

$x = \dfrac{25}{3}$

$DC = 8\dfrac{1}{3}$

b. $\dfrac{DC}{AC} = \dfrac{AC}{BC}$

Let $BD = x$ and $BC = x + 4$

$\dfrac{4}{5}$ or $\dfrac{2}{3} = \dfrac{10}{x + 4}$

$2(x + 4) = 50$

$2x + 8 = 50$

$2x = 42$

$x = 21$

$BD = 21$

c. $\dfrac{BD}{BA} = \dfrac{BA}{BC}$

Let $BA = x$.

$\dfrac{2}{x} = \dfrac{x}{6}$

$x^2 = 12$

$x = \sqrt{12} = 2\sqrt{3}$

$BA = 2\sqrt{3} \approx 3.46$

d. $\dfrac{DA}{AC} = \dfrac{AC}{BC}$

Let $DC = x$ and $BC = x + 3$.

$\dfrac{x}{3\sqrt{2}} = \dfrac{3\sqrt{2}}{x+3}$

$x(x+3) = 18$

$x^2 + 3x - 18 = 0$

$(x+6)(x-3) = 0$

$x = -6$ or $x = 3$; reject $x = -6$

$DC = 3$.

31. a. $\dfrac{AD}{BD} = \dfrac{BD}{DC}$

Let $DC = x$.

$\dfrac{9}{12}$ or $\dfrac{3}{4} = \dfrac{12}{x}$

$3x = 48$

$x = 16$

$DC = 16$

b. $\dfrac{DC}{BC} = \dfrac{BC}{AC}$

Let $AD = x$ and $AC = x + 5$.

$\dfrac{5}{15}$ or $\dfrac{1}{3} = \dfrac{15}{x+5}$

$x + 5 = 45$

$x = 40$

$AD = 40$

c. $\dfrac{AD}{AB} = \dfrac{AB}{AC}$

Let $AB = x$ and $AC = 10$.

$\dfrac{2}{x} = \dfrac{x}{10}$

$x^2 = 20$

$x = \sqrt{20} = 2\sqrt{5}$

$AB = 2\sqrt{5} \approx 4.47$

d. $\dfrac{AD}{AB} = \dfrac{AB}{AC}$

Let $AD = x$ and $AC = x + 2$.

$\dfrac{x}{2\sqrt{6}} = \dfrac{2\sqrt{6}}{x+2}$

$x(x+2) = 24$

$x^2 + 2x - 24 = 0$

$(x+6)(x-4) = 0$

$x = -6$ or $x = 4$; reject $x = -6$

$AD = 4$.

32. a. $x = 30$. Since the leg is half of the hypotenuse, the angle opposite the leg must be 30°.

b. Half of the base is 10. In the right △, 1 side has length 10 and the hypotenuse has length 26. The other side has length 24 since (10, 24, 26) is a multiple of (5, 12, 13).

c. $x^2 = 12^2 + 16^2$

$x^2 = 144 + 256$

$x^2 = 400$

$x = 20$

or (12, 16, 20) is a multiple of (3, 4, 5).

d. The unknown length of the right △ is 8 using the Triple (8, 15, 17).

$x = 16$.

33. In rect. *ABCD*, $BC = 24$ and since *E* is a midpoint, $BE = 12$ and $EC = 12$. $CD = 16$ and $FD = 7$. There are three right triangles for which the Pythagorean Triples apply. $AE = 20$ using (12, 16, 20) which is a multiple of (3, 4, 5). $EF = 15$ using (9, 12, 15) which is also a multiple of (3, 4, 5). $AF = 25$ using the Triple (7, 24, 25).

34. In a square there are two 45-45-90 △ s. If the length of the side of the square is 4 inches, then the length of the diagonal is $4\sqrt{2} \approx 5.66$ inches.

35. In a square there are two 45°-45°-90° △ s. If the length of the diagonal is 6, then $6 = a\sqrt{2}$. Solving for a gives

$a = \dfrac{6}{\sqrt{2}} = \dfrac{6\sqrt{2}}{2} = 3\sqrt{2}$

Hence, the length of a side is $3\sqrt{2} \approx 4.24$ cm.

36. Since the diagonals of a rhombus are perpendicular and bisect each other, there are 4 right triangles formed whose sides are the lengths 24 cm and 7 cm. The hypotenuse must then have a length of 25. Since they hypotenuse of a right triangle is the side of the rhombus, the side has length 25 cm.

37. The altitude to one side of an equilateral triangle divides it into two 30°-60°-90° △ s.

The altitude is the side opposite the 60 degree angle and is equal in length to one-half the length of the hypotenuse times $\sqrt{3}$. Hence, the altitude has length $5\sqrt{3} \approx 8.66$ in.

38. The altitude to one side of an equilateral triangle divides it into two 30°-60°-90° △ .

The altitude is the side opposite the 60 degree angle and is equal in length to one-half the length of the hypotenuse times $\sqrt{3}$. If H represents the length of the hypotenuse, then

$$6 = \frac{1}{2} \cdot H \cdot \sqrt{3}$$
$$12 = H \cdot \sqrt{3}$$
$$H = \frac{12}{\sqrt{3}} \cdot \frac{\sqrt{3}}{\sqrt{3}} = \frac{12\sqrt{3}}{3} = 4\sqrt{3}$$

The length of the sides of the △ is $4\sqrt{3} \approx 6.93$ in.

39. The altitude to the side of length 14 separates it into two parts the lengths of these are given by x and $14 - x$.

If the length of the altitude is H, we can use the Pythagorean Theorem on the two right triangles to get $x^2 + H^2 = 13^2$ and $(14 - x)^2 + H^2 = 15^2$. Subtracting the first equation from the second, we have

$$196 - 29x + x^2 + H^2 = 225$$
$$\underline{ x^2 + H^2 = 169}$$
$$196 - 28x = 56$$
$$-28x = -140$$
$$x = 5$$

Now we use x to find H.

$x^2 + H^2 = 13^2$ becomes
$$5^2 + H^2 = 169$$
$$H^2 = 144$$
$$H = 12$$

The length of the altitude is 12 cm.

40. a. Let the length of the hypotenuse common to both △ s be H.

$$\frac{1}{2} \cdot H \cdot \sqrt{3} = 9\sqrt{3}$$
$$H \cdot \sqrt{3} = 18\sqrt{3}$$
$$H = 18$$
$$y = \frac{1}{2} \cdot 18 = 9$$
$$x = 9\sqrt{2} \approx 12.73$$

b. $y = 6$ using the Triple (6, 8, 10). Since the length of the altitude to the hypotenuse is 6, 6 is the geometric mean for x and 8. That is,

$$\frac{x}{6} = \frac{6}{8}$$
$$8x = 36$$
$$x = \frac{36}{8} = \frac{9}{2} = 4\frac{1}{4}.$$

c. 6 is the geometric mean for y and x. But since $x = y + 9$, we have

$$\frac{y}{6} = \frac{6}{y+9}$$
$$y(y+9) = 36$$
$$y^2 + 9y - 36 = 0$$
$$(y+12)(y-3) = 0$$
$$y = -12 \text{ or } y = 3; \text{ reject } y = -12$$
$$\therefore y = 3 \text{ and } x = 12.$$

d. $4^2 + x^2 = \left(6\sqrt{2}\right)^2$
$$16 + x^2 = 72$$
$$x^2 = 56$$
$$x = \sqrt{56} = 2\sqrt{14} \approx 7.48$$
$$y = 13$$

41.

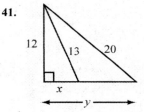

$x = 5$ using the Triple (5, 12, 13).
$y = 16$ using the Triple (12, 16, 20).
The ships are 11 km apart.

42. **a.** $14^2 < 12^2 + 13^2$ ∴ acute △

    b. $11 + 5 \not> 18$ ∴ no △

    c. $18^2 > 9^2 + 15^2$ ∴ obtuse △

    d. $10^2 = 6^2 + 8^2$ ∴ right △

    e. $8 + 7 \not> 16$ ∴ no △

    f. $8^2 < 7^2 + 6^2$ ∴ acute △

    g. $13^2 > 8^2 + 9^2$ ∴ obtuse △

    h. $4^2 > 2^2 + 3^2$ ∴ obtuse △

CHAPTER TEST

1. **a.** 3:5 or $\dfrac{3}{5}$

    b. $\dfrac{25 \text{ mi}}{\text{gal}}$

2. **a.** $\dfrac{x}{5} = \dfrac{8}{13}$
$$13x = 40$$
$$x = \dfrac{40}{13}$$

    b. $\dfrac{x+1}{5} = \dfrac{16}{x-1}$
$$(x+1)(x-1) = 80$$
$$x^2 - 1 = 80$$
$$x^2 = 81$$
$$x = 9 \text{ or } -9$$

3. 15° and 75°

4. **a.** $m\angle W \cong m\angle T$. Let $m\angle T = x$
$$m\angle T + m\angle R + m\angle S = 180°$$
$$x + 67 + 21 = 180$$
$$x = 92$$
$$m\angle W = 92°$$

    b. $\dfrac{UW}{RT} = \dfrac{WV}{TS}$
$$\dfrac{6}{4} = \dfrac{x}{8}$$
$$48 = 4x$$
$$x = 12$$
$$WV = 12$$

5. **a.** SAS~

    b. AA

6. △ABC ~ △ACD ~ △CBD

7. **a.** $c = \sqrt{a^2 + b^2}$
$$c = \sqrt{5^2 + 4^2}$$
$$c = \sqrt{25 + 16}$$
$$c = \sqrt{41}$$

    b. $a^2 + b^2 = c^2$
$$a^2 = c^2 - b^2$$
$$a = \sqrt{c^2 - b^2}$$
$$a = \sqrt{8^2 - 6^2}$$
$$a = \sqrt{64 - 36}$$
$$a = \sqrt{28} = 2\sqrt{7}$$

8. **a.** $a^2 + b^2 = 15^2 + 8^2 = 225 + 64 = 289$
$$c^2 = 17^2 = 289$$
      Yes

    b. $a^2 + b^2 = 11^2 + 8^2 = 121 + 64 = 185$
$$c^2 = 15^2 = 225$$
      No

9. $(AC)^2 = (AB)^2 + (BC)^2$
$$AC = \sqrt{4^2 + 3^2}$$
$$AC = \sqrt{16 + 9}$$
$$AC = \sqrt{25} = 5$$
$$(DA)^2 = (AC)^2 + (DC)^2$$
$$DA = \sqrt{5^2 + 8^2}$$
$$DA = \sqrt{25 + 64}$$
$$DA = \sqrt{89}$$

10. **a.** In the 45-45-90 △, $XZ = 10$ and $YZ = 10$ so $XY = 10\sqrt{2}$ in.

    b. In the 45-45-90 △, $XY = 8\sqrt{2}$ so $XZ = 8$ cm.

11. **a.** In the 30-60-90 △, $EF = 10$ so $DE = 5$ m .

    b. In the 30-60-90 △, $DF = 6\sqrt{3}$ so $EF = 12$ ft .

12. Let $EC = x$. Then $AC = 9 + x$.
$$\dfrac{AB}{AD} = \dfrac{AC}{AE}$$
$$\dfrac{6+8}{6} = \dfrac{9+x}{9}$$
$$6(9 + x) = 126$$
$$54 + 6x = 126$$
$$6x = 72$$
$$x = 12$$
$$EC = 12$$

13. Let $PQ = x$. Then $QM = 10 - x$.

$$\frac{PQ}{PN} = \frac{QM}{MN}$$

$$\frac{x}{6} = \frac{10 - x}{9}$$

$$9x = 6(10 - x)$$

$$9x = 60 - 6x$$

$$15x = 60$$

$$x = 4$$

$$PQ = 4$$

$$QM = 10 - 4 = 6$$

14. 1

15. If $\angle 1 \cong \angle C$ and $\angle B \cong \angle B$,

then $\triangle ACB \sim \triangle MDB$. By CPSTP,

$$\frac{CB}{DB} = \frac{AB}{MB} \quad \text{or} \quad \frac{12}{x} = \frac{14 + x}{6}$$

$14x + x^2 = 72$

$x^2 + 14x - 72 = 0$

$(x + 18)(x - 4) = 0$

$x = -18$ or $x = 4$; reject $= -18$

$\therefore DB = 4$

16. **S1.** $\overline{MN} \parallel \overline{QR}$

R1. Given

R2. Corresponding $\angle$ s are $\cong$.

S3. $\angle P \cong \angle P$

R4. AA

17. **R1.** Given

R2. Identity

R3. Given

R5. Substitution

R6. SAS~

S7. $\angle PRC \cong \angle B$

Chapter 6: Circles

SECTION 6.1: Circles and Related Segments and Angles

1. 29°

2. 46°

3. 47.6°

4. 28.2°

5. 56.6°

6. 48.3°

7. 313°

8. 48°

9. a. 90°

   b. 270°

   c. 135°

   d. 135°

10.

    Draw in $\overline{QT}$ forming equilateral triangle SQT. Each angle of $\triangle SQT$ measures 60°.

    a. 60°

    b. 120°

    c. 180°

    d. 60°

11. Since the $\text{m}\widehat{AB} : \text{m}\widehat{BC} : \text{m}\widehat{CA} = 2:3:4$, we can write the equation $2x + 3x + 4x = 360$. Solving for x we get $9x = 360$ or $x = 40$.

    a. 80°

    b. 120°

    c. 160°

    d. 80°

    e. 120°

    f. 160°

    g. 10°

    h. 50°

    i. 30°

12. $\text{m}\angle DOF = 104°$ and $\text{m}\angle GOF = 98°$

    a. 76°

    b. 104°

    c. 38°

    d. 38°

    e. 93°

    f. Yes

13. a. 72°

    b. 144°

    c. 36°

    d. 72°

    e. Draw in $\overline{OA}$. In $\triangle BOA$, $\text{m}\angle BOA = 144°$; therefore the $\text{m}\angle ABO = 18°$

14.

    a. $OA < AB$

    b. $AC < AB$

    c. Can't be determined.

15. a. 12

    b. $6\sqrt{2}$

16. a. $QW = 4$; $WV = 3$; therefore $QV = 7$. Using the Pythagorean Theorem on $\triangle QRV$, we have
    $$4^2 + (RV)^2 = 7^2$$
    $$16 + (RV)^2 = 49$$
    $$(RV)^2 = 33$$
    $$RV = \sqrt{33}$$

    b. $TV = 2\sqrt{33}$

17. $RV = 4$ and let $RQ = x$.
    Using the Pythagorean Theorem, we have
    $$x^2 + 4^2 = (x+2)^2$$
    $$x^2 + 16 = x^2 + 4x + 4$$
    $$12 = 4x$$
    $$x = 3$$
    $$RQ = 3$$

129

18. Draw in $\overline{AO}$, $\overline{BO}$, $\overline{AQ}$, and $\overline{BQ}$. *BOAQ* is a rhombus. Therefore $\overline{AB}$ and $\overline{OQ}$ are perpendicular bisectors of each other. If $AR = 6$ and $AQ = 10$, then $RQ = 8$ using the Pythagorean Triple (6, 8, 10); $OQ = 16$.

19. Draw in $\overline{AO}$, $\overline{BO}$, $\overline{AQ}$, and $\overline{BQ}$. $\triangle OAQ \cong \triangle OBQ$ by SSS. If $\angle AOB \cong \angle BOQ$ by CPCTC, then $\triangle AOR \cong \triangle BOR$ by SAS. $\overline{AR} \cong \overline{BR}$ and $\angle QRA \cong \angle QRB$ by CPCTC. Hence, $\overline{OQ}$ is the perpendicular bisector of $\overline{AB}$. In right triangle *OAR*, $AR = 3$ and $OA = 4$. Using the Pythagorean Theorem, we have
$$3^2 + (OR)^2 = 4^2$$
$$9 + (OR)^2 = 16$$
$$(OR)^2 = 7$$
$$OR = \sqrt{7}$$
In rt. $\triangle QAR$, $AQ = 6$ and $AR = 3$. Using the Pythagorean Theorem again, we have
$$3^2 + (RQ)^2 = 6^2$$
$$9 + (RQ)^2 = 36$$
$$(RQ)^2 = 27$$
$$RQ = \sqrt{27} = 3\sqrt{3}$$
$$OQ = \sqrt{7} + 3\sqrt{3}.$$

20. 120°; Equilateral triangle

21. 90°; Square

22. Regular pentagon; Regular pentagon with *n* sides

23. a. The measure of an arc equals the measure of its corresponding central angle. Therefore, congruent arcs would have to have congruent central angles.

b. The measure of a central angle equals the measure of its intercepted arc. Therefore, congruent central angles have congruent arcs.

c. Draw the radii to the endpoints of the congruent chords. The two triangles formed are congruent by SSS. The central angles of each triangle are congruent by CPCTC. Therefore, the corresponding arcs to the central angles are also congruent. Hence, congruent chords have congruent arcs.

d. Draw the four radii to the endpoints of the congruent arcs. Also draw the chords corresponding to the congruent arcs. The central angles corresponding to the congruent arcs are also congruent. Therefore, the triangles are congruent by SAS. The chords are congruent by CPCTC. Hence, congruent arcs have congruent chords.

e. Congruent central angles will have congruent arcs (from b). Congruent arcs have congruent chords (from d). Hence, congruent central angles have congruent chords.

f. Congruent chords have congruent arcs (from c). Congruent arcs have congruent central angles (from a). Therefore, congruent chords will have congruent central angles.

24. a.

At 1:30 PM, the hour hand is half the distance from 1 to the 2. Therefore, the angle measure is found by adding 120 and 15. The angle is 135°.

b.

At 2:20 AM the hour hand is $\frac{1}{3}$ the distance from the 2 to the 3. Therefore, the angle measure is found by adding 30 and 20. The angle is 50°.

25. a.

At 6:30 PM, the hour hand is half the distance from 6 to the 7. Therefore, the angle measure is 15°.

b.

At 5:40 AM the hour hand is $\frac{2}{3}$ the distance from 5 to 6. Therefore, the angle measure is found by adding 60 and 10. The angle is 70°.

26. 72°

27. 72°

28. 60°

29. 45°

30. 1. Diameters $\overline{AB}$ and $\overline{CD}$ intersecting at E in $\odot E$.

2. Vertical angles are $\cong$.

3. If 2 $\angle$s are $\cong$, then their measures are equal.

4. The degree measures of a central $\angle$ equals the degree measure of its arc.

5. Substitution

6. $\overset{\frown}{AC} \cong \overset{\frown}{DB}$

31. 1. $\overline{MN} \parallel \overline{OP}$ in $\odot O$

2. If 2 $\parallel$ lines are cut by a transversal, then the alt. int. $\angle$s are $\cong$.

3. If 2 $\angle$s are $\cong$, then their measures are =.

4. The measure of an inscribed $\angle$ equals $\dfrac{1}{2}$ the measure of its intercepted arc.

5. The measure of a central $\angle$ equals the measure of its arc.

6. Substitution

32. Proof: Since $\overline{RS}$ and $\overline{TV}$ are diameters of $\odot W$, they are $\cong$. Also, $\angle$s RTS and VST are right $\angle$s and are therefore $\cong$. With $\overline{TS} \cong \overline{TS}$, by HL $\triangle RST \cong \triangle VTS$.

33. Proof: Using the chords $\overline{AB}$, $\overline{BC}$, $\overline{CD}$ and $\overline{AD}$ in $\odot O$ as sides of inscribed angles, $\angle B \cong \angle D$ and $\angle A \cong \angle C$ since they are inscribed angles intercepting the same arc. $\triangle ABE \sim \triangle CED$ by AA.

34. Prove: Congruent chords are at the same distance from the center of a circle.

Given: $\overline{AB} \cong \overline{DC}$ in circle O;
$\overline{OE} \perp \overline{AB}$ and $\overline{OF} \perp \overline{DC}$

Prove: $\overline{OE} \cong \overline{OF}$

Proof: In circle O draw in radii $\overline{OB}$ and $\overline{OC}$. Because $\overline{OE} \perp \overline{AB}$ and $\overline{OF} \perp \overline{DC}$, triangles OEB and OFC are right triangles. $\overline{OB} \cong \overline{OC}$ and $\overline{AB} \cong \overline{DC}$. Both $\overline{AB}$ and $\overline{DC}$ are bisected because a radius perpendicular to a chord bisects the chord. Therefore, E and F are midpoints of $\overline{AB}$ and $\overline{DC}$, respectively. $\overline{EB} \cong \overline{FC}$ because if 2 segments are $\cong$, then their midpoints separate these segments into four congruent segments. $\triangle OEB \cong \triangle OFC$ by HL. $\overline{OE} \cong \overline{OF}$ by CPCTC.

35. Prove: A radius perpendicular to a chord bisects the arc of that chord.

Given: $\overline{OC} \perp \overline{AB}$ in $\odot O$

Prove: $\overline{OC}$ bisects $\overset{\frown}{AB}$

Proof: If $\overline{OC} \perp \overline{AB}$ in $\odot O$, then $\overline{OC}$ bisects $\overline{AB}$ giving $\overline{AD} \cong \overline{DB}$. Draw in radii $\overline{OA}$ and $\overline{OB}$ which are congruent. Using $\overline{OD} \cong \overline{OD}$, $\triangle ODA \cong \triangle ODB$ by SSS. Therefore, $\angle AOC \cong \angle BOC$ by CPCTC. $\overset{\frown}{AC} \cong \overset{\frown}{CB}$ since congruent central angles will have congruent arcs. Hence, $\overline{OC}$ bisects $\overset{\frown}{AB}$.

36. Prove: An angle inscribed in a semicircle is a right angle.

Given: $\odot O$ with diameter $\overline{RT}$

Prove: $\angle RST$ is a right angle.

Proof: in $\odot O$ with diameter $\overline{RT}$, $m\overset{\frown}{RVT} = 180$ since it is half of the circle. Therefore $m\angle RST = \frac{1}{2}m\overset{\frown}{RVT} = 90$. Hence, $\angle RST$ is a right angle.

37. Prove: If two inscribed angles intercept the same arc, then these angles are congruent.

Given: A circle with inscribed angles A and D intercepting $\overset{\frown}{BC}$.

Prove: $\angle A \cong \angle D$

Proof: Since both inscribed angles, A and D, intercept $\overset{\frown}{BC}$, $m\angle A = \frac{1}{2}m\overset{\frown}{BC}$ and $m\angle D = \frac{1}{2}m\overset{\frown}{BC}$. Therefore, $m\angle A = m\angle D$ which means $\angle A \cong \angle D$.

38. Draw diagonal $\overline{NQ}$ trapezoid $MNPQ$. If $\overline{MN} \parallel \overline{PQ}$, then $\angle MNQ \cong \angle NQP$ since they are alt. int. $\angle$s for parallel lines. If $\cong$ inscribed $\angle$s intercept $\cong$ arcs, then $\overset{\frown}{MQ} \cong \overset{\frown}{NP}$. If arcs of a circle are $\cong$, then their chords are $\cong$. Hence, $\overline{MQ} \cong \overline{NP}$ and $MNPQ$ is an isosceles trapezoid.

39. If $\overset{\frown}{ST} \cong \overset{\frown}{TV}$, $\overline{ST} \cong \overline{TV}$ since $\cong$ arcs in a circle have $\cong$ chords. $\triangle STV$ is an isosceles $\triangle$ because it has two $\cong$ sides.

40. Given: $\odot O$ with chords $\overline{AB}$ and $\overline{BC}$; also radii $\overline{AO}$ and $\overline{OC}$ as shown.

Prove: $m\angle ABC < m\angle AOC$

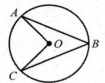

Proof: With chords $\overline{AB}$ and $\overline{BC}$ and radii $\overline{AO}$ and $\overline{OC}$ in $\odot O$, we know $m\angle AOC = m\overset{\frown}{AC}$ and $m\angle ABC = \frac{1}{2} \cdot m\overset{\frown}{AC}$. Therefore, $m\angle ABC = \frac{1}{2} \cdot m\angle AOC$. Since the measure of $\angle ABC$ is half the measure of $\angle AOC$, $m\angle ABC < m\angle AOC$.

41. Given: $\odot O$ with inscribed $\angle RSW$ and diameter $\overline{ST}$

Prove: $m\angle RSW = \frac{1}{2} \cdot m\overset{\frown}{RW}$

Proof: In $\odot O$, diameter $\overline{ST}$ is one side of inscribed $\angle RST$ and one side of inscribed $\angle TSW$. Using Case (1), $m\angle RST = \frac{1}{2} \cdot m\overset{\frown}{RT}$ and $m\angle TSW = \frac{1}{2} \cdot m\overset{\frown}{TW}$. By the Addition Property of Equality, $m\angle RST + m\angle TSW = \frac{1}{2} \cdot m\overset{\frown}{RT} + \frac{1}{2} \cdot m\overset{\frown}{TW}$. But since $m\angle RSW = m\angle RST + m\angle TSW$, we have $m\angle RSW = \frac{1}{2} \cdot m\overset{\frown}{RT} + \frac{1}{2} \cdot m\overset{\frown}{TW}$. Factoring the $\frac{1}{2}$ out, we have $m\angle RSW = \frac{1}{2}\left(m\overset{\frown}{RT} + m\overset{\frown}{TW}\right)$. But $m\overset{\frown}{RT} + m\overset{\frown}{TW} = m\overset{\frown}{RW}$. Therefore $m\angle RSW = \frac{1}{2} \cdot m\overset{\frown}{RW}$.

42. Given: $\odot O$ with inscribed $\angle RSV$

and diameter $\overline{ST}$

Prove: $m\angle RSV = \frac{1}{2} \cdot m\widehat{RV}$

Proof: In $\odot O$, diameter $\overline{ST}$ is one side of inscribed $\angle RST$ and one side of inscribed $\angle VST$. Using Case (1), $m\angle RST = \frac{1}{2} \cdot m\widehat{RT}$ and $m\angle VST = \frac{1}{2} \cdot m\widehat{VT}$. By the Subtraction Property of Equality,

$m\angle RST - m\angle VST = \frac{1}{2} \cdot m\widehat{RT} - \frac{1}{2} \cdot m\widehat{VT}$. But $m\angle RST = m\angle RSV + m\angle VST$ or $m\angle RST - m\angle VST = m\angle RSV$. By substitution then $m\angle RSV = \frac{1}{2} \cdot m\widehat{RT} - \frac{1}{2} \cdot m\widehat{VT}$. Factoring the $\frac{1}{2}$ out, we have $m\angle RSV = \frac{1}{2}\left(m\widehat{RT} + m\widehat{VT}\right)$. But $m\widehat{RT} = m\widehat{RV} + m\widehat{VT}$ or $m\widehat{RT} - m\widehat{VT} = m\widehat{RV}$. By substitution, we have $m\angle RSV = \frac{1}{2} \cdot m\widehat{RV}$.

43. The Given information leads to XO = 5; XY = 10;

YZ = 8 (6, 8, 10 right Δ). Let WZ = x, then

YW = XZ = 8 • x. In right Δ XZW,

$x^2 + 6^2 = (8 \cdot x)^2$

$x^2 + 36 = 64 \cdot 16x + x^2$

$\bullet 28 = \bullet 16x$

$x = \dfrac{28}{16} = \dfrac{7}{4} = 1.75$; WZ = 1.75

SECTION 6.2: More Angle Measures in the Circle

1. If $m\widehat{AB} = 92°$, $m\widehat{DA} = 114°$, and $m\widehat{BC} = 138°$, then $m\widehat{DC} = 16°$.

   a. $m\angle 1 = \frac{1}{2}(16) = 8°$

   b. $m\angle 2 = \frac{1}{2}(92) = 46°$

   c. $m\angle 3 = \frac{1}{2}(92 - 16) = \frac{1}{2}(76) = 38°$

   d. $m\angle 4 = \frac{1}{2}(92 + 16) = \frac{1}{2}(108) = 54°$

   e. $m\angle 5 = 180 - 54 = 126°$ or

       $m\angle 5 = \frac{1}{2}(114 + 138) = \frac{1}{2}(252) = 126°$

2. If $m\widehat{DC} = 30°$ and $\widehat{DABC}$ is trisected at points A and B, then $m\widehat{DA} = m\widehat{BC} = m\widehat{CB} = 110°$.

   a. $m\angle 1 = \frac{1}{2}(30) = 15°$

   b. $m\angle 2 = \frac{1}{2}(110) = 55°$

   c. $m\angle 3 = \frac{1}{2}(110 - 30) = \frac{1}{2}(80) = 40°$

   d. $m\angle 4 = \frac{1}{2}(110 + 30) = \frac{1}{2}(140) = 70°$

   e. $m\angle 5 = \frac{1}{2}(110 + 110) = \frac{1}{2}(220) = 110°$

3. a. 90°

   b. 13°

   c. 103°

4. $m\angle RSW = 90°$

Let $m\angle RST = x$.

$\dfrac{m\angle RST}{m\angle RSW} = \dfrac{1}{5}$

$\dfrac{x}{90} = \dfrac{1}{5}$

$x = \dfrac{90}{5} = 18°$

$m\angle RST = 18°$

$m\angle RST = \frac{1}{2}\left(m\widehat{RT}\right)$

$18° = \frac{1}{2}\left(m\widehat{RT}\right)$

$m\widehat{RT} = 36°$

5. Let $m\widehat{RT} = x$, then $m\widehat{TS} = 4x$

$x + 4x = 180$

$5x = 180$

$x = 36$

$m\widehat{RT} = 36°$

$m\angle RST = \frac{1}{2}\left(m\widehat{RT}\right)$

$m\angle RST = \frac{1}{2}(36)$

$m\angle RST = 18°$

6. a. No

   b. Yes

7. If $m\widehat{MP} = 112°$ and $m\widehat{MN} = 60°$, then
   $m\widehat{NP} = 52°$. If $\overline{PV}$ is a diameter in $\odot Q$, then
   $m\widehat{MV} = 68°$. If $m\widehat{MT} = 46°$, then $m\widehat{TV} = 22°$.

   a. $m\angle MRP = \frac{1}{2}(112 - 68) = \frac{1}{2}(44) = 22°$

   b. $m\angle 1 = \frac{1}{2}(60 - 46) = \frac{1}{2}(14) = 7°$

   c. $m\angle 2 = \frac{1}{2}(52 - 22) = \frac{1}{2}(30) = 15°$

8. If $m\widehat{BC} = 126°$ in $\odot O$ then $m\widehat{BDC} = 234°$.

   a. $m\angle A = \frac{1}{2}(234 - 126) = \frac{1}{2}(108) = 54°$

   b. $m\angle ABC = \frac{1}{2}(126) = 63°$

   c. $m\angle ACB = \frac{1}{2}(126) = 63°$

9. a. $m\angle ACB = \frac{1}{2}(m\widehat{BC})$ or $68 = \frac{1}{2}(m\widehat{BC})$ or
   $m\widehat{BC} = 136°$.

   b. $m\widehat{BDC} = 360 - 136 = 224°$

   c. $m\angle ABC = \frac{1}{2}(136) = 68°$

   d. $m\angle A = \frac{1}{2}(224 - 136) = \frac{1}{2}(88) = 44°$

10. a. $72° = \frac{1}{2}(m\widehat{AB} + 34)$ or $144° = m\widehat{AB} + 34$ or
   $m\widehat{AB} = 110°$.

   b. $m\angle 2 = \frac{1}{2}(110 - 34) = \frac{1}{2}(76) = 38°$

11. $m\angle 2 = \frac{1}{2}(m\widehat{AB} - m\widehat{DC})$

   $36 = \frac{1}{2}(4x - x)$

   $36 = \frac{1}{2}(3x)$

   $72 = 3x$

   $24 = x$

   a. $m\widehat{AB} = 4(24) = 96°$

b. $m\angle 1 = \frac{1}{2}(96 + 24)$

   $= \frac{1}{2}(120)$

   $= 60°$

12. Let $m\widehat{RT} = x$, then $m\widehat{RST} = 360 - x$

   $42 = \frac{1}{2}((360 - x) - x)$

   $84 = 360 - 2x$

   $-276 = -2x$

   $x = 138°$

   a. $m\widehat{RT} = 138°$

   b. $m\widehat{RST} = 222°$

13. a. $m\widehat{RT} = 120°$

   b. $m\widehat{RST} = 240°$

   c. $m\angle 3 = \frac{1}{2}(240 - 120) = \frac{1}{2}(120) = 60°$

14. $63 = \frac{1}{2}((3x + 6) + x)$

   $126 = 4x + 6$

   $120 = 4x$

   $x = 30°$

   $m\widehat{RS} = 3(30) + 6 = 90 + 6 = 96°$

15. If $m\angle 2 = 124°$, then $m\angle 1 = 56°$ because they are
   supplementary $\angle s$.

   $56 = \frac{1}{2}(1x + 1 + 3(x + 1))$

   $112 = 1x + 1 + 3x + 3$

   $108 = 4x$

   $x = 27°$

   $m\widehat{TV} = 27 + 1 = 28°$

16. Let $m\widehat{CE} = x$ and $m\widehat{BD} = y$.

   $71 = \frac{1}{2}(x + y)$

   $33 = \frac{1}{2}(x - y)$

   $142 = x + y$

   $\underline{66 = x - y}$

   $208 = 2x$

   $104 = x$

   $y = 38$

   $m\widehat{CE} = 104°$

   $m\widehat{BD} = 38°$

17. Let $m\overset{\frown}{CE} = x$ and $m\overset{\frown}{BD} = y$.

$$62 = \frac{1}{2}(x + y)$$
$$26 = \frac{1}{2}(x - y)$$

$$124 = x + y$$
$$\underline{52 = x - y}$$
$$176 = 2x$$
$$88 = x$$

$$m\overset{\frown}{CE} = 88°$$
$$y = 36$$
$$m\overset{\frown}{BD} = 36°$$

18. a. Supplementary

b. 68°

19. a. Supplementary

b. 107°

20. a. Rhombus

b. Square

21. 1. $\overline{AB}$ and $\overline{AC}$ are tangents to $\odot O$ from A

2. The measure of an $\angle$ formed by a tangent and a chord equals $\frac{1}{2}$ the arc measure.

3. Substitution

4. If two $\angle$s are $=$ in measure, they are $\cong$.

5. $\overline{AB} \cong \overline{AC}$

6. $\triangle ABC$ is isosceles

22. 1. Given

2. If 2 $\parallel$ lines are cut by a transversal, then the alt. int. $\angle$s are $\cong$.

3. $m\angle S = m\angle T$

4. The measure of an inscribed $\angle = \frac{1}{2}$ the arc measure.

5. Same as 4.

6. Substitution

8. $\overset{\frown}{RT} \cong \overset{\frown}{SQ}$

23. Given: Tangent $\overline{AB}$ to $\odot O$ at point B;

$$m\angle A = m\angle B$$

Prove: $m\overset{\frown}{BD} = 2 \cdot m\overset{\frown}{BC}$

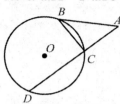

Proof: $m\angle BCD = m\angle A + m\angle B$; but because $m\angle A = m\angle B$, $m\angle BCD = m\angle B + m\angle B$ or $m\angle BCD = 2 \cdot m\angle B$. $m\angle BCD$ also $= \frac{1}{2}m\overset{\frown}{BD}$ since it is an inscribed $\angle$. Therefore, $\frac{1}{2}m\overset{\frown}{BD} = 2 \cdot m\angle B$ or $m\overset{\frown}{BD} = 4 \cdot m\angle B$. But if $\overline{AB}$ is a tangent to $\odot O$ at B, $m\angle B = \frac{1}{2}m\overset{\frown}{BC}$.

By substitution, $m\overset{\frown}{BD} = 4\left(\frac{1}{2}m\overset{\frown}{BC}\right)$ or

$m\overset{\frown}{BD} = 2 \cdot m\overset{\frown}{BC}$.

24. Given: Diameter $\overline{AB} \perp \overline{CE}$ at D

Prove: CD is the geometric mean of AD and DB.

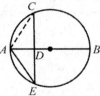

Proof: Draw in $\overline{AC}$. If $\overline{AB}$ is a diameter, then $\angle ACB$ is a rt. Angle and $\triangle ACB$ is a rt. $\triangle$. Since $\overline{AB} \perp \overline{CE}$, then CD is the geometric mean of AD and DB. (The length of the altitude to the hypotenuse of a right $\triangle$ is the geometric mean of the lengths of the segments of the hypotenuse.)

25. If $m\overset{\frown}{AB} = x$, then $m\overset{\frown}{ADB} = 360 - x$. Then

$$m\angle 1 = \frac{1}{2}\left(m\overset{\frown}{ADB} - m\overset{\frown}{AB}\right)$$
$$= \frac{1}{2}(360 - x - x)$$
$$= \frac{1}{2}(360 - 2x)$$
$$= 180° - x$$

26. $m\angle 1 = 180 - 104 = 76°$

27. The hypotenuse of a right $\triangle$ has a length of 4003. Let the length of the third side be x. Then

$$x^2 + 4000^2 = 4003^2$$
$$x^2 = 4003^2 - 4000^2$$
$$x \approx 154.95 \text{ miles}$$

28. The radius of the circle in feet is $4000 \cdot 5280$. The hypotenuse then has a length of $4000 \cdot 5280 + 80$. Let the length of the third side be x.

$$x^2 + (4000 \cdot 5280)^2 = (4000 \cdot 5280 + 80)^2$$
$$x^2 = (4000 \cdot 5280 + 80)^2 - (4000 \cdot 5280)^2$$
$$x \approx 38,131 \text{ feet or } \approx 11 \text{ miles}$$

29. Each arc of the circle is $72°$.

$$m\angle 1 = \frac{1}{2}(72) = 36°$$
$$m\angle 2 = \frac{1}{2}(144 + 72) = \frac{1}{2}(216) = 108°$$

30. $m\angle 1 = 60°$
        $m\angle 2 = 120°$

31. a. $30°$

    b. $60°$

    c. $\frac{1}{2}(360 - 60) = 150°$

32. $\angle 1 \cong \angle 2$; $\angle R \cong \angle W$; also, $\angle RST \cong \angle WVT$

33. $\angle X \cong \angle X$; $\angle R \cong \angle W$; also, $\angle RVW \cong \angle WSX$

34. $m\angle DOE = 60°$ and $m\angle FOE = 30°$.

$m\angle OEF = 60°$. Use right $\triangle OFE$ (see larger drawing)

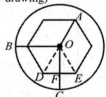

$OE = OA = 5$. $FE = \frac{1}{2}(OE) = \frac{1}{2}(5) = \frac{5}{2}$.

$OF = \frac{1}{2} \cdot OE \cdot \sqrt{3} = \frac{1}{2}(5)\sqrt{3} = \frac{5}{2}\sqrt{3}$.

$FC = 10 - \frac{5}{2}\sqrt{3}$ mm.

35. Using the given information, we know that $\angle ACB$ is a right $\angle$. Let $AM = MC = x$ and $CN = NB = y$. Using the Pythagorean Theorem we have,

$$x^2 + (2y)^2 + (\sqrt{73})^2 \text{ and}$$
$$(2x)^2 + y^2 = (2\sqrt{13})^2$$

$$x^2 + 4y^2 = 73 \quad \text{(Multiply by } -4)$$
$$4x^2 + y^2 = 52$$

$$\begin{array}{r} -4x^2 - 16y^2 = -292 \\ 4x^2 + y^2 = 52 \\ \hline -15y^2 = -240 \\ y^2 = 16 \\ y = 4 \end{array}$$

$$x^2 + 4(4^2) = 73$$
$$x^2 + 4(16) = 73$$
$$x^2 = 9$$
$$x = 3$$

$AM = MC = 3$ and $CN = NB = 4$
Therefore, $AC = 6$ and $CB = 8$, $AB = 10$ using the Pythagorean Triple (6, 8, 10).

36.

Draw in the segments are indicated. Let the length of the radius of the circle be x. The side opposite the $60°$ angle is $x\sqrt{3}$. Therefore,

$$x\sqrt{3} = 45$$
$$x = \frac{45}{\sqrt{3}} \cdot \frac{\sqrt{3}}{\sqrt{3}} = \frac{45\sqrt{3}}{3}$$
$$x = 15\sqrt{3}$$

The diameter has length $30\sqrt{3}$ feet.

37. Draw a segment from the center of the larger circle through the center of the smaller circle to the vertex of the square. Draw a radius from the center of the larger circle to the point of tangency on the right side of the square. The hypotenuse of a triangle formed is $2\sqrt{2}$. The diameter of the smaller circle is $\left(2\sqrt{2} - 2\right)$. The radius of the

smaller circle is $\frac{1}{2}\left(2\sqrt{2} - 2\right) = \left(\sqrt{2} - 1\right)$ cm.

38. In circle R draw $\overline{TR}$. If QS = 2(PT), then

QR = RS = PT = TR.

If $m\angle$ P = 23, then $m\angle$ TRP = 23;

$m\angle$ PTR = 134; $m\angle$ RTV = $m\angle$ RVT = 46;

$m\angle$ TRV = 88;

$m\angle$ VRS = 180 − (23 + 88) = 69°.

39. If 2 parallel lines intersect a circle, then the intercepted arcs between these lines are congruent.
Given: $\overline{BC} \parallel \overline{AD}$

Prove: $\overarc{AB} \cong \overarc{CD}$

Proof: Draw $\overline{AC}$. If $\overline{BC} \parallel \overline{AD}$, then $\angle 1 \cong \angle 2$
or m$\angle 1 = m\angle 2$. m$\angle 1 = \frac{1}{2}m\overarc{AB}$ and
m$\angle 2 = \frac{1}{2}$m$\overarc{CD}$. Therefore, $\frac{1}{2}$m$\overarc{AB} = \frac{1}{2}m\overarc{CD}$ or
m$\overarc{AB} = m\overarc{CD}$. $\overarc{AB} \cong \overarc{CD}$ since they are in the same circle and have equal measures.

40. The line joining the centers of two circles, which intersect in two points, is the perpendicular bisector of the common chord.
Given: $\odot$ s A and B intersect at C and D
Prove: $\overline{AB}$ is the $\perp$ bisector of $\overline{CD}$.

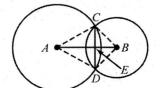

Proof: In $\odot$ s A and B intersect at C and D, draw $\overline{AC}$, $\overline{AD}$, $\overline{BC}$ and $\overline{BD}$. $\overline{AC} \cong \overline{AD}$ and $\overline{BC} \cong \overline{BD}$ because they are radii in the same circle. Using $\overline{AB} \cong \overline{AB}$, $\triangle ACB \cong \triangle ADB$ by SSS. By CPCTC, $\angle CAB \cong \angle DAB$. Using $\overline{AE} \cong \overline{AE}$, $\triangle CAE \cong \triangle DAE$ by SAS. $\overline{CE} \cong \overline{ED}$ and $\angle CEA \cong \angle DEA$ by CPCTC. Therefore, $\overline{AB}$ must be $\perp$ $\overline{CD}$ and $\overline{AB}$ bisects $\overline{CD}$.

41. If a trapezoid is inscribed in a circle, then it is an isosceles trapezoid.
Given: $ABCD$ is an inscribed trapezoid.
Prove: $ABCD$ is an isosceles trapezoid.

Proof: If $ABCD$ is a trapezoid, then $\overline{BC} \parallel \overline{AD}$. If 2 $\parallel$ lines intersect a circle, then the intercepted arcs between these lines are congruent. Therefore $\overarc{AB} \cong \overarc{CD}$, which means $\overline{AB} \cong \overline{CD}$. If the nonparallel sides of a trapezoid are congruent, then trapezoid $ABCD$ is an isosceles trapezoid.

42. If a parallelogram is inscribed in a circle, then it is a rectangle.
Given: $ABCD$ is a parallelogram inscribed in circle O.
Prove: $ABCD$ is a rectangle.

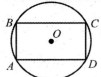

Proof: If $ABCD$ is a parallelogram inscribed in $\odot O$, then m$\angle B + m\angle D = 180°$. Also, m$\angle B = m\angle D$ because opposite $\angle$s of a parallelogram are equal in measure. By substitution, m$\angle B = 90°$. Angle B is a right angle and hence $ABCD$ is a rectangle.

43. If one side of an inscribed triangle is a diameter, then the triangle is a right triangle.
Given: $\triangle ACB$ inscribed in $\odot O$ with $\overline{AB}$ a diameter
Prove: $\triangle ABC$ is a right $\triangle$

Proof: If $\triangle ACB$ is inscribed in $\odot O$ and $\overline{AB}$ is a diameter, then $\angle ACB$ must be a right angle because an angle inscribed in a semicircle is a right angle. $\triangle ACB$ is a right triangle since it contains a right angle.

44. Given: $\overline{AC}$ is a diameter in $\odot O$ and

$\overline{CD}$ is a tangent.

Prove: $m\angle BCD = \frac{1}{2}m\overset{\frown}{BC}$

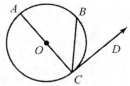

Proof: If $\overline{AC}$ is a diameter in $\odot O$ and $\overline{CD}$ is a

tangent, then by Case (1), $m\angle ACD = \frac{1}{2}m\overset{\frown}{ABC}$.

$m\angle ACD = m\angle ACB + m\angle BCD$
   (Angle Addition Postulate)

$m\angle ACB + m\angle BCD = \frac{1}{2}m\overset{\frown}{ABC}$
   (Substitution)

$m\overset{\frown}{ABC} = m\overset{\frown}{AB} + m\overset{\frown}{BC}$
   (Arc Addition Postulate)

$m\angle ACB + m\angle BCD = \frac{1}{2}\left(m\overset{\frown}{AB} + m\overset{\frown}{BC}\right)$
   (Substitution)

$m\angle ACB + m\angle BCD = \frac{1}{2}m\overset{\frown}{AB} + \frac{1}{2}m\overset{\frown}{BC}$
   (Distributive)

But $m\angle ACB = \frac{1}{2}m\overset{\frown}{AB}$
   (Inscribed Angle)

$m\angle BCD = \frac{1}{2}m\overset{\frown}{BC}$
   (Subtraction)

45. Given: $\overline{AC}$ is a diameter in $\odot O$ and

$\overline{CD}$ is a tangent.

Prove: $m\angle BCD = \frac{1}{2}m\overset{\frown}{BAC}$

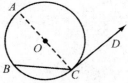

Proof: If $\overline{AC}$ is a diameter in $\odot O$ and $\overline{CD}$ is a

tangent.

$m\angle BCD = m\angle BCA + m\angle ACD$
   (Angle Addition Postulate)

$m\angle ACD = \frac{1}{2}m\overset{\frown}{AC}$ (Case (1))

$m\angle BCA = \frac{1}{2}m\overset{\frown}{BA}$ (Inscribed $\angle$)

$m\angle BCD = \frac{1}{2}m\overset{\frown}{BA} + \frac{1}{2}m\overset{\frown}{AC}$

$\qquad = \frac{1}{2}\left(m\overset{\frown}{BA} + m\overset{\frown}{AC}\right)$

   (Substitution and Distributive)

$m\overset{\frown}{BA} + m\overset{\frown}{AC} = m\overset{\frown}{BAC}$
   (Arc-Addition Postulate)

$m\angle BCD = \frac{1}{2}m\overset{\frown}{BAC}$ (Substitution)

46. With $O\text{-}Y\text{-}P$, $OP = OY + YP$. Since $YP > 0$,
$OP > OY$. (If $a > b$, then $a = b + k$, where k is a
positive number.)

47. Given: Quad. *RSTV* inscribed in $\odot Q$

Prove: $m\angle R + m\angle T = m\angle V + m\angle S$

Proof: $m\angle R = \frac{1}{2}m\overset{\frown}{VTS}$ and $m\angle T = \frac{1}{2}m\overset{\frown}{VRS}$

$\therefore m\angle R + m\angle T = \frac{1}{2}m\overset{\frown}{VTS} + \frac{1}{2}m\overset{\frown}{VRS}$

$\qquad = \frac{1}{2}\left(m\overset{\frown}{VTS} + m\overset{\frown}{VRS}\right)$

$\qquad = \frac{1}{2}(360°)$

$\qquad = 180°$

Similarly,

$m\angle V + m\angle S = \frac{1}{2}m\overset{\frown}{RST} + \frac{1}{2}m\overset{\frown}{RVT}$

$\qquad = \frac{1}{2}\left(m\overset{\frown}{RST} + m\overset{\frown}{RVT}\right)$

$\qquad = \frac{1}{2}(360°)$

$\qquad = 180°$

$\therefore m\angle R + m\angle T = m\angle V + m\angle S$

SECTION 6.3: Line and Segment Relationships in the Circle

1. $\triangle OCD$ is an equilateral triangle with
   $m\angle COD = 60°$. Since $\overline{OE} \perp \overline{CD}$, $\overline{OF}$ bisects
   $\overline{CD}$. $m\widehat{CF} = m\widehat{FD}$ and
   $m\angle COF = m\angle FOD = 30°$. $m\widehat{CF}$ must equal
   30°.

2. Since $\overline{OE} \perp \overline{CD}$ in $\odot O$, $\overline{OE}$ bisects $\overline{CD}$ so
   that $CE = ED$. Using Pythagorean Theorem on
   $\triangle OEC$, we have
   $$6^2 + (CE)^2 = 8^2$$
   $$36 + (CE)^2 = 64$$
   $$(CE)^2 = 28$$
   $$CE = \sqrt{28} = 2\sqrt{7}$$
   $$CD = 2(2\sqrt{7}) = 4\sqrt{7}$$

3. If $OV = 9$, then OR also equals 9. Since
   $\overline{OV} \perp \overline{RS}$, $\overline{OV}$ bisects $\overline{RS}$ which means
   $RT = TS$. Using the Pythagorean Theorem in rt.
   $\triangle RTO$, we have
   $$(RT)^2 + 6^2 = 9^2$$
   $$(RT)^2 + 36 = 81$$
   $$(RT)^2 = 45$$
   $$RT = \sqrt{45} = 3\sqrt{5}$$
   $$RS = 2(3\sqrt{5}) = 6\sqrt{5}$$

4. Draw in $\overline{RO}$ and $\overline{SO}$. If V is the midpoint of
   $\widehat{RS}$, then $\widehat{RV} \cong \widehat{VS}$ and $\angle ROV \cong \angle SOV$. If
   $m\angle VSR = 15$, then $m\widehat{VS} = m\widehat{VR} = 30$ and
   $m\angle VOR = 30 = m\angle VOS$. If $\overline{RO} \cong \overline{OS}$,
   $\triangle RTO \cong \triangle STO$ by SAS. By CPCTC
   $\angle RTO \cong \angle STO$ which means $\angle RTO$ is a rt.
   angle and measures 90°. The $m\angle TRO$ must be
   60°. In rt. $\triangle RTO$, the side opposite the 60° angle
   is 6. Let $OR = 2x$ which means $RT = x$ and
   $OT = x\sqrt{3}$.
   Therefore, $6 = x\sqrt{3}$
   $$x = \frac{6}{\sqrt{3}} \cdot \frac{\sqrt{3}}{\sqrt{3}} = \frac{6\sqrt{3}}{3}$$
   $$x = 2\sqrt{3}$$
   OR must be $2(2\sqrt{3}) = 4\sqrt{3}$.

5. a.

   b.

   c.

   d.

   e.

6. $ABCD$ is a square because the diagonals are $\cong$
   and they bisect each other.

7. Let $EC = x$. Then
   $$6 \cdot 4 = 8 \cdot x$$
   $$24 = 8x$$
   $$x = 3$$
   $$EC = 3$$

8. Let $EB = x$. Then
   $$12 \cdot 5 = 8 \cdot x$$
   $$60 = 8x$$
   $$x = 7\frac{1}{2}$$
   $$EB = 7\frac{1}{2}$$

9. Let $DE = x$ and $EC = 16 - x$. Then
$$8 \cdot 6 = x(16 - x)$$
$$48 = 16x - x^2$$
$$x^2 - 16x - 48 = 0$$
$$(x - 4)(x - 12) = 0$$
$$x = 4 \text{ or } x = 12$$
$$DE = 4 \text{ and } EC = 12 \text{ OR}$$
$$DE = 12 \text{ and } EC = 4$$

10. Let $DE = x$ and $EC = 12 - x$. Then
$$7 \cdot 5 = x(12 - x)$$
$$35 = 12x - x^2$$
$$x^2 - 12x + 35 = 0$$
$$(x - 5)(x - 7) = 0$$
$$x = 5 \text{ or } x = 7$$
$$DE = 7 \text{ and } EC = 5 \text{ OR}$$
$$DE = 5 \text{ and } EC = 7.$$

11. $\angle A \cong \angle C$ since they are inscribed $\angle$s intercepting the same arc. For the same reason, $\angle D \cong \angle B$. By AA, $\triangle AED \sim \triangle CEB$. Hence,
$$\frac{AE}{EC} = \frac{AD}{CB}$$
$$\frac{6}{3} = \frac{8}{CB}$$
$$\frac{2}{1} = \frac{8}{CB}$$
$$2 \cdot CB = 8$$
$$CB = 4$$

12. $\angle A \cong \angle C$ since they are inscribed angles intercepting the same arc. For the same reason, $\angle D \cong \angle B$. By AA, $\triangle AED \sim \triangle CEB$. Hence,
$$\frac{AD}{BC} = \frac{AE}{EC}$$
$$\frac{10}{4} = \frac{7}{EC}$$
$$\frac{5}{2} = \frac{7}{EC}$$
$$5 \cdot EC = 14$$
$$EC = 2\frac{4}{5}$$

13. $\dfrac{x}{2} \cdot 12 = \dfrac{x + 6}{3} \cdot 9$

$6x = 3(x + 6)$

$6x = 3x + 18$

$3x = 18$

$x = 6; \ AE = 3$

14. $\dfrac{x}{2} \cdot \dfrac{x}{3} = \dfrac{5x}{6} \cdot 6$

$\dfrac{x^2}{6} = 5x$

$x^2 = 30x$

$x^2 \bullet 30x = 0$

$x(x \bullet 30) = 0$

$x = 0 \text{ or } x = 30; \text{ reject } x = 0$

$x = 30; \ DE = \dfrac{5}{6} \cdot 30 = 25$

15. Let $EC = x$, then $DE = 2x$.
$$9 \cdot 8 = 2x \cdot x$$
$$72 = 2x^2$$
$$36 = x^2$$
$$x^2 - 36 = 0$$
$$(x - 6)(x + 6) = 0$$
$$x = 6 \text{ or } x = -6; \text{ reject } x = -6$$
$$EC = 6$$
$$DE = 12$$

16. Let $EC = x$, then $DE = 3x$.
$$6 \cdot 4 = 3x \cdot x$$
$$24 = 3x^2$$
$$8 = x^2$$
$$x = \sqrt{8} = 2\sqrt{2}$$
$$EC = 2\sqrt{2}$$
$$DE = 3(2\sqrt{2}) = 6\sqrt{2}$$

17. If $AB = 6$ and $BC = 8$, then $AC = 14$.
Let $DE = x$ and $AD = 15 - x$.
$$6 \cdot 14 = (15 - x) \cdot 15$$
$$84 = 225 - 15x$$
$$-141 = -15x$$
$$x = 9\frac{2}{3}$$
$$DE = 9\frac{2}{5}$$

18. Let $AD = x$. Then
$$6 \cdot 12 = x \cdot 14$$
$$72 = 14x$$
$$x = 5\frac{1}{7}$$
$$AD = 5\frac{1}{7}$$

19. If $AB = 4$ and $BC = 5$, then $AC = 9$.
Let $DE = x$ and $AE = x + 3$.
$$4 \cdot 9 = 3(x + 3)$$
$$36 = 3x + 9$$
$$27 = 3x$$
$$x = 9$$
$$DE = 9$$

20. If $AB = 5$ and $BC = 6$, then $AC = 11$.
Let $AE = x$.
$$5 \cdot 11 = 6 \cdot x$$
$$55 = 6x$$
$$x = 9\frac{1}{6}$$
$$AE = 9\frac{1}{6}$$

21. Let $RT = x$.
$$8^2 = x \cdot 12$$
$$64 = 12x$$
$$x = 5\frac{1}{3}$$
$$RT = 5\frac{1}{3}$$

22. If $RT = 4$ and $TV = 6$, then $RV = 10$.
Let $RS = x$
$$x^2 = 4 \cdot 10$$
$$x^2 = 40$$
$$x = \sqrt{40} = 2\sqrt{10}$$
$$RS = 2\sqrt{10}$$

23. Let $RS = TV = x$ and $RV = 6 + x$.
$$x^2 = 6(6 + x)$$
$$x^2 = 36 + 6x$$
$$x^2 - 6x - 36 = 0$$
Since the quadratic won't factor, we must use the quadratic formula.
$$x = \frac{-b \pm \sqrt{b^2 - 4ac}}{2a}$$
$$x = \frac{6 \pm \sqrt{36 - 4(1)(-36)}}{2(1)}$$
$$x = \frac{6 \pm \sqrt{36 + 144}}{2}$$
$$x = \frac{6 \pm \sqrt{180}}{2}$$
$$x = \frac{6 \pm 6\sqrt{5}}{2}$$
$$x = 3 + 3\sqrt{5} \text{ or } 3 - 3\sqrt{5}; \text{ reject } 3 - 3\sqrt{5}$$
$$RS = 3 + 3\sqrt{5}$$

24. Let $RT = x$, $RS = 2x$ and $RV = x + 9$.
$$(2x)^2 = x(x + 9)$$
$$4x^2 = x^2 + 9x$$
$$3x^2 - 9x = 0$$
$$3x(x - 3) = 0$$
$$x = 0 \text{ or } x = 3$$
$$RT = 3$$

25. a. None

b. One

c. 4

26. a. 3

b. 2

c. None

27. If $\overline{AF}$ is tangent to $\odot O$ and $\overline{AC}$ is a secant to $\odot O$, then $(AF)^2 = AC \cdot AB$. If $\overline{AF}$ is a tangent to $\odot Q$ and $\overline{AE}$ is a secant to $\odot Q$, then $(AF)^2 = AE \cdot AD$. By substitution, $AC \cdot AB = AE \cdot AD$.

28. In $\odot O$, if $\overline{OM} \perp \overline{AB}$, $\overline{ON} \perp \overline{BC}$, and $\overline{OM} \cong \overline{ON}$, then $\overline{AB} \cong \overline{BC}$. (Chords at the same distance from the center of the circle are congruent.) $\triangle ABC$ is isosceles because two sides in the triangle are congruent.

29. Let M, N, P, and Q be the pts. Of tangency for $\overline{DC}$, $\overline{DA}$, $\overline{AB}$, and $\overline{BC}$, respectively. Because tangent segments from an ext. point are $\cong$, $AP = AN$, $PB = BQ$, $CM = CQ$, and $MD = DN$. Thus, $AP + PB + CM + MD = AN + BQ + CQ + DN$. Reordering and associating, $(AP + PB) + (CM + MD) = (AN + DN) + (BQ + CQ)$
$$AB + CD = DA + BC$$

30. With $\overline{AB} \cong \overline{DC}$ in $\odot P$, $\overset{\frown}{ADB} \cong \overset{\frown}{DBC}$ and $m\overset{\frown}{ADB} = m\overset{\frown}{DBC}$. But $m\overset{\frown}{ADB} = m\overset{\frown}{AD} + m\overset{\frown}{DB}$ and $m\overset{\frown}{DBC} = m\overset{\frown}{DB} + m\overset{\frown}{BC}$ by the Arc Addition Postulate. By substitution, $m\overset{\frown}{AD} + m\overset{\frown}{DB} = m\overset{\frown}{DB} + m\overset{\frown}{BC}$. By the Subtraction Prop. of Eq. $m\overset{\frown}{AD} = m\overset{\frown}{BC}$ which means $\overset{\frown}{AD} \cong \overset{\frown}{BC}$. It follows that $\overline{AD} \cong \overline{BC}$ and using $\overline{DB} \cong \overline{DB}$, we have $\triangle ABD \cong \triangle CDB$ by SSS.

31. Yes; $\overline{AE} \cong \overline{CE}$; $\overline{DE} \cong \overline{EB}$

32.

Since T is the midpoint of $\overset{\frown}{RTS}$, $\overline{RT} \cong \overline{TS}$ and $\overline{RT} \cong \overline{TS}$. Draw in $\overline{TO}$. $\overline{TO} \cong \overline{RO}$. Let $m\overline{TO} = x = m\overline{RO}$. $m\overline{TR} = x\sqrt{2}$.

$$\frac{RT}{RS} = \frac{x\sqrt{2}}{2x\sqrt{2}} = \frac{1}{2}$$

$$\frac{RT}{RO} = \frac{x\sqrt{2}}{x} = \frac{\sqrt{2}}{1}$$

33. $m\angle D = \frac{1}{2}(200 - 160) = 20°$

34. $m\angle D = \frac{1}{2}\left(m\overset{\frown}{ABC} - m\overset{\frown}{AC}\right)$
$= \frac{1}{2}(36)$
$= 18°$

35. Let $AM = x$, then $MB = 14 - x$.
Let $BN = y$, then $NC = 16 - y$.
Let $PC = z$, then $AP = 12 - z$.
If tangent segments to a circle from an external point are congruent, $AM = AP$, $BN = MB$, and $PC = NC$ or
$$\begin{cases} x = 12 - z \\ y = 14 - x \\ z = 16 - y \end{cases} \text{ or } \begin{cases} x + z = 12 \\ x + y = 14 \\ y + z = 16 \end{cases}$$
Subtracting the first equation from the 2nd equation and using the 3rd equation, we have
$y - z = 2$
$y + z = 16$
Adding gives $2y = 18$ or $y = 9$. Solving for x and z we have $x = 5$ and $z = 7$. Therefore, $AM = 5$; $PC = 7$; $BN = 9$.

36. If $\odot Q$ is inscribed in isosceles right $\triangle RST$, then $\overline{RT}$, $\overline{RS}$, and $\overline{TS}$ are tangent to the circle. If the perimeter is $8 + 4\sqrt{2}$, then $RS = 4\sqrt{2}$, $RT = 4$, and $TS = 4$. Let $TM = x = TN$ and $RM = 4 - x = NS$. Let $PS = y$ and $RP = 4\sqrt{2} - y$. Since tangent segments to a circle from an external point are congruent, $MB = RP$ and $PS = NS$. That is,
$4 - x = 4\sqrt{2} - y \;\rightarrow\; 4 - 4\sqrt{2} = x - y$
$\quad y = 4 - x \quad\;\rightarrow\qquad\quad 4 = x + y$
Add the 2 equations on the right to get
$8 - 4\sqrt{2} = 2x$
$\qquad x = 4 - 2\sqrt{2}$
Hence, $TM = 4 - 2\sqrt{2}$.

37. Draw in $\overline{AO}$, $\overline{BQ}$, and $\overline{OQ}$. Since $\overline{AO} \perp \overline{AB}$ and $\overline{BQ} \perp \overline{AB}$, $ABQO$ is a trapezoid. Now draw a segment from O perpendicular to $\overline{BQ}$. Call the point of intersection R. Now $ABRO$ is a rectangle. If $OC = OA = 4$, and $BQ = CQ = 9$, then $OQ = 13$ and $RQ = 5$. But $\triangle ORQ$ is a right $\triangle$ and $OR = 12$ by the Pythagorean Triple (5, 12, 13). AB must also be 12 since $ABRO$ is a rectangle.

38. $OA = 3$; $BP = 9$; $OD = x$; $DP = 20 - x$.
$\frac{3}{x} = \frac{9}{20 - x}$ or $60 - 3x = 9x$. Solve to get $x = 5$.
$\therefore OD = 5$; $DP = 15$; $AD = 4$ and $DB = 11$ so $AB = 16$ in.

39. $OA = 2$; $BP = 3$; $OD = x$; $DP = 10 - x$.
$\frac{2}{x} = \frac{3}{10 - x}$ or $20 - 2x = 3x$. Solve to get $x = 4$.
$\therefore OD = 4$; $DP = 6$; $AD = 2\sqrt{3}$ and $DB = 3\sqrt{3}$ so $AB = 5\sqrt{3}$ or $AB \approx 8.7$ in.

40. a. $OP = 5$, $PQ = 4$, $OQ = 3$
Right

b. $OP = 5$, $PQ = 5$, $OQ = 4$
Isosceles

41. a. $OP = 7$, $PQ = 5$, $OQ = 4$
Obtuse

b. $OP = 4$, $PQ = 4$, $OQ = 4$
Equilateral

42. Let x represent the angle measure of the smaller gear. It is intuitively obvious that the
$$\frac{\text{number of teeth in the larger gear}}{\text{number of teeth in the smaller gear}} = \frac{\text{angle measure in smaller gear}}{\text{angle measure in larger gear}}.$$
The proportion becomes
$\frac{5}{3} = \frac{x}{60}$
$3x = 300$
$x = 100°$

43. Let x represent the angle measure of the larger gear. It is intuitively obvious that the
$$\frac{\text{number of teeth in the larger gear}}{\text{number of teeth in the smaller gear}} = \frac{\text{angle measure in smaller gear}}{\text{angle measure in larger gear}}.$$
The proportion becomes
$\frac{2}{1} = \frac{90}{x}$
$2x = 90$
$x = 45°$

44. Given: ⊙ A with $\overline{AB} \perp \overline{CD}$

Prove: $\overrightarrow{AB}$ bisects $\overline{CD}$ and $\overset{\frown}{CD}$

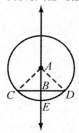

Proof: ⊙ A with $\overline{AB} \perp \overline{CD}$ draw in $\overline{AC}$ and $\overline{AD}$ which are congruent since they are radii of the circle. Using $\overline{AB} \cong \overline{AB}$, the right triangles ACB and ADB are congruent by HL. By CPCTC, $\overline{CB} \cong \overline{BD}$ and $\angle CAB \cong \angle DAB$. It follows that $\overset{\frown}{CE} \cong \overset{\frown}{ED}$ and hence $\overrightarrow{AB}$ bisects $\overline{CD}$ and $\overset{\frown}{CD}$.

45. Given: $\overrightarrow{AB}$ contains O, the center of the circle and $\overrightarrow{AB}$ contains M, the midpoint of $\overline{RS}$.

Prove: $\overrightarrow{AB} \perp \overline{RS}$

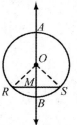

Proof: If M is the midpoint of $\overline{RS}$ in ⊙ O, then $\overline{RM} \cong \overline{MS}$. Draw $\overline{RO}$ and $\overline{OS}$ which are $\cong$ because they are radii in the same circle. Using $\overline{OM} \cong \overline{OM}$, $\triangle ROM \cong \triangle SOM$ by SSS. By CPCTC, $\angle OMS \cong \angle OMR$ and hence $\overrightarrow{AB} \perp \overline{RS}$.

46. Given: $\overline{AB}$ and $\overline{AC}$ are secants

Prove: $AB \cdot RA = AC \cdot TA$

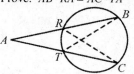

Proof: With secants $\overline{AB}$ and $\overline{AC}$, draw in $\overline{TB}$ and $\overline{RC}$. $\angle B \cong \angle C$ since they are inscribed angles intercepting the same arc. Also, $\angle A \cong \angle A$. $\triangle ABT \sim \triangle ACR$ by AA and it follows that $\dfrac{AB}{AC} = \dfrac{TA}{RA}$. Hence $AB \cdot RA = AC \cdot TA$.

47. Given: $\overline{TX}$ is a secant segment and $\overline{TV}$ is a tangent at V

Prove: $(TV)^2 = TW \cdot TX$

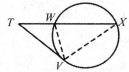

Proof: With secant $\overline{TX}$ and tangent $\overline{TV}$, draw in $\overline{WV}$ and $\overline{VX}$. $m\angle X = \dfrac{1}{2}m\overset{\frown}{WV}$ since $\angle X$ is an inscribed angle. $m\angle TVW = \dfrac{1}{2}m\overset{\frown}{WV}$ because it is formed by a tangent and a chord. By substitution, $m\angle TVW = m\angle X$ or $\angle TVW \cong \angle X$. $\angle T \cong \angle T$ and $\triangle TVW \sim \triangle TXV$. It follows that $\dfrac{TV}{TW} = \dfrac{TX}{TV}$ or $(TV)^2 = TW \cdot TX$.

SECTION 6.4: Some Constructions and Inequalities for the Circle

1. m∠CQD < m∠AQB

2. CD < AB

3. QM < QN

4. m∠A < m∠C

5. CD < AB

6. QM < QN

7. QM > QN

8. m∠$\widehat{AB}$ < m∠$\widehat{CD}$

9.
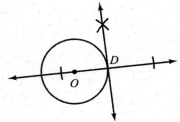

10.
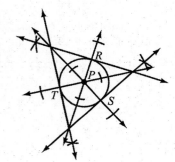

11. No, the angles are not congruent.

12.
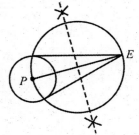

13.
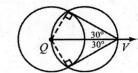

The measure of the angle formed by the tangents at *V* is 60°.

14. **a.** Kite

b. Rhombus

15. $\overline{AB}$; $\overline{GH}$ for a circle containing unequal chords, the chord nearest the center has the greatest length and the chord at the greatest distance from the center has the least length.

16. $\overline{MN}$; $\overline{TV}$; for a circle containing unequal chords, the chord nearest the center has the greatest length and the chord at the greatest distance from the center is the shortest chord.

17. **a.** $\overline{OT}$

b. $\overline{OD}$

18. **a.** m∠1 > m∠2

b. m$\widehat{RS}$ > m$\widehat{TV}$

19. **a.** m$\widehat{MN}$ > m$\widehat{QP}$

b. m$\widehat{MPN}$ < m$\widehat{PMQ}$

20. **a.** m∠1 > m∠2

b. m$\widehat{XY}$ > m$\widehat{YZ}$

21. Obtuse

22. Isosceles trapezoid

23. **a.** m∠AOB < m∠BOC

b. AB > BC

24. **a.** m∠AOB > m∠BOC

b. m$\widehat{AB}$ > m$\widehat{BC}$

25. **a.** m$\widehat{AB}$ > m$\widehat{BC}$

b. AB > BC

26. **a.** $\widehat{AC}$

b. $\overline{AC}$

27. **a.** ∠C

b. $\overline{AC}$

28. a. m$\widehat{AC}$

    b. $\overline{AC}$

29. a. $\angle B$

    b. $\overline{AC}$

30.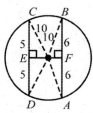

The radius $\perp$ to each chord bisects the chord. In $\triangle BOF$, $OF = 8$ using the Pythagorean triple $(6, 8, 10)$. In $\triangle DOE$, m$\angle DOE = 30°$ since DE is $\frac{1}{2}OD$. That means $OE = 5\sqrt{3}$ using the $30°$-$60°$-$90°$ $\triangle$. Hence, $\overline{AB}$ is $5\sqrt{3} - 8$ cm closer to point O than $\overline{CD}$.

31.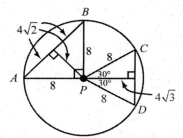

The distance from P to $\overline{AB}$ is $4\sqrt{2}$.
The distance from P to $\overline{CD}$ is $4\sqrt{3}$.
$\overline{AB}$ is $\left(4\sqrt{3} - 4\sqrt{2}\right)$ closer than $\overline{CD}$.

32.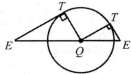

$\angle T$ is the largest angle and $\overline{EQ}$ is the longest side. The smallest side and angle depend on the location of E.

33.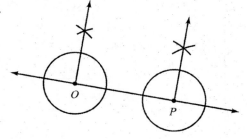

34. The longer chord corresponds to the greater minor arc leaving the lesser major arc.

35. Given: $\odot O$ with m$\widehat{AB}$ > m$\widehat{CD}$

    Prove: m$\angle AOB$ > m$\angle COD$

Proof: In $\odot O$, m$\angle AOB =$ m$\widehat{AB}$ and m$\angle COD =$ m$\widehat{CD}$. If m$\widehat{AB}$ > m$\widehat{CD}$, then by substitution, m$\angle AOB$ > m$\angle COD$.

36. Given: $\odot O$ with $AB > CD$

    Prove: m$\angle AOB$ > m$\angle COD$

Proof: If in $\odot O$, $AB > CD$, then m$\widehat{AB}$ > m$\widehat{CD}$. (In a circle containing two unequal chords, the longer chord corresponds to the greater <u>minor</u> arc.) It follows that m$\angle AOB$ > m$\angle COD$ using the theorem in Problem 27.

37. Draw in $\overline{OB}$ to form rt. $\triangle OMB$. Since $MB = 12$ and $OB = 13$, $OM = 5$. Draw in $\overline{OD}$ to form rt. $\triangle OND$. Since $ND = 5$ and $OD = 13$, $ON = 12$. $MN = ON - OM$; $MN = 12 - 5 = 7$.

38. The exact value is $8\sqrt{3} - 8 \approx 5.86$

CHAPTER REVIEW

1. (9, 12, 15) is a multiple of the Pythagorean Triple (3, 4, 5). Therefore, the distance from the center of the circle to the chord is 9 mm.

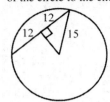

2. (8, 15, 17) is a Pythagorean Triple. Therefore, the length of half of the chord is 15 and the length of the chord is 30 cm.

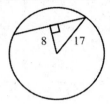

3. $r^2 = 5^2 + 4^2$
   $r^2 = 25 + 16$
   $r^2 = 41$
   $r = \sqrt{41}$ in.

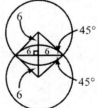

4. The radius of each circle has a length of $6\sqrt{2}$ cm.

5. $m\angle B = \frac{1}{2}\left(m\widehat{AD} - m\widehat{AC}\right)$
   $25 = \frac{1}{2}\left(140 - m\widehat{AC}\right)$
   $50 = 140 - m\widehat{AC}$
   $m\widehat{AC} = 90°$
   $m\widehat{DC} = 360 - (140 + 90) = 130°$

6. $m\widehat{AC} = 360 - (140 + 155) = 65°$
   $m\angle B = \frac{1}{2}\left(m\widehat{AD} - m\widehat{AC}\right)$
   $m\angle B = \frac{1}{2}(155 - 65) = \frac{1}{2}(90) = 45°$

7. If $m\angle EAD = 70°$ then $m\widehat{AD} = 140°$.
   $m\angle B = \frac{1}{2}\left(m\widehat{AD} - m\widehat{AC}\right)$
   $30 = \frac{1}{2}\left(140 - m\widehat{AC}\right)$
   $60 = 140 - m\widehat{AC}$
   $m\widehat{AC} = 80°$

8. If $m\angle D = 40°$ then $m\widehat{AC} = 80°$.
   $m\widehat{AD} = 360 - (80 + 130) = 150°$
   $m\angle B = \frac{1}{2}\left(m\widehat{AD} - m\widehat{AC}\right)$
   $m\angle B = \frac{1}{2}(150 - 80)$
   $m\angle B = \frac{1}{2}(70) = 35°$

9. Let $m\widehat{AC} = m\widehat{CD} = x$. Then $m\widehat{AD} = 360 - 2x$.
   $m\angle B = \frac{1}{2}\left(m\widehat{AD} - m\widehat{AC}\right)$
   $40 = \frac{1}{2}(360 - 2x - x)$
   $80 = 360 - 3x$
   $-280 = -3x$
   $x = 93\frac{1}{3}$
   $m\widehat{AC} = m\widehat{DC} = 93\frac{1}{3}°$
   $m\widehat{AD} = 173\frac{1}{3}°$

10. Let $m\widehat{AC} = x$; $m\widehat{AD} = 290 - x$
    $m\angle B = \frac{1}{2}\left(m\widehat{AD} - m\widehat{AC}\right)$
    $35 = \frac{1}{2}(290 - x - x)$
    $70 = 290 - 2x$
    $-220 = -2x$
    $x = 110$
    $m\widehat{AC} = 110°$ and $m\widehat{AD} = 80°$

11. If $m\angle 1 = 46°$, then $m\widehat{BC} = 92°$.
    If $\overline{AC}$ is a diameter, $m\widehat{AB} = 88°$.
    $m\angle 2 = 44°$; $m\angle 3 = 90°$; $m\angle 4 = 46°$;
    $m\angle 5 = 44°$.

12. If $m\angle 5 = 40°$, then $m\widehat{AB} = 80°$.
    If $\overline{AC}$ is a diameter, $m\widehat{BC} = 100°$.
    $m\angle 1 = 50°$; $m\angle 2 = 40°$; $m\angle 3 = 90°$;
    $m\angle 4 = 50°$.

13. (12, 16, 20) is a multiple of the Pythagorean Triple (3, 4, 5). Hence, half of the chord has a length of 12 and the chord has length 24.

14. The radius of the circle has length 10 using the Pythagorean Triple (6, 8, 10).

15. A

16. S

17. N

18. S

19. A

20. N

21. A

22. N

23. a. $m\angle AEB = \frac{1}{2}\left(m\widehat{AB} + m\widehat{CD}\right)$

$75 = \frac{1}{2}\left(80 + m\widehat{CD}\right)$

$150 = 80 + m\widehat{CD}$

$m\widehat{CD} = 70°$

b. $m\angle BED = \frac{1}{2}\left(m\widehat{AC} + m\widehat{BD}\right)$

$45 = \frac{1}{2}\left(62 + m\widehat{BD}\right)$

$90 = 62 + m\widehat{BD}$

$m\widehat{BD} = 28°$

c. $m\angle P = \frac{1}{2}\left(m\widehat{AB} - m\widehat{CD}\right)$

$24 = \frac{1}{2}\left(88 - m\widehat{CD}\right)$

$48 = 88 + m\widehat{CD}$

$m\widehat{CD} = 40°$

$m\angle CED = \frac{1}{2}\left(m\widehat{AB} + m\widehat{CD}\right)$

$m\angle CED = \frac{1}{2}(88 + 40) = \frac{1}{2}(128) = 64°$

d. $m\angle CED = \frac{1}{2}\left(m\widehat{AB} + m\widehat{CD}\right)$

$41 = \frac{1}{2}\left(m\widehat{AB} + 20\right)$

$82 = m\widehat{AB} + 20$

$m\widehat{AB} = 62°$

$m\angle P = \frac{1}{2}\left(m\widehat{AB} - m\widehat{CD}\right)$

$m\angle P = \frac{1}{2}(62 - 20) = \frac{1}{2}(42) = 21°$

e. $m\angle AEB = \frac{1}{2}\left(m\widehat{AB} + m\widehat{CD}\right)$ and

$m\angle P = \frac{1}{2}\left(m\widehat{AB} - m\widehat{CD}\right).$

$65 = \frac{1}{2}\left(m\widehat{AB} + m\widehat{CD}\right)$

$25 = \frac{1}{2}\left(m\widehat{AB} - m\widehat{CD}\right)$

$130 = m\widehat{AB} + m\widehat{CD}$

$\underline{50 = m\widehat{AB} - m\widehat{CD}}$

$180 = 2 \cdot m\widehat{AB}$

$m\widehat{AB} = 90°; \ m\widehat{CD} = 40°$

f. $m\angle CED = \frac{1}{2}\left(m\widehat{AB} - m\widehat{CD}\right)$

$50 = \frac{1}{2}\left(m\widehat{AB} - m\widehat{CD}\right)$

$100 = \left(m\widehat{AB} - m\widehat{CD}\right)$

$m\widehat{AC} + m\widehat{BD} = 360 - 100 = 260°$

24. a. Let $BC = x$.

$6^2 = 12 \cdot x$

$36 = 12x$

$x = 3$

$BC = 3$

b. Let $DG = x$.

$4 \cdot 6 = x \cdot 3$

$24 = 3x$

$x = 8$

$DG = 8$

c. Let $CE = x$.

$3 \cdot x = 4 \cdot 12$

$3x = 48$

$x = 16$

$CE = 16$

d. Let $GE = x$.

$10 \cdot x = 5 \cdot 8$

$10x = 40$

$x = 4$

$GE = 4$

148

Chapter 6: *Circles*

e. Let $BC = x$ and $CA = x + 5$.

$6^2 = x(x+5)$

$36 = x^2 + 5x$

$0 = x^2 + 5x - 36$

$0 = (x+9)(x-4)$

$x = -9$ or $x = 4$; reject $x = -9$.

$BC = 4$.

f. Let $DG = x$ and $AG = 9 - x$.

$x(9-x) = 4 \cdot 2$

$9x - x^2 = 8$

$0 = x^2 - 9x + 8$

$0 = (x-8)(x-1)$

$x = 8$ or $x = 1$;

$GD = 8$ or $GD = 1$.

g. Let $CD = ED = x$ and $CE = 2x$.

$x(2x) = 3 \cdot 30$

$2x^2 = 90$

$x^2 = 45$

$x = \sqrt{45} = 3\sqrt{5}$

$ED = 3\sqrt{5}$

h. Let $CD = x$ and $CE = x + 12$

$x(x+12) = 5 \cdot 9$

$x^2 + 12x = 45$

$x^2 + 12x - 45 = 0$

$(x+15)(x-3) = 0$

$x = -15$ or $x = 3$; reject $x = -15$;

$CD = 3$.

i. Let $FC = x$

$x^2 = 4 \cdot 12$

$x^2 = 48$

$x = \sqrt{48} = 4\sqrt{3}$

$FC = 4\sqrt{3}$

j. Let $CD = x$ and $CE = x + 9$.

$x(x+9) = 6^2$

$x^2 + 9x = 36$

$x^2 + 9x - 36 = 0$

$(x+12)(x-3) = 0$

$x = -12$ or $x = 3$; reject $x = -12$;

$CD = 3$

25. $5x + 4 = 2x + 19$

$3x = 15$

$x = 5$

$OE = 5(5) + 4 = 29$

26.
$$x(x-2) = x + 28$$
$$x^2 - 2x - x - 28 = 0$$
$$x^2 - 3x - 28 = 0$$
$$(x-7)(x+4) = 0$$

$x = 7$ or $x = -4$. If $x = 7$, then

$AC = 7 + 28 = 35$; $DE = 17\frac{1}{2}$.

If $x = -4$, then $AC = 24$; $DE = 12$.

27. Given: $\overline{DC}$ is tangent to circles B and A at points D and C, respectively.

Prove: $AC \cdot ED = CE \cdot BD$

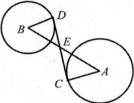

Proof: If $\overline{DC}$ is tangent to circles B and A at points D and C, then $\overline{BD} \perp \overline{DC}$ and $\overline{AC} \perp \overline{DC}$. $\angle$s D and C are congruent since they are right angles. $\angle DEB \cong \angle CEA$ because of vertical angles. $\triangle BDE \sim \triangle ACE$ by AA. It follows that $\dfrac{AC}{CE} = \dfrac{BD}{ED}$ because corresponding sides are proportional. Hence, $AC \cdot ED = CE \cdot BD$.

28. Given: $\odot O$ with $\overline{EO} \perp \overline{BC}$, $\overline{DO} \perp \overline{BA}$, $\overline{EO} \cong \overline{OD}$

Prove: $\overparen{BC} \cong \overparen{BA}$

Proof: In $\odot O$, if $\overline{EO} \perp \overline{BC}$, $\overline{DO} \perp \overline{BA}$, and $\overline{EO} \cong \overline{OD}$, then $\overline{BC} \cong \overline{BA}$. (Chords equidistant from the center of the circle are congruent.) It follows then that $\overparen{BC} \cong \overparen{BA}$.

© 2011 Cengage Learning. All Rights Reserved. May not be copied, scanned, or duplicated, in whole or in part, except for use as permitted in a license distributed with a certain product or service or otherwise on a password-protected website for classroom use.

29. Given: $\overline{AP}$ and $\overline{BP}$ are tangent to $\odot Q$

at A and B; C is the midpoint of $\overarc{AB}$.

Prove: $\overrightarrow{PC}$ bisects $\angle APB$

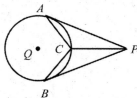

Proof: If $\overline{AP}$ and $\overline{BP}$ are tangent to $\odot Q$ at A and B, then $\overline{AP} \cong \overline{BP}$. $\overarc{AC} \cong \overarc{BC}$ because C is the midpoint of $\overarc{AB}$. It follows that $\overline{AC} \cong \overline{BC}$ and, using $\overline{CP} \cong \overline{CP}$, we have $\triangle ACP \cong \triangle BCP$ by SSS. $\angle APC \cong \angle BCP$ by CPCTC and hence $\overrightarrow{PC}$ bisects $\angle APB$.

30. If $m\overarc{AD} = 136°$ and $\overline{AC}$ is a diameter, then $m\overarc{DC} = 44°$. If $m\overarc{BC} = 50°$, then $m\overarc{AB} = 130°$.

$m\angle 1 = 93°$; $m\angle 2 = 25°$; $m\angle 3 = 43°$;

$m\angle 4 = 68°$; $m\angle 5 = 90°$; $m\angle 6 = 22°$;

$m\angle 7 = 68°$; $m\angle 8 = 22°$; $m\angle 9 = 50°$;

$m\angle 10 = 112°$

31. Each side of the square has length $6\sqrt{2}$.

Therefore, the perimeter is $24\sqrt{2}$ cm.

32. The perimeter of the triangle is $15 + 5\sqrt{3}$ cm.

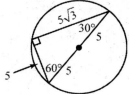

33.
$$(35-x)^2 + (6+x)^2 = 29^2$$
$$1225 - 70x + x^2 + 36 + 12x + x^2 = 841$$
$$2x^2 - 58x + 420 = 0$$
$$x^2 - 29x + 210 = 0$$
$$(x-15)(x-14) = 0$$

$x = 15$ or $x = 14$

The lengths of the segments on the hypotenuse are 14 cm and 15 cm.

34. Let $AD = x = AF$; $BE = y = DB$;

$FC = z = CE$, then

$$x + y \quad = 9$$
$$x \quad + z = 10$$
$$\quad y + z = 13$$

Subtracting the second equation from the first we get $y - z = 1$. Using this one along with the third equation, we have

$$y - z = -1$$
$$y + z = 13.$$

Adding, we get $2y = 12$ or $y = 6$.

Solving for x and z, $x = 3$ and $z = 7$.

$AD = 3$; $BE = 6$; $FC = 7$.

35. a. $AB > CD$

b. $QP < QR$

c. $m\angle A < m\angle C$

36. a.

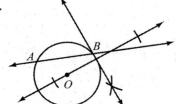

b.

37.

38.

CHAPTER TEST

1. a. 272°

    b. $m\widehat{ACB} = 360 - m\widehat{AB} = 360 - 92 = 268°$
        $m\widehat{AC} = \frac{1}{2}m\widehat{ACB} = \frac{1}{2}(268) = 134°$

2. a. 69°

    b. $m\angle BAC = \frac{1}{2}m\widehat{BC} = \frac{1}{2}(64) = 32°$

3. a. $m\angle BAC = \frac{1}{2}m\widehat{BC}$
        $m\widehat{BC} = 2(24) = 48°$

    b. Isosceles

4. a. Right

    b. Congruent

5. a. $m\angle 1 = \frac{1}{2}(106 + 32) = \frac{1}{2}(138) = 69°$

    b. $m\angle 2 = \frac{1}{2}(106 - 32) = \frac{1}{2}(74) = 37°$

6. a. 214°

    b. $m\angle 3 = \frac{1}{2}(214 - 146) = \frac{1}{2}(68) = 34°$

7. $m\angle 3 = \frac{1}{2}\left(m\widehat{RST} - m\widehat{RT}\right)$

    $46 = \frac{1}{2}\left(m\widehat{RST} - m\widehat{RT}\right)$

    $92 = m\widehat{RST} - m\widehat{RT}$

    $360 = m\widehat{RST} + m\widehat{RT}$

    Adding the above 2 equations gives

    $452 = 2 \cdot m\widehat{RST}$ or $m\widehat{RST} = 226$

    a. $m\widehat{RST} = 226°$ b. $m\widehat{RT} = 134°$

8. a. Concentric

    b. $(QV)^2 = (QR)^2 + (RV)^2$
        $(RV)^2 = (QV)^2 - (QR)^2$
        $(RV)^2 = 5^2 - 3^2$
        $(RV)^2 = 25 - 9$
        $(RV)^2 = 16$
        $RV = 4$
        $TV = 8$

9. AB = 6; OC = AO = 5; AC = 10

    In rt. Δ ABC, BC = 8. If M is the midpoint, then

    MB = MC = 4. In rt. Δ MBA,

    $(AM)^2 = 6^2 + 4^2$

    $(AM)^2 = 36 + 16 = 52$

    AM = $\sqrt{52} = \sqrt{4 \cdot 13} = 2\sqrt{13}$

10. a. 1

    b. 2

11. a. $HP = 4$, $PJ = 5$, and $PM = 2$.
        Let $LP = x$.
        $4 \cdot 5 = 2 \cdot x$
        $20 = 2x$
        $x = 10$
        $LP = 10$

    b. $HP = x + 1$, $PJ = x - 1$, $LP = 8$, and
        $PM = 3$.
        $(x+1)(x-1) = 8 \cdot 3$
        $x^2 - 1 = 24$
        $x^2 - 25 = 0$
        $(x-5)(x+5) = 0$
        $x = 5$ or $x = -5$; reject $x = -5$.

12. If TX = 3 and XW = 5, then TW = 8.

    If $\Delta TVW \sim \Delta TXV$, then

    $\frac{TV}{TX} = \frac{TW}{TV}$ or $\frac{TV}{3} = \frac{8}{TV}$ or

    $(TV)^2 = 24$

    TV = $\sqrt{24} = \sqrt{4 \cdot 6} = 2\sqrt{6}$

13.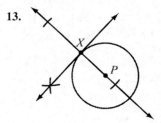

14. a. $m\angle AQB > m\angle CQD$

   b. $AB > CD$

15. a. 1

   b. 7

16. S1. In $\odot O$, chords $\overline{AD}$ and $\overline{BC}$ intersect at E

   R1. Given

   R2. Vertical angles are congruent

   R4. AA

   S5. $\dfrac{AE}{CE} = \dfrac{BE}{DE}$

Chapter 7: Locus and Concurrence

SECTION 7.1: Locus of Points

1. A, C, E

2. F, H, K

3.
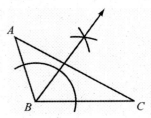

4.
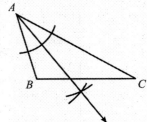

5.
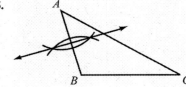

6.
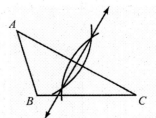

7.
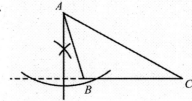

8.
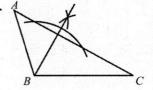

9.
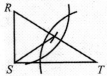

10.
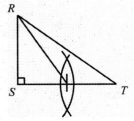

11. The locus of points at a given distance from a fixed line is two parallel lines on either side of the fixed line at the same (given) distance from the fixed line.

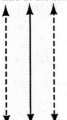

12. The locus of points equidistant from two parallel lines is another parallel line in the middle of the given lines.

13. The locus of points at a distance of 3 inches from point O is a circle with center O and radius 3 in.

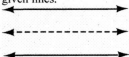

14. The locus of points equidistant from two fixed points A and B is perpendicular bisector of $\overline{AB}$.

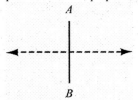

15. The locus of points equidistant from the three noncollinear points D, E, and F is the circumcenter of $\triangle DEF$.

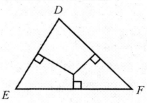

16. The locus of the midpoints of the radii of circle O whose radius has length 8 cm is another circle whose radius has a length of 4 cm.

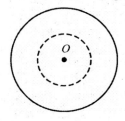

17. The locus of the midpoints of the chords in $\odot Q$ parallel to diameter $\overline{PR}$ is the perpendicular bisector of $\overline{PR}$.

18. The locus of points in the interior of a 6"-8"-10" right triangle at a distance of 1" from the triangle is another triangle similar to the first one.

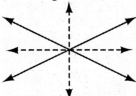

19. The locus of points equidistant from two given intersecting lines are two perpendicular lines which bisect the angles formed by the 2 intersecting lines.

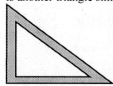

20. The locus of points equidistant from a fixed line and a point not on that line is a parabola.

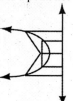

21. The locus of points 1 cm from line p and 2 cm from line q are the four points A, B, C, and D as shown.

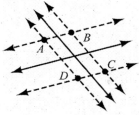

22. The locus of points 1 inch from each circle are the seven points shown.

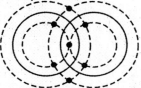

23. The locus of points at a given distance from a fixed line is a cylinder (like a tin can without a lid or base).

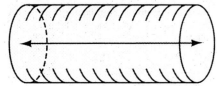

24. The locus of points equidistant from two fixed points is the plane that is the perpendicular bisector of the segment joining the two fixed points.

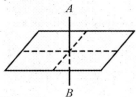

25. The locus of points at a distance of 2 cm from a sphere whose radius is 5 cm is two concentric spheres with the same center. The radius of one sphere is 3 cm and the radius of the other sphere is 7 cm.

26. The locus of points at a given distance from a given plane is 2 parallel planes on either side of the given plane at the given distance from the given plane.

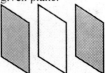

27. The locus is another sphere with the same center and a radius of length 2.5 meters.

28. The locus of points equidistant from three noncollinear points *D*, *E*, and *F* is the line through the circumcenter of the triangle, perpendicular to the plane containing the triangle.

29. The locus of points equidistant from an 8 foot ceiling and the floor is a parallel plane in the middle.

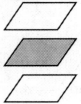

30. The locus of points equidistant from all points on the surface of a sphere is the center of the given sphere.

31. By the method of construction and the fact that "all radii of a circle are equal in length," we know that $\overline{AC} \cong \overline{BC}$ and $\overline{AD} \cong \overline{BD}$. Also $\overline{CD} \cong \overline{CD}$ and it follows that $\triangle CAD \cong \triangle CBD$ by SSS. Then $\angle ACD \cong \angle BCD$ by CPCTC. Using $\overline{CE} \cong \overline{CE}$, $\triangle ACE \cong \triangle BCE$ by SAS. If follows that $\overline{AE} \cong \overline{EB}$ and $\angle AEC \cong \angle BEC$ by CPCTC. Hence, $\overleftrightarrow{CD}$ is the perpendicular bisector of $\overline{AB}$.

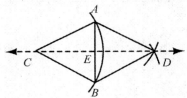

32. By the method of construction and the fact that "all radii of a circle are equal in length," we know that $\overline{AC} \cong \overline{BC}$ and $\overline{AD} \cong \overline{BD}$. Using $\overline{CD} \cong \overline{CD}$, we have $\triangle CAD \cong \triangle CBD$ by SSS. By CPCTC, $\angle ACD \cong \angle BCD$. Using $\overline{CE} \cong \overline{CE}$, it follows that $\triangle CAE \cong \triangle CBE$ by SAS. By CPCTC, $\angle CEA \cong \angle CEB$ and hence $\overleftrightarrow{CD} \perp \overline{AB}$.

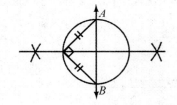

33.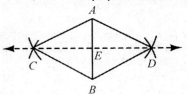

34.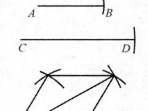

35.

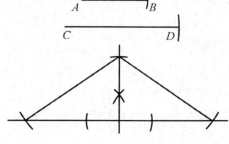

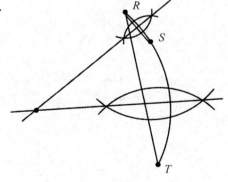

36.

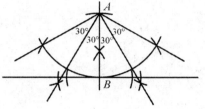

37.

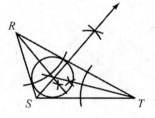

38.

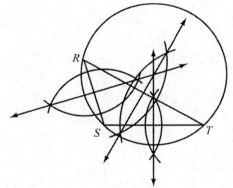

39.

40.

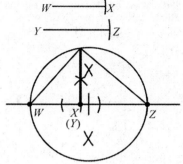

41.

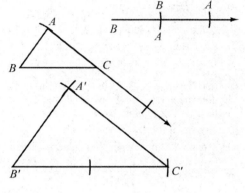

42. **(*i*)** If a point is on the perpendicular bisector, then it is equidistant from the two fixed points.

Given: $\overleftrightarrow{DC} \perp$ bisector of $\overline{AB}$

Prove: $\overline{AD} \cong \overline{DB}$

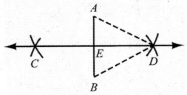

Proof: If $\overleftrightarrow{DC}$ is the $\perp$ bisector of $\overline{AB}$, then $\overline{AE} \cong \overline{EB}$ and $\angle DEA \cong \angle DEB$. Using $\overline{DE} \cong \overline{DE}$, it follows that $\triangle AED \cong \triangle BED$ by SAS. Hence, $\overline{AD} \cong \overline{DB}$ by CPCTC.

(*ii*) If a point is equidistant from two fixed points, then the point is on the perpendicular bisector of the segment joining the two points.

Given: $\overline{AD} \cong \overline{DB}$

Prove: D is on the perpendicular bisector of $\overline{AB}$

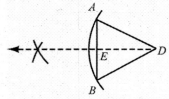

Proof: From D construct the perpendicular to $\overline{AB}$. Call the point of intersection E. $\angle$s DEA and DEB are right angles. Using $\overline{DE} \cong \overline{DE}$, it follows that $\triangle DEA \cong \triangle DEB$ by HL. $\overline{AE} \cong \overline{EB}$ by CPCTC and hence D is on the perpendicular bisector of $\overline{AB}$.

SECTION 7.2: Concurrence of Lines

1. Yes

2. Point A

3. Incenter

4. Circumcenter

5. Circumcenter

6. Centroid

7. **a.** Angle bisectors

   b. Perpendicular bisectors of sides

   c. Altitudes

   d. Medians

8. No

9. No

10. No

11. Equilateral triangle

12. Vertex of the right angle

13. Midpoint of the hypotenuse

14. Yes

15.

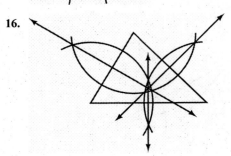

16.

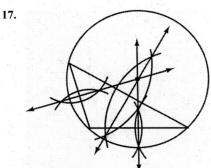

17.

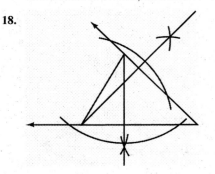

18.

19.

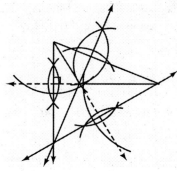

20.

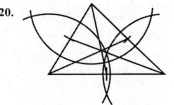

21.

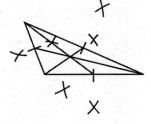

22. Yes

23. No

24. The hypotenuse of the right triangle has length 10 using the Pythagorean Triple (6, 8, 10). Using the figure as marked, we know that

$$6 - x + 8 - x = 10$$
$$14 - 2x = 10$$
$$-2x = -4$$
$$x = 2$$

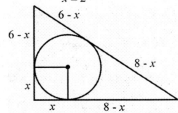

Hence, the radius has a length of 2.

25. Using the figure as marked, we know that in the 30°-60°-90° triangle, the side opposite the 60 degree angle is $x\sqrt{3}$. Therefore, $x\sqrt{3} = 5$ or

$$x = \frac{5}{\sqrt{3}} \cdot \frac{\sqrt{3}}{\sqrt{3}} = \frac{5\sqrt{3}}{3}.$$

The radius would be $2 \cdot \dfrac{5\sqrt{3}}{3}$ or $\dfrac{10\sqrt{3}}{3}$.

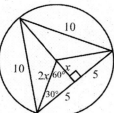

26. $\triangle ABC$ is inscribed in circle O and $AB = BC = 6$. $\overline{OB}$ must be the perpendicular bisector of $\overline{AC}$. $\triangle BDC$ is a 30°-60°-90° triangle. Since $OB = OC$, and $m\angle OBC = m\angle OCB = 60°$, $m\angle BOC$ must also be 60°. Therefore, $\triangle OBC$ is equilateral and $OB = OC = BC = 6$.

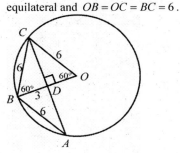

27. $RZ = 15$ using the Pythagorean Triple (8, 15, 17). $RQ = \dfrac{2}{3} \cdot 15 = 10$.

In right $\triangle QZS$, $QZ = 5$ and $ZS = 8$. Using the Pythagorean Theorem, we have

$$(SQ)^2 = 8^2 + 5^2$$
$$(SQ)^2 = 64 + 25$$
$$(SQ)^2 = 89$$
$$SQ = \sqrt{89}$$

28. $RZ = 6$ using the Pythagorean Triple (6, 8, 10). $RQ = \dfrac{2}{3} \cdot 6 = 4$.

In right $\triangle QZS$, $QZ = 2$ and $ZT = 8$. Using the Pythagorean Theorem, we have

$$(QT)^2 = 2^2 + 8^2$$
$$(QT)^2 = 4 + 64$$
$$(QT)^2 = 68$$
$$QT = \sqrt{68} = 2\sqrt{7}$$

29. **a.** 4

    b. 6

    c. 10.5

30. **a.** 4.1

    b. 7

    c. 13.8

31.

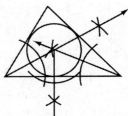

32.

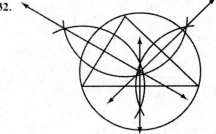

33. Equilateral

34. **a.** No

    b. Yes

35. **a.** Yes

    b. Yes

36. **a.** Yes

    b. Yes

37. **a.** Yes

    b. No

38. **a.** No

    b. Yes

39.

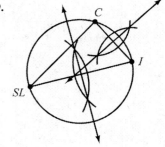

40. The agency would be located at the intersection of the ⊥ bisectors of $\overline{WO}$, $\overline{WT}$, and $\overline{OT}$ which is the circumcenter. (See construction from exercise 39.)

41. Draw isosceles $\triangle ABC$ with $AB = BC = 10$. Base $AC = 12$. Let circle O be the inscribed circle. Draw the altitude $\overline{BF} \perp \overline{AC}$. Because the $\triangle$ is isosceles $\overline{BF}$ will contain point O.

    $BF = 8$. Let $OF = r$ and $OB = 8 - r$. If a circle is inscribed in a $\triangle$, then the center of the circle is equidistant from the sides of the $\triangle$. If a point is equidistant from the sides of an angle, then it is on the angle bisector. $\therefore \overrightarrow{AO}$ bisects $\angle$ BAF in $\triangle$ BAF and we can use the proportion

$$\frac{AB}{AF} = \frac{OB}{OF}$$

$$\frac{10}{6} = \frac{8 - r}{r}$$

$$\frac{5}{3} = \frac{8 - r}{r}$$

$$5r = 24 - 3r$$

$$8r = 24$$

$$r = 3; \text{ radius} = 3 \text{ in.}$$

SECTION 7.3: More About Regular Polygons

1. First, construct the angle-bisectors of two consecutive angles, say *A* and *B*. The point of intersection, *O*, is the center of the inscribed circle.

   Second, construct the line segment $\overline{OM}$ which is perpendicular to $\overline{AB}$. Then, using the radius $r = OM$, construct the inscribed circle with the center *O*.

2. If two opposite angles (say *B* and *D*) are right angles, then a circle can be circumscribed about kite *ABCD*.

3. Draw the diagonals (angle-bisectors) $\overline{JL}$ and $\overline{MK}$. These determine center *O* of the inscribed circle. Now construct the line segment $\overline{OR} \perp \overline{MJ}$. Use *OR* as the length of the radius of the inscribed circle.

4. If the legs are congruent (the trapezoid is isosceles), then a circle can be circumscribed about the trapezoid.

5. In $\odot O$, draw diameter $\overline{AB}$.

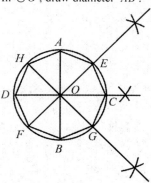

Now construct the diameter $\overline{CD}$ which is $\perp$ to $\overline{AB}$ at O. Construct the angle bisectors for $\angle$s AOC and BOC, and extend these to form diameters $\overline{EF}$ and $\overline{GH}$. Joining in the order A, E, C, G, B, F, D, and H, determines a regular octagon inscribed in $\odot O$.

6. Using the radius of $\odot O$, mark off 6 congruent arcs on the circle as shown. Now join every other point (like A to C, C to E, and E to A). The triangle ACE is equilateral and is inscribed in $\odot O$.

7. In $\odot Q$, draw in a diameter $\overline{AB}$. Now construct a diameter $\overline{CD}$ which is $\perp$ to $\overline{AB}$.

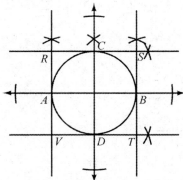

Construct tangents to $\odot Q$ at points A, C, B, and D. This is accomplished by extending each diameter into the exterior of $\odot Q$, and then constructing segments $\perp$ to the diameter at that point. Extend the tangents until they meet as shown: $RSTV$ is a circumscribed square.

8. Using the radius of $\odot Q$, mark off 6 congruent arcs in the circle as shown.

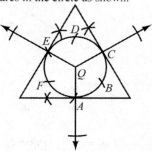

Through every other point (say A, C, and E), draw an extended radius. Now construct line segments perpendicular to $\overline{QA}$, $\overline{QC}$ and $\overline{QE}$. Extend these until they meet at points X, Y, and Z. Now $\triangle XYZ$ is circumscribed equilateral $\triangle$ for $\odot Q$.

9. $P = 8(3.4) = 27.2$ in.

10. $130 = n(6.5)$
$n = 20$ sides

11. $99.6 = 12s$
$s = 8.3$ cm

12. If the apothem length = 5, then the side length = 10. $\therefore$ the perimeter = 40 cm.

13. In square $ABCD$, apothem $a = 5$ in. (using the $45°$-$45°$-$90°$ relationship).

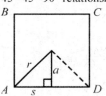

Also radius $r = 5\sqrt{2}$ in.

14.

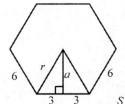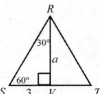

In equilateral $\triangle RST$, we see that $SV = 3$, $RV = 3\sqrt{3}$, and $RS = 6$. (Using the $30°$-$60°$-$90°$ relationship). Then apothem $a = 3\sqrt{3}$ cm and radius $r = 6$ cm.

15.

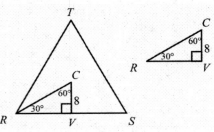

In $\triangle CRV$, $RV = 8\sqrt{3}$ and $CR = 16$ (by the 30°-60°-90° relationship). Now side $RS = 2(RV)$ so $RS = 16\sqrt{3}$ ft, while radius $CR = 16$ ft.

16.

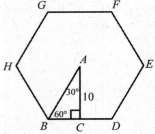

In $\triangle ABC$, $(BC)\sqrt{3} = 10$,

$\therefore BC = \dfrac{10}{\sqrt{3}}$

$BC = \dfrac{10}{\sqrt{3}} \cdot \dfrac{\sqrt{3}}{\sqrt{3}} = \dfrac{10\sqrt{3}}{3}$.

Then $AB = 2(BC) = \dfrac{20\sqrt{3}}{3}$.

Side $BD = 2(BC)$ so that the side and radius

each have the length $\dfrac{20\sqrt{3}}{3}$ meters.

17. $c = \dfrac{360}{n}$

   a. 120°

   b. 90°

   c. 72°

   d. 60°

18. $c = \dfrac{360}{n}$

   a. 45°

   b. 36°

   c. 40°

   d. 30°

19. $c = \dfrac{360}{n}$ or $n = \dfrac{360}{c}$

   a. 4

   b. 8

   c. 6

   d. 15

20. $c = \dfrac{360}{n}$ or $n = \dfrac{360}{c}$

   a. 12

   b. 5

   c. 10

   d. 18

21. $c = \dfrac{360}{n} \Rightarrow n = \dfrac{360}{c}$; ext. $\angle = \dfrac{360}{n}$

   a. n = 9; ext. $\angle = 40$; int. $\angle = 140°$

   b. n = 8; ext. $\angle = 45$; int. $\angle = 135°$

   c. n = 6; ext. $\angle = 60$; int. $\angle = 120°$

   d. n = 4; ext. $\angle = 90$; int. $\angle = 90°$

22. $c = \dfrac{360}{n} \Rightarrow n = \dfrac{360}{c}$; ext. $\angle = \dfrac{360}{n}$

   a. n = 12; ext. $\angle = 30°$

   b. n = 9; ext. $\angle = 40°$

   c. n = 8; ext. $\angle = 45°$

   d. n = 3; ext. $\angle = 120°$

23. The difference between the measures of the interior angle and the central angle = 60.

$$\dfrac{(n-2)\cdot 180}{n} - \dfrac{360}{n} = 60$$

$$180n - 360 - 360 = 60n$$

$$120n = 720$$

$$n = 6$$

24. The difference between the measures of the interior angle and the central angle = 90.

$$\frac{(n-2)\cdot 180}{n} - \frac{360}{n} = 90$$

$$180n - 360 - 360 = 90n$$

$$90n = 720$$

$$n = 8$$

25. $c = \dfrac{360}{n}$

    a. $n = 9$; yes

    b. $n \neq$ an integer; no

    c. $n = 6$; yes

    d. $n \neq$ an integer; no

26.

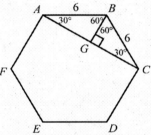

Using the 30°-60°-90° relationship,

$$AG = GC = 3\sqrt{3}$$

$$\therefore AC = 2(3\sqrt{3}) = 6\sqrt{3}$$

27.

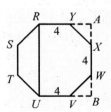

$$\triangle YAX \cong \triangle WBV$$

$$\overline{YA} \cong \overline{AX} = \frac{4}{\sqrt{2}} \cdot \frac{\sqrt{2}}{\sqrt{2}} = \frac{4\sqrt{2}}{2} = 2\sqrt{2} \text{ (using the }$$

45°-45°-90° relationship.)

$$RU = 2\sqrt{2} + 4 + 2\sqrt{2}$$

$$= 4 + 4\sqrt{2}$$

28. a. Isosceles   **b.** Concave kite

29.

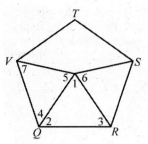

$$m\angle 1 = m\angle 2 = m\angle 3 = 60°$$

$$m\angle VQR = \frac{(5-2)180}{5} = 108°;$$

So $m\angle 4 = 108 - 60 = 48°$.

With $\overline{VQ} \cong \overline{QR}$ and $\overline{PQ} \cong \overline{QR}$, $\overline{VQ} \cong \overline{PQ}$,

$$m\angle 7 = m\angle 5$$

$$\therefore m\angle 5 = 66°$$

Similarly, $m\angle 6 = 66°$.

$$m\angle VPS = 360 - (m\angle 5 + m\angle 1 + m\angle 6)$$

$$m\angle VPS = 168°$$

30. In regular pentagon *JKLMN*, the measure of each interior angle is $\dfrac{(5-2)180}{5} = 108°$.

$$m\angle M = 108°.$$

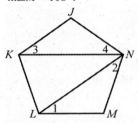

Because $\overline{LM} \cong \overline{NM}$, $\angle 1 \cong \angle 2$.

Now $m\angle 1 + m\angle 2 + m\angle M = 180°$

$$2(m\angle 2) + 108 = 180$$

$$2(m\angle 2) = 72$$

$$m\angle 2 = 36°$$

Similarly, $m\angle 4 = 36°$.

Now $m\angle JNM = m\angle 2 + m\angle 4 + m\angle LNK$

$$108 = 36 + 36 + m\angle LNK$$

$$108 = 72 + m\angle LNK$$

$$m\angle LNK = 36°$$

31. If a circle is divided into *n* congruent arcs $(n \geq 3)$, the chords determined by joining consecutive endpoints of these arcs form a regular polygon.

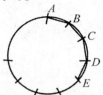

Proof: Let A, B, C, D, E, be the points which determine congruent arcs $\overset{\frown}{AB}$, $\overset{\frown}{BC}$, $\overset{\frown}{CD}$, $\overset{\frown}{DE}$, ... Now $\overline{AB} \cong \overline{BC} \cong \overline{CD} \cong \overline{DE} \cong ...$ since congruent arcs have congruent chords. Because

$\text{m}\overset{\frown}{ABC} = \text{m}\overset{\frown}{AB} + \text{m}\overset{\frown}{BC} = 2\text{m}\overset{\frown}{AB} = 2\text{m}\overset{\frown}{BC}$,

$\text{m}\overset{\frown}{BCD} = \text{m}\overset{\frown}{BC} + \text{m}\overset{\frown}{CD} = 2\text{m}\overset{\frown}{BC} = 2\text{m}\overset{\frown}{CD}$

$\text{m}\overset{\frown}{CDE} = \text{m}\overset{\frown}{CD} + \text{m}\overset{\frown}{DE} = 2\text{m}\overset{\frown}{CD} = 2\text{m}\overset{\frown}{DE}$

it follows that

$\text{m}\overset{\frown}{ABC} = \text{m}\overset{\frown}{BCD} = \text{m}\overset{\frown}{CDE} = ...$

Now

$\text{m}\overset{\frown}{AEC} = 360° - \text{m}\overset{\frown}{ABC}$

$\text{m}\overset{\frown}{BED} = 360° - \text{m}\overset{\frown}{BCD}$

$\text{m}\overset{\frown}{CAE} = 360° - \text{m}\overset{\frown}{CDE}$

So that $\text{m}\overset{\frown}{AEC} = \text{m}\overset{\frown}{BED} = \text{m}\overset{\frown}{CAE} = ...$

But $\text{m}\angle B = \text{m}\overset{\frown}{AEC}$

$\quad \text{m}\angle C = \text{m}\overset{\frown}{BED}$

$\quad \text{m}\angle D = \text{m}\overset{\frown}{CAE} = ...$

so that $\text{m}\angle B = \text{m}\angle C = \text{m}\angle D = ...$

Thus the polygon is a regular polygon.

32. If a circle is divided into *n* congruent arcs $(n \geq 3)$, the tangents drawn at the endpoints of these arcs form a regular polygon.

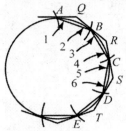

Proof: Let A, B, C, D, E, ... be the points which determine congruent arcs $\overset{\frown}{AB}$, $\overset{\frown}{BC}$, $\overset{\frown}{CD}$, $\overset{\frown}{DE}$, ...

Let Q, R, S, T, ... be the points from which tangents are drawn so that A, B, C, D, E, ... are points of tangency.

Now $\overline{AB} \cong \overline{BC} \cong \overline{CD} \cong \overline{DE} \cong ...$ since congruent arcs have congruent chords. $\text{m}\angle 1 = \frac{1}{2}\text{m}\overset{\frown}{AB}$ and

$\text{m}\angle 2 = \frac{1}{2}\text{m}\overset{\frown}{AB}$ so that $\angle 1 \cong \angle 2$. Similarly

$\angle 3 \cong \angle 4$, $\angle 5 \cong \angle 6$, etc. But since $\overset{\frown}{AB} \cong \overset{\frown}{BC} \cong \overset{\frown}{CD} \cong ...,$

$\angle 1 \cong \angle 2 \cong \angle 3 \cong \angle 4 \cong \angle 5 \cong \angle 6$, ...

Then $\triangle AQB \cong \triangle BRC \cong \triangle CSD \cong ...$

It follows that $\angle Q \cong \angle R \cong \angle S \cong \angle T \cong ...$

Also $\overline{AQ} \cong \overline{QB} \cong \overline{BR} \cong \overline{RC} \cong \overline{CS} \cong ...$

Then $AQ = QB = BR = RC = CS = ...$

so $QB + BR = RC + CS = SD + DT = ...$

and $QR = RS = ST = ...$

Then $\overline{QR} \cong \overline{RS} \cong \overline{ST} \cong ...$

Because $\angle$s are congruent and sides are also congruent, the circumscribed polygon is a regular polygon.

CHAPTER REVIEW

1.

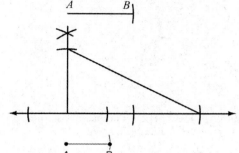

2.

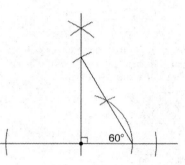

3.

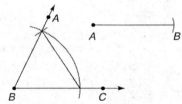

4.

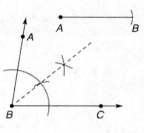

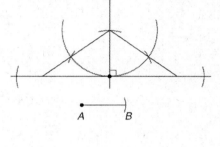

5.

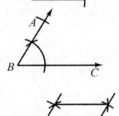

6.

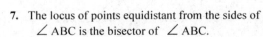

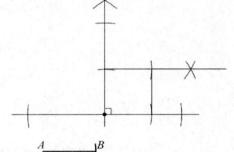

7. The locus of points equidistant from the sides of ∠ ABC is the bisector of ∠ ABC.

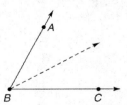

8. The locus of points that are 1 inch from point B is a circle with center B and radius length 1 inch.

9. The locus of points equidistant from points D and E is the perpendicular bisector of $\overline{DE}$.

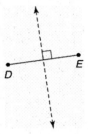

10. The locus of points $\frac{1}{2}$ inch from $\overleftrightarrow{DE}$ are 2 parallel lines on either side of $\overleftrightarrow{DE}$ $\frac{1}{2}$ inch from $\overleftrightarrow{DE}$.

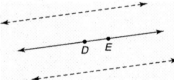

11. The locus of the midpoints of the radii of a circle is a concentric circle with radius half the length of the given radius.

12. The locus of the centers of all circles passing through two given points is the perpendicular bisector of the segment joining the 2 given points.

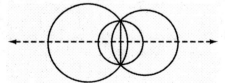

13. The locus of the centers of a penny that rolls around a half-dollar is a circle.

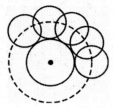

14. The locus of points in space 2 cm from point A is a sphere with center A and radius of length 2 cm.

15. The locus of points 1 cm from a given plane is 2 parallel planes on either side of the given plane at a distance of 1 cm.

16. The locus of points in space less than three units from a given point is the interior of a sphere.

17. The locus of points equidistant from two parallel planes is a parallel plane midway between the two planes.

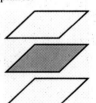

18.

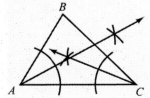

19.

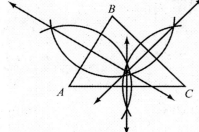

20.

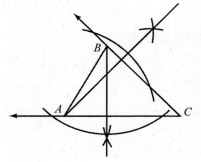

21.

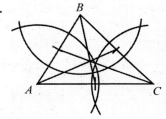

22.

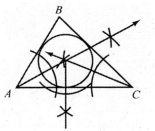

23.

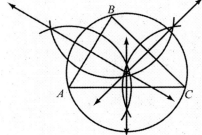

24. **a.** $BG = \frac{2}{3}(BF) = \frac{2}{3}(18) = 12$

b. $AG = \frac{2}{3}(AE)$

$4 = \frac{2}{3}(AE)$

$AE = \frac{3}{2}(4) = 6$

$GE = 2$

c. $CG = \frac{2}{3}(DC)$

$4\sqrt{3} = \frac{2}{3}(DC)$

$DC = \frac{3}{2}(4\sqrt{3}) = 6\sqrt{3}$

$DG = 2\sqrt{3}$

25. $AG = 2(GE)$ and $BG = 2(GF)$

$2x + 2y = 2(2x - y)$ and $3y + 1 = 2(x)$.

Simplifying: $2x + 2y = 4x - 2y$ and $3y + 1 = 2x$.

$-2x + 4y = 0$ and $2x - 3y = 1$.

Adding the above two equations gives $y = 1$.

Solving for x gives

$-2x + 4 = 0$

$-2x = -4$

$x = 2$

$BF = BG + GF = 4 + 2 = 6;$

$AE = AG + GE = 6 + 3 = 9.$

26. **a.** $c = \frac{360}{5} = 72°$

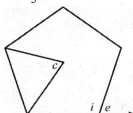

b. $i = \frac{(5-2)180}{5} = \frac{3(180)}{5} = \frac{540}{5} = 108°$

c. $e = 180° - 108° = 72°$

27. **a.** $c = \frac{360}{10} = 36°$

b. $i = \frac{(10-2)180}{10} = \frac{8(180)}{10} = \frac{1440}{10} = 144°$

c. $e = 180° - 144° = 36°$

28. a. $c = \dfrac{360}{n}$

         $45 = \dfrac{360}{n}$

         $45n = 360$

         $n = 8$

  b. $P = n(s)$

       $P = 8(5)$

       $P = 40$

29. a. The radius of the regular polygon is $3\sqrt{2}$. A central angle must measure 90. Using

$c = \dfrac{360}{n}$, n = 4. ∴ the perimeter = 24 in.

  b. The radius length is $3\sqrt{2}$ in.

30. a. No

  b. No

  c. Yes

  d. Yes

31. a. No.

  b. Yes

  c. No

  d. Yes

32. If the radius of the inscribed circle is 7 in., then the length of the radius of the triangle is 14 in.

33. Draw the circle inscribed in the regular hexagon. Now draw in 2 consecutive radii of the hexagon forming an equilateral triangle. Now draw the height of the equilateral triangle (which is a radius

of the circle). In the 30-60-90 triangle, the side opposite the 30°angle is *a*, the side opposite

the 60°angle is $a\sqrt{3}$. $10 = a\sqrt{3}$ ⇒

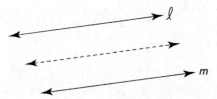

$a = \dfrac{10}{\sqrt{3}} = \dfrac{10\sqrt{3}}{3}$. The side of the equilateral

$\Delta = \dfrac{20\sqrt{3}}{3}$. The perimeter of the hexagon

$= 6 \cdot \dfrac{20\sqrt{3}}{3} = 40\sqrt{3}$ cm.

CHAPTER TEST

1. The locus of points equidistant from parallel lines ℓ and *m* is a line parallel to ℓ and *m* and midway between them.

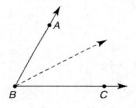

2. The locus of points equidistant from the sides of ∠ ABC is the angle bisector of ∠ ABC.

3. The locus of points equidistant from the endpoints

   of $\overline{DE}$ is the perpendicular bisector of $\overline{DE}$.

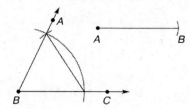

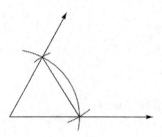

13. $c = \dfrac{360}{n}$

$36 = \dfrac{360}{n}$

$n = 10$

14. Side = 10 ∴ P = 80 cm

15. **a.** $4\sqrt{3}$ in.

    b. 8 in.

4. The locus of points in a plane that are at a distance of 3 cm from P is a circle with center P and radius of length 3 cm.

5. The locus of points in space that are at a distance of 3 cm from P is a sphere with center P and radius of length 3 cm.

6. **a.** Incenter   **b.** Centroid

7. **a.** Circumcenter   **b.** Orthocenter

8. Equilateral Δ

9. Angle bisectors and medians

10. **a.** True   **b.** True

    c. False   **d.** False

11. **a.** 1.5 in.   **b.** $3\sqrt{3}$ in.

12. **a.** $c = \dfrac{360}{n} = \dfrac{360}{5} = 72°$

    b. $i = \dfrac{(n-2) \cdot 180}{n} = \dfrac{(5-2) \cdot 180}{5} = 108°$

Chapter 8: Areas of Polygons and Circles

SECTION 8.1: Area and Initial Postulates

1. Two triangles with equal areas are not necessarily congruent.

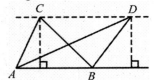

$\triangle ABC \not\cong \triangle ABD$

Two squares with equal areas must be congruent because the sides will be congruent.

2. The area does not equal 42 because the 2 figures overlap. The area will be less than 42.

3. $A = (12+30) - 5$
   $A = 37$ units^2

4. Because a rhombus is a parallelogram, use $A = bh$.

5. The altitudes to $\overline{PN}$ and to $\overline{MN}$ are congruent.

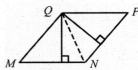

This follows from the fact that $\triangle$s QMN and QPN are congruent. Corresponding altitudes of $\cong$ $\triangle$s are $\cong$.

6. The four small triangles are congruent and have equal areas. The area of each small triangle is one-fourth the area of the rhombus.

7. Areas are equal.

8. No

9. $A = bh$
   $A = 6 \cdot 9$
   $A = 54$ cm^2

10. $c^2 = a^2 + b^2$
    $29^2 = 20^2 + b^2$
    $841 = 400 + b^2$
    $b = \sqrt{441} = 21$

$A = \dfrac{1}{2}bh$
$A = \dfrac{1}{2} \cdot 21 \cdot 20$
$A = 210$ in^2

11. $A = \dfrac{1}{2}bh$
    In a 45°-45°-90° triangle, $b = h = 6$
    $A = \dfrac{1}{2} \cdot 6 \cdot 6$
    $A = \dfrac{1}{2} \cdot 36$
    $A = 18$ m^2

12. $A = \dfrac{1}{2}bh$
    $A = \dfrac{1}{2} \cdot 15 \cdot 8$
    $A = 60$ in^2

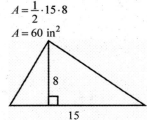

13. $A = bh$
    $A = 12 \cdot 6$
    $A = 72$ in^2

14. In rt. $\triangle EJH$,

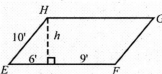

$h = 8$ using the Pythagorean Triple, (6, 8, 10).
$A = bh$
$A = (15)(8)$
$A = 120$ ft^2

15. $A = bh$
    $A = 10 \cdot 10$
    $A = 100$ in^2

16. $A = A_\triangle + A_{\text{RECT.}}$

$A = \dfrac{1}{2} \cdot 10 \cdot 4 + 10 \cdot 9$

$A = 20 + 90$

$A = 110 \text{ ft}^2$

17. Using the Pythagorean Triple, (5, 12, 13), $b = 12$.

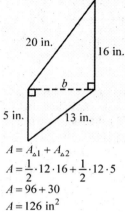

$A = A_{\triangle 1} + A_{\triangle 2}$

$A = \dfrac{1}{2} \cdot 12 \cdot 16 + \dfrac{1}{2} \cdot 12 \cdot 5$

$A = 96 + 30$

$A = 126 \text{ in}^2$

18. $A = A_{\text{LARGE RECT.}} - A_{\text{SMALL RECT.}}$

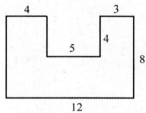

$A = 8 \cdot 12 - 5 \cdot 4$

$A = 96 - 20$

$A = 76 \text{ units}^2$

19. $A = A_{\text{LARGE RECT.}} - A_{\text{SMALL RECT.}}$

$A = (20)(30) - (14)(24)$

$A = 600 - 336$

$A = 264 \text{ units}^2$

20. $A = A_{\text{RECT.}} - A_\triangle$

$A = (12)(6) - \dfrac{1}{2}(12)(6)$

$A = 72 - 36$

$A = 36 \text{ units}^2$

21. In the right $\triangle$, $h = 8$, using the Pythagorean Triple (6, 8, 10).

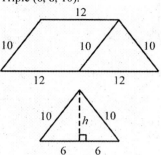

$A = A_{\text{PARALLELOGRAM}} + A_\triangle$

$A = 12 \cdot 8 + \dfrac{1}{2} \cdot 12 \cdot 8$

$A = 96 + 48$

$A = 144 \text{ units}^2$

22. $A = A_{\text{LARGE }\triangle} - A_{\text{SMALL }\triangle}$

Since A and B are midpoints, the small $\triangle$ is a (3, 4, 5) $\triangle$. The larger $\triangle$ is a (6, 8, 10) $\triangle$.

$A = \dfrac{1}{2} \cdot 6 \cdot 8 - \dfrac{1}{2} \cdot 3 \cdot 4$

$A = 24 - 6$

$A = 18 \text{ units}^2$

23. $A = \dfrac{1}{2} bh$

$A = \dfrac{1}{2} \cdot 16 \cdot 24$

$A = 192 \text{ ft}^2$

24.

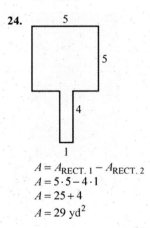

$A = A_{\text{RECT. 1}} - A_{\text{RECT. 2}}$

$A = 5 \cdot 5 - 4 \cdot 1$

$A = 25 + 4$

$A = 29 \text{ yd}^2$

25. $A = \frac{1}{2}bh + bh$

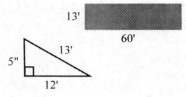

a. $A = \frac{1}{2} \cdot 24 \cdot 5 + 24 \cdot 10$

$A = 300 \text{ ft}^2$

b. 3 gallons

c. \$46.50

26.

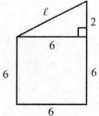

a. $A = 2 \cdot A_{\text{RECT.}}$
$A = 2(13 \times 60)$
$A = 2(780)$
$A = 1560 \text{ ft}^2$

b. 15.6 squares
16 squares to be purchased.

c. $17 \times \$22.50 = \$382.50$

27. $A = A_{\text{TOP}} + A_{\text{BACK}} + 2 \cdot A_{\text{SIDES}}$

$\ell^2 = 6^2 + 2^2$
$\ell^2 = 36 + 4$
$\ell^2 = 40$
$\ell = \sqrt{40} = 2\sqrt{10}$

$A = \left(2\sqrt{10}\right)(12) + 6(12) + 2\left[(6)(6) + \frac{1}{2}(6)(2)\right]$
$A = 24\sqrt{10} + 72 + 2[36 + 6]$
$A = 24\sqrt{10} + 72 + 2[42]$
$A = 24\sqrt{10} + 72 + 84$
$A = \left(156 + 24\sqrt{10}\right) \text{ ft}^2$

28. a. $A = 12 \cdot 10 + 10 \cdot 10$
$A = 120 + 100$
$A = 220 \text{ ft}^2$

b. $\text{Cost} = 220 \times \$3.20$
$\text{Cost} = \$704.00$

29. a. 3 ft = 1 yd ∴ 9 sq ft = 1 sq yd

b. 36 in. = 1 yd ∴ 1296 sq in. = 1 sq yd

30.

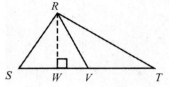

a. If $\overline{RV}$ is the median to $\overline{ST}$, then V is the midpoint of $\overline{ST}$. Therefore, $SV = VT$. Draw the altitude from R to $\overline{ST}$. This altitude length is the same for both $\triangle RSV$ and $\triangle RVT$. The two triangles have the same base length and the same altitude length. Hence, their areas are equal.

b. Since $A_{RSV} = A_{RVT}$ and $A_{RST} = 40.8 \text{ cm}^2$, then $A_{RSV} = 20.4 \text{ cm}^2$.

31. $A_{RYTX} = 24 \text{ cm}^2$

32. $A_{RSTV} = 27 \text{ in}^2$

33. Given: $\triangle ABC$ with midpoints M, N, and P
Explain why $A_{ABC} = 4 \cdot A_{MNP}$

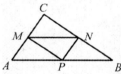

Explanation: $\overline{MN}$ joins the midpoints of $\overline{CA}$ and $\overline{CB}$ so $MN = \frac{1}{2}(AB)$. ∴ $\overline{AP} \cong \overline{PB} \cong \overline{MN}$.

$\overline{PN}$ joins the midpoints of $\overline{CB}$ and $\overline{AB}$ so $PN = \frac{1}{2}(AC)$. ∴ $\overline{AM} \cong \overline{MC} \cong \overline{PN}$.

$\overline{MP}$ joins the midpoints of $\overline{AB}$ and $\overline{AC}$ so $MP = \frac{1}{2}(BC)$. ∴ $\overline{CN} \cong \overline{NB} \cong \overline{MP}$. The four triangles are all $\cong$ by SSS. Therefore, the area of each triangle is the same. Hence the area of the big triangle is the same as four times the area of one of the smaller triangles.

34. Let x and $(x + 2)$ represent the lengths of the legs of the right triangle.

$$\frac{1}{2}x(x + 2) = 3(x + 2)$$

Mult. by 2, $x(x + 2) = 6(x + 2)$

$$x^2 + 2x = 6x + 12$$
$$x^2 - 4x - 12 = 0$$
$$(x - 6)(x + 2) = 0$$

$x - 6 = 0$ or $x + 2 = 0$

$x = 6$ or $x = -2$; reject -2

The legs have lengths of 6 and 8 units.

35. Given: Square $HJKL$ with $LJ = d$.

Prove: $A_{HJKL} = \dfrac{d^2}{2}$

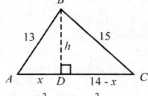

Proof: $A = (LH)(HJ) = s^2$

$s^2 + s^2 = d^2$ by the Pythagorean Theorem.

$2s^2 = d^2$

$s^2 = \dfrac{d^2}{2}$

$\therefore A = \dfrac{d^2}{2}$.

36. Given: Parallelogram $RSTV$ with $\overline{VW} \cong \overline{VT}$

Prove: $A_{RSTV} = (RS)^2$

Proof: $A_{RSTV} = bh = (RS)(VW)$

But $\overline{VW} \cong \overline{VT}$ and $\overline{VT} \cong \overline{RS}$. Then $\overline{VW} \cong \overline{RS}$ so that $VW = RS$. Now $A_{RSTV} = (RS)(RS) = (RS)^2$.

37. $A = \dfrac{1}{2}bh$

$40 = \dfrac{1}{2} \cdot x(x + 2)$

Multiplying by 2,

$80 = x(x + 2)$

$80 = x^2 + 2x$

$0 = x^2 + 2x - 80$

$0 = (x + 10)(x - 8)$

$x + 10 = 0$ or $x - 8 = 0$

$x = -10$ or $x = 8$ in.

Reject $x = -10$.

38. Let x and $(x + 2)$ represent the lengths of the legs of the right triangle.

$$\frac{1}{2}x(x + 2) = 3(x + 2)$$

Mult. by 2, $x(x + 2) = 6(x + 2)$

$$x^2 + 2x = 6x + 12$$
$$x^2 - 4x - 12 = 0$$
$$(x - 6)(x + 2) = 0$$

$x - 6 = 0$ or $x + 2 = 0$

$x = 6$ or $x = -2$; reject -2

The legs have lengths of 6 and 8 units.

39. a. Let $BD = h$.

$$h^2 + x^2 = 13^2 \text{ and}$$
$$h^2 + (14 - x)^2 = 15^2$$

Then $h^2 = 169 - x^2$, so

$$(169 - x^2) + (14 - x)^2 = 225$$
$$169 - x^2 + 196 - 28x + x^2 = 225$$
$$-28x + 365 = 225$$
$$-28x = -140$$
$$x = 5$$

Because $h^2 = 169 - x^2$

$$h^2 = 169 - 25$$
$$h^2 = 144$$
$$h = 12 \text{ in.}$$

b. $A_{ABC} = \dfrac{1}{2}bh$

$A_{ABC} = \dfrac{1}{2} \cdot 14 \cdot 12$

$\therefore A_{ABC} = 84 \text{ in}^2$

40. a. Let $BD = h$.

$$h^2 + x^2 = 10^2 \text{ and}$$
$$h^2 + (21-x)^2 = 17^2$$

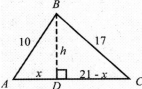

Then $h^2 = 100 - x^2$, so

$$(100 - x^2) + (21-x)^2 = 289$$
$$100 - x^2 + 441 - 42x + x^2 = 289$$
$$-42x + 541 = 289$$
$$-42x = -252$$
$$x = 6$$

Because $h^2 = 100 - x^2$

$$h^2 = 100 - 36$$
$$h^2 = 64$$
$$h = 8 \text{ cm}$$

b. $A_{ABC} = \dfrac{1}{2}bh$

$$A_{ABC} = \dfrac{1}{2} \cdot 21 \cdot 8$$
$$A_{ABC} = 84 \text{ cm}^2$$

41.
$$A_{\text{RECT.}} = bh$$
$$A_{\text{LARGE RECT.}} = (b + 0.2b)(h + 0.3h)$$
$$= (1.2b)(1.3h) = 1.56bh$$
$$A_{\text{LARGE RECT.}} - A_{\text{RECT.}} = 1.56bh - bh = 0.56bh$$
The area is increased by 56%.

42.
$$A_{\text{RECT.}} = bh$$
$$A_{\text{2nd RECT.}} = (b + 0.2b)(h - 0.3h)$$
$$= (1.2b)(0.7h) = 0.84bh$$
$$A_{\text{2nd RECT.}} - A_{\text{RECT.}} = 0.84bh - bh = -0.16bh$$
There is a decrease in area of 16%.

43.

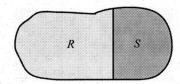

By the Area-Addition Postulate,
$$A_{R \cup S} = A_R + A_S$$
Now $A_{R \cup S}$, A_R, and A_S are all positive numbers.
Let p represent the area of region S, so that
$$A_{R \cup S} = A_R + p.$$
By the definition of inequality, $A_R < A_{R \cup S}$ or
$$A_{R \cup S} > A_R.$$

44.

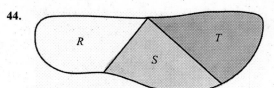

Because $R \cup S$ and T do not overlap,
$$A_{R \cup S \cup T} = A_{R \cup T} + A_T.$$
But $A_{R \cup S} = A_R + A_S$, so that
$$A_{R \cup S \cup T} = A_R + A_S + A_T.$$

45. $(a+b)(c+d) = ac + ad + bc + bd$

46. $(a+b)^2 = (a+b)(a+b)$
$$= a^2 + ab + ba + b^2 \text{ or } a^2 + 2ab + b^2$$

47. Using $c^2 = a^2 + b^2$
$$c^2 = 5^2 + 12^2$$
$$c^2 = 169$$
$$c = 13$$

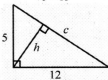

Using the 12" side as base, the length of its

altitude is 5". $\therefore A = \dfrac{1}{2} \cdot 12 \cdot 5$
$$A = 30 \text{ in}^2$$

Also, $A = \dfrac{1}{2}ch$
$$A = \dfrac{1}{2} \cdot 13 \cdot h$$
$$A = \dfrac{13}{2}h$$

Then $\dfrac{13}{2}h = 30$.

Mult. by $\dfrac{2}{13}$, $\dfrac{2}{13} \cdot \dfrac{13}{2}h = \dfrac{2}{13} \cdot 30$
$$h = \dfrac{60}{13} \text{ or } 4\dfrac{8}{13} \text{ in.}$$

48. Let h = length of the altitude to the 20 cm side; and H = length of altitude to the 13 cm side. The area is unique, so that
$$\dfrac{1}{2} \cdot 21 \cdot 12 = \dfrac{1}{2} \cdot 20 \cdot h = \dfrac{1}{2} \cdot 13 \cdot H$$
$$126 = 10h = \dfrac{13}{2}H$$

$10h = 126$ and $\dfrac{13}{2}H = 126$

$h = 12.6$ and $H = \dfrac{2}{13}(126)$

$h = 12\dfrac{3}{5} \text{ cm}$ and $H = \dfrac{252}{13} \text{ or } 19\dfrac{5}{13} \text{ cm}$

49.

$A_{MNPQ} = (QR)(MN)$
But $MN = QP = 12$
$\therefore A_{MNPQ} = 6(12) = 72$ units^2

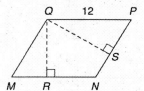

$A_{MNPQ} = (QS)(PN)$
But $PN = QM = 9$ so
$A_{MNPQ} = (QS)9$
$72 = 9(QS)$
$QS = 8$ units

50.

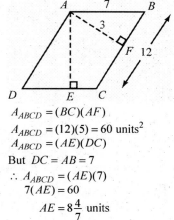

$A_{ABCD} = (BC)(AF)$
$A_{ABCD} = (12)(5) = 60$ units^2
$A_{ABCD} = (AE)(DC)$
But $DC = AB = 7$
$\therefore A_{ABCD} = (AE)(7)$
$7(AE) = 60$
$AE = 8\frac{4}{7}$ units

51. $xy = 48 \rightarrow y = \dfrac{48}{x}$

$P = 2x + 2y$

$P = 2x + 2\left(\dfrac{48}{x}\right)$

$P = 2x + \dfrac{96}{x}$

52. $2x + 2y = 32 \rightarrow x + y = 32 \rightarrow y = 16 - x$

$A = xy$

$A = x(16 - x)$

$A = 16x - x^2$

53. Let each side length of the square = x.

$\triangle ADG \sim \triangle FEB$

$\dfrac{AD}{DG} = \dfrac{FE}{EB}$

$\dfrac{6}{x} = \dfrac{x}{8}$

$x^2 = 48$

$A_{DEFG} = 48$ un^2

54. 1st)

$\dfrac{ST}{RT} = \dfrac{SV}{RV}$

$\dfrac{6}{9} = \dfrac{SV}{RV}$

$\dfrac{2}{3} = \dfrac{SV}{RV}$

$2 \cdot RV = 3 \cdot SV$

$RV = \dfrac{3}{2} \cdot SV$

2nd) Let h represent the $\perp$ distance from T to $\overline{RS}$ or the extension of $\overline{RS}$. This is the height of $\triangle SVT$ with base $\overline{SV}$ and for $\triangle TVR$ with base $\overline{VR}$.

$A_{RST} = A_{SVT} + A_{TVR}$

$25 = \dfrac{1}{2} \cdot SV \cdot h + \dfrac{1}{2} \cdot RV \cdot h$

$25 = \dfrac{1}{2} \cdot SV \cdot h + \dfrac{1}{2} \cdot \dfrac{3}{2} \cdot SV \cdot h$

$25 = \dfrac{1}{2} \cdot SV \cdot h + \dfrac{3}{4} \cdot SV \cdot h$

$100 = 2 \cdot SV \cdot h + 3 \cdot SV \cdot h$

$100 = 5 \cdot SV \cdot h$

$20 = SV \cdot h$

$A_{SVT} = \dfrac{1}{2} \cdot SV \cdot h$

$A_{SVT} = \dfrac{1}{2} \cdot 20 = 10$ m^2

55. a. 10

   b. 26

   c. 18

   d. No

56. a. 12

   b. 20

   c. 16

   d. Yes

SECTION 8.2: Perimeter and Area of Polygons

1. $c = 13$ using the Pythagorean Triple (5, 12, 13).

$P = a + b + c$
$P = 5 + 12 + 13$
$P = 30$ in.

2. Using the Pythagorean Triple (6, 8, 10), $AB = 10$.

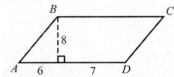

$P = 2b + 2s$
$P = 2(13) + 2(10)$
$P = 26 + 20$
$P = 46$ in.

3.

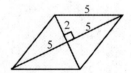

Let the length of each side of the rhombus be s.

Then $s^2 = 2^2 + 5^2$
$s^2 = 4 + 25$
$s^2 = 29$
$s = \sqrt{29}$

In turn, $P = 4\sqrt{29}$ m.

4.

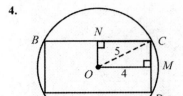

Using the Pythagorean Theorem, $CM = 3$; also $NC = 4$. The inscribed parallelogram must be a rectangle.

$CD = 2(CM) = 2(3) = 6$ and
$BC = 2(NC) = 2(4) = 8$.

$\therefore P_{ABCD} = 2b + 2h$
$P_{ABCD} = 2(8) + 2(6)$
$P_{ABCD} = 16 + 12$
$P_{ABCD} = 28$ units.

5.

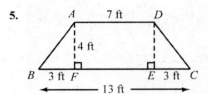

Draw the altitude from D to $\overline{BC}$. $FE = 7$ and $BF = ED = 3$. $AB = DC = 5$. Therefore, the perimeter of isosceles trapezoid $ADCB$ with altitudes $\overline{AF}$ and $\overline{DE}$

$P = 7 + 5 + 5 + 13 = 30$ ft.

6.

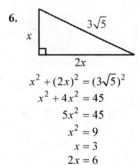

$x^2 + (2x)^2 = (3\sqrt{5})^2$
$x^2 + 4x^2 = 45$
$5x^2 = 45$
$x^2 = 9$
$x = 3$
$2x = 6$

$P = 3 + 6 + 3\sqrt{5}$
$P = 9 + 3\sqrt{5}$ units

7.

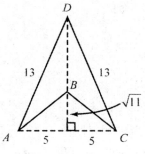

$(AB)^2 = 5^2 + (\sqrt{11})^2$
$(AB)^2 = 25 + 11$
$(AB)^2 = 36$
$AB = 6$
$P = 2(AD) + 2(AB)$
$P = 2(13) + 2(6)$
$P = 26 + 12$
$P = 38$ units

8.

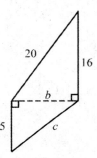

In the upper rt. $\triangle$,
$b^2 + 16^2 = 20^2$
$b^2 + 256 = 400$
$b^2 = 144$
$b = 12$
Now, $b^2 + 5^2 = c^2$
$144 + 25 = c^2$
$169 = c^2$
$c = \sqrt{169}$
$c = 13$
Now $P = 5 + 20 + 16 + 13$
$P = 54$ cm

9. $A = \sqrt{s(s-a)(s-b)(s-c)}$ where
$a = 13, b = 14, c = 15$ and
$s = \frac{1}{2}(13 + 14 + 15)$
$s = \frac{1}{2}(42) = 21$ ∴
$A = \sqrt{21(21-13)(21-14)(21-15)}$
$A = \sqrt{21(8)(7)(6)}$
$A = \sqrt{(3 \cdot 7) \cdot (2 \cdot 4) \cdot 7 \cdot (2 \cdot 3)}$
$A = \sqrt{2^2 \cdot 3^2 \cdot 2^2 \cdot 7^2}$
$A = 2 \cdot 3 \cdot 2 \cdot 7$
$A = 84$ in^2

10. $A = \sqrt{s(s-a)(s-b)(s-c)}$ where
$a = 10, b = 17, c = 21$ and
$s = \frac{1}{2}(10 + 17 + 21)$
$s = \frac{1}{2}(48) = 24$ ∴
$A = \sqrt{24(24-10)(24-17)(24-21)}$
$A = \sqrt{24(14)(7)(3)}$
$A = \sqrt{(2^3 \cdot 3) \cdot (2 \cdot 7)(7)(3)}$
$A = \sqrt{2^4 \cdot 3^2 \cdot 7^2}$
$A = 2^2 \cdot 3 \cdot 7$
$A = 84$ cm^2

11. $s = \frac{1}{2}(a + b + c + d)$
$s = \frac{1}{2}(39 + 52 + 25 + 60)$
$s = 88$
$A = \sqrt{(s-a)(s-b)(s-c)(s-d)}$
$A = \sqrt{(88-39)(88-52)(88-25)(88-60)}$
$A = \sqrt{(49)(36)(63)(28)}$
$A = \sqrt{7^2 \cdot 6^2 \cdot (3^2 \cdot 7)(2^2 \cdot 7)}$
$A = 7 \cdot 6 \cdot 3 \cdot 2 \cdot 7$
$A = 1764$ mm^2

12. $s = \frac{1}{2}(a + b + c + d)$
$s = \frac{1}{2}(6 + 7 + 2 + 9)$
$s = 12$
$A = \sqrt{(s-a)(s-b)(s-c)(s-d)}$
$A = \sqrt{(12-6)(12-7)(12-2)(12-9)}$
$A = \sqrt{(6)(5)(10)(3)}$
$A = \sqrt{2^2 \cdot 3^2 \cdot 5^2}$
$A = 2 \cdot 3 \cdot 5$
$A = 30$ cm^2

13. $A = \frac{1}{2}h(b_1 + b_2)$
$A = \frac{1}{2} \cdot 4(7 + 13)$
$A = \frac{1}{2} \cdot 4(20)$
$A = 40$ ft^2

14. $A = \frac{1}{2}h(b_1 + b_2)$
$A = \frac{1}{2} \cdot 15(12 + 20)$
$A = \frac{1}{2} \cdot 15(32)$
$A = 240$ m^2

15. $ABCD$ is a rhombus

$$A = \frac{1}{2}d_1 \cdot d_2$$

$$A = \frac{1}{2}(10)(16)$$

$$A = 80 \text{ units}^2$$

16. $\overline{BC} \cong \overline{CD}$ and $\overline{BC} \cong \overline{AD}$

$\therefore AD = 6$ while its altitude measures 5 units.

$$A = 5 \cdot 6$$

$$A = 30 \text{ units}^2$$

17.

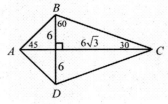

$$A = \frac{1}{2} \cdot d_1 \cdot d_2$$

$$A = \frac{1}{2} \cdot 12\left(6 + 6\sqrt{3}\right)$$

$$A = 6\left(6 + 6\sqrt{3}\right)$$

$$A = \left(36 + 36\sqrt{3}\right) \text{ units}^2$$

18.

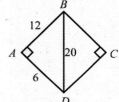

$$12^2 + b^2 = 20^2$$

$$144 + b^2 = 400$$

$$b^2 = 256$$

$$b = 16$$

$$A_{ABCD} = 2 \cdot A_{ABD}$$

$$= 2\left(\frac{1}{2} \cdot 12 \cdot 16\right)$$

$$= 192 \text{ units}^2$$

19. Let x = length of second side of triangle.

$2x$ = length of first side of triangle.

$x + 12$ = length of third side of triangle.

$$P = a + b + c$$

$$76 = x + 2x + (x + 12)$$

$$76 = 4x + 12$$

$$4x = 64$$

$$x = 16 \text{ in.}$$

$$2x = 32 \text{ in.}$$

$$x + 12 = 28 \text{ in.}$$

20.
$$A = \frac{1}{2}bh$$

$$72 = \frac{1}{2} \cdot 8 \cdot h$$

$$72 = 4 \cdot h$$

$$h = 18 \text{ in.}$$

21. $A = \frac{1}{2}h\left(b_1 + b_2\right)$

$$96 = \frac{1}{2} \cdot 8(b + 9)$$

$$96 = 4(b + 9)$$

$$96 = 4b + 36$$

$$60 = 4b$$

$$b = 15 \text{ cm}$$

22.
$$s^2 - 4s = 32$$

$$s^2 - 4s - 32 = 0$$

$$(s - 8)(s + 4) = 0$$

$$s - 8 = 0 \quad \text{or} \quad s + 4 = 0$$

$$s = 8 \quad \text{or} \quad s = -4; \text{ reject } s = -4$$

23. **a.** $\dfrac{A_1}{A_2} = \left(\dfrac{s_1}{s_2}\right)^2 = \left(\dfrac{3}{2}\right)^2 = \dfrac{9}{4}$

b. $\dfrac{A_1}{A_2} = \left(\dfrac{s_1}{s_2}\right)^2 = \left(\dfrac{2}{1}\right)^2 = \dfrac{4}{1}$ or 4

24. **a.** $\dfrac{A_1}{A_2} = \left(\dfrac{s_1}{s_2}\right)^2 = \left(\dfrac{2}{5}\right)^2 = \dfrac{4}{25}$

b. $\dfrac{A_1}{A_2} = \left(\dfrac{s_1}{s_2}\right)^2 = \left(\dfrac{3}{2}\right)^2 = \dfrac{9}{4}$

25. Using Heron's Formula, the semiperimeter is $\frac{1}{2}(3s)$ or $\frac{3s}{2}$. Then

$$A = \sqrt{\frac{3s}{2}\left(\frac{3s}{2} - s\right)\left(\frac{3s}{2} - s\right)\left(\frac{3s}{2} - s\right)}$$

$$A = \sqrt{\frac{3s}{2}\left(\frac{s}{2}\right)\left(\frac{s}{2}\right)\left(\frac{s}{2}\right)}$$

$$A = \sqrt{\frac{3s^4}{16}} = \frac{\sqrt{3} \cdot \sqrt{s^4}}{\sqrt{16}}$$

$$A = \frac{s^2\sqrt{3}}{4}$$

26. Using Heron's Formula, the semiperimeter is

$$\frac{1}{2}(2a + 2s) = a + s$$

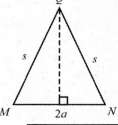

$$A = \sqrt{(a+s)((a+s)-s)((a+s)-s)((a+s)-2a)}$$
$$A = \sqrt{(a+s)a \cdot a \cdot (s-a)}$$
$$A = \sqrt{a^2(s+a)(s-a)}$$
$$A = \sqrt{a^2} \cdot \sqrt{s^2 - a^2}$$
$$A = a\sqrt{s^2 - a^2}$$

27. $OA = 5$
$AC = 10$
$\angle$s B and D are right angles (inscribed in semicircles.)

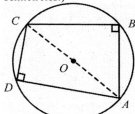

In rt. $\triangle ABC$, $(AC)^2 = (AB)^2 + (BC)^2$
$$10^2 = (AB)^2 + 6^2$$
$$100 = (AB)^2 + 36$$
$$(AB)^2 = 64$$
$$AB = 8$$

In rt. $\triangle ADC$, $(AC)^2 = (AD)^2 + (CD)^2$
$$10^2 = (AD)^2 + 4^2$$
$$100 = (AD)^2 + 16$$
$$(AD)^2 = 84$$
$$AB = \sqrt{84} = 2\sqrt{21}$$

Now $A_{ABCD} = A_{ABC} + A_{ADC}$
$$A_{ABCD} = \frac{1}{2}(6)(8) + \frac{1}{2}(4)(2\sqrt{21})$$
$$A_{ABCD} = (24 + 4\sqrt{21}) \text{ units}^2$$

28. Using the Pythagorean Theorem, the altitude of trapezoid $WXTV$ is 4.

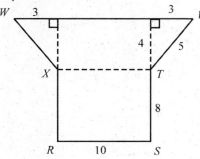

$$A_{RSTVWX} = A_{RECT} + A_{TRAP}$$
$$A_{RSTVWX} = (8)(10) + \frac{1}{2} \cdot 4(10 + 16)$$
$$A_{RSTVWX} = 80 + 2(26)$$
$$A_{RSTVWX} = 80 + 52 = 132 \text{ units}^2$$

29. In $\triangle ABC$, $AC = 13$ (by using the Pythagorean Theorem). Now $EC = 12$.

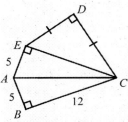

Using the 45°-45°-90° relationship,
$$DE \cdot \sqrt{2} = 12$$
$$DE = \frac{12}{\sqrt{2}} \cdot \frac{\sqrt{2}}{\sqrt{2}} = \frac{12\sqrt{2}}{2} = 6\sqrt{2}$$
$\therefore DC = 6\sqrt{2}$ (since $\overline{DC} \cong \overline{DE}$)
$$A_{ABCDE} = A_{ABC} + A_{AEC} + A_{EDC}$$
$$A_{ABCDE} = \frac{1}{2} \cdot 5 \cdot 12 + \frac{1}{2} \cdot 5 \cdot 12 + \frac{1}{2} \cdot (6\sqrt{2})(6\sqrt{2})$$
$$A_{ABCDE} = 30 + 30 + \frac{1}{2}(36)(2)$$
$$A_{ABCDE} = 30 + 30 + 36 = 96 \text{ units}^2$$

30. Using the 45°-45°-90° triangle,

$VT = TS = WV = WR = 8$

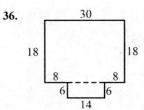

$A_{RSTVW} = A_{RSV} + A_{STV} + A_{VWR}$

$A_{RSTVW} = \dfrac{(8\sqrt{2})^2}{4}\sqrt{3} + \dfrac{1}{2}\cdot 8 \cdot 8 + \dfrac{1}{2}\cdot 8 \cdot 8$

$A_{RSTVW} = \dfrac{128}{4}\sqrt{3} + 32 + 32$

$A_{RSTVW} = (32\sqrt{3} + 64) \text{ units}^2$

31. $A = bh$ and $P = 2b + 2h$

$bh = 48$ and $2b + 2h = 28$

$b + h = 14$

$b = 14 - h$

$\therefore bh = 48$ becomes $(14 - h)\cdot h = 48$

$14h - h^2 = 48$

$h^2 - 14h + 48 = 0$

$(h - 6)(h - 8) = 0$

$h - 6 = 0$ or $h - 8 = 0$

$h = 6$ or $h = 8$

If $h = 6$, then $b = 8$ and vice versa. The dimensions of the garden are 6 yd by 8 yd.

32. $a + b + c = 12$

$a + b + 5 = 12$

$a + b = 7$

$b = 7 - a$

$a^2 + b^2 = 5^2$

$a^2 + b^2 = 25$

$a^2 + (7 - a)^2 = 25$

$a^2 + 49 - 14a + a^2 = 25$

$2a^2 - 14a + 24 = 0$

$2(a^2 - 7a + 12) = 0$

$2(a - 3)(a - 4) = 0$

$a - 3 = 0$ or $a - 4 = 0$

$a = 3$ or $a = 4$

The lengths of the legs of the rt. △ are 3 m and 4 m.

33. a. $P = 2b + 2h$

$P = 2(245) + 2(140)$

$P = 490 + 280$

$P = 770$ ft

b. Cost = ($0.59)(770)

Cost = $454.30

34. a. $3(x) + 2(2x) = 770$

$3x + 4x = 770$

$4x = 770$

$x = 100$

$2x = 220$

The partitioned rectangle is 110 ft by 220 ft.

b. $A = bh$

$A = 110 \times 220 = 24{,}200 \text{ ft}^2$

35. $A = A_{\text{RECT. }\#1} + A_{\text{RECT. }\#2}$

$A = (18)(30) + (6)(14)$

$A = 540 + 84$

$A = 624 \text{ ft}^2$

36.

$P = 30 + 2(18) + 2(8) + 2(6) + 14$

$P = 30 + 36 + 16 + 12 + 14$

$P = 108$ ft

37. The largest area occurs when the rectangle is a square with sides of length 10 inches.

38. The smallest perimeter occurs when the rectangle is a square with each side of length 6 in. The smallest perimeter is 24 in.

39. The 4 ≅ ∆s have sides of length 5, 12, 13.

    a. Perimeter = 52 units

    b. Area = 169 units^2

40. The 4 ≅ ∆s have sides of length 8, 15, 17.

    a. Perimeter = 68 units

    b. Area = 289 units^2

41.

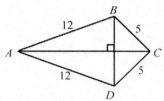

Using Pythagorean Triple (5, 12, 13), $AC = 13$.

$A_{\triangle ABC} = \sqrt{s(s-a)(s-b)(s-c)}$ where

$a = 5$, $b = 12$, $c = 13$ and

$s = \dfrac{1}{2}(5+12+13)$

$s = \dfrac{1}{2}(30) = 15 \therefore$

$A_{\triangle ABC} = \sqrt{15(15-5)(15-12)(15-13)}$

$A_{\triangle ABC} = \sqrt{15(10)(3)(2)}$

$A_{\triangle ABC} = \sqrt{(3 \cdot 5) \cdot (2 \cdot 5) \cdot 3 \cdot 2}$

$A_{\triangle ABC} = \sqrt{2^2 \cdot 3^2 \cdot 5^2}$

$A_{\triangle ABC} = 2 \cdot 3 \cdot 5$

$A_{\triangle ABC} = 30$ in^2

Since $A_{\triangle ABC} \cong A_{\triangle ADC}$, then

$A_{ABCD} = A_{\triangle ABC} + A_{\triangle ADC}$

      $= 30 + 30 = 60$ in^2

42.

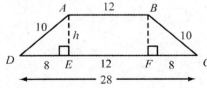

$AB = EF = 12$

$DE = FC = 8$

Using Pythagorean Triple (6, 8, 10),

$AE = BF = h = 6$.

$A_{\text{TRAP } ABCD} = A_{\triangle ADE} + A_{\triangle BCF} + A_{\square ABFE}$

$A_{\text{TRAP } ABCD} = \dfrac{1}{2}(8)(6) + \dfrac{1}{2}(8)(6) + 12(6)$

$A_{\text{TRAP } ABCD} = 24 + 24 + 72$

$A_{\text{TRAP } ABCD} = 120$ cm^2

43. **a.** No

    b. Yes

44. **a.** Yes

    b. No

45. The area of a trapezoid $= \dfrac{1}{2}h(b_1 + b_2)$

             $= h \cdot \dfrac{1}{2}(b_1 + b_2)$

             $= h \cdot m$

since the median, m, of a trapezoid $= \dfrac{1}{2}(b_1 + b_2)$.

46. $A = h \cdot m = 4.2(6.5) = 27.3$ m^2

47. $A = h \cdot m = 5\dfrac{1}{3} \cdot 2\dfrac{1}{4} = \dfrac{16}{3} \cdot \dfrac{9}{4} = 12$ ft^2

48. A square has ≅ diagonals that are ⊥.

    $\therefore A_{\text{SQUARE}} = \dfrac{1}{2}d_1 \cdot d_2$ or $\dfrac{1}{2}d^2$.

49. $A = \dfrac{1}{2}d^2 = \dfrac{1}{2}(\sqrt{10})^2 = \dfrac{1}{2}(10) = 5$ in^2

50. $A = \dfrac{1}{2}d^2 = \dfrac{1}{2}(14.5)^2 = 105.125$ cm^2

51. $\qquad A_{\text{TRAP}} = A_{\text{BIG }\triangle} - A_{\text{SMALL }\triangle}$

    $\dfrac{1}{2} \cdot h(b_1 + b_2) = 24 - 6$

    $\dfrac{1}{2} \cdot h(5+10) = 18$

    So $h = 2.4$.

52. Use the Given to draw the described trapezoid.

Also, draw $\overline{OE} \perp \overline{AB}$. EB = 3; OB = 5

$\therefore$ OE = 4.

$A = \dfrac{1}{2}h(b_1 + b_2)$

$A = \dfrac{1}{2} \cdot 4(6+10)$

$A = 2(16)$

$A = 32$ units^2

53. Draw the figure described in the Given.

$A_{VWSY} = b \cdot h$

$16 = x \cdot 8$

$x = 2; VW = 2$ units

SECTION 8.3: Regular Polygons and Area

1. a. $A = s^2 = (3.5)^2 = 12.25$ cm^2

b. If $a = 4.7$, then $s = 9.4$. $A = (9.4)^2 = 88.36$ in^2

2. a. $14.8 = 4s \rightarrow s = 3.7$ $A = (3.7)^2 = 13.69$ cm^2

b. $r = 4\sqrt{2} \rightarrow s = 8$ $A = 8^2 = 64$ in^2

3. a. $A = \dfrac{s^2}{4}\sqrt{3} = \dfrac{(2.5)^2}{4}\sqrt{3} = 1.5625\sqrt{3}$ m^2

b. If $a = 3$, then $s = 6\sqrt{3}$. $A = \dfrac{(6\sqrt{3})^2}{4}\sqrt{3} = 27\sqrt{3}$ in^2

4. a. If $P = 24.6$, then $s = 8.2$.

$A = \dfrac{s^2}{4}\sqrt{3} = \dfrac{(8.2)^2}{4}\sqrt{3} = 16.81\sqrt{3}$ cm^2

b. If $r = 4$, then $s = 4\sqrt{3}$. $A = \dfrac{(4\sqrt{3})^2}{4}\sqrt{3} = 12\sqrt{3}$ in^2

5. $c = \dfrac{360}{n}$

$30 = \dfrac{360}{n}$

$n = 12$; $P = 12(5.7) = 68.4$ in.

6. If each int. $\angle = 135$, then each ext. $\angle = 45$.

Ext. $\angle = \dfrac{360}{n} \rightarrow 45 = \dfrac{360}{n}$

$n = 8$; $P = 8(4.2) = 33.6$ cm.

7. Let $r =$ the length of the radius of the circle.

$10 = \dfrac{1}{2}\sqrt{3} \rightarrow 20 = r\sqrt{3}$

$r = \dfrac{20}{\sqrt{3}} = \dfrac{20\sqrt{3}}{3}$ cm

8. $r = 6\sqrt{3}$ in.

9. Regular hexagon

10. Square

11. Square

12. $A = \dfrac{1}{2}aP$

$P = \dfrac{1}{2}aP$

$1 = \dfrac{1}{2}a$

$a = 2$

13. $A = \dfrac{1}{2}aP$

$A = \dfrac{1}{2}(3.2)(25.6)$

$A = 40.96$ cm^2

14. $A = \dfrac{1}{2}aP$

$A = \dfrac{1}{2}(3.2)(19.2\sqrt{3})$

$A = 30.72\sqrt{3}$ cm^2

15. $A = \dfrac{1}{2}aP$

$A = \dfrac{1}{2}(4.6)(27.6\sqrt{3})$

$A = 63.48\sqrt{3}$ in.^{2}

16. $A = \dfrac{1}{2}aP$

$A = \dfrac{1}{2}(8.2)(65.6)$

$A = 268.96$ ft^2

17. $A = \frac{1}{2}aP = \frac{1}{2}(5.2)(37.5) = 97.5 \text{ cm}^2$

18. $A = \frac{1}{2}aP = \frac{1}{2}(6.5)(47) = 152.75 \text{ in}^2$

19. $A = \frac{1}{2}aP = \frac{1}{2}(9.8)(64.8) = 317.52 \text{ in}^2$

20. $A = \frac{1}{2}aP = \frac{1}{2}(7.9)(5) = 205.4 \text{ ft}^2$

21.

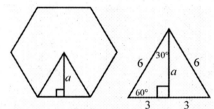

The length of the apothem is $a = 3\sqrt{3}$ (using the $30°$-$60°$-$90°$ relationship).

$A = \frac{1}{2}aP$ becomes

$A = \frac{1}{2} \cdot 3\sqrt{3} \cdot 36$

$A = 54\sqrt{3} \text{ cm}^2$

22. If $a = 5$, then the length of the side of the square is 10.

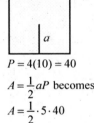

$P = 4(10) = 40$

$A = \frac{1}{2}aP$ becomes

$A = \frac{1}{2} \cdot 5 \cdot 40$

$A = 100 \text{ cm}^2$

23.

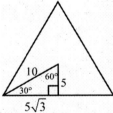

Given the radius length 10, the apothem is $a = 5$.

Because each side measures $10\sqrt{3}$, the perimeter is $30\sqrt{3}$.

$A = \frac{1}{2}aP$ becomes

$A = \frac{1}{2} \cdot 5 \cdot 30\sqrt{3}$

$A = 75\sqrt{3} \text{ in}^2$

24.

$P = 5(8.9) = 44.5$

$A = \frac{1}{2}aP$

$A = \frac{1}{2} \cdot 6 \cdot (44.5)$

$A = 133.5 \text{ in}^2$

25.

$\dfrac{a}{s} = \dfrac{6}{5} \rightarrow 6s = 5a \rightarrow s = \dfrac{5}{6}a$

$P = 8\left(\dfrac{5}{6}a\right) = \dfrac{20}{3}a = \dfrac{20}{3}(15) = 100$

$A = \dfrac{1}{2}P$

$A = \dfrac{1}{2}(15)(100)$

$A = 750 \text{ cm}^2$

26. $\dfrac{a}{s} = \dfrac{15}{8}$

$8a = 15s \rightarrow a = \dfrac{15}{8}s$

$a = \dfrac{15}{8}(12) = 22.5$

$P = 12(12) = 144$

$A = \dfrac{1}{2}aP$

$A = \dfrac{1}{2}(22.5)(144)$

$A = 1620 \text{ ft}^2$

27.　$\dfrac{a}{s} = \dfrac{15}{8}$

$$15s = 8a \rightarrow s = \dfrac{8}{15}a$$

$$s = \dfrac{8}{15}(12) = 6.4$$

$$P = 12(6.4) = 76.8$$

$$A = \dfrac{1}{2}aP$$

$$A = \dfrac{1}{2}(12)(76.8)$$

$$A = 460.8 \text{ ft}^2$$

28.　$\dfrac{a}{s} = \dfrac{6}{5}$

$$5a = 6s \rightarrow a = \dfrac{6}{5}s$$

$$a = \dfrac{6}{5}(15) = 18$$

$$P = 8(15) = 120$$

$$A = \dfrac{1}{2}aP$$

$$A = \dfrac{1}{2}(18)(120)$$

$$A = 1080 \text{ ft}^2$$

29.　$P = 12(2) = 24$
$A = \dfrac{1}{2}aP$
$A = \dfrac{1}{2}(2 + \sqrt{3})24$
$A = 12(2 + \sqrt{3})$
$A = (24 + 12\sqrt{3}) \text{ in}^2$

30.　$P = 8 \cdot 8(\sqrt{2} - 1)$
$P = 64(\sqrt{2} - 1)$
$A = \dfrac{1}{2}aP$
$A = \dfrac{1}{2} \cdot 4 \cdot 64(\sqrt{2} - 1)$
$A = 128(\sqrt{2} - 1)$
$A = (128\sqrt{2} - 128) \text{ cm}^2$

31.

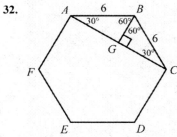

Where r is the radius of the circle, the side of the circumscribed square is $2r$ and the side of the inscribed square is $r\sqrt{2}$.

$$\dfrac{A_{ABCD}}{A_{EFGH}} = \dfrac{(2r)^2}{(r\sqrt{2})^2} = \dfrac{2}{1}$$

32.

Using the 30°-60°-90° relationship,
$AG = GC = 3\sqrt{3}$
$\therefore AC = 2(3\sqrt{3}) = 6\sqrt{3}$

Draw $\overline{FD}$.

$$A_{ACDF} = 6\left(6\sqrt{3}\right) = 36\sqrt{3}$$

$$A_{EFD} = A_{ABC} = \dfrac{1}{2}\left(6\sqrt{3}\right)(3) = 9\sqrt{3}$$

$$A_{ACDEF} = 36\sqrt{3} + 9\sqrt{3} = 45\sqrt{3} \text{ units}^2$$

33. In octagon RSTUVWXY draw $\overline{SP} \perp \overline{RU}$

Δ RPS is an isosceles right Δ.

$\therefore$ SP $= \dfrac{4}{\sqrt{2}} \cdot \dfrac{\sqrt{2}}{\sqrt{2}} = \dfrac{4\sqrt{2}}{2} = 2\sqrt{2}$

a, the apothem, $= 2\sqrt{2} + 2$ and RU $= 4 + 4\sqrt{2}$

$A_{RYXWVU} = A_{OCTAGON} - A_{RSTU}$

$\quad = \dfrac{1}{2} aP - \dfrac{1}{2}(b_1 + b_2)$

$\quad = \dfrac{1}{2}\left(2\sqrt{2}+2\right)(32) - \dfrac{1}{2}\left(2\sqrt{2}\right)\left(4+4\sqrt{2}+4\right)$

$\quad = \left(\sqrt{2}+1\right)(32) - \sqrt{2}\left(8+4\sqrt{2}\right)$

$A_{RYXWVU} = 32\sqrt{2} + 32 - 8\sqrt{2} - 8$

$A_{RYXWVU} = 24\sqrt{2} + 24 \text{ units}^2$

34. $A_{SQUARE} < A_{OCTAGON} < A_{CIRCLE}$

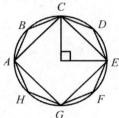

The side of the square measures $\left(\dfrac{7}{2}\sqrt{2}\right)\sqrt{2} = 7$.

$A_{SQUARE} = s^2 = 7^2 = 49$

$A_{CIRCLE} = \pi r^2$

$\quad = \pi\left(\dfrac{7}{2}\sqrt{2}\right)^2$

$\quad = \dfrac{22}{7} \cdot \dfrac{49}{4} \cdot 2$

$\quad = 77$

The area of the octagon is between 49 cm^2 and 77 cm^2.

35. $A_{RSTVQ} = \dfrac{1}{2} P = \dfrac{1}{2}(12)(50)$

Let h = height of ΔPVQ

$h = \sqrt{10^2 - (4.1)^2}$

$h = \sqrt{100 - 16.81}$

$h = \sqrt{83.19}$

$h \approx 9.12$

$A_{PRS} = A_{PVQ} \approx \dfrac{1}{2}(8.2)(9.12) \approx 37.39$

$A_{PQR} = \dfrac{s^2}{4}\sqrt{3} = \dfrac{10^2}{4}\sqrt{3} = 25\sqrt{3} \approx 43.25$

$A_{VPST} = A_{RSTVQ} - \left(A_{PQR} + A_{PVQ} + A_{PRS}\right)$

$A_{VPST} \approx 300 - (43.25 + 37.39 + 37.39)$

$A_{VPST} \approx 182 \text{ units}^2$

36. Draw the pentagon as described. Now draw the circumscribed circle. $\angle RFQ \cong \angle VTQ$ because inscribed angles intercepting the same arc are congruent. $\angle RFQ \cong \angle TFV$ (Vertical angles are congruent.) Therefore, $\Delta RFQ \sim \Delta TFV$. It follows by CSSTP that

$\dfrac{FQ}{FR} = \dfrac{VF}{TF}$ and $VF \cdot FR = TF \cdot FQ$

37. In octagon RSTUVWXY draw $\overline{SP} \perp \overline{RU}$

$\triangle$ RPS is an isosceles right $\triangle$.

$\therefore$ SP $= \dfrac{4}{\sqrt{2}} \cdot \dfrac{\sqrt{2}}{\sqrt{2}} = \dfrac{4\sqrt{2}}{2} = 2\sqrt{2}$

a, the apothem, $= 2\sqrt{2} + 2$ and RU $= 4 + 4\sqrt{2}$

$A_{RYXWVU} = A_{OCTAGON} - A_{RSTU}$

$= \dfrac{1}{2}aP - \dfrac{1}{2}\left(b_1 + b_2\right)$

$= \dfrac{1}{2}\left(2\sqrt{2} + 2\right)(32) - \dfrac{1}{2}\left(2\sqrt{2}\right)\left(4 + 4\sqrt{2} + 4\right)$

$= \left(\sqrt{2} + 1\right)(32) - \sqrt{2}\left(8 + 4\sqrt{2}\right)$

$A_{RYXWVU} = 32\sqrt{2} + 32 - 8\sqrt{2} - 8$

$A_{RYXWVU} = 24\sqrt{2} + 24 \text{ units}^2$

SECTION 8.4: Circumference and Area of a Circle

1. $C = 2\pi r \qquad A = \pi r^2$
$C = 2 \cdot \pi \cdot 8 \qquad A = \pi \cdot 8^2$
$C = 16\pi \text{ cm} \qquad A = 64\pi \text{ cm}^2$

2. If $d = 10''$, then $r = 5''$.
$C = 2\pi r \qquad A = \pi r^2$
$C = 2 \cdot \pi \cdot 5 \qquad A = \pi \cdot 5^2$
$C = 10\pi \text{ in} \qquad A = 25\pi \text{ in}^2$

3. $C = 2\pi r \qquad A = \pi r^2$
$C = 2 \cdot \dfrac{22}{7} \cdot \dfrac{21}{2} \quad A = \dfrac{22}{7} \cdot \dfrac{21}{2} \cdot \dfrac{21}{2}$
$C = 66 \text{ in.} \qquad A = \dfrac{693}{2} = 346\dfrac{1}{2} \text{ in}^2$

4. If $d = 20$cm, then $r = 10$cm.
$C = 2\pi r \qquad A = \pi r^2$
$C = 2(3.14)(10) \quad A = (3.14)(10)^2$
$C = 62.8 \text{ cm} \qquad A = 314 \text{ cm}^2$

5. a. $C = 2\pi r$
$44\pi = 2\pi r$
$\dfrac{44\pi}{2\pi} = r$
$r = 22 \text{ in.}$
$\therefore d = 44 \text{ in.}$

    b. $C = 2\pi r$
$60\pi = 2\pi r$
$\dfrac{60\pi}{2\pi} = r$
$r = 30 \text{ ft}$
$\therefore d = 60 \text{ ft}$

6. a. $C = 2\pi r$
$88\pi = 2 \cdot \dfrac{22}{7} r$
$88 = \dfrac{44}{7} r$
$\dfrac{7}{44} \cdot 88 = \dfrac{7}{44} \cdot \dfrac{44}{7} r$
$r = 14 \text{ in.}$
$\therefore d = 28 \text{ in.}$

    b. $C = 2\pi r$
$157 = 2(3.14)r$
$157 = 6.28r$
$\dfrac{157}{6.28} = r$
$r = 25 \text{ m}$
$\therefore d = 50 \text{ m}$

7. a. $A = \pi r^2$
$25\pi = \pi r^2$
$r^2 = 25$
$r = 5 \text{ in.}$
$\therefore d = 10 \text{ in.}$

    b. $A = \pi r^2$
$2.25\pi = \pi r^2$
$r^2 = 2.25$
$r = 1.5 \text{ cm}$
$\therefore d = 3.0 \text{ cm}$

8. a. $A = \pi r^2$
$36\pi = \pi r^2$
$r^2 = 36$
$r = 6 \text{ m}$
$C = 2\pi r$
$C = 2 \cdot \pi \cdot 6$
$C = 12\pi \text{ m}$

    b. $A = \pi r^2$
$6.25\pi = \pi r^2$
$r^2 = 6.25$
$r = 2.5 \text{ ft}$
$C = 2\pi r$
$C = 2\pi(2.5)$
$C = 5\pi \text{ ft}$

9. $\ell = \dfrac{m}{360} \cdot C$

$\ell = \dfrac{60}{360} \cdot 2 \cdot \pi \cdot 8$

$\ell = \dfrac{1}{6} \cdot 16\pi$

$\ell = \dfrac{8}{3}\pi$ in.

10. $\ell = \dfrac{m}{360} \cdot C$

$\ell = \dfrac{135}{360} \cdot 2\pi \cdot 12$

$\ell = \dfrac{3}{8}(24\pi)$

$\ell = 9\pi$ cm

11. $C = 2\pi r$

$C = 2\pi(12.38)$

$C \approx 77.79$

12. $A = \pi r^2$

$A = \pi(12.38)^2$

$A \approx 481.49$ cm

13. $A = \pi r^2$

$143 = \pi r^2$

$\dfrac{143}{\pi} = r^2$

$r \approx 6.7$ cm

14. $C = 2\pi r$

$5.48 = 2\pi r$

$r = \dfrac{5.48}{2\pi}$

$r \approx 0.9$

15. $\ell = \dfrac{60}{360} \cdot 2\pi r$

$\ell = \dfrac{1}{6} \cdot 2\pi \cdot 7$

$\ell \approx 7.33$ in.

16. $A = \pi r^2$

$56.35 = \pi r^2$

$r^2 = \dfrac{56.35}{\pi}$

$r \approx 4.24$

$d \approx 8.47$

17. The maximum area of a rectangle occurs when it is a square. $\therefore A = 16$ sq in.

18. Because the length of the third side of the triangle must be less than the sum of 5 and 7, the third side is less than 12. Similarly, s is greater than 2. $\therefore 2 < s < 12$.

19. $\overline{AN}$ can be no longer than the hypotenuse in length. That is, AN is less than or equal to 13 units. Of course $AN > AB$ so AN is greater than 5 units. Hence, $5 < AN < 13$.

20. The largest measure of $\angle RTS$ occurs as T moves toward $\overline{RS}$. The smallest measure for $\angle RTS$ occurs as T moves toward the circle. $90° < m\angle RTS < 180°$.

21. $A = A_{\text{CIRCLE}} - A_{\text{SQUARE}}$

$A = \pi\left(4\sqrt{2}\right)^2 - 8^2$

$A = (32\pi - 64)$ in^2

22. $A = A_{\text{CIRCLE}} - A_{\text{RECTANGLE}}$

$A = \pi \cdot 5^2 - 6 \cdot 8$

$A = (25\pi - 48)$ ft^2

23. $A = A_{\text{RHOMBUS}} - A_{\text{CIRCLE}}$

$A = \dfrac{1}{2} \cdot d_1 \cdot d_2 - \pi r^2$

$A = \dfrac{1}{2}(30)(40) - \pi(12)^2$

$A = (600 - 144\pi)$ ft^2

24. $A = A_{\text{CIRCLE}} - 6A_{\text{EQ. }\triangle}$

$A = \pi r^2 - 6 \cdot \dfrac{s^2}{4}\sqrt{3}$

$A = \pi \cdot 6^2 - 6 \cdot \dfrac{6^2}{4}\sqrt{3}$

$A = \left(36\pi - 54\sqrt{3}\right)$ cm^2

25. $A = \pi r^2$

$154 = \pi r^2$

$r^2 = \dfrac{154}{\pi}$

$r \approx 7$ cm

26. $C = \pi d$

$157 = \pi d$

$d = \dfrac{157}{\pi}$

$d \approx 50$ in.

27. $\ell = \dfrac{m}{360} \cdot C$

$4\pi = \dfrac{90}{360} \cdot 2\pi r$

$4\pi = \dfrac{1}{2}\pi r$

Mult. by 2,

$8\pi = \pi r$

$\therefore r = 8$ in.

28. Let R be the radius of the larger circle and r be the radius of the smaller circle.

$\dfrac{2\pi R}{2\pi r} = \dfrac{2}{1}$

$\dfrac{R}{r} = \dfrac{2}{1}$

$R = 2r$

$\dfrac{A_L}{A_S} = \dfrac{\pi R^2}{\pi r^2}$

$\dfrac{A_L}{A_S} = \dfrac{\pi(2r)^2}{\pi r^2} = \dfrac{4\pi r^2}{\pi r^2} = \dfrac{4}{1}$

That is, $A_L : A_S = 4 : 1$.

29. Given: Concentric circles with radii of lengths R and r, where $R > r$.

Explain: $A_{\text{RING}} = \pi(R+r)(R-r)$

$A = A_{\text{LARGER CIRCLE}} - A_{\text{SMALLER CIRCLE}}$

$A = \pi R^2 - \pi r^2$

$A = \pi\left(R^2 - r^2\right).$

But $R^2 - r^2$ is a difference of 2 squares, so that

$A = \pi(R+r)(R-r)$.

30. Given: A circle with diameter of lengths d.

Explain: $A_{\text{CIRCLE}} = \dfrac{1}{4}\pi d^2$

$A = \pi r^2$

But $r = \dfrac{1}{2}d$, so

$A = \pi\left(\dfrac{1}{2}d\right)^2$

$A = \pi \cdot \dfrac{1}{4}d^2$

$A = \dfrac{1}{4}\pi d^2$

31. Let r and $(r+1)$ represent the lengths of radii of the 2 circles.

$\pi(r+1)^2 - \pi r^2 = 7\pi$

$\pi\left(r^2 + 2r + 1\right) - \pi r^2 = 7\pi$

$(2r+1)\pi = 7\pi$

Dividing by π ,

$2r + 1 = 7$

$2r = 6$

$r = 3$

The radii of the concentric circles measure 3 in. and 4 in.

32. **a.** $C = \pi d$

$C = \pi(18)$

$C \approx 56.52$ ft

b. $\dfrac{56.52}{6} = 9.42$

Thus, 10 metal strips are needed.

c. $6 \times 10 \times \$1.59 = \$95.40$

33. **a.** $A = \pi r^2$

$A = \pi\left(8^2\right)$

$A \approx 201.06$ ft^2

b. $\dfrac{201.06}{70} \approx 2.87$ pints

Thus, 3 pints need to be purchased.

c. $3 \times \$2.95 = \$8.85$

34. $440 - 200 = 240$ yards for the 2 semicircles.

$\therefore 2\left(\dfrac{1}{2} \cdot 2\pi r\right) = 240$

$2\pi r = 240$

$r = \dfrac{240}{2\pi}$

$r \approx 38.2$ yd

35. **a.** $A = \pi r^2$

$A = \pi\left(20^2\right)$

$A \approx 1256$ ft^2

b. $\dfrac{1256}{60} = 20.93$

Thus, 21 pounds of seed are needed.

c. $21 \times \$1.65 = \$34.65$

36. $A_{\text{POLYGON}} \approx A_{\text{CIRCLE}}$

$A \approx \pi r^2$

$A \approx \pi \cdot 7^2$

$A \approx 153.94$ cm^2

37. $P_{\text{POLYGON}} \approx C_{\text{CIRCLE}}$

$P \approx 2\pi r$

$P \approx 2 \cdot \pi \cdot 7$

$P \approx 43.98$ cm

38. $C = 2\pi r$
$C = 2\pi(6)$
$C = 37.70$
Pulley $\approx 20 + 20 + 37.70 \approx 77.70$ in.

39. $C = 2\pi(4)$
$C = 8\pi$
Let the distance between the centers be d.
Chain length $= C + 2d$
$54 = 8\pi + 2d$
$54 - 8\pi = 2d$
$d = \dfrac{54 - 8\pi}{2}$
$d \approx 14.43$ in.

40. $A = \pi r^2$
$A = \pi(12)^2$
$A \approx 452.39$ sq in.
Price per sq in. $= \dfrac{\$6.95}{452.39} \approx \$0.0154$

$A = \pi r^2$
$A = \pi(16)^2$
$A \approx 804.25$ sq in.
Price per sq in. $= \dfrac{\$9.95}{804.25} \approx \$0.124$
The 16 in. pizza is a better buy.

41. $C = 2\pi r$
$C = 2\pi(4375)$
$C \approx 27,488.94$ miles

42. $\dfrac{12 \text{ rev}}{3 \text{ min}} = \dfrac{12 \text{ rev} \cdot 2\pi(40) \text{ ft/rev}}{3 \text{ min}(60 \text{ sec/min})}$

$= \dfrac{960\pi \text{ ft}}{180 \text{ sec}} = \dfrac{\frac{960\pi}{180} \text{ ft}}{1 \text{ sec}} \approx \dfrac{16.76 \text{ ft}}{\text{sec}}$

43. $C = \pi d = \pi \cdot 30 \approx 94.25$ ft

In one revolution, rate $= \dfrac{94.25}{6} = 15.7$ ft/sec

44.

$A_{LEAVES} = A_{SEMICIRCLE} - A_{TRAPEZOID}$

$A_{LEAVES} = \dfrac{1}{2}\pi r^2 - \dfrac{1}{2}h(b_1 + b_2)$

$A_{LEAVES} = \dfrac{1}{2}\pi r^2 - \dfrac{1}{2}\left(\dfrac{1}{2}r\sqrt{3}\right)(2r + r)$

$A_{LEAVES} = \dfrac{1}{2}\pi r^2 - \dfrac{1}{4}r\sqrt{3}\,(3r)$

$A_{LEAVES} = \dfrac{1}{2}\pi r^2 - \dfrac{3}{4}r^2\sqrt{3}$

$A_{LEAVES} = r^2\left(\dfrac{1}{2}\pi - \dfrac{3}{4}\sqrt{3}\right)$

% increase $=$

$\dfrac{A_{LEAVES}}{A_{TRAPEZOID}} = \dfrac{r^2\left(\dfrac{1}{2}\pi - \dfrac{3}{4}\sqrt{3}\right)}{\dfrac{3}{4}r^2\sqrt{3}} =$

$\dfrac{\dfrac{1}{2}\pi - \dfrac{3}{4}\sqrt{3}}{\dfrac{3}{4}\sqrt{3}} =$

$\dfrac{2\pi - 3\sqrt{3}}{3\sqrt{3}} \approx 0.209 \approx 21\%$

45.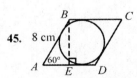

8 cm

$BE = 4\sqrt{3}$ cm (using the
30°-60°-90° relationship).
$\overline{BE}$ is the same as the diameter of the circle, so
then the radius of the circle $= 2\sqrt{3}$ cm .

$A_{CIRCLE} = \pi r^2 = \pi\left(2\sqrt{3}\right)^2 = \pi \cdot 4 \cdot 3 = 12\pi$ cm^2

SECTION 8.5: More Area Relationships in the Circle

1. $P_{SECTOR} = 10 + 10 + 14 = 34$ in.

2. $A_{SECTOR} = \dfrac{90}{360} \cdot 360 = 90$ in^2

3. $A_{SECTOR} = \dfrac{m}{360} \cdot A_{CIRCLE}$

$50 = \dfrac{120}{360} \cdot A_{CIRCLE}$

$50 = \dfrac{1}{3} \cdot A_{CIRCLE}$

$A_{CIRCLE} = 150$ cm^2

4. $40 - 16 = 24$ cm^2

5. $A_\triangle = \dfrac{1}{2} rP$

$A_\triangle = \dfrac{1}{2} r(3s)$

$A_\triangle = \dfrac{3}{2} rs$

6.

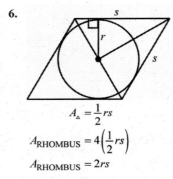

$A_\triangle = \dfrac{1}{2} rs$

$A_{RHOMBUS} = 4\left(\dfrac{1}{2} rs\right)$

$A_{RHOMBUS} = 2rs$

7. $P = 24 + 30 = 54$ mm

8. $P_{SECTOR} = 2r + \ell_{ARC}$

$30 = 2r + 12$

$18 = 2r$

$r = 9$ in.

9. $A_\triangle = \dfrac{1}{2} rP$

$A_\triangle = \dfrac{1}{2}(2)(6 + 8 + 10)$

$A_\triangle = 24$ sq in.

10. $A_\triangle = \dfrac{1}{2} rP$

$A_\triangle = \dfrac{1}{2}(2)(5 + 12 + 13)$

$A_\triangle = 30$ sq in.

11. $A_\triangle = \dfrac{1}{2} rP$

$6 = \dfrac{1}{2} r(3 + 4 + 5)$

$12 = r(12)$

$r = 1$ in.

12. $A_\triangle = \dfrac{1}{2} rP$

$7.48 = \dfrac{1}{2} r(3 + 4 + 5)$

$15.96 = r(14)$

$r = 1.07$ in.

13. $P = 2r + \ell$

$P = 2(8) + \dfrac{8}{3}\pi$

$P = \left(16 + \dfrac{8}{3}\pi\right)$ in.

$A = \dfrac{m}{360} \cdot \pi r^2$

$A = \dfrac{60}{360} \cdot \pi\left(8^2\right)$

$A = \dfrac{1}{6} \cdot 64\pi$

$A = \dfrac{32}{3}\pi$ in^2

14. $P = 2r + \ell$

$P = 2(12) + 9\pi$

$P = (24 + 9\pi)$ cm

$A = \dfrac{m}{360} \cdot \pi r^2$

$A = \dfrac{135}{360} \cdot \pi\left(12^2\right)$

$A = \dfrac{3}{8}(144\pi)$

$A = 54\pi$ cm^2

15. $P = 2r + \ell$

$P = 2(9) + \dfrac{80}{360}(2)(\pi)(9)$

$P = 18 + \dfrac{2}{9}(18\pi)$

$P = 18 + 4\pi$

$P \approx 30.57$ in.

16. $A = \dfrac{m}{360} \cdot \pi r^2$

$A = \dfrac{80}{360} \cdot \pi\left(9^2\right)$

$A = \dfrac{2}{9}(81\pi)$

$A \approx 56.55$ in^2

17. $P = AB + \ell \overarc{AB}$

$P = 12 + \dfrac{60}{360} \cdot 2\pi(12)$

$P = 12 + \dfrac{1}{6}(24\pi)$

$P = (12 + 4\pi)$ in.

$A = A_{\text{SECTOR}} - A_{\triangle}$

$A = \dfrac{1}{6}(\pi)(12^2) - \dfrac{12^2}{4}\sqrt{3}$

$A = \dfrac{1}{6}(144\pi) - \dfrac{144}{4}\sqrt{3}$

$A = \left(24\pi - 36\sqrt{3}\right)$ in^2

18. $P = AB + \ell \overarc{AB}$

$P = 10 + \dfrac{120}{360} \cdot 2\pi \cdot \dfrac{10}{\sqrt{3}}$

$P = 10 + \dfrac{1}{6} \cdot 2\pi \cdot \dfrac{10\sqrt{3}}{3}$

$P = \left(10 + \dfrac{20\pi\sqrt{3}}{9}\right)$ in.

$A = A_{\text{SECTOR}} - A_{\triangle}$

$A = \dfrac{120}{360} \cdot \pi \cdot 10^2 - \dfrac{1}{2} \cdot 10 \cdot \dfrac{5}{\sqrt{3}}$

$A = \dfrac{1}{3}(100\pi) - \dfrac{1}{2}(10)\left(\dfrac{5\sqrt{3}}{3}\right)$

$A = \dfrac{100\pi}{3} - \dfrac{25\sqrt{3}}{3}$ or

$A = \left(\dfrac{100\pi - 25\sqrt{3}}{3}\right)$ in^2

19. $A = A_{\text{EQ. }\triangle} - 3 \cdot A_{\text{SECTOR}}$

$A = \dfrac{s^2}{4}\sqrt{3} - 3 \cdot \dfrac{m}{360} \cdot \pi r^2$

$A = \dfrac{10^2}{4}\sqrt{3} - 3 \cdot \dfrac{60}{360} \cdot \pi \cdot (5^2)$

$A = \left(25\sqrt{3} - \dfrac{25}{2}\pi\right)$ cm^2

20. $A = A_{\text{SQUARE}} - 4 \cdot A_{\text{SECTOR}}$

$A = 12^2 - 4 \cdot \dfrac{90}{360} \cdot \pi(6^2)$

$A = 144 - 4 \cdot \dfrac{1}{4} \cdot \pi \cdot 36$

$A = (144 - 36\pi)$ m^2

21. $A = \dfrac{m}{360} \cdot \pi r^2$

$\dfrac{9}{4}\pi = \dfrac{40}{360} \cdot \pi r^2$

$\dfrac{9}{4}\pi = \dfrac{1}{9}\pi r^2$

Multiply by 9

$\dfrac{81}{4}\pi = \pi r^2$

$r^2 = \dfrac{81}{4}$

$r = \dfrac{9}{2}$ cm

22. $A = A_{\text{SECTOR}} - A_{\text{EQ. }\triangle}$

$A = \dfrac{m}{360} \cdot \pi r^2 - \dfrac{1}{2}bh$

$A = \dfrac{120}{360} \cdot \pi(6^2) - \dfrac{1}{2}(6\sqrt{3})(3)$

$A = \dfrac{1}{3}(36\pi) - 9\sqrt{3}$

$A = \left(12\pi - 9\sqrt{3}\right)$ in^2

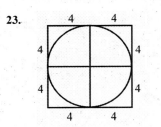

23.

$A = \pi r^2$

$A = \pi(6^2)$

$A = 36\pi$ units^2

24.

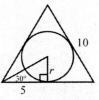

In the 30°-60°-90° $\triangle$,

$r\sqrt{3} = 5$

$r = \dfrac{5}{\sqrt{3}}$

$r = \dfrac{5\sqrt{3}}{3}$

$\therefore A = \pi \cdot \left(\dfrac{5\sqrt{3}}{3}\right)^2$

$A = \pi \cdot \dfrac{75}{9}$

$A = \dfrac{75}{9}\pi$ units^2

25. $\ell = \dfrac{m}{360} \cdot 2\pi r$

$6\pi = \dfrac{m}{360} \cdot 2\pi(12)$

$6\pi = \dfrac{m}{360} \cdot 24\pi$

Dividing by 24π, we get

$\dfrac{1}{4} = \dfrac{m}{360}$

Multiplying by 360, we get $m = 90°$.

26. $\$3.40 + \$2.20 = \$5.60$
Dividing by 6, gives 93¢ per share.

27. $\$1.25 \cdot 6$ slices $= \$7.50$ per pizza
$\$0.95 \cdot 8$ slices $= \$7.60$ per pizza
Better to cut the pizza into 8 slices at $0.95 per slice.

28. $A = A_{\text{SQUARE}} - A_{\text{CIRCLE}}$

$A = s^2 - \pi\left(\dfrac{1}{2}s\right)^2$

$A = s^2 - \pi\dfrac{1}{4}(s^2)$

$A = s^2 - \dfrac{\pi}{4}s^2$

29. Draw in two radii to consecutive vertices of the square. Then

$r^2 + r^2 = s^2$

$2r^2 = s^2$

$r^2 = \dfrac{s^2}{2}$

$r = \dfrac{s}{\sqrt{2}} = \dfrac{s\sqrt{2}}{2}$

$A = A_{\text{CIRCLE}} - A_{\text{SQUARE}}$

$A = \pi r^2 - s^2$

$A = \pi\left(\dfrac{s\sqrt{2}}{2}\right)^2 - s^2$

$A = \pi \cdot \dfrac{s^2 \cdot 2}{4} - s^2$

$A = \left(\dfrac{\pi}{2}\right)s^2 - s^2$

30. $A = \dfrac{1}{4}\left(\pi R^2 - \pi r^2\right)$

$A = \dfrac{1}{4}\pi\left(R^2 - r^2\right)$

$A = \dfrac{\pi}{4}\left(R^2 - r^2\right)$

31. $A_{\triangle} = \dfrac{1}{2}bh$

$A_{\triangle} = \dfrac{1}{2}(10)(12)$

$A_{\triangle} = 60$

$A_{\triangle} = \dfrac{1}{2}rP$

$60 = \dfrac{1}{2}r(36)$

$60 = 18r$

$r = 3\dfrac{1}{3}$ ft or 3 ft 4 in.

32.

$A_{\triangle} = \dfrac{1}{2}bh$

$A_{\triangle} = \dfrac{1}{2}ba$

$A_{\triangle} = \dfrac{1}{2}ab$

$A_{\triangle} = \dfrac{1}{2}rP$

So $\dfrac{1}{2}ab = \dfrac{1}{2}r(a + b + c)$.

Solve for r.

$r = \dfrac{ab}{a + b + c}$

33. $A_\Delta = \sqrt{s(s-a)(s-b)(s-c)}$

Also, $A_\Delta = \frac{1}{2}rP$ or $A_\Delta = \frac{1}{2}r(a+b+c)$.

So $\frac{1}{2}r(a+b+c) = \sqrt{s(s-a)(s-b)(s-c)}$.

Solve for r.

$r = \dfrac{2\sqrt{s(s-a)(s-b)(s-c)}}{a+b+c}$

34. a. $r = \dfrac{ab}{a+b+c}$

$r = \dfrac{8(15)}{8+15+17}$

$r = 3$

b. $r = \dfrac{2\sqrt{s(s-a)(s-b)(s-c)}}{a+b+c}$

$r = \dfrac{2\sqrt{14(7)(5)(2)}}{7+9+12}$

$r = \dfrac{2\sqrt{14(14)(5)}}{28}$

$r = \dfrac{2(14)\sqrt{5}}{28} = \sqrt{5}$

35. a. $r = \dfrac{ab}{a+b+c}$

$r = \dfrac{7(24)}{7+24+25}$

$r = 3$

b. $r = \dfrac{2\sqrt{s(s-a)(s-b)(s-c)}}{a+b+c}$

$r = \dfrac{2\sqrt{18(9)(8)(1)}}{9+10+17}$

$r = \dfrac{2\sqrt{(9)(2)(9)(8)}}{28}$

$r = \dfrac{2(36)}{36} = 2$

37. $A = \dfrac{120}{360} \cdot \pi\left(18^2 - 4^2\right)$

$A = \dfrac{1}{3} \cdot \pi \cdot (324 - 16)$

$A = \dfrac{\pi}{3}(308)$

$A = \dfrac{308\pi}{3} \approx 322.54$ sq in.

38.

$A = \dfrac{1}{2} \cdot \pi(12^2) + \dfrac{1}{4} \cdot \pi(6^2)$

$A = \dfrac{1}{2}(\pi)(144) + \dfrac{1}{4}(\pi)(36)$

$A = 72\pi + 9\pi$

$A = 81\pi \approx 254.47$ sq ft

39. $A = \dfrac{1}{4}\left(\pi R^2 - \pi r^2\right)$

$A = \dfrac{1}{4}\left(\pi(380)^2 - \pi(370)^2\right)$

$A = \dfrac{1}{4}\pi\left(380^2 - 370^2\right)$

$A = \dfrac{1}{4}\pi(7500)$

$A = 1875\pi \approx 5890$ ft^2

40. If AB = 12, BC = 6, and AC = $6\sqrt{3}$.

$A_\Delta = \dfrac{1}{2}bh = \dfrac{1}{2}(6\sqrt{3})6 = 18\sqrt{3}$

$A_\Delta = \dfrac{1}{2}rP$ (r = radius length of inscribed $\odot$)

$18\sqrt{3} = \dfrac{1}{2}r\left(6 + 6\sqrt{3} + 12\right)$

$18\sqrt{3} = \dfrac{1}{2}r\left(18 + 6\sqrt{3}\right)$

$36\sqrt{3} = r(18 + 6\sqrt{3})$

$r = \dfrac{36\sqrt{3}}{18 + 6\sqrt{3}} = \dfrac{6\sqrt{3}}{3 + \sqrt{3}}$

41. A diameter of the circumscribed circle is a hypotenuse of the (6, 8, 10) inscribed triangle. Draw the circumscribed circle, the right triangle, and the circle inscribed in the right triangle. Draw the segment between the centers of the circles. Let the length of that segment be x.

$$A_{Rt.\Delta} = \frac{1}{2}bh = \frac{1}{2}(6)(8) = 24$$

$$A_{Rt.\Delta} = \frac{1}{2}rP$$

$$24 = \frac{1}{2}r(6+8+10)$$

$$24 = \frac{1}{2}r(24)$$

$$24 = 12r$$

$r = 2$; radius of the inscribed $\odot = 2$

From the center of the inscribed circle, draw a radius to each point of tangency. A square is formed with side length equal to the radius length, 2. Because a side length of the inscribed triangle is 6 and the side of the square has length 2, the tangent segment length is 4.

If tangent segments from an external point are congruent,

the other tangent segment is also 4. In the little right triangle with hypotenuse length x, side length 2, the third side has length 1.

$x^2 = 2^2 + 1^2$ or $x^2 = 5$ or $x = \sqrt{5} \approx 2.2$ cm

CHAPTER REVIEW

1.

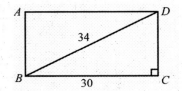

Using the Pythagorean Theorem,

$$(34)^2 = (30)^2 + (DC)^2$$
$$1156 = 900 + (DC)^2$$
$$256 = (DC)^2$$
$$DC = 16$$
$$A = 30(16) = 480 \text{ units}^2$$

2. a. $A = 10(4) = 40 \text{ units}^2$

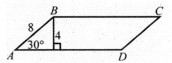

b. $A = 10(4\sqrt{3}) = 40\sqrt{3} \text{ units}^2$

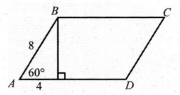

c. $A = 10(4\sqrt{2}) = 40\sqrt{2} \text{ units}^2$

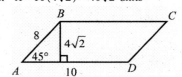

3. Using the 45°-45°-90° relationship,
$AB = DB = 5\sqrt{2}$.
$\therefore A_{ABCD} = bh$
$A_{ABCD} = (5\sqrt{2})(5\sqrt{2})$
$A_{ABCD} = 50 \text{ units}^2$

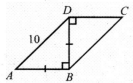

4. $A = \sqrt{s(s-a)(s-b)(s-c)}$ where

$s = \frac{1}{2}(17+25+26)$

$s = \frac{1}{2}(68)$

$s = 34$

$A = \sqrt{34(34-26)(34-25)(34-17)}$

$A = \sqrt{34(8)(9)(17)}$

$A = \sqrt{2^4 \cdot 3^2 \cdot 17^2}$

$A = 2^2 \cdot 3 \cdot 17$

$A = 204 \text{ units}^2$

5. $A = \sqrt{s(s-a)(s-b)(s-c)}$ where

$s = \frac{1}{2}(26+28+30)$

$s = \frac{1}{2}(84)$

$s = 42$

$A = \sqrt{42(42-26)(42-28)(42-30)}$

$A = \sqrt{42(16)(14)(12)}$

$A = \sqrt{2^8 \cdot 3^2 \cdot 7^2}$

$A = 2^4 \cdot 3 \cdot 7$

$A = 336 \text{ units}^2$

6. Using the (3, 4, 5) Pythagorean Triple,
$BH = 4$

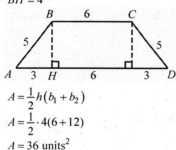

$A = \frac{1}{2}h(b_1+b_2)$

$A = \frac{1}{2} \cdot 4(6+12)$

$A = 36 \text{ units}^2$

7.

C 8 B
6   $3\sqrt{2}$ $3\sqrt{2}$
$45°$ 8 $45°$
D $3\sqrt{2}$ $3\sqrt{2}$ A

a. $A = \frac{1}{2}h(b_1+b_2)$

$A = \frac{1}{2} \cdot 3\sqrt{2}\left(8 + (8+6\sqrt{2})\right)$

$A = \frac{1}{2} \cdot 3\sqrt{2}\left(16+6\sqrt{2}\right)$

$A = 3\sqrt{2}\left(8+3\sqrt{2}\right)$

$A = \left(24\sqrt{2}+18\right) \text{ units}^2$

b. $A = \frac{1}{2} \cdot 3\left(8 + (8+6\sqrt{3})\right)$

$A = \frac{3}{2}\left(16+6\sqrt{3}\right)$

$A = \left(24+9\sqrt{3}\right) \text{ units}^2$

C 8 B
6   8   6
$30°$ 8
D $3\sqrt{3}$ $3\sqrt{3}$ A

c. $A = \frac{1}{2} \cdot 3\sqrt{3}\,(8+14)$

$A = \frac{1}{2}\left(3\sqrt{3}\right)(22)$

$A = 33\sqrt{3} \text{ units}^2$

C 8 B
6   $3\sqrt{3}$ 6
$60°$ 8
D 3   3 A

8. $A = \frac{1}{2}d_1 \cdot d_2$

$A = \frac{1}{2}(18)(24)$

$A = 216 \text{ in}^2$

9   12
12   9

Using the (9, 12, 15) Pythagorean Triple,
$P = 4(15) = 60 \text{ in.}$

9. a. $A = (140)(160) - \left[(80)(35)+(30)(20)\right]$

$A = 22{,}400 - \left[2800+600\right]$

$A = 22{,}400 - 3400$

$A = 19{,}000 \text{ ft}^2$

b. $\frac{19{,}000}{5000} = 3.8 \text{ bags}$

Tom needs to buy 4 bags.

c. $\text{Cost} = 4 \cdot \$18 = \$72$

10. a. $A = (9 \cdot 8) + (12 \cdot 8)$

$A = 72 + 96$

$A = 168 \text{ ft}^2$

$\frac{168}{60} = 2.8 \text{ double rolls}$

3 double rolls are needed.

b. $P = 2a + 2b$

$P = 2(9) + 2(12)$

$P = 18 + 24$

$P = 42 \text{ ft or } 14 \text{ yd}$

$\frac{14}{5} = 2.8 \text{ rolls}$

3 rolls of border are needed.

11.

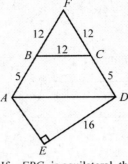

If $\triangle FBC$ is equilateral, then so is $\triangle FAD$.

$\therefore \quad AD = 17$

$$(AD)^2 = (AE)^2 + (ED)^2$$
$$(17)^2 = (AE)^2 + (16)^2$$
$$28 = (AE)^2 + 256$$
$$(AE)^2 = 33$$
$$AE = \sqrt{33}$$

a. $A_{EAFD} = A_{FAD} + A_{AED}$

$$A_{EAFD} = \frac{17^2}{4}\sqrt{3} + \frac{1}{2}(16)\sqrt{33}$$
$$A_{EAFD} = \left(\frac{289}{4}\sqrt{3} + 8\sqrt{33}\right) \text{ units}^2$$

b. $P_{EAFD} = AF + FD + DE + AE$

$$P_{EAFD} = 17 + 17 + 16 + \sqrt{33}$$
$$P_{EAFD} = \left(50 + \sqrt{33}\right) \text{ units}$$

12.

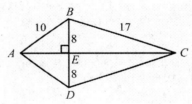

$AE = 6$
(using the 6-8-10 Pythagorean Triple)
$EC = 15$
(using the 8-15-17 Pythagorean Triple)

$$A = \frac{1}{2}d_1 \cdot d_2$$
$$A = \frac{1}{2}(BD)(AC)$$
$$A = \frac{1}{2}(16)(6 + 15)$$
$$A = 8(21)$$
$$A = 168 \text{ units}^2$$

13.

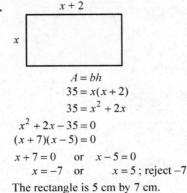

$$A = bh$$
$$35 = x(x + 2)$$
$$35 = x^2 + 2x$$
$$x^2 + 2x - 35 = 0$$
$$(x + 7)(x - 5) = 0$$
$$x + 7 = 0 \quad \text{or} \quad x - 5 = 0$$
$$x = -7 \quad \text{or} \quad x = 5 \text{ ; reject } -7$$

The rectangle is 5 cm by 7 cm.

14. $P = a + b + c$

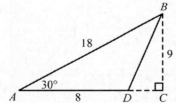

a. $\quad 60 = x + (x + 10) + (x + 5)$

$$60 = 3x + 15$$
$$3x = 45$$
$$x = 15$$
$$x + 10 = 25$$
$$x + 5 = 20$$

The three sides have lengths 15 cm, 25 cm, and 20 cm.

b. (15, 20, 25) is a Pythagorean Triple in which 25 is the length of the hypotenuse.

$$A = \frac{1}{2}bh$$
$$A = \frac{1}{2}(20)(15)$$
$$A = 150 \text{ cm}^2$$

15.

Using the 30°-60°-90° relationship, $BC = 9$.

$$A = \frac{1}{2}bh$$
$$A = \frac{1}{2}(8)(9)$$
$$A = 36 \text{ units}^2$$

16. $A = \dfrac{s^2}{4}\sqrt{3}$

$A = \dfrac{12^2}{4}\sqrt{3}$

$A = \dfrac{144}{4}\sqrt{3}$

$A = 36\sqrt{3} \text{ cm}^2$

17.

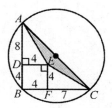

$A = A_{ABC} - \left(A_{ADE} + A_{BDEF} + A_{EFC} \right)$

$A = \dfrac{1}{2}(11)(12) - \left[\dfrac{1}{2}(8)(4) + 4^2 + \dfrac{1}{2}(4)(7) \right]$

$A = 66 - [16 + 16 + 14]$

$A = 66 - 46$

$A = 20 \text{ units}^2$

18. a. $c = \dfrac{360}{5} = 72°$

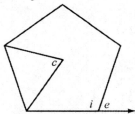

b. $i = \dfrac{(5-2)180}{2} = \dfrac{3(180)}{5} = \dfrac{540}{5} = 108°$

c. $e = 180° - 108° = 72°$

19.

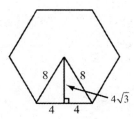

$A = \dfrac{1}{2}aP$

$A = \dfrac{1}{2}\left(4\sqrt{3}\right)(6 \cdot 8)$

$A = 96\sqrt{3} \text{ ft}^2$

20. $P = 3\left(12\sqrt{3}\right) = 36\sqrt{3}$

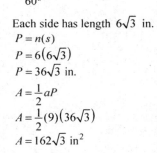

$A = \dfrac{1}{2}aP$

$108\sqrt{3} = \dfrac{1}{2} \cdot a \cdot 36\sqrt{3}$

$108\sqrt{3} = \left(18\sqrt{3}\right)a$

$a = 6 \text{ in.}$

21. $x \cdot \sqrt{3} = 9$

$x = \dfrac{9}{\sqrt{3}}$

$x = \dfrac{9}{\sqrt{3}} \cdot \dfrac{\sqrt{3}}{\sqrt{3}} = \dfrac{9\sqrt{3}}{3} = 3\sqrt{3}$

Each side has length $6\sqrt{3}$ in.

$P = n(s)$

$P = 6\left(6\sqrt{3}\right)$

$P = 36\sqrt{3} \text{ in.}$

$A = \dfrac{1}{2}aP$

$A = \dfrac{1}{2}(9)\left(36\sqrt{3}\right)$

$A = 162\sqrt{3} \text{ in}^2$

22. a. $c = \dfrac{360}{n}$

$45 = \dfrac{360}{n}$

$45n = 360$

$n = 8$

b. $P = n(s)$

$P = 8(5)$

$P = 40$

$A = \dfrac{1}{2}aP$

$A \approx \dfrac{1}{2}(6)(40)$

$A \approx 120 \text{ cm}^2$

23. a. No. ⊥ bisectors of sides of a parallelogram are not necessarily concurrent.

   b. No. ⊥ bisectors of sides of a rhombus are not concurrent.

   c. Yes. ⊥ bisectors of sides of a rectangle are concurrent.

   d. Yes. ⊥ bisectors of sides of a square are concurrent.

24. a. No. ∠ bisectors of a parallelogram are not necessarily concurrent.

   b. Yes. ∠ bisectors of a rhombus are concurrent.

   c. No. ∠ bisectors of a rectangle are not necessarily concurrent.

   d. Yes. ∠ bisectors of a square are concurrent.

25. If the radius of the inscribed circle is 7 in., then the length of each side of the triangle is $14\sqrt{3}$ in.

$$A_{\triangle} = \frac{1}{2}rP$$
$$A_{\triangle} = \frac{1}{2}(7)(3 \cdot 14\sqrt{3})$$
$$A_{\triangle} = 147\sqrt{3}$$
$$A_{\triangle} \approx 254.61 \text{ sq in.}$$

26. a. $A = (20)(30) - (12)(24)$
   $$A = 600 - 288$$
   $$A = 312 \text{ ft}^2$$

   b. $\frac{312}{9} = 34\frac{2}{3} \text{ yd}^2$

   35 yd^2 should be purchased.

   c. $35 \cdot \$9.97 = \$348.95$

27. $A = A_{\text{SQUARE}} - 4 \cdot A_{\text{SECTOR}}$
$$A = 8^2 - 4 \cdot \left[\frac{90}{360}(\pi \cdot 4^2)\right]$$
$$A = 64 - 4\left[\frac{1}{4}(16\pi)\right]$$
$$A = (64 - 16\pi) \text{ units}^2$$

28. $A = A_{\text{SEMICIRCLE}} - A_{\text{TRIANGLE}}$
$$A = \frac{1}{2}(\pi \cdot 7^2) - \frac{1}{2}(7)(7\sqrt{3})$$
$$A = \left(\frac{49}{2}\pi - \frac{49}{2}\sqrt{3}\right) \text{ units}^2$$

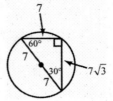

29. $A_{\text{SEGMENT}} = A_{\text{SECTOR}} - A_{\text{TRIANGLE}}$
$$A_{\text{SEGMENT}} = \frac{60}{360} \cdot \pi \cdot 4^2 - \frac{4^2}{4}\sqrt{3}$$
$$A_{\text{SEGMENT}} = \left(\frac{8}{3}\pi - 4\sqrt{3}\right) \text{ units}^2$$

30.

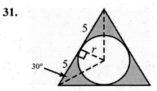

$A = A_{\text{RECT}} - 2 \cdot A_{\text{CIRCLE}}$
$$A = (12)(24) - 2 \cdot (\pi \cdot 6^2)$$
$$A = (288 - 72\pi) \text{ units}^2$$

31.

The radius of the circle is r.
$$r\sqrt{3} = 5$$
$$r = \frac{5}{\sqrt{3}} = \frac{5\sqrt{3}}{3}$$
$$A = A_{\text{EQ.}\triangle} - A_{\text{CIRCLE}}$$
$$A = \frac{10^2}{4}\sqrt{3} - \pi\left(\frac{5\sqrt{3}}{3}\right)^2$$
$$A = 25\sqrt{3} - \pi \cdot \frac{75}{9}$$
$$A = \left(25\sqrt{3} - \frac{25}{3}\pi\right) \text{ units}^2$$

32.

$$\ell = \frac{m}{360}(2\pi r)$$
$$\ell = \frac{40}{360}\left(2 \cdot \pi \cdot 3\sqrt{5}\right)$$
$$\ell = \frac{1}{9}\left(6\pi\sqrt{5}\right)$$
$$\ell = \frac{2\pi\sqrt{5}}{3} \text{ cm}$$
$$A = \frac{m}{360}\left(\pi r^2\right)$$
$$A = \frac{40}{360}\left(\pi \cdot \left(3\sqrt{5}\right)^2\right)$$
$$A = \frac{1}{9}(\pi \cdot 45)$$
$$A = 5\pi \text{ cm}^2$$

33. a.
$$C = \pi d$$
$$66 = \frac{22}{7} \cdot d$$
$$\frac{7}{22} \cdot 66 = \frac{7}{22} \cdot \frac{22}{7}d$$
$$d = 21 \text{ ft}$$

b. $d = 21$, $r = \frac{21}{2}$
$$A = \pi r^2$$
$$A = \frac{22}{7}\left(\frac{21}{2}\right)^2$$
$$A = \frac{693}{2} \approx 346\frac{1}{2} \text{ ft}^2$$

34. a. $A_{\text{SECTOR}} = \frac{m}{360}\left(\pi r^2\right)$
$$A = \frac{80}{360}(27\pi)$$
$$A = \frac{2}{9}(27\pi)$$
$$A = 6\pi \text{ ft}^2$$

b. Since $\pi r^2 = 27\pi$,
$$r^2 = 27$$
$$r = \sqrt{27}$$
$$r = 3\sqrt{3}$$

$$\ell = \frac{m}{360}(2\pi r)$$
$$\ell = \frac{80}{360}\left(2\pi \cdot 3\sqrt{3}\right)$$
$$\ell = \frac{2}{9}\left(6\pi\sqrt{3}\right)$$
$$\ell = \frac{4\pi}{3}\sqrt{3}$$
$$P = 2r + \ell$$
$$P = 2\left(3\sqrt{3}\right) + \frac{4\pi}{3}\sqrt{3}$$
$$P = \left(6\sqrt{3} + \frac{4\pi}{3}\sqrt{3}\right) \text{ ft}$$

35.

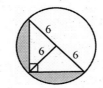

$$A_{\text{SHADED}} = A_{\text{SEMICIRCLE}} - A_{\triangle}$$
$$A_{\text{SHADED}} = \frac{1}{2} \cdot \left(\pi \cdot 6^2\right) - \frac{1}{2} \cdot 6 \cdot 12$$
$$A_{\text{SHADED}} = 18\pi - 36$$

The area sought is one-half the shaded area.
$$A = \frac{1}{2}(18\pi - 36)$$
$$A = (9\pi - 18) \text{ in}^2$$

36. Given: Concentric circles with radii of lengths R and r with $R > r$; O is the center of the circles.

Prove: $A_{\text{RING}} = \pi(BC)^2$

Proof: By an earlier theorem,

$$A_{\text{RING}} = \pi R^2 - \pi r^2$$
$$= \pi(OC)^2 - \pi(OB)^2$$
$$= \pi\left[(OC)^2 - (OB)^2\right]$$

In rt. $\triangle OBC$,

$$(OB)^2 + (BC)^2 = (OC)^2$$
$$\therefore (OC)^2 - (OB)^2 = (BC)^2$$

In turn, $A_{\text{RING}} = \pi(BC)^2$

37. The area of a circle circumscribed about a square is twice the area of the circle inscribed within the square.

Proof: Let r represent the length of radius of the inscribed circle.
Using the 45°-45°-90° relationship, the radius of the larger circle is $r\sqrt{2}$.
Now,

$$A_{\text{INSCRIBED CIRCLE}} = \pi r^2$$
$$A_{\text{CIRCUMSCRIBED CIRCLE}} = \pi\left(r\sqrt{2}\right)^2$$
$$= \pi \cdot \left(r^2 \cdot 2\right)$$
$$= 2\left(\pi r^2\right)$$
$$= 2\left(A_{\text{INSCRIBED CIRCLE}}\right)$$

38. If semicircles are constructed on each of the sides of a right triangle, then the area of the semicircle on the hypotenuse is equal to the sum of the areas of the semicircles on the two legs.

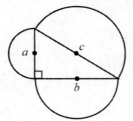

Proof: The radii of the semicircles are $\frac{1}{2}a$, $\frac{1}{2}b$, and $\frac{1}{2}c$. The area of the semicircle on the hypotenuse is

$$A = \frac{1}{2}\left[\pi\left(\frac{1}{2}c\right)^2\right]$$
$$= \frac{1}{2}\cdot\pi\left(\frac{1}{4}c^2\right)$$
$$= \frac{1}{2}\pi\left[\frac{1}{4}\left(a^2+b^2\right)\right] \quad \left(c^2 = a^2 + b^2 \text{ by the}\right.$$
$$\text{Pythagorean Theorem.)}$$
$$= \frac{1}{2}\pi\left[\frac{1}{4}a^2 + \frac{1}{4}b^2\right]$$
$$= \frac{1}{2}\pi\left(\frac{1}{4}a^2\right) + \frac{1}{2}\pi\left(\frac{1}{4}b^2\right)$$
$$= \frac{1}{2}\pi\left(\frac{1}{2}a\right)^2 + \frac{1}{2}\pi\left(\frac{1}{2}b\right)^2$$
$$= \frac{1}{2}\left[\pi\left(\frac{1}{2}a\right)^2\right] + \frac{1}{2}\left[\pi\left(\frac{1}{2}b\right)^2\right]$$

which is the sum of areas of the semicircles on the two legs.

39. a. $A = (18)(15) - \left[\frac{1}{2}(3.14)\cdot 3^2 + \frac{1}{4}(3.14)\cdot 3^2\right]$

$A = 270 - 21.2$

$A = 248.8 \text{ ft}^2$

The approx. number of yd^2 of carpeting needed is $\frac{248.8}{9} \approx 28 \text{ yd}^2$.

b. From (a), the number of ft^2 to be tiled is 21.2 ft^2.

40. a. $A = \frac{1}{2}\left[\pi R^2 - \pi r^2\right]$

$A = \frac{1}{2}\left[(3.14)(30)^2 - (3.14)(18)^2\right]$

$A = \frac{1}{2}[1808.64]$

$A = 904.32 \text{ ft}^2 \approx 905 \text{ ft}^2$

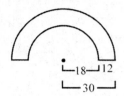

|—18—|—12

|———30———|

b. Cost = (905)($0.18)

Cost = $162.90

c. Length = $\frac{1}{2}(2\pi R) + \frac{1}{2}(2\pi r)$

|—17—|

|———31———|

$= \frac{1}{2}[2(3.14)(31)] + \frac{1}{2}[2(3.14)(17)]$

$= 97.34 + 52.38$

$= 150.72$

Approximately 151 flowers.

CHAPTER TEST

1. a. square inches

b. equal

2. a. $A = s^2$

b. $C = 2\pi r$

3. a. True

b. False

4. 23 cm^2

5.

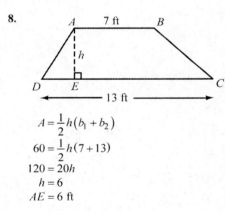

2 yd = 6 ft; 3 yd = 9 ft

$10^2 = 6^2 + x^2$

$x^2 = 10^2 - 6^2$

$x = \sqrt{100 - 36}$

$x = \sqrt{64} = 8$

$A_{EFGH} = bh = (6 + 9)(8) = 120 \text{ ft}^2$

6. $A_{MNPQ} = \frac{1}{2}d_1 d_2 = \frac{1}{2}(8)(6) = 24 \text{ ft}^2$

7. $s = \frac{1}{2}(4 + 13 + 15) = 16$

$A = \sqrt{s(s-a)(s-b)(s-c)}$

$A = \sqrt{16(16-4)(16-13)(16-15)}$

$A = \sqrt{16(12)(3)(1)}$

$A = \sqrt{4^2 \cdot 3^2 \cdot 2^2}$

$A = 4 \cdot 3 \cdot 2$

$A = 24 \text{ cm}^2$

8.

A ———7 ft——— B, h, D E, |———13 ft———|

$A = \frac{1}{2}h(b_1 + b_2)$

$60 = \frac{1}{2}h(7 + 13)$

$120 = 20h$

$h = 6$

$AE = 6 \text{ ft}$

9. a. $P = ns = 5(5.8) = 29 \text{ in.}$

b. $A = \frac{1}{2}aP = \frac{1}{2}(4.0)(29) = 58 \text{ in}^2$

10. a. $C = 2\pi r = 2\pi(5) = 10\pi \text{ in.}$

b. $A = \pi r^2 = \pi(5)^2 = 25\pi \text{ in}^2$

11. $\ell \widehat{AC} = \frac{m\widehat{AC}}{360} \cdot 2\pi r$

$\ell \widehat{AC} = \frac{45}{360} \cdot 2\left(\frac{22}{7}\right)(7)$

$\ell \widehat{AC} = \frac{1}{8} \cdot 44$

$\ell \widehat{AC} = \frac{11}{2} = 5\frac{1}{2} \text{ in.}$

12. $d = 2r$
   $20 = 2r$
   $r = 10$ cm
   $A = \pi r^2$
   $A = (3.14)(10)^2 = 314$ cm^2

13. By the 45°-45°-90° relationship, the radius of the circle is 4.

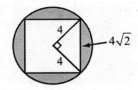

$A_{\text{SHADED}} = A_{\text{CIRCLE}} - A_{\text{SQUARE}}$

$A_{\text{SHADED}} = (\pi \cdot r^2) - s^2$

$A_{\text{SHADED}} = (\pi \cdot 4^2) - (4\sqrt{2})^2$

$A_{\text{SHADED}} = (16\pi - 32)$ in^2

14. $A = \dfrac{m}{360}\pi r^2$

   $A = \dfrac{135}{360} \cdot \pi \cdot 12^2$

   $A = \dfrac{3}{8} \cdot \pi \cdot 144$

   $A = 54\pi$ cm^2

15.

$A_{\text{SHADED}} = A_{\text{SECTOR}} - A_{\text{TRIANGLE}}$

$A_{\text{SHADED}} = \dfrac{m}{360}\pi r^2 - \dfrac{1}{2}bh$

$A_{\text{SHADED}} = \dfrac{90}{360} \cdot \pi \cdot 12^2 - \dfrac{1}{2}(12)(12)$

$A_{\text{SHADED}} = \dfrac{1}{4} \cdot \pi \cdot 144 - 72$

$A_{\text{SHADED}} = (36\pi - 72)$ in^2

16. $P = a + b + c$
   $P = 5 + 12 + 13$
   $P = 30$

   $A = \dfrac{1}{2}rP$

   $30 = \dfrac{1}{2}r(30)$

   $1 = \dfrac{1}{2}r$

   $r = 2$ in.

Chapter 9: Surfaces and Solids

SECTION 9.1: Prisms, Area, and Volume

1. a. Yes
    b. Oblique
    c. Hexagon
    d. Oblique hexagonal prism
    e. Parallelogram

2. a. Yes
    b. Right
    c. Triangular
    d. Right triangular prism
    e. Rectangle

3. a. 12
    b. 18
    c. 8

4. a. 6
    b. 9
    c. 5

5. a. cm^2
    b. cm^3

6. a. ft^2
    b. ft^3

7. $T = 2(12) + 6(18)$
    $T = 132$ cm^2

8. $T = 2(3.4) + 3(4.6)$
    $T = 20.6$ cm^2

9. $V = bh$
    $V = 12(10)$
    $V = 120$ cm^3

10. $V = bh$
    $V = (3.4)(1.2)$
    $V = 4.08$ cm^3

11. a. 16
    b. 8
    c. 16

12. a. 10
    b. 5
    c. 10

13. a. $2n$
    b. n
    c. $2n$
    d. $3n$
    e. n
    f. 2
    g. $n + 2$

14. a. $L = hP$
    $L = 10(5 \cdot 6)$
    $L = 300$ in^2

    b. $T = L + 2B$
    $T = 300 + 2\left(\frac{1}{2}bh\right)$
    $T = 300 + (4.1)(5 \cdot 6)$
    $T = 423$ in^2

    c. $V = Bh$
    $V = \left(\frac{1}{2}aP\right)(10)$
    $V = \frac{1}{2}(4.1)(30)(10)$
    $V = 615$ in^3

15. a. $L = hP$
    $L = (14.6)(5 \cdot 9.2)$
    $L = 671.6$ cm^2

    b. $T = L + 2B$
    $T = 671.6 + 2\left(\frac{1}{2}aP\right)$
    $T = 671.6 + (6.3)(5 \cdot 9.2)$
    $T = 961.4$ cm^2

    c. $V = Bh$
    $V = \left(\frac{1}{2}aP\right)(14.6)$
    $V = \frac{1}{2}(6.3)(5 \cdot 9.2)(14.6)$
    $V = 2115.54$ cm^3

16. a. $L = hP$
$L = 7(4 + 5 + 6)$
$L = 105 \text{ m}^2$

b. $B = \sqrt{s(s-a)(s-b)(s-c)}$
$B = \sqrt{7.5(7.5-4)(7.5-5)(7.5-6)}$
$B \approx 9.92$
$T = L + 2B$
$T = 105 + 2(9.92)$
$T = 124.84 \text{ m}^2$

c. $V = Bh$
$V = (9.92)(7)$
$V = 69.44 \text{ m}^3$

17. a. $L = hP$
$L = (6)(3 + 4 + 5)$
$L = 72 \text{ ft}^2$

b. $T = L + 2B$
$T = 72 + 2\left(\frac{1}{2}bh\right)$
$T = 72 + 4 \cdot 3$
$T = 84 \text{ ft}^2$

c. $V = Bh$
$V = \left(\frac{1}{2}bh\right) \cdot 6$
$V = \left(\frac{1}{2} \cdot 4 \cdot 3\right)(6)$
$V = 36 \text{ ft}^3$

18. $(100)(100)(100) = 1{,}000{,}000 \text{ cm}^3 = 1 \text{ m}^3$

19. $(12)(12)(12) = 1728 \text{ in}^3 = 1 \text{ ft}^3$

20. $V = Bh$
$V = (8 \cdot 2) \cdot 10$
$V = 160 \text{ in}^3$
$T = L + 2B$
$T = hP + 2(\ell w)$
$T = 10 \cdot (2 \cdot 8 + 2 \cdot 2) + 2 \cdot (2 \cdot 8)$
$T = 10 \cdot (16 + 4) + 2 \cdot 16$
$T = 232 \text{ in}^2$

21.

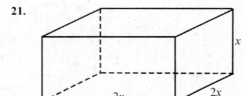

$V = l \cdot w \cdot h$
$108 = 2x \cdot 2x \cdot x$
$108 = 4x^3$
$x^3 = 27$
$x = 3 \rightarrow 2x = 6$
The figure is 6 in. by 6 in. by 3 in.

22. $L = 4 \cdot x + 4(x + 2) + 4 \cdot x + 4(x + 2)$
$96 = 4x + 4x + 8 + 4x + 4x + 8$
$96 = 16x + 16$
$80 = 16x$
$x = 5$
$x + 2 = 7$
The width of the base is 5 meters. The length of the base is 7 meters.

23. $T = 4x + 4(x+2) + x(x+2) + 4x + 4(x+2) + x(x+2)$
$94 = 4x + 4x + 8 + x^2 + 2x + 4x + 4x + 8 + x^2 + 2x$
$94 = 2x^2 + 20x + 16$
$0 = 2x^2 + 20x - 78$
$0 = 2\left(x^2 + 10x - 39\right)$
$0 = 2(x + 13)(x - 3)$
$x + 13 = 0$ or $x - 3 = 0$
$\quad\quad x = -13$ or $\quad\quad x = 3$
reject $x = -13$

24. $V = \ell \cdot w \cdot h$
$252 = (x + 2) \cdot x \cdot 4$
$0 = 4x^2 + 8x - 252$
$0 = 4\left(x^2 + 2x - 63\right)$
$0 = 4(x + 9)(x - 7)$
$x + 9 = 0$ or $x - 7 = 0$
$\quad\quad x = -9$ or $\quad\quad x = 7$
reject $x = -9$

25. 1 foot equals 12 inches.
$L = 5 \cdot 6 + 12 \cdot 6 + 5 \cdot 6 + 12 \cdot 6$
$L = 30 + 72 + 30 + 7$
$L = 204 \text{ in}^2$
$B = 5 \cdot 12 = 60 \text{ in}^2$
The area of both bases is 120 in².
Cost = $0.01(204) + $0.02(120)
Cost = $2.04 + $2.40
Cost = $4.44

26. $V = Bh$
$V = \left(32 \cdot 1\frac{3}{8}\right) \cdot 80$
$V = 3520 \text{ in}^3$

27. V = Volume of rectangular prism
$\quad\quad$ + Volume of triangular prism
$V = 8 \cdot 10 \cdot 7 + \frac{1}{2} \cdot 8 \cdot 2 \cdot 10$
$V = 560 + 80$
$V = 640 \text{ ft}^3$

28. Use the trapezoid shown as the base; the height is 8'.

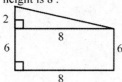

$V = Bh$

$V = \left(\frac{1}{2} \cdot 2 \cdot 8 + 6 \cdot 8\right) \cdot 8$

$V = (8 + 48) \cdot 8$

$V = 448 \text{ ft}^3$

29. **a.** $T = L + 2B$

$T = hP + 2(e \cdot e)$

$T = e(4e) + 2e^2$

$T = 4e^2 + 2e^2$

$T = 6e^2$

b. $T = 6e^2$

$T = 6 \cdot 4^2$

$T = 96 \text{ cm}^2$

c. $V = Bh$

$V = e^2 \cdot e$

$V = e^3$

d. $V = e^3$

$V = 4^3 = 64 \text{ cm}^3$

30. **a.** $T = 6e^2$

$T = 6 \cdot (5.3)^2$

$T = 168.54 \text{ ft}^2$

b. $V = e^3$

$V = (5.3)^3$

$V = 148.88 \text{ ft}^3$

31. Let x = the length of the side of the original cube. The difference in volumes of the two cubes = 61.

$(x + 1)^3 - x^3 = 61$

$(x + 1)(x^2 + 2x + 1) - x^3 = 61$

$x^3 + 2x^2 + x + x^2 + 2x + 1 - x^3 - 61 = 0$

$3x^2 + 3x - 60 = 0$

$x^2 + x - 20 = 0$

$(x + 5)(x - 4) = 0$

$x = -5$ or $x = 4$; reject $x = -5$

The length of the edge of the original cube is

4 cm.

32. Let the length of each edge of the cube = x.

$x^3 = 6x^2$

$x^3 - 6x^2 = 0$

$x(x^2 - 6) = 0$

$x = 0$ or $x = 6$; reject $x = 0$

Each edge length = 6 units.

33. The diagonal of a base is $e\sqrt{2}$.
Let the diagonal of the cube be D.

$D = \sqrt{\left(e\sqrt{2}\right)^2 + e^2}$

$D = \sqrt{e^2 \cdot 2 + e^2}$

$D = \sqrt{3e^2}$

$D = e\sqrt{3}$

34. $V = (36' \cdot 30') \cdot \frac{2}{3}'$

$V = 720 \text{ ft}^3$

$1 \text{ yd}^3 = 27 \text{ ft}^3$

$V = 720 \text{ ft}^3 \div \frac{27 \text{ ft}^3}{1 \text{ yd}^3}$

$V = 26\frac{2}{3} \text{ yd}^3$

35. $V = 15' \cdot 12' \cdot 2'$

$V = 360 \text{ ft}^3$

$1 \text{ yd}^3 = 27 \text{ ft}^3$

$V = 360 \text{ ft}^3 \div \frac{27 \text{ ft}^3}{1 \text{ yd}^3}$

$V = 13\frac{1}{3} \text{ yd}^3$

$\text{Cost} = 13\frac{1}{3} \text{ yd}^3 \cdot \frac{\$9.60}{1 \text{ yd}^3} = \$128$

36. $V = 18 \text{ yd} \cdot 12 \text{ yd} \cdot 3 \text{ yd} = 648 \text{ yd}^3$

37. $V = 12 \cdot 12 \cdot 6 = 864 \text{ in}^3$

38. $V = 18 \cdot 8 \cdot 6 = 864 \text{ in}^3$

39. $V = 2 \cdot 1 \cdot \frac{2}{3} = \frac{4}{3} \text{ ft}^3$

# of gallons $= \frac{4}{3} \cdot 7.5 = 10 \text{ gal}$

40. $V = 2 \cdot \frac{5}{3} \cdot \frac{3}{4} = \frac{5}{2} \text{ ft}^3$

# of gallons $= \frac{5}{2} \cdot 7.5 = 18\frac{3}{4} \text{ gal}$

41. $L = 5 \cdot A_{\text{PARALLELOGRAM}}$

$L = 5 \cdot bh$

$L = 5 \cdot 12 \cdot 12$

$L = 720 \text{ cm}^2$

42. $T = L + 2B$

$T = L + 2\left(\dfrac{1}{2}aP\right)$

$T = 720 + (8.2)(12 \cdot 5)$

$T = 720 + 492$

$T = 1212 \text{ cm}^2$

43. $V = Bh$

$V = \left(\dfrac{1}{2}aP\right) \cdot 12$

$V = \dfrac{1}{2} \cdot 8.2 \cdot (12 \cdot 5) \cdot 12$

$V = 2952 \text{ cm}^3$

44. $d = \sqrt{\ell^2 + w^2 + h^2}$

$d = \sqrt{(12)^2 + 4^2 + 3^2}$

$d = \sqrt{144 + 16 + 9}$

$d = \sqrt{169}$

$d = 13 \text{ in.}$

SECTION 9.2: Pyramids, Area, and Volume

1. a. Right pentagonal prism

  b. Oblique pentagonal prism

2. a. Right hexagonal prism

  b. Oblique hexagonal prism

3. a. Regular square pyramid

  b. Oblique square pyramid

4. a. Right hexagonal pyramid

  b. Oblique hexagonal pyramid

5. a. Pyramid

  b. E

  c. $\overline{EA}$, $\overline{EB}$, $\overline{EC}$, $\overline{ED}$

  d. $\triangle EAB$, $\triangle EBC$, $\triangle ECD$, $\triangle EAD$

  e. No

6. a. V

  b. $\overline{MN}$, $\overline{NP}$, $\overline{PQ}$, $\overline{QR}$, $\overline{RS}$, $\overline{SM}$

  c. Yes

  d. Yes

7. a. 5

  b. 8

  c. 5

8. a. 7

  b. 12

  c. 7

9. $T = 12 + 16 + 12 + 10 + 16$

$T = 66 \text{ in}^2$

10. $T = 6(20) + 41.6$

$T = 161.6 \text{ cm}^2$

11. $V = \dfrac{1}{3}Bh$

$V = \dfrac{1}{3}(16)(6)$

$V = 32 \text{ cm}^3$

12. $V = \dfrac{1}{3}Bh$

$V = \dfrac{1}{3}(41.6)(3.7)$

$V = 51.31 \text{ cm}^3$

13. a. $n + 1$

  b. n

  c. n

  d. $2n$

  e. n

  f. $n + 1$

14. 1a, 2a

15. 3a, 4a

16. a. Slant height

  b. Lateral edge

17. a. Slant height

  b. Lateral edge

18. $\ell^2 = a^2 + h^2$

$\ell^2 = 4^2 + 8^2$

$\ell^2 = 16 + 64$

$\ell^2 = 80$

$\ell = \sqrt{80} = 4\sqrt{5} \approx 8.94 \text{ in.}$

19. $\ell^2 = a^2 + h^2$

$5^2 = 3^2 + h^2$

$h^2 = 5^2 - 3^2$

$h^2 = 16$

$h = 4 \text{ in.}$

20. Using a lateral face with the slant height drawn, we have

$$\ell^2 + 3^2 = 8^2$$
$$\ell^2 = 64 - 9$$
$$\ell^2 = 55$$
$$\ell = \sqrt{55}$$

a. $L = \frac{1}{2}\ell P$

$$L = \frac{1}{2}\left(\sqrt{55}\right)(30)$$
$$L = 15\sqrt{55} \approx 111.24 \text{ in}^2$$

b. $T = L + B$

$$T = 11.24 + \frac{1}{2}(4.1)(6.5)$$
$$T = 172.74 \text{ in}^2$$

21. a. $B = \frac{1}{2}aP$

$$B = \frac{1}{2}(6.3)(5 \cdot 9.2)$$
$$B = 144.9 \text{ cm}^2$$

b. $V = \frac{1}{3}Bh$

$$V = \frac{1}{3}(144.9)(14.6)$$
$$V = 705.18 \text{ cm}^3$$

22. Using a lateral face with the slant height drawn, we have

$$\ell^2 + 5^2 = 13^2$$
$$\ell^2 = 169 - 25$$
$$\ell^2 = 144$$
$$\ell = 12$$

a. $L = \frac{1}{2}\ell P$

$$L = \frac{1}{2}(12)(10.4)$$
$$L = 240 \text{ m}^2$$

b. $T = L + B$

$$T = 240 + 100$$
$$T = 340 \text{ m}^2$$
$$\ell^2 = a^2 + h^2$$
$$12^2 = 5^2 + h^2$$
$$h^2 = 144 - 25$$
$$h = \sqrt{119} \text{ m}$$

c. $V = \frac{1}{3}Bh$

$$V = \frac{1}{3}(100)\left(\sqrt{119}\right)$$
$$V = \frac{100\sqrt{119}}{3} \approx 363.62 \text{ m}^3$$

23. $\ell^2 = a^2 + h^2$
$$\ell^2 = 3^2 + 4^2$$
$$\ell^2 = 9 + 16$$
$$\ell^2 = 25$$
$$\ell = 5$$

a. $L = \frac{1}{2}\ell P$

$$L = \frac{1}{2}(5)(6 \cdot 4)$$
$$L = 60 \text{ ft}^2$$

b. $T = L + B$
$$T = 60 + (6 \cdot 6)$$
$$T = 96 \text{ ft}^2$$

c. $V = \frac{1}{3}Bh$
$$V = \frac{1}{3}(36)(4)$$
$$V = 48 \text{ ft}^3$$

24. The apothem, a, of the base is $3\sqrt{3}$.

$$\ell^2 = a^2 + h^2$$
$$\ell^2 = \left(3\sqrt{3}\right)^2 + 8^2$$
$$\ell^2 = 27 + 64$$
$$\ell^2 = 91$$
$$\ell = \sqrt{91}$$

a. $L = \frac{1}{2}\ell P$

$$L = \frac{1}{2}\left(\sqrt{91}\right)(6 \cdot 6)$$
$$L = 18\sqrt{91} \approx 171.71 \text{ ft}^2$$

b. $T = L + B$

$$T = 171.71 + \frac{1}{2}aP$$
$$T = 171.71 + \frac{1}{2}\left(3\sqrt{3}\right)(6 \cdot 6)$$
$$T = 171.71 + 54\sqrt{3}$$
$$T \approx 171.71 + 93.53$$
$$T \approx 265.24 \text{ ft}^2$$

c. $V = \frac{1}{3}Bh$

$V = \frac{1}{3}(54\sqrt{3})(8)$

$V = 144\sqrt{3} \approx 249.42 \text{ ft}^3$

25. $V = \frac{1}{3}Bh$

$72 = \frac{1}{3} \cdot x^2 \cdot x$

$72 = \frac{1}{3}x^3$

$x^3 = 216$

$x = 6$

$\ell^2 = a^2 + h^2$

$\ell^2 = 3^2 + 6^2$

$\ell^2 = 45$

$\ell = \sqrt{45} = 3\sqrt{5}$

$L = \frac{1}{2}\ell P$

$L = \frac{1}{2}(3\sqrt{5})(4 \cdot 6)$

$L = 36\sqrt{5}$

$T = L + B$

$T = 36\sqrt{5} + (6 \cdot 6)$

$T = 36\sqrt{5} + 36 \approx 116.5 \text{ in}^2$

26. $L = \frac{1}{2}\ell P$

$200 = \frac{1}{2} \cdot e \cdot 4e$ (*e* is the base edge length)

$200 = 2e^2$

$100 = e^2$

$e = 10$

$\ell^2 = a^2 + h^2$

$10^2 = 5^2 + h^2$

$h^2 = 100 - 25$

$h^2 = 75$

$h = \sqrt{75} = 5\sqrt{3} \text{ in.}$

$V = \frac{1}{3}Bh$

$V = \frac{1}{3}(10 \cdot 10)(5\sqrt{3})$

$V = \frac{500\sqrt{3}}{3} \approx 288.68 \text{ in}^3$

27. $L = \frac{1}{2}\ell P$

$L = \frac{1}{2}(15)(16 \cdot 4)$

$L = 480 \text{ ft}^2$

28. $\ell^2 = a^2 + h^2$

$15^2 = 8^2 + h^2$

$h^2 = 225 - 64$

$h^2 = 161$

$h = \sqrt{161}$

$V = \frac{1}{3}Bh$

$V = \frac{1}{3}(16 \cdot 16)(\sqrt{161})$

$V = \frac{256\sqrt{161}}{3} \approx 1082.76 \text{ ft}^3$

29. $V = \frac{1}{3}Bh$

$V = \frac{1}{3}\left(\frac{1}{2}aP\right)(15)$

$V = \frac{1}{3} \cdot \frac{1}{2} \cdot (7.5)(12 \cdot 4)(15)$

$V = 900 \text{ ft}^3$

30. $\ell^2 = a^2 + h^2$

$\ell^2 = (7.5)^2 + 15^2$

$\ell^2 = 281.25$

$\ell = \sqrt{281.25}$

$L = \frac{1}{2}\ell P$

$L = \frac{1}{2}(\sqrt{281.25})(4 \cdot 12)$

$L = 24\sqrt{281.25} \approx 402.49 \text{ ft}^2$

31. Let the altitude length = base edge length = x

The apothem length $= \frac{1}{2}x\sqrt{3}$

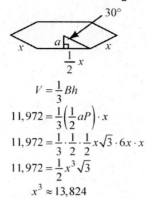

$$V = \frac{1}{3}Bh$$
$$11,972 = \frac{1}{3}\left(\frac{1}{2}aP\right)\cdot x$$
$$11,972 = \frac{1}{3}\cdot\frac{1}{2}\cdot\frac{1}{2}x\sqrt{3}\cdot 6x\cdot x$$
$$11,972 = \frac{1}{2}x^3\sqrt{3}$$
$$x^3 \approx 13,824$$
$$x \approx 24 \text{ ft}$$

32.
$$L = \frac{1}{2}aP$$
$$800 = \frac{1}{2}\cdot\ell\cdot(8\cdot 10)$$
$$80 = \ell\cdot 40$$
$$\ell = 20$$

$$\ell^2 = a^2 + h^2$$
$$20^2 = 12^2 + h^2$$
$$h^2 = 20^2 - 12^2$$
$$h^2 = 256$$
$$h = 16 \text{ ft}$$

33. $V = V_{\text{TALLER PYRAMID}} - V_{\text{SHORTER PYRAMID}}$
$$V = \frac{1}{3}B_1 h_1 - \frac{1}{3}B_2 h_2$$
$$V = \frac{1}{3}(6\cdot 6)(32) - \frac{1}{3}(3\cdot 3)(16)$$
$$V = 384 - 48$$
$$V = 336 \text{ in}^3$$

34. $V = V_{\text{TALLER PYRAMID}} - V_{\text{SHORTER PYRAMID}}$
$$V = \frac{1}{3}B_1 h_1 - \frac{1}{3}B_2 h_2$$
$$V = \frac{1}{3}(6\cdot 6)(24) - \frac{1}{3}(4\cdot 4)(16)$$
$$V = 288 - 85\frac{1}{3}$$
$$V = 202\frac{2}{3} \text{ in}^3$$

35. a. $A_{\text{EQ}_\triangle} = \dfrac{s^2\sqrt{3}}{4} = \dfrac{e^2\sqrt{3}}{4}$

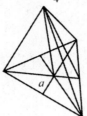

b. $T = L + B$

$$T = 3\left(\frac{e^2\sqrt{3}}{4}\right) + \frac{e^2\sqrt{3}}{4} = e^2\sqrt{3}$$

36. $\ell = \frac{1}{2}e\sqrt{3}$

$$\therefore a = \frac{1}{3}\left(\frac{1}{2}e\sqrt{3}\right)$$
$$a = \frac{1}{6}e\sqrt{3}$$

a.
$$\ell^2 = a^2 + h^2$$
$$\left(\frac{1}{2}e\sqrt{3}\right)^2 = \left(\frac{1}{6}e\sqrt{3}\right)^2 + h^2$$
$$h^2 = \frac{3}{4}e^2 - \frac{1}{2}e^2$$
$$h^2 = \left(\frac{9}{12} - \frac{1}{12}\right)e^2$$
$$h^2 = \frac{2}{3}e^2$$
$$h = \frac{\sqrt{2}}{\sqrt{3}}e$$

h \qquad $\ell = \frac{1}{2}e\sqrt{3}$

$a = \frac{1}{6}e\sqrt{3}$

b. $V = \frac{1}{3}Bh$
$$V = \frac{1}{3}\left(\frac{e^2\sqrt{3}}{4}\right)\left(\frac{\sqrt{2}}{\sqrt{3}}e\right)$$
$$V = \frac{\sqrt{2}e^3}{12}$$

c. $V = \dfrac{\sqrt{2}e^3}{12}$
$$V = \frac{\sqrt{2}}{12}(4)^3 = \frac{\sqrt{2}}{12}\cdot 64$$
$$V = \frac{16\sqrt{2}}{3} \approx 7.54 \text{ in}^3$$

37.

$$l^2 + 9 = 34$$
$$l^2 = 25$$
$$l = 5$$

$T = B + L$
$T = 36 + \frac{1}{2} \cdot 24 \cdot 5$
$T = 36 + 60$
$T = 96 \text{ in}^2$

38.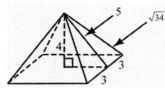

$V = \frac{1}{3}Bh$
$V = \frac{1}{3} \cdot 36 \cdot 4$
$V = 48 \text{ in}^3$

39. $\dfrac{V_1}{V_2} = \left(\dfrac{e_1}{e_2}\right)^3 = \left(\dfrac{4}{2}\right)^3 = \dfrac{2^3}{1^3} = \dfrac{8}{1}$ or 8 : 1.

40. $\dfrac{V_1}{V_2} = \left(\dfrac{e_1}{e_2}\right)^3 = \left(\dfrac{2}{6}\right)^3 = \dfrac{1^3}{3^3} = \dfrac{1}{27}$ or 1 : 27

41.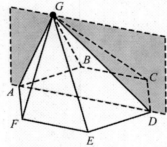

$V_{ABCD} = V_{DEFA}$
$V_{ABCDEF} = V_{ABCD} + V_{DEFA}$
$V_{ABCDEF} = 19.7 + 19.7 = 39.4 \text{ in}^3$

SECTION 9.3: Cylinders and Cones

1. a. Yes

   b. Yes

   c. Yes

2. a. Yes

   b. Yes

   c. Yes

3. a. $L = 2\pi r h$
      $L = 2\pi \cdot 5 \cdot 6$
      $L = 60\pi \approx 188.5 \text{ in}^2$

   b. $T = L + 2B$
      $T = 60\pi + 2\pi \cdot 5^2$
      $T = 60\pi + 50\pi$
      $T = 110\pi \approx 345.58 \text{ in}^2$

   c. $V = \pi r^2 h$
      $V = \pi \cdot 5^2 \cdot 6$
      $V = 150\pi \approx 471.24 \text{ in}^3$

4. a. $L = 2\pi r h$
      $L = 2\pi \cdot 12 \cdot 15$
      $L = 360\pi \approx 1130.97 \text{ cm}^2$

   b. $T = L + 2B$
      $T = 360\pi + 2\pi \cdot 12^2$
      $T = 360\pi + 288\pi$
      $T = 648\pi \approx 2035.75 \text{ cm}^2$

   c. $V = \pi r^2 h$
      $V = \pi \cdot 12^2 \cdot 15$
      $V = 2160\pi \approx 6785.84 \text{ cm}^3$

5. $L = 2\pi r h$
   $L = 2\pi(1.5)(4.25)$
   $L = 12.75\pi \text{ in}^2$

   $B = \pi r^2$
   $B = \pi(1.5)^2$
   $B = 2.25\pi$

   $T = L + 2B$
   $T = 12.75\pi + 2(2.25\pi)$
   $T = 17.25\pi \approx 54.19 \text{ in}^3$

6. $V = \pi r^2 h$

$V = \pi \cdot (1.05)^2 (4.25)$

$V = 9.5625\pi \approx 30.04$ cm^3

$$\frac{\text{Weight of Smaller}}{\text{Volume of Smaller}} = \frac{\text{Weight of Larger}}{\text{Volume of Larger}}$$

$$\frac{16}{9.5625\pi} = \frac{20}{V}$$

$$16V = 20(9.5625\pi)$$

$$16V = 191.25\pi$$

$$V \approx 37.55 \text{ in}^3$$

7. $V = \pi r^2 h$

$200\pi = \pi \cdot r^2 \cdot 8$

$r^2 = \dfrac{200\pi}{8\pi} = 25$

$r = 5$ cm

8. $V = \pi r^2 h$

$d = \dfrac{3}{4} h$

$2r = \dfrac{3}{4} h$

$r = \dfrac{3}{8} h$

$9\pi = \pi \cdot \left(\dfrac{3}{8} h\right)^2 h$

$9\pi = \dfrac{9}{64} \pi h^3$

$h^3 = \dfrac{9\pi}{\frac{9}{64}\pi}$

$h^3 = 9 \cdot \dfrac{64}{9}$

$h^3 = 64$

$h = 4$ in.

9. $L = 2\pi r h$

$12\pi = 2\pi r(4+1)$

$12\pi = 2\pi(r^2 + r)$

$\dfrac{12\pi}{2\pi} = \dfrac{2\pi(r^2 + r)}{2\pi}$

$r^2 + r = 6$

$r^2 + r - 6 = 0$

$(r+3)(r-2) = 0$

$r + 3 = 0$ or $r - 2 = 0$

$r = -3$ or $r = 2$; reject -3

The radius has a length of 2 inches and the altitude has a length of 3 inches.

10. $C = 2\pi r$

$6\pi = 2\pi r$

$r = \dfrac{6\pi}{2\pi} = 3$

$V = \pi r^2 h$

$81\pi = \pi \cdot 3^2 \cdot h$

$81\pi = 9\pi h$

$h = \dfrac{81\pi}{9\pi}$

$h = 9$ m

11. Using the 45-45-90 relationship,

$h\sqrt{2} = 8\sqrt{2}$

$h = \dfrac{8\sqrt{2}}{\sqrt{2}}$

$h = 8$ in.

$V = \pi r^2 h$

$V = \pi \cdot 2^2 \cdot 8$

$V = 32\pi \approx 100.53$ in^3

12. $L = 2\pi r h$

$L = 2\pi(1)(3)$

$L = 6\pi \approx 18.85$ in^2

$B = \pi r^2$

$B = \pi(1)^2$

$B \approx 3.14$ in^2

so $2B \approx 6.28$ in^2

Cost $= (0.5)(6.28) + (0.2)(18.85)$

$= 6.91 \approx 7$ cents

13. $r^2 + h^2 = \ell^2$

$4^2 + 6^2 = \ell^2$

$\ell^2 = 52$

$\ell = \sqrt{52} = 2\sqrt{13} \approx 7.21$ cm

14. $r^2 + h^2 = \ell^2$

$(5.2)^2 + (3.9)^2 = \ell^2$

$\ell^2 = 42.25$

$\ell = 6.5$ ft

15. $r^2 + h^2 = \ell^2$

$(4.8)^2 + h^2 = (5.2)^2$

$h^2 = (5.2)^2 - (4.8)^2$

$h^2 = 4$

$h = 2$ m

16. $r^2 + h^2 = \ell^2$

$r^2 + 6^2 = 8^2$

$r^2 = 8^2 - 6^2$

$r^2 = 28$

$r = \sqrt{28} = 2\sqrt{7} \approx 5.29$ yd

17. $r^2 + h^2 = \ell^2$

$6^2 + h^2 = (2h)^2$

$3h^2 = 36$

$h^2 = 12$

$h = 2\sqrt{3}$

$\ell = 2h = 2(2\sqrt{3}) = 4\sqrt{3} \approx 6.93$ in.

18. $r^2 + h^2 = \ell^2$

$r^2 + (3r)^2 = 12^2$

$r^2 + 9r^2 = 144$

$10r^2 = 144$

$r^2 = 14.4$

$r = \sqrt{14.4} \approx 3.79$ in.

19. Let x = the length of the axis of the cone.

$x^2 = 3^2 + 6^2$

$x^2 = 45$

$x = \sqrt{45} = 3\sqrt{5} \approx 6.71$ cm

20. **a.** $\ell^2 = r^2 + h^2$

$\ell^2 = 4^2 + 6^2$

$\ell^2 = 52$

$\ell = \sqrt{52} = 2\sqrt{13}$

$L = \frac{1}{2}\ell C$

$L = \frac{1}{2} \cdot 2\sqrt{13} \cdot 2\pi r$

$L = \frac{1}{2} \cdot 2\sqrt{13} \cdot 2\pi \cdot 4$

$L = 8\pi\sqrt{13} \approx 90.62$ m^2

b. $T = L + B$

$T = 8\pi\sqrt{13} + \pi r^2$

$T = 8\pi\sqrt{13} + \pi \cdot 4^2$

$T = 8\pi\sqrt{13} + 16\pi \approx 140.88$ m^2

c. $V = \frac{1}{3}Bh$

$V = \frac{1}{3}\pi r^2 h$

$V = \frac{1}{3} \cdot \pi \cdot 4^2 \cdot 6$

$V = 32\pi \approx 100.53$ m^3

21. $\ell^2 = r^2 + h^2$

$\ell^2 = 7^2 + 6^2$

$\ell^2 = 85$

$\ell = \sqrt{85}$

a. $L = \frac{1}{2}\ell C$

$L = \frac{1}{2}\sqrt{85} \cdot 2\pi r$

$L = \frac{1}{2}\sqrt{85} \cdot 2 \cdot \pi \cdot 6$

$L = 6\pi\sqrt{85} \approx 173.78$ in^2

b. $T = L + B$

$T = 6\pi\sqrt{85} + \pi r^2$

$T = 6\pi\sqrt{85} + \pi \cdot 6^2$

$T = 6\pi\sqrt{85} + 36\pi \approx 286.88$ in^2

c. $V = \frac{1}{3}Bh$

$V = \frac{1}{3}\pi r^2 \cdot 7$

$V = \frac{1}{3} \cdot \pi \cdot 6^2 \cdot 7$

$V = 84\pi \approx 263.89$ in^3

22. $V = \frac{1}{3}Bh$

$V = \frac{1}{3}\pi \cdot r^2 \cdot 15$

$V = \frac{1}{3} \cdot \pi \cdot 6^2 \cdot 15$

$V = 180\pi \approx 565.49$ ft^3

23. The solid formed is a cylinder with $r = 3$ and $h = 6$.

$V = Bh$

$V = \pi r^2 h$

$V = \pi \cdot 3^2 \cdot 6$

$V = 54\pi$ in^3

24. The solid formed is a cylinder with $r = 6$ and $h = 3$.

$V = Bh$

$V = \pi r^2 h$

$V = \pi \cdot 6^2 \cdot 3$

$V = 108\pi$ in^3

25. The solid formed is a cone with $r = 20$ and $h = 15$.

$V = \frac{1}{3}Bh$

$V = \frac{1}{3}\pi r^2 h$

$V = \frac{1}{3} \cdot \pi \cdot 20^2 \cdot 15$

$V = 2000\pi \text{ cm}^3$

26. The solid formed is a cone with $r = 15$ and $h = 20$.

$V = \frac{1}{3}Bh$

$V = \frac{1}{3}\pi r^2 h$

$V = \frac{1}{3} \cdot \pi \cdot 15^2 \cdot 20$

$V = 1500\pi \text{ cm}^3$

27. The solid formed consists of two cones sharing the same base with $r = 12$. The height of one cone is 16 and the height of the other cone is 9.

$V = \frac{1}{3}Bh_1 + \frac{1}{3}Bh_2$

$V = \frac{1}{3}\pi r^2 h_1 + \frac{1}{3}\pi r^2 h_2$

$V = \frac{1}{3}\pi r^2 (h_1 + h_2)$

$V = \frac{1}{3} \cdot \pi \cdot 12^2 \cdot (16 + 9)$

$V = \frac{1}{3} \cdot \pi \cdot 12^2 \cdot 25$

$V = 1200\pi \text{ cm}^3$

28. $V = \frac{4}{3}\pi r^3$

$V = \frac{4}{3} \cdot \pi \cdot 3^3$

$V = 36\pi \text{ cm}^3$

29. $d = 10 \therefore r = 5$

$V = \frac{1}{3}Bh$

$V = \frac{1}{3}\pi r^2 h$

$100\pi = \frac{1}{3} \cdot \pi \cdot 5^2 \cdot h$

$100\pi = \frac{25\pi}{3} \cdot h$

$h = 12$

$L = \frac{1}{2}\ell C$

$L = \frac{1}{2} \cdot 13 \cdot 2\pi r$

$L = \frac{1}{2} \cdot 13 \cdot 2\pi \cdot 5$

$L = 65\pi \approx 204.2 \text{ cm}^2$

30. $L = \frac{1}{2}\ell C$

$96\pi = \frac{1}{2} \cdot 12 \cdot 2\pi r$

$96\pi = 12\pi r$

$r = 8 \text{ ft}$

$\ell^2 = r^2 + h^2$

$12^2 = 8^2 + h^2$

$h^2 = 144 - 64$

$h^2 = 80$

$h = \sqrt{80} = 4\sqrt{5}$

$V = \frac{1}{3}Bh$

$V = \frac{1}{3}\pi r^2 \cdot 4\sqrt{5}$

$V = \frac{1}{3} \cdot \pi \cdot 8^2 \cdot 4\sqrt{5}$

$V = \frac{256\pi\sqrt{5}}{3} \approx 599.45 \text{ ft}^3$

31. $V = V_{\text{CYLINDER}} - V_{\text{CONE}}$

$V = Bh - \frac{1}{3}Bh$

$V = \frac{2}{3}Bh$

$V = \frac{2}{3} \cdot \pi r^2 \cdot h$

$V = \frac{2}{3} \cdot \pi \cdot 6^2 \cdot 8$

$V = 192\pi \approx 603.19 \text{ in}^3$

32. $T = L + 2B$

$T = hC + 2\pi r^2$

$T = h \cdot 2\pi r + 2\pi r^2$

$T = 2\pi rh + 2\pi r^2$

$T = 2\pi r(h + r)$

$T = 2\pi r(r + h)$

33. $V = V_{\text{LARGE CYLINDER}} - V_{\text{SMALL CYLINDER}}$

$V = \pi R^2 h - \pi r^2 h$

$V = \pi h(R^2 - r^2)$

$V = \pi h(R - r)(R + r)$

34. Let the length of the radius of the base = x.
The length of the slant height will then = $2x$.

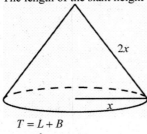

$$T = L + B$$
$$T = \frac{1}{2}\ell C + \pi r^2$$
$$48\pi = \frac{1}{2} \cdot 2x \cdot 2\pi r + \pi \cdot x^2$$
$$48\pi = \frac{1}{2} \cdot 2x \cdot 2\pi \cdot x + \pi \cdot x^2$$
$$48\pi = 2\pi x^2 + \pi x^2$$
$$48\pi = 3\pi x^2$$
$$x^2 = 16$$
$$x = 4 \text{ in.}$$
$$\ell = 8 \text{ in.}$$

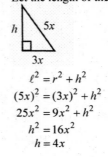

$$\ell^2 = r^2 + h^2$$
$$8^2 = 4^2 + h^2$$
$$h^2 = 64 - 16$$
$$h^2 = 48$$
$$h = \sqrt{48} = 4\sqrt{3} \approx 6.93 \text{ in.}$$

35. Let the length of the radius of the base = $3x$
Let the length of the slant height = $5x$.

$$\ell^2 = r^2 + h^2$$
$$(5x)^2 = (3x)^2 + h^2$$
$$25x^2 = 9x^2 + h^2$$
$$h^2 = 16x^2$$
$$h = 4x$$

$$V = \frac{1}{3}Bh$$
$$96\pi = \frac{1}{3} \cdot \pi r^2 \cdot 4x$$
$$96\pi = \frac{1}{3} \cdot \pi \cdot (3x)^2 \cdot 4x$$
$$96\pi = 12\pi x^3$$
$$x^3 = 8$$
$$x = 2$$
$$r = 3x = 3(2) = 6 \text{ in.}$$
$$\ell = 5x = 5(2) = 10 \text{ in.}$$

$$L = \frac{1}{2}\ell C$$
$$L = \frac{1}{2} \cdot 10 \cdot 2\pi r$$
$$L = \frac{1}{2} \cdot 10 \cdot 2\pi \cdot 6$$
$$L = 60\pi \approx 188.5 \text{ in}^2$$

36. Let r and h represent the dimensions of the smaller cylinder while $2r$ and $2h$ represent those of the larger cylinder.

Volume of smaller $= Bh = \pi r^2 h$

Volume of larger $= Bh = \pi(2r)^2(2h) = 8\pi r^2 h$

$$\frac{\text{Volume of larger}}{\text{Volume of smaller}} = \frac{8\pi r^2 h}{\pi r^2 h} = \frac{8}{1} \text{ or } 8 : 1.$$

37. Lateral area of smaller $= 2\pi rh$

Lateral area of larger $= 2\pi(2r)(2h) = 8\pi rh$

$$\frac{\text{Lateral area of larger}}{\text{Lateral area of smaller}} = \frac{8\pi rh}{2\pi rh} = \frac{4}{1} \text{ or } 4:1$$

38. For the given cone,
$$V = \frac{1}{3}Bh$$
$$V = \frac{1}{3} \cdot \pi r^2 \cdot h$$
$$V = \frac{1}{3} \cdot \pi \cdot 6^2 \cdot 8$$
$$V = 96\pi \text{ cm}^3$$
For the second one,
$$V = \frac{1}{3}Bh$$
$$V = \frac{1}{3} \cdot \pi r^2 \cdot h$$
$$V = \frac{1}{3} \cdot \pi \cdot 12^2 \cdot 4$$
$$V = 192\pi \text{ cm}^3$$
The volumes are unequal; the second cone has a volume equal to twice that of the first cone.

39. $V = Bh$
$$V = \pi r^2 h$$
$$V = \pi \cdot 2^2 \cdot 5$$
$$V = 20\pi$$
Capacity $= 20\pi \cdot 7.5 \approx 471.24$ gallons

40. $T = L + 2B$
$$T = hC + 2 \cdot \pi r^2$$
$$T = 5 \cdot 2\pi r + 2 \cdot \pi \cdot 2^2$$
$$T = 5 \cdot 2 \cdot \pi \cdot 2 + 2 \cdot \pi \cdot 2^2$$
$$T = 20\pi + 8\pi$$
$$T = 28\pi \approx 87.96 \text{ ft}^2$$
The number of pints required to paint the tank is
$$\frac{87.96}{50} \approx 1.76 \text{ pints.}$$
Two pints of paint need to be purchased.

41. $V = V_{\text{LARGER CONE}} - V_{\text{SMALLER CONE}}$
$$V = \frac{1}{3}\pi R^2 h - \frac{1}{3}\pi r^2 h$$

42. $V = V_{\text{LARGER CONE}} - V_{\text{SMALLER CONE}}$
$$V = \frac{1}{3}\pi R^2 H - \frac{1}{3}\pi r^2 h$$
$$V = \frac{1}{3}\pi (7^2)\left(32\frac{2}{3}\right) - \frac{1}{3}\pi (5.5^2)(26)$$
$$V \approx 852.59 \text{ cm}^3$$

43. $V = V_{\text{LARGER CONE}} - V_{\text{SMALLER CONE}}$
$$V = \frac{1}{3}\pi R^2 H - \frac{1}{3}\pi r^2 h$$
$$V = \frac{1}{3}\pi (4^2)(30) - \frac{1}{3}\pi (3^2)(22.5)$$
$$V \approx 290.60 \text{ cm}^3$$

44. $V = \pi r^2 h$
$$V = \pi \cdot 10^2 \cdot 16$$
$$V = 1600\pi$$
$$V \approx 5026.548 \text{ ft}^3$$
# of gallons $= 5026.548 \cdot 7.5 \approx 37,700$ gal

45. $V = \pi r^2 h$
$$V = \pi \cdot (1.5)^2 \cdot 6$$
$$V = 13.5\pi$$
$$V \approx 42.4115 \text{ ft}^3$$
# of gallons $= 42.4115 \cdot 7.5 \approx 318$ gal

46. $L = \dfrac{240}{360} \cdot \pi r^2 = \dfrac{2}{3} \cdot \pi \cdot (6.4)^2 \approx 85.8 \text{ in}^2$

47. 18 in. = 1.5 ft
$$L = 2\pi r h$$
$$L = 2\pi(1.5)(4)$$
$$L = 12\pi \approx 38 \text{ ft}^2$$

SECTION 9.4: Polyhedrons and Spheres

1. Polyhedron *EFGHIJK* is concave.

2. Polyhedron *ABCD* has 4 faces (F), 4 vertices (V), and 6 edges (E).
$$V + F = E + 2$$
$$4 + 4 = 6 + 2$$

3. Polyhedron *EFGHIJK* has 9 faces (F), 7 vertices (V), and 14 edges (E).
$$V + F = E + 2$$
$$7 + 9 = 14 + 2$$

4. A regular tetrahedron has 4 faces (F), 4 vertices (V), and 6 edges (E).
$$V + F = E + 2$$
$$4 + 4 = 6 + 2$$

5. A regular hexahedron has 6 faces (F), 8 vertices (V), and 12 edges (E).
$$V + F = E + 2$$
$$8 + 6 = 12 + 2$$

6. a. $V + F = E + 2$
$$8 + F = 12 + 2$$
$$F = 14 - 8 = 6$$
Six faces

b. Regular hexahedron or cube

7. a. $V + F = E + 2$
$$6 + F = 12 + 2$$
$$F = 14 - 6 = 8$$
Eight faces

b. Regular octahedron

8. $V + F = E + 2$
$$10 + 7 = E + 2$$
$$E = 17 - 2 = 15$$
Fifteen edges

9. Nine faces

10. a. $\dfrac{1}{6}$

   b. $\dfrac{3}{6} = \dfrac{1}{2}$

   c. $\dfrac{4}{6} = \dfrac{2}{3}$

11. a. $\dfrac{6}{12} = \dfrac{1}{2}$

   b. $\dfrac{5}{12}$

   c. $\dfrac{10}{12} = \dfrac{5}{6}$

12. a. $\dfrac{10}{20} = \dfrac{1}{2}$

   b. $\dfrac{8}{20} = \dfrac{2}{5}$

   c. $\dfrac{18}{20} = \dfrac{9}{10}$

13.

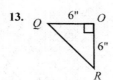

   a. Using the 45°-45°-90° relationship,
$QR = 6\sqrt{2} \approx 8.49$ in.

   b.

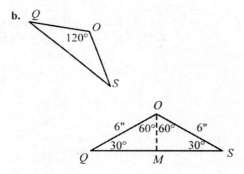

Where M is the midpoint of $\overline{QS}$, $OM = 3$ and
$QM = 3\sqrt{3}$ by the 30°-60°-90° relationship.
$QS = 2(QM) = 2\left(3\sqrt{3}\right) = 6\sqrt{3}$.
That is, $QS = 6\sqrt{3} \approx 10.39$ in.

14. $S = 4\pi r^2$
$S = 4\pi \cdot 6^2$
$S = 144\pi \approx 452.39$ in^2
$V = \dfrac{4}{3}\pi r^3$
$V = \dfrac{4}{3}\pi \cdot 6^3$
$V = 288\pi \approx 904.79$ in^3

15. $S = 8(5.5)^2 = 44$ in^2

16. $S = 12(6.4)^2 = 76.8$ cm^2

17. $S = 6(4.2)^2 = 105.84$ cm^2

18. $S = 4 \cdot \dfrac{s^2\sqrt{3}}{4} = 6^2\sqrt{3} = 36\sqrt{3}$ in^2

19. a. $\dfrac{105.84}{6} = 17.64$ m^2

   b. $s^2 = 17.64$
$s = 4.2$ m

20. a. $\dfrac{32\sqrt{3}}{8}$

   b. $\dfrac{s^2\sqrt{3}}{4} = 4\sqrt{3}$
$s^2 = 16$
$s = 4$ ft

21. a. $A = 34.9(12) + 52.5(20) = 1468.8$ cm^2

   b. Cost $= 1468.8(\$0.006) = \$8.81$

22. a. $A = 27.5(12) = 330$ cm^2

   b. Cost $= 330(\$0.008) = \$2.64$

23. a. For the cylinder, the radius measures r and the
altitude is $2r$.
$T = L + 2B$
$T = hC + 2B$
$T = h \cdot 2\pi r + 2 \cdot \pi r^2$
$T = (2r) \cdot 2\pi \cdot r + 2\pi r^2$
$T = 4\pi r^2 + 2\pi r^2$
$T = 6\pi r^2$

For the sphere, $S = 4\pi r^2$.
The ratio is $\dfrac{6\pi r^2}{4\pi r^2} = \dfrac{3}{2}$ or 3 : 2.

b. For the cylinder,

$V = Bh$

$V = \pi r^2 h$

$V = \pi r^2 (2r)$

$V = 2\pi r^3$

For the sphere,

$V = \dfrac{4}{3}\pi r^3$.

The ratio is

$\dfrac{2\pi r^3}{\frac{4}{3}\pi r^3} = \dfrac{2}{\frac{4}{3}} = \dfrac{3}{2}$ or 3 : 2.

24.

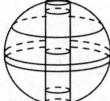

As the radius or the height of the cylinder become smaller, so does the volume, Bh. ∴ the cylinder's volume will approach 0.

25.

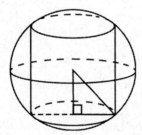

$h = d$ or $h = 2r$

In the triangle shown, $\dfrac{h}{2} = r$.

Then,

$r^2 + r^2 = 6^2$

$2r^2 = 36$

$r^2 = 18$

$r = \sqrt{18} = 3\sqrt{2} \approx 4.24$ in.

$h = 6\sqrt{2} \approx 8.49$ in.

26. The maximum volume for the polyhedron is the volume of the sphere.

$V = \dfrac{4}{3}\pi r^3$

$V = \dfrac{4}{3}\pi \cdot 6^3$

$V = 288\pi \approx 904.79$ in^3

27.

 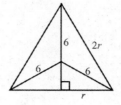

$\ell = d = 2r$

a. Using the 30°-60°-90° relationship,

$r = 3\sqrt{3} \approx 5.20$.

b. The altitude of the cone is of length

$6 + 3 = 9$ in.

28.

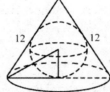 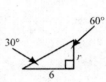

Using the 30°-60°-90° relationship,

$r\sqrt{3} = 6$

$r = \dfrac{6}{\sqrt{3}} = \dfrac{6\sqrt{3}}{3} = 2\sqrt{3} \approx 3.46$ cm.

29. a. $S = 4\pi r^2$

$S = 4\pi \cdot 3^2$

$S = 36\pi \approx 113.1$ m^2

b. $V = \dfrac{4}{3}\pi r^3$

$V = \dfrac{4}{3}\pi \cdot 3^3$

$V = 36\pi \approx 113.1$ m^3

30. a. $S = 4\pi r^2$

$S = 4\pi \cdot 7^2$

$S = 196\pi \approx 615.75$ cm^2

b. $V = \dfrac{4}{3}\pi r^3$

$V = \dfrac{4}{3}\pi \cdot 7^3$

$V = \dfrac{1372\pi}{3} = 457\dfrac{1}{3}\pi \approx 1436.76$ cm^3

31. $V = \dfrac{4}{3}\pi r^3$

$\dfrac{99}{7} = \dfrac{4}{3} \cdot \dfrac{22}{7} \cdot r^3$

$r^3 = \dfrac{99}{7} \cdot \dfrac{21}{88}$

$r^3 = \dfrac{27}{8}$

$r = \dfrac{3}{2}$ or 1.5 in.

32. $S = 4\pi r^2$

$154 = 4 \cdot \dfrac{22}{7} \cdot r^2$

$r^2 = 154 \cdot \dfrac{7}{88}$

$r^2 = \dfrac{49}{4}$

$r = \sqrt{\dfrac{49}{4}}$

$r = \dfrac{7}{2}$ or 3.5 in.

33. $S = 4\pi r^2$

$S = 4\pi \cdot 3^2$

$S = 36\pi \approx 113.1 \text{ ft}^2$

The number of pints of paint needed to paint the

tank is $\dfrac{113.1}{40} = 2.836$ pints. 3 pints of paint

would have to be purchased.

34. Surface area = Lateral area of cylinder

+ Surface area of hemisphere.

$S = hC + \dfrac{1}{2}(4\pi r^2)$

$S = h \cdot 2\pi r + 2\pi r^2$

$S = 30 \cdot 2\pi \cdot 14 + 2\pi \cdot 14^2$

$S = 840\pi + 392\pi$

$S = 1232\pi \approx 3870.44 \text{ ft}^2$

The number of gallons for a single coat is

$\dfrac{3870.44}{300} = 12.90$ or 13 gallons. If the second coat

of coverage requires the same amount of paint,
then 26 gallons of paint need to be purchased.

35.

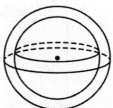

Smaller radius is $r = 4.25$ in.
Larger radius is $R = 4.35$ in.

$V = \dfrac{4}{3}\pi R^3 - \dfrac{4}{3}\pi r^3$

$V = \dfrac{4}{3}\pi \cdot (4.35)^3 - \dfrac{4}{3}\pi \cdot (4.25)^3$

$V = 7.4\pi \approx 23.24 \text{ in}^3$ of leather.

36. The hemisphere and cone must have radius = 1 in.

$V = V_{\text{CONE}} + V_{\text{HEMISPHERE}}$

$V = \dfrac{1}{3}Bh + \dfrac{1}{2}\left(\dfrac{4}{3}\pi r^3\right)$

$V = \dfrac{1}{3}\pi r^2 h + \dfrac{2}{3}\pi r^3$

$V = \dfrac{1}{3} \cdot \pi \cdot 1^2 \cdot 3 + \dfrac{2}{3} \cdot \pi \cdot 1^3$

$V = \pi + \dfrac{2}{3}\pi$

$V = \dfrac{5}{3}\pi \approx 5.24 \text{ in}^3$

37. a. Yes

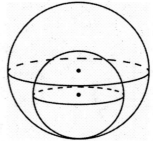

b. Yes

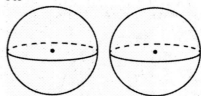

38. A slice of the intersection is a circle.

39. Parallel

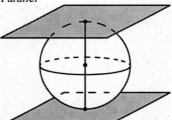

40. Perpendicular

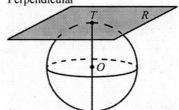

41. Congruent

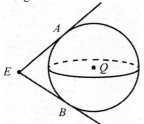

42. One

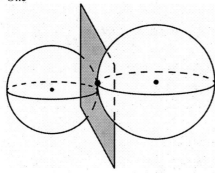

43. The solid formed is a sphere.

$$S = 4\pi r^2$$
$$S = 4\pi \cdot 3^2$$
$$S = 36\pi \text{ units}^2$$

$$V = \frac{4}{3}\pi r^3$$
$$V = \frac{4}{3}\pi \cdot 3^3$$
$$V = 36\pi \text{ units}^3$$

44. The solid formed is a sphere.

$$S = 4\pi r^2$$
$$S = 4\pi \cdot 2^2$$
$$S = 16\pi \text{ units}^2$$

$$V = \frac{4}{3}\pi r^3$$
$$V = \frac{4}{3}\pi \cdot 2^3$$
$$V = \frac{32\pi}{3} \text{ units}^3$$

45.

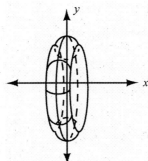

The solid of revolution looks like an inner tube.

46.

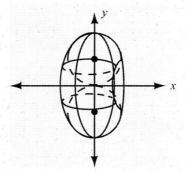

47. $V = V_{\text{LARGER SHPERE}} - V_{\text{SMALLER SHPERE}}$

$$\therefore V = \frac{4}{3}\pi R^3 - \frac{4}{3}\pi r^3$$

48. Area = Surface Area of Larger Sphere + Surface Area of Smaller Sphere

$$A = 4\pi R^2 + 4\pi r^2$$
$$A = 4\pi(R^2 + r^2)$$

CHAPTER REVIEW

1. $L = hP$
$L = 12(8 \cdot 7)$
$L = 672 \text{ in}^2$

2. $L = hP$
$L = 11(7 + 8 + 12)$
$L = 297 \text{ cm}^2$

3.

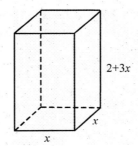

$L = hP$
$480 = (2 + 3x) \cdot 4x$
$480 = 8x + 12x^2$
$0 = 12x^2 + 8x - 480$
$0 = 3x^2 + 2x - 120$
$0 = (3x + 20)(x - 6)$
$3x + 20 = 0 \quad$ or $\quad x - 6 = 0$
$\quad x = -\dfrac{20}{3} \quad$ or $\quad x = 6$; reject $x = -\dfrac{20}{3}$

Dimensions are 6 in. by 6 in. by 20 in.

$V = Bh$
$V = (6 \cdot 6)(20)$
$V = 720 \text{ in}^3$

4.

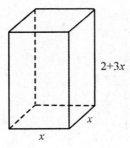

$2+3x$

x

x

$$L = 12(4x+6)$$
$$360 = 48x + 72$$
$$48x = 288$$
$$x = 6$$

The dimensions of the box are $l = 9$ cm,
$w = 6$ cm, $h = 12$ cm.

$$T = L + 2B$$
$$T = 360 + 2(9 \cdot 6)$$
$$T = 360 + 108$$
$$T = 468 \text{ cm}^2$$

$$V = l \cdot w \cdot h$$
$$V = 9 \cdot 6 \cdot 12$$
$$V = 648 \text{ cm}^3$$

5. The base of the prism is a right triangle since
$$15^2 = 9^2 + 12^2$$

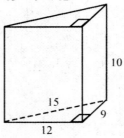

10

15

9

12

a. $L = hP$
$$L = 10(9 + 12 + 15)$$
$$L = 360 \text{ in}^2$$

b. The area of the base is
$$B = \frac{1}{2}bh$$
$$B = \frac{1}{2} \cdot 12 \cdot 9$$
$$B = 54 \text{ in}^2$$

$$T = L + 2B$$
$$T = 360 + 2 \cdot 54$$
$$T = 468 \text{ in}^2$$

c. $V = Bh$
$$V = 54 \cdot 10$$
$$V = 540 \text{ in}^3$$

6. a. $L = hP$
$$L = 13(6 \cdot 8)$$
$$L = 624 \text{ cm}^2$$

b. Using the 30°-60°-90° relationship, the
apothem of the base is $4\sqrt{3}$.

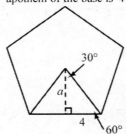

30°

a

4

60°

The area of the base is then equal to
$$B = \frac{1}{2}aP$$
$$B = \frac{1}{2} \cdot 4\sqrt{3} \cdot (6 \cdot 8)$$
$$B = 96\sqrt{3} \text{ cm}^2$$

$$T = L + 2B$$
$$T = 624 + 2 \cdot 96\sqrt{3}$$
$$T = 624 + 192\sqrt{3}$$
$$T \approx 956.55 \text{ cm}^2$$

c. $V = Bh$
$$V = \left(96\sqrt{3}\right) \cdot 13$$
$$V = 1248\sqrt{3} \approx 2161.6 \text{ cm}^3$$

7. $l^2 = a^2 + h^2$
$$l^2 = 5^2 + 8^2$$
$$l^2 = 89$$
$$l = \sqrt{89} \approx 9.43 \text{ cm}$$

8. $l^2 = a^2 + h^2$
$$12^2 = 9^2 + h^2$$
$$h^2 = 144 - 81$$
$$h^2 = 63$$
$$h = \sqrt{63} = 3\sqrt{7} \approx 7.94 \text{ in.}$$

9. $l^2 = r^2 + h^2$
$$l^2 = 5^2 + 7^2$$
$$l^2 = 74$$
$$l = \sqrt{74} \approx 8.60 \text{ in.}$$

10. $l^2 = r^2 + h^2$
$$(2r)^2 = r^2 + 6^2$$
$$4r^2 = r^2 + 36$$
$$3r^2 = 36$$
$$r^2 = 12$$
$$r = \sqrt{12} = 2\sqrt{3} \approx 3.46 \text{ cm}$$

11.

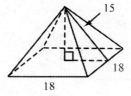

15
18
18

a. $L = \frac{1}{2} l P$

$L = \frac{1}{2} \cdot 15 \cdot (4 \cdot 18)$

$L = 540 \text{ in}^2$

b. $T = L + B$

$T = 540 + 18^2$

$T = 540 + 324$

$T = 864 \text{ in}^2$

c.

h 15
9

$l^2 = a^2 + h^2$

$15^2 = 9^2 + h^2$

$h^2 = 225 - 81$

$h^2 = 144$

$h = 12 \text{ in.}$

$V = \frac{1}{3} B h$

$V = \frac{1}{3} \cdot 18^2 \cdot 12$

$V = 1296 \text{ in}^3$

12. a. Using the 30°-60°-90° relationship, the apothem is $a = 2\sqrt{3}$ cm.

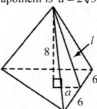

8   l
6
a
6

$l^2 = a^2 + h^2$

$l^2 = \left(2\sqrt{3}\right)^2 + 8^2$

$l^2 = 12 + 64$

$l^2 = 76$

$l = \sqrt{76} = 2\sqrt{19} \text{ cm}$

$L = \frac{1}{2} l P$

$L = \frac{1}{2} \cdot 2\sqrt{19} \cdot (12 \cdot 3)$

$L = 36\sqrt{19} = 156.92 \text{ cm}^2$

b. $T = L + B$

$T = 36\sqrt{19} + \frac{s^2 \sqrt{3}}{4}$

$T = 36\sqrt{19} + \frac{12^2 \sqrt{3}}{4}$

$T = 36\sqrt{19} + 36\sqrt{3} \approx 219.27 \text{ cm}^2$

c. $V = \frac{1}{3} B h$

$V = \frac{1}{3}\left(36\sqrt{3}\right)(8)$

$V = 96\sqrt{3} \approx 166.28 \text{ cm}^3$

13. a. $L = hC$

$L = h \cdot 2\pi r$

$L = 10 \cdot 2\pi \cdot 6$

$L = 120\pi \text{ in}^2$

b. $T = L + 2B$

$T = 120\pi + 2\pi r^2$

$T = 120\pi + 2\pi \cdot 6^2$

$T = 120\pi + 72\pi$

$T = 192\pi \text{ in}^2$

c. $V = Bh$

$V = \pi r^2 h$

$V = \pi \cdot 6^2 \cdot 10$

$V = 360\pi \text{ in}^3$

14. a. $V = \frac{1}{2} B h$

$V = \frac{1}{2} \pi r^2 h$

$V \approx \frac{1}{2} \cdot 3.14 \cdot 4^2 \cdot 14$

$V \approx 351.68 \text{ ft}^3$

b. The inside area and outside area represent the total area of the cylinder.

$T = L + 2B$

$T \approx 2(3.14)(4)(14) + 2(3.14) \cdot 4^2$

$T \approx 351.68 + 100.48$

$T \approx 452.16 \text{ ft}^2$

15. a.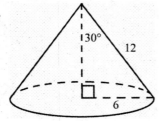

$$L = \frac{1}{2}lC$$
$$L = \frac{1}{2}l \cdot 2\pi r$$
$$L = l \cdot \pi r$$
$$L = 12 \cdot \pi \cdot 6$$
$$L = 72\pi \approx 226.19 \text{ cm}^2$$

b. $T = L + B$
$$T = 72\pi + \pi r^2$$
$$T = 72\pi + \pi \cdot 6^2$$
$$T = 72\pi + 36\pi$$
$$T = 108\pi \approx 339.29 \text{ cm}^2$$

c. $V = \frac{1}{3}Bh$
$$V = \frac{1}{3} \cdot \pi r^2 \cdot h$$
$$V = \frac{1}{3} \cdot \pi \cdot 6^2 \cdot 6\sqrt{3}$$
$$V = 72\pi\sqrt{3} \approx 391.78 \text{ cm}^3$$

16.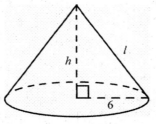

$$V = \frac{1}{3}Bh$$
$$V = \frac{1}{3}\pi r^2 \cdot h$$
$$96\pi = \frac{1}{3} \cdot \pi \cdot 6^2 \cdot h$$
$$96\pi = 12\pi h$$
$$h = \frac{96\pi}{12\pi} = 8$$

$l = 10$ using the Pythagorean Triple (6, 8, 10).

17. $S = 4\pi r^2$
$$S \approx 4 \cdot \frac{22}{7} \cdot 7^2$$
$$S \approx 616 \text{ in}^2$$

18. $V = \frac{4}{3}\pi r^3$
$$V \approx \frac{4}{3}(3.14) \cdot 6^3$$
$$V \approx 904.32 \text{ cm}^3$$

19.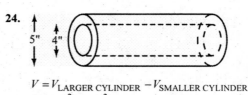

$$V = V_{\text{HEMISPHERE}} + V_{\text{CYLINDER}} + V_{\text{CONE}}$$
$$V = \frac{1}{2}\left(\frac{4}{3}\pi r^3\right) + Bh + \frac{1}{3}Bh$$
$$V = \frac{1}{2}\left(\frac{4}{3}\pi r^3\right) + \pi r^2 h + \frac{1}{3}\pi r^2 h$$
$$V = \frac{1}{2}\left(\frac{4}{3}\pi \cdot 3^3\right) + \pi \cdot 3^2 \cdot 10 + \frac{1}{3}\pi \cdot 3^2 \cdot 4$$
$$V = 18\pi + 90\pi + 12\pi$$
$$V = 120\pi \text{ units}^3$$

20. Let r equal the radius of the smaller sphere while $3r$ is the radius of the larger sphere.

$$\frac{\text{Surface Area of Smaller}}{\text{Surface Area of Larger}} = \frac{4\pi r^2}{4\pi(3r)^2} = \frac{r^2}{9r^2} = \frac{1}{2}$$

$$\frac{\text{Volume of Smaller}}{\text{Volume of Larger}} = \frac{\frac{4}{3}\pi r^3}{\frac{4}{3}\pi(3r)^3} = \frac{r^3}{27r^3} = \frac{1}{27}$$

21. The solid formed is a cone.
$$V = \frac{1}{3}Bh$$
$$V = \frac{1}{3} \cdot \pi r^2 \cdot h$$
$$V \approx \frac{1}{3} \cdot \frac{22}{7} \cdot 5^2 \cdot 7$$
$$V \approx 183\frac{1}{3} \text{ in}^3$$

22. The solid formed is a cylinder.
$$V = Bh$$
$$V = \pi r^2 h$$
$$V = \pi \cdot 6^2 \cdot 8$$
$$V = 288\pi \text{ cm}^3$$

23. The solid formed is a sphere.
$$V = \frac{4}{3}\pi r^3$$
$$V = \frac{4}{3}\pi \cdot 2^3$$
$$V = \frac{32\pi}{3} \text{ in}^3$$

24.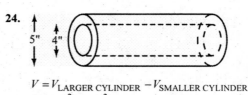

$$V = V_{\text{LARGER CYLINDER}} - V_{\text{SMALLER CYLINDER}}$$
$$V = \pi R^2 h - \pi r^2 h$$
$$V \approx (3.14)(5^2)(36) - (3.14)(4^2)(36)$$
$$V \approx 2826 - 1808.64$$
$$V \approx 1017.36 \text{ in}^3$$

25. $V = V_{CUBE} - V_{SPHERE}$

$$V = e^3 - \frac{4}{3}\pi r^3$$

$$V = 14^3 - \frac{4}{3}\pi \cdot 7^3$$

$$V = \left(2744 - \frac{1372\pi}{3}\right) \text{ in}^3$$

26. a. An octahedron has eight faces which are equilateral triangles.

b. A tetrahedron has four faces which are equilateral triangles.

c. A dodecahedron has twelve faces which are regular pentagons.

27. $V = V_{CYLINDER} + V_{2\ HEMISPHERES} - V_{SPHERE}$

Because the volume of the 2 hemispheres equals the volume of a sphere, we have

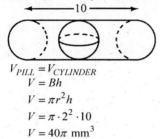

$V_{PILL} = V_{CYLINDER}$

$V = Bh$

$V = \pi r^2 h$

$V = \pi \cdot 2^2 \cdot 10$

$V = 40\pi \text{ mm}^3$

28. a. $V = 16$, $E = 24$, $F = 10$

$V + F = E + 2$

$16 + 10 = 24 + 2$

b. $V = 4$, $E = 6$, $F = 4$

$V + F = E + 2$

$4 + 4 = 6 + 2$

c. $V = 6$, $E = 12$, $F = 8$

$V + F = E + 2$

$6 + 8 = 12 + 2$

29. $V = 10 \cdot 3 \cdot 4 - 2 \cdot (1 \cdot 1 \cdot 3)$

$V = 120 - 6$

$V = 114 \text{ in}^3$

30. a. $\dfrac{4}{8} = \dfrac{1}{2}$

b. $\dfrac{5}{8}$

31. a. $A = 6.5(12) = 78 \text{ in}^2$

b. $A = 4\left(\dfrac{s^2\sqrt{3}}{4}\right) = 4\left(\dfrac{4^2\sqrt{3}}{4}\right) = 16\sqrt{3} \text{ cm}^2$

32. Right triangle (3-4-5)

CHAPTER TEST

1. a. 15

b. 7

2. a. $P = 5 \cdot 3.2 = 16$ cm

$A = \dfrac{1}{2}aP$

$= \dfrac{1}{2}(2 \cdot 16)$

$= 16 \text{ cm}^2$

b. $L = hP = 5 \cdot 16 = 80$

$T = L + 2B$

$T = 80 + 2\left(\dfrac{1}{2}aP\right)$

$T = 80 + 2(16)$

$T = 112 \text{ cm}^2$

c. $V = Bh$

$V = \left(\dfrac{1}{2}aP\right)(5)$

$V = 16 \cdot 5$

$V = 80 \text{ cm}^3$

3. a. 5

b. 4

4.

$6^2 = 2^2 + l^2$

$l^2 = 32$

$l = \sqrt{32} = 4\sqrt{2}$ ft

a. $L = \dfrac{1}{2}lP$

$L = \dfrac{1}{2}(4\sqrt{2})(16)$

$L = 32\sqrt{2} \text{ ft}^2$

b. $T = B + L$

$T = 16 + 32\sqrt{2} \approx 61.25 \text{ ft}^2$

5.

$17^2 = 8^2 + l^2$

$l^2 = 225$

$l = 15$ ft

6.

$5^2 = 4^2 + l^2$

$l^2 = 9$

$l = 3$ in.

7. $V = \dfrac{1}{3}Bh$

$V = \dfrac{1}{3}(5 \cdot 5)(6)$

$V = 50$ ft^3

8. a. False

b. True

9. a. True

b. True

10. $V = 6$, $F = 8$

$V + F = E + 2$

$6 + 8 = E + 2$

$E = 12$

11.

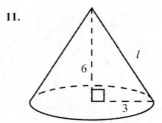

$l^2 = 3^2 + 6^2$

$l^2 = 45$

$l = \sqrt{45} = 3\sqrt{5}$ cm

12. a. $L = 2\pi rh$

$L = 2\pi \cdot 4 \cdot 6$

$L = 48\pi$ cm^2

b. $V = \pi r^2 h$

$V = \pi \cdot 4^2 \cdot 6$

$V = 96\pi$ cm^3

13.

$V = \dfrac{1}{3}\pi r^2 h$

$32\pi = \dfrac{1}{3}\pi \cdot 4^2 \cdot h$

$h = 6$ in.

14. a. $\dfrac{4}{8} = \dfrac{1}{2}$

b. $\dfrac{3}{8}$

15. a. $S = 4\pi r^2$

$S = 4\pi \cdot 10^2$

$S = 400\pi \approx 1256.6$ ft^2

b. $V = \dfrac{4}{3}\pi r^3$

$V = \dfrac{4}{3}\pi \cdot 10^3$

$V = \dfrac{4000}{3}\pi \approx 4188.8$ ft^3

16. $V = \dfrac{4}{3}\pi r^3$

$V = \dfrac{4}{3}\pi(10)^3$

$V = \dfrac{4000}{3}\pi$ ft^3

Volume $=$ Rate $\cdot$ Time

Time $=$ Volume $\div$ Rate

Time $= \dfrac{4000}{3}\pi$ $ft^3 \div 8\pi \dfrac{ft^3}{min}$

Time $= \dfrac{4000}{3}\pi$ $ft^3 \cdot \dfrac{1}{8\pi}\dfrac{min}{ft^3}$

Time $=$

$\dfrac{500}{3}$ min $= 166\dfrac{2}{3}$ or 2 hours 47 minutes

Chapter 10: Analytic Geometry

SECTION 10.1: The Rectangular Coordinate System

1.

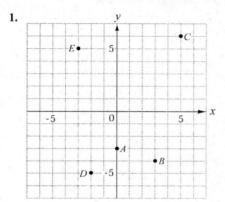

2. $A = (-5, 3)$ in Quadrant II
$B = (6, 2)$ in Quadrant I
$C = (0, -3)$ on the y-axis
$D = (-6, -2)$ in Quadrant III
$E = (5, -2)$ in Quadrant IV

3. a. The segment is vertical so
$d = y_2 - y_1$ if $y_2 > y_1$
$d = 1 - (-3) = 4$

b. The segment is horizontal so
$d = x_2 - x_1$ if $x_2 > x_1$
$d = 5 - (-3) = 8$

c. The segment is vertical so
$d = y_2 - y_1$ if $y_2 > y_1$
$d = 2 - (-3) = 5$

d. The segment is horizontal so
$d = x_2 - x_1$ if $x_2 > x_1$
$d = 7 - (-2) = 9$

4. Because the line segment is vertical,
$d = a - 3$ if $a > 3$.
$\therefore a - 3 = 5$
$\quad a = 8$
$d = 3 - a$ if $3 > a$.
$\therefore 3 - a = 5$
$\quad -a = 2$
$\quad a = -2$

5. The segment is horizontal so $d = 7 - b$ if $7 > b$
$\therefore 7 - b = 3.5$
$\quad -b = -3.5$
$\quad b = 3.5$
If $b > 7$, then $d = b - 7$.
$\therefore b - 7 = 3.5$
$\quad b = 10.5$

6. The line segment is vertical and $b > c$.
$\therefore d = b - c$.

7. a. $d = \sqrt{(x_2 - x_1)^2 + (y_2 - y_1)^2}$
$d = \sqrt{(4-0)^2 + (0-(-3))^2}$
$d = \sqrt{4^2 + 3^2}$
$d = \sqrt{16 + 9}$
$d = \sqrt{25} = 5$

b. $d = \sqrt{(4-(-2))^2 + (-3-5)^2}$
$d = \sqrt{6^2 + (-8)^2}$
$d = \sqrt{36 + 64}$
$d = \sqrt{100} = 10$

c. $d = \sqrt{(5-3)^2 + (-2-2)^2}$
$d = \sqrt{2^2 + (-4)^2}$
$d = \sqrt{4 + 16}$
$d = \sqrt{20} = 2\sqrt{5}$

d. $d = \sqrt{(0-a)^2 + (b-0)^2}$
$d = \sqrt{(-a)^2 + b^2}$
$d = \sqrt{a^2 + b^2}$

8. a. $d = \sqrt{(2-(-3))^2 + (6-(-7))^2}$
$d = \sqrt{5^2 + 12^2}$
$d = \sqrt{25 + 144}$
$d = \sqrt{169} = 13$

b. $d = \sqrt{(-2-0)^2 + (6-0)^2}$
$d = \sqrt{(-2)^2 + 6^2}$
$d = \sqrt{4 + 36}$
$d = \sqrt{40} = 2\sqrt{10}$

c. $d = \sqrt{(a-(-a))^2 + (b-(-b))^2}$
$d = \sqrt{(2a)^2 + (2b)^2}$
$d = \sqrt{4a^2 + 4b^2}$
$d = \sqrt{4(a^2 + b^2)}$
$d = 2\sqrt{a^2 + b^2}$

d. Where D represents the distance,
$D = \sqrt{(2c - 2a)^2 + (2d - 2b)^2}$
$D = \sqrt{4(c-a)^2 + 4(d-b)^2}$
$D = \sqrt{4\left[(c-a)^2 + (d-b)^2\right]}$
$D = 2\sqrt{(c-a)^2 + (d-b)^2}$

9. a. $M = \left(\dfrac{x_1 + x_2}{2}, \dfrac{y_1 + y_2}{2} \right)$

$M = \left(\dfrac{0+4}{2}, \dfrac{(-3)+0}{2} \right)$

$M = \left(\dfrac{4}{2}, -\dfrac{3}{2} \right) = \left(2, -\dfrac{3}{2} \right)$

b. $M = \left(\dfrac{(-2)+4}{2}, \dfrac{5+(-3)}{2} \right)$

$M = \left(\dfrac{2}{2}, \dfrac{3}{2} \right)$

$M = (1, 1)$

c. $M = \left(\dfrac{3+5}{2}, \dfrac{2+(-2)}{2} \right)$

$M = \left(\dfrac{8}{2}, \dfrac{0}{2} \right)$

$M = (4, 0)$

d. $M = \left(\dfrac{a+0}{2}, \dfrac{0+b}{2} \right)$

$M = \left(\dfrac{a}{2}, \dfrac{b}{2} \right)$

10. a. $M = \left(\dfrac{(-3)+2}{2}, \dfrac{(-7)+5}{2} \right)$

$M = \left(\dfrac{-1}{2}, \dfrac{-2}{2} \right)$

$M = \left(-\dfrac{1}{2}, -1 \right)$

b. $M = \left(\dfrac{0+(-2)}{2}, \dfrac{0+6}{2} \right)$

$M = \left(\dfrac{-2}{2}, \dfrac{6}{2} \right)$

$M = (-1, 3)$

c. $M = \left(\dfrac{(-a)+a}{2}, \dfrac{(-b)+b}{2} \right)$

$M = \left(\dfrac{0}{2}, \dfrac{0}{2} \right)$

$M = (0, 0)$

d. $M = \left(\dfrac{2a+2c}{2}, \dfrac{2b+2d}{2} \right)$

$M = (a+c, b+d)$

11. a. $(-3, 4)$

b. $(0, -2)$

c. $(-a, 0)$

d. $(-b, -c)$

12. a. $(1, 10)$

b. $(4, 4)$

c. $(-1, 6)$

d. $(4 - a, 6 - b)$

13. a. $\left(4, -\dfrac{5}{2} \right)$

b. $(0, 4)$

c. $\left(\dfrac{7}{2}, -1 \right)$

d. (a, b)

14. a. $(3, 4)$

b. $(0, -2)$

c. $(0, -a)$

d. $(b, -c)$

15. a. $(5, -1)$

b. $(0, -5)$

c. $(2, -a)$

d. $(b, -c)$

16. a. $(-1, 1)$

b. $(4, 5)$

c. $(10, a)$

d. $(4 - b, c)$

17. a. $(-3, -4)$

b. $(-2, 0)$

c. $(-a, 0)$

d. $(-b, c)$

18. a. x-axis

b. y-axis

c. y-axis

d. x-axis

19. a. $x = 4$

b. $y = b$

c. $x = 2$

d. $y = 3$

20. $\quad M = \left(\dfrac{x_1 + x_2}{2}, \dfrac{y_1 + y_2}{2} \right)$

$(3, -4) = \left(\dfrac{x+(5)}{2}, \dfrac{y+7}{2} \right)$

$\therefore \dfrac{x-5}{2} = 3 \quad$ and $\quad \dfrac{y+7}{2} = -4$

$x - 5 = 6 \qquad\qquad y + 7 = -8$

$x = 11 \qquad\qquad\quad y = -15$

$B = (11, -15)$

21. $M = \left(\dfrac{x_1 + x_2}{2}, \dfrac{y_1 + y_2}{2} \right)$

$(2.1, -5.7) = \left(\dfrac{x + 1.7}{2}, \dfrac{y + 2.3}{2} \right)$

$\dfrac{x+1.7}{2} = 2.1$ and $\dfrac{y+2.3}{2} = -5.7$

$x + 1.7 = 4.2$ and $y + 2.3 = -11.4$

$x = 2.5$ and $y = -13.7$

$B = (2.5, -13.7)$

22. The circle's center is the midpoint of the diameter.

$(-2, 3) = \left(\dfrac{x+3}{2}, \dfrac{y-5}{2} \right)$

$\dfrac{x+3}{2} = -2$ and $\dfrac{y-5}{2} = 3$

$x + 3 = -4 \qquad y - 5 = 6$

$x = -7 \qquad y = 11$

$(-7, 11)$

23. $D = (2, 3)$

$A = 4 \cdot 4 = 16$

24. $D = (a, b)$

$A = a \cdot b = ab$

25. a. $AB = 4 - 0 = 4$

$BC = \sqrt{(2-4)^2 + (5-0)^2}$

$= \sqrt{(-2)^2 + 5^2}$

$= \sqrt{4 + 25} = \sqrt{29}$

$AC = \sqrt{(2-0)^2 + (5-0)^2}$

$= \sqrt{2^2 + 5^2}$

$= \sqrt{4 + 25} = \sqrt{29}$

Because $BC = AC$, $\triangle ABC$ is isosceles.

b. $DE = 4 - 0 = 4$

$DF = \sqrt{(2-0)^2 + \left(2\sqrt{3} - 0\right)^2}$

$= \sqrt{2^2 + \left(2\sqrt{3}\right)^2}$

$= \sqrt{4 + 12} = \sqrt{16} = 4$

$EF = \sqrt{(2-4)^2 + \left(2\sqrt{3} - 0\right)^2}$

$= \sqrt{(-2)^2 + \left(2\sqrt{3}\right)^2}$

$= \sqrt{4 + 12} = \sqrt{16} = 4$

Because $DE = DF = EF$, $\triangle DEF$ is equilateral.

c. $GH = \sqrt{(-2 - [-5])^2 + (6 - 2)^2}$

$= \sqrt{3^2 + 4^2}$

$= \sqrt{9 + 16} = \sqrt{25} = 5$

$GK = \sqrt{(2 - [-5])^2 + (3 - 2)^2}$

$= \sqrt{7^2 + 1^2}$

$= \sqrt{49 + 1} = \sqrt{50} = 5\sqrt{2}$

$HK = \sqrt{(2 - [-2])^2 + (3 - 6)^2}$

$= \sqrt{4^2 + (-3)^2}$

$= \sqrt{16 + 9} = \sqrt{25} = 5$

Because $GH = HK$ and $(GH)^2 + (HK)^2 = (GK)^2$, $\triangle GHK$ is an isosceles right triangle.

26. Let $X = (x, y)$ represent a point on the line.

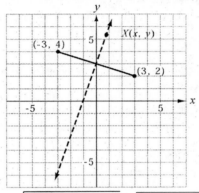

$\sqrt{(x - (-3))^2 + (y - 4)^2} = \sqrt{(x - 3)^2 + (y - 2)^2}$

$\sqrt{(x + 3)^2 + (y - 4)^2} = \sqrt{(x - 3)^2 + (y - 2)^2}$

$(x + 3)^2 + (y - 4)^2 = (x - 3)^2 + (y - 2)^2$

$x^2 + 6x + 9 + y^2 - 8y + 16 = x^2 - 6x + 9 + y^2 - 4y + 4$

$6x - 8y + 25 = -6x - 4y + 13$

$12x - 4y = -12$

Divide by 4, $3x - y = -3$.

Alternately, $-3x + y = 3$.

27. Let $X = (x, y)$ be a point on the line.

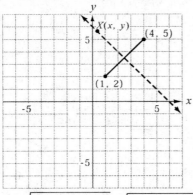

$$\sqrt{(x-1)^2 + (y-2)^2} = \sqrt{(x-4)^2 + (y-5)^2}$$
$$(x-1)^2 + (y-2)^2 = (x-4)^2 + (y-5)^2$$
$$x^2 - 2x + 1 + y^2 - 4y + 4 = x^2 - 8x + 16 + y^2 - 10y + 25$$
$$-2x - 4y + 5 = -8x - 10y + 41$$
$$6x + 6y = 36$$

Divide by 6, $x + y = 6$.

28. Because $AC = AB + BC$, the points A, B, and C are collinear.

29. Call the third vertex (a, b). Because the three sides must be of the same length and $AB = 2a$, we have

$$\sqrt{(a-0)^2 + (b-0)^2} = 2a$$
$$\sqrt{a^2 + b^2} = 2a$$

Squaring, $a^2 + b^2 = 4a^2$
$$b^2 = 3a^2$$
$$b = \pm\sqrt{3a^2}$$
$$b = \pm a\sqrt{3}$$

The third vertex is $(a, a\sqrt{3})$ or $(a, -a\sqrt{3})$.

30. $AC = \sqrt{(a-0)^2 + (b-0)^2}$
$$= \sqrt{a^2 + b^2}$$
$$BD = \sqrt{(a-0)^2 + (0-b)^2}$$
$$= \sqrt{a^2 + (-b)^2}$$
$$= \sqrt{a^2 + b^2}$$

31. Call the point on the y-axis $(0, b)$. Then

$$\sqrt{(0-3)^2 + (b-1)^2} = 6$$
$$\sqrt{(-3)^2 + (b-1)^2} = 6$$
$$\sqrt{9 + (b-1)^2} = 6$$

Squaring, $9 + (b-1)^2 = 36$
$$b^2 - 2b + 1 + 9 = 36$$
$$b^2 - 2b - 26 = 0$$
$$b = \frac{2 \pm \sqrt{4 - 4(1)(-26)}}{2}$$
$$b = \frac{2 \pm \sqrt{108}}{2}$$
$$b = \frac{2 \pm 6\sqrt{3}}{2} = \frac{2(1 \pm 3\sqrt{3})}{2}$$
$$b = 1 \pm 3\sqrt{3}$$

The points are $(0,\ 1 + 3\sqrt{3})$ and $(0, 1 - 3\sqrt{3})$.

32. Call the point on the x-axis $(a, 0)$. Then

$$\sqrt{(a-3)^2 + (0-1)^2} = 6$$
$$\sqrt{(a-3)^2 + 1} = 6$$

Squaring, $(a-3)^2 + 1 = 36$
$$a^2 - 6a + 9 + 1 = 36$$
$$a^2 - 6a - 26 = 0$$
$$a = \frac{6 \pm \sqrt{(-6)^2 - 4(1)(-26)}}{2}$$
$$a = \frac{6 \pm \sqrt{36 + 104}}{2}$$
$$a = \frac{6 \pm \sqrt{140}}{2}$$
$$a = \frac{6 \pm 2\sqrt{35}}{2} = \frac{2(3 \pm \sqrt{35})}{2}$$
$$a = 3 \pm \sqrt{35}$$

The points are $(3 + \sqrt{35},\ 0)$ and $(3 - \sqrt{35}, 0)$.

33.

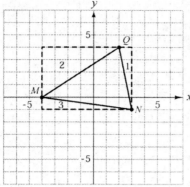

$A_{MNQ} = A_{\text{RECT}} - \left(A_{\Delta 1} + A_{\Delta 2} + A_{\Delta 3} \right)$

$A = (7)(5) - \left[\dfrac{1}{2}(1)(5) + \dfrac{1}{2}(6)(4) + \dfrac{1}{2}(7)(1) \right]$

$A = 35 - \left[\dfrac{5}{2} + 12 + \dfrac{7}{2} \right]$

$A = 35 - 18$

$A = 17$

34.

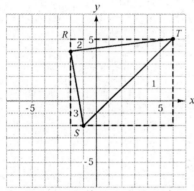

$A_{RST} = A_{\text{RECT}} - \left(A_{\Delta 1} + A_{\Delta 2} + A_{\Delta 3} \right)$

$A = 8 \cdot 7 - \left[\dfrac{1}{2}(7)(7) + \dfrac{1}{2}(8)(1) + \dfrac{1}{2}(1)(6) \right]$

$A = 56 - \left[\dfrac{49}{2} + 4 + 3 \right]$

$A = 56 - 31\dfrac{1}{2}$

$A = 24\dfrac{1}{2}$

35. $A_\Delta = \dfrac{1}{2}bh$ where $b = 3 - (-3) = 6$
                          and $h = 5 - 2 = 3$

$A_\Delta = \dfrac{1}{2} \cdot 6 \cdot 3$

$A_\Delta = 9$

36. $A_\Delta = \dfrac{1}{2}bh$ where $b = 5 - (-5) = 10$
                          and $h = 3 - 1 = 2$

$A_\Delta = \dfrac{1}{2} \cdot 10 \cdot 2$

$A_\Delta = 10$

37. a. A cone is formed; $r = 9, h = 5$

$V = \dfrac{1}{3}\pi r^2 h$

$V = \dfrac{1}{3}\pi \cdot 9^2 \cdot 5$

$V = 135\pi \text{ units}^3$

b. A cone is formed; $r = 5, h = 9$

$V = \dfrac{1}{3}\pi r^2 h$

$V = \dfrac{1}{3}\pi \cdot 5^2 \cdot 9$

$V = 75\pi \text{ units}^3$

38. a. A cone is formed.
$r = 4$ and $h = 6$

$V = \dfrac{1}{3}\pi r^2 h$

$V = \dfrac{1}{3}\pi \cdot 4^2 \cdot 6$

$V = 32\pi \text{ units}^3$

b. A solid is formed for which

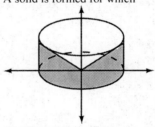

$V = V_{\text{CYLINDER}} - V_{\text{CONE}}$

$V = \pi r^2 h - \dfrac{1}{3}\pi r^2 h$

$V = \dfrac{2}{3}\pi r^2 h$

$V = \dfrac{2}{3}\pi \cdot 6^2 \cdot 4$

$V = 96\pi \text{ units}^3$

39. a. A cylinder is formed.
$r = 4$ and $h = 6$

$V = \pi r^2 h$

$V = \pi \cdot 4^2 \cdot 6$

$V = 96\pi \text{ units}^3$

b. A cylinder is formed.
$r = 6$ and $h = 4$

$V = \pi r^2 h$

$V = \pi \cdot 6^2 \cdot 4$

$V = 144\pi \text{ units}^3$

40. a. A cylinder is formed.
$r = 5$ and $h = 9$
$V = \pi r^2 h$
$V = \pi \cdot 5^2 \cdot 9$
$V = 225\pi$ units^3

b. A cylinder is formed.
$r = 9$ and $h = 5$
$V = \pi r^2 h$
$V = \pi \cdot 9^2 \cdot 5$
$V = 405\pi$ units^3

41. a. $L = 2\pi rh$
$L = 2\pi \cdot 5 \cdot 9$
$L = 90\pi$ units^2

b. $L = 2\pi rh$
$L = 2\pi \cdot 9 \cdot 5$
$L = 90\pi$ units^2

42. $V = V_{\text{LARGE CONE}} - V_{\text{SMALL CONE+CYLINDER}}$
$V = \frac{1}{3}\pi r^2 h - \left(\frac{1}{3}\pi r^2 h + \pi r^2 h\right)$
$V = \frac{1}{3}\pi \cdot 4^2 \cdot 8 - \left(\frac{1}{3}\pi \cdot 2^2 \cdot 4 + \pi \cdot 2^2 \cdot 4\right)$
$V = \frac{128}{3}\pi - \frac{16}{3}\pi - \frac{48}{3}\pi$
$V = \frac{64}{3}\pi$ in^3

43. Other points on the ellipse are (0, 4), (0, -4), and (-5, 0).

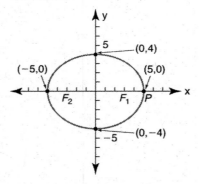

44. Other points on the hyperbola are (-3, 0), (4, 3), (4, -3), (-4, 3), and (-4, -3).

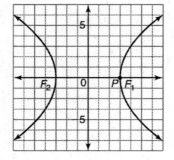

45. a. $(-3, -1)$

b. $(1, -3)$

c. $(3, 1)$

46. a. $(-b, a)$

b. $(-a, -b)$

c. (a, b)

47. a. $(5, 4)$

b. $(5, 8)$

c. $(3, 2)$

SECTION 10.2: Graphs of Linear Equations and Slope

1. $3x + 4y = 12$ has intercepts (4, 0) and (0, 3).

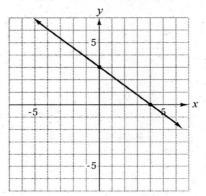

2. $3x + 5y = 15$ has intercepts (5, 0) and (0, 3).

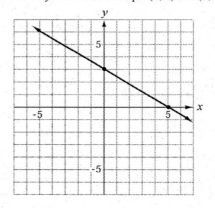

3. $x - 2y = 5$ has intercepts $(5, 0)$ and $\left(0, -\dfrac{5}{2}\right)$.

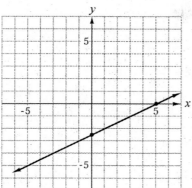

4. $x - 3y = 4$ has intercepts $(4, 0)$ and $\left(0, -\dfrac{4}{3}\right)$.

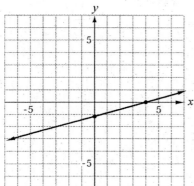

5. $2x + 6 = 0$ is equivalent to $x = -3$. It is a vertical line with x-intercept $(-3, 0)$.

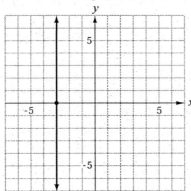

6. $3y - 9 = 0$ is equivalent to $y = 3$. It is a horizontal line with y-intercept $(0, 3)$.

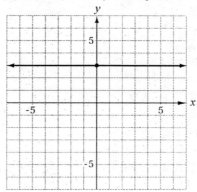

7. $\dfrac{1}{2}x + y = 3$ Multiply by 2,

$x + 2y = 6$ has intercepts $(6, 0)$ and $(0, 3)$.

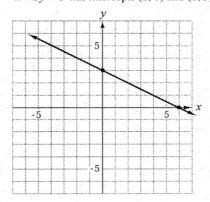

8. $\dfrac{2}{3}x - y = 1$ Multiply by 3,

$2x - 3y = 3$ The intercepts are $\left(\dfrac{3}{2}, 0\right)$ and $(0, -1)$.

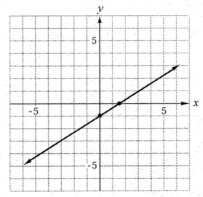

9. a. $m = \dfrac{y_2 - y_1}{x_2 - x_1}$

     $m = \dfrac{5 - (-3)}{4 - 2}$

     $m = \dfrac{8}{2}$

     $m = 4$

b. $m = \dfrac{7 - (-2)}{3 - 3} = \dfrac{9}{0}$

     m is undefined.

c. $m = \dfrac{-2 - (-1)}{2 - 1}$

     $m = \dfrac{-1}{1}$

     $m = -1$

d. $m = \dfrac{5 - 5}{(-1.3) - (-2.7)}$

     $m = \dfrac{0}{1.4}$

     $m = 0$

e. $m = \dfrac{d - b}{c - a}$

f. $m = \dfrac{b - 0}{0 - a}$

     $m = -\dfrac{b}{a}$

10. a. $m = \dfrac{2 - (-5)}{-1 - 3}$

     $m = \dfrac{7}{-4}$

     $m = -\dfrac{7}{4}$

b. $m = \dfrac{(-7) - (-3)}{(-5) - (-2)}$

     $m = \dfrac{-4}{-3}$

     $m = \dfrac{4}{3}$

c. $m = \dfrac{5\sqrt{6} - (-3\sqrt{6})}{3\sqrt{2} - 2\sqrt{2}}$

     $m = \dfrac{8\sqrt{6}}{\sqrt{2}} = 8 \cdot \sqrt{\dfrac{6}{3}}$

     $m = 8\sqrt{3}$

d. $m = \dfrac{\sqrt{3} - \sqrt{7}}{\sqrt{2} - \sqrt{2}}$

     $m = \dfrac{\sqrt{3} - \sqrt{7}}{0}$

     m is undefined.

e. $m = \dfrac{c - 0}{(a + b) - a}$

     $m = \dfrac{c}{b}$

f. $m = \dfrac{-a - b}{-b - a}$

     $m = \dfrac{-a - b}{-a - b}$

     $m = 1$

11. a. $m = \dfrac{y_2 - y_1}{x_2 - x_1}$

     $1 = \dfrac{5 - (-3)}{x - 2}$

     $1 = \dfrac{8}{x - 2}$

     Multiply by $x - 2$,

     $x - 2 = 8$

     $x = 10$

b. $m = \dfrac{y_2 - y_1}{x_2 - x_1}$

     $-0.5 = \dfrac{5 - (-1)}{3 - x}$

     $\dfrac{-1}{2} = \dfrac{6}{3 - x}$

     Using the Means-Extremes Property,

     $-1(3 - x) = 2 \cdot 6$

     $-3 + x = 12$

     $x = 15$

12. a. $m = \dfrac{y_2 - y_1}{x_2 - x_1}$

     $\dfrac{3}{2} = \dfrac{y - (-3)}{4 - 2}$

     $\dfrac{3}{2} = \dfrac{y + 3}{2}$

     $2(y + 3) = 3 \cdot 2$

     $2y + 6 = 6$

     $2y = 0$

     $y = 0$

b. $m = \dfrac{y_2 - y_1}{x_2 - x_1}$

     $-\dfrac{2}{3} = \dfrac{y - (-4)}{3 - (-1)}$

     $-\dfrac{2}{3} = \dfrac{y + 4}{4}$

     $-2 \cdot 4 = 3(y + 4)$

     $-8 = 3y + 12$

     $-20 = 3y$

     $y = -\dfrac{20}{3}$ or $-6\dfrac{2}{3}$

13. a. $m_{\overline{AB}} = \dfrac{2-5}{0-(-2)}$

$m_{\overline{AB}} = -\dfrac{3}{2}$

$m_{\overline{BC}} = \dfrac{-4-2}{4-0}$

$m_{\overline{BC}} = \dfrac{-6}{4}$

$m_{\overline{BC}} = -\dfrac{3}{2}$

Because $m_{\overline{AB}} = m_{\overline{BC}}$, the points A, B and C are collinear.

b. $m_{\overline{DE}} = \dfrac{-2-(-1)}{2-(-1)}$

$m_{\overline{DE}} = -\dfrac{1}{3}$

$m_{\overline{EF}} = \dfrac{-5-(-2)}{5-2}$

$m_{\overline{EF}} = \dfrac{-3}{3}$

$m_{\overline{EF}} = -1$

Because $m_{\overline{DE}} \neq m_{\overline{EF}}$, the points D, E and F are noncollinear.

14. a. $m_{\overline{AB}} = \dfrac{2-(-2)}{3-(-1)}$

$m_{\overline{AB}} = \dfrac{4}{4}$

$m_{\overline{AB}} = 1$

$m_{\overline{BC}} = \dfrac{5-2}{5-3}$

$m_{\overline{BC}} = \dfrac{3}{2}$

Because $m_{\overline{AB}} \neq m_{\overline{BC}}$, the points A, B and C are noncollinear.

b. $m_{\overline{DE}} = \dfrac{c-(c-d)}{b-a}$

$m_{\overline{DE}} = \dfrac{d}{b-a}$

$m_{\overline{EF}} = \dfrac{(c+d)-c}{(2b-a)-b}$

$m_{\overline{EF}} = \dfrac{d}{b-a}$

Because $m_{\overline{DE}} = m_{\overline{EF}}$, the points D, E and F are collinear.

15. For ℓ_1 to be parallel to ℓ_2, the slopes m_1 and m_2 must be equal.

a. $m_1 = \dfrac{3}{4}$; $m_2 = \dfrac{3}{4}$

b. $m_1 = -\dfrac{5}{3}$; $m_2 = -\dfrac{5}{3}$

c. $m_1 = -2$; $m_2 = -2$

d. $m_1 = \dfrac{a-b}{c}$; $m_2 = \dfrac{a-b}{c}$

16. a. $m_1 = \dfrac{4}{5}$; $m_2 = \dfrac{4}{5}$

b. $m_1 = -\dfrac{1}{5}$; $m_2 = -\dfrac{1}{5}$

c. $m_1 = 3$; $m_2 = 3$

d. $m_1 = \dfrac{f+g}{h+j}$; $m_2 = \dfrac{f+g}{h+j}$

17. a. 2

b. $-\dfrac{4}{3}$

c. $-\dfrac{1}{3}$

d. $-\dfrac{h+j}{f+g}$

18. For ℓ_1 to be perpendicular to ℓ_2, m_1 and m_2 must be negative reciprocals.

a. $m_1 = 5$; $m_2 = -\dfrac{1}{5}$

b. $m_1 = -\dfrac{5}{3}$; $m_2 = \dfrac{3}{5}$

c. $m_1 = -\dfrac{1}{2}$; $m_2 = 2$

d. $m_1 = \dfrac{a-b}{c}$; $m_2 = -\dfrac{c}{a-b}$ or $m_2 = \dfrac{c}{b-a}$

19. $2x + 3y = 6$ contains the points $(3, 0)$ and $(0, 2)$ so that its slope is $m_1 = \dfrac{2-0}{0-3} = -\dfrac{2}{3}$.

$3x - 2y = 12$ contains $(6, 0)$ and $(0, -4)$, so that its slope is $m_2 = \dfrac{-4-0}{0-6} = \dfrac{-4}{-6} = \dfrac{2}{3}$.

None of these.

20. $2x + 3y = 6$ contains the points $(3, 0)$ and $(0, 2)$ so that its slope is $m_1 = \dfrac{2-0}{0-3} = -\dfrac{2}{3}$.

$4x + 6y = -12$ contains $(-3, 0)$ and $(0, -2)$, so that its slope is $m_2 = \dfrac{-2-0}{0-(-3)} = -\dfrac{2}{3}$.

With different intercepts but the same slope, these lines are parallel.

21. $2x + 3y = 6$ contains $(3, 0)$ and $(0, 2)$ so that its

slope is $m_1 = \dfrac{2-0}{0-3} = -\dfrac{2}{3}$.

$3x - 2y = 12$ contains $(4, 0)$ and $(0, -6)$ so that its

slope is $m_2 = \dfrac{-6-0}{0-4} = \dfrac{-6}{-4} = \dfrac{3}{2}$.

Because $m_1 \cdot m_2 = -1$, these lines are
perpendicular.

22. $2x + 3y = 6$ contains $(3, 0)$ and $(0, 2)$ so that its

slope is $m_1 = \dfrac{2-0}{0-3} = -\dfrac{2}{3}$.

$4x + 6y = -12$ contains $(3, 0)$ and $(0, 2)$.
Because the intercepts are the same, these lines
are the same line.

23. Points A, B, and C are collinear if $m_{\overline{AB}} = m_{\overline{BC}}$.

$m_{\overline{AB}} = \dfrac{3-5}{2-x} = \dfrac{-2}{2-x}$

$m_{\overline{BC}} = \dfrac{-5-3}{4-2} = \dfrac{-8}{2} = \dfrac{-4}{1}$ or -4

$\dfrac{-2}{2-x} = 4$

Multiply by $2 - x$,

$-2 = -4(2 - x)$

$-2 = -8 + 4x$

$4x = 6$

$x = \dfrac{3}{2}$

24. Points A, B, and C are collinear if $m_{\overline{AB}} = m_{\overline{BC}}$.

$m_{\overline{AB}} = \dfrac{5-3}{4-1} = \dfrac{-2}{3}$

$m_{\overline{BC}} = \dfrac{a-5}{a-4}$

$\dfrac{a-5}{a-4} = \dfrac{2}{3}$

$3(a - 5) = 2(a - 4)$

$3a - 15 = 2a - 8$

$a = 7$

25. The 2 lines are perpendicular if $m_1 \cdot m_2 = -1$.

$m_1 = \dfrac{2-(-3)}{3-2} = \dfrac{5}{1} = 5$

$m_2 = \dfrac{-1-4}{x-(-2)} = \dfrac{-5}{x+2}$

$\dfrac{5}{1} \cdot \dfrac{-5}{x+2} = -1$

$\dfrac{-25}{x+2} = -1$

$-25 = -1(x + 2)$

$-25 = -1x - 2$

$-23 = -1x$

$x = 23$

26. The 2 lines are parallel if $m_1 = m_2$.

$m_1 = \dfrac{2-(-3)}{3-2} = \dfrac{5}{1} = 5$

$m_2 = \dfrac{-1-4}{x-(-2)} = \dfrac{-5}{x+2}$

$\dfrac{-5}{x+2} = 5$

Multiply by $x + 2$,

$-5 = 5(x + 2)$

$-5 = 5x + 10$

$-15 = 5x$

$-3 = x$

27. First plot the point $(3, -2)$. If $m = 2$ or $m = \dfrac{2}{1}$,

then a change in y of 2 corresponds to a change in
x of 1.

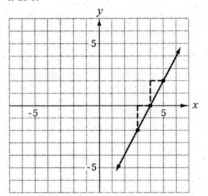

28. First plot $(-2, -5)$. If $m = \dfrac{5}{7}$, then a change in y of

5 corresponds to a change in x of 7.

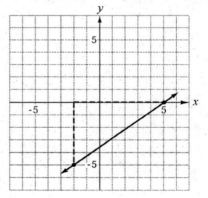

29. First plot $(0, 5)$. If $m = -\dfrac{3}{4}$, then $m = \dfrac{-3}{4}$; a change in y of -3 corresponds to a change in x of 4.

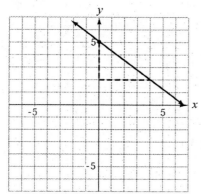

30. First plot $(-3, 0)$. If $m = 0.25$, then $m = \dfrac{1}{4}$; a change in y of 1 corresponds to a change in x of 4.

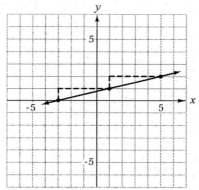

31. The line $2x - y = 6$ contains $(3, 0)$ and $(0, -6)$, so its slope is $m = \dfrac{-6 - 0}{0 - 3} = \dfrac{-6}{-3} = 2$.

Plot the point $(-2, 1)$. Then draw the line for which a change of 2 in y corresponds to a change of 1 in x.

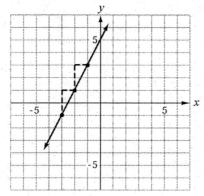

32. The line with intercepts $a = -2$ and $b = 3$ contains $(-2, 0)$ and $(0, 3)$. Its slope is $m_1 = \dfrac{3 - 0}{0 - (-2)} = \dfrac{3}{2}$. A line perpendicular to one with slope $\dfrac{3}{2}$ has the slope $m_2 = \dfrac{-2}{3}$. Plot the point $(-2, 1)$. Now draw the line for which a change in y of -2 corresponds to a change in x of 3.

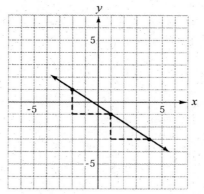

33. Let $A = (6, 5)$, $B = (-3, 0)$, and $C = (4, -2)$.
$$m_{\overline{AB}} = \frac{0 - 5}{-3 - 6} = \frac{-5}{-9} = \frac{5}{9}$$
$$m_{\overline{BC}} = \frac{-2 - 0}{4 - (-3)} = \frac{-2}{7}$$
$$m_{\overline{AC}} = \frac{-2 - 5}{4 - 6} = \frac{-7}{-2} = \frac{7}{2}$$
Because $m_{\overline{BC}} \cdot m_{\overline{AC}} = -1$, $\overline{BC} \perp \overline{AC}$ and $\triangle ABC$ is a right triangle.

34. If rt. $\triangle ABC$ has a right angle at vertex C, then $\overline{AC} \perp \overline{BC}$.
$$m_{\overline{AC}} = \frac{x - 2}{4 - 2} = \frac{x - 2}{2}$$
$$m_{\overline{BC}} = \frac{x - 3}{4 - 7} = \frac{x - 3}{-3}$$
$m_{\overline{AC}} \cdot m_{\overline{BC}} = -1$ becomes
$$\frac{x - 2}{2} \cdot \frac{x - 3}{-3} = -1$$
$$\frac{(x - 2)(x - 3)}{-6} = -1$$
$$(x - 2)(x - 3) = 6$$
$$x^2 - 5x + 6 = 6$$
$$x^2 - 5x = 0$$
$$x(x - 5) = 0$$
$x = 0$ or $x - 5 = 0$
$x = 0$ or $ x = 5$

35. As shown, possible locations are $P_1 = (4, 7)$, $P_2 = (0, -1)$, and $P_3 = (10, -3)$.

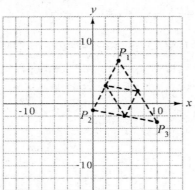

36. With $A = (-5, 1)$ and $B = (-2, -3)$,

$$m_{\overline{AB}} = \frac{(-3) - 1}{(-2) - (-5)} = \frac{-4}{3}$$

$$m_{\overline{BC}} = \frac{y - (-3)}{6 - (-2)} = \frac{y + 3}{8}$$

Because $\overline{AB} \perp \overline{BC}$, $m_{\overline{AB}} \cdot m_{\overline{BC}} = -1$.

$$\frac{-4}{3} \cdot \frac{y + 3}{8} = -1$$

$$\frac{-4(y + 3)}{24} = -1$$

$$-4(y + 3) = -24$$

$$-4y - 12 = -24$$

$$-4y = -12$$

$$y = 3$$

The fourth vertex is $D = (3, 7)$.

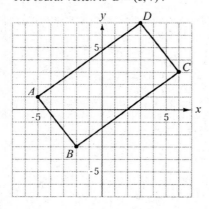

37. $m_{\overline{VT}} = \dfrac{e - e}{(c - d) - (a + d)} = \dfrac{0}{c - a - 2d} = 0$

$m_{\overline{RS}} = \dfrac{b - b}{c - a} = \dfrac{0}{c - a} = 0$

$\therefore \overline{VT} \parallel \overline{RS}$

$RV = \sqrt{[(a + d) - a]^2 + (e - b)^2}$

$\quad = \sqrt{d^2 + (e - b)^2}$

$\quad = \sqrt{d^2 + e^2 - 2be + b^2}$

$ST = \sqrt{[c - (c - d)]^2 + (b - e)^2}$

$\quad = \sqrt{d^2 + (b - e)^2}$

$\quad = \sqrt{d^2 + b^2 - 2be + e^2}$

$\therefore \overline{RV} \parallel \overline{ST}$

$RSTV$ is an isosceles trapezoid.

38. $m_{\overline{AB}} = \dfrac{0 - 0}{a - 0} = \dfrac{0}{a} = 0$

$m_{\overline{DC}} = \dfrac{c - c}{(a + b) - b} = \dfrac{0}{a} = 0$

$\therefore \overline{AB} \parallel \overline{DC}$

$m_{\overline{AD}} = \dfrac{c - 0}{b - 0} = \dfrac{c}{b}$

$m_{\overline{BC}} = \dfrac{c - 0}{(a + b) - a} = \dfrac{c}{b}$

$\therefore \overline{AD} \parallel \overline{BC}$

$ABCD$ is a parallelogram.

39. $m_{\overline{EH}} = \dfrac{2c - 0}{2b - 0} = \dfrac{2c}{2b} = \dfrac{c}{b}$

$m_{\overline{FG}} = \dfrac{c - 0}{(a + b) - a} = \dfrac{c}{b}$

Since one pair of opposite sides are parallel, $EFGH$ is a trapezoid.

40. $\overline{AC} \perp \overline{BC}$ so that $m_{\overline{AC}} \cdot m_{\overline{BC}} = -1$.

$m_{\overline{AC}} = \dfrac{d - b}{c - a}$

$m_{\overline{BC}} = \dfrac{b - d}{e - c}$

Then

$$\frac{d - b}{c - a} \cdot \frac{b - d}{e - c} = -1$$

$$\frac{(d - b)(b - d)}{(c - a)(e - c)} = -1$$

$$(d - b)(b - d) = -1(c - a)(e - c)$$

$$-b^2 + 2bd - d^2 = -ce + c^2 + ae - ac$$

or

$$b^2 - 2bd + d^2 = ce - c^2 - ae + ac$$

or
some equivalent form.

41. If $l_1 \parallel l_2$, then $\angle A \cong \angle D$.

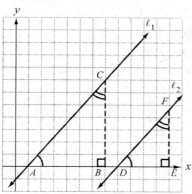

With $\overline{CB} \perp \overline{AB}$ and $\overline{FE} \perp \overline{DE}$, $\overline{CB} \parallel \overline{FE}$

(both $\perp$ to the x-axis). Then $\angle B \cong \angle E$ (all rt. $\angle s$ are $\cong$). By AA, $\triangle ABC \sim \triangle DEF$.

Then $\dfrac{CB}{FE} = \dfrac{AB}{DE}$ since corr. sides of $\sim \triangle$s are proportional. By a property of proportions,

$\dfrac{CB}{AB} = \dfrac{FE}{DE}$ (means were interchanged).

But $m_1 = \dfrac{CB}{AB}$ and $m_2 = \dfrac{FE}{DE}$.

Then $m_1 = m_2$ and the slopes are equal.

42. Let $\overline{AB}$ and $\overline{CD}$ be horizontal while $\overline{BC}$ and $\overline{ED}$ are vertical (as shown).

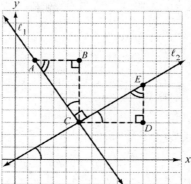

Then $\angle B \cong \angle D$. Because $\ell_1 \perp \ell_2$, $\angle ACE$ is a rt. $\angle$. Then $\angle$s BCA and BCE are complementary. Also $\angle$s BCE and ECD are complementary.

$\therefore \angle BCA \cong \angle ECD$ ($\angle$s comp. to the same $\angle$ are $\cong$.)

By AA, $\triangle ABC \sim \triangle EDC$. Then by $\dfrac{BC}{AB} = \dfrac{CD}{ED}$.

By the Means-Extremes Property,

$BC \cdot ED = AB \cdot CD$.

Now $m_1 = \dfrac{-(BC)}{AB}$ since the slope is negative

while $m_2 = \dfrac{ED}{CD}$.

Then $m_1 \cdot m_2 = \dfrac{-(BC)}{AB} \cdot \dfrac{ED}{CD}$

$= \dfrac{-(BC)(ED)}{(AB)(CD)}$

$= -\dfrac{(AB)(CD)}{(AB)(CD)} = -1$

43. The vertices of the triangle are $(0, 0)$, $(0, b)$, and $(a, 0)$.

$$m = -\frac{b}{a}$$

$$am = -b$$

$$a = -\frac{b}{m}$$

$$A_\Delta = \frac{1}{2} base \cdot height$$

$$A_\Delta = \frac{1}{2} \cdot a \cdot b$$

$$A_\Delta = \frac{1}{2} \cdot -\frac{b}{a} \cdot b$$

$$A_\Delta = -\frac{b^2}{2m}$$

44. The vertices of the trapezoid are $(0, 0)$, $(0, b)$, $(a, 0)$, and $(a, ma + b)$.

$$A_{TRAP} = \frac{1}{2} ht \cdot (b_1 + b_2)$$

$$A_{TRAP} = \frac{1}{2} a(b + ma + b)$$

$$A_{TRAP} = \frac{1}{2} a(ma + 2b)$$

$$A_{TRAP} = \frac{1}{2} ma^2 + ab$$

SECTION 10.3: Preparing to Do Analytic Proofs

1. a. $d = \sqrt{(x_2 - x_1)^2 + (y_2 - y_1)^2}$

$d = \sqrt{(0 - a)^2 + (a - 0)^2}$

$d = \sqrt{(-a)^2 + a^2}$

$d = \sqrt{a^2 + a^2}$

$d = \sqrt{2a^2} = a\sqrt{2}$ if $a > 0$

b. $m = \dfrac{y_2 - y_1}{x_2 - x_1}$

$m = \dfrac{d - b}{c - a}$

2. a. $M = \left(\dfrac{x_1 + x_2}{2}, \dfrac{y_1 + y_2}{2} \right)$

$M = \left(\dfrac{a + 0}{2}, \dfrac{0 + b}{2} \right) = \left(\dfrac{a}{2}, \dfrac{b}{2} \right)$

b. $M = \left(\dfrac{2a + 0}{2}, \dfrac{0 + 2b}{2} \right) = (a, b)$

3. a. $m = \dfrac{a - 0}{0 - a} = \dfrac{a}{-a} = -1$

b. $m = \dfrac{b - 0}{0 - a} = -\dfrac{b}{a}$

4. a. $m_1 = \dfrac{b - 0}{0 - a} = -\dfrac{b}{a}$

The slope of any line parallel to the given line has slope $m_2 = -\dfrac{b}{a}$.

b. $m_1 = -\dfrac{b}{a}$

The slope of any line perpendicular to the given line has slope $m_2 = \dfrac{a}{b}$.

5. $\overline{AB}$ is horizontal and $\overline{BC}$ is vertical.
∴ $\overline{AB} \perp \overline{BC}$. Hence $\angle B$ is a right $\angle$ and $\triangle ABC$ is a right triangle.

6. Using the Distance Formula,

$RT = \sqrt{(0 - (-a))^2 + (b - 0)^2}$

$RT = \sqrt{a^2 + b^2}$

$TS = \sqrt{(a - 0)^2 + (0 - b)^2}$

$TS = \sqrt{a^2 + b^2}$

If $RT = TS$, then $\triangle RTS$ is an isosceles $\triangle$.

7. $m_{\overline{QM}} = \dfrac{c - 0}{b - 0} = \dfrac{c}{b}$

$m_{\overline{PN}} = \dfrac{c - 0}{(a + b) - a} = \dfrac{c}{b}$

∴ $\overline{QM} \parallel \overline{PN}$

$m_{\overline{QP}} = \dfrac{c - c}{(a + b) - b} = \dfrac{0}{a} = 0$

$m_{\overline{MN}} = \dfrac{0 - 0}{a - 0} = \dfrac{0}{a} = 0$

∴ $\overline{QM} \parallel \overline{MN}$

Since both pairs of opposite sides are parallel, $MNPQ$ is a parallelogram.

8. $m_{\overline{DC}} = \dfrac{c - c}{b - d} = \dfrac{0}{b - d} = 0$

$m_{\overline{AB}} = \dfrac{0 - 0}{a - 0} = \dfrac{0}{a} = 0$

∴ $\overline{DC} \parallel \overline{AB}$

Since $ABCD$ has one pair of parallel sides, $ABCD$ is a trapezoid.

9. $m_{\overline{MN}} = 0$ and $m_{\overline{QP}} = 0$. $\therefore \overline{MN} \parallel \overline{QP}$

$\overline{QM}$ and $\overline{PN}$ are both vertical;

$\therefore \overline{QM} \parallel \overline{PN}$. Hence, $MQPN$ is a parallelogram.

Since $\overline{QM}$ is vertical and $\overline{MN}$ is horizontal, $\angle QMN$ is a right angle. Because parallelogram $MQPN$ has a right $\angle$, it is also a rectangle.

10. $\overline{VT} \parallel \overline{RS}$ since both are horizontal.

$\overline{VR} \parallel \overline{TS}$ since both are vertical.

Hence, $RSTV$ is a parallelogram.

If $\overline{VR}$ is vertical and $\overline{RS}$ is horizontal, then $\angle VRS$ is a right angle. Hence, $RSTV$ is a rectangle. $RS = a$ and $VR = a$. Since two adjacent sides of a rectangle are congruent, $RSTV$ is a square.

11. $A = (0, 0); B = (a, 0); C = (a, b)$

12. $D = (0, 0); E = (2a, 0); F = (a, b)$

13. $M = (0, 0); N = (r, 0); P = (r + s, t)$

14. $A = (0, 0); B = (a, 0); C = (a, a); D = (0, a)$

15. $A = (0, 0); B = (a, 0); C = (a - c, d)$

16. $R = (0, 0); S = (s, 0); T = (s, t); V = (0, t)$

17. **a.** Square

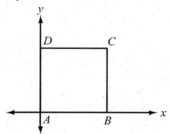

$A = (0, 0); B = (a, 0); C = (a, a); D = (0, a)$

b. Square (with midpoints of sides)
$A = (0, 0); B = (2a, 0)$
$C = (2a, 2a); D = (0, 2a)$

18. **a.** Rectangle

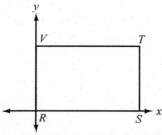

$R = (0, 0); S = (a, 0); T = (a, b); V = (0, b)$

b. Rectangle (with midpoints of sides)
$R = (0, 0); S = (2a, 0)$
$T = (2a, 2b); V = (0, 2b)$

19. **a.** Parallelogram

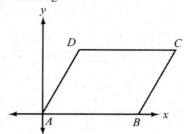

$A = (0, 0); B = (a, 0); C = (a + b, c);$
$D = (b, c)$
Note: D chosen before C

b. Parallelogram (with midpoints of sides)
$A = (0, 0); B = (2a, 0)$
$C = (2a + 2b, 2c); D = (2b, 2c)$

20. **a.** Triangle

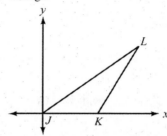

$J = (0, 0); K = (a, 0); L = (b, c)$

b. Triangle (with midpoints)
$J = (0, 0); K = (2a, 0); L = (2b, 2c)$

21. **a.** Isosceles triangle

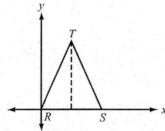

$R = (0, 0); S = (2a, 0); T = (a, b)$

b. Isosceles triangle (with midpoints)
$R = (0, 0); S = (4a, 0); T = (2a, 2b)$

22. a. Trapezoid

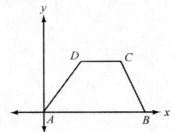

$A = (0, 0)$; $B = (a, 0)$; $C = (d, c)$; $D = (b, c)$
Note: D chosen before C

b. Trapezoid (with midpoints)
$A = (0, 0)$; $B = (2a, 0)$;
$C = (2d, 2c)$; $D = (2b, 2c)$

23. $MNPQ$ is a rhombus.
$MN = r - 0 = r$
$MQ = \sqrt{(s-0)^2 + (t-0)^2}$
$MQ = \sqrt{s^2 + t^2}$

$MN = MQ$, so $r = \sqrt{s^2 + t^2}$.

Squaring, $r^2 = s^2 + t^2$.

24. Parallelogram $RSTV$ with $RT = VS$.
$RT = \sqrt{((s+t)-0)^2 + (v-0)^2}$
$\quad = \sqrt{(s+t)^2 + v^2}$
$VS = \sqrt{(s-t)^2 + (0-v)^2}$
$\quad = \sqrt{(s-t)^2 + v^2}$
If $RT = VS$, then
$\sqrt{(s+t)^2 + v^2} = \sqrt{(s-t)^2 + v^2}$
Squaring,
$\quad (s+t)^2 + v^2 = (s-t)^2 + v^2$
$s^2 + 2st + t^2 + v^2 = s^2 - 2st + t^2 + v^2$
$\quad\quad\quad 2st = -2st$
$\quad\quad\quad 4st = 0$
$\quad\quad\quad s \cdot t = 0$
Note: This can also be expressed by the disjunction $s = 0$ or $t = 0$.

25. Parallelogram $ABCD$ with $\overline{AC} \perp \overline{DB}$
$m_{\overline{AC}} = \dfrac{c-0}{a+b-0} = \dfrac{c}{a+b}$

$m_{\overline{DB}} = \dfrac{0-c}{a-b} = \dfrac{-c}{a-b}$

$\therefore \dfrac{c}{a+b} \cdot \dfrac{-c}{a-b} = -1$

$\dfrac{-c^2}{a^2-b^2} = -1$

$-c^2 = -(a^2 - b^2)$

$c^2 = a^2 - b^2$

26. Quad. $RSTV$
$m_{\overline{RV}} = \dfrac{r-0}{q-0} = \dfrac{r}{q}$

$m_{\overline{ST}} = \dfrac{p-0}{n-m} = \dfrac{p}{n-m}$

If $\overline{RV} \parallel \overline{ST}$, then $m_{\overline{RV}} = m_{\overline{ST}}$ and

$\dfrac{r}{q} = \dfrac{p}{n-m}$
$r(n-m) = pq$
$rn - rm = pq$

27. Equilateral $\triangle ABC$.
$AB = 2a - 0 = 2a$

Because $\quad AC = \sqrt{(a-0)^2 + (b-0)^2}$
$\quad\quad\quad = \sqrt{a^2 + b^2}$
$\sqrt{a^2 + b^2} = 2a$
Squaring,
$a^2 + b^2 = 4a^2$
$\quad b^2 = 3a^2$

28. Isos. $\triangle RST$.
$RS = s - 0 = s$
$RS = \sqrt{(t-0)^2 + (v-0)^2}$
$RT = \sqrt{t^2 + v^2}$
$\overline{RS} \cong \overline{RT}$ so $RS = RT$.
$s = \sqrt{t^2 + v^2}$
Squaring,
$s^2 = t^2 + v^2$

29. a. a is positive

b. $-a$ is negative

c. $AB = a - (-a) = 2a$

30. a. r is negative

b. $RS = s - r$

c. $t = s - r$

31. a. Slope Formula (and $m_1 \cdot m_2 = -1$)

b. Distance Formula

c. Midpoint Formula

d. Slope Formula (and $m_1 = m_2$)

32. a. Midpoint Formula

b. Slope Formula

c. Slope Formula (and $m_1 = m_2$)

d. Distance Formula

33. The line segment joining the midpoints of the two nonparallel sides of a trapezoid is parallel to the bases of the trapezoid.

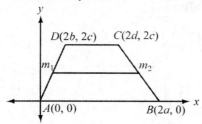

34. If the midpoints of the sides of a quadrilateral are joined in order, the resulting quadrilateral is a parallelogram.

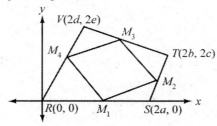

35. The diagonals of a rectangle are equal in length.

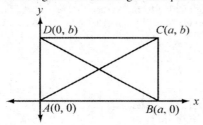

36. The diagonals of a rhombus are $\perp$ and $a = \sqrt{b^2 + c^2}$.

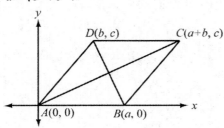

37. Let the coordinates of T be (x, 0). Because the angle is bisected, we can use a proportion.

$$\frac{2a}{a} = \frac{2-x}{a-2}$$

$$2 = \frac{2-x}{a-2}$$

$$2a - 4 = 2 - x$$

$$x = 2 + 4 - 2a$$

$$x = 6 - 2a$$

$$T(6 - 2a, 0)$$

SECTION 10.4: Analytic Proofs

1. The diagonals of a rectangle are equal in length. Proof: Let rectangle *ABCD* have vertices as shown.

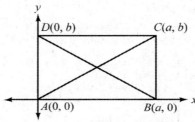

Then $AC = \sqrt{(a-0)^2 + (b-0)^2}$
$= \sqrt{a^2 + b^2}$

Also $DB = \sqrt{(a-0)^2 + (0-b)^2}$
$= \sqrt{a^2 + (-b)^2} = \sqrt{a^2 + b^2}$

Then $AC = DB$, and the diagonals of the rectangle are equal in length.

2. The opposite sides of a parallelogram are equal in length.
Proof: Let parallelogram $RSTV$ have vertices are shown.

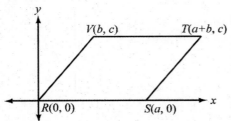

Then $RS = a - 0 = a$ and $VT = (a + b) - b = a$.
$\therefore RS = VT$.

$$RV = \sqrt{(b - 0)^2 + (c - 0)^2}$$
$$\quad = \sqrt{b^2 + c^2}$$

$$ST = \sqrt{((a + b) - a)^2 + (c - 0)^2}$$
$$\quad = \sqrt{b^2 + c^2}$$

$\therefore RV = ST$, and both pairs of opposite sides of the parallelogram are equal in length.

3. The diagonals of a square are perpendicular bisectors of each other.
Proof: Let square $RSTV$ have the vertices shown.

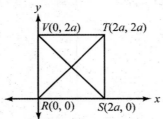

Then the midpoints of the diagonals are $M_{\overline{RT}} = (a, a)$ and $M_{\overline{VS}} = (a, a)$. Also, $m_{\overline{RT}} = 1$ and $m_{\overline{VS}} = -1$. Because the two diagonals share the midpoint (a, a) and the product of their slopes is -1, they are perpendicular bisectors of each other.

4. The diagonals of an isosceles trapezoid are equal in length.
Proof: The trapezoid $WXYZ$ with vertices as shown is isosceles because $WZ = XY$ (proven earlier).

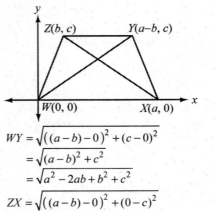

$$WY = \sqrt{((a - b) - 0)^2 + (c - 0)^2}$$
$$\quad = \sqrt{(a - b)^2 + c^2}$$
$$\quad = \sqrt{a^2 - 2ab + b^2 + c^2}$$

$$ZX = \sqrt{((a - b) - 0)^2 + (0 - c)^2}$$
$$\quad = \sqrt{(a - b)^2 + c^2}$$
$$\quad = \sqrt{a^2 - 2ab + b^2 + c^2}$$

Because $WY = ZX$, the diagonals of an isosceles trapezoid are equal in length.

5. The median from the vertex of an isosceles triangle to the base is perpendicular to the base.

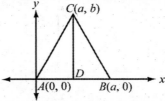

Proof: The triangle ABC with vertices as shown is isosceles because $AC = BC$.

Let D be the midpoint of $\overline{AB}$.

$$D = \left(\frac{0 + 2a}{2}, \frac{0 + 0}{2} \right) = (a, 0).$$

$m_{\overline{AB}} = \dfrac{0 - 0}{2a - 0} = 0$; that is $\overline{AB}$ is horizontal.

$m_{\overline{CD}} = \dfrac{b - 0}{a - a} = \dfrac{b}{0}$ which is undefined; that is $\overline{CD}$ is vertical.

Then $\overline{CD} \perp \overline{AB}$ and the median to the base of the isosceles triangle is perpendicular to the base.

6. The medians to the congruent sides of an isosceles triangle are equal in length.

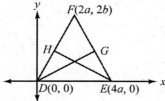

Proof: $\triangle DEF$, with vertices as shown, is isosceles because $DF = EF$. Let H and G name the midpoints of $\overline{DF}$ and $\overline{EF}$ respectively.

Then $H = \left(\dfrac{0+2a}{2}, \dfrac{0+2b}{2}\right) = (a, b)$ and

$\qquad G = \left(\dfrac{2a+4a}{2}, \dfrac{0+2b}{2}\right) = (3a, b)$

Now $DB = \sqrt{(3a-0)^2 + (b-0)^2}$

$\qquad\quad = \sqrt{(3a)^2 + b^2}$

$\qquad\quad = \sqrt{9a^2 + b^2}$

$\quad HE = \sqrt{(4a-a)^2 + (0-b)^2}$

$\qquad\quad = \sqrt{(3a)^2 + (-b)^2}$

$\qquad\quad = \sqrt{9a^2 + b^2}$

Now $DB = HE$, so the medians to the congruent sides of the isosceles triangle are equal in length.

7. The segments which join the midpoints of the consecutive sides of a quadrilateral from a parallelogram.

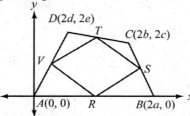

Proof: The midpoints, as shown, of the sides of a quad. $ABCD$ are

$R = \left(\dfrac{0+2a}{2}, \dfrac{0+0}{2}\right) = (a, 0)$

$S = \left(\dfrac{2a+2b}{2}, \dfrac{0+2c}{2}\right) = (a+b, c)$

$T = \left(\dfrac{2d+2b}{2}, \dfrac{2e+2c}{2}\right) = (d+b, e+c)$

$V = \left(\dfrac{0+2d}{2}, \dfrac{0+2e}{2}\right) = (d, e)$

Now we determine slopes as follows.

$m_{\overline{RS}} = \dfrac{c-0}{(a+b)-a} = \dfrac{c}{b}$

$m_{\overline{ST}} = \dfrac{(e+c)-c}{(d+b)-(a+b)} = \dfrac{e}{d-a}$

$m_{\overline{TV}} = \dfrac{(e+c)-e}{(d+b)-d} = \dfrac{c}{b}$

$m_{\overline{VR}} = \dfrac{e-0}{d-a} = \dfrac{e}{d-a}$

Because $m_{\overline{RS}} = m_{\overline{TV}}$, $\overline{RS} \parallel \overline{TV}$. Also

$m_{\overline{ST}} = m_{\overline{VR}}$ so that $\overline{RT} \parallel \overline{VR}$. Then $RSTV$ is a parallelogram.

8. The segments which join the midpoints of the opposite sides of a quadrilateral bisect each other.

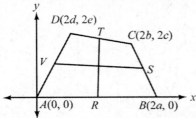

Proof: With $ABCD$ as shown the midpoints are
$R = (a, 0)$
$S = (a + b, c)$
$T = (d + b, e + c)$
$V = (d, e)$

The midpoint of $\overline{RT}$ is
$$\left(\frac{a + (d + b)}{2}, \frac{0 + (e + c)}{2} \right) \text{ or } \left(\frac{a + d + b}{2}, \frac{c + e}{2} \right).$$

The midpoint of $\overline{VS}$ is $\left(\frac{(a + b) + d}{2}, \frac{c + e}{2} \right)$ or

$\left(\frac{a + d + b}{2}, \frac{c + e}{2} \right).$

Because $\overline{RT}$ and $\overline{VS}$ share a common midpoint, these line segments bisect each other.

9. The segments which join the midpoints of the consecutive sides of a rectangle form a rhombus.

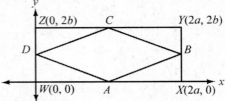

Proof: With vertices as shown, $WXYZ$ is a rectangle.
Midpoints of the sides of the rect. Are
$$A = \left(\frac{0 + 2a}{2}, \frac{0 + 0}{2} \right) = (a, 0)$$
$$B = \left(\frac{2a + 2a}{2}, \frac{0 + 2b}{2} \right) = (2a, b)$$
$$C = \left(\frac{0 + 2a}{2}, \frac{2b + 2b}{2} \right) = (a, 2b)$$
$$D = \left(\frac{0 + 0}{2}, \frac{0 + 2b}{2} \right) = (0, b)$$
$$m_{\overline{AB}} = \frac{b - 0}{2a - a} = \frac{b}{a} \text{ and}$$
$$m_{\overline{DC}} = \frac{b - a}{0 - a} = \frac{-b}{-a} = \frac{b}{a}, \text{ so } \overline{AB} \parallel \overline{DC}.$$

$$m_{\overline{DA}} = \frac{b - 0}{0 - a} = \frac{b}{-a} \text{ and}$$
$$m_{\overline{CB}} = \frac{2b - b}{a - 2a} = \frac{-b}{-a} = \frac{b}{a}, \text{ so } \overline{DA} \parallel \overline{CB}.$$
Then $ABCD$ is a parallelogram.
We need to show that 2 adjacent sides are congruent (equal in length).
$$AB = \sqrt{(2a - a)^2 + (b - 0)^2} = \sqrt{a^2 + b^2}$$
$$BC = \sqrt{(a - 2a)^2 + (2b - b)^2}$$
$$= \sqrt{(-a)^2 + b^2} = \sqrt{a^2 + b^2}$$

10. The segments which join the midpoints of the consecutive sides of a rhombus form a rectangle.

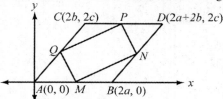

Proof: As shown, $ABCD$ is a parallelogram. To have $ABCD$ be a rhombus, it is necessary that $AB = AC$. Now $AB = 2a - 0 = 2a$ while

$$AC = \sqrt{(2b-0)^2 + (2c-0)^2}$$
$$= \sqrt{4b^2 + 4c^2}$$
$$= 2\sqrt{b^2 + c^2}$$

If $AB = AC$, then $2a = 2\sqrt{b^2 + c^2}$
$$a = \sqrt{b^2 + c^2}$$
$$a^2 = b^2 + c^2 \ (*)$$

The midpoints are

$$M = \left(\frac{0+2a}{2}, \frac{0+0}{2}\right) = (a, 0)$$
$$N = \left(\frac{2a+(2a+2b)}{2}, \frac{0+2c}{2}\right) = (2a+b, c)$$
$$P = \left(\frac{2b+(2a+2b)}{2}, \frac{2c+2c}{2}\right) = (a+2b, 2c)$$
$$Q = \left(\frac{0+2b}{2}, \frac{0+2c}{2}\right) = (b, c)$$

We see that

$$m_{\overline{MN}} = \frac{c-0}{(2a+b)-a} = \frac{c}{a+b}$$
$$m_{\overline{PN}} = \frac{2c-c}{(a+2b)-(2a+b)} = \frac{c}{-a+b}$$
$$= \frac{c}{b-a}$$
$$m_{\overline{PQ}} = \frac{2c-c}{(a+2b)-b} = \frac{c}{a+b}$$
$$m_{\overline{QM}} = \frac{c-0}{b-a} = \frac{c}{b-a}$$

Then $\overline{MN} \parallel \overline{PQ}$ since $m_{\overline{MN}} = m_{\overline{PQ}}$; also

$\overline{PN} \parallel \overline{QM}$ since $m_{\overline{PN}} = m_{\overline{QM}}$. Then $MNPQ$ is a parallelogram. For $MNPQ$ to be a rectangle, we need to show that any 2 adjacent sides are $\perp$ (and form a right angle).

Because $m_{\overline{MN}} = \frac{c}{a+b}$ and $m_{\overline{PN}} = \frac{c}{b-a}$, their

product is $m_{\overline{MN}} \cdot m_{\overline{PN}} = \frac{c}{a+b} \cdot \frac{c}{b-a}$
$$= \frac{c^2}{b^2 - a^2}$$
$$= \frac{c^2}{b^2 - (b^2 + c^2)} \ (*)$$
$$= \frac{c^2}{-c^2} = -1$$

Then $\overline{MN} \perp \overline{PN}$, and $MNPQ$ is a rectangle.

11. The midpoint of the hypotenuse of a right triangle is equidistant from the three vertices of the triangle.

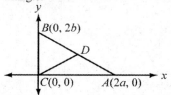

Proof: Let rt. $\triangle ABC$ have vertices as shown. Then D, the midpoint of the hypotenuse, is given

by $D = \left(\frac{0+2a}{2}, \frac{2b+0}{2}\right) = (a, b)$.

Now $BD = DA = \sqrt{(2a-a)^2 + (0-b)^2}$
$$= \sqrt{a^2 + (-b)^2} = \sqrt{a^2 + b^2}$$

Also, $CD = \sqrt{(a-0)^2 + (b-0)^2} = \sqrt{a^2 + b^2}$
Then D is equidistant from A, B, and C.

12. The median of a trapezoid is parallel to the bases of the trapezoid and has a length equal to one-half the sum of the lengths of the two bases.

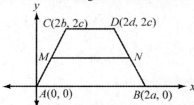

Proof: Let trapezoid $ABCD$ have vertices as shown. With M and N the midpoints of $\overline{AC}$ and $\overline{DB}$.

$$M = \left(\frac{0+2b}{2}, \frac{0+2c}{2}\right) = (b, c)$$
$$N = \left(\frac{2a+2d}{2}, \frac{0+2c}{2}\right) = (a+d, c)$$
$$m_{\overline{AB}} = \frac{0-0}{2a-0} = \frac{0}{2a} = 0; \ m_{\overline{MN}} = \frac{c-c}{(a+d)-b} = 0$$
$$m_{\overline{CD}} = \frac{2c-2c}{2d-2b} = \frac{0}{2d-2b} = 0$$

Then $\overline{MN} \parallel \overline{AB}$ and $\overline{MN} \parallel \overline{CD}$. The median is parallel to both bases.
Because each segment is horizontal, use
$d = x_2 - x_1 \ (x_2 > x_2)$ to find the length.
$$CD = 2d - 2b$$
$$MN = (a+d) - b = a + d - b$$
$$AB = 2a - 0 = 2a$$
$$\frac{1}{2}(AB + CD) = \frac{1}{2}(2a + (2d - 2b))$$
$$= a + d - b$$
$$= MN$$

That is, $MN = \frac{1}{2}(AB + CD)$. The median has a

length equal to one-half the sum of the lengths of the two bases.

13. The segment which joins the midpoints of 2 sides of a triangle is parallel to the third side and has a length equal to one-half the length of the third side.

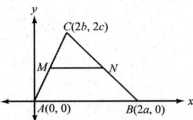

Proof: Let $\triangle ABC$ have vertices as shown. With M and N the midpoints of $\overline{AC}$ and $\overline{BC}$ respectively,

$$M = \left(\frac{0+2b}{2}, \frac{0+2c}{2}\right) = (b, c) \text{ and}$$

$$N = \left(\frac{2a+2b}{2}, \frac{0+2c}{2}\right) = (a+b, c).$$

Now $m_{\overline{MN}} = \dfrac{c-c}{(a+b)-b} = \dfrac{0}{a} = 0$ and

$$m_{\overline{AB}} = \frac{0-0}{2a-0} = \frac{0}{2a} = 0$$

Then $\overline{MN} \parallel \overline{AB}$.

Also $MN = (a+b) - b = a$
$\qquad AB = 2a - 0 = 2a$

Then $MN = \dfrac{1}{2}(AB)$

That is, the segment $\left(\overline{MN}\right)$ which joins the midpoints of 2 sides of the triangle is parallel to the third side and equals one-half its length.

14. The perpendicular bisector of the base of an isosceles triangle contains the vertex of the triangle.

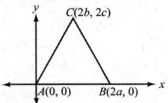

Proof: let the vertices of a triangle be as shown. If $\overline{AC} \cong \overline{BC}$, then $\triangle ABC$ is isosceles. The perpendicular bisector of the base $\overline{AB}$ has an undefined slope because $m_{\overline{AB}} = \dfrac{0-0}{2a-0} = \dfrac{0}{2a} = 0$.

Also the perpendicular bisector of the base contains M, the midpoint of the base. Since

$M = \left(\dfrac{0+2a}{2}, \dfrac{0+0}{2}\right) = (a, 0)$, the equation of the

perpendicular bisector is $x = a$.

Recalling that $AC = BC$, we have

$$\sqrt{(2b-0)^2 + (2c-0)^2} = \sqrt{(2b-2a)^2 + (2c-0)^2}$$
$$\sqrt{4b^2 + 4c^2} = \sqrt{4b^2 - 8ab + 4a^2 + 4c^2}$$

Squaring

$$4b^2 + 4c^2 = 4b^2 - 8ab + 4a^2 + 4c^2$$
$$0 = 4a^2 - 8ab$$
$$0 = 4a(a-b)$$

$4a = 0 \quad$ or $\quad a - 2b = 0$
$\ a = 0 \quad$ or $\qquad a = 2b$

Since a cannot equal 0 (points B and C would coincide), $a = 2b$. Then the point $(2b, 2c)$

becomes $(a, 2c)$ which satisfies the equation

$x = a$. Then the vertex of the isosceles triangles lies on the perpendicular bisector of the base.

15. If the midpoint of one side of a rectangle is joined to the endpoints of the opposite sides, an isosceles triangle is formed.

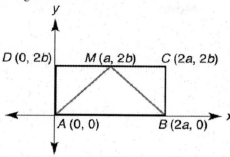

Proof: Let rectangle $ABCD$ have endpoints as shown.

With M the midpoint of $\overline{DC}$,

$$M = \left(\frac{0+2a}{2}, \frac{2b+2b}{2}\right) = (a, 2b).$$

$$MA = \sqrt{(a-0)^2 + (2b-0)^2} = \sqrt{a^2 + 4b^2}$$

$$MB = \sqrt{(a-2a)^2 + (2b-0)^2} = \sqrt{a^2 + 4b^2}$$

Since $MA = MB$, $\triangle AMB$ is isosceles.

16. If the median to one side of a triangle is also an altitude of the triangle, then the triangle is isosceles.

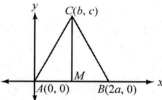

Proof: Let the vertices of $\triangle ABC$ be as shown. Then M, the midpoint of $\overline{AB}$ is

$$M = \left(\frac{0+2a}{2}, \frac{0+0}{2}\right) = (a, 0).$$

$\overline{CM}$ is the median from C to $\overline{AB}$. Since $\overline{AB}$ is a horizontal line for which $m_{\overline{AB}} = 0$, $m_{\overline{CM}}$ must be undefined if $\overline{CM}$ is also an altitude of $\triangle ABC$.

But $m_{\overline{CM}} = \frac{c-0}{b-a} = \frac{c}{b-a}$. $m_{\overline{CM}}$ is undefined if $b - a = 0$, which leads to $a = b$.

If $a = b$, then $C = (a, c)$.

Now $AC = \sqrt{(a-0)^2 + (c-0)^2} = \sqrt{a^2 + c^2}$

Also $BC = \sqrt{(2a-a)^2 + (0-c)^2} = \sqrt{a^2 + c^2}$.

Because $AC = BC$, $\triangle ABC$ is isosceles.

17. If the diagonals of a parallelogram are perpendicular, then the parallelogram is a rhombus.

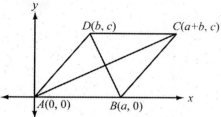

Proof: Let parallelogram $ABCD$ have vertices as shown. If $\overline{AC} \perp \overline{DB}$, then $m_{\overline{AC}} \cdot m_{\overline{DB}} = -1$.

Because $m_{\overline{AC}} = \frac{c-0}{(a+b)-0} = \frac{c}{a+b}$ and

$m_{\overline{DB}} = \frac{0-c}{a-b} = \frac{-c}{a-b}$, it follows that

$$\frac{c}{a+b} \cdot \frac{-c}{a-b} = -1$$

$$\frac{-c^2}{a^2 - b^2} = -1$$

$$-c^2 = -1(a^2 - b^2)$$

$$-c^2 = -a^2 + b^2$$

$$a^2 = b^2 + c^2 \ (*)$$

For $ABCD$ to be a rhombus, we must show that two adjacent sides are congruent. $AB = a - 0 = a$

and $AD = \sqrt{(b-0)^2 + (c-0)^2} = \sqrt{b^2 + c^2}$.

Because $a^2 = b^2 + c^2 (*)$, it follows that

$a = \sqrt{b^2 + c^2}$ and $AB = AD$. Then parallelogram $ABCD$ is a rhombus.

18. Let parallelogram $ABCD$ have the indicated vertices. Also let $H, J, K,$ and L represent the midpoints of the sides.

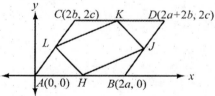

The Midpoint Formula leads to $H = (a, 0)$,

$J = (2a+b, c)$, $K = (a+2b, 2c)$, and $L = (b, c)$.

In turn, the slopes of the sides of quad. $HJKL$ are

$$m_{\overline{LH}} = \frac{c-0}{(2a+b)-a} = \frac{c}{a+b}$$

$$m_{\overline{JK}} = \frac{2c-c}{(a+2b)-(2a+b)} = \frac{c}{b-a}$$

$$m_{\overline{HJ}} = \frac{2c-c}{(a+2b)-b} = \frac{c}{a+b}$$

$$m_{\overline{LK}} = \frac{c-0}{b-a} = \frac{c}{b-a}$$

Because $m_{\overline{LH}} = m_{\overline{JK}}$, $\overline{LH} \parallel \overline{JK}$. Also

$m_{\overline{HJ}} = m_{\overline{LK}}$, so that $\overline{HH} \parallel \overline{LK}$. Then $HJKL$ is a parallelogram.

19. Let vertices of $\triangle ABC$ be as shown so that $\overline{AC} \cong \overline{BC}$.

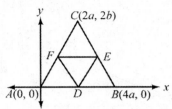

Then the midpoints of the sides are $D = (2a, 0)$, $E = (3a, b)$, and $F = (a, b)$.

$$DE = \sqrt{(3a - 2a)^2 + (b - 0)^2} = \sqrt{a^2 + b^2}$$
$$EF = \sqrt{(a - 3a)^2 + (b - b)^2} = \sqrt{4a^2} = 2a$$
$$FD = \sqrt{(a - 2a)^2 + (b - 0)^2} = \sqrt{a^2 + b^2}$$

Because $DE = FD$, the $\triangle DEF$ is also isosceles.

20. $Ax + By = C$
$$By = -Ax + C$$
$$y = -\frac{A}{B}x + \frac{C}{B}$$

So $m_1 = -\dfrac{A}{B}$

$Ax + By = D$
$$By = -Ax + D$$
$$y = -\frac{A}{B}x + \frac{D}{B}$$

So $m_2 = -\dfrac{A}{B}$

Since $m_1 = m_2 = -\dfrac{A}{B}$, then the lines are parallel.

21. $Ax + By = C$
$$By = -Ax + C$$
$$y = -\frac{A}{B}x + \frac{C}{B}$$

So $m_1 = -\dfrac{A}{B}$

$Bx - Ay = D$
$$-Ay = -Bx + D$$
$$y = \frac{B}{A}x - \frac{D}{A}$$

So $m_2 = \dfrac{B}{A}$

Since $m_1 \cdot m_2 = -\dfrac{A}{B} \cdot \dfrac{B}{A} = -1$, then the lines are perpendicular.

22. $2x + 3y = D$
$$2(4) + 3(5) = D$$
$$23 = D$$
$$2x + 3y = 23$$

23. $3x - 2y = D$
$$3(4) - 2(5) = D$$
$$2 = D$$
$$3x - 2y = 2$$

24. Using the distance formula,
$$r = \sqrt{(x - 0)^2 + (y - 0)^2}$$
$$r = \sqrt{x^2 + y^2}$$
$$r^2 = x^2 + y^2$$
or $x^2 + y^2 = r^2$.

25. $x^2 + y^2 = r^2$
$$x^2 + y^2 = 3^2$$
$$x^2 + y^2 = 9$$

26. $x^2 + y^2 = r^2$
$$3^2 + 4^2 = r^2$$
$$9 + 16 = r^2$$
$$25 = r^2$$
$$x^2 + y^2 = 25$$

27. The slope of the radius to the point of tangency, (a, b) is $\dfrac{b}{a}$. $\therefore$ the slope of the tangent is $-\dfrac{a}{b}$.

28. The slope of the radius to the point of tangency, (c, d) is $\dfrac{d - k}{c - h}$. $\therefore$ the slope of the tangent is

$$-\frac{c - h}{d - k} \ or \ \frac{h - c}{d - k}.$$

29. The theorem remains true. The quadrilateral which results is a parallelogram.

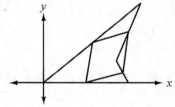

30. If $c^2 = a^2 + b^2$, then the triangle ABC is a right triangle.

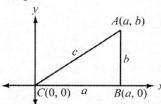

Proof: With the triangle as shown

$c = AC = \sqrt{(r-0)^2 + (s-0)^2} = \sqrt{r^2 + s^2}$

$a = BC = a - 0 = a$ and

$b = AB = \sqrt{(r-a)^2 + (s-0)^2}$

$\quad = \sqrt{(r-a)^2 + s^2}$.

If $c^2 = a^2 + b^2$, then

$\left(\sqrt{r^2 + s^2}\right)^2 = a^2 + \left(\sqrt{(r-a)b + s^2}\right)^2$

$r^2 + s^2 = a^2 + (r-a)^2 + s^2$

$r^2 + s^2 = a^2 + 4^2 - 2ar + a^2 + s^2$

$0 = 2a^2 - 2ar$

$0 = 2a(a-r)$

Now either $a = 0$ or $a - r = 0$.

$a \neq 0$ for point B would coincide with point C.

If $a - r = 0$, then $a = r$. Then $A = (r, s) = (a, s)$

and $\overline{AB}$ is a vertical line. Then $\overline{AB} \perp \overline{CB}$ and there is a right angle at B.

$\therefore \triangle ABC$ is a right triangle.

SECTION 10.5: Equations of Lines

1. Dividing by 8, $8x + 16y = 48$ becomes

$x + 2y = 6$.

Then $\quad 2y = -1x + 6$

$\quad \frac{1}{2}(2y) = \frac{1}{2}(-1x + 6)$

$\quad y = -\frac{1}{2}x + 3$

2. Dividing by 5, $15x - 35y = 105$ becomes

$3x - 7y = 21$

$\quad -7y = -3x + 21$

$-\frac{1}{7}(-7y) = -\frac{1}{7}(-3x + 21)$

$\quad y = \frac{3}{7}x - 3$

3. Dividing by 6, $-6x + 18y = -240$ becomes

$-x + 3y = -40$

$\quad 3y = x - 40$

$\frac{1}{3}(3y) = \frac{1}{3}(x - 40)$

$\quad y = \frac{1}{3}x - \frac{40}{3}$

4. Dividing by 9, $27x - 36y = 108$ becomes

$3x - 4y = 12$

Then $\quad -4y = -3x + 12$

$\quad -\frac{1}{4}(-4y) = -\frac{1}{4}(-3x + 12)$

$\quad y = \frac{3}{4}x - 3$

5. $y = 2x - 3$ has $m = 2$ and $b = -3$. Plot the point $(0, -3)$. Then draw the line for which an increase of 2 in y corresponds to an increase of 1 in x.

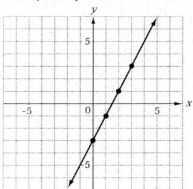

6. $y = -2x + 5$ has $m = -2$ and $b = 5$. Plot the point $(0, 5)$. Then draw the line for which a decrease of 2 in y corresponds to an increase of 1 in x.

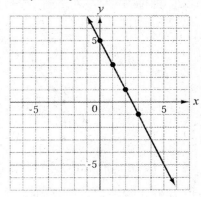

7. $\frac{2}{5}x + y = 6$ becomes $y = \frac{-2}{5}x + 6$.

$m = \frac{-2}{5}$ and $b = 6$. Plot the point (0, 6). Then draw the line for which a decrease of 2 in y corresponds to an increase of 5 in x.

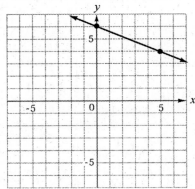

8. $3x - 2y = 12$
    $-2y = -3x + 12$
    $-\frac{1}{2}(-2y) = -\frac{1}{2}(-3x + 12)$
    $y = \frac{3}{2}x - 6$

    Then $m = \frac{3}{2}$ and $b = -6$. Plot the point $(0, -6)$.

    Now draw the line so that an increase of 3 in y corresponds to an increase of 2 in x.

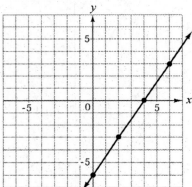

9. Using $y = mx + b$,
    $$y = -\frac{2}{3}x + 5$$
    $$3y = -2x + 15$$
    $$2x + 3y = 15$$

10. Using $y = mx + b$,
    $$y = -3x - 2$$
    $$3x + y = -2$$

11. $m = \frac{6-4}{0-2} = \frac{2}{-2} = -1$

    Using $y = mx + b$,
    $$y = -1x + 6$$
    $$x + y = 6$$

12. $m = \frac{-1-5}{2-(-2)} = \frac{-6}{4} = \frac{-3}{2}$

    Using $y - y_1 = m(x - x_1)$ and the point $(2, -1)$,
    $$y - (-1) = \frac{-3}{2}(x - 2)$$
    $$y + 1 = \frac{-3}{2}(x - 2)$$

    Mult. by 2,
    $$2(y + 1) = -3(x - 2)$$
    $$2y + 2 = -3x + 6$$
    $$3x + 2y = 4$$

13. $m = \frac{1-(-1)}{3-0} = \frac{2}{3}$

    Using $y = mx + b$, $y = \frac{2}{3}x - 1$.

    Mult. by 3,
    $$3y = 2x - 3$$
    $$-2x + 3y = -3$$

14. $m = \frac{3-0}{4-(-2)} = \frac{3}{6} = \frac{1}{2}$

    Using $y - y_1 = m(x - x_1)$ and the point $(-2, 0)$,
    $$y - 0 = \frac{1}{2}(x - (-2))$$
    $$y = \frac{1}{2}(x + 2)$$

    Mult. by 2,
    $$2y = x + 2$$
    $$-x + 2y = 2$$

15. $m = \frac{b-0}{0-a} = -\frac{b}{a}$

    Using $y = mx + b$
    $$y = -\frac{b}{a}x + b$$
    $$ay = -bx + ab$$
    $$bx + ay = ab$$

16. Using $y - y_1 = m(x - x_1)$
    $$y - c = d(x - b)$$
    $$y - c = dx - bd$$
    $$dx - y = bd - c$$

17. The graph contains (2, 0) and (0, −2).

    $m = \frac{-2-0}{0-2} = \frac{-2}{-2} = 1$.

    Using $y = mx + b$,
    $$y = 1x + 2$$
    $$-x + y = -2$$

18. The graph contains $(-3, 0)$ and $(0, 5)$.

$$m = \frac{5-0}{0-(-3)} = \frac{5}{3}$$

Using $y = mx + b$

$$y = \frac{5}{3}x + 5$$

Mult. by 3,

$$3y = 5x + 15$$
$$-5x + 3y = 15$$

19. The equation $5x + 2y = 10$ is equivalent to

$y = -\frac{5}{2}x + 5$. The line described has slope

$$m = \frac{-5}{2}.$$

Using $y - y_1 = m(x - x_1)$

$$y - 5 = -\frac{5}{2}(x - (-1))$$

$$y - 5 = -\frac{5}{2}(x + 1)$$

Mult. by 2, $2(y - 5) = -5(x + 1)$

$$2y - 10 = -5x - 5$$
$$5x + 2y = 5$$

20. Because $3x + y = 7$ is equivalent to $y = -3x + 7$,

the desired line has slope $m = -3$.

Using $\quad y = mx + b$

$$y = -3x + 3$$
$$3x + y = 3$$

21. The line $y = \frac{3}{4}x - 5$ has slope $m_1 = \frac{3}{4}$. The

desired line has $m_2 = -\frac{4}{3}$. Using $y = mx + b$,

$y = -\frac{4}{3}x - 4$. Mult. by 3,

$$3y = -4x - 12$$
$$4x + 3y = -12$$

22. $2x - 3y = 6$ changes to $y = \frac{2}{3}x - 2$ and the

desired line has slope $m_2 = -\frac{3}{2}$.

Using $\quad y - y_1 = m(x - x_1)$

$$y - (-3) = -\frac{3}{2}(x - 2)$$

$$y + 3 = \frac{-3}{2}(x - 2)$$

Mult. by 2,

$$2(y + 3) = -3(x - 2)$$
$$2y + 6 = -3x + 6$$
$$3x + 2y = 0$$

23. The midpoint of the line segment joining $(3, 5)$

and $(5, -1)$ is

$$M = \left(\frac{3+5}{2}, \frac{5+(-1)}{2}\right)$$
$$M = (4, 2)$$

The slope of the given line segment is

$$m_1 = \frac{-1-5}{5-3} = \frac{-6}{2} = -3.$$

The perpendicular bisector has the slope $m_2 = \frac{1}{3}$.

Using $y - y_1 = m(x - x_1)$

$$y - 2 = \frac{1}{3}(x - 4).$$

Multiply by 3,

$$3(y - 2) = x - 4$$
$$3y - 6 = x - 4$$
$$-x + 3y = 2.$$

24. The midpoint of the given line segment joining

$(-4, 5)$ and $(1, 1)$ is

$$M = \left(\frac{(-4)+1}{2}, \frac{5+1}{2}\right) = \left(\frac{-3}{2}, 3\right).$$

The slope of this line segment is

$$m_1 = \frac{1-5}{1-(-4)} = \frac{-4}{5}$$

The slope of the $\perp$ bisector is $m_2 = \frac{5}{4}$.

Using $y - y_1 = m(x - x_1)$

$$y - 3 = \frac{5}{4}\left(x - \left(\frac{-3}{2}\right)\right)$$

$$y - 3 = \frac{5}{4}\left(x + \frac{3}{2}\right)$$

$$y - 3 = \frac{5}{4}x + \frac{15}{8}$$

Mult. by 8, $\quad 8y - 24 = 10x + 15$

$$-10x + 8y = 39$$

25. Perpendicular slope is $-\frac{b}{a}$.

$$y - h = -\frac{b}{a}(x - g)$$

$$y = h = -\frac{b}{a}x + \frac{bg}{a}$$

$$y = -\frac{b}{a}x + \frac{bg + ha}{a}$$

26. Parallel slope is $\frac{a}{b}$

$$y - h = \frac{a}{b}(x - g)$$

$$y - h = \frac{a}{b}x - \frac{ag}{b}$$

$$y = \frac{a}{b}x + \frac{bh - ag}{b}$$

27.

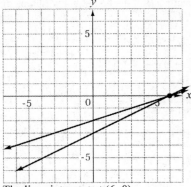

The lines intersect at (6, 0).

28.

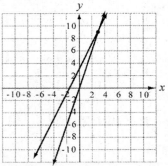

The lines intersect at (3, 9).

29. $2x + y = 6$
$\qquad y = -2x + 6$
$3x - y = 19$
$\qquad y = 3x - 19$

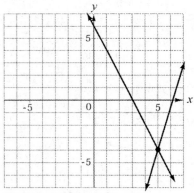

The lines intersect at (5, −4).

30. $\dfrac{1}{2}x + y = -3$
$\qquad y = \dfrac{-1}{2}x - 3$
$\dfrac{3}{4}x - y = 8$
$\qquad y = \dfrac{3}{4}x - 8$

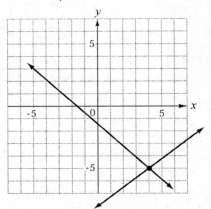

The lines intersect at $(4, -5)$.

31. $4x + 3y = 18$
$\qquad y = \dfrac{-4}{3}x + 6$
$x - 2y = 10$
$\qquad y = \dfrac{1}{2}x - 5$

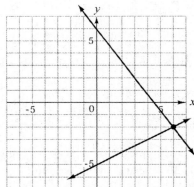

The lines intersect at $(6, -2)$.

32. $2x + 3y = 3$

$$y = \frac{-2}{3}x + 1$$

$$3x - 2y = 24$$

$$y = \frac{3}{2}x - 12$$

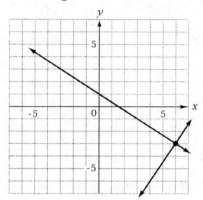

The lines intersect at $(6, -3)$.

33. $2x + y = 8$

$$\frac{3x - y = 7}{5x = 15}$$

$$x = 3$$

$$2(3) + y = 8$$

$$6 + y = 8$$

$$y = 2$$

The point of intersection is $(3, 2)$.

34. $2x + 3y = 7$

$x + 3y = 2$ \qquad Multiply by -1

$$2x + 3y = 7$$

$$\frac{-1x - 3y = -2}{1x = 5}$$

$$5x + 3y = 2$$

$$3y = -3$$

$$y = -1$$

The point of intersection is $(5, -1)$.

35. $2x + y = 11$ \qquad Multiply by -2

$$3x + 2y = 16$$

$$-4x - 2y = -22$$

$$\frac{3x + 2y = 16}{-1x = -6}$$

$$x = 6$$

$$2(6) + y = 11$$

$$12 + y = 11$$

$$y = -1$$

The point of intersection is $(6, -1)$.

36. $x + y = 1$ \qquad Multiply by 2

$$4x - 2y = 1$$

$$2x + 2y = 2$$

$$\frac{4x - 2y = 1}{6x = 3}$$

$$x = \frac{1}{2}$$

$$2\left(\frac{1}{2}\right) + 2y = 2$$

$$1 + 2y = 2$$

$$2y = 1$$

$$y = \frac{1}{2}$$

The point of intersection is $\left(\frac{1}{2}, \frac{1}{2}\right)$.

37. $2x + 3y = 4$ \qquad Multiply by -3

$3x - 4y = 23$ \qquad Multiply by 2

$$-6x - 9y = -12$$

$$\frac{6x - 8y = 46}{-17y = 34}$$

$$y = -2$$

$$2x + 3(-2) = 4$$

$$2x - 6 = 4$$

$$2x = 10$$

$$x = 5$$

The point of intersection is $(5, -2)$.

38. $5x - 2y = -13$ \qquad Multiply by 5

$3x + 5y = 17$ \qquad Multiply by 2

$$25x - 10y = -65$$

$$\frac{6x + 10y = 34}{31x = -31}$$

$$x = -1$$

$$3(-1) + 5y = 17$$

$$-3 + 5y = 17$$

$$5y = 20$$

$$y = 4$$

The point of intersection is $(-1, 4)$.

39. $\frac{1}{2}x - 3 = \frac{1}{3}x - 2$

Multiply by 6

$$3x - 18 = 2x - 12$$

$$x = 6$$

$$y = \frac{1}{2}(6) - 3$$

$$y = 0$$

$(6, 0)$

40. $2x + 3 = 3x$

$$x = 3$$

$$y = 3(3) = 9$$

$(3, 9)$

41. $bx + c = a$

$bx = a - c$

$x = \dfrac{a - c}{b}$

and $y = a$.

$\left(\dfrac{a-c}{b}, a \right)$

42. $x = d$ so $y = fx + g$ becomes

$y = fd + g$

$(d, df + g)$

43. The altitude from C is vertical with equation $x = b$.

To find the equation for the altitude from A, find the slope of $\overline{BC}$. $m_{\overline{BC}} = \dfrac{-c}{a - b}$. $\therefore$ the slope of the altitude from A to $\overline{BC}$ is $\dfrac{a - b}{c}$. The equation for that altitude is $y = \dfrac{a - b}{c} x$. If $x = b$, then

$y = \dfrac{a - b}{c} \cdot b = \dfrac{ab - b^2}{c}$.

$\left(b, \dfrac{ab - b^2}{c} \right)$

44. One median lies on the y-axis so the equation is $x = 0$. If M is the midpoint of $\overline{NQ}$, $M = (a, b)$.

The slope of $\overline{PM}$ is $m = \dfrac{b - 0}{a - (-2a)} = \dfrac{b}{3a}$. Using

$(-2a, 0)$ and $m = \dfrac{b}{3a}$,

$y - 0 = \dfrac{b}{3a}(x - (-2a))$

$y = \dfrac{b}{3a} x + \dfrac{b}{3a} \cdot 2a$

$y = \dfrac{b}{3a} x + \dfrac{2}{3} b$

If $x = 0$, then $y = \dfrac{2}{3} b$.

Coordinates of the centroid are $\left(0, \dfrac{2}{3}b \right)$.

45. The altitudes of a triangle are concurrent.

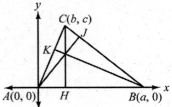

Proof: For $\triangle ABC$, let $\overline{CH}$, $\overline{AJ}$, and $\overline{BK}$ name the altitudes. Because $\overline{AB}$ is horizontal $\left(m_{\overline{AB}} = 0 \right)$, $\overline{CH}$ is vertical and has the equation $x = b$. Because $m_{\overline{BC}} = \dfrac{c - 0}{b - a} = \dfrac{c}{b - a}$, the slope of altitude $\overline{AJ}$ is $m_{\overline{AJ}} = -\dfrac{b - a}{c} = \dfrac{a - b}{c}$. Since $\overline{AJ}$ contains $(0, 0)$, its equation is $y = \dfrac{a - b}{c} x$. The intersection of altitudes $\overline{CH}$ ($x = b$) and $\overline{AJ}$ $\left(y = \dfrac{a - b}{c} x \right)$ is at $x = b$ so that

$y = \dfrac{a - b}{c} \cdot b = \dfrac{b(a - b)}{c} = \dfrac{ab - b^2}{c}$. That is, $\overline{CH}$ and $\overline{AJ}$ intersect at $\left(b, \dfrac{ab - b^2}{c} \right)$. The remaining altitude is $\overline{BK}$. Since $m_{\overline{AC}} = \dfrac{c - 0}{b - 0} = \dfrac{c}{b}$,

$m_{\overline{BK}} = -\dfrac{b}{c}$. Because $\overline{BK}$ contains $(a, 0)$, its equation is $y - 0 = -\dfrac{b}{c}(x - a)$ or $y = \dfrac{-b}{c}(x - a)$.

For the three altitudes to be concurrent, $\left(b, \dfrac{ab - b^2}{c} \right)$ must lie on the line $y = \dfrac{-b}{c}(x - a)$.

Substitution leads to

$\dfrac{ab - b^2}{c} = \dfrac{-b}{c}(b - a)$

$\dfrac{ab - b^2}{c} = \dfrac{-b(b - a)}{c}$

$\dfrac{ab - b^2}{c} = \dfrac{-b^2 + ab}{c}$, which is true.

Therefore, the three altitudes are concurrent.

46. The perpendicular bisectors of the sides of a triangle are concurrent.

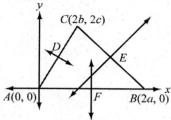

Proof: Let the $\triangle ABC$ have vertices as shown. If D, E, and F are midpoints of the sides $\overline{AC}$, $\overline{CB}$, and $\overline{AB}$ respectively, then

$$D = \left(\frac{0+2b}{2}, \frac{0+2c}{2}\right) = (b, c)$$

$$E = \left(\frac{2a+2b}{2}, \frac{0+2c}{2}\right) = (a+b, c)$$

$$F = \left(\frac{0+2a}{2}, \frac{0+0}{2}\right) = (a, 0)$$

Because $\overline{AB}$ is horizontal $\left(m_{\overline{AB}} = 0\right)$, the equation of the perpendicular bisector of $\overline{AB}$ is $x = a$.

Now, $m_{\overline{AC}} = \frac{2c-0}{2b-0} = \frac{2c}{2b} = \frac{c}{b}$; the slope of the perpendicular bisector of $\overline{AC}$ is $-\frac{b}{c}$. Its equation is $y - c = \frac{-b}{c}(x - b)$. The perpendicular bisectors of $\overline{AB}$ and $\overline{AC}$ intersect at a point for which $x = a$. Then

$$y - c = \frac{-b}{c}(a - b)$$

$$y - c = \frac{-ab}{c} + \frac{b^2}{c}$$

$$y = \frac{-ab}{c} + \frac{b^2}{c} + \frac{c^2}{c^2}$$

$$y = \frac{b^2 + c^2 - ab}{c}$$

That is, the perpendicular bisectors of $\overline{AB}$ and $\overline{AC}$ intersect at $\left(a, \frac{b^2 + c^2 - ab}{c}\right)$. Because $m_{\overline{BC}} = \frac{2c-0}{2b-2a} = \frac{2c}{2b-2a} = \frac{c}{b-a}$, the slope of the perpendicular bisector of $\overline{BC}$ is $-\frac{b-a}{c}$ or $\frac{a-b}{c}$. Since the perpendicular bisector of $\overline{BC}$ contains $E = (a+b, c)$, its equation is $y - c = \frac{a-b}{c}(x - (a+b))$. But $\left(a, \frac{b^2 + c^2 - ab}{c}\right)$ is also a solution for this equation since

$\frac{b^2 + c^2 - ab}{c} - c = \frac{a-b}{c}(a - (a+b))$. That is,

$$\frac{b^2 + c^2 - ab}{c} - \frac{c^2}{c} = \frac{a-b}{c}(-b)$$

$$\frac{b^2 - ab}{c} = \frac{-ab + b^2}{c}$$

The point, $\left(a, \frac{b^2 + c^2 - ab}{c}\right)$ lies on each of the three perpendicular bisectors. Thus the three perpendicular bisectors are concurrent at that point.

47.

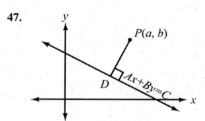

1st: Find the slope of $Ax + By = C$.

2nd: Use the result in (1) to find $m_{\overline{PD}}$.

3rd: Form the equation for $\overline{PD}$, which contains (a, b).

4th: Solve the system of equations, using $Ax + By = C$ and the equation of (3).

5th: Having determined the point of intersection of the two lines in (4), use The Distance Formula to find the distance between point P and the point of intersection.

CHAPTER REVIEW

1. a. $d = y_2 - y_1$ (if $y_2 > y_1$) $= 4 - (-3) = 7$

    b. $d = x_2 - x_1$ (if $x_2 > x_1$) $= 1 - (-5) = 6$

    c. $d = \sqrt{(x_2 - x_1)^2 + (y_2 - y_1)^2}$

       $d = \sqrt{(7 - (-5))^2 + (-3 - 2)^2}$

       $d = \sqrt{12^2 + (-5)^2} = \sqrt{144 + 25} = \sqrt{169} = 13$

    d. $d = \sqrt{(x - (x-3))^2 + ((y-2) - (y+2))^2}$

       $d = \sqrt{3^2 + (-4)^2} = \sqrt{9 + 16} = \sqrt{25} = 5$

2. a. $d = y_2 - y_1$ (if $y_2 > y_1$) $= 5 - (-3) = 8$

b. $d = x_2 - x_1$ (if $x_2 > x_1$) $= 3 - (-7) = 10$

c. $d = \sqrt{(4-(-4))^2 + (5-1)^2}$

$d = \sqrt{8^2 + 4^2} = \sqrt{64+16} = \sqrt{80} = 4\sqrt{5}$

d. $d = \sqrt{((x+4)-(x-2))^2 + ((y+5)-(y-3))^2}$

$d = \sqrt{6^2 + 8^2} = \sqrt{36+64} = \sqrt{100} = 10$

3. a. $M = \left(\dfrac{x_1 + x_2}{2}, \dfrac{y_1 + y_2}{2} \right)$

$M = \left(\dfrac{6+6}{2}, \dfrac{4+(-3)}{2} \right) = \left(6, \dfrac{1}{2} \right)$

b. $M = \left(\dfrac{1+(-5)}{2}, \dfrac{4+4}{2} \right) = (-2, 4)$

c. $M = \left(\dfrac{(-5)+7}{2}, \dfrac{2+(-3)}{2} \right) = \left(1, -\dfrac{1}{2} \right)$

d. $M = \left(\dfrac{(x-3)+x}{2}, \dfrac{(y+2)+(y-2)}{2} \right)$

$M = \left(\dfrac{2x-3}{2}, y \right)$

4. a. $M = \left(\dfrac{2+2}{2}, \dfrac{(-3)+5}{2} \right) = (2, 1)$

b. $M = \left(\dfrac{3+(-7)}{2}, \dfrac{(-2)+(-2)}{2} \right) = (-2, -2)$

c. $M = \left(\dfrac{(-4)+4}{2}, \dfrac{1+5}{2} \right) = (0, 3)$

d. $M = \left(\dfrac{(x-2)+(x+4)}{2}, \dfrac{(y-3)+(y+5)}{2} \right)$

$M = (x+1, y+1)$

5. a. $m = \dfrac{y_2 - y_1}{x_2 - x_1}$

$m = \dfrac{(-3)-4}{6-6} = \dfrac{-7}{0}$ m is undefined.

b. $m = \dfrac{4-4}{-5-1} = \dfrac{0}{-6} = 0$

c. $m = \dfrac{-3-2}{7-(-5)} = \dfrac{-5}{12}$

d. $m = \dfrac{(y-2)-(y+2)}{x-(x-3)} = \dfrac{-4}{3}$

6. a. $m = \dfrac{5-(-3)}{2-2} = \dfrac{8}{0}$ m is undefined.

b. $m = \dfrac{-2-(-2)}{-7-3} = \dfrac{0}{-10} = 0$

c. $m = \dfrac{5-1}{4-(-4)} = \dfrac{4}{8} = \dfrac{1}{2}$

d. $m = \dfrac{(y+5)-(y-3)}{(x+4)-(x-2)} = \dfrac{8}{6} = \dfrac{4}{3}$

7. $M = \left(\dfrac{x_1 + x_2}{2}, \dfrac{y_1 + y_2}{2} \right)$

$(2,1) = \left(\dfrac{8+x}{2}, \dfrac{10+y}{2} \right)$

$\dfrac{8+x}{2} = 2$ and $\dfrac{10+y}{2} = 1$

$8+x = 4$ and $10+y = 2$

$x = -4$ and $y = -8$

$B = (-4, -8)$

8. Due to symmetry, $R = (3, 7)$.

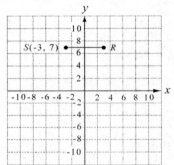

9. $m = \dfrac{y_2 - y_1}{x_2 - x_1}$

$-3 = \dfrac{3-1}{x-2}$

$-3 = \dfrac{2}{x-2}$

$-3(x-2) = 2$

$-3x + 6 = 2$

$-3x = -4$

$x = \dfrac{4}{3}$

10. $m = \dfrac{y_2 - y_1}{x_2 - x_1}$

$\dfrac{-6}{7} = \dfrac{y-2}{2-(-5)}$

$\dfrac{-6}{7} = \dfrac{y-2}{7}$

$-6 = y-2$

$y = -4$

11. a. $x + 3y = 6$

$$y = -\frac{1}{3}x + 2$$

$$m = -\frac{1}{3}$$

$$3x - y = -7$$

$$y = 3x + 7$$

$$m = 3$$

Since $m_1 \cdot m_2 = -1$, the lines are perpendicular.

b. $2x - y = -3$

$$y = 2x + 3$$

$$m = 2 \text{ and } b = 3$$

$$y = 2x - 14$$

$$m = 2 \text{ and } b = -14$$

Since $m_1 = m_2$, the lines are parallel.

c. $y + 2 = -3(x - 5)$

$$y = -3x + 13$$

$$m = -3$$

$$2y = 6x + 11$$

$$y = 3x + \frac{11}{2}$$

$$m = 3$$

The lines are neither parallel nor perpendicular.

d. $0.5x + y = 0$

$$y = -\frac{1}{2}x$$

$$m = -\frac{1}{2}$$

$$2x - y = 10$$

$$y = 2x - 10$$

$$m = 2$$

Since $m_1 \cdot m_2 = -1$, the lines are perpendicular.

12. Let $A = (-6, 5)$, $B = (1, 7)$, and $C = (16, 10)$.
The points would be collinear if

$$m_{\overline{AB}} = m_{\overline{BC}}$$

$$m_{\overline{AB}} = \frac{7 - 5}{1 - (-6)} = \frac{2}{7}$$

$$m_{\overline{BC}} = \frac{10 - 7}{16 - 1} = \frac{3}{15} = \frac{1}{5}$$

The points are not collinear.

13. Let $A = (-2, 3)$, $B = (x, 6)$, and $C = (8, 8)$. If $m_{\overline{AB}} = m_{\overline{BC}}$, then A, B, and C are collinear.

$$m_{\overline{AB}} = \frac{6 - 3}{x - (-2)} = \frac{3}{x + 2}$$

$$m_{\overline{BC}} = \frac{8 - x}{8 - x} = \frac{2}{8 - x}$$

$$\frac{3}{x + 2} = \frac{2}{8 - x}$$

$$3(8 - x) = 2(x + 2)$$

$$24 - 3x = 2x + 4$$

$$20 = 5x$$

$$x = 4$$

14. Intercepts are (7, 0) and (0, 3).

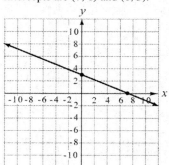

15. $4x - 3y = 9$

$$-3y = -4x + 9$$

$$y = \frac{4}{3}x - 3$$

First, plot the point (0, −3). Then locate a second point for which an increase of 4 in y corresponds to an increase of 3 in x.

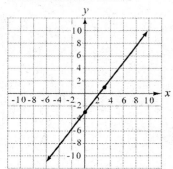

16. $y + 2 = \frac{-2}{3}(x - 1)$

$y - (-2) = \frac{-2}{3}(x - 1)$ is a line which contains

$(1, -2)$ and has slope $m = \frac{-2}{3}$. First plot

$(1, -2)$. Then from that point draw a line which

has $m = \frac{-2}{3}$.

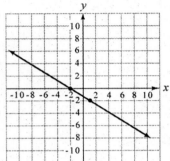

17. a. $m = \frac{6 - 3}{-3 - 2} = \frac{3}{-5}$ or $\frac{-3}{5}$

$y - 3 = \frac{-3}{5}(x - 2)$

$5(y - 3) = -3(x - 2)$

$5y - 15 = -3x + 6$

$3x + 5y = 21$

b. $m = \frac{-9 - (-3)}{8 - 6} = \frac{-6}{2} = -3$

$y - (-1) = -3(x - (-2))$

$y + 1 = -3(x + 2)$

$y + 1 = -3x - 6$

$3x + y = -7$

c. $x + 2y = 4$

$y = \frac{-1}{2}x + 2$

Since $m_1 = \frac{-1}{2}$, the desired line has $m_2 = 2$.

$y - (-2) = 2(x - 3)$

$y + 2 = 2x + 6$

$-2x + y = -8$

d. A line parallel to the x-axis has the form

$y = b$. $\therefore y = 5$

18. Let $A = (-2, -3)$, $B = (4, 5)$, and $C = (-4, 1)$.

$m_{\overline{AB}} = \frac{5 - (-3)}{4 - (-2)} = \frac{8}{6} = \frac{4}{3}$

$m_{\overline{BC}} = \frac{1 - 5}{-4 - 4} = \frac{-4}{-8} = \frac{1}{2}$

$m_{\overline{AC}} = \frac{1 - (-3)}{-4 - (-2)} = \frac{4}{-2} = -2$

Because $m_{\overline{AC}} \cdot m_{\overline{BC}} = -1$, $\overline{AC} \perp \overline{BC}$ and $\angle C$ is

a rt. $\angle$. The triangle is a right triangle.

19. Let $A = (3, 6)$, $B = (-6 \, 4)$, and $C = (1, -2)$.

$AB = \sqrt{(-6 - 3)^2 + (4 - 6)^2}$

$= \sqrt{(-9)^2 + (-2)^2} = \sqrt{81 + 4} = \sqrt{85}$

$BC = \sqrt{(1 - (-6))^2 + (-2 - 4)^2}$

$= \sqrt{(-9)^2 + (-2)^2} = \sqrt{49 + 36} = \sqrt{85}$

$AC = \sqrt{(1 - 3)^2 + (-2 - 6)^2}$

$= \sqrt{(-2)^2 + (-8)^2} = \sqrt{4 + 64}$

$= \sqrt{68} = 2\sqrt{17}$

Because $AB = BC$, the triangle is isosceles.

20. $R = (-5, -3)$, $S = (1, -11)$, $T = (7, -6)$, and

$V = (1, 2)$.

$m_{\overline{RS}} = \frac{-11 - (-3)}{1 - (-5)} = \frac{-8}{6} = \frac{-4}{3}$

$m_{\overline{ST}} = \frac{-6 - (-11)}{7 - 1} = \frac{5}{6}$

$m_{\overline{TV}} = \frac{2 - (-6)}{1 - 7} = \frac{8}{-6} = \frac{-4}{3}$

$m_{\overline{RV}} = \frac{2 - (-3)}{1 - (-5)} = \frac{5}{6}$

$\therefore \overline{RS} \parallel \overline{VT}$ and $\overline{RV} \parallel \overline{ST}$ and $RSTV$ is a

parallelogram.

21. Solution by graphing:

$4x - 3y = -3$

$y = \frac{4}{3}x + 1$

$x + 2y = 13$

$y = -\frac{1}{2}x + \frac{13}{2}$

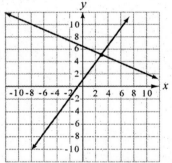

The graphs (lines) intersect at (3, 5).

22. Solution by graphing:

$$y = x + 3$$
$$y = 4x$$

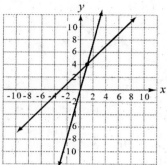

The graphs (lines) intersect at $(1, 4)$.

23. Solution by Substitution:

$$4x - 3y = -3$$
$$x + 2y = 13$$
$$x = 13 - 2y$$
$$4(13 - 2y) - 3y = -3$$
$$52 - 8y - 3y = -3$$
$$-11y = -55$$
$$y = 5$$
$$x = 13 - 2(5) = 3$$

$(3, 5)$

24. Solution by Substitution:

$$4x = x + 3$$
$$3x = 3$$
$$x = 1$$
$$y = 4(1) = 4$$

$(1, 4)$

25.

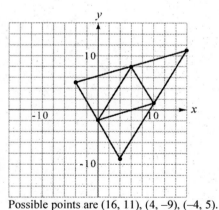

Possible points are $(16, 11)$, $(4, -9)$, $(-4, 5)$.

26. **a.** $D = M_{\overline{AC}} = (7, 2)$

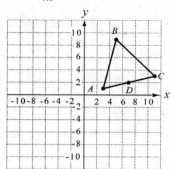

The length of $\overline{BD}$ is

$$\sqrt{(7-5)^2 + (2-9)^2} = \sqrt{2^2 + (-7)^2}$$
$$= \sqrt{4 + 49} = \sqrt{53}$$

b. $m_{\overline{AC}} = \dfrac{3-1}{11-3} = \dfrac{2}{8} = \dfrac{1}{4}$.

Then the slope of the altitude to $\overline{AC}$ is -4.

c. Since $m_{\overline{AC}} = \dfrac{1}{4}$, the slope of any line parallel

to $\overline{AC}$ is also $\dfrac{1}{4}$.

27. $A = (-a, 0)$
$B = (0, b)$
$C = (a, 0)$

28. $D = (0, 0)$
$E = (a, 0)$
$F = (a, 2a)$
$G = (0, 2a)$

29. $R = (0, 0)$
$U = (0, a)$
$T = (a, a + b)$

30. $M = (0, 0)$
$N = (a, 0)$
$Q = (a + b, c)$
$P = (b, c)$

31. a. The midpoint of $\overline{AB}$ is
$M_{\overline{AB}} = (a + c, b + d)$. Then

$$CM = \sqrt{(a + c - 0)^2 + (b + d - 2e)^2}$$
$$= \sqrt{(a + c)^2 + (b + d - 2e)^2}$$

b. $m_{\overline{AC}} = \dfrac{2e - 2b}{0 - 2a} = \dfrac{e - b}{-a}$ or $\dfrac{b - e}{a}$

Then the slope of the altitude to $\overline{AC}$ is

$-\dfrac{a}{b - e}$ or $\dfrac{a}{e - b}$.

c. The altitude from B to $\overline{AC}$ contains the point

$(2c, 2d)$ and has slope $m = \dfrac{a}{e - b}$ from part

(b). $y - 2d = \dfrac{a}{e - b}(x - 2c)$.

32. See Section 10.4, #18.

33. If the diagonals of a rectangle are perpendicular, then the rectangle is a square.

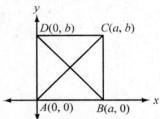

Proof: Let rect. *ABCD* have vertices as shown.
If $\overline{DB} \perp \overline{AC}$, then $m_{\overline{DB}} \cdot m_{\overline{AC}} = -1$. But

$m_{\overline{DB}} = \dfrac{0 - b}{a - 0} = \dfrac{-b}{a}$ and $m_{\overline{AC}} = \dfrac{b - 0}{a - 0} = \dfrac{b}{a}$. Then

$\dfrac{-b}{a} \cdot \dfrac{b}{a} = -1$

$\dfrac{-b^2}{a^2} = -1$

$-b^2 = -a^2$

$b^2 = a^2$

Since a and b are both positive, $a = b$. Then
$AB = a - 0 = a$ and $AD = b - 0 = b$. Since $a = b$,
$AB = AD$. If $AB = AD$, then *ABCD* is a square.

34. If the diagonals of a trapezoid are equal in length, then the trapezoid is an isosceles trapezoid.

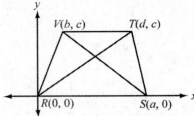

Proof: Let trap. *RSTV* have vertices as shown.
If $RT = VS$, then

$$\sqrt{(d - 0)^2 + (c - 0)^2} = \sqrt{(a - b)^2 + (0 - c)^2}$$
$$\sqrt{d^2 + c^2} = \sqrt{(a - b)^2 + (-c)^2}$$
$$\sqrt{d^2 + c^2} = \sqrt{(a - b)^2 + c^2}$$
Squaring, $d^2 + c^2 = (a - b)^2 + c^2$
$$d^2 = (a - b)^2$$
$$d = (a - b$$

Comparing the lengths of $\overline{RV}$ and $\overline{ST}$,

$RV = \sqrt{(b - 0)^2 + (c - 0)^2} = \sqrt{b^2 + c^2}$
$ST = \sqrt{(a - d)^2 + (0 - c)^2} = \sqrt{(a - d)^2 + c^2}$

Now *RV* would equal *ST* if
$b^2 + c^2 = (a - d)^2 + c^2$
$$b^2 = (a - d)^2$$
$$b = a - d$$
Because $d = a - b$ leads to $b = a - d$, so
$RV = ST$. Then *RSTV* is isosceles.

35. If two medians of a triangle are equal in length, then the triangle is isosceles.

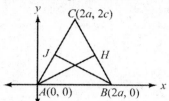

Proof: Let $\triangle ABC$ has vertices as shown, so that the midpoint of $\overline{AC}$ is $J = (b, c)$ and the midpoint of $\overline{BC}$ is $H = (a + b, c)$. If $AH = BJ$, then

$$\sqrt{(a + b - 0)^2 + (c - 0)^2} = \sqrt{(2a - b)^2 + (0 - c)^2}$$
$$\sqrt{(a + b)^2 + c^2} = \sqrt{(2a - b)^2 + c^2}$$

Squaring, $(a + b)^2 + c^2 = (2a - b)^2 + c^2$
$$(a + b)^2 = (2a - b)^2$$

Taking the principal of square roots,
$a + b = 2a - b$
$2b = a$

Then point $C = (a, 2c)$.

Now $AC = \sqrt{(a - 0)^2 + (2c - 0)^2}$
$= \sqrt{a^2 + (2c)^2} = \sqrt{a^2 + 4c^2}$

and $BC = \sqrt{(2a - a)^2 + (0 - 2c)^2}$
$= \sqrt{a^2 + (-2c)^2} = \sqrt{a^2 + 4c^2}$

Because $AC = BC$, the triangle is isosceles.

36. The segments joining the midpoints of consecutive sides of an isosceles trapezoid form a rhombus.

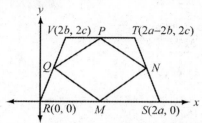

Proof: Let trapezoid $RSTV$ have vertices as shown so that $RV = TS$. Where M, N, P, and Q are the midpoints of the sides,

$$M = \left(\frac{0 + 2a}{2}, \frac{0 + 0}{2}\right) = (a, 0)$$
$$N = \left(\frac{(2a - 2b) + 2a}{2}, \frac{0 + 2c}{2}\right) = (2a - b, c)$$
$$P = \left(\frac{(2a - 2b) + 2b}{2}, \frac{2c + 2c}{2}\right) = (a, 2c)$$
$$Q = \left(\frac{0 + 2b}{2}, \frac{0 + 2c}{2}\right) = (b, c)$$

By an earlier theorem, $MNPQ$ is a parallelogram. We must show that two adjacent sides of parallelogram $MNPQ$ are equal in length.

$$QM = \sqrt{(a - b)^2 + (0 - c)^2}$$
$$= \sqrt{(a - b)^2 + (-c)^2} = \sqrt{(a - b)^2 + c^2}$$
$$MN = \sqrt{(2a - b - a)^2 + (c - 0)^2} = \sqrt{(a - b)^2 + c^2}$$

Now $QM = MN$, so $MNPQ$ is a rhombus.

CHAPTER TEST

1. a. $(5, -3)$

b. $(0, -4)$

2.

3. $d = \sqrt{(-6 - 0)^2 + (1 - 9)^2} = \sqrt{(-6)^2 + (-8)^2}$
$= \sqrt{36 + 64} = \sqrt{100} = 10$

4. $M = \left(\dfrac{x_1+x_2}{2}, \dfrac{y_1+y_2}{2}\right) = \left(\dfrac{-6+0}{2}, \dfrac{1+9}{2}\right)$

     $= (-3, 5)$

5.

x	0	3	0	9
y	4	2	4	-2

6. Graph of $2x + 3y = 12$,

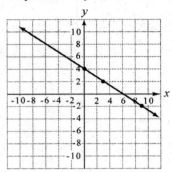

7. a. $m = \dfrac{-6-3}{2-(-1)} = \dfrac{-9}{3} = -3$

     b. $m = \dfrac{d-b}{c-a}$

8. a. $\dfrac{2}{3}$

     b. $-\dfrac{3}{2}$

9. $AB = \sqrt{(0-0)^2 + (a-0)^2} = \sqrt{a^2} = a$

     $BC = \sqrt{(a+b-a)^2 + (c-0)^2} = \sqrt{b^2+c^2}$

     $CD = \sqrt{(b-(a+b))^2 + (c-c)^2} = \sqrt{(-a)^2} = a$

     $AD = \sqrt{(b-0)^2 + (c-0)^2} = \sqrt{b^2+c^2}$

Since $\overline{AB} = \overline{CD}$ and $\overline{BC} = \overline{AD}$, $ABCD$ is a parallelogram.

10. $AB = \sqrt{(0-0)^2 + (a-0)^2} = \sqrt{a^2} = a$

     $AD = \sqrt{(b-0)^2 + (c-0)^2} = \sqrt{b^2+c^2}$

If $\overline{AB} = \overline{AD}$, then $a = \sqrt{b^2+c^2}$ or $a^2 = b^2 + c^2$.

11. a. Isosceles triangle

     b. Trapezoid

12. a. Slope Formula

     b. Distance Formula

13. Let $D = (0, 0)$ and $E = (2a, 0)$, then $F = (a, b)$.

14. (b)

15. Since $RSTV$ is a parallelogram, then $m_{\overline{VR}} = m_{\overline{TS}}$.

     $m_{\overline{VR}} = \dfrac{v-0}{0-r} = -\dfrac{v}{r}$

     $m_{\overline{TS}} = \dfrac{v-0}{t-s} = \dfrac{v}{t-s}$

     So $-\dfrac{v}{r} = \dfrac{v}{t-s}$

         $rv = -v(t-s)$

         $r = -t + s$

     or $s = r + t$ or $t = -r + s$.

16. a. $m = \dfrac{6-4}{2-0} = \dfrac{2}{2} = 1$

         $y - 4 = 1(x-0)$

         $y - 4 = x$

         $y = x + 4$

     b. $m = \dfrac{3}{4}$, $b = -3$

         $y = \dfrac{3}{4}x - 3$

17. The slope of the perpendicular line $m = c$.

     $y - b = c(x-a)$

     $y - b = cx - ac$

         $y = cx + (b - ac)$

18. $x + 2y = 6$

     $x = -2y + 6$

     Use substitution,

         $2x - y = 7$

     $2(-2y+6) - y = 7$

       $-4y + 12 - y = 7$

           $-5y = -5$

             $y = 1$

         $x = -2(1) + 6 = 4$

     (4, 1)

19. $5x - 2y = -13$ Multiply by 5

     $3x + 5y = 17$ Multiply by 2

     $25x - 10y = -65$

     $\dfrac{6x + 10y = 34}{31x = -31}$

          $x = -1$

     $3(-1) + 5y = 17$

        $-3 + 5y = 17$

           $5y = 20$

            $y = 4$

     (-1, 4)

20. $M = (a+b, c)$ and $N = (a, 0)$.

     Then $m_{\overline{AC}} = \dfrac{2c-0}{2b-0} = \dfrac{c}{b}$.

     Also $m_{\overline{MN}} = \dfrac{c-0}{a+b-a} = \dfrac{c}{b}$.

     With $m_{\overline{AC}} = m_{\overline{MN}}$, it follows that $\overline{AC} \parallel \overline{MN}$.

Chapter 11: Introduction to Trigonometry

SECTION 11.1: The Sine Ratio and Applications

1. $\sin\alpha = \dfrac{\text{opposite}}{\text{hypotenuse}} = \dfrac{5}{13}$

   $\sin\beta = \dfrac{12}{13}$

2. $\sin\alpha = \dfrac{6}{10} = \dfrac{3}{5}$

   $\sin\beta = \dfrac{8}{10} = \dfrac{4}{5}$

3. Using the Pythagorean Triple, (8, 15, 17), $a = 8$.

   $\therefore \sin\alpha = \dfrac{8}{17}$; $\sin\beta = \dfrac{15}{17}$

4. $a^2 + b^2 = c^2$

   $\left(\sqrt{5}\right)^2 + b^2 = 3^2$

   $5 + b^2 = 9$

   $b^2 = 4$

   $b = 2$

   $\sin\alpha = \dfrac{\sqrt{5}}{3}$; $\sin\beta = \dfrac{2}{3}$

5. $a^2 + b^2 = c^2$

   $\left(\sqrt{2}\right)^2 + \left(\sqrt{3}\right)^2 = c^2$

   $2 + 3 = c^2$

   $5 = c^2$

   $\sqrt{5} = c$

   $\sin\alpha = \dfrac{\sqrt{3}}{\sqrt{5}} = \dfrac{\sqrt{3}}{\sqrt{5}} \cdot \dfrac{\sqrt{5}}{\sqrt{5}} = \dfrac{\sqrt{15}}{5}$

   $\sin\beta = \dfrac{\sqrt{2}}{\sqrt{5}} = \dfrac{\sqrt{2}}{\sqrt{5}} \cdot \dfrac{\sqrt{5}}{\sqrt{5}} = \dfrac{\sqrt{10}}{5}$

6. $a^2 + b^2 = c^2$

   $3^2 + b^2 = \left(\sqrt{13}\right)^2$

   $9 + b^2 = 13$

   $b^2 = 4$

   $b = 2$

   $\sin\alpha = \dfrac{3}{\sqrt{13}} = \dfrac{3}{\sqrt{13}} \cdot \dfrac{\sqrt{13}}{\sqrt{13}} = \dfrac{3\sqrt{13}}{13}$

   $\sin\beta = \dfrac{2}{\sqrt{13}} = \dfrac{2}{\sqrt{13}} \cdot \dfrac{\sqrt{13}}{\sqrt{13}} = \dfrac{2\sqrt{13}}{13}$

7. $\sin 90° = 1$

8. $\sin 0° = 0$

9. $\sin 17° = 0.2924$

10. $\sin 23° = 0.3907$

11. $\sin 82° = 0.9903$

12. $\sin 46° = 0.7193$

13. $\sin 72° = 0.9511$

14. $\sin 57° = 0.8387$

15. $\sin 35° = \dfrac{a}{12}$

    $a = 12\sin 35°$

    $a \approx 12(0.5736)$

    $a \approx 6.9$ in.

    $\sin 55° = \dfrac{b}{12}$

    $b = 12\sin 55°$

    $b \approx 12(0.8192)$

    $b \approx 9.8$ in.

16. $\sin 43° = \dfrac{a}{20}$

    $a = 20\sin 43°$

    $a \approx 20(0.6820)$

    $a \approx 13.6$ m

    $\sin 47° = \dfrac{b}{20}$

    $b = 20\sin 47°$

    $b \approx 20(0.7314)$

    $b \approx 14.6$ m

17. $\sin 43° = \dfrac{a}{16}$

    $a = 16\sin 43°$

    $a \approx 16(0.6820)$

    $a \approx 10.9$ ft

    $\sin 47° = \dfrac{b}{16}$

    $b = 16\sin 47°$

    $b \approx 16(0.7314)$

    $b \approx 11.7$ ft

18. $\sin 58° = \dfrac{12}{c}$

    $c \cdot \sin 43° = 12$

    $c = \dfrac{12}{\sin 58}$

    $c \approx \dfrac{12}{0.8480}$

    $c \approx 14.2$ in.

    $\sin 32° = \dfrac{d}{c}$

    $d = c \cdot \sin 32°$

    $d \approx (14.2)(0.5299)$

    $d \approx 7.5$ in.

261

19. $\sin 17° = \dfrac{c}{30}$

$c = 30\sin 17°$

$c \approx 30(0.2924)$

$c \approx 8.8$ cm

$\sin 73° = \dfrac{d}{30}$

$d = 30\sin 73°$

$d \approx 30(0.9563)$

$d \approx 28.7$ cm

20. $\sin 52° = \dfrac{15}{c}$

$c = \dfrac{15}{\sin 52}$

$c \approx \dfrac{15}{0.7880}$

$c \approx 19.0$ cm

$\sin 38° = \dfrac{d}{c}$

$d = c \cdot \sin 38°$

$d \approx (19.0)(0.6157)$

$d \approx 11.7$ cm

21. $\sin \alpha = \dfrac{12}{25} = 0.4800$

$\alpha \approx 29°$

$\beta \approx 90° - 29°$ or $\beta \approx 61°$

22. $\sin \alpha = \dfrac{14}{20} = 0.7000$

$\alpha \approx 44°$

$\beta \approx 90° - 44°$ or $\beta \approx 46°$

23. $\sin \alpha = \dfrac{3}{10} = 0.3000$

$\alpha \approx 17°$

$\beta \approx 90° - 17°$ or $\beta \approx 73°$

24. $\sin \alpha = \dfrac{5}{12} = 0.4167$

$\alpha \approx 25°$

$\beta \approx 90° - 25°$ or $\beta \approx 65°$

25. $\sin \alpha = \dfrac{x}{3x} = \dfrac{1}{3} \approx 0.3333$

$\alpha \approx 19°$

$\beta \approx 90° - 19°$ or $\beta \approx 71°$

26. $\sin \beta = \dfrac{2x}{3x} = \dfrac{2}{3} \approx 0.6667$

$\beta \approx 42°$

$\alpha \approx 90° - 42°$ or $\alpha \approx 48°$

27. Using the Pythagorean Triple, (5, 12, 13), $c = 13$.

$\therefore \ \sin \alpha = \dfrac{5}{13} \approx 0.3846$

$\alpha \approx 23°$

28. Let h represent height of the kite.

$\sin 67° = \dfrac{h}{100}$

$h = 100\sin 67°$

$h \approx 100(0.9205)$

$h \approx 92.1$ ft

29. Let d represent the distance between Danny and the balloon.

$\sin 75° = \dfrac{100}{d}$

$d \cdot \sin 75° = 100$

$d = \dfrac{100}{\sin 75°}$

$d \approx \dfrac{100}{0.9659}$

$d \approx 103.5$ ft

30. $\sin \alpha = \dfrac{100}{2000} \approx 0.0500$

$\alpha \approx 3°$

31. Let d represent the distance between the person and auto. Because alt. int. $\angle$s are $\cong$,

$\sin 23° = \dfrac{50}{d}$

$d \cdot \sin 23° = 50$

$d = \dfrac{50}{\sin 23°}$

$d \approx \dfrac{50}{0.3907}$

$d \approx 128.0$ ft

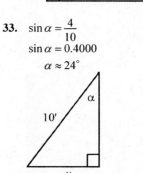

32. $\sin \alpha = \dfrac{4}{12}$

$\sin \alpha = 0.3333$

$\alpha \approx 19°$

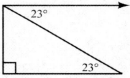

33. $\sin \alpha = \dfrac{4}{10}$

$\sin \alpha = 0.4000$

$\alpha \approx 24°$

34. Let h represent the gain in altitude in 1 second.

$$\sin 10° = \frac{h}{350}$$
$$h = 350 \sin 10°$$
$$h \approx 350(0.1736)$$
$$h \approx 60.76 \text{ ft}$$

Over 15 seconds, the increase in altitude is approximately $15(60.76) = 911.4 \text{ ft}$.

35.

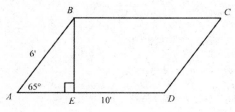

a. $\sin 65° = \dfrac{BE}{6}$

$$BE = 6 \sin 65°$$
$$BE \approx 6(0.9063)$$
$$BE \approx 5.4 \text{ ft}$$

b. $A_{ABCD} = AD \cdot BE$
$$A \approx (10)(5.4)$$
$$A \approx 54 \text{ ft}^2$$

36.

a. $\sin 35° = \dfrac{a}{20}$

$$a = 20 \cdot \sin 35$$
$$a \approx 20(0.5736)$$
$$a \approx 11.5 \text{ in.}$$

b. $\sin 55° = \dfrac{b}{20}$

$$b = 20 \cdot \sin 55$$
$$b \approx 20(0.8192)$$
$$b \approx 16.4 \text{ in.}$$

c. $A_{\triangle ABC} \approx \dfrac{1}{2}(11.5)(16.4)$

$$A_{\triangle ABC} \approx 94.3 \text{ in}^2$$

37.

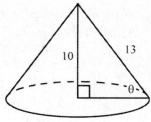

$$\sin \theta = \frac{10}{13} \approx 0.7692$$
$$\theta \approx 50°$$

38.

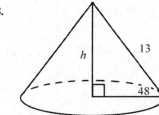

$$\sin 48° = \frac{h}{13}$$
$$h = 13 \cdot \sin 48$$
$$h \approx 13(0.4695)$$
$$h \approx 9.7 \text{ cm}$$

39. **a.** Draw the described pentagon using the Given. Name the altitude of $\triangle ABC$, $\overline{BF}$.

If the interior angle of the pentagon is 108, then $m\angle FBC = 54$ and $m\angle FCB = 36$.

$$\sin 36 = \frac{h}{s} \text{ or } h = s \cdot \sin 36$$

b.

$$\sin 54 = \frac{\frac{1}{2}d}{s}$$

$$\frac{1}{2}d = s \cdot \sin 54$$

$$d = 2s \cdot \sin 54$$

SECTION 11.2: The Cosine Ratio and Applications

1. $\cos\alpha = \dfrac{\text{adjacent}}{\text{hypotenuse}} = \dfrac{12}{13}$

$\cos\beta = \dfrac{5}{13}$

2. $\cos\alpha = \dfrac{8}{17}$; $\cos\beta = \dfrac{15}{17}$

3. $a = 8$ using the Pythagorean Triple (6, 8, 10).

$\cos\alpha = \dfrac{6}{10} = \dfrac{3}{5}$; $\cos\beta = \dfrac{8}{10} = \dfrac{4}{5}$

4. $a^2 + b^2 = c^2$

$a^2 + \left(\sqrt{5}\right)^2 = 3^2$

$a^2 + 5 = 9$

$a^2 = 4$

$a = 2$

$\cos\alpha = \dfrac{\sqrt{5}}{3}$; $\cos\beta = \dfrac{2}{3}$

5. $a^2 + b^2 = c^2$

$\left(\sqrt{3}\right)^2 + \left(\sqrt{2}\right)^2 = c^2$

$3 + 2 = c^2$

$5 = c^2$

$\sqrt{5} = c$

$\cos\alpha = \dfrac{\sqrt{2}}{\sqrt{5}} = \dfrac{\sqrt{2}}{\sqrt{5}} \cdot \dfrac{\sqrt{5}}{\sqrt{5}} = \dfrac{\sqrt{10}}{5}$

$\cos\beta = \dfrac{\sqrt{3}}{\sqrt{5}} = \dfrac{\sqrt{3}}{\sqrt{5}} \cdot \dfrac{\sqrt{5}}{\sqrt{5}} = \dfrac{\sqrt{15}}{5}$

6. $a^2 + b^2 = c^2$

$3^2 + b^2 = \left(\sqrt{13}\right)^2$

$9 + b^2 = 13$

$b^2 = 4$

$b = 2$

$\cos\alpha = \dfrac{2}{\sqrt{13}} = \dfrac{2}{\sqrt{13}} \cdot \dfrac{\sqrt{13}}{\sqrt{13}} = \dfrac{2\sqrt{13}}{13}$

$\cos\beta = \dfrac{3}{\sqrt{13}} = \dfrac{3}{\sqrt{13}} \cdot \dfrac{\sqrt{13}}{\sqrt{13}} = \dfrac{3\sqrt{13}}{13}$

7. a. $\sin\alpha = \dfrac{\text{leg opposite } \alpha}{\text{hypotenuse}} = \dfrac{a}{c}$

$\cos\beta = \dfrac{\text{leg adjacent to } \beta}{\text{hypotenuse}} = \dfrac{a}{c}$

$\therefore \sin\alpha = \cos\beta$

b. $\cos\alpha = \dfrac{\text{leg adjacent to } \alpha}{\text{hypotenuse}} = \dfrac{b}{c}$

$\sin\beta = \dfrac{\text{leg opposite } \beta}{\text{hypotenuse}} = \dfrac{b}{c}$

$\therefore \cos\alpha = \sin\beta$

8. $\sin\alpha = \dfrac{5}{13}$ and $\cos\beta = \dfrac{12}{13}$

$\sin^2\alpha + \cos^2\alpha = \left(\dfrac{5}{13}\right)^2 + \left(\dfrac{12}{13}\right)^2$

$= \dfrac{25}{169} + \dfrac{144}{169}$

$= \dfrac{25 + 144}{169}$

$= \dfrac{169}{169}$ or 1

9. $\cos 23° \approx 0.9205$

10. $\cos 0° = 1.0000$

11. $\cos 17° \approx 0.9563$

12. $\cos 73° \approx 0.2924$

13. $\cos 90° = 0$

14. $\cos 42° \approx 0.7431$

15. $\cos 82° \approx 0.1392$

16. $\cos 7° \approx 0.9925$

17. $\cos 32° = \dfrac{a}{100}$

$a = 100\cos 32°$

$a \approx 100(0.8480)$

$a \approx 84.8$ ft

$\sin 32° = \dfrac{b}{100}$

$b = 100\sin 32°$

$b \approx 100(0.5299)$

$b \approx 53.0$ ft

18. $\cos 57° = \dfrac{5}{c}$

$c = \dfrac{5}{\cos 57°}$

$c \approx \dfrac{5}{0.5446}$

$c \approx 9.2$ in.

$\sin 57° = \dfrac{d}{c}$

$d = c \cdot \sin 57°$

$d \approx (9.2)(0.8387)$

$d \approx 7.7$ in.

19. $\cos 45° = \dfrac{b}{5\sqrt{2}}$

$b = 5\sqrt{2}\cos 45°$

$b \approx 5\sqrt{2}(0.7071)$

$b \approx 5$ cm

In the 45°-45°-90° triangle, $a = b$ so that $a \approx 5$ cm. Note: $a = b = 5$ cm are exact values.

20. $\cos 60° = \dfrac{x}{20}$

$x = 20 \sin 60°$

$x \approx 20(0.5000)$

$x \approx 10$ ft

$\sin 60° = \dfrac{y}{20}$

$y = 20 \sin 60°$

$y \approx 20(0.8660)$

$y \approx 17.3$ ft

<u>Note</u>: In the 30°-60°-90° triangle, $x = 10$ ft and
$y = 10\sqrt{3}$ ft .

21. $\cos 51° = \dfrac{12}{c}$

$c = \dfrac{12}{\cos 51°}$

$c \approx \dfrac{12}{0.6293}$

$c \approx 19.1$ in.

$\sin 51° = \dfrac{d}{c}$

$d = c \cdot \sin 51°$

$d \approx (19.1)(0.7771)$

$d \approx 14.8$ in.

22. $\sin 17° = \dfrac{10}{x}$

$x = \dfrac{10}{\sin 17°}$

$x \approx \dfrac{10}{0.2924}$

$x \approx 34.2$ ft

$\cos 17° = \dfrac{y}{x}$

$y = x \cdot \cos 17°$

$y \approx (34.2)(0.9563)$

$y \approx 32.7$ ft

23. $\cos \alpha = \dfrac{5}{10} = 0.5000$

$\alpha = 60°$ (exact)

$\beta = 90° - 60°$

$\beta = 30°$ (exact)

24. $\cos \alpha = \dfrac{7}{10} = 0.7000$

$\alpha \approx 46°$

$\beta \approx 90° - 46°$

$\beta \approx 44°$

25. $a^2 + b^2 = c^2$

$\left(\sqrt{3}\right)^2 + \left(\sqrt{2}\right)^2 = c^2$

$3 + 2 = c^2$

$5 = c^2$

$\sqrt{5} = c$

$\cos \alpha = \dfrac{\sqrt{2}}{\sqrt{5}} = \sqrt{\dfrac{2}{5}} = \sqrt{0.4} \approx 0.6325$

$\alpha \approx 51°$

$\cos \beta \approx 90° - 51°$

$\beta \approx 39°$

26. $\cos \phi = \dfrac{\sqrt{5}}{5} \approx \dfrac{2.2361}{5} \approx 0.4472$

$\phi \approx 63°$

$\theta \approx 90° - 63°$

$\theta \approx 27°$

27. $\cos \alpha = \dfrac{5}{12} \approx 0.4167$

$\alpha \approx 65°$

$\beta \approx 90° - 65°$

$\beta \approx 25°$

28. $AD = CB = 8$

$DB = 10$ using the Pythagorean Triple (6, 8, 10).

$\cos \alpha = \dfrac{6}{10} = 0.6000$

$\alpha \approx 53°$ so $\phi \approx 53°$

(alt. int. $\angle$s for $\parallel$ lines)

$\beta \approx 90° - 53°$

$\beta \approx 37°$

so $\theta \approx 37°$

(alt. int. $\angle$s for $\parallel$ lines)

29. $\cos \theta = \dfrac{10}{12} \approx 0.8333$

$\theta \approx 34°$

30. $\sin \theta = \dfrac{2}{12} \approx 0.1667$

$\theta \approx 10°$

31. Because alt. int. $\angle$s are $\cong$,

$\sin 5° = \dfrac{100}{x}$

$x = \dfrac{100}{\sin 5°}$

$x \approx \dfrac{100}{0.0872}$

$x \approx 1147.4$ ft

32. $\sin 37° = \dfrac{h}{x}$ while $\cos 37° = \dfrac{200}{x}$. Then

$$\frac{\sin 37°}{\cos 37°} = \frac{\dfrac{h}{x}}{\dfrac{200}{x}} = \frac{h}{200}$$

$$h = 200 \cdot \frac{\sin 37°}{\cos 37°}$$

$$h \approx 200 \cdot \frac{0.6018}{0.7986}$$

$$h \approx 150.7 \text{ ft}$$

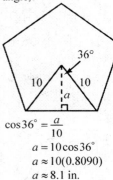

33. Let c represent the measure of the central angle of the regular pentagon. Then $c = \dfrac{360°}{5} = 72°$.

Because the apothem shown bisects the central angle,

$$\cos 36° = \frac{a}{10}$$

$$a = 10\cos 36°$$

$$a \approx 10(0.8090)$$

$$a \approx 8.1 \text{ in.}$$

34. $\cos \alpha = \dfrac{10}{30} \approx 0.3333$

$\alpha \approx 71°$

35. Let c represent the measure of the central angle of the regular decagon.

$$c = \frac{360°}{10} = 36°$$

The apothem bisects the central angle so that $\alpha = 18°$.

Now, $\cos 18° = 12.5$

$$r = \frac{12.5}{\cos 18°}$$

$$r \approx \frac{12.5}{0.9511}$$

$$r \approx 13.1 \text{ cm}$$

36. Let d represent distance from helicopter to man in raft.

$$\cos 78° = \frac{200}{d}$$

$$d = \frac{200}{\cos 78°}$$

$$d \approx \frac{200}{0.2079}$$

$$d \approx 962.0 \text{ ft}$$

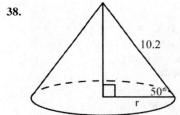

37. Let d represent the length of the diagonal of the base and x the length of an edge of the cube. By the Pythagorean Theorem,

$$d^2 = x^2 + x^2$$

$$d^2 = 2x^2.$$

Let D represent the Pythagorean Theorem again,

$$x^2 + d^2 = D^2$$

$$x^2 + 2x^2 = D^2$$

so that

$$D^2 = 3x^2$$

$$D = \sqrt{3x^2}$$

$$D = x\sqrt{3}$$

Now, $\cos \alpha = \dfrac{\text{adjacent}}{\text{hypotenuse}} = \dfrac{x}{x\sqrt{3}} = \dfrac{1}{\sqrt{3}}$

$$\cos \alpha \approx 0.5774$$

$$\alpha \approx 55°$$

38.

a. $\cos 50° = \dfrac{r}{10.2}$

$$r = 10\cos 50°$$

$$r \approx 6.6 \text{ cm}$$

b. $L = \pi r \ell$

$$L \approx \pi(6.6)(10.2)$$

$$L \approx 67.32\pi \approx 211.5 \text{ cm}^2$$

39.

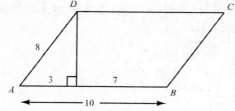

a. $\cos A = \dfrac{3}{8}$

$m\angle A = 68°$

b. $m\angle B = 180 - 68 = 112°$

40.

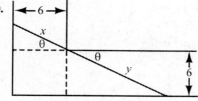

$\cos\theta = \dfrac{6}{x}$ $\sin\theta = \dfrac{6}{y}$

$x\cos\theta = 6$ $y\sin\theta = 6$

$x = \dfrac{6}{\cos\theta}$ $y = \dfrac{6}{\sin\theta}$

$L = x + y$

$L = \dfrac{6}{\cos\theta} + \dfrac{6}{\sin\theta}$

$L = \dfrac{6}{\sin\theta} + \dfrac{6}{\cos\theta}$

41.

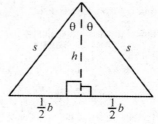

$\sin\theta = \dfrac{\frac{1}{2}b}{s}$

$s \cdot \sin\theta = \dfrac{1}{2}b$

$b = 2s \cdot \sin\theta$

$\cos\theta = \dfrac{h}{s}$

$h = s \cdot \cos\theta$

$A_\triangle = \dfrac{1}{2}bh$

$A_\triangle = \dfrac{1}{2}(2s \cdot \sin\theta)(s \cdot \cos\theta)$

$A_\triangle = s^2 \cdot \sin\theta \cdot \cos\theta$

42. Let the side length of the pentagon be s. Name the center of the pentagon P. Draw $\overline{PF} \perp \overline{BC}$. (Could be $\perp$ to any side.) $m\angle BCD = 108$ and $m\angle FCP = 54$. FC $= \dfrac{1}{2}s$.

$\cos 54 = \dfrac{\frac{1}{2}s}{r}$

$r \cdot \cos 54 = \dfrac{1}{2}s$

$s = 2r \cdot \cos 54$

Perimeter $= 10r \cdot \cos 54$

43. Use the information from Exercise 42.

Let $PF = a$, the apothem length. Find a

in terms of r. $\sin 54 = \dfrac{a}{r}$ or $a = r \cdot \sin 54$

$A = \dfrac{1}{2}aP$

$A = \dfrac{1}{2} \cdot r \cdot \sin 54 \cdot 10r \cdot \cos 54$

$A = 5r^2 \cdot \sin 54 \cdot \cos 54$

Alternate Solution:

In an isosceles Δ formed by 2 radii and a side of the pentagon, draw the height of the Δ to the side.

$\sin 54 = \dfrac{h}{r}$

$h = r \cdot \sin 54$

$\cos 54 = \dfrac{\dfrac{1}{2}s}{r}$

$\dfrac{1}{2}s = r \cdot \cos 54$

$s = 2r \cdot \cos 54$

$A_{1\Delta} = \dfrac{1}{2} \cdot s \cdot r \cdot \sin 54$

$A_{1\Delta} = \dfrac{1}{2} \cdot 2r \cdot \cos 54 \cdot r \cdot \sin 54$

$A_{1\Delta} = r^2 \cdot \sin 54 \cdot \cos 54$

$A_{PENTAGON} = 5r^2 \cdot \sin 54 \cdot \cos 54$

SECTION 11.3: The Tangent Ratio and Other Ratios

1. $\tan \alpha = \dfrac{\text{opposite}}{\text{adjacent}} = \dfrac{3}{4}$

$\tan \beta = \dfrac{4}{3}$

2. Using the Pythagorean Triple (8, 15, 17), $b = 8$.

$\tan \alpha = \dfrac{15}{8};\ \tan \beta = \dfrac{8}{15}$

3. $a^2 + b^2 = c^2$

$a^2 + 4^2 = 6^2$

$a^2 + 16 = 36$

$a^2 = 20$

$a = \sqrt{20} = 2\sqrt{5}$

$\tan \alpha = \dfrac{2\sqrt{5}}{4} = \dfrac{\sqrt{5}}{2}$

$\tan \beta = \dfrac{4}{2\sqrt{5}} = \dfrac{2}{\sqrt{5}} = \dfrac{2}{\sqrt{5}} \cdot \dfrac{\sqrt{5}}{\sqrt{5}} = \dfrac{2\sqrt{5}}{5}$

4. $BC = DA = \sqrt{3}$

$a^2 + b^2 = c^2$

$\left(\sqrt{3}\right)^2 + b^2 = \left(\sqrt{7}\right)^2$

$3 + b^2 = 7$

$b^2 = 4$

$b = 2$

$\tan \alpha = \dfrac{\sqrt{3}}{2}$

$\tan \beta = \dfrac{2}{\sqrt{3}} = \dfrac{2}{\sqrt{3}} \cdot \dfrac{\sqrt{3}}{\sqrt{3}} = \dfrac{2\sqrt{3}}{3}$

5. Using the Pythagorean Triple, (5, 12, 13), $b = 12$.

$\sin \alpha = \dfrac{\text{opposite}}{\text{hypotenuse}} = \dfrac{5}{13}$

$\cos \alpha = \dfrac{\text{adjacent}}{\text{hypotenuse}} = \dfrac{12}{13}$

$\tan \alpha = \dfrac{\text{opposite}}{\text{adjacent}} = \dfrac{5}{12}$

$\cot \alpha = \dfrac{\text{adjacent}}{\text{opposite}} = \dfrac{12}{5}$

$\sec \alpha = \dfrac{\text{hypotenuse}}{\text{adjacent}} = \dfrac{13}{12}$

$\csc \alpha = \dfrac{\text{hypotenuse}}{\text{opposite}} = \dfrac{13}{5}$

6.
$$a^2 + b^2 = c^2$$
$$a^2 + \left(\sqrt{5}\right)^2 = 4^2$$
$$a^2 + 5 = 16$$
$$a^2 = 11$$
$$a = \sqrt{11}$$

$$\sin\alpha = \frac{\sqrt{11}}{4}$$
$$\cos\alpha = \frac{\sqrt{5}}{4}$$
$$\tan\alpha = \frac{\sqrt{11}}{\sqrt{5}} = \frac{\sqrt{11}}{\sqrt{5}} \cdot \frac{\sqrt{5}}{\sqrt{5}} = \frac{\sqrt{55}}{5}$$
$$\cot\alpha = \frac{\sqrt{5}}{\sqrt{11}} = \frac{\sqrt{5}}{\sqrt{11}} \cdot \frac{\sqrt{11}}{\sqrt{11}} = \frac{\sqrt{55}}{11}$$
$$\sec\alpha = \frac{4}{\sqrt{5}} = \frac{4}{\sqrt{5}} \cdot \frac{\sqrt{5}}{\sqrt{5}} = \frac{4\sqrt{5}}{5}$$
$$\csc\alpha = \frac{4}{\sqrt{11}} = \frac{4}{\sqrt{11}} \cdot \frac{\sqrt{11}}{\sqrt{11}} = \frac{4\sqrt{11}}{11}$$

7. $\quad \sin\alpha = \dfrac{a}{c} \qquad \cot\alpha = \dfrac{b}{a}$

$\quad \cos\alpha = \dfrac{b}{c} \qquad \sec\alpha = \dfrac{c}{b}$

$\quad \tan\alpha = \dfrac{a}{b} \qquad \csc\alpha = \dfrac{c}{a}$

8. $\quad \sin\alpha = \dfrac{y}{\sqrt{x^2 + y^2}}$

$$= \frac{y}{\sqrt{x^2 + y^2}} \cdot \frac{\sqrt{x^2 + y^2}}{\sqrt{x^2 + y^2}}$$
$$= \frac{y\sqrt{x^2 + y^2}}{x^2 + y^2}$$
$$\cos\alpha = \frac{x}{\sqrt{x^2 + y^2}}$$
$$= \frac{x}{\sqrt{x^2 + y^2}} \cdot \frac{\sqrt{x^2 + y^2}}{\sqrt{x^2 + y^2}}$$
$$= \frac{x\sqrt{x^2 + y^2}}{x^2 + y^2}$$
$$\tan\alpha = \frac{y}{x}$$
$$\cot\alpha = \frac{x}{y}$$
$$\sec\alpha = \frac{\sqrt{x^2 + y^2}}{x}$$
$$\csc\alpha = \frac{\sqrt{x^2 + y^2}}{y}$$

9.
$$a^2 + b^2 = c^2$$
$$x^2 + b^2 = \left(\sqrt{x^2 + 1}\right)^2$$
$$x^2 + b^2 = x^2 + 1$$
$$b^2 = 1$$
$$b = 1$$

$$\sin\alpha = \frac{x}{\sqrt{x^2 + 1}}$$
$$= \frac{x}{\sqrt{x^2 + 1}} \cdot \frac{\sqrt{x^2 + 1}}{\sqrt{x^2 + 1}}$$
$$= \frac{x\sqrt{x^2 + 1}}{x^2 + 1}$$
$$\cos\alpha = \frac{1}{\sqrt{x^2 + 1}}$$
$$= \frac{1}{\sqrt{x^2 + 1}} \cdot \frac{\sqrt{x^2 + 1}}{\sqrt{x^2 + 1}}$$
$$= \frac{\sqrt{x^2 + 1}}{x^2 + 1}$$
$$\tan\alpha = \frac{x}{1}$$
$$\cot\alpha = \frac{1}{x}$$
$$\sec\alpha = \frac{\sqrt{x^2 + 1}}{1} = \sqrt{x^2 + 1}$$
$$\csc\alpha = \frac{\sqrt{x^2 + 1}}{x}$$

10. $a^2 + b^2 = c^2$
$x^2 + 2^2 = c^2$
$c^2 = x^2 + 4$
$c = \sqrt{x^2 + 4}$

$\sin\alpha = \dfrac{x}{\sqrt{x^2 + 4}}$

$= \dfrac{x}{\sqrt{x^2 + 4}} \cdot \dfrac{\sqrt{x^2 + 4}}{\sqrt{x^2 + 4}}$

$= \dfrac{x\sqrt{x^2 + 4}}{x^2 + 4}$

$\cos\alpha = \dfrac{2}{\sqrt{x^2 + 4}}$

$= \dfrac{2}{\sqrt{x^2 + 4}} \cdot \dfrac{\sqrt{x^2 + 4}}{\sqrt{x^2 + 4}}$

$= \dfrac{2\sqrt{x^2 + 4}}{x^2 + 4}$

$\tan\alpha = \dfrac{x}{2}$

$\cot\alpha = \dfrac{2}{x}$

$\sec\alpha = \dfrac{\sqrt{x^2 + 4}}{2}$

$\csc\alpha = \dfrac{\sqrt{x^2 + 4}}{x}$

11. $\tan 15° = 0.2679$

12. $\tan 45° = 1.0000$

13. $\tan 57° = 1.5399$

14. $\tan 78° = 4.7046$

15. $\tan 32° = \dfrac{x}{12}$
$x = 12\tan 32°$
$x \approx 12(0.6249)$
$x \approx 7.5$
$\cos 32° = \dfrac{12}{z}$
$z \cdot \cos 32° = 12$
$z = \dfrac{12}{\cos 32°}$
$z \approx \dfrac{12}{0.8480}$
$z \approx 14.2$

16. $\sin 37° = \dfrac{y}{15}$
$y = 15\sin 37°$
$y \approx 15(0.6018)$
$y \approx 9.0$
$\cos 37° = \dfrac{x}{15}$
$x = 15\cos 37°$
$x \approx 15(0.7986)$
$x \approx 12.0$

17. $\cos 58° = \dfrac{y}{10}$
$y = 10\cos 58°$
$y \approx 10(0.5299)$
$y \approx 5.3$
$\sin 58° = \dfrac{z}{10}$
$z = 10\sin 58°$
$z \approx 10(0.8480)$
$z \approx 8.5$

18. $\tan 52° = \dfrac{20}{a}$
$a \cdot \tan 52° = 20$
$a = \dfrac{20}{\tan 52°}$
$a \approx \dfrac{20}{1.2799}$
$a \approx 15.6$
$\sin 52° = \dfrac{20}{c}$
$c \cdot \sin 52° = 20$
$c = \dfrac{20}{\sin 52°}$
$c \approx \dfrac{20}{0.7880}$
$c \approx 25.4$

19. The angle inscribed in the semicircle is a right angle.

$$\cos 36° = \frac{d}{10}$$
$$d = 10\cos 36°$$
$$d \approx 10(0.8090)$$
$$d \approx 8.1$$

20. $DA = CB = w$

$$\sin 30° = \frac{w}{12}$$
$$w = 12\sin 30°$$
$$w = 12(0.5000)$$
$$w = 6$$
$$\cos 30° = \frac{\ell}{12}$$
$$\ell = 12\cos 30°$$
$$\ell \approx 12(0.8660)$$
$$\ell \approx 10.4$$

21. $\tan \alpha = \dfrac{3}{4} = 0.7500$

$$\alpha \approx 37°$$
$$\beta \approx 90° - 37° \text{ or } \beta \approx 53°$$

22. $\tan \alpha = \dfrac{3}{4} = 0.7500$

$$\alpha \approx 37°$$
$$\beta \approx 90° - 37° \text{ or } \beta \approx 53°$$

23. $\sin \alpha = \dfrac{5}{6} = 0.8333$

$$\alpha \approx 56°$$
$$\gamma \approx 90° - 56° \text{ or } \gamma \approx 34°$$

24. $\sin \theta = \dfrac{5}{6} \approx 0.8333$

$$\theta \approx 37°$$
$$\gamma \approx 90° - 56° \text{ or } \gamma \approx 34°$$

25. $\tan \alpha = \dfrac{\sqrt{5}}{4} \approx \dfrac{2.2361}{4} \approx 0.5590$

$$\alpha \approx 29°$$
$$\beta \approx 90° - 29° \text{ or } \beta \approx 61°$$

26. $\tan \beta = \dfrac{\sqrt{6}}{\sqrt{3}} = \sqrt{\dfrac{6}{3}} = \sqrt{2} \approx 1.414$

$$\beta \approx 55°$$
$$\alpha \approx 90° - 55° \text{ or } \alpha \approx 35°$$

27. $\cot 34° = \dfrac{1}{\tan 34°} \approx \dfrac{1}{0.6745} \approx 1.4826$

28. $\sec 15° = \dfrac{1}{\cos 15°} \approx \dfrac{1}{0.9659} \approx 1.0353$

29. $\csc 30° = \dfrac{1}{\sin 30°} = \dfrac{1}{0.5} = 2.0000 \text{ (exact)}$

30. $\cot 67° = \dfrac{1}{\tan 67°} \approx \dfrac{1}{2.3559} \approx 0.4245$

31. $\sec 42° = \dfrac{1}{\cos 42°} \approx \dfrac{1}{0.7431} \approx 1.3456$

32. $\csc 72° = \dfrac{1}{\csc 72°} \approx \dfrac{1}{0.9511} \approx 1.0515$

33. **a.** $\sin \alpha = \dfrac{a}{c}$ and $\cos \alpha = \dfrac{b}{c}$

Then $\dfrac{\sin \alpha}{\cos \alpha} = \sin \alpha \div \cos \alpha = \dfrac{a}{c} \div \dfrac{b}{c}$.

In turn, $\dfrac{\sin \alpha}{\cos \alpha} = \dfrac{a}{c} \cdot \dfrac{c}{b} = \dfrac{a}{b} = \tan \alpha$.

b. $\tan 23° \approx 0.4245$

$$\dfrac{\sin 23°}{\cos 23°} \approx \dfrac{0.39073}{0.92050} \approx 0.4245 \approx \tan 23°$$

34. **a.** $\sin \alpha = \dfrac{a}{c}$ and $\cos \alpha = \dfrac{b}{c}$

Then $\dfrac{\cos \alpha}{\sin \alpha} = \cos \alpha \div \sin \alpha = \dfrac{b}{c} \div \dfrac{a}{c}$.

In turn, $\dfrac{\cos \alpha}{\sin \alpha} = \dfrac{b}{c} \cdot \dfrac{c}{a} = \dfrac{b}{a} = \dfrac{1}{\frac{a}{b}} = \dfrac{1}{\tan \alpha} = \cot \alpha$.

b. $\cot 57° \approx 0.6494$

$$\dfrac{\cos 57°}{\sin 57°} \approx \dfrac{0.5446}{0.8387} \approx 0.6493 \approx \cot 57°$$

35. **a.** $\cos \alpha = \dfrac{b}{c}$

Then $\dfrac{1}{\cos \alpha} = \dfrac{1}{\frac{b}{c}} = \dfrac{c}{b} = \sec \alpha$

b. $\sec 82° \approx 7.1853$

$$\dfrac{1}{\cos 82°} \approx \dfrac{1}{0.1392} \approx 7.1853 \approx \sec 82°$$

36. **a.** $\sin \alpha = \dfrac{a}{c}$

Then $\dfrac{1}{\sin \alpha} = \dfrac{1}{\frac{a}{c}} = \dfrac{c}{a} = \csc \alpha$

b. $\csc 12.3° \approx 7.1853$

$$\frac{1}{\cos 82°} \approx \frac{1}{0.1392} \approx 7.1853 \approx \sec 82°$$

37. $\sin 5° = \dfrac{120}{x}$

$x \cdot \sin 5° = 120$

$\quad x = \dfrac{120}{\sin 5°}$

$\quad x \approx \dfrac{120}{0.0872} \approx 1376.8 \text{ ft}$

38. Let h represent the height of the tower.

$\tan 37° = \dfrac{h}{270}$

$\quad h = 270 \cdot \tan 37°$

$\quad h \approx 200(0.7536)$

$\quad h \approx 203.5 \text{ ft}$

39. The apothem bisects the 72° central angle and the 6" side. Now

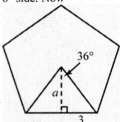

$\tan 36° = \dfrac{3}{a}$

$a \cdot \tan 36° = 3$

$\quad a = \dfrac{3}{\tan 36°}$

$\quad a \approx \dfrac{3}{0.7265} \approx 4.129 \text{ or } 4.1 \text{ in.}$

40. If x is the length of each edge of the cube, then $x\sqrt{2}$ is the length of the diagonal of the base. Now,

$\tan \alpha = \dfrac{x}{x\sqrt{2}} = \dfrac{1}{\sqrt{2}}$

$\tan \alpha \approx 0.7071$

$\quad \alpha \approx 35°$

41.

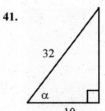

$\cos \alpha = \dfrac{10}{32}$

$\cos \alpha = 0.3125$

$\quad \alpha \approx 72°$

42. Let r = horizontal distance to rescue boat (in feet).
Let ℓ = horizontal distance to lifeboat (in feet)

$\tan 14° = \dfrac{1000}{r}$

$r \cdot \tan 14° = 1000$

$\quad r = \dfrac{1000}{\tan 14°}$

$\quad r \approx \dfrac{1000}{0.2493}$

$\quad r \approx 4011 \text{ feet}$

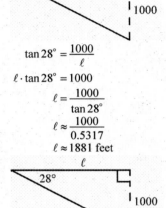

$\tan 28° = \dfrac{1000}{\ell}$

$\ell \cdot \tan 28° = 1000$

$\quad \ell = \dfrac{1000}{\tan 28°}$

$\quad \ell \approx \dfrac{1000}{0.5317}$

$\quad \ell \approx 1881 \text{ feet}$

Because $4011 - 1881 = 2130$, the distance between the rescue boat and the lifeboat is approximately 2130 feet.

43. Let x represent the distance from the base of the tower to the fire. Then

$\tan 12° = \dfrac{200}{x}$

$x \cdot \tan 12° = 200$

$\quad x = \dfrac{200}{\tan 12°}$

$\quad x \approx \dfrac{200}{0.2126}$

$\quad x \approx 941 \text{ feet}$

Note the position of α in $\triangle ABC$.

$\tan \alpha \approx \dfrac{1000}{941}$

$\tan \alpha \approx 1.0627$

$\quad \alpha \approx 47°$

The heading may be described as N 47° W.

44. a.
$$\tan 43° = \frac{12.6}{x}$$
$$x \cdot \tan 43° = 12.6$$
$$x = \frac{12.6}{\tan 43°}$$
$$x \approx 13.5 \text{ units}$$

b.
$$\tan 36° = \frac{12.6}{y}$$
$$y \cdot \tan 36° = 12.6$$
$$y = \frac{12.6}{\tan 36°}$$
$$y \approx 17.3 \text{ units}$$

c.
$$A = \frac{1}{2}bh$$
$$A \approx \frac{1}{2}(13.5 + 17.3)(12.6)$$
$$A \approx 194.04 \text{ units}^2$$

45.

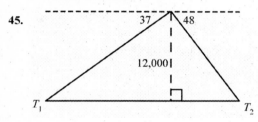

$$\tan 37 = \frac{12,000}{x}$$
$$x \cdot \tan 37 = 12,000$$
$$x = \frac{12,000}{\tan 37}$$
$$x \approx 15,924.5$$

$$\tan 48 = \frac{12,000}{y}$$
$$y \cdot \tan 48 = 12,000$$
$$y = \frac{12,000}{\tan 48}$$
$$y \approx 10,804.8$$

$$\text{Distance} \approx 15,924.5 + 10,804.8$$
$$\approx 26,729.3 \approx 26,730 \text{ feet}$$

46.

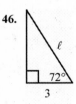

a.
$$\cos 72° = \frac{3}{\ell}$$
$$\ell \cdot \cos 72 = 3$$
$$\ell = \frac{3}{\cos 72}$$
$$\ell \approx 9.7 \text{ units}$$

b.
$$L = \frac{1}{2}\ell P$$
$$L \approx \frac{1}{2}(9.7)(24)$$
$$L \approx 116.4 \text{ units}^2$$

47. a.
$$\tan 72° = \frac{h}{3}$$
$$h = 3\tan 72$$
$$h \approx 9.2 \text{ units}$$

b.
$$V = \frac{1}{3}Bh$$
$$V \approx \frac{1}{3}(36)(9.2)$$
$$V \approx 110.4 \text{ units}^3$$

SECTION 11.4: Applications to Acute Triangles

1. a.
$$A = \frac{1}{2}ab\sin\gamma$$
$$A = \frac{1}{2} \cdot 5 \cdot 6 \cdot \sin 78°$$

b.
$$\alpha + \beta + \gamma = 180°$$
$$36° + 88° + \gamma = 180°$$
$$124 + \gamma = 180$$
$$\gamma = 56°$$
$$A = \frac{1}{2}ab\sin\gamma$$
$$A = \frac{1}{2} \cdot 5 \cdot 7 \cdot \sin 56°$$

2. a.
$$A = \frac{1}{2}(7.3)(8.6)\sin 38°$$

b.
$$A = \frac{1}{2}(5.3)(8.4)\sin\left(180° - (36° + 87°)\right)$$
$$A = \frac{1}{2}(5.3)(8.4)\sin 57°$$

3. a.
$$\frac{\sin\beta}{8} = \frac{\sin 40°}{5}$$

b.
$$\frac{\sin 41°}{5.3} = \frac{\sin 87°}{c}$$

4. a.
$$\frac{\sin\beta}{8.1} = \frac{\sin 86°}{8.4}$$

b.
$$\frac{\sin 40°}{5.3} = \frac{\sin\left(180° - (40° + 80°)\right)}{c}$$
$$\frac{\sin 40°}{5.3} = \frac{\sin 60°}{c}$$

5. a. $c^2 = a^2 + b^2 - 2ab\cos\gamma$
$c^2 = (5.2)^2 + (7.9)^2 - 2(5.2)(7.9)\cos 83°$

b. $a^2 = b^2 + c^2 - 2bc\cos\alpha$
$6^2 = 9^2 + 10^2 - 2(9)(10)\cos\alpha$

6. a. $b^2 = (5.7)^2 + (8.2)^2 - 2(5.7)(8.2)\cos 79°$

b. $8^2 = 6^2 + 9^2 - 2(6)(9)\cos\beta$

7. a. $\dfrac{\sin\alpha}{a} = \dfrac{\sin\beta}{b}$

b. $a^2 = b^2 + c^2 - 2bc\cos\alpha$

8. a. $b^2 = a^2 + c^2 - 2ac\cos\beta$

b. $\dfrac{\sin\alpha}{a} = \dfrac{\sin\beta}{b}$

9. a. $(3, 4, 5)$ is a Pythagorean Triple. γ lies opposite the longest side and must be a right angle.

b. $90°$

10. a. The sum of the three angles of any triangle is $180°$. When two angles are know, the third is found by subtracting the sum of the two angles from $180°$.

b. $\gamma = 180° - (57° + 84°) = 39°$

11. Using $A = \dfrac{1}{2}ab\sin\gamma$
$A = \dfrac{1}{2} \cdot 4 \cdot 8 \cdot \sin 30°$
$A = \dfrac{1}{2} \cdot 4 \cdot 8 \cdot \dfrac{1}{2}$
$A = 8 \text{ in}^2$

12. $A = \dfrac{1}{2} \cdot 8 \cdot 12 \cdot \sin 60°$
$A = \dfrac{1}{2} \cdot 8 \cdot 12 \cdot \dfrac{\sqrt{3}}{2}$
$A = 24\sqrt{3} \text{ cm}^2 \quad (\text{exact})$

13. With measures of angles shown, the third angle measures $70°$. Then the triangle is isosceles, with sides as shown.

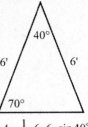

$A = \dfrac{1}{2} \cdot 6 \cdot 6 \cdot \sin 40°$
$A \approx \dfrac{1}{2} \cdot 6 \cdot 6 \cdot (0.6428)$
$A \approx 11.6 \text{ ft}^2$

14. $A = \dfrac{1}{2} \cdot 4 \cdot 10 \cdot \sin 64°$
$A \approx \dfrac{1}{2} \cdot 4 \cdot 10 \cdot (0.8988)$
$A \approx 18.0 \text{ m}^2$

15. All sides have length 6 feet.
$A_{\triangle QMN} = \dfrac{1}{2} \cdot 6 \cdot 6 \cdot \sin 25°$
$\approx \dfrac{1}{2} \cdot 6 \cdot 6 \cdot (0.4226)$
$\approx 7.6 \text{ ft}^2$

Now the area of the rhombus is $2(7.6) \approx 15.2 \text{ ft}^2$

16.

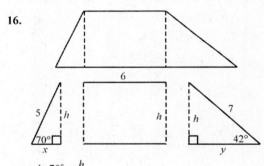

$\sin 70° = \dfrac{h}{5}$
$h = 5\sin 70°$
$h \approx 4.7 \text{ in.}$

$\cos 70° = \dfrac{x}{5}$
$x = 5\cos 70°$
$x \approx 1.7 \text{ in.}$

$\cos 42° = \dfrac{y}{7}$
$y = 7\cos 42°$
$y \approx 5.2 \text{ in.}$

$A = A_{\triangle 1} + A_{\text{RECT.}} + A_{\triangle 2}$
$A \approx \dfrac{1}{2}(1.7)(4.7) + 6(4.7) + \dfrac{1}{2}(5.2)(4.7)$
$A \approx 4.0 + 28.2 + 12.2$
$A \approx 44.4 \text{ in}^2$

17.
$$\frac{\sin\alpha}{a} = \frac{\sin\beta}{b}$$
$$\frac{\sin 60°}{x} = \frac{\sin 70°}{12}$$
$$\frac{0.8660}{x} = \frac{0.9397}{12}$$
$$x(0.9397) = 12(0.8660)$$
$$x \approx 11.1 \text{ in.}$$

18.
$$\frac{\sin\alpha}{6} = \frac{\sin 65°}{10}$$
$$\frac{\sin\alpha}{6} = \frac{0.9063}{10}$$
$$10(\sin a) = 6(0.9063)$$
$$\sin\alpha \approx 0.5438$$
$$\alpha \approx 33°$$

19.
$$\frac{\sin 35°}{y} = \frac{\sin 75°}{15}$$
$$\frac{0.5736}{y} = \frac{0.9659}{15}$$
$$0.9659 y = 15(0.5736)$$
$$y \approx 8.9 \text{ m}$$

20. $\beta = 40°$
(no need to use the Law of Sines; the triangle is isosceles.)

21.
$$\frac{\sin\gamma}{10} = \frac{\sin 80°}{12}$$
$$\frac{\sin\gamma}{10} = \frac{0.9397}{12}$$
$$12(\sin\gamma) = 10(0.9848)$$
$$\sin\gamma \approx 0.8207$$
$$\gamma \approx 55°$$

22. The third angle measures 45°.
$$\frac{\sin 70°}{x} = \frac{\sin 45°}{5}$$
$$\frac{0.9397}{x} = \frac{0.7071}{5}$$
$$0.7071x = 5(0.9397)$$
$$x \approx 6.6 \text{ ft}$$

23.
$$a^2 = b^2 + c^2 - 2bc\cos\alpha$$
$$7^2 = 5^2 + 9^2 - 2\cdot 5\cdot 9\cdot\cos\alpha$$
$$49 = 25 + 81 - 90\cos\alpha$$
$$90\cos\alpha = 57$$
$$\cos\alpha = \frac{57}{90} \approx 0.6333$$
$$\alpha \approx 51°$$

24.
$$b^2 = a^2 + c^2 - 2ac\cos\beta$$
$$10^2 = 6^2 + 8^2 - 2\cdot 6\cdot 8\cdot\cos\beta$$
$$100 = 36 + 64 - 96\cos\beta$$
$$96\cos\beta = 0$$
$$\cos\beta = 0$$
$$\beta \approx 90°$$
((6, 8, 10) is a Pythagorean Triple)

25.
$$x^2 = 8^2 + 12^2 - 2\cdot 8\cdot 12\cos 60°$$
$$x^2 = 64 + 144 - 192\cos 60°$$
$$x^2 = 208 - 192(0.5)$$
$$x^2 = 112$$
$$x = \sqrt{112} \approx 10.6$$

26.
$$x^2 = 9^2 + 10^2 - 2\cdot 9\cdot 10\cos 40°$$
$$x^2 = 81 + 100 - 180(0.766)$$
$$x^2 = 181 - 137.9$$
$$x^2 = 43.1$$
$$x \approx 6.6$$

27.
$$6^2 = x^2 + 4^2 - 2\cdot x\cdot 4\cos 60°$$
$$36 = x^2 + 16 - 8x(0.5)$$
$$36 = x^2 + 16 - 4x$$
$$0 = x^2 - 4x - 20$$
$$x = \frac{-(-4)\pm\sqrt{(-4)^2 - 4(1)(-20)}}{2(1)}$$
$$x = \frac{4\pm\sqrt{96}}{2}$$
$$x = \frac{4\pm 4\sqrt{6}}{2}$$
$$x = \frac{2(2\pm 2\sqrt{6})}{2}$$
$$x = 2 + 2\sqrt{6} \quad (\text{Reject } 2 - 2\sqrt{6})$$
$$x \approx 6.9$$

28. Let $\beta = 2\cdot\alpha$ so that $m\angle PMN = \beta$.
$$6^2 = 5^2 + 7^2 - 2\cdot 5\cdot 7\cdot\cos\beta$$
$$36 = 25 + 49 - 70\cos\beta$$
$$70\cos\beta = 38$$
$$\cos\beta = \frac{38}{70}$$
$$\cos\beta = 0.5429$$
$$\beta \approx 57.1° \text{ so } \alpha \approx 29°$$

29. a. $x^2 = 150^2 + 180^2 - 2(150)(180)\cos 80°$
$$x^2 = 22,500 + 32,400 - 54,000(0.1736)$$
$$x^2 = 44,525.6$$
$$x = \sqrt{44,525.6}$$
$$x \approx 213.4 \text{ feet}$$

b. $A = \frac{1}{2}(150)(180)\sin 80°$
$$A \approx \frac{1}{2}(150)(180)(0.9848)$$
$$A \approx 13,294.9 \text{ ft}^2$$

30. The third angle measures 68°.

$$\frac{\sin 47°}{x} = \frac{\sin 68°}{500}$$
$$500 \sin 47° = x(\sin 68°)$$
$$0.9272x = 500(0.7314)$$
$$x \approx 394.4 \text{ ft}$$

31. Let x represent the distance from aircraft to enemy headquarters.

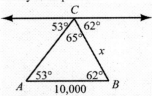

Using the Law of Sines,

$$\frac{\sin 53°}{x} = \frac{\sin 65°}{10,000}$$
$$x(\sin 65°) = 10,000 \sin 53°$$
$$0.9063x = 10,000(0.7986)$$
$$x \approx 8812 \text{ m}$$

32. Using the Law of Cosines,

$$26^2 = 24^2 + 10^2 - 2(24)(10)\cos \alpha$$
$$676 = 576 + 100 - 480 \cos \alpha$$
$$-480 \cdot \cos \alpha = 0$$
$$\cos \alpha = 0$$
$$\alpha = 90°$$

33. The third angle measures 85°.
Using the Law of Sines,

$$\frac{\sin 85°}{x} = \frac{\sin 30°}{8}$$
$$\frac{0.9962}{x} = \frac{0.5}{8}$$
$$0.5x = 8(0.9962)$$
$$x \approx 15.9 \text{ ft}$$

34. The third angle measures 80°.
Using the Law of Sines,

$$\frac{\sin 80°}{120} = \frac{\sin 30°}{x}$$
$$\frac{0.9848}{120} = \frac{0.5}{x}$$
$$0.9848x = 0.5(120)$$
$$x \approx 60.9 \text{ m}$$

35.
$$A_\triangle = \frac{1}{2}ab\sin \gamma$$
$$18\sqrt{3} = \frac{1}{2}(x)(2x)(\sin 60°)$$
$$18\sqrt{3} = x^2 \cdot \sin 60°$$
$$18\sqrt{3} = x^2 \left(\frac{\sqrt{3}}{2}\right)$$
$$x^2 = 36$$
$$x = 6$$

36.
$$(2\sqrt{3})^2 = 2^2 + b^2 - 2(2)(b)\cos 60°$$
$$12 = 4 + b^2 - 4b\left(\frac{1}{2}\right)$$
$$12 = 4 + b^2 - 2b$$
$$0 = b^2 - 2b - 8$$
$$0 = (b-4)(b+2)$$
$$b = 4 \text{ or } b = -2; \text{ reject } b = -2$$

37.
$$a^2 = 27^2 + 27^2 - 2(27)(27)\cos 30°$$
$$a^2 = 729 + 729 - 2(729) \cdot \frac{\sqrt{3}}{2}$$
$$a^2 \approx 195.33$$
$$a \approx 13.97 \approx 14.0 \text{ feet}$$

38.
$$a^2 = 27^2 + 27^2 - 2(27)(27)\cos 30°$$
$$a^2 = 729 + 729 - 2(729) \cdot \frac{\sqrt{3}}{2}$$
$$a^2 \approx 195.33$$
$$a \approx 13.97 \approx 14.0 \text{ ft}$$

39. Let $\gamma = 90°$

Then $c^2 = a^2 + b^2 - 2ab\cos \gamma$

becomes $c^2 = a^2 + b^2 - 2 \cdot a \cdot b \cdot \cos 90°$.

But $\cos 90° = 0$.

$\therefore c^2 = a^2 + b^2 - 2 \cdot a \cdot b \cdot 0$ or
$$c^2 = a^2 + b^2$$

40. $A = 8 \cdot 12 \cdot \sin 70° = 90.2 \text{ cm}^2$

41. $A = (6.3)(8.9)\sin 67.5°$
$A = 51.8 \text{ cm}^2$

42. $A_{\text{PARALLELOGRAM}} = ab\sin \gamma$
In a rhombus consecutive sides are $\cong$ (both $= a$).
Then $A_{\text{RHOMBUS}} = a \cdot a \sin \theta$ or $a^2 \sin \theta$.

43. $\dfrac{1}{2}ab$

CHAPTER REVIEW

1. sine;
$$\sin 40° = \frac{a}{16}$$
$$a = 16 \sin 40°$$
$$a \approx 10.3 \text{ in.}$$

2. sine;
$$\sin 70° = \frac{d}{8}$$
$$d = 8 \sin 70°$$
$$d \approx 7.5 \text{ ft}$$

3. cosine;

$$\cos 80° = \frac{4}{c}$$

$$c = \frac{4}{\cos 80°}$$

$$c \approx \frac{4}{0.1736}$$

$$c \approx 23.0 \text{ in.}$$

4. sine;

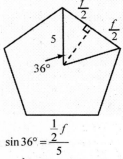

$$\sin 36° = \frac{\frac{1}{2}f}{5}$$

$$\frac{1}{2}f = 5(\sin 36°)$$

$$\frac{1}{2}f \approx 5(0.5878)$$

$$\frac{1}{2}f \approx 2.939$$

$$f \approx 5.9 \text{ ft}$$

5. tangent;

$$\tan \alpha = \frac{13}{14}$$

$$\tan \alpha \approx 0.9286$$

$$\alpha \approx 43°$$

6. cosine;

$$\cos \theta = \frac{8}{15}$$

$$\cos \theta \approx 0.5333$$

$$\theta \approx 58°$$

7. sine;

$$\sin \alpha = \frac{9}{12}$$

$$\sin \alpha \approx 0.7500$$

$$\alpha \approx 49°$$

8. tangent;

$$\tan \beta = \frac{7}{24}$$

$$\tan \beta \approx 0.2917$$

$$\beta \approx 16°$$

9. Law of Sines

$$\frac{\sin 57°}{x} = \frac{\sin 49°}{8}$$

$$x(\sin 49°) = 8(\sin 57°)$$

$$x(0.7547) = 8(0.8387)$$

$$x \approx 8.9 \text{ units}$$

10. Law of Cosines

$$15^2 = 14^2 + 16^2 - 2(14)(16)\cos \alpha$$

$$225 = 196 + 256 - 448 \cos \alpha$$

$$448 \cos \alpha = 227$$

$$\cos \alpha = \frac{227}{448}$$

$$\cos \alpha \approx 0.5067$$

$$\alpha \approx 60°$$

11. The third angle measures 80°.
Law of Sines

$$\frac{\sin 40°}{y} = \frac{\sin 80°}{20}$$

$$y(\sin 80°) = 20(\sin 40°)$$

$$y(0.9848) = 20(0.6428)$$

$$y \approx 13.1 \text{ units}$$

12. Law of Cosines

$$w^2 = 14^2 + 21^2 - 2(14)(21)\cos 60°$$

$$w^2 = 196 + 441 - 294$$

$$w^2 = 343$$

$$w = \sqrt{343}$$

$$w \approx 18.5 \text{ units}$$

13. The remaining angles of the triangle measure 47° and 74°.

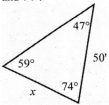

Using the Law of Sines,

$$\frac{\sin 47°}{x} = \frac{\sin 59°}{50}$$

$$\frac{0.7314}{x} = \frac{0.8572}{50}$$

$$x(0.8572) = 50(0.7314)$$

$$x \approx 42.7 \text{ feet}$$

14. Let d be the length of the shorter diagonal.

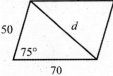

Law of Cosines

$$d^2 = 50^2 + 70^2 - 2(50)(70)\cos 75°$$

$$d^2 = 2500 + 4900 - 7000(0.2588)$$

$$d^2 = 2500 + 4900 - 1811.6$$

$$d^2 = 5588.4$$

$$d = \sqrt{5588.4}$$

$$d \approx 74.8 \text{ cm}$$

15. Law of Cosines

$$6^2 = 6^2 + 11^2 - 2(6)(11)\cos\alpha$$
$$36 = 366 + 121 - 132\cos\alpha$$
$$132\cos\alpha = 121$$
$$\cos\alpha = \frac{121}{132}$$
$$\cos\alpha \approx 0.9167$$
$$\alpha \approx 23.6°$$

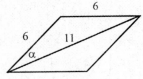

The acute angle of the rhombus measures $2\alpha \approx 47°$.

16.

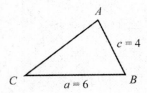

$$A = \frac{1}{2}ac\sin B$$
$$9.7 = \frac{1}{2}(6)(4)\sin B$$
$$9.7 = 12\sin B$$
$$\sin B = \frac{9.7}{12} \approx 0.8083$$
$$B \approx 54°$$

17.

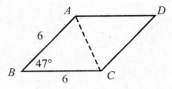

If the acute angle measures 47°, then

$A = \frac{1}{2}ab\sin 47°$ gives one-half the desired area.

$$A = \frac{1}{2} \cdot 6 \cdot 6 \cdot \sin 47°$$
$$A \approx 13.16 \text{ in}^2$$

for $\triangle ABC$. The area of rhombus $ABCD$ is approximately 26.3 in².

18. If $m\angle R = 45°$,

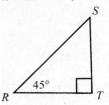

then $m\angle S = 45°$ also. Then $\overline{RT} = \overline{ST}$. Let $RT = ST = x$. Now, $\tan R = \tan 45° = \frac{x}{x} = 1$.

19. If $m\angle S = 30°$,

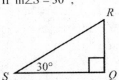

then the sides of $\triangle RQS$ can be represented by $RQ = x$, $RS = 2x$, and $SQ = x \cdot \sqrt{3}$.

$\sin S = \sin 30° = \frac{x}{2x} = \frac{1}{2}$.

20. If $m\angle T = 60°$,

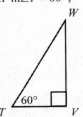

then the sides of $\triangle TVW$ can be represented by $TV = x$, $TW = 2x$, and $VW = x\sqrt{3}$.

$\sin T = \sin 60° = \frac{x\sqrt{3}}{2x} = \frac{\sqrt{3}}{2}$.

21. Because alt. int. $\angle$s are $\cong$,

$$\tan 55° = \frac{12}{x}$$
$$x(\tan 55°) = 12$$
$$x = \frac{12}{\tan 55°} \approx \frac{12}{1.4281}$$
$$x \approx 8.4 \text{ ft}$$

22.
$$\sin 60° = \frac{x}{200}$$
$$x = 200\sin 60°$$
$$x \approx 200(0.866)$$
$$x \approx 173.2$$

If the rocket rises 173.2 feet per second, then its altitude after 5 seconds will be approximately 866 feet.

23.
$$\cos\alpha = \frac{3}{4}$$
$$\cos\alpha = 0.75$$
$$\alpha \approx 41°$$

24. $\sin\alpha = \dfrac{300}{2200}$

$\sin\alpha = 0.1364$

$\alpha \approx 8°$

25. Let x represent one-half the length of a side of a regular pentagon.

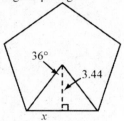

$\tan 36° = \dfrac{x}{3.44}$

$x = 3.44(\tan 36°)$

$x \approx 3.44(0.7265)$

$x \approx 2.50$

Then the length of each side is approximately 5.0 cm.

26.

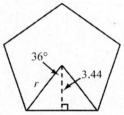

$\cos 36° = \dfrac{3.44}{r}$

$r = \dfrac{3.44}{\cos 36°}$

$r \approx \dfrac{3.44}{0.8090}$

$r \approx 4.3$ cm

27. The altitude bisects the base where β represents the measure of the base angle,

$\cos\beta = \dfrac{15}{40}$

$\cos\beta = 0.375$

$\beta \approx 68°$

28. The measure of acute angle α is one-half the desired angle's measure.

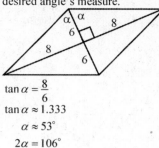

$\tan\alpha = \dfrac{8}{6}$

$\tan\alpha \approx 1.333$

$\alpha \approx 53°$

$2\alpha = 106°$

29. $\tan 23° = \dfrac{a}{b}$

$\tan 23° = \dfrac{3}{b}$

$b(\tan 23°) = 3$

$b = \dfrac{3}{\tan 23°}$

$b \approx \dfrac{3}{0.4245} \approx 7$

The grade of the hill is 3 to 7 (or 3:7).

30. Let S_1 represent the distance to the nearer ship and S_2 represent the distance to the farther ship.

$\tan 32° = \dfrac{2500}{S_2}$ and $\tan 44° = \dfrac{2500}{S_1}$

$S_2 = \dfrac{2500}{\tan 32°}$ $\qquad S_1 = \dfrac{2500}{\tan 44°}$

$S_2 \approx 4000.8$ $\qquad S_1 \approx 2588.8$

The distance between the ships is
4000.8 − 2588.8 or approximately 1412.0 meters.

31. $\sin\theta = \dfrac{7}{25}$

Using $\sin^2\theta + \cos^2\theta = 1$,

$\left(\dfrac{7}{25}\right)^2 + \cos^2\theta = 1$

$\dfrac{49}{625} + \cos^2\theta = 1$

$\cos^2\theta = 1 - \dfrac{49}{625}$

$\cos^2\theta = \dfrac{576}{625}$

$\cos\theta = \sqrt{\dfrac{576}{625}} = \dfrac{\sqrt{576}}{\sqrt{625}} = \dfrac{24}{25}$

Because $\sec\theta = \dfrac{1}{\cos\theta}$,

$\sec\theta = \dfrac{1}{\frac{24}{25}} = \dfrac{25}{24}$.

32. $\tan\theta = \dfrac{11}{60}$

Using $\tan^2\theta + 1 = \sec^2\theta$,

$$\left(\frac{11}{60}\right)^2 + 1 = \sec^2\theta$$

$$\frac{121}{3600} + 1 = \sec^2\theta$$

$$\frac{3721}{3600} = \sec^2\theta$$

$$\sec\theta = \sqrt{\frac{3721}{3600}} = \frac{\sqrt{3721}}{\sqrt{3600}} = \frac{61}{60}$$

Because $\cot\theta = \dfrac{1}{\tan\theta}$,

$$\cot\theta = \frac{1}{\frac{11}{60}} = \frac{60}{11}.$$

33. $\cot\theta = \dfrac{21}{20}$

Using $\cot^2\theta + 1 = \csc^2\theta$,

$$\left(\frac{21}{20}\right)^2 + 1 = \csc^2\theta$$

$$\frac{841}{400} = \csc^2\theta$$

$$\csc\theta = \sqrt{\frac{841}{400}} = \frac{\sqrt{841}}{\sqrt{400}} = \frac{29}{20}$$

Because $\sin\theta = \dfrac{1}{\csc\theta}$,

$$\sin\theta = \frac{1}{\frac{29}{20}} = \frac{20}{29}.$$

34.

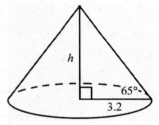

$$\tan 65° = \frac{h}{3.2}$$
$$h = 3.2 \cdot \tan 65$$
$$h \approx 6.9 \text{ feet}$$

$$V = \frac{1}{3}Bh$$
$$V = \frac{1}{3}\pi r^2 h$$
$$V \approx \frac{1}{3}\pi \cdot (3.2)^2 \cdot (6.9)$$
$$V \approx 74.0 \text{ ft}^3$$

CHAPTER TEST

1. a. $\sin\alpha = \dfrac{a}{c}$

   b. $\tan\beta = \dfrac{b}{a}$

2. a. $\cos\beta = \dfrac{6}{10} = \dfrac{3}{5}$

   b. $\sin\alpha = \dfrac{6}{10} = \dfrac{3}{5}$

3. a. $\tan 45° = \dfrac{1}{1} = 1$

   b. $\tan 60° = \dfrac{\sqrt{3}}{2}$

4. a. $\sin 23° \approx 0.3907$

   b. $\cos 79° \approx 0.1908$

5. $\sin\theta = 0.6691$
    $\theta \approx 42°$

6. a. $\tan 26°$

   b. $\cos 47°$

7.

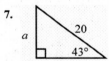

$$\sin 43° = \frac{a}{20}$$
$$a = 20\sin 43°$$
$$a \approx 20(0.6820)$$
$$a \approx 14$$

8.

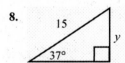

$$\sin 37° = \frac{y}{15}$$
$$y = 15\sin 37°$$
$$y \approx 15(0.6018)$$
$$y \approx 9$$

9.

$$\sin\theta = \frac{5}{6}$$
$$\sin\theta \approx 0.8333$$
$$\theta \approx 56°$$

10.   **a.** $\cos\beta = \dfrac{a}{c} = \sin\alpha$

       True

     b.   True

11. $\sin 67° = \dfrac{x}{100}$

       $x = 100\sin 67°$
       $x \approx 100(0.9205)$
       $x \approx 92$ feet

12. $\sin\theta = \dfrac{2}{12}$
    $\sin\theta \approx 0.1667$
     $\theta \approx 10°$

13.   **a.** $\csc\alpha = \dfrac{1}{\sin\alpha} = \dfrac{1}{\frac{1}{2}} = 2$

     b. $\sin\alpha = \dfrac{1}{2}$
       $\sin\alpha = 0.5$
        $\alpha = 30°$

14.   **a.**

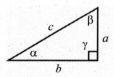

$$\cos\beta = \frac{a}{c}$$
$$\sin\alpha = \frac{a}{c}$$

     b.

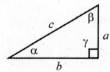

$$\cos\beta = \frac{a}{c}$$
$$\sec\beta = \frac{1}{\cos\beta}$$
$$\sec\beta = \frac{1}{\frac{a}{c}} = \frac{c}{a}$$

15. $A = \dfrac{1}{2}bc\sin\alpha$

      $A = \dfrac{1}{2}(8)(12)\sin 60°$
      $A \approx 48(0.8660)$
      $A \approx 42$ cm^2

16.

$$\frac{\sin\alpha}{a} = \frac{\sin\beta}{b} = \frac{\sin\gamma}{c}$$

17.

$$a^2 = b^2 + c^2 - 2bc\cos\alpha$$

18.   Law of Sines

$$\frac{\sin\alpha}{a} = \frac{\sin\beta}{b}$$
$$\frac{\sin 65°}{10} = \frac{\sin\alpha}{6}$$
$$10\sin\alpha = 6\sin 65$$
$$\sin\alpha = \frac{6\sin 65}{10}$$
$$\sin\alpha \approx 0.5438$$
$$\alpha \approx 33°$$

19.   Law of Cosines

$$x^2 = 12^2 + 8^2 - 2(12)(8)\cos 60°$$
$$x^2 = 144 + 64 - 192(0.5)$$
$$x^2 = 112$$
$$x = \sqrt{112}$$
$$x \approx 11$$

20. In an isosceles triangle formed by 2 radii and a side of the pentagon, draw the height of the triangle to the side. This is the apothem with length, a. If *s* represents the side length of the pentagon (the base of the isosceles triangle), then

$$\tan 54 = \frac{a}{\frac{1}{2}s}$$

$$\frac{1}{2}s \cdot \tan 54 = a$$

$$s = \frac{2a}{\tan 54}$$

$$A_{1\triangle} = \frac{1}{2} \cdot \frac{2a}{\tan 54} \cdot a$$

$$A_{1\triangle} = \frac{a^2}{\tan 54}$$

$$A_{ABCDE} = \frac{5a^2}{\tan 54}$$

Appendix A: Algebra Review

SECTION A.1: Algebraic Expressions

1. Undefined terms, definitions, axioms or postulates, theorems

2. Algebra; geometry

3. a. Reflexive
   b. Transitive
   c. Substitution
   d. Symmetric

4. a. $2 = 2$
   b. If $2 = x$, then $x = 2$.
   c. If $x = 2$ and $2 = y$, then $x = y$.
   d. If $2 + 5 = 7$ and $7 + y = z$, then $2 + 5 + y = z$.

5. a. 12
   b. -2
   c. 2
   d. -12

6. a. 8
   b. -8
   c. -22
   d. 1

7. a. 35
   b. -35
   c. -35
   d. 35

8. a. -84
   b. 84
   c. -84
   d. 84

9. No; Commutative Axiom for Multiplication

10. a. Commutative Axiom for Multiplication
    b. Associative Axiom for Addition
    c. Commutative Axiom for Addition
    d. Associative Axiom for Multiplication

11. a. 9
    b. -9
    c. 8
    d. -8

12. $(-3) - 7$

13. a. -4
    b. -36
    c. 18
    d. $-\dfrac{1}{4}$

14. 5 feet divided by 10 spaces $= \dfrac{1}{2}$ ft per space. Or since 5 feet = 60 inches, 60 inches divided by 10 spaces = 6 inches per space.

15. $-\$60$

16. $25(2) + 30(2) = 50 + 60 = \$110$

17. a. $30 + 35 = 65$
    b. $28 - 12 = 16$
    c. $\dfrac{7}{2} + \dfrac{11}{2} = \dfrac{18}{2} = 9$
    d. $8x$

18. a. $54 - 24 = 30$
    b. $3(4 + 8) = 12 + 24 = 36$
    c. $7y - 2y = (7 - 2)y = 5y$
    d. $(16 + 8)x = 24x$

19. a. $(6 + 4)\pi = 10\pi$
    b. $(8 + 3)\sqrt{2} = 11\sqrt{2}$
    c. $(16 - 9)x^2 y = 7x^2 y$
    d. $(9 - 2)\sqrt{3} = 7\sqrt{3}$

20. a. $(1 + 2)\pi r^2 = 3\pi r^2$
    b. $(7 + 3)xy = 10xy$
    c. $7x^2 y + 3xy^2$
    d. $(1 + 1)x + y = 2x + y$

21. a. $2 + 12 = 14$

    b. $5 \cdot 4 = 20$

    c. $2 + 3 \cdot 4 = 2 + 12 = 14$

    d. $2 + 6^2 = 2 + 36 = 38$

22. a. $9 + 16 = 25$

    b. $7^2 = 49$

    c. $9 + 6 \div 3 = 9 + 2 = 11$

    d. $[9 + 6] \div 3 = 15 \div 3 = 5$

23. a. $\dfrac{6}{-6} = -1$

    b. $\dfrac{8 - 6}{6 \cdot 3} = \dfrac{2}{18} = \dfrac{1}{9}$

    c. $\dfrac{10 - 18}{9} = \dfrac{-8}{9}$

    d. $\dfrac{5 - 12 + (-3)}{4 + 16} = \dfrac{-10}{20} = \dfrac{-1}{2}$

24. a. $8 + 10 + 12 + 15 = 45$

    b. $42 + 7 - 12 - 2 = 35$

25. a. $15 - 6 - 5 + 2 = 6$

    b. $12x^2 - 15x + 8x - 10 = 12x^2 - 7x - 10$

26. a. $10x^2 - 35x + 6x - 21 = 10x^2 - 39x - 21$

    b. $6x^2 - 10xy + 3xy - 5y^2 = 6x^2 - 7xy - 5y^2$

27. $5x + 2y$

28. $2xy + 2yz + 2xz$

29. $10x + 5y$

30. $xy + xz + y^2 + yz$; the total of the areas of the four smaller plots is also $xy + y^2 + xz + yz$.

31. $10x$

32. $9\pi + 48\pi + 9\pi = 66\pi$

SECTION A.2: Formulas and Equations

1. $5x + 8$

2. $-1x + 8$

3. $2x - 2$

4. $4x - 2$

5. $2x + 2 + 3x + 6 = 5x + 8$

6. $6x + 15 - 6x + 2 = 17$

7. $x^2 + 4x + 3x + 12 = x^2 + 7x + 12$

8. $x^2 - 7x - 5x + 35 = x^2 - 12x + 35$

9. $6x^2 - 4x + 5x - 10 = 6x^2 + 11x - 10$

10. $6x^2 + 9x + 14x + 21 = 6x^2 + 23x + 21$

11. $(a + b)(a + b) + (a - b)(a - b)$
$= a^2 + ab + ab + b^2 + a^2 - ab - ab + b^2$
$= 2a^2 + 2b^2$

12. $(x + 2)(x + 2) - (x - 2)(x - 2)$
$= x^2 + 2x + 2x + 4 - \left(x^2 - 2x - 2x + 4\right)$
$= x^2 + 4x + 4 - \left(x^2 - 4x + 4\right)$
$= x^2 + 4x + 4 - x^2 + 4x - 4$
$= 8x$

13. $4 \cdot 3 \cdot 5 = 60$

14. $5^2 + 7^2 = 35 + 49 = 74$

15. $2 \cdot 13 + 2 \cdot 7 = 26 + 14 = 40$

16. $6 \cdot 16 \div 4 = 96 \div 4 = 24$

17. $S = 2 \cdot 6 \cdot 4 + 2 \cdot 4 \cdot 5 + 2 \cdot 6 \cdot 5$
$S = 48 + 40 + 60$
$S = 148$

18. $A = \left(\dfrac{1}{2}\right)2(6 + 8 + 10)$
$A = 1(24)$
$A = 24$

19. $V = \left(\dfrac{1}{3}\right)\pi(3)^2 \cdot 4$
$V = \dfrac{1}{3} \cdot \pi \cdot 9 \cdot 4$
$V = 12\pi$

20. $S = 4\pi r^2$
$S = 4\pi r(2)^2$
$S = 4\pi \cdot 4$
$S = 16\pi$

21. $2x = 14$
 $x = 7$

22. $3x = -3$
 $x = -1$

23. $\dfrac{y}{-3} = 4$
 $y = -12$

24. $7y = -21$
 $y = -3$

25. $2a + 2 = 26$
 $2a = 24$
 $a = 12$

26. $\dfrac{3b}{2} = 27$
 $3b = 54$
 $b = 18$

27. $2x + 2 = 30 - 6x + 12$
 $2x + 2 = 42 - 6x$
 $8x = 40$
 $x = 5$

28. $2x + 2 + 3x + 6 = 22 + 40 - 4x$
 $5x + 8 = 62 - 4x$
 $9x = 54$
 $x = 6$

29. Multiply equation by 6 to get
 $2x - 3x = -30$
 $-x = -30$
 $x = 30$

30. Multiply equation by 12 to get
 $6x + 4x + 3x = 312$
 $13x = 312$
 $x = 24$

31. Multiply equation by n to get
 $360 + 135n = 180n$
 $360 = 45n$
 $8 = n$

32. Multiply equation by n to get
 $(n - 2)180 = 150n$
 $180n - 360 = 150n$
 $-360 = -30n$
 $12 = n$

33. $148 = 2 \cdot 5 \cdot w + 2 \cdot w \cdot 6 + 2 \cdot 5 \cdot 6$
 $148 = 10w + 12w + 60$
 $88 = 22w$
 $4 = w$

34. $156 = \left(\dfrac{1}{2}\right) \cdot 12 \cdot (b + 11)$
 $156 = 6(b + 11)$
 $156 = 6b + 66$
 $90 = 6b$
 $15 = b$

35. $23 = \left(\dfrac{1}{2}\right)(78 - y)$
 $46 = 78 - y$
 $-32 = -y$
 $32 = y$

36. $\dfrac{-3}{2} = \dfrac{Y - 1}{2 - (-2)}$
 $\dfrac{-3}{2} = \dfrac{Y - 1}{4}$
 $2Y - 2 = -12$
 $2Y = -10$
 $Y = -5$

SECTION A.3: Inequalities

1. The length of $\overline{AB}$ is greater than the length of $\overline{CD}$.

2. $e < f;\ f > e$

3. The measure of angle ABC is greater than the measure of angle DEF.

4. $x = 6,\ x = 9,\ x = 12$

5. **a.** $p = 4$

 b. $p = 10$

6. Yes

7. $AB > IJ$

8. The measure of angle JKL is greater than the measure of angle ABC.

9. **a.** False

 b. True

 c. True

 d. False

10. **a.** True

 b. False

 c. True

 d. False

11. The measure of the second angle must be greater than $148°$ and less than $180°$.

12. The length of the second board must be less than 5 feet.

13. **a.** $-12 \le 20$

  b. $-10 \le -2$

  c. $18 \ge -30$

  d. $3 \ge -5$

14. **a.** $2 > -1$

  b. $12 < 18$

  c. $-12 > -18$

  d. $2 < 3$

15.

No Change	No Change
No Change	No Change
No Change	CHANGE
No Change	CHANGE

16. $5x \le 30$
  $x \le 6$

17. $2x \le 14$
  $x \le 7$

18. $4x > 20$
  $x > 5$

19. $-4x > 20$
  $x < -5$

20. $10 - 5x \le 30$
  $-5x \le 20$
   $x \ge -4$

21. $5x < 200 - 5x$
 $10x < 200$
  $x < 20$

22. $5x + 10 < 54 - 6x$
  $11x < 44$
   $x < 4$

23. $2x - 3x \le 24$
  $-x \le 24$
   $x \ge -24$

24. $2x - 3 < -35$
  $2x < -32$
   $x < -16$

25. $x^2 + 4x \le x^2 - 5x - 18$
  $9x \le -18$
   $x \le -2$

26. $x^2 + 2x < 2x - x^2 + 2x^2$
  $x^2 + 2x < x^2 + 2x$
  No solution or $\varnothing$.

27. Not true if $c < 0$.

28. Not true if $c = 0$.

29. Not true if $a = -3$ and $b = -2$.

30. Not true if $a = c$.

SECTION A.4: Quadratic Equations

1. a. 3.61

   b. 2.83

   c. −5.39

   d. 0.77

2. a. 4.12

   b. 20

   c. −2.65

   d. 1.26

3. a, c, d, f

4. a, b, c, e

5. a. $\sqrt{8} = \sqrt{4 \cdot 2} = 2\sqrt{2}$

   b. $\sqrt{45} = \sqrt{9 \cdot 5} = 3\sqrt{5}$

   c. $\sqrt{900} = 30$

   d. $\left(\sqrt{3}\right)^2 = 3$

6. a. $\sqrt{28} = \sqrt{4 \cdot 7} = 2\sqrt{7}$

   b. $\sqrt{32} = \sqrt{16 \cdot 2} = 4\sqrt{2}$

   c. $\sqrt{54} = \sqrt{9 \cdot 6} = 3\sqrt{6}$

   d. $\sqrt{200} = \sqrt{100 \cdot 2} = 10\sqrt{2}$

7. a. $\sqrt{\dfrac{9}{16}} = \dfrac{\sqrt{9}}{\sqrt{16}} = \dfrac{3}{4}$

   b. $\sqrt{\dfrac{25}{49}} = \dfrac{\sqrt{25}}{\sqrt{49}} = \dfrac{5}{7}$

   c. $\sqrt{\dfrac{7}{16}} = \dfrac{\sqrt{7}}{\sqrt{16}} = \dfrac{\sqrt{7}}{4}$

   d. $\sqrt{\dfrac{6}{9}} = \dfrac{\sqrt{6}}{\sqrt{9}} = \dfrac{\sqrt{6}}{3}$

8. a. $\sqrt{\dfrac{1}{4}} = \dfrac{\sqrt{1}}{\sqrt{4}} = \dfrac{1}{2}$

   b. $\sqrt{\dfrac{16}{9}} = \dfrac{\sqrt{16}}{\sqrt{9}} = \dfrac{4}{3}$

   c. $\sqrt{\dfrac{5}{36}} = \dfrac{\sqrt{5}}{\sqrt{36}} = \dfrac{\sqrt{5}}{6}$

   d. $\sqrt{\dfrac{3}{16}} = \dfrac{\sqrt{3}}{\sqrt{16}} = \dfrac{\sqrt{3}}{4}$

9. a. $\sqrt{54} \approx 7.35$ and $3\sqrt{6} \approx 7.35$

   b. $\sqrt{\dfrac{5}{16}} \approx 0.56$ and $\dfrac{\sqrt{5}}{4} \approx 0.56$

10. a. $\sqrt{48} \approx 6.93$ and $4\sqrt{3} \approx 6.93$

    b. $\sqrt{\dfrac{7}{9}} \approx 0.88$ and $\dfrac{\sqrt{7}}{3} \approx 0.88$

11.
$$x^2 - 6x + 8 = 0$$
$$(x - 4)(x - 2) = 0$$
$$x - 4 = 0 \quad \text{or} \quad x - 2 = 0$$
$$x = 4 \quad \text{or} \quad x = 2$$

12.
$$x^2 + 4x = 21$$
$$x^2 + 4x - 21 = 0$$
$$(x + 7)(x - 3) = 0$$
$$x + 7 = 0 \quad \text{or} \quad x - 3 = 0$$
$$x = -7 \quad \text{or} \quad x = 3$$

13.
$$3x^2 - 51x + 180 = 0$$
$$3\left(x^2 - 17x + 60\right) = 0$$
$$3(x - 12)(x - 5) = 0$$
$$x - 12 = 0 \quad \text{or} \quad x - 5 = 0$$
$$x = 12 \quad \text{or} \quad x = 5$$

14.
$$2x^2 + x - 6 = 0$$
$$(2x - 3)(x + 2) = 0$$
$$2x - 3 = 0 \quad \text{or} \quad x + 2 = 0$$
$$2x = 3 \quad \text{or} \quad x = -2$$
$$x = \frac{3}{2} \quad \text{or} \quad x = -2$$

15.
$$3x^2 = 10x + 8$$
$$3x^2 - 10x - 8 = 0$$
$$(3x + 2)(x - 4) = 0$$
$$3x + 2 = 0 \quad \text{or} \quad x - 4 = 0$$
$$3x = -2 \quad \text{or} \quad x = 4$$
$$x = -\frac{2}{3} \quad \text{or} \quad x = 4$$

16.
$$8x^2 + 40x - 112 = 0$$
$$8\left(x^2 + 5x - 14\right) = 0$$
$$8(x + 7)(x - 2) = 0$$
$$x + 7 = 0 \quad \text{or} \quad x - 2 = 0$$
$$x = -7 \quad \text{or} \quad x = 2$$

17.
$$6x^2 = 5x - 1$$
$$6x^2 - 5x + 1 = 0$$
$$(3x - 1)(2x - 1) = 0$$
$$3x - 1 = 0 \quad \text{or} \quad 2x - 1 = 0$$
$$3x = 1 \quad \text{or} \quad 2x = 1$$
$$x = \frac{1}{3} \quad \text{or} \quad x = \frac{1}{2}$$

18.
$$12x^2 + 10x = 12$$
$$12x^2 + 10x - 12 = 0$$
$$2(6x^2 + 5x - 6) = 0$$
$$2(3x - 2)(2x + 3) = 0$$
$$3x - 2 = 0 \quad \text{or} \quad 2x + 3 = 0$$
$$3x = 2 \quad \text{or} \quad 2x = -3$$
$$x = \frac{2}{3} \quad \text{or} \quad x = -\frac{3}{2}$$

19. $x^2 - 7x + 10 = 0$
$a = 1, \ b = -7, \ c = 10$
$$x = \frac{-b \pm \sqrt{b^2 - 4ac}}{2a}$$
$$x = \frac{7 \pm \sqrt{49 - 4(1)(10)}}{2(1)}$$
$$x = \frac{7 \pm \sqrt{49 - 40}}{2}$$
$$x = \frac{7 \pm \sqrt{9}}{2}$$
$$x = \frac{7 + 3}{2} \text{ or } x = \frac{7 - 3}{2}$$
$$x = 5 \text{ or } 2$$

20. $x^2 + 7x + 12 = 0$
$a = 1, \ b = 7, \ c = 12$
$$x = \frac{-b \pm \sqrt{b^2 - 4ac}}{2a}$$
$$x = \frac{-7 \pm \sqrt{49 - 4(1)(12)}}{2(1)}$$
$$x = \frac{-7 \pm \sqrt{49 - 48}}{2}$$
$$x = \frac{-7 \pm \sqrt{1}}{2}$$
$$x = \frac{-7 + 1}{2} \text{ or } x = \frac{-7 - 1}{2}$$
$$x = -3 \text{ or } -4$$

21.
$$x^2 + 9 = 7x$$
$$x^2 - 7x + 9 = 0$$
$a = 1, \ b = -7, \ c = 9$
$$x = \frac{-b \pm \sqrt{b^2 - 4ac}}{2a}$$
$$x = \frac{7 \pm \sqrt{49 - 4(1)(9)}}{2(1)}$$
$$x = \frac{7 \pm \sqrt{49 - 36}}{2}$$
$$x = \frac{7 \pm \sqrt{13}}{2} \approx 5.30 \text{ or } 1.70$$

22.
$$2x^2 + 3x = 6$$
$$2x^2 + 3x - 6 = 0$$
$a = 2, \ b = 3, \ c = -6$
$$x = \frac{-b \pm \sqrt{b^2 - 4ac}}{2a}$$
$$x = \frac{-3 \pm \sqrt{9 - 4(2)(-6)}}{2(2)}$$
$$x = \frac{-3 \pm \sqrt{9 + 48}}{4}$$
$$x = \frac{-3 \pm \sqrt{57}}{4} \approx 1.14 \text{ or } -2.64$$

23. $x^2 - 4x - 8 = 0$
$a = 1, \ b = -4, \ c = -8$
$$x = \frac{-b \pm \sqrt{b^2 - 4ac}}{2a}$$
$$x = \frac{4 \pm \sqrt{16 - 4(1)(-8)}}{2(1)}$$
$$x = \frac{4 \pm \sqrt{16 + 32}}{2}$$
$$x = \frac{4 \pm \sqrt{48}}{2}$$
$$x = \frac{4 \pm 4\sqrt{3}}{2} \approx 5.46 \text{ or } -1.46$$

24. $x^2 - 6x - 2 = 0$
$a = 1, \ b = -6, \ c = -2$
$$x = \frac{-b \pm \sqrt{b^2 - 4ac}}{2a}$$
$$x = \frac{6 \pm \sqrt{36 - 4(1)(-2)}}{2(1)}$$
$$x = \frac{6 \pm \sqrt{36 + 8}}{2}$$
$$x = \frac{6 \pm \sqrt{44}}{2}$$
$$x = \frac{6 \pm 2\sqrt{11}}{2}$$
$$x = 3 \pm \sqrt{11} \approx 6.32 \text{ or } -0.32$$

25.
$$5x^2 = 3x + 7$$
$$5x^2 - 3x - 7 = 0$$
$a = 5, \ b = -3, \ c = -7$
$$x = \frac{-b \pm \sqrt{b^2 - 4ac}}{2a}$$
$$x = \frac{3 \pm \sqrt{9 - 4(5)(-7)}}{2(5)}$$
$$x = \frac{3 \pm \sqrt{9 + 140}}{10}$$
$$x = \frac{3 \pm \sqrt{149}}{10} \approx 1.52 \text{ or } -0.92$$

26.
$$2x^2 = 8x - 1$$
$$2x^2 - 8x + 1 = 0$$
$$a = 2, \quad b = -8, \quad c = 1$$
$$x = \frac{-b \pm \sqrt{b^2 - 4ac}}{2a}$$
$$x = \frac{8 \pm \sqrt{64 - 4(2)(1)}}{2(2)}$$
$$x = \frac{8 \pm \sqrt{64 - 8}}{4}$$
$$x = \frac{8 \pm \sqrt{56}}{4}$$
$$x = \frac{8 \pm 2\sqrt{14}}{4}$$
$$x = \frac{4 \pm \sqrt{14}}{2} \approx 3.87 \text{ or } 0.13$$

27.
$$2x^2 = 14$$
$$x^2 = 7$$
$$x = \pm\sqrt{7}$$
$$x \approx \pm 2.65$$

28.
$$2x^2 = 14x$$
$$2x^2 - 14x = 0$$
$$2x(x - 7) = 0$$
$$2x = 0 \quad \text{or} \quad x - 7 = 0$$
$$x = 0 \quad \text{or} \quad x = 7$$

29.
$$4x^2 - 25 = 0$$
$$4x^2 = 25$$
$$x^2 = \frac{25}{4}$$
$$x = \pm\frac{5}{2}$$

30.
$$4x^2 - 25x = 0$$
$$x(4x - 25) = 0$$
$$x = 0 \quad \text{or} \quad 4x - 25 = 0$$
$$x = 0 \quad \text{or} \quad 4x = 25$$
$$x = 0 \quad \text{or} \quad x = \frac{25}{4}$$

31.
$$ax^2 - bx = 0$$
$$x(ax - b) = 0$$
$$x = 0 \quad \text{or} \quad ax - b = 0$$
$$x = 0 \quad \text{or} \quad ax = b$$
$$x = 0 \quad \text{or} \quad x = \frac{b}{a}$$

32.
$$ax^2 - b = 0$$
$$ax^2 = b$$
$$x^2 = \frac{b}{a}$$
$$x = \pm\sqrt{\frac{b}{a}}$$
$$x = \pm\frac{\sqrt{ab}}{a}$$

33. Let the length $= x + 3$ and width $= x$. The area is then:
$$x(x + 3) = 40$$
$$x^2 + 3x = 40$$
$$x^2 + 3x - 40 = 0$$
$$(x + 8)(x - 5) = 0$$
$$x + 8 = 0 \quad \text{or} \quad x - 5 = 0$$
$$x = -8 \quad \text{or} \quad x = 5$$

Reject $x = -8$ because the length cannot be negative. The rectangle is 5 by 8.

34.
$$x \cdot (x + 5) = (x + 1) \cdot 4$$
$$x^2 + 5x = 4x + 4$$
$$x^2 + 1x - 4 = 0$$
$$a = 1, \quad b = 1, \quad c = -4$$
$$x = \frac{-b \pm \sqrt{b^2 - 4ac}}{2a}$$
$$x = \frac{-1 \pm \sqrt{1 - 4(1)(-4)}}{2(1)}$$
$$x = \frac{-1 \pm \sqrt{1 + 16}}{2}$$
$$x = \frac{-1 \pm \sqrt{17}}{2}$$
$$CP = \frac{-1 + \sqrt{17}}{2} \approx 1.56$$

$\dfrac{-1 - \sqrt{17}}{2}$ is rejected because it is a negative number.

35.
$$D = \frac{n(n - 3)}{2}$$
$$9 = \frac{n(n - 3)}{2}$$
$$18 = n^2 - 3n$$
$$0 = n^2 - 3n - 18$$
$$0 = (n - 6)(n - 3)$$
$$n = 6 \text{ or } n = -3$$
$$n = 6 \text{ reject } n = -3 .$$

36. $D = \dfrac{n(n-3)}{2}$

$n = \dfrac{n(n-3)}{2}$

$2n = n^2 - 3n$

$0 = n^2 - 5n$

$0 = n(n-5)$

$n = 0 \quad \text{or} \quad n - 5 = 0$

$n = 0 \quad \text{or} \qquad n = 5$

$n = 5 \ \text{reject} \ n = 0$.

37. $c^2 = a^2 + b^2$

$c^2 = 3^2 + 4^2$

$c^2 = 9 + 16$

$c^2 = 25$

$c = \pm 5$

$c = 5; \ \text{reject} \ c = -5$

38. $c^2 = a^2 + b^2$

$10^2 = 6^2 + b^2$

$100 - 36 = b^2$

$64 = b^2$

$b = \pm 8$

$b = 8; \ \text{reject} \ b = -8$